# Human–Computer Interaction Series

**Editors-in-Chief**

Jean Vanderdonckt, Louvain School of Management, Université catholique de Louvain, Louvain-La-Neuve, Belgium

Q. Vera Liao, Microsoft Research Canada, Montréal, Canada

*The Human – Computer Interaction Series,* launched in 2004, publishes books that advance the science and technology of developing systems which are effective and satisfying for people in a wide variety of contexts. Titles focus on theoretical perspectives (such as formal approaches drawn from a variety of behavioural sciences), practical approaches (such as techniques for effectively integrating user needs in system development), and social issues (such as the determinants of utility, usability and acceptability).

HCI is a multidisciplinary field and focuses on the human aspects in the development of computer technology. As technology becomes increasingly more pervasive the need to take a human-centred approach in the design and development of computer-based systems becomes ever more important.

Titles published within the Human–Computer Interaction Series are included in Thomson Reuters' Book Citation Index, The DBLP Computer Science Bibliography and The HCI Bibliography.

Michele Geronazzo · Stefania Serafin
Editors

# Sonic Interactions
# in Virtual Environments

 Springer

*Editors*
Michele Geronazzo
Department of Engineering
and Management
University of Padova
Padova, Italy

Dyson School of Design Engineering
Imperial College London
London, UK

Department of Humanities and Cultural
Heritage
University of Udine
Udine, Italy

Stefania Serafin
Aalborg University
København SV, Denmark

Nordic SMC University Hub, NordForsk, Stensberggata 27, 0170 Oslo, Norway represented by: Hans Jørgen Andersen, Professor
Università degli Studi di Udine, Dipartimento di Studi Umanistici e del Patrimonio Culturale, Vicolo Florio n. 2/B, 33100 Udine, Italy represented by: Prof. Andrea Zannini, Department Director
EU project SONICOM, funded by the Horizon 2020 research and innovation programme (grant agreement No 101017743), represented by: Dr. Lorenzo Picinali, Reader

ISSN 1571-5035          ISSN 2524-4477  (electronic)
Human–Computer Interaction Series
ISBN 978-3-031-04023-8          ISBN 978-3-031-04021-4  (eBook)
https://doi.org/10.1007/978-3-031-04021-4

This Springer imprint is published by the registered company Springer Nature Switzerland AG
The registered company address is: Gewerbestrasse 11, 6330 Cham, Switzerland

*Between stimulus and response there is a space. In that space is our power to choose our response. In our response lies our growth and our freedom.*

*—Viktor E. Frankl*

# Preface

Sonic Interaction Design (SID) is the study and exploitation of sound being one of the principal channels conveying information, meaning, esthetic, and emotional qualities in interactive contexts. The field of *Sonic Interactions in Virtual Environments* (SIVE) extends SID to immersive media, i.e., virtual/augmented/mixed reality (XR). Considering a virtuality continuum, this book mainly focused on virtual reality (VR) also facing occasionally mixed and hybrid reality settings.

The basic and most obvious assumption that motivates this volume is: it is hard to live in a world without sound and it is hard in virtual environments (VE) too. VR without plausible and convincing sounds feels unnatural to users. Auditory information is a powerful omnidirectional source of learning for our interaction in real and virtual environments. The good news brought by this book is that VR finally sounds plausible. Advances in several fields are now able to provide an immersive listening experience that is perceptually indistinguishable from reality which means that immersive sounds could make interaction intrinsically natural. Auralization and spatial audio technologies play a fundamental role in providing immersion and presence in VR applications at an unprecedented level. The combination of recent developments in VR headsets and earables further strengthens the perceptual validity of multimodal virtual environments and experiences.

We can therefore promote a true audio-centered and audio-first design for VR with levels of realism and immersiveness that can even surpass the visual counterpart. Visuals, although rightly emphasized by many studies and products, are often not very effectively enhanced and strengthened by sound. The final result is a weakening of multisensory integration and the corresponding VR potentials that strongly determine the quality and durability of the experience.

The editors would like to identify two starting points in the past 10 years that have given rise and awareness to the SIVE research area and studies. The first episode is symbolic: we would like to anecdotally bring back from our memories the first meeting between us, the two editors of the book. The year was 2011, exactly 10 years ago. Michele had recently started his Ph.D. at the Sound and Music Computing Group of the Department of Information Engineering at the University of Padua, under the supervision of Dr. Avanzini. The Italian Association of Musical Informatics

(AIMI) organized the workshop "Sound and Music Computing for Human-Computer Interaction" at the ninth edition of the Biannual Conference of the Italian ACM SIGCHI Chapter (CHItaly) at the beautiful Alghero in Sardinia in early September. A great period for the seaside.

Michele was asked to write his first conference paper to be presented at the workshop entitled "Customized 3D Sound for Innovative Interaction Design," An article with a high-sounding title that promises a lot but provides little: in short, an article of which not to be proud. On the other hand, there were some valuable references to the *egocentric audio perspective* that will be formalized in the introductory chapter of this book. However, the reason why we tell this anecdote is that at his first presentation at a scientific conference for the Ph.D. student Michele Geronazzo, among the very small audience, there was Dr. Stefania Serafin. Ten years ago, we began to discuss issues that connected sonic interaction design with immersive 3D audio in VR. The AIMI president of that time failed to get the workshop's contributions included in the official ACM CHItaly proceedings despite a regular peer-review process. The poor Ph.D. student Michele found himself without an official publication, at his first conference, in an unknown scientific community. We like to think that at that event and with that meeting started something much more relevant and impactful: SIVE. We are here to give it a shape in this book edited and structured together.

Another temporal coincidence brings us to connect this story with the second and official starting point of this adventure. Michele's unpublished conference paper was finally published within his doctoral thesis, defended in 2014, the year in which the *IEEE Virtual Reality* workshop series "*Sonic Interactions in Virtual Environments (SIVE)*" started (https://sive.create.aau.dk/). The mission of IEEE VR SIVE was to increase among the virtual reality community and junior researchers the awareness of the importance of sonic elements when designing immersive XR environments. However, we can also identify a certain degree of reciprocity while considering the fragmented nature and specificity of those studies aim at developing immersive XR environments for sound and music. First, we, therefore, refer to our beloved Sound and Music Computing (SMC) network, and then we consider the International Community for Auditory Display (ICAD), the Audio Engineering Society (AES), and the communities linked to the International Conference on New Interfaces for Musical Expression (NIME), the Digital Audio Effects (DAFX), and the Sonic Interaction Design COST Action (COST-SID IC601, ended in 2012). All these communities address aspects of the SIVE topics according to their specificities. No institutional nor contextual references that collect technological developments, best practices, and creative efforts related to the peculiarities of immersive VEs existed before the SIVE workshop. The book follows a similar philosophy trying to give an exhaustive view of those multidisciplinary topics already mentioned in our two recent reviews.[1] It features state-of-the-art research on real-time auralization, sonic

---

[1] S. Serafin, M. Geronazzo, N. C. Nilsson, C. Erkut, and R. Nordahl, "Sonic interactions in virtual reality: state of the art, current challenges and future directions," IEEE Computer Graphics and Applications, vol. 38, no. 2, pp. 31–43, 2018.

   S. Serafin et al., "Reflections from five years of Sonic Interactions in Virtual Environments workshops," Journal of New Music Research, vol. 49, no. 1, pp. 24–34, Jan. 2020.

interaction design in VR, quality of the experience in multimodal environments, and applications. We aim to provide an organized starting point on which to develop a new generation of immersive experiences and applications. Since the editors are aware of the very fast social transformation by the acceleration in the development of digital technologies, all chapters should be read as entry points. Future scenarios and solutions will necessarily evolve by combining emerging research areas such as artificial intelligence, ubiquitous and pervasive computing, quantum technologies, as well as continuous discoveries in the neuroscientific field and anthropological reflections on the authenticity of the experience in VR.

For this reason, contributing authors and editors include interdisciplinary experts from the fields of computer science, engineering, acoustics, psychology, design, humanities, and beyond. So that we can give to the reader a broad view and a clear introduction to the state-of-the-art technologies and design principles, and to the challenges that might be awaiting us in the future.

Through an overview of emerging topics, theories, methods, tools, and practices in sonic interactions in virtual environments research, the book aims to establish the basis for further development of this new research area. The authors were invited to contribute to specific topics according to their well-known expertise. They followed a predefined structure outlined by the editors.

The book is divided into four parts:

**Part I, Introduction:** this theoretical part frames the background and the key themes in SIVE. The editors address several phenomenological foundational issues intending to shape a new research field from an archipelago of studies scattered in different research communities.

**Part II, Interactive and Immersive Audio:** we cover the system requirement part with four chapters introducing and analyzing audio-related technological aspects and challenges. With some overlaps and connections, the four chapters deal with the plausibility of an immersive rendering able to tackle the computational burden. To do so, we deal with methods and algorithms for real-time rendering considering sound production, propagation, and spatialization, respectively. Finally, the reproduction and evaluation phase allows closing the development loop of new audio technologies.

**Part III, Sonic Interactions:** a sonic interaction design part devoted to emphasizing the peculiar aspects of sound in immersive media. In particular, spatial interactions are important where we would like to produce and transform ideas and actions to create meaning with VR, as well as the virtual auditory space is an information container that could be shaped by users. As the VR systems enter people's lives, manufacturers, developers, and creators should carefully consider an embodied experience ready to share a common space with peers, collaboratively.

**Part IV, Sonic Experiences:** the last part focuses on multimodal integration for sonic experiences in VR with the help of several case studies. Starting from a literature review of multimodal experiments and experiences with sound, this last part offers some reflections on the concept of audio-visual immersion and audio-haptic integration able to form our ecology of everyday or musical sounds. Finally, the potentials of VR to transport artists and spectators into a world of imagination and unprecedented expression is taken as an exemplar of what multimodal and immersive experiences can elicit in terms of emotional and rational engagement.

In the following, a summary for each chapter is provided to help the reader to follow the proposed narrative structure.

## Part I

Chapter 1 illustrates the editors' vision of the SIVE research field. The main concept introduced here is the egocentric audio perspective in a technologically mediated environment. The listeners should be entangled with their auditory digital twins in a participatory and enacted exploration for sense-making characterized by a personalized and multisensory first-person spatial reference frame. Intra-actions between humans and non-human agents/actors dynamically and fluidly determine immersion and coherence of the experience, participatively. SID aims to facilitate the diffraction of knowledge in different tasks and contexts.

## Part II

Chapter 2 addresses the first building block of SIVE, i.e., the modeling and synthesis of sound sources, focusing on procedural approaches. Special emphasis is placed on physics-based sound synthesis methods and their potential for improved interactivity concerning the sense of presence and embodiment of a user in a virtual environment.

In Chap. 3, critical challenges in auralization systems in virtual reality and games are identified, including progressing from modeling enclosures to complex, general scenes such as a city block with both indoor and outdoor areas. The authors provide a general overview of real-time auralization systems, their historical design and motivations, and how novel systems have been designed to tackle the new challenges.

Chapter 4 deals with the concepts of adaptation in a binaural audio context, considering first the adaptation of the rendering system to the acoustic and perceptual properties of the user, and second the adaptation of the user to the rendering quality of the system. The authors introduce the topics of head-related transfer function (HRTF) selection (system-to-user adaptation) and HRTF accommodation (user-to-system adaptation).

Finally, Chap. 5 concludes the second part of the book by introducing audio reproduction techniques for virtual reality, the concepts of audio quality, and quality of the experience in VR.

# Part III

Chapter 6 opens the third part of the book devoted to SID within virtual environments. In particular, it deals with space, a fundamental feature of VR systems, and more generally, human experience. In this chapter, the authors propose a typology of VR interactive audio systems, focusing on the function of systems and the role of space in their design. Spatial categories are proposed to be able to analyze the role of space within existing interactive audio VR products.

Chapter 7 promotes the following great opportunities offered by VR systems: to bring experiences, technologies, and users' physical and experiential bodies (soma) together, and to study and teach these open-ended relationships of enaction and meaning-making in the framework of soma design. In this chapter, the authors introduce soma design and focus on design exemplars that come from physical rehabilitation applied to sonic interaction strategies.

Then, Chap. 8 investigates how to design the user experience without being detrimental to the creative output, and how to design spatial configurations to support both individual creativity and collaboration. The authors examine user experience design for collaborative music-making in shared virtual environments, giving design implications for the auditory information and the collaborative facilitation.

Finally, Chap. 9 explores the possibilities in content creation like spatial music mixing, be it in virtual spaces or for surround sound in film and music, offered by the development of VR systems and multimodal simulations. Authors present some design aspects for mixing in VR, investigating existing virtual music mixing products, and creating a framework for a virtual spatial-music mixing tool.

# Part IV

Chapter 10 helps the reader to understand how sound enhances, substitutes, or modifies the way we perceive and interact with the world. This is an important element when designing interactive multimodal experiences. In this chapter, Stefania presents an overview of sound in a multimodal context, ranging from basic experiments in multimodal perception to more advanced interactive experiences.

Chapter 11 focuses on audiovisual experiences, by discussing the idea of immersion, and by providing an experimental paradigm that can be used for assessing immersion. The authors highlight the factors that can influence immersion and they differentiate immersion from the quality of experience (QoE). The theoretical implications for conducting experiments on these aspects are presented, and the authors provide a case study for subjective evaluation after assessing the merits and demerits of subjective and objective measures.

Chapter 12 focuses on audio-haptic experiences, being concerned with haptic augmentations having effects on auditory perception, for example, about how different vibrotactile cues may affect the perceived sound quality. The authors review the results of different experiments showing that the auditory and somatosensory channels together can produce constructive effects resulting in a measurable perceptual enhancement.

Finally, Chap. 13 examines the special case of virtual music experiences, with particular emphasis on the performance with Immersive Virtual Musical Instruments (IVMI) and the relation between musicians and spectators. The authors assess in detail the several technical and conceptual challenges linked to the composition of IVMI performances on stage (i.e., their scenography), providing a new critical perspective.

We hope the reader finds this book informative and useful for both research and practice with sound.

Udine, Copenhagen                                                                        Michele Geronazzo
September 2021                                                                               Stefania Serafin

# Acknowledgements

We would like to thank all authors and people involved in the book for their time and effort. In particular, the co-organizers of the IEEE Virtual Reality Workshop SIVE participated, in different ways, in this book project. Special thanks to Helen Desmond (Springer Computer Science Editor) and the Springer team for allowing us to prepare this volume.

**Michele:** I take my place, I have been creating my place in SIVE. This book project closes my first 10 years of academic activities, It has allowed me to reflect on my path and interdisciplinary education, challenging my knowledge extraction process. I went through the three "HCI waves" with my own time: ergonomics and engineering in Padova, psychology, and cognition in Verona, embodied design and UX in Copenhagen. I found recognition and maturity in London, and, finally, Udine gave me the time to find my identity. I would like to thank all my mentors and peers who made me grow in the research jungle, on numerous occasions and at different moments in my life. A big thanks go to my beloved family who supports me and always brings me back down to earth.

New challenges in VR are on the horizon and I am ready to make resonate our audio perspective!

**Stefania:** This year I have been recognized with the Danish Sound Award, for being pivotal in securing Denmark's role as a leader in fields such as sonic interaction design, sound, and music computing and developing the role of sound in international virtual reality research. This award and this book would not have been possible without the wonderful colleagues and students of the Multisensory Experience Lab at Aalborg University in Copenhagen, who keep me motivated and inspired on a daily basis. It was a pleasure to host Michele as a postdoc in the lab for 2 years, and this book is a result of that. The lab is my second family, that wonderfully complements my first beloved family, both in Italy and in Denmark, that I thank with all my heart for everything they mean to me.

**List of expert readers:** we thank the following researchers to be our first critical readers, providing valuable comments for specific chapters within their area of expertise:

Roberto Barumerli, Acoustics Research Institute, Vienna, Austria
Braxton Boren, American University, Washington, DC, US
Enzo De Sena, University of Surrey, Guildford, Surrey, UK
Michele Ducceschi, University of Bologna, Bologna, Italy
Isaac Engel, Imperial College London, London, UK
Floriana Ferro, University of Udine, Udine, Italy
Amalia de Götzen, Aalborg University Copenhagen, Copenhagen, Denmark
Marcella Mandanici, Music Conservatory "Luca Marenzio", Brescia, Italy
Raul Masu, Universidade NOVA de Lisboa, Lisbon, Spain
Catarina Mendonça, University of Azores, Ponta Delgada, Portugal
Fabio Morreale, University of Auckland, Auckland, New Zealand
Niels Christian Nilsson, Aalborg University Copenhagen, Copenhagen, Denmark
Dan Overholt, Aalborg University Copenhagen, Copenhagen, Denmark
Archontis Politis, Tampere University, Tampere, Finland
Sebastian Prepelita, Facebook Reality Labs, Redmond, WA, US
Giorgio Presti, University of Milano, Milano, Italy
Davide Rocchesso, University of Palermo, Palermo, Italy
Lauri Savioja, Aalto University, Espoo, Finland
Bernhard Seeber, Technische Universität München, Munich, Germany
Ana Tajadura-Jiménez, University College London, London, UK
Maarten Van Walstijn, Queen's University Belfast, Belfast, UK
Silvin Willemsen, Aalborg University Copenhagen, Copenhagen, Denmark

## Open Access Funding

This book project was supported by

- the Nordic Sound and Music Computing Network (NordicSMC)—University hub by Nordforsk (Norway),
- the Department of Humanities and Cultural Heritage—University of Udine (Italy) with the recognition of "Department of Excellence" by the Ministry of Education, University and Research (MIUR) of Italy

that cover the majority of the open-access publishing costs. We are grateful to the EU project SONICOM (grant number: 101017743, RIA action of Horizon 2020) for its sponsorship that contributes to the full transition to open access.

# Contents

**Part I  Introduction**

1   Sonic Interactions in Virtual Environments:
    The Egocentric Audio Perspective of the Digital Twin ............. 3
    Michele Geronazzo and Stefania Serafin

**Part II  Interactive and Immersive Audio**

2   Procedural Modeling of Interactive Sound Sources in Virtual
    Reality ...................................................... 49
    Federico Avanzini

3   Interactive and Immersive Auralization ........................ 77
    Nikunj Raghuvanshi and Hannes Gamper

4   System-to-User and User-to-System Adaptations in Binaural
    Audio ...................................................... 115
    Lorenzo Picinali and Brian F. G. Katz

5   Audio Quality Assessment for Virtual Reality ................... 145
    Fabian Brinkmann and Stefan Weinzierl

**Part III  Sonic Interactions**

6   Spatial Design Considerations for Interactive Audio in Virtual
    Reality ...................................................... 181
    Thomas Deacon and Mathieu Barthet

7   Embodied and Sonic Interactions in Virtual Environments:
    Tactics and Exemplars ........................................ 219
    Sophus Béneé Olsen, Emil Rosenlund Høeg, and Cumhur Erkut

8   Supporting Sonic Interaction in Creative, Shared Virtual
    Environments ................................................ 237
    Liang Men and Nick Bryan-Kinns

9    Spatial Audio Mixing in Virtual Reality ........................ 269
     Anders Riddershom Bargum, Oddur Ingi Kristjánsson,
     Péter Babó, Rasmus Eske Waage Nielsen,
     Simon Rostami Mosen, and Stefania Serafin

Part IV   Sonic Experiences

10   Audio in Multisensory Interactions: From Experiments
     to Experiences ............................................... 305
     Stefania Serafin

11   Immersion in Audiovisual Experiences ........................ 319
     Sarvesh R. Agrawal and Søren Bech

12   Augmenting Sonic Experiences Through Haptic Feedback ........ 353
     Federico Fontana, Hanna Järveläinen, and Stefano Papetti

13   From the Lab to the Stage: Practical Considerations
     on Designing Performances with Immersive Virtual Musical
     Instruments ................................................. 383
     Victor Zappi, Dario Mazzanti, and Florent Berthaut

Index ........................................................... 425

# Editors and Contributors

## About the Editors

**Michele Geronazzo** Ph.D., is an Associate Professor at the University of Padova—Dept. of Management and Engineering, and part of the coordination unit of the EU-H2020 project SONICOM at Imperial College London. He received his M.S. degree in Computer Engineering (2009) and his Ph.D. degree in Information & Communication Technologies (2014) from the University of Padova. Between 2014 and 2021, he worked as an Assistant Professor in Digital Media at the University of Udine and a postdoctoral researcher at Imperial College London, Aalborg University, and the University of Verona in the fields of neurosciences and simulations of complex human–machine systems. His main research interests involve binaural spatial audio modeling and synthesis, virtual/augmented reality, and sound in human–computer interaction.

He is an IEEE Senior Member and part of the organizing committee of the IEEE VR Workshop on Sonic Interactions for Virtual Environments since 2015 (chair of the 2018 and 2020 editions). From September 2019, he has been appointed as an Editorial Board member for Frontiers in Virtual Reality, and he served as guest editor for Wireless Communications and Mobile Computing (John Wiley & Sons and Hindawi publishers, 2019). He is a co-recipient of six best paper/poster awards and co-author of more than 70 scientific publications. In 2015, his Ph.D. thesis was honored by the Acoustic Society of Italy (AIA) with the "G. Sarcedote" award.

**Stefania Serafin** is a Professor of Sonic interaction design at Aalborg University in Copenhagen and the leader of the Multisensory Experience Lab together with Rolf Nordahl. She was previously appointed as Associate Professor (2006–2013) and Assistant Professor (2003–2006) in the same University. She has been visiting researcher at the University of Cambridge and KTH in Stockholm (2003) and visiting professor at the University of Virginia (2002). Since 2014, she is the President of the Sound and Music Computing association, and since 2018, the Project Leader of the Nordic Sound and Music Computing network supported by Nordforsk. She has been a part of the organizing committee of the IEEE VR Workshop on Sonic Interactions for Virtual Environments since the first edition. She is also the coordinator of the Sound and music computing Master at Aalborg University. She received her Ph.D. entitled "The sound of friction: computer models, playability and musical applications" from Stanford University in 2004, supervised by Professor Julius Smith III. She is the co-author of more than 300 papers in the fields of sound and music computing, sound for virtual and augmented reality, sonic interaction design, and new interfaces for musical expression.

# Contributors

**Agrawal Sarvesh R.** Bang & Olufsen, Struer, Denmark;
Technical University of Denmark, Department of Photonics Engineering, Lyngby, Denmark

**Avanzini Federico** Laboratory of Music Informatics, Department of Computer Science, University of Milano, Milano, Italy

**Babó Péter** Department of Architecture, Design, and Media Technology, Aalborg University Copenhagen, Copenhagen, Denmark

**Barthet Mathieu** Centre for Digital Music, Queen Mary University of London, London, United Kingdom

**Bech Søren** Bang & Olufsen, Struer, Denmark;
Department of Electronic Systems, Aalborg University, Aalborg, Denmark

**Berthaut Florent** University of Lille, Lille, France

**Brinkmann Fabian** Audio Communication Group, Technical University of Berlin, Berlin, Germany

**Bryan-Kinns Nick** Queen Mary University of London, London, United Kingdom

**Deacon Thomas** Media and Arts Technology CDT, Queen Mary University of London, London, United Kingdom

**Erkut Cumhur** Multisensory Experience Lab, Aalborg University Copenhagen, Copenhagen, Denmark

**Eske Waage Nielsen Rasmus** Department of Architecture, Design, and Media Technology, Aalborg University Copenhagen, Copenhagen, Denmark

**Fontana Federico** Department of Mathematics, Computer Science and Physics, University of Udine, Udine, Italy

**Gamper Hannes** Microsoft Research, Redmond, USA

**Geronazzo Michele** Department of Engineering and Management, University of Padova, Padova, Italy;
Dyson School of Design Engineering, Imperial College London, London, UK;
Department of Humanities and Cultural Heritage, University of Udine, Udine, Italy

**Høeg Emil Rosenlund** Multisensory Experience Lab, Aalborg University Copenhagen, Copenhagen, Denmark

**Ingi Kristjánsson Oddur** Department of Architecture, Design, and Media Technology, Aalborg University Copenhagen, Copenhagen, Denmark

**Järveläinen Hanna** Institute for Computer Music and Sound Technology, Zurich University of the Arts, Zurich, Switzerland

**Katz Brian F. G.** Sorbonne Université, CNRS, UMR 7190, Institut Jean Le Rond d'Alembert, Paris, France

**Mazzanti Dario** Independent researcher, Genoa, Italy

**Men Liang** Liverpool John Moores University, Liverpool, United Kingdom

**Olsen Sophus Béneé** Multisensory Experience Lab, Aalborg University Copenhagen, Copenhagen, Denmark

**Papetti Stefano** Institute for Computer Music and Sound Technology, Zurich University of the Arts, Zurich, Switzerland

**Picinali Lorenzo** Imperial College London, London, UK

**Raghuvanshi Nikunj** Microsoft Research, Redmond, USA

**Riddershom Bargum Anders** Department of Architecture, Design, and Media Technology, Aalborg University Copenhagen, Copenhagen, Denmark

**Rostami Mosen Simon** Department of Architecture, Design, and Media Technology, Aalborg University Copenhagen, Copenhagen, Denmark

**Serafin Stefania** Department of Architecture, Design, and Media Technology, Aalborg University Copenhagen, Copenhagen, Denmark

**Weinzierl Stefan** Audio Communication Group, Technical University of Berlin, Berlin, Germany

**Zappi Victor** Northeastern University, Boston, MA, United States

# Part I
# Introduction

# Chapter 1
# Sonic Interactions in Virtual Environments: The Egocentric Audio Perspective of the Digital Twin

Michele Geronazzo and Stefania Serafin

**Abstract** The relationships between the listener, physical world, and virtual environment (VE) should not only inspire the design of natural multimodal interfaces but should be discovered to make sense of the mediating action of VR technologies. This chapter aims to transform an archipelago of studies related to sonic interactions in virtual environments (SIVE) into a research field equipped with a first theoretical framework with an inclusive vision of the challenges to come: the egocentric perspective of the auditory digital twin. In a VE with immersive audio technologies implemented, the role of VR simulations must be enacted by a participatory exploration of sense-making in a network of human and non-human agents, called actors. The guardian of such locus of agency is the auditory digital twin that fosters intra-actions between humans and technology, dynamically and fluidly redefining all those configurations that are crucial for an immersive and coherent experience. The idea of entanglement theory is here mainly declined in an egocentric spatial perspective related to emerging knowledge of the listener's perceptual capabilities. This is an actively transformative relation with the digital twin potentials to create movement, transparency, and provocative activities in VEs. The chapter contains an original theoretical perspective complemented by several bibliographical references and links to the other book chapters that have contributed significantly to the proposal presented here.

M. Geronazzo (✉)
Department of Engineering and Management, University of Padova, Padova, Italy
e-mail: michele.geronazzo@unipd.it

Dyson School of Design Engineering, Imperial College London, London, UK

Department of Humanities and Cultural Heritage, University of Udine, Udine, Italy

S. Serafin
Department of Architecture, Design, and Media Technology, Aalborg University Copenhagen, Copenhagen, Denmark
e-mail: sts@create.aau.dk

© The Author(s) 2023
M. Geronazzo and S. Serafin (eds.), *Sonic Interactions in Virtual Environments*,
Human—Computer Interaction Series, https://doi.org/10.1007/978-3-031-04021-4_1

## 1.1  Introduction

Our daily auditory experience is characterized by immersion from the very beginning of our life inside the womb, actively listening to sounds surrounding us from different positions in space. Auditory information takes the form of a binaural continuous stream of messages to the left and right ears, conveying a compact representation of the omnidirectional source of learning for our existence [19, 48]. Both temporal and spatial activity of sounds of interest (e.g., dialogues, alarms, etc.) allow us to localize and encode the contextual information and intentions of our social interaction [1].

The hypothesis that our daily listening experience of sounding objects with certain physical characteristics dynamically shapes the acoustic features for which we ascribe meaning to our auditory world is supported by one of the key concepts in Husserl's phenomenology *"Meaning-bestowal"* ("Sinngebung" in German [73]) and by studies in ecological acoustics such as [48, 54, 96]. In particular, the idea of acoustic invariant as a complex pattern of change for a real-world sound interaction is strongly related to human perceptual learning and a socio-cultural mediation dictated by the real world. For some surveys of classical studies on the topic of ecological acoustics refer to [112].

From this perspective, acoustic invariants are learned on an individual basis through experiential learning. Hence, there is the need to trace their development over multiple experiences and to formalize a common ground for a dynamic expansion of individual knowledge. Any emerging understanding should be transferred to a technological system able to provide an immersive and interactive simulation of a sonic virtual environment (VE). Such a process must be adaptive and dynamic to ensure a level of coupling between user and technology in such a way that the active listening experience is considered authentic.

Immersive virtual reality (here we generically referred to as VR) technologies allow immense flexibility and increasing possibilities for the creation of VEs with relationships or interactions that might be ontologically relevant even if radically different from the physical world. This can be evident by referring to the distinction between naturalistic and magical interactions, where the latter can be considered observable system configurations in the domain of artificial illusions, incredibly expanding the spectrum of possible digital experiences [13, 127].

One of the main research topics in the VR and multimedia communities is rendering. For decades, computer-aided design applications have favored—in the first place—the development of computer graphics algorithms. Some of these approaches, e.g., geometric ray-tracing methods, have been adapted to model sound propagation in complex VEs (see Chap. 3 for more details). However, there has been a clear tendency to prioritize resources and research on the visual side of virtual reality, confining auditory information to a secondary and ancillary role [158]. Although sound is an essential component of the grammar of digital immersion, relatively little compared to the visual side of things has been done to investigate the role of auditory space and environments. Nowadays, there is increasing consensus toward the essential contribution of spatial sound, also in (VR) simulations [9, 102, 145].

Technologies for **spatial audio rendering** are now able to convey perceptually plausible simulations with stimuli that are reconstructed from real-life recordings [18] or historical archives, as for the Cathédrale Notre-Dame de Paris before and after the 2019 fire [79], getting closer to a virtual version indistinguishable from the natural reality [77]. This is made possible by a high level of personalization in modeling user morphology and acoustic transformations caused by the human body interacting with the sound field generated in room acoustic computer simulations [17, 78, 114].

Nowadays, the boundary between technology and humans has increasingly blurred thanks to recent developments in research areas such as virtual and augmented reality, artificial intelligence, cyber-physical systems, and neuro-implants. It is not possible to easily distinguish where the human ends and the technology begins. For this reason, we embrace the idea of [10] who sees technology as a lens for the understanding of what it means to be human in a changing world. We can therefore consider the *phenomenal transparency* [94] where technology takes on the role of a transparent mediator for self-knowledge. According to Loomis [88], the **phenomenology of presence** between physical and virtual environments places the internal listener representation created by the spatial senses and the brain on the same level. Human-technology-reality relations are thus created by enactivity that allows a fluid and dynamic entanglement of all the involved actors.

In this chapter, we initially adopt Slater's definition of presence for an immersive VR system [135] embracing the recent revision by Skarbez [134]. The concepts of plausibility illusion and place illusion are central to capturing the subjective internal states. While the plausibility illusion determines the overall credibility of a VE in terms of subjective expectations, the place illusion establishes the quality of having sensations of being in a real place. They are both fundamental in providing credibility to a digital simulation based on individual experience and expectations concerning an internal frame of reference for scenes, environments, and events.[1]

We propose a theoretical framework for the new field of study, namely Sonic Interactions in Virtual Environments (SIVE). We suggest from now on a unified reading of this chapter with references and integrations from all chapters of the corresponding book [49]. Each chapter provides state-of-the-art challenges and case studies for specific SIVE-related topics curated by internationally renowned scientists and their collaborators. The provided point of view focuses on the relations between real auditory experience and technologically mediated experiences in immersive VR. The first is characterized by individuality to confer immersiveness within a physical world. It is important to emphasize the omnidirectionally of auditory information that allows the listener to collect both the whole and the parts at 360°. The individualized auditory signals are the result of the acoustic transformations made by the head, ear, and torso of the listener that act as a spatial fingerprint for a complex spatio-temporal signal. Familiarity, and therefore previous experience with sounds, shape spatial localization capabilities with high intersubjectivity. Finally, studies on

---

[1] For a dedicated discussion on the basic notions related to presence, please refer also to Chap. 11 in this volume.

neural plasticity of the human brain confirm continuous adaptability of listening with impaired physiological functions, e.g., a hearing loss, and with electrical stimulation, e.g., via cochlear implants [82].

The **mediated VR experience** is often characterized by the user's digital counterpart called avatar. It allows the creation of an embodied and situated experience in digital VEs. The scientific literature supports the idea that the manipulation of VR simulations can induce changes at the cognitive level [124], such as in educational [34] and therapeutic [106] positive effects. The ability of VR technologies to mediate within the immersive environment in embodied and situated relations gives immersive technologies the opportunities to change one's self [151].

For these reasons, we believe it is time to coin, at the terminological level, a new perspective that relates the two listening experiences (i.e., real and virtual), called **egocentric audio perspective**. In particular, we refer to the term audio to identify an auditory sensory component, implicitly recalling those technologies capable of immersive and interactive rendering. The term egocentric refers to the perceptual reference system for the acquisition of multisensory information in immersive VR technologies as well as the sense of subjectivity and perceptual/cognitive individuality that shape the self, identity, or consciousness. In accordance with Husserl's phenomenology, the human body can be philosophically defined as a "Leib", a living body, and a "Nullpunkt", a zero-point of reference and orientation [73].

This perspective aims to extend the discipline of Sonic Interaction Design [44] by taking into account not only the importance of sound as the main channel conveying information, meaning, aesthetic, and emotional qualities, but rather an egocentric perspective of entanglement between the perceiving subject and the computer simulating the perceived environment. In the first instance, this can be described by processes of personalization, adaptation, and mutual relations to maintain the immersive illusion. However in this chapter, we will try to argue that it is much more than that. We hope that our vision will guide the development of new immersive audio technologies and conscious use of sound design within VEs.

The starting point of this theoretical framework is an ecologically egocentric perspective. The foundational phenomenological assumption considers a self-propelled entity with agency and intentionality [47]. It can interact with the VE being aware of its activities in a three-dimensional space. The active immersion in a simulated acoustic field provides it meaningful experiences through sound.

Therefore, it is important to introduce a terminological characterization of what is the **listener**, not a user in this context, as a human being with prior experience and subjective auditory perception. A closely related entity is the **auditory digital twin**, which differs from the most common avatar. The idea of an avatar within a digital simulation co-located with objects, places, and other avatars [126] requires a user taking control of any form of virtual bodies which might be noticeably different from that of the listenerâŁ™s physical body. On the other hand, the digital twin cannot disregard an egocentric perspective of the listener for whom it is created. This means that the relations with the VEs should consider personalization techniques on the virtual body closely linked to the listener's biological body. This mediation is essential for the interactions between the listener and all the diegetic sounds, whether they are produced by the avatar's gestures or by sound sources in the VE.

In such a context, immersiveness is a dynamic relationship between physical and meaningful actions by the listener in the VE. Specifically, having performed bodily practices such as walking, sitting, talking, grasping, etc. provide meaning to virtual places, objects, and avatars [59]. Accordingly, the sense of embodiment can be considered a subjective internal feeling which is an expression of the relationship between one's self and such VE. In this regard, Kilteni et al. [80] identified the sense of embodiment for an artificial body (i.e., avatar) in the mediation between the avatar's properties and their processing by the user's biological properties.

We now introduce the technological mediation in the form of an auditory digital twin which is a guardian and facilitator of (i) the sense of self-location, (ii) plausibility, (iii) body ownership, and (iv) agency for the listener. In the first instance, a performative view might make us see realities as " a doing", enacting practical actions [6, 104]. Similarly, the listener and the avatar cannot be considered fixed and independent interacting entities, but constituent parts of emergent, multiple and dynamic phenomena resulting from entangled social, cognitive, and perceptual elements. This **intra-systemic action** of entangled elements dynamically constructs identities and properties of the immersive listening experience. The illusory permanence of auditory immersion lies in the boundaries between situationally entangled elements in fluid and dynamic situations. They can be seen as confrontations occurring exactly in the auditory digital twin that facilitates the phenomenon. The auditory digital twin is the meeting and shared place between the listener and a virtual body identity, communicating in a non-discursive (performative) way according to the quality level of the digital simulation.

In an immersive VE, the listeners cannot exist without their auditory digital twin and vice versa. Through the digital twin characterization, the acoustic signals generated by the VE are filtered exclusively for the listeners, according to their ability to extract meaningful information. It is worthwhile to mention the **participatory nature** of such entanglement process between listener and digital twin, as a joint exploration of the listener's attentional process in selecting meaningful information, e.g., the cocktails party effect [20]. We might speculate by considering a simulation that interacts within the digital twin to provide the best pattern or to discover it in order to attract the listener's attention. The decision-making process will then be the result of intra-action in and of the auditory digital twin.

This chapter has three main sections. Section 1.2 gathers the different souls that characterize the research and artistic works in SIVE. Section 1.3 holds a central position by defining the constitutive elements of our proposed egocentric audio perspective in SIVE: spatial centrality and entanglement between human and computer in the digital twin. In Sect. 1.4, we attempt incorporating this theoretical framework by adapting Milgram and Kishino's well-known taxonomy for VR [95], with an audio-first perspective. Finally, Sect. 1.5 concludes this chapter by encouraging a new starting point for SIVE. We suggest an inclusive approach to the next paradigm shift in the field of human-computer interaction (HCI) discipline.

## 1.2   SIVE: From an Archipelago to a Research Field

This chapter aims to provide an interpretation to an archipelago of researches from different communities such as

- Sound and Music Computing (SMC) network, a point of convergence for different research disciplines mainly related to digital processing of musical information.[2]
- International Community for Auditory Display (ICAD), a point of convergence for different areas of research with digital processing of non-musical audio information and the idea of sonification in common.[3]
- The Audio Engineering Society (AES), the main community for institutions and companies devoted to the world of audio technologies.[4]
- The research community gathered by the International Conference on New Interfaces for Musical Expression (NIME), devoted to interactions with new interfaces with the aim at facilitating the human creative process.[5]
- The Digital Audio Effects community (DAFX) aiming at designing technological-based simulations of sonic phenomena.[6]

We employ here the metaphor of an archipelago because it well describes a context in which all these communities address aspects of VR according to their specificities, influencing each other. After all, they share the same "waters". They are relatively close to each other but feeling distant from a VR community at the same time, like the islands of an archipelago in the open sea. Thus, we affirm the need to unify the fragmentary and specificity of those studies and to fill the gap with their visual counterpart's aiming at developing immersive VR environments for sound and music. To achieve this goal, the editors have pursued the following spontaneous path that is characterized by three main steps.

1. The first review article related to SIVE topics, dated back to 2018 [128], focused on the technological components characterizing an immersive potential for interactive sound environments. In that work, the editors and their collaborators produced a first compact survey including sound synthesis, propagation, rendering, and reproduction with a focus on the ongoing development of headphone technologies.
2. Two years later, we published a second review paper together with all the organizers of the past five editions of the IEEE Virtual Reality's SIVE workshop [129]. In this paper, we analyzed the contributions presented at the various editions highlighting the emerging aspects of interaction design, presence, and evaluation. An inductive approach was adopted, supported by a posteriori analysis of the characterizing categories of SIVE so far.

---

[2] https://smcnetwork.org/

[3] https://icad.org/

[4] https://www.aes.org/

[5] https://nime.org

[6] https://www.dafx.de/

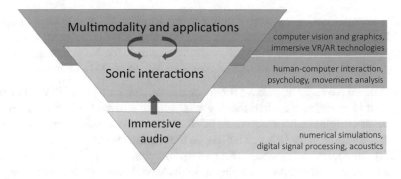

**Fig. 1.1** The SIVE inverse pyramid. Arrows indicate high-level relational hierarchies

3. Finally, this book and, in particular, this chapter want to raise the bar further
   with an organic and structured narrative of an emerging discipline. We aim to
   provide a theoretical framework for interpreting and accompanying the evolution
   of SIVE, focusing on the close relationship between physically real and virtual
   auditory experiences described in terms of immersive, coherent, and entangled
   features.

This chapter is the result of the convergence of two complementary analytical
strategies: (i) a *top-down* approach describing the structure given by the editors to
the book originated from the studies experienced by the editors themselves, and
(ii) a *bottom-up* approach drawing on the knowledgeable insights of the contributing
authors of this book on several specialist and interdisciplinary aspects. Consequently,
we will constantly refer to these chapters in an attempt to provide a unified and long-
term vision for SIVE.

Our proposal for the definition of a new research field starts from a simple layer
structure without claiming to be exhaustive. The graphical representation in Fig. 1.1
is capable of giving an overview and a rough inter-relation of the multidisciplinarity
involved in SIVE. We suggest a hierarchical structure for the various disciplines in
the form of an inverted pyramid representation. SIVE research can be conceptually
organized in three levels:

i **Immersive audio** concerns the computational aspects of the acoustical-space
  properties of technologies. It involves the study of acoustic aspects, psychoacoustic, computational, and algorithmic representation of the auditory information, and the development of enabling audio technologies;
ii **Sonic interaction** refers to human-computer interplay through auditory feedback in 3D environments. It comprises the study of vibroacoustic information
  and its interaction with the user to provide abstract meanings, specific indicators
  of the state for a process or activity in interactive contexts;

iii The **integration** of immersive audio in multimodal VR/AR systems impacts different application domains. This third and final level collects all the studies regarding the integration of virtual environments in different application domains such as rehabilitation, health, psychology, music, to name but a few.

The immersive audio layer is a strongly characterizing element of SIVE. For such a reason, it is placed as the tip of the inverse pyramid, where all SIVE development opportunities originate. In other words, SIVE cannot exist without sound spatialization technologies, and the research built upon them is intrinsically conditioned by the level of technological development (for more arguments on this issue see Sect. 1.3.2).

In particular, spatial audio rendering through headphones involves the computation of binaural room impulse responses (BRIRs) to capture/render sound sources in space (see Fig. 1.2). BRIRs can be separated into two distinct components: the room impulse response (RIR), which defines room acoustic properties, and the head-related impulse response (HRIR) or head-related transfer function (HRTF, i.e., the HRIR in the frequency domain), which acoustically describes the individual contributions of the listener's head, pinna, torso, and shoulders. The former describes the acoustic space and environment, while the latter prepares this information into perceptually relevant spatial acoustic cues for the auditory system, taking advantage of the flexibility of **immersive binaural synthesis through headphones** and state-of-the-art consumer head-mounted displays (HMDs) for VR. The perceptually coherent auralization with lifelike acoustic phenomena, taking into account the effects of near-field acoustics and listener specificity in user and headphones acoustics, is a key technological matter here [11, 21, 68].

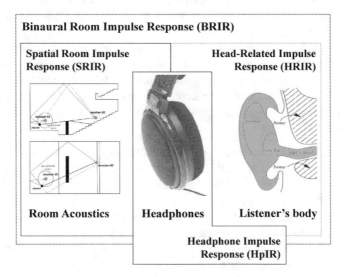

**Fig. 1.2** High-level acoustic components for immersive audio with a focus on spatial room acoustics and headphone reproduction

The visual component of spatial immersion is so evident that it may seem that the sensation of immersion is exclusively dependent on it, but the aural aspect has as much or even more relevance. We can simulate an interactive listening experience within VR using standard components such as headsets, digital signal processors (DSPs), inertial sensors, and handheld controllers. Immersive audio technologies have the potential to revolutionize the way we interact socially within VR environments and applications. Users can navigate immersive content employing head motions and translations in 3D space with 6 degrees of freedom (DoF). When immersive auditory feedback is provided in an ecologically valid interactive multisensory experience, a perceptually plausible scheme for developing sonic interactions is practically convenient [128], yet still efficient in computational power, memory, and latency (refer to Chap. 3 for further details). The trade-off between accuracy and plausibility is complex and finding algorithms that can parameterize sound rendering remains challenging [62]. The creation of an immersive sonic experience requires

- *Action sounds*: sound produced by the listener that changes with movement,
- *Environmental sounds*: sounds produced by objects in the environment, referred to as soundscapes,
- *Sound propagation*: acoustic simulation of the space, i.e., room acoustics,
- *Binaural rendering*: user-specific acoustics that provides for auditory localization.

These are the virtual acoustics and auralization key elements [153] at the basis of auditory feedback design that draws on user attention and enhances the sensation of place and space in virtual reality scenarios [102].

The two upper layers of the SIVE inverse pyramid, i.e., sonic interactions and multimodal experiences, are not clearly distinguishable and we propose the following interpretation: we differentiate the interaction from the experience layer when we intend to extrapolate design rules for the sonic component with a different meaning for the designer, system, users, etc. . In both cases, embodiment and proprioception are essential, naturally supporting multimodality in the VR presence. This leads us to a certain difficulty in generalizations which is well-grounded by our egocentric audio perspective. In our proposal of theoretical framework, the hierarchies initially identified can change dynamically.

Ernst and Bülthoff's theory [41] suggests how our brain combines and merges different sources of sensory information. The authors described two main strategies: sensory combination and integration. The former aims at maximizing the information extraction from each modality in a non-redundant manner. The second aims at finding congruence and reducing variability in the redundant sensory information in search of greater perceptual reliability. Both strategies consider a bottom-up approach to sensory integration. In particular, the concept of *dominance* is associated with perceptual reliability from each specific sensory modality given the specific stimulus. This means that the main research challenge for SIVE is not only to foster research aimed at understanding how humans process information from different sensory channels (psychophysics and neuroscience domains), but especially how multimodal VEs should distribute the information load to obtain the best experience for each individual. Accordingly, we assume that each listener has **personal**

**optimization strategies** to extract meaning from redundant sensory information distributions. The VR technology can improve if and only if it can have a sort of dialogue with the listener to understand such a natural mixture of information.

The design process of multimodal VEs must also constantly take into account the limitations, i.e., the characterization, of the VR technologies with the aim at creating real-time interactions with the listener. According to Pai [108], interaction models can be described as a trade-off between accuracy and responsiveness. Increasing the descriptive power and thus the accuracy of a model for a certain phenomenon leads to processing more information before providing an output in response to a parametric configuration. It comes at the price of higher latency for the system. For **multisensory models** that should synchronize different sensory channels, this is crucial and has to be carefully balanced with many other concurrent goals.

Understanding interactions between humans and their everyday physical world should not only inspire the design of natural multimodal interfaces but should be directly explored into VE models and simulation algorithms. This message is strongly supported by Chap. 10 and our theoretical framework fully integrates this vision by trying to further extend this perspective to non-human agents. The role of the digital simulation and the computer behind it is participation and discovery for the listener. They constitute a complex system whose interactions contribute to the dynamic definition of non-linear narratives and causal relationships that are crucial for immersive experiences. The application contexts of the interactive simulations instruct the trade-off between the accuracy and responsiveness models. Hence, the knowledge of the perceptual-cognitive listener capabilities emerges as active transformations in multimodal digital VR experiences.

## 1.3   Egocentric Audio

A large body of research in computational acoustics focused on the technical challenges of quantitative accuracy characterizing engineering applications, simulations for acoustic design, and treatment in concert halls. Such simulations are very expensive in terms of computational resources and memory, so it is not surprising that the central role of perception in rendering has gradually come into play. The search for lower bounds such as the perceptually authentic audio-visual renderings can be achieved (see Chap. 5 for a more detailed discussion). Continuous knowledge exchange between psychophysical research and interactive algorithms development allows to test new hypotheses and propose responsive VR solutions. It is worthwhile to mention the topic of artificial reverberations and modeling of the reverberation time aiming to provide a sense of presence through the main spatial qualities of a room, e.g., its size [83, 147].

In the context of SIVE, we could review and adapt the three paradigm shifts, or "waves" in HCI mentioned by Harrison [64], which still coexist and are at the center of research agendas for different scientific communities. The first wave considers the optimization of interaction in terms of the human factor in an engineered system.

We could mention as an example the ergonomic, but generic, " one fits all" solutions of dummy-heads and binaural microphones for capturing acoustic scenes [110]. The second wave introduces a connection between man and machine in terms of information exchange, looking for similarities and common ground in decision-making processes, e.g., memory and cognition. The structural inclusion of non-linearities and auditory Just-Noticeable Differences (JNDs) to determine the amount of information to be encoded for gesture sonification is an example of this direction [38]. Finally, the third paradigm shift considers interaction as a situated, embodied, and social experience, characterized by emotions and complex relations encountered in everyday life. We could place here many of the case studies collected in this volume (Parts III and IV). To this regard, the extracted patterns or best practices are often very specific to each study and listeners' groups, e.g., musician vs. non-musician (Chap. 9).

From developments in phenomenological [93] and, more recently, post-phenomenological thinking [74, 150], we will therefore develop the egocentric audio perspective. The key principle is the shift between interaction between defined objects to intra-action within a phenomenon whose main actors are human and non-human agents. Boundaries between actors are fluidly determined, similarly to the Gibsonian ecological theory of perception [54, 55]. Even though this is a shift from an anthropocentric and user-centered view toward a system of enactive relations and associations in the immersive world of sounds, we chose the term egocentric to emphasize the **spatial anchoring** between humans and technology in the self-knowledge constitution.

It would be useful also referring to the concept of *ambiguity* by the philosopher Maurice Merleau-Ponty that says that all experiences are ambiguous, composed of things that do not have defined, identifiable essence, but rather by open or flexible styles or patterns of interactions and developments [93, 123]. Starting from an egocentric spatial perspective of immersive VR, the learning and transformation processes of the listeners occur when their attention is guided toward external virtual sounds, e.g., the out-of-the-head and externalized stimuli. This allows them to achieve meaningful discoveries also for their auditory digital twins. Accordingly, the experience mediated by a non-self, i.e., auditory simulation of VEs, is shaped (i) by the past experience of the listener and the digital twin indistinctly acquired from a physical or cybernetic world in a constructivist sense, (ii) by the physical-acoustic imprinting induced or simulated by the body, head and ears, and (iii) by active and adaptive processes of perceptual re-learning [57, 160] induced by **a symbiosis with technology**. Figure 1.3 schematizes and simplifies this relationship between man-technology-world from which the listener acquires meaning. As pointed out by Vindenes and Wasson [151], experiences are mediated in a situated way from the subjectivity of the listener which constitutes herself in relation to the objectivity of the VE. Having placed the physical and virtual worlds at the same level yields to similar internal representations for the listener and her digital twin, allowing us to promote the transformative role of VR experiences for a human-reality relationship altered after exposure.

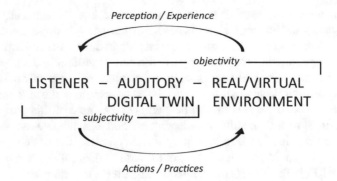

*Perception / Experience*

*objectivity*

LISTENER  –  AUDITORY  –  REAL/VIRTUAL
             DIGITAL TWIN  ENVIRONMENT

*subjectivity*

*Actions / Practices*

**Fig. 1.3** Technological mediation of the auditory digital twin (adapted from Hauser et al. [66])

The core of our framework is an ideal **auditory digital twin**: an essential mediator and existential mirror for an egocentric audio perspective. Technology is the mediator of this intentional relationship co-constituting both the listener and her being in the world. From this post-phenomenological perspective of SIVE, we are interested in understanding how the VE relates to the listener and what is the meaning of the VEs for the listener, at the same time. Our main goal is to characterize the mediating action between the listener and the VE by an auditory digital twin. This guardian can reveal the listener's ongoing reconfiguration through the human-world relationship occurring outside the VR experience.

In the remainder of this chapter, we will motivate the opportunity to refer to this non-human entity other than the self and aspiring to be the mediator for the self. This first philosophical excursus of hermeneutical nature allows us to take a forward-looking vision for the SIVE discipline, framing the current state of the art but also including the rapid technological developments and ethical challenges due to the digital transformation.

### 1.3.1  Spatial Centrality

The three-dimensionality of the action space is one of the founding characteristics of immersive VE. Considering such space of transmission, propagation, and reception of virtually simulated sounds, sonic experiences can assume different meanings and open up to many opportunities.

Immersive audio in VR can be reproduced both through headphones and loud-speaker arrays determining a differentiation between listener- and loudspeaker-centric perspectives. The latter seems to decentralize the listener role in favor of a strong correlation between virtual and physical (playback) space. In particular, sound in VEs is decoded for the specific loudspeaker arrangements in the physical world (for a summary of the playback systems refer to Chap. 5). This setup allows the coexistence of several listeners in the controlled playback space, depending on the so-called sweet spot. However, the VE and the listener-avatar mapping is intrinsically egocentric and multisensory, subordinating a loudspeaker-centric perspective for the simulation of the auditory field to a listener-centric one. Let us try to clarify this idea with a practical example: head movements and the navigation system, e.g., redirected walking [101], determine the spatial reference changes for the real/virtual environment mapping corresponding to the listener's dynamic exploration. The tracking system could trigger certain algorithmic decisions to maintain the place and plausibility illusions of the immersive audio experience.

### 1.3.1.1 First Person Point of View

In this theoretical framework, we focus on the listener's perspective, where sound is generated from the first-person point of view (generally referred to as 1PP). Virtual sounds are shaped by spatial hearing models: auralization takes into account the individual everyday listening experience both in physical-acoustic and non-acoustic terms. Contextual information relate spatial positions between sound events and objects with the avatar virtual body, creating a sense of proximity and meaningful relations for the listener.

It is relevant to stress the connection between the egocentric audio perspective and the research field of egocentric vision that has more than twenty-year history. The latter is a subfield of computer vision that involves the analysis of images and videos captured by wearable cameras, e.g., Narrative Clips[7] and GoPro[8], considering an approximation of the visual field due to a 1PP. From this source of information, spatio-temporal visual features can be extracted to conduct various types of recognition tasks, e.g., of objects or activities [100], and analysis of social interactions [2]. The egocentric audio perspective originates from the same 1PP in which both space and time of events play a fundamental role in the analysis and synthesis of sonic interactions. Furthermore, we stress the idea that all hypotheses and evaluations in both egocentric vision and audition are individually shaped around a human actor. However, our vision does not focus exclusively on the analysis of the listener behaviors but includes **generative aspects** thanks to the technological mediation of the spatial relations between humans and VEs (these aspects will be extensively discussed in Sect. 1.3.2).

Using a simplification adopted in Chap. 2 concerning the work by Stockburger [140] on sounds in video games, we can distinguish two categories for sound effects: (i) those related to the avatar's movements and actions (e.g., footsteps, knocking on a door, clothing noises, etc.) and (ii) the remaining effects produced by the VE. In this simple distinction, it is important to note that all events are echoic, i.e., they produce delays and resonances imprinted by the spatial arrangements of the avatar-VE configurations depending on the acoustical characteristics of the simulated space.

---

[7] http://getnarrative.com/
[8] https://gopro.com/

Moreover, all events should be interpreted by the listener's memory which is shaped by the natural everyday reality.

Finally, it is worthwhile to notice that egocentric 1PP poses novel challenges in the field of cinematic VR narration or more generally of storytelling in VR. Gödde et al. [56] identified immersive audio as an essential element able to capture attention on events/objects outside the field of view. The distinction between the active role of the listener interacting with the narrative or passive role as an observer raises interesting questions about the spatial and temporal positioning of scenic elements. The balance between environment, action, and narration is delicate. Citing Gödde and collaborators, one *"can only follow a narrative sufficiently when temporal and spatial story density are aligned with each other"*. Hence, the spatio-temporal alignment of sound is crucial.

For most researchers interested in sound, from the neurological to the aesthetic-communicative level, it is clear that while the visual object exists primarily in space, the auditory stimulus occurs in time. Therefore, it is not surprising that in order to speak of spatial centrality in audio we need to consider presence, the central attribute for a VR experience. In his support of a representational view of it, Loomis [88] cites two scientists with two opposite opinions: Willian Warren and Pavel Zahorik, the first an expert in visual VR and the latter in acoustic VR. The former supports a rationalist view of representational realism and direct perception [154], while the latter supports the ecological perspective in the **fluidity in perception-action** [159].[9] The second perspective supports the concept of enaction such that it is impossible to separate perception from action in a systematic way. Perception is inherently active and reflexive in the self. Recalling Varela, another leading supporter of this perspective [148], experience does not happen within the listener but is instead enacted by the listener by exploring the environment. Accordingly, we consider an embodied, environmentally situated perceiver where sensory and motor processes are inseparable from the exploratory action in space. At first glance, such a view restricts experiences to only those generated by specific motor skills which are in turn induced by biological, psychological, and cultural context. However, it is generally not true in a digital-twin-driven VE (see Sect. 1.4.3).

### 1.3.1.2   Binaural Hearing

The geometric and material features of the environment are constituent elements of the virtual world that must be simulated in a plausible way for that specific listener. First of all, the listener-environment coupling is unavoidable and must guarantee as good sound localization performances as to maintain immersiveness. It has to especially avoid the inside-the-head spatial collapse, i.e., when the virtual sound stimuli are perceived inside the head, a condition opposite to the natural listening experience of outside-the-head localization for surrounding sound sources, also

---

[9] Atherton and Wang [4] recently developed a similar view point comparison and proposed a set of design principles for VR, born from the contrast between "doing vs, being".

called externalization [131]. Externalization can be considered a necessary but not sufficient condition for the place illusion, being immersed in that virtual acoustic space. For a recent review of the literature on this topic, Best et al. [8] suggest that ambient reverberation and sensorimotor contingencies are key indicators for eliciting a sense of externalization, whereas HRTF personalization and consistent visual information may reinforce the illusion under specific circumstances. However, the intra-action between these factors is so complex that **no univocal priority principles** can be applied. Accordingly, we should explore dynamic relations depending on specific links between evolving states of the listener-VE system during the VR experiences. Moreover, huge individual-based differences in the perception of externalization require in-depth exploration of several individual factors such as monaural and binaural HRTF spectral features, temporal processes of adaptation [27, 65, 146].

Binaural audio and spatial hearing have been well-established research fields for more than 100 years and have received relevant contributions from information and communications technologies (ICT) and in particular from digital signal processing. Progress in digital simulations has made it possible to replicate with increasing accuracy the acoustic transformation by the body of a specific listener with very high spatial resolution up to sub-millimeter grids for the outer ear [113, 114]. This process generates acoustically personalized HRTFs so that the rendering of immersive audio matches the listener's acoustic characterization (*System-to-User adaptation* in Chap. 4). On the opposite side, the VE can train and guide the listener in a process of *User-to-System adaptation* by designing ad-hoc procedures for continuous interaction with the VE to induce a persistent **recalibration of the auditory system** to non-individual HRTFs.[10] These two approaches can be considered two poles between which one can define several mixed solutions. This dualism is brilliantly exposed and analyzed in Chap. 4.

### 1.3.1.3   Quality of the Mediated Experience

Since our theoretical framework aims to go beyond user-centricity, we approach the space issue from different perspectives, both user and technology perspectives, respectively. However, all points of view remain ecologically anchored to the egocentric 1PP of the listener giving rise to a fundamental question: how can we obtain high-quality sonic interactions for a specific listener-technology relation? In principle, many **quality assessment procedures** might be applied to immersive VR systems. However, there is no adequately in-depth knowledge of the technical-psychological-cognitive relationship regarding spatial hearing and multisensory integration processes linked to plausibility and technological mediation.

On the other hand, a good level of standardization has been achieved for the perceptual evaluation of audio systems. For instance, the ITU recommendations focus on the technical properties of the system and signal processing algorithms. Chapter 5 introduces the *Basic Audio Qualities* used for telecommunications and audio codecs,

---

[10] The HRTF selection process can potentially result from a random choice [139].

commonly adopted in the evaluation of spatial audio reproduction systems. On the other hand, the evaluation of the listening experience quality, called *Overall Listening Experience* [125], is also introduced, considering not only system technical performances but also listeners' expectations, personality, and their current state. All these factors influence the listening of specific audio content. A related measure can be the level of audio detail (LOAD) [39] that attempts to manage the available computational power, the variation of spatio-temporal auditory resolution in complex scenes, and the perceptual outcome expected by the listener, in a dynamically adaptive way.

Chapter 2 provides an original discussion on audio "quality scaling" in VR simulations, drawing the following conclusion: there is neither an unambiguous definition nor established models for such issues. It suggests that understanding the listener-simulation-playback relations is an open challenge, extremely relevant to SIVE. In general, the most commonly used approach is the **differential diagnosis**, allowing the qualities of VR systems to emerge from different quantitative and qualitative measurements. Several taxonomies for audio qualities or sound spatialization have given rise to several attribute collections, e.g., semantic analysis of expert surveys and expert focus groups (see Chap. 5 on this). It is worthwhile to mention that a substantial body of research in VR is devoted to explore the connections between VR properties such as authenticity, immersion, sense of presence and neurophysiological measurements, e.g., electroencephalogram, electromyography, electrocardiogram, and behavioral measurements, e.g., reaction time, kinematic analysis.

To summarize, this differentiation tries to capture all those factors that lead to a high level of presence: sensory plausibility, naturalness in the interactions, meaning and relevance of the scene, etc. Moreover, the sense of presence in a VR will remain limited if the experience is irrelevant to the listener. If the listener-environment relation is weak, the mediating action of the immersive technology might result in a break in presence that can hardly be restored after a pause [136]. These cognitive illusions depend, for example, on the level of hearing training, familiarity with a stimulus/sound environment. All these aspects reinforce the term egocentric again, grounding auditory information to a reference system that is naturally processed and interpreted in 1PP. However, SIVE challenges go far beyond two opposing points of view, i.e., user-centered and technology-centered. In this chapter, we offer a first attempt at a systemic interpretation of the phenomenon.

## 1.3.2 Entanglement HCI

Heidegger's phenomenology aims to overcome mind-body dualism by introducing the notion of "Dasein" which requires an embodied mind to be in the world [67]. The concept of embodiment became central to the third wave of HCI, e.g., in relation to mobile and tangible user interfaces [64]. More recently, the bodily element has been incorporated into the theoretical framework of somaesthetics to explain aesthetic experiences of interaction and into **design principles for bodily interac-**

tion [71]. Designers are encouraged to participate with their lived, sentient, subjective, purposive bodies in the process of creating human-computer interactions, either by improving their design skills and sensibilities, or by providing an added value of aesthetic pleasure, lasting satisfaction, and enjoyment to users. These elements are summarized in Chap. 7, which provides a useful distinction of perspectives for interaction design: the first-person, second-person, and third person design perspective. The latter is equivalent to an observer approach to design such as considering the common practices, e.g., interview administration, subjective evaluations, and data analysis acquired from a variety of sensors. The second-person is equivalent to the user-centered and co-design approach between the user's perspective and the designer's attempt to step into the shoes of someone else. On the other hand, soma design principles embrace a first-person perspective, we would argue egocentric, even for designers, who are actively involved with their bodies during each step of the interaction design process of an artifact or simulation. They explicitly become actors themselves with the result of shaping a felt and lived experience for other actors.

In the movement computing work by Loke and Robertson [87], the authors introduced another perspective distinction relevant here. The mover (first-person perspective) and the observer (third-person perspective) are explicitly joined by **the machine perspective**. The role of technology is pivotal for the interactions with digital movement information and, in particular, for the process of attributing meaning based on user input. This perspective requires mapping data from sensing technologies into meaningful representations for the observer and the mover. It is worthwhile to note that machines capture the qualities of movement with considerable losses in terms of spatial, temporal, or range resolution, making the comprehension of such limitations on interaction design essential. We need to explore the various perspectives, not in a mutually exclusive way, but dynamically managing the analysis of the various points of view in every immersive experience.

According to Verbeek [150], human-world relations are enacted through technology. Thus, man and technology constitute themselves as actors in a **fluid reconfiguration**. A practical example in the field of music perception considers a drummer who changes her latency perception the more she plays the musical instrument [86]. The action of playing the drum changes the relationships that she has with the instrument itself, with the self, and with temporal aspects of the world, e.g., reaction times and synchronizations.

The recent proposal of a post-phenomenological framework by Vindenes [151] is based on Verbeek's concept of technological mediation, which identifies several human-technology relationships including immersion in smart environments, ambient intelligence, or persuasive technologies. In particular, for the latter case, VR plays a central role co-participating within a mixed intentionality between humans and technology. Accordingly, Verbeek introduced the idea of composite intentionality for cyborgs [149], a cooperation between human and technological intentionality with the aim to reveal a (virtual) reality that can only be experienced by technologies, by **making accessible technological intentionalities to human intentionality**. We can argue that the world and the technology become one in the immersive simulation that knows the listeners and actively interacts with them. This configuration becomes bidirectional: humans are directed toward technology and technology is directed toward them. Moreover, listeners have the opportunity to access reflective relationships with themselves through VEs. For example, Osimo et al. provided experience of the self through virtual body-swapping in the embodied perspective-taking [106]. We must decentralize humans as the sole source of activity and attribute to the material/technological world an active role in revealing new and unprecedented relational actions.

This approach opens up new opportunities for "reflexive intentionality" of the human beings about themselves through the active relation with simulations [5]. About this, Verbeek [150] classifies the technological influence on humans according to two dimensions: visibility and strength. Some mediations can be hidden but induce strong limitations, while others can be manifest but have a weak impact on humans. There is a deep entanglement between humans and machines to the extent that there is no human experience that is not mediated through some kind of technology that shapes who we are and what we do in the world. Considering immersive VR technologies, we must speculate on what is a **locus of agency**: the understanding of the active contributions of each tool in the listener's actions in VEs. Such an infrastructure must be enactive and re-interpretive of each actor in each circumstance. In other words, there is the opportunity of becoming different actors depending on an active inter-dependence.

At this point, recalling the work of Orlikowski [105] is twofold. First, she gave the name of *entanglement* theories to those heterogeneous theories that have in common the recognition of the active inter-dependence between socio-technological-material configurations with the consequence of promoting studies of man and technology in a unitary way. Secondly, Orlikowski supported her position with an experimental example of social VR, the Sun Microsystems' Project Wonderland developed more than a decade ago and, nowadays, it seems more relevant than ever due to the COVID-19 pandemic. We will analyze a similar case in SIVE, supporting our taxonomy in Sect. 1.4. In this section, we focus on entanglement theories that are foundational for our egocentric perspective.

The entanglement is the deep connection between men and their tools, having relevant repercussions in the field of human-computer interaction. In [45], Frauenberger provided the following interpretative key: we cannot design computers or interactions, we can work on facilitating certain configurations that enact certain phenomena. Both configurations and phenomena are situated and fluid, but not random. They are causally connected within **hybrid networks in which human and non-human actors interact**. However, it must be made clear that these actors do not possess fixed representations of their entities, but they exist only in their situated intra-action. This means that their relations and configurations are dynamically defined by the so-called *agential cuts* that draw the boundaries between entities during phenomena. In this network of associations, each configuration change is equivalent to a newly enacted phenomenon where new agential cuts are redefined or create new actors. Hence, the term agency refers to a performative mechanism of boundary definition and constitution of the self. Together with the post-phenomenological notion of technological mediation, entangled HCI provides a lens able to interpret the increasingly fuzzy boundaries between humans, machines, and their distribution of agency.

The sonic information from intentional active listening is anchored to an egocentric perspective of spatiality that allows the understanding of an acoustic scene transformed by the listener's actions/movements. This process can be mathematically formalized with the active inference approach by Karl Friston and colleagues [46] and their recent enactive interpretation [115]. Their computational framework quantitatively integrates sensation and prediction through probability and generative models optimizing the so-called *free-energy principle*, i.e., an optimization problem of a function of the beliefs and expectations. Following this line of thought both philosophically and mathematically, we argue that immersive audio technologies are capable of contributing to the listener's internal representation in both spatial and semantic terms, eliciting a strong sense of presence in VR [12]. Just as we cannot clearly distinguish between listener and real environment, the more we cannot distinguish between listener and VE.

Therefore, the sonic interaction design in VEs is an intra-action between technology, concepts, visions, designers, and listeners that produce certain configurations and agential cuts. According to the sociological actor-network theory [28, 85], the network of associations characterizes the ways in which materials join together to generate themselves. Prior knowledge also becomes an actor in such a network that shapes, constrains, enables, or promotes certain activities. For example, modeling the listener's acoustic contribution with measurements from a dummy head induces a cut that shapes the use cases and VR experiences. Similarly, agential cuts are performed based on knowledge from other studies. For instance, the auditory feedback supports the plausibility of footstep synthesis or the strategies employed in the definition of time windows for synchronous and embodied sensory integration [122]. Moreover, the physical and design features of the technology also contribute to determining what is feasible: e.g., the differentiation of playback systems for spatial audio results in differentiation in the quality of the experience (see Chap. 11).

In the entanglement within the relational network of listener-reality-simulation, configurations and actors are dynamically defined in a situated and embodied manner. In the process of configuring and reconfiguring actors, designing various aspects, and operating agential cuts **new knowledge is produced** that causally links the enactment of the technological design to the phenomenon created [45]. This means that this knowledge has several forms, one resides in the technological artifact itself, i.e., in the VR simulation. In a more general sense, we could argue that exploring the evolution in the network configurations and actors enables an active search for the egocentrically meaningful experience. In line with this, agency and its responsibilities are not the prerogative of the listener or the technology but reside in their intra-actions.

### 1.3.3 Auditory Digital Twin

From entanglement theories, we inherit a series of open questions that guides our reflection on the SIVE research field. Let's consider the immersive VR simulation as the digital artifact co-defining itself with the listener who experiences it.

How can certain transformative actions and interactions be programmed?

Who/what is the mediator, if any, in the relationship between the physical world and the VE?

How should such a mediator act?

Of particular interest here is Schultze's interpretation of the avatar [126]: a dynamic self-representation for the user, a form of situated presence that is variably implemented. Sometimes the avatar is seen as a separate entity, behaving independently of the user. Sometimes the listener inhabits the avatar, merging with it to such an extent that they feel completely immersed and present in the virtual space. From this variety of instances, definitions of identity (avatar vs. self), agency (technology vs. human), and the world (physical vs. virtual) are fluid and enacted depending on the situation. Moreover, we argue that avatars and listeners know very little about each other. Such consideration strengthens the individual experience that determines one tendency over the other (separation vs. union with an avatar) with difficult predictions and poorly generalizable interpretations. Consequently, the user characterization in human-centered design is somehow included here [76]. However, our view promotes meaningful human-technology relationships in a bidirectional manner: not only personalized user experiences, but **experiences able to shape who we really want to be**.

The communication between the avatar and the listener, the virtual and the physical is challenging. Considering the avatar as part of a VE configuration, we can formulate one of the initial questions: if we can handle mediation, where/who is in charge of that?

Our performative perspective is questioning the a priori and fixed distinctions of certain representationalism between avatar and self, technology agency and listener, physical reality, and virtuality. These boundaries have to be drawn in situated and embodied action, which makes them dynamic and temporary. The exploration of how, when, and why agential cuts define boundaries of identity, agency, and environments is the core of our theoretical framework.

We want to give a digital form to the philosophical question of the *locus of agency*: we envision a meta-environment with technological-digital nature, which is the guardian, careful observer, and lifeblood for the dialogue and participation of each actor. Its name is the **auditory digital twin**. In an egocentric perspective, it takes shape around the listener, i.e., the natural world that is meaningful to her. Why twin? Because this term recalls the idea of the deep connection between two different and distant entities or persons, commonly grounded by similarities, e.g., the DNA or a close friendship. Although the adjective auditory would seem to restrict our idea to the sound component, the framework ecologically extends to the multisensory domain by considering the intrinsic multisensory nature of VR. For these reasons, we will provide an audio-first perspective, sometimes sacrificing the term auditory in favor of a more readable and synthetic expression without loss of information, i.e., (auditory) digital twin.

Technical aspects of an artifact can be used to recreate a virtualized version or digital simulation of the artifact itself in the so-called virtual prototyping process [90]. Similarly, perceptual and cognitive aspects might serve to obtain digital replicas of biological systems, also referred to as a bio-digital twin in the field of personalized medicine [23]. The real person/machine provides the data that gives shape to the virtual one. In the case of humans, the process of **quantified self** [89] supports the modeling of the virtual digital twin, an algorithmic assistant in decision-making. Implications of the digital twin paradigm are already envisioned in [40]. They range from the continuous monitoring of patient health to the management of the agency in a potentially immortal virtual agent.

In the scientific literature, the most common definition of a digital twin is related to a digital replica. However, we would like to provide a significant imprint to our idea of the auditory digital twin as a **psycho-socio-cultural-material objectified actor-network with agential participation**. As depicted in Fig. 1.4, all digitally objectifiable configurations related to listener profile, VE, HW/SW technology, design, ethical impact, etc. are made available to the digital twin so that it can actively participate intra-acting with system states.

To understand the central role of the digital twin in SIVE, we provide some practical examples:

- **Links to setup configurations**—Body movement tracking opens up numerous opportunities for dynamic rendering and customization of the listener's acoustic contribution in harmony between the real and the virtual body, i.e., the avatar's body. Real-time monitoring of the motion sensors is crucial to avoid a negative impact on responsiveness.
- **Links to listener configurations**—Adaptation and accommodation processes are strongly situated in the task. Assuming the unavailability of individual HRTF measurements, the best HRTF model requires a dynamic analysis of each task/context in a mutual learning perspective between the listener and the digital twin.
- **Links to environment configurations**—Persuasion of a VE for a listener behavioral change depends on social and cultural resonances within the listener. The distribution of agency in a music-induced mood has to be analyzed with particular attention. Again, certain immersive gaming experiences or role-playing may be beneficial for some listeners, to be avoided for others.
- **Links to configurations of others**—Other entities, e.g., virtual agents or avatars guided by other listeners, populate VEs. To manage confrontation and sharing activities, the intra-action between a larger number of digital twins must be consciously encouraged.

All these configurations are not independent but are always interconnected with each other. Of particular relevance here, we can consider the externalization of sound sources. The level of externalization depends on customization techniques of the spatial audio rendering, the acoustic information of the virtual room, the sensory

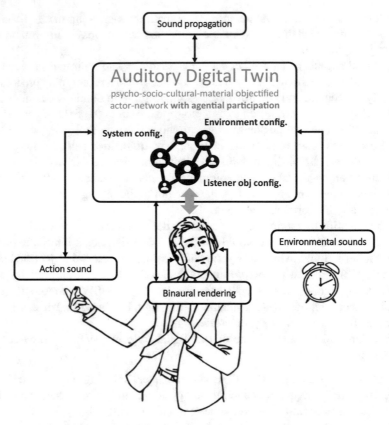

**Fig. 1.4** A schematic representation of the different sound elements needed to create an immersive sonic experience. Colored lines identify the differences compared to the scheme proposed in [128]. In particular, this representation focuses on the central role of the auditory digital twin as a quantifiable *locus of agency* in an active relationship with all actors of a VR experience. The green arrow identifies the participatory relationship between the listener and the digital twin in its performative formation of individual self-knowledge

coherence and synchronicity, and the familiarity with the situation [8]. A coordination action of setup, environment, and listener(s) is needed. The presence in VR experiences will be the result of all these fluid intra-connections.

Suchman posed a highly relevant question in [141]: how can we consider all these configurations in such a way that we can act responsibly and productively with and through them? To answer, we must deal with the participation issues for all involved actors.

The egocentric perspective requires us to start from the listener and her experience. The scientific literature already tells us that memory, comprehension, and human performance benefit considerably from these VEs, especially in guided or supervised tasks involving human or digital agents [29]. Let us focus on the series of actions triggered by an active role of agents. In [31], Collins analyzed the player role in the audio design of video games. The participatory nature of video games potentially leads to the creation of additional or completely new meanings compared to those originally intended by the creators and their storytelling. Hence, there is a change not only in the reception but also in the transmission in the communication of auditory information. The player becomes a co-transmitter of information introducing non-linearities in the experience that propagate throughout the agents' chain of activity, triggering feedback and generating further non-linearities.

In this respect, Frauenberger's entanglement HCI (Sect. 1.3.2) suggests abandoning a user-centered design of the digital artifact in favor of participatory, speculative, and agonistic methods with the ultimate goal of obtaining meaningful relationships and not merely optimized processes relating to the human or the machine pole, or their interaction. It is useful to briefly recall these methods. The agonistic and **adversarial design** employs processes and creates spaces to foster vigorous but polite disputes involving designers' participation in order to constructively identify inspiring elements of friction [36]. On the other hand, the participation in a speculative process through designing **prototypes** aims to provoke a discussion about the technological and cultural future by considering creative, political, and controversial aspects [117].

The more degrees of freedom in the network configurations, the more behaviors can potentially be stimulated. The relational network should not be hardly controlled because its expressive potential can be exploited through its differentiation. In our opinion, the current immersive audio technologies are struggling to emerge, because they often introduce static agential cuts, justified by audio quality assessments conducted in a reductionistic way. On the contrary, the main goal of the digital twin is to favor the participation of all available configurations. Specific configurations and agential cuts emerge in a speculative, agonistic, and provocative manner so that all actors can benefit from different attempts following **knowledge diffraction** [6]. The learning in such fluid and dynamic evolution from one configuration to another is a continuous flow of knowledge that informs the digital twin's activity. In other words, the digital twin continuously proposes new agential cuts to record and analyze the overall results. A relevant example in SIVE is the co-determination of the attentional focus in selecting the meaningful auditory information for a digital twin facing the cocktail-party effect [20]. The digital twin must be able to guide an active participation with the VE considering listener's available knowledge extracted by previously experienced and stored scenarios (and agential cuts).

The continuous intra-action within the digital twin in relation to a shared and immersive experience is of strong practical relevance within the proposed theoretical framework. This issue offers concrete possibilities for radically changing the way we interact socially in the future, by using digital tools equipped with computational intelligence and **artificial intelligence** (AI) algorithms able to manage complex systems [107]. The decision-making phase of intelligent algorithms will improve over time, thanks to a dynamic identification and classification of configurations and links in the actor-network. The knowledge can be continuously extracted as a result of computational intra-actions of the *human-in-the-loop* type where the listener can be seen as an agent directly involved in the learning phase, step-by-step influencing cost functions and all other measures [69]. More in general, the reinforcement learning paradigm focuses on long-term goals, defining a formal framework for the interaction between a learning agent and its environment in terms of states, actions, and rewards, hence no explicit definition of desired behavior might be required [35]. This process can be accomplished during exposure to a continuous stream of multimodal information like in the case of lifelong learning [109], or via interactive annotations and labeling [81].

## 1.4 A Taxonomy for SIVE

An important contribution to the design in VEs comes from practice, e.g., professional reports and testimonials, best practices, or reviews and interpretations of lessons learned in the industry (see Chap. 6 and [76]). Taking into account all these inputs, academic studies, new technologies, and commercial user feedback, different communities draw support for their specific users and domains of interest. Within the SIVE field, there is still much work to be done. There is a lack of recommendations and design analysis on creating interfaces, interactions, and environments that fully exploit egocentric sonic information. To unlock such potential, our suggestion is to start from a multi and interdisciplinary work resulting in these foundational questions: does a development path exist for the SIVE field? Is an *ad-hoc* theoretical approach necessary? Without going into the details of the epistemological crisis that is affecting the HCI field, we would try to avoid discussions on what is called in the HCI community *intermediate knowledge* [72] where positivist and constructivist perspectives are constantly clashing [45]. Examples of intermediate knowledge are all patterns/best practices proposed for certain aspects of the immersive experience.

There exist several classifications attempting to describe virtual spaces for sound and music purposes. The recent formulation in [4] distinguished three aspects:

- Immersive audio—the VE should provide the feeling of being surrounded by a world of sounds.
- Interactive audio—the VE allows the user to influence the virtual world in some meaningful way.
- Virtual audio—the virtual world must be dynamically simulated.

They have already been extensively discussed in the previous sections and many of the existing taxonomies for VR [95, 134, 157] prioritizing the system (or simulation) or the user, not the close relationship with the listener. In this section, we propose an **audio-centered taxonomy** that does not distinguish between user and system, listener and simulation. Our theoretical framework uses an egocentric audio perspective by emphasizing the situated, embodied, enactive dimensions of the listener's experiences with their different actors involved. An emphasis on the entanglement between humans and technology assumes that the listener's internal states are directly inaccessible to a non-intrusive and external technology, i.e., focused on exteroceptive sense [134]. Accordingly, we will motivate the selection of three dimensions able to describe a technological mediation in VR: **immersion**, **coherence**, and **entan-**

**glement**. The qualitative description in this section leaves as a future challenge a quantification of the performative processes introduced here.

Referring to the autobiographical element introduced in the book preface, the first meeting of the two chapter authors at the ACM CHItaly 2011, the biennial conference of the Italian HCI community, has also a scientific meaning for the proposed taxonomy. The paper by Geronazzo et al. [50] was presented more than 10 years ago, as one of the first tasks of the first author's doctoral program. He attempted to adapt the *virtuality continuum* of Milgram and Kishino [95] in the context of spatial audio personalization technologies for VR/AR. His main motivation was to overcome his difficulty in fitting the strong acoustic relationship (i.e., HRTF customization) between listener and technology into a taxonomy created for visual displays in 1994.

That paper proposes a characterization that uses a simplified two-dimensional parameter space defined in terms of the *degree of immersion* (DI) and *coordinate system deviation* (CSD) from the physical world. It is a simplification of Milgram's three-dimension space, summarized in the following:

- Extent of World Knowledge (EWK): knowledge held by the system about virtual and physical worlds.
- Reproduction Fidelity (RF)—virtual object rendering: quality of the stimuli presented by the system, in terms of multimodal congruency with their real counterpart.
- Extent of Presence Metaphor (EPM)—subject sensations: this dimension takes into account the observer's sense of presence.

CSD matches EWK with the distinction that a low CSD means a high EWK: the system knows everything about the material world and can render the synthetic environment in a unified mixed world. From an ecological perspective, the system knows and dynamically fosters the overlap between real and virtual. On the other hand, EPM and RF are not entirely orthogonal and the definition of DI follows this idea: when a listener is surrounded by a real sound, all his/her body interacts with the acoustic waves propagating in the environment, i.e., a technology with high presence can monitor the whole listener's embodiment and actions (high DI).

Recently Skarbez et al. [134] have proposed a revised version of Milgram's virtuality continuum introducing two distinctive elements. First, the consideration of only two instead of three Milgram's dimensions similarly to [50]: Immersion and Extent of World Knowledge. In particular, Immersion is exactly based on the same idea as DI. Second, they introduced a discontinuity in the RF and EPM dimensions considering the absence of any display at the left side of the spectrum: the physical world without mediation is inherently different from the highest level of realism achievable through VR technologies that stimulate exteroceptive senses (i.e., sight, hearing, touch, smell, and taste). The latter consideration propagates to Immersion.

The rough taxonomy of Geronazzo *et. al.* missed the idea of coherence between simulation and human behavior, which is well identified as the third analytical dimension of Skarbez et al. [134]: *coherence*. It takes into account both plausibility and expectation of technological behaviors for the user in cognitive, social, and cultural terms. However, the three proposed dimensions cannot and do not claim to describe such a relationship between the user and the system as emphasized by the authors in their system-centered taxonomy. The work of Skarbez and colleagues is once again anchored to the distinction between user and system which generates several issues in framing the intra-actions of actors/factors in VR/AR sonic experiences.

To support the SIVE theoretical framework, we focus on purely VR only. This means that our discussion will not consider the CSD/EWK dimension assuming that there are no anchors to the physical world. However, since we are emphasizing the influence of human-real-world relationships on experience in VE and vice versa, we have decided not to make the world configurations explicit thus considering them as a whole with the listener. Extensions to mixed reality will be an object of future studies in a reviewed version of our theoretical framework.

Starting from the previously identified dimensions of Immersion [50] and Coherence [134], we suggest **three top-level categories** that need to be addressed through interdisciplinary design work. A schematic representation can be found in Fig. 1.5.

**Immersion:** the digital information related to the listener-digital twin relationship supporting an increasing number of actions in VEs. It measures the technological level and its enactive potential between listener and auditory digital twin.

**Coherence:** the digital information related to the digital-twin-VE relationship that allows the plausible rendering of an increasing number of behaviors in VEs. It measures the effectiveness of sonic interaction design in VEs.

**Entanglement:** represents the overall effectiveness of the actor-network and its agential cuts that are dynamically, individually, and adaptively created. It measures participation in the locus of agency and its consequent phenomenological description.

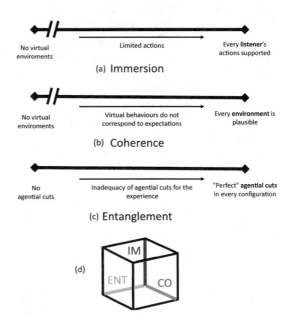

**Fig. 1.5** Three-dimensional taxonomy for SIVE, (a) Immersion, (b) Coherence, (c) Entanglement, and their relations in (d)

The auditory digital twin actively proposes new relations favoring redefinitions in the agential cuts, i.e., the mutual transformative actions between listener and technology.

To support our proposed taxonomy for SIVE, we introduce a case study on a fictitious and purely theoretical artifact along the lines of *Flow* [45]. It allows us to decline the various facets of the framework in a flexible example.

*Spritz!* is an interactive and immersive VR simulation supported by full-body tracking, stereoscopic vision, and headphone auralization. It is designed to address the *cocktail-party effect*. The human selective attention requires different contributions and levels of perception in supporting the ability to segregate signals-also referred to as auditory signal analysis [15, 20]. When confronted with multiple simultaneous stimuli (speech or non-linguistic stimuli), it is necessary to segregate relevant auditory information from concurrent background sounds and to focus the attention on the source of interest. This action is related to the principles of auditory scene analysis that require a stream of auditory information filtered and grouped into many perceptually distinct and coherent auditory objects. In multi-talker situations, auditory object formation and selection together with attentional allocation contribute to defining a model of cocktail-party listening [75, 132]. The design of *Spritz!* aims to give shape to an auditory digital twin able to detect listener intent, i.e., identify the relevance of a sound compared to other overlapping events. It can instantaneously determine the attentional balance within an auditory space. Its main goal is to promote the listener's well-being through manipulations of the sound scene in a participatory way respecting the listener's desires.

## *1.4.1  Immersion*

According to Murray [98], the term **immersion** comes from the physical experience of being immersed in water. In a psychologically immersive experience, one aims at experiencing the feeling of being surrounded by a medium that is a reality other than the physical one, able to capture our attention and all our senses. Therefore, it has an important element of continuity with our framework by identifying a mediating action of VR experiences. According to Slater and Wilbur [137], the term **immersion is tightly linked to the technology**, the mediator, to elicit the sense of presence. Technological systems for immersive VR count several combinations of equipment and techniques, such as HMD, multimodal feedback, high frame rates, and large tracking areas. Such a heterogeneous arsenal is a complex system of functional elements that have an immediate impact on the listener's experience. Initially, technical specifications were reasonably identified as the main constraints for a VR experience. However, other elements were considered with a large-scale diffusion of VR technologies. The design of VEs became critical in those details that ensure a plurality of actions with virtual objects, the surrounding virtual world, and their representations. As discussed in [30], the effects of all these components are highly interconnected with each other. Moreover, the absence or misuse of any of them can produce immediate disruptions in the sense of presence or cybersickness [33], such as low headset quality [16] or unfiltered noise caused by sound sources external to the VR setup [136].

The strong connection between immersion and equipment means that different VR solutions hold an intrinsic level of immersion regardless of the actual applications performed with them [120]. This is evident when considering basic audio quality vs. quality of the listening experience. For instance, considering projected screens offers designers of VEs the opportunity to combine real and virtual elements in the tracked area (Chap. 13 offers an interesting reflection on artistic performances mediated by VR/AR technologies). However, the overall sense of presence experienced by the listener depends on the specific combination of the HW/SW setup. Such setups support a certain type of action within the VE. The **Immersion "I"** dimension takes into account these features as the starting point of an enactive potential for the auditory digital twin. Such a potential intrinsically limits the development and creation of new actions.

Furthermore, the enactive egocentric perspective of Sect. 1.3.1 provides a solid theoretical framework for considering the importance of ecologically valid auditory information in eliciting a sense of presence in a VR-mediated experience. First of all, it should be mentioned that there is a lack of research related to the effects of interactive sound on the sense of body ownership and agency (refer to the discussion in Chap. 2). The vast majority of studies addressing presence from an auditory perspective focus on place illusion and spatial attributes. This should not come as a surprise, since many of these binaural attributes are perceived by applying sensory-motor contingencies and embodied multisensory integrations. A simple example in spatial audio technologies is the importance of head movements data that are acquired by three degree-of-freedom head-trackers, allowing listeners to exploit binaural cues for resolving the so-called *front-back confusion* [22]. However, computational models for binaural cues are usually parameterized by the head radius or circumference, or ears position [52]. This example suggests that synchronization and plausible interactive variations, i.e., occurring in reaction to the digital twin's gestures in coherence with sensorimotor contingencies, can positively influence the sense of agency. In addition, other studies demonstrate how the **sound of action** and an active exploration can support haptic sensations and vice versa in a co-located and simultaneous manner. For instance, Chap. 12 analyzes the impact of sound in an audio-tactile identification of everyday materials from a bouncing ball.

Regarding spatial hearing, there is a huge differentiation in accuracy between more (experienced) and less (naive) reliable listeners [3, 51]. More generally, the distinction between categories of listeners is still challenging and is made based on several factors such as multisensory calibration and integration (see Chap. 12 for audio-haptics), familiarity with immersive/spatial audio technologies, musical background [152], or audio mixing experience (as in Chap. 9), etc. Both acoustic (i.e., acoustic transformations of the body) and non-acoustic (i.e., everything else) factors are highly individual and depend on the relationship between the listener and the real-world which is mediated by technology in a general sense (not only in the digital domain, e.g., games, musical instruments, etc.).

All **objectifiable information regarding the listener** are known configurations. For example, bottom-up approaches for modeling psychophysical phenomena of spatial hearing and multisensory integration fall into this category. Such knowledge has to be integrated into the immersive system, explicitly contributing to the actor-network managed by the digital twin.

Coming back to our *Spritz!* simulation, the level of **I** is expected to be high due to state-of-the-art technological components. The digital twin can recognize and manage several full-body skeletal configurations as well as near-field acoustics algorithms that take into account the acoustic coupling of the main joints such as the head and shoulders. This last aspect is usually largely underestimated in virtual acoustics systems [17]. The customization based on anthropometry allows the digital twin to guide the acoustic rendering of movements considering head tilt and torso shadowing in real-time. Furthermore, binaural and spectral cues might be personalized and weighted according to the listener's level of uncertainty, allowing the digital twin to predict which sound sources are most likely to be segregated based on an egocentric direction-of-arrival perspective.

The contribution of the **I** dimension can be summarized as follow: **I** is the digital information related to the listener-digital twin relationship limited by a specific technological setup. The support of an increasing number of actions in VEs is a consequence of technological improvements (both HW/SW) and/or an increasing objectification of the listener's configurations. Considering the idea of immersive potential of Chap. 11, limitations in enaction determine which changes are significant after technological manipulation. The level of reconfigurability within the digital twin accounts for the constant dialogue with the listener to explore her state and tendency to immersion in every moment of the experience (see also Sect. 1.4.3).

## 1.4.2 Coherence

The VR simulation must be able to make the digital twin freely interact with the VE, eliciting a plausible experience for the listener who is always aware of the mediated nature of the experience. In other words, the interaction design must support functionally and plausible actions, the 'doing' in [43]. This means that possible configurations of the technical setup and the listener (the objectification in the digital-twin, see Sect. 1.4.1) constitute the enactive potential of immersion and must be balanced within the sonic interactions.

In this section, we focus on the *coherence* of the digital-twin/environment relationship. On the other hand, Sect. 1.4.3 provides an interpretation of the dialogue with the *immersion* dimension.

VE simulations can create fictional worlds, exploiting opportunities for both naturalistic and magical interactions [13]. Designers can experiment with defining rules that only apply in the virtual domain, such as scale, perspective, and time. The philosophical discussion of the dualism "Doing vs. Being" in [4] provides interesting insights into our egocentric auditory perspective: simulation can have different levels of interactivity suggesting different action spaces for the digital twin in the virtual worlds.

Interacting with the VE, avatar included, consists of **altering the states of 3D elements** that have been created at different levels of proximity: the virtual body (i.e., avatar), the foreground (i.e., peripersonal object manipulation space), and in the background (i.e., extra-personal virtual world space). Existing researches on 3D interaction focuses on the spatial aspects of the following main categories: selection, manipulation, navigation, and application control (the latter involving menus and other VE configuration widgets). Selection techniques allow users to indicate an object or a group of objects. According to the classification of Bowman et al. [14], one can consider selection techniques based on object indication (occlusion, object touch, pointing, indirect selection), activation method (event, gesture, voice command), and feedback type (text, acoustic, visual, force/tactile). Manipulation techniques allow the digital twin to modify all virtual objects configurations that are made accessible to it: e.g., the spatial transformation of objects, i.e., roto-translation and scaling, surface properties such as material texture and acoustic properties, or 3D shape and structure manipulations. For the variety of interaction metaphors for selection, we refer to a recent review in [92]. Finally, navigation techniques allow digital twins to move within the VE to explore areas and virtual worlds. Typical movements include walking and virtual transportation, including flight experiences. In particular, walking is fundamental to humans, and supporting natural locomotion is not always feasible on a limited tracked space. Accordingly, there are other interaction metaphors such as walk-in-place [42], teleportation, or semi-automatic movements between control points [61]. It is worthwhile to mention the self-motion illusions. In circular vection [116], moving sounds surrounding the listeners facilitate the perception of being in motion when in fact they are not. For spatial design considerations in sonic interactions, Chap. 6 provides a comprehensive analysis and a typology of VR interactive audio systems.

These configurations must be plausible and the digital twin should support a dynamic transition from one to another. This is crucial to avoid irreparable breaks in presence. Therefore, **coherence "C"** describes the degrees of freedom introduced by the sonic interaction design in VEs based on the active dialogue between the digital-twin and the VE, established experience after experience.

In this section, we are particularly interested in the plausibility illusion determined by the overall credibility of a VE concerning subjective expectations. It is not only a coherence between external events not directly caused by listeners but an objective feature of the VE [134]. Its reconfigurability includes an **internal logical coherence and a behavioral consistency** considering prior knowledge. Sound conveys ecological information relevant to the expectation toward VE behaviors compared to the listener's everyday experience: embodied, and situated in a socio-cultural context. The environment configurations (avatars and virtual worlds) intertwine with the known listener configurations held in the digital twin. Once again, the digital twin has a central and active role following an egocentric audio perspective (see Fig. 1.4

for this foundational idea). Dimension **C** advocates a top-down approach to inter-actions, constituted of cognitive and socio-cultural influences based on listener real life.

Moreover, coherence does not presuppose physical realism. It fosters interactions in coherent virtual magic worlds. The dynamic dialogue between VE and digital-twin makes it possible. For example, let's consider a cartoon world where simplified descriptions of sound phenomena exaggerate certain features [118]. It may be plau-sible as long as it conveys relevant ecological information. Audio procedural mod-els are based on simplifications in properties and behavior of a the corresponding real object, i.e., simplified configurations. Such parameterization can be informed by auditory perception and cognition maintaining ecological validity of a fictional sonic world while reinforcing the listener's sense of agency. Digital information regarding the relationship between the digital twin and VE allows the creation of an increasing number of plausible behaviors in VR.

Considering once again the distinction among avatar, peri- and extra-personal spaces, neurophysiological research on body ownership and multisensory integration suggests the existence of a fluid boundary in the **perceived space by subjects** [60]. It is worth noticing that the neuronal activity sensitive to the appearance of stimuli within the personal space is multisensory in nature and involves neurons located in the frontoparietal area. In this area, neuronal activity is related to action preplanning particularly for reacting to potential threats [130] and elicits defensive movements when stimulated [32]; these multimodal neurons combine somatosensory with body position information [58]. Bufacchi and Iannetti [24] suggested that the personal space should be described as a series of action fields that spatially and dynamically define possible responses and create contact-prediction functions with objects. Such fields may vary in location and size, depending on the body interaction within the environment and its actual and predicted location. Space is also modulated in response to external stimuli and internal states of the subject, defining a relationship between listener, environment, and tools [119].

Of particular interest for our framework are modulations due to the **proxemics**. The term was introduced by Hall [63] and concerns implicit social rules of interper-sonal distance among people conveying different social meanings. The cooperation in a socially shared interpersonal space [144] requires to support the transition from individual to collaborative spaces [142]. In Chap. 8, the design of sound intensity (or sound attenuation) as a function of the proximity from a sound source is addressed. Different configurations of personal and public spaces were tested in a shared VE for collaborative music composition. Interestingly, rigid boundaries in the transition between spaces forced listeners to take a **social distance** and isolate with a nega-tive impact on the collaborative aspects of the composition process. Therefore, the separation between public and personal space should be fluid rather than rigid. The VE should be configurable in the social aspects that emerge from the strong inter-connection between configurations made available to the digital twin, increasing the fluidity and better supporting collaboration in shared experiences.

In *Spritz!*, we should identify the VE's abilities in shaping the simulation within the digital twin. First, *Spritz!* has multiple configurations accounting for different strategies of the level of audio details. The radial distance with an egocentric reference can drive the dynamic definition of three partially overlapping levels of detail associated with proximity profiles: avatar, personal and public. The avatar's movement sounds are rendered through procedural approaches with individualized configurations based on listener acoustics; in the personal space, *Spritz!* can manipulate sound behavior with simplified models taking into account security and privacy levels required by the situated and embodied states of the digital twin. Finally, sounds in the public space can be clustered, grouped, or attenuated by implementing plausible statistical behavior, e.g., using audio impostor replacement such as audio samples.

The *Spritz!* environment should facilitate resolutions of the cocktail-party problem in crowded situations. Accordingly, it should be able to apply noise suppression of negligible information in the public space or vice versa to operate audio enhancements supporting attentive focus. This dynamic connection between VE and digital twin should be able to maintain *coherence* in the induced behaviors, supporting the plausibility of actions while bending the space around the listener.

A meaningful manipulation of virtual spaces is crucial and creative. Since SIVE naturally includes researches in music composition, a VE must foster the development of individual or collaborative creative ideas through dynamic control of its configurations within and by the digital twin. In particular, results in Chap. 8 support VE spatial design as the creation of "magical" exploratory opportunities, adding original dynamics to collaborative work in VEs. The digital twin has a pivotal role in such space modulations that allow tracing boundaries performatively and eliciting internal emotional states following the listener/composer's expectations.

## 1.4.3   Entanglement

The listener's susceptibility to immersive VE experiences is usually determined by administering questionnaires [155, 156]. The experimenters' aim is usually to perform a screening test to distinguish who can and will be able to easily immerse in a VR-mediated situation. Furthermore, this separation is assumed to remain constant throughout a short-enough experiment. However, the immersive tendency can change over time due to training, learning, experience, mood changes and personality, etc. (see Chap. 11 for further details). For such reasons, common recommendations for VR experiments suggest conducting single experimental sessions. However, studying the impact of the aforementioned dynamic changes opens to the third and last dimension of our taxonomy: **entanglement**, which is the knowledge extraction from the evolution of an actor-network able to reveal multiple facets of the egocentric experience in time, space, and intra-actions.

The first step requires describing the available configurations. Starting from the idea of immersive tendency, VR simulation would benefit from the **knowledge of the listener's susceptibility** toward configurations of setup and environment to modify or avoid non-significant experiences, e.g., getting a break in illusion. In other words, (quantifiable) listener configurations must be defined, discovered, and actively explored by the digital twin. For example, the way sound samples are engineered is very interesting here. A sliding friction sample, e.g., squeaking, rubbing, etc., requires a large amount of data and randomization techniques to avoid repetition. Sounds should be consistent with the listener's expectations in response to complex and continuous motor actions. For this reason, procedural audio approaches can tightly connect the sound to complex and continuous motor actions.

The **Entanglement** dimension ("**E**") aims to provide a phenomenological characterization of actors' evolution and activities based on their performativity and participation in a locus of agency. We realize the high complexity of such a descriptive and formal process, but we believe that an attempt in capturing the **transformative potential of VR** in mediated experiences is worthwhile to be conducted for the SIVE discipline. Of great importance here is the idea of **monad** by sociologists Tarde and Latour [84, 143]: *"A monad is not a part of a whole, but a point of view on all the entities taken severally and not as a totality"*.One can consider a monad as a relational perspective of each actor, shifting the emphasis from aggregation of the whole to movement between different points of view. The main purpose of any perspective is the structural analysis of the network and its configurations and, at a later stage, to derive knowledge and understanding of its dynamics. The inherently egocentric local perspective of the locus of agency, i.e., digital twin, is again emphasized as opposed to a global view. Egocentric networks built around specific nodes such as the listener configurations can support the exploration of intra-activated dynamics. Configurations and links can be discovered and/or modified during different mediated experiences.

The **collaboration among actors is vital in integrating different points of view**, creating opportunities for meaningful experiences. In shared VEs (Chap. 8), listeners are co-present with other human participants interacting in an interpersonal way. Research interests of computing-supported cooperative work can provide interesting insights into prioritizing collaboration [99]. The choice of collaborative models fostering the design of active VEs for meaningful and creative experiences is of particular relevance to entangled SIVE.

Intentionality and gesture support can be achieved through continuous network reconfiguration. Identifying common goals through inter-actor communication are fundamental requirements to increase the digital-twin enactive potential. We argue that this area of research is absolutely new for SIVE, especially in these collaborative aspects. Many fundamental and critical questions for SIVE are waiting to be answered.

Digital transformation promotes ubiquitous and pervasive interconnected data sets with the opportunity to offer new ways of navigating and extracting knowledge. Dork et al. [37] explored the visualization of relational information spaces, incorporating both the individual and the whole in a monadic perspective. The authors' goal was to exploit the rich semantic connections to design new exploration methods for interconnected elements. There is an increasing interest in more exploratory forms of information retrieval without specific needs/constraints, sustained by the **desire to learn, play and discover** openly [91]. In analogy with these practices, the digital twin should curiously move between nodes, configurations, and connections experimenting and manipulating the actor-network for sense-making. To encourage surprising discoveries and interest within experiences, the digital twin should offer unconventional and appealing views with the agency.

The auditory digital twin actively proposes new relationships and encourages agential cuts under the mutual transformative action between listener and technology. In the monadic perspective of the digital twin, the distinctive qualities of each actor within a VE should emerge in each situated experience. Differentiation among configurations is not an a priori actor property but it is identified by its uniqueness in the network. Each actor imprints its particular identity on an ever-changing relational world. In other words, the digital twin is looking for differences in each actor by considering different monadic perspectives. VR simulations allow us to take the point of view of each element thanks to a shared virtual world knowledge.

In the area of AI agents, i.e., non-human entities capable of interacting with ecological behaviors [109], intelligent algorithms would have the predictive potential on the listener's action program. Their ability in monitoring and predicting listeners' behavioral responses could enable the digital twin to determine listeners' expectations and cognitive and psychological capabilities [25]. Moreover, AI algorithms could propose exploration paths to the listener within VEs. Therefore, the capabilities of safely navigating through temporary, transient, and overlapping configurations are definitely complimentary to their predictive power.

In line with the emerging research area called **immersive analytics,** humans and AI can support each other in decision-making based on the navigation in shared thinking spaces [133]. Meetings between the listener and her digital twin can take place in a virtual meta-environment where configurations and connections of an experience can be a posteriori analyzed, collaboratively. The unique personal supervision of the AI algorithms implemented in the digital twin could reflect the listener's traits and interests. Understanding the listener's preferences and assessing their impact on the predictive performance of AI algorithms can help to propose adaptive and customizable systems with a certain level of memory of past VR-mediated experiences [103].

Finally, how can we measure the overall effectiveness of an actor-network and its agential cuts that the digital twin dynamically, individually, and adaptively creates? This question corresponds to Latour et al.'s challenge to take into account long-term features, indicative of a systemic order that might be learned navigating overlapping perspectives (monads) [84]. Such an emphasis on navigation gives a unique role to **movement/exploration** as a way of experiencing relationships and differences between configurations. Therefore, we suggest that the digital twin should navigate along with different and novel perspectives for sense-making. The dynamic relational quality of each actor's unique position in network space, i.e., agential cuts, reflects the exploration potential shaping and creating meaning for the listener.

We argue that the VR-mediated experience is never solitary, considering both human and non-human actors. Any actor cooperates within a shared VE, e.g., to perform a musical performance (Chap. 13) or a spatialized audio mixing (Chap. 9). Collaboration takes place on a common task, which has a huge impact on the intra-action dynamics. In addition to the exploratory movements, technological transparency introduced in Sect. 1.3 is a key factor influencing "E" measures. In analogy with the sense of presence, **co-presence** [26], i.e., the feeling of sharing a VE with others, has been shown to strongly depend on avatar appearance and its realism, as well as on the cooperation level in task completion [111]. Another aspect worth mentioning here is the **awareness** [7] which is the action understanding of other actors, especially with non-human agents. This latter concept strongly relates to trustworthy AI issues and explainable AI [70].

A further "E" measure in SIVE can be inspired by the River and MacTavish's framework [117]. They proposed to generate low-level prototypes of an artifact from simplified attributes. The more extreme the change in such attributes, the more likely the change will be to provoke and reveal hidden assumptions in the design process. In our taxonomy, we call it generative potential in explorative movements and network changes, and technological transparency.

The final example in our fictitious case study *Spritz!* considers the meaningful prediction of the listener's intentionality and the understanding of any sources of interest, e.g., avatar's gestures or other avatars' action. *Spritz!* should be able to support attentional focus. A virtual ray/cone pointer projected by the avatar through the VE or a virtual cursor/hand mapped to the listener's body movements might facilitate the selection of points of interest. Gesture analysis could provide *Spritz!* relevant information for a semi-automatic focus support. This scenario opens to the experimentation and development of "magic" interactions of virtual superhuman hearing tools such as a dual audio beamformer guided by the avatar's body [52]. *Spritz!* should be free to propose novel ways of interaction and exploration within VEs. This dynamic dialogue can be considered a form of **virtual provotyping** that has to guarantee *coherence* with all available sensorimotor contingencies, having a positive effect on the listener's sense of agency in any proposed behavior.

## 1.5   Conclusion

This chapter aims at emphasizing how the SIVE book was born and developed in a constantly evolving situation in the field of human-computer interaction. We invite the reader to explore all its chapters with this shared and dynamic tension that we, as editors, have tried to formalize in what we have called the egocentric perspective of the auditory digital twin. The co-transformation of man and technology seems to us a central theme that will surely help us to enter the $4^{th}$ HCI wave, consciously.

The proposed taxonomy focuses on action, behavior, and sense-making because we believe it is a meaningful way for authentic auditory experiences in VR. In particular, the last aspect of sense-making turns out to be the most challenging. The idea of diffraction and exploration of differences and discoveries requires novel ways of scientific investigation in SIVE. The most crucial aspect might be the level of personalization that future technologies will require to acquire from the listeners. New paradigms for artificial and immersive interaction between humans and VE will have to be proposed. The attribution of agency to a digital twin is a network effect that will have relevant ethical implications, as well as complexity in its analysis.

How much would the listener trust her digital twin? Its intermediary role, sometimes provocative, in search of differences can elicit strong reactions in the listeners. Will the listener accept and share this perspective? The affective information strongly links sound to meaning [138], creating empathy between listener and her digital twin. This aspect will be carefully considered for its ethical implications.

How can one quantify and classify the various actor networks in the proposed three dimensions? Surely, this is an open challenge of this first proposed theoretical framework for SIVE. Visualizing and representing transitions and agential cuts are relevant issues toward an objective description of any mediation phenomenon. Creating multiple ontologies in "magical" interaction metaphors allows to transcend reality and immerse into unique experiences within VEs. Since VR is not yet able to fully replicate natural reality and may not be able to do so, its current features actually allow listeners to do and be things that are impossible in the real world. This is the very essence of knowledge diffraction: the digital twin should explore such differences that are impossible to test in the physical world, extracting meaning for the listener. Of particular interest here, the ideas of superhuman powers and virtual prototyping [52] reflect human desire to increase her capabilities. They are receiving increasing attention thanks to the post-humanism and human enhancement manifestos [97]. Following this line of thought, Sadeghian et al. [121] proposed to VR designers to explore new forms of interaction without necessarily imitating the physical world. VR's limitations in creating realistic interactions are replaced by a focus on experiences that are impossible to have in the real world, such as superhuman powers of flying, X-ray vision, shape-shifting, super memory, etc. Limitations obviously occurred while differentiating VEs before confusion invades the listener. Indeed, a balance in ecological and familiar stimulation should guide the creation of a "safety net" or "comfort zone" for the listener—the digital twin's exploration of agonistic and provocative knowledge opportunities without drawbacks.

This chapter aims to shape the SIVE research field, **sonic interactions in VEs**, that is now ready to welcome wide-ranging reflections on what might be called

**sonic intra-actions in VEs**.

# References

1. Adavanne, S., Politis, A., Nikunen, J., Virtanen, T.: Sound Event Localization and Detection of Overlapping Sources Using Convolutional Recurrent Neural Networks. IEEE Journal of Selected Topics in Signal Processing **13**, 34-48 (2019).
2. Alletto, S., Serra, G., Calderara, S., Cucchiara, R.: Understanding social relationships in egocentric vision. en. Pattern Recognition **48**, 4082-4096 (2015).
3. Andéol, G., Simpson, B. D.: Editorial: How, and Why, Does Spatial-Hearing Ability Differ among Listeners? What is the Role of Learning and Multisensory Interactions? Frontiers in Neuroscience **10** (2016).
4. Atherton, J., Wang, G.: Doing vs. Being: A philosophy of design for artful VR. Journal of New Music Research **49**, 35-59 (2020).
5. Aydin, C., González Woge, M., Verbeek, P.-P.: Technological Environmentality: Conceptualizing Technology as a Mediating Milieu. en. Philosophy & Technology **32**, 321-338 (2019).

6. Barad, K.: Meeting the Universe Halfway: Quantum Physics and the Entanglement of Matter and Meaning en (Duke University Press, 2007).
7. Benford, S., Bowers, J., Fahlén, L. E., Greenhalgh, C.: Managing mutual awareness in collaborative virtual environments in Proceedings of the conference on Virtual reality software and technology (World Scientific Publishing Co., Inc., USA, 1994), 223-236.
8. Best, V., Baumgartner, R., Lavandier, M., Majdak, P., Kop?o, N.: Sound Externalization: A Review of Recent Research. en. Trends in Hearing **24** (2020).
9. Bharitkar, S., Kyriakakis, C.: Immersive audio signal processing English (Springer, New York, NY, 2006).
10. Blackwell, A.: Interacting with an inferred world: the challenge of machine learning for humane computer interaction. en (2015).
11. Boren, B., Geronazzo, M., Brinkmann, F., Choueiri, E.: Coloration metrics for headphone equalization in Proc. of the 21st Int. Conf. on Auditory Display (ICAD 2015) (Graz, Austria, 2015), 29-34.
12. Bormann, K.: Presence and the Utility of Audio Spatialization. Presence **14**, 278-297 (2005).
13. Bowman, D. et al.: 3D User Interfaces: New Directions and Perspectives. Computer Graphics and Applications, IEEE **28**, 20-36 (2008).
14. Bowman, D. A., Hodges, L. F.: Formalizing the Design, Evaluation, and Application of Interaction Techniques for Immersive Virtual Environments. Journal of Visual Languages & Computing **10**, 37-53 (1999).
15. Bregman, A. S.: Auditory scene analysis: the perceptual organization of sound (MIT Press, Cambridge, Mass., 1990).
16. Breves, P., Dodel, N.: The influence of cybersickness and the media devices' mobility on the persuasive effects of 360° commercials. en. Multimedia Tools and Applications **80**, 27299-27322 (2021).
17. Brinkmann, F., Roden, R., Lindau, A., Weinzierl, S.: Audibility and interpolation of head-above-torso orientation in binaural technology. IEEE Journal of Selected Topics in Signal Processing PP, 1-1 (2015).
18. Brinkmann, F., Lindau, A., Weinzierl, S.: On the authenticity of individual dynamic binaural synthesis. en. The Journal of the Acoustical Society of America **142**, 1784-1795 (2017).
19. Broadbent, D. E.: Perception and Communication en (Scientific Book Guild,1958).
20. Bronkhorst, A. W.: The cocktail-party problem revisited: early processing and selection of multi-talker speech. Attention, Perception & Psychophysics **77**, 1465-1487 (2015).
21. Brungart, D. S.: Near-Field Virtual Audio Displays. Presence **11**, 93-106 (2002).
22. Brungart, D. S. et al.: The interaction between head-tracker latency, source duration, and response time in the localization of virtual sound sources en. In In Proc. International Conference on Auditory Display 2004 (2004), 7.
23. Bruynseels, K., Santoni de Sio, F., van den Hoven, J.: Digital Twins in Health Care: Ethical Implications of an Emerging Engineering Paradigm. Frontiers in Genetics **9**, 31 (2018).
24. Bufacchi, R. J., Iannetti, G. D.: An Action Field Theory of Peripersonal Space. Trends in Cognitive Sciences **22**, 1076-1090 (2018).
25. Cadet, L. B., Chainay, H.: Memory of virtual experiences: Role of immersion, emotion and sense of presence. en. International Journal of Human-Computer Studies **144**, 102506 (2020).
26. Casanueva, J., Blake, E.: en. in Virtual Environments 2000 (eds Hansmann, W., Purgathofer, W., Sillion, F., Mulder, J., van Liere, R.) 85-94 (Springer Vienna, Vienna, 2000).
27. Catic, J., Santurette, S., Buchholz, J. M., Gran, F., Dau, T.: The effect of interaural-level-difference fluctuations on the externalization of sound. The Journal of the Acoustical Society of America **134**, 1232-1241 (2013).
28. in. Advances in Social Theory and Methodology (RLE Social Theory) (eds Cetina, K. K., Cicourel, A. V.) (Routledge, 2014).
29. Understanding learning in virtual worlds en (eds Childs, M., Peachey, A.) (Springer, London, 2013).
30. Cho, D. et al.: The dichotomy of presence elements: the where and what in IEEE Virtual Reality, 2003. Proceedings. (2003), 273-274.

31. Collins, K. in Essays on Sound and Vision (eds Richardson, J., Hawkins, S.) 263-298 (Helsinki University Press, Helsinki, 2007).
32. Cooke, D. F., Taylor, C. S. R., Moore, T., Graziano, M. S. A.: Complex movements evoked by microstimulation of the ventral intraparietal area. Proceedings of theNationalAcademy of Sciences of theUnited States of America **100**, 6163-6168 (2003).
33. Davis, S., Nesbitt, K., Nalivaiko, E.: A Systematic Review of Cybersickness en. in Proceedings of the 2014 Conference on Interactive Entertainment - IE2014 (ACM Press, Newcastle, NSW, Australia, 2014), 1-9.
34. Degli Innocenti, E. et al.: Mobile virtual reality for musical genre learning in primary education. Computers & Education **139**, 102-117 (2019).
35. Den Hengst, F., Grua, E. M., el Hassouni, A., Hoogendoorn, M.: Reinforcement learning for personalization: A systematic literature review. en. Data Science **3**, 107-147 (2020).
36. DiSalvo, C.: Adversarial Design en (eds Friedman, K., Stolterman, E.) (MIT Press, Cambridge, MA, USA, 2012).
37. Dörk, M., Comber, R., Dade-Robertson, M.: Monadic exploration: seeing the whole through its parts in Proceedings of the SIGCHI Conference on Human Factors in Computing Systems (Association for Computing Machinery, New York, NY, USA, 2014), 1535-1544.
38. Dubus, G., Bresin, R.: A Systematic Review of Mapping Strategies for the Sonification of Physical Quantities. PLoS ONE **8**, e82491 (2013).
39. Durr, G., Peixoto, L., Souza, M., Tanoue, R., Reiss, J. D.: Implementation and Evaluation of Dynamic Level ofAudio Detail English. in (Audio Engineering Society, 2015).
40. El Saddik, A.: Digital Twins: The Convergence of Multimedia Technologies. IEEE MultiMedia **25**, 87-92 (2018).
41. Ernst, M. O., Bülthoff, H. H.: Merging the senses into a robust percept. Trends in Cognitive Sciences **8**, 162-169 (2004).
42. Feasel, J., Whitton, M. C., Wendt, J. D.: LLCM-WIP: Low-latency, continuous-motionwalking-in-place in 3D User Interfaces, 2008. 3DUI 2008. IEEE Symposium on (IEEE, 2008), 97-104.
43. Flach, J. M., Holden, J. G.: The Reality of Experience: Gibson's Way. en. Presence: Teleoperators and Virtual Environments **7**, 90-95 (1998).
44. Franinovic, K., Serafin, S.: Sonic Interaction Design en (MIT Press, 2013).
45. Frauenberger, C.: Entanglement HCI The NextWave? ACM Transactions on Computer-Human Interaction **27**, 2:1-2:27 (2019).
46. Friston, K., FitzGerald, T., Rigoli, F., Schwartenbeck, P., Pezzulo, G.: Active Inference: A Process Theory. Neural Computation **29**, 1-49 (2017).
47. Gallagher, S., Zahavi, D.: The Phenomenological Mind 3rd ed. (Routledge, London, 2020).
48. Gaver, W. W.: What in the World Do We Hear?: An Ecological Approach to Auditory Event Perception. Ecological Psychology **5**, 1-29 (1993).
49. Sonic Interactions in Virtual Environments (eds Geronazzo, M., Serafin, S.) (Springer International Publishing, 2022).
50. Geronazzo, M., Spagnol, S., Avanzini, F.: Customized 3D Sound for Innovative Interaction Design in Proc. SMC-HCI Work., CHItaly 2011 Conf. (Alghero, Italy, 2011).
51. Geronazzo, M., Spagnol, S., Avanzini, F.: Do we need individual head-related transfer functions for vertical localization? The case study of a spectral notch distance metric. IEEE/ACM Transactions on Audio, Speech, and Language Processing **26**, 1243-1256 (2018).
52. Geronazzo, M., Tissieres, J. Y., Serafin, S.: A Minimal Personalization of Dynamic Binaural Synthesis with Mixed Structural Modeling and Scattering Delay Networks in Proc. IEEE Int. Conf. on Acoust. Speech Signal Process. (ICASSP 2020) (Barcelona, Spain, 2020), 411-415.
53. Geronazzo, M., Vieira, L. S., Nilsson, N. C., Udesen, J., Serafin, S.: Superhuman Hearing - Virtual Prototyping of Artificial Hearing: a Case Study on Interactions and Acoustic Beamforming. IEEE Transactions on Visualization and Computer Graphics **26**, 1912-1922 (2020).
54. Gibson, E. J., Pick, A. D.: An Ecological Approach to Perceptual Learning and Development en (Oxford University Press, New York, NY, 2000).

55. Gibson, J. J.: The Ecological Approach to Visual Perception: Classic Edition (Psychology Press, New York, 2014).
56. Gödde, M., Gabler, F., Siegmund, D., Braun, A.: Cinematic Narration in VR - Rethinking Film Conventions for 360 Degrees en. in Virtual, Augmented and Mixed Reality: Applications in Health, Cultural Heritage, and Industry (eds Chen, J. Y., Fragomeni, G.) (Springer International Publishing, Cham,2018), 184-201.
57. Goldstone, R. L.: Perceptual Learning. Annual Review of Psychology **49**, 585-612 (1998).
58. Graziano, M. S., Yap, G. S., Gross, C. G.: Coding of visual space by premotor neurons. en. Science **266**, 1054-1057 (1994).
59. Graziano, M. S. A., Taylor, C. S. R., Moore, T.: Complex Movements Evoked by Microstimulation of Precentral Cortex. Neuron **34**, 841-851 (2002).
60. Grivaz, P., Blanke, O., Serino, A.: Common and distinct brain regions processing multisensory bodily signals for peripersonal space and body ownership. NeuroImage **147**, 602-618 (2017).
61. Hachet, M., Decle, F., Knodel, S., Guitton, P.: Navidget for Easy 3D Camera Positioning from 2D Inputs in 2008 IEEE Symposium on 3D User Interfaces (2008), 83-89.
62. Hacihabiboglu, H., De Sena, E., Cvetkovic, Z., Johnston, J., Smith III, J. O.:Perceptual SpatialAudioRecording, Simulation, andRendering: An overview of spatial-audio techniques based on psychoacoustics. IEEE Signal Processing Magazine **34**, 36-54 (2017).
63. Hall, E. T. et al.: Proxemics [and Comments and Replies]. Current Anthropology **9**, 83-108 (1968).
64. Harrison, S., Tatar, D., Sengers, P.: The Three Paradigms of HCI. en, 22 (2007).
65. Hartmann, W. M., Wittenberg, A.: On the externalization of sound images. The Journal of theAcoustical Society of America **99**, 3678-3688 (1996).
66. Hauser, S., Oogjes, D.,Wakkary, R.,Verbeek, P.-P.: AnAnnotated Portfolio on Doing Postphenomenology Through Research Products in Proceedings of the 2018 Designing Interactive Systems Conference (Association for Computing Machinery, New York, NY, USA, 2018), 459-471.
67. Heidegger, M.: Being and Time en (Blackwell, 1967).
68. Hiipakka, M., Kinnari, T., Pulkki, V.: Estimating head-related transfer functions of human subjects from pressure-velocity measurements. The Journal of the Acoustical Society of America **131**, 4051-4061 (2012).
69. Holzinger, A.: Interactive machine learning for health informatics: when do we need the human-in-the-loop? en. Brain Informatics **3**, 119-131 (2016).
70. Holzinger, A.: From Machine Learning to Explainable AI in 2018 World Symposium on Digital Intelligence for Systems and Machines (DISA) (2018), 55-66.
71. Höök, K.: Designing with the Body: Somaesthetic Interaction Design en (MIT Press, 2018).
72. Höök, K., Löwgren, J.: Strong concepts: Intermediate-level knowledge in interaction design research. ACM Transactions on Computer-Human Interaction **19**, 23:1-23:18 (2012).
73. Husserl, E.: Ideas Pertaining to a Pure Phenomenology and to a Phenomenological Philosophy en (Springer Netherlands, 1982).
74. Ihde, D.: Technology and the Lifeworld: From Garden to Earth Inglese (Indiana Univ Pr, Bloomington, 1990).
75. Ihlefeld, A., Shinn-Cunningham, B.: Disentangling the effects of spatial cues on selection and formation of auditory objects. J. Acoust. Soc. Am. **124**, 2224-2235 (2008).
76. Jerald, J.: The VR Book: Human-Centered Design for Virtual Reality (Association for Computing Machinery and Morgan & Claypool, New York, NY, USA, 2016).
77. Kanade, T., Rander, P., Narayanan, P. J.: Virtualized reality: constructing virtual worlds from real scenes. IEEE MultiMedia **4**, 34-47 (1997).
78. Katz, B. F. G.: Boundary Element Method Calculation of Individual Head- Related Transfer Function. I. Rigid Model Calculation. The Journal of Acoustical Society of America **110**, 2440-2448 (2001).
79. Katz, B. F. G.,Weber, A.: An Acoustic Survey of the Cathédrale Notre-Dame de Paris before and after the Fire of 2019. en. Acoustics **2**, 791-802 (2020).

80. Kilteni, K., Groten, R., Slater, M.: The Sense of Embodiment in Virtual Reality. Presence **21**, 373-387 (2012).
81. Kim, B., Pardo, B.: A Human-in-the-Loop System for Sound Event Detection and Annotation. ACMTransactions on Interactive Intelligent Systems **8**, 13:1-13:23 (2018).
82. Laback, B., Majdak, P.: Binaural jitter improves interaural time-difference sensitivity of cochlear implantees at high pulse rates. en. Proceedings of the National Academy of Sciences **105**, 814-817 (2008).
83. Larsson, P., Västfjäll, D., Kleiner, M.: Effects of auditory information consistency and room acoustic cues on presence in virtual environments. en. Acoustical Science and Technology **29**, 191-194 (2008).
84. Latour, B., Jensen, P., Venturini, T., Grauwin, S., Boullier, D.: 'The whole is always smaller than its parts' - a digital test of Gabriel Tardes' monads. en. The British Journal of Sociology **63**, 590-615 (2012).
85. Law, J.: Notes on the theory of the actor-network: Ordering, strategy, and heterogeneity. en. Systems practice **5**, 379-393 (1992).
86. Lester, M., Boley, J.: The effects of latency on live sound monitoring in Proc. 123 Audio Engin. Soc. Convention (New York, 2007).
87. Loke, L., Robertson, T.: Moving and making strange: An embodied approach to movement-based interaction design. ACM Transactions on Computer-Human Interaction **20**, 7:1-7:25 (2013).
88. Loomis, J. M.: Presence in Virtual Reality and Everyday Life: Immersion within a World of Representation. en. Presence: Teleoperators and Virtual Environments **25**, 169-174 (2016).
89. Lupton, D.: The Quantified Self en (John Wiley & Sons, 2016).
90. Virtual Reality & Augmented Reality in Industry en (eds Ma, D., Gausemeier, J., Fan, X., Grafe, M.) (Springer-Verlag, Berlin Heidelberg, 2011).
91. Marchionini, G.: Exploratory search: from finding to understanding. Communications of the ACM **49**, 41-46 (2006).
92. Mendes, D., Caputo, F. M., Giachetti, A., Ferreira, A., Jorge, J.: A Survey on 3D Virtual Object Manipulation: From the Desktop to Immersive Virtual Environments. en. Computer Graphics Forum **38**, 21-45 (2019).
93. Merleau-Ponty, M.: Phenomenology of Perception 1st edition. Inglese (Routledge, Abingdon, Oxon ; New York, 2013).
94. Metzinger, T. K.: Why Is Virtual Reality Interesting for Philosophers? Frontiers in Robotics and AI **5**, 101 (2018).
95. Milgram, P., Kishino, F.: A Taxonomy of Mixed Reality Visual Displays. en. undefined (1994).
96. M?ynarski, W., McDermott, J. H.: Ecological origins of perceptual grouping principles in the auditory system. en. Proceedings of the National Academy of Sciences (2019).
97. Moore, P.: Enhancing Me: The Hope and the Hype of Human Enhancement 1st edition. English (Wiley, Chichester, England ; Hoboken, NJ, 2008).
98. Murray, J. H.: Hamlet on the Holodeck: The Future of Narrative in Cyberspace Updated Edition. en (MIT Press, Cambridge, MA, USA, 2017).
99. Nassiri, N., Powell, N., Moore, D.: Human interactions and personal space in collaborative virtual environments. Virtual Reality **14**, 229-240 (2010).
100. Nguyen, T.-H.-C., Nebel, J.-C., Florez-Revuelta, F.: Recognition of Activities of Daily Living with Egocentric Vision: A Review. en. Sensors **16**, 72 (2016).
101. Nilsson,N. C. et al.: 15Years of Research on RedirectedWalking in Immersive Virtual Environments. IEEE Computer Graphics and Applications **38**, 44-56 (2018).
102. Nordahl, R., Nilsson, N. C.: The Sound of Being There: Presence and Interactive Audio in Immersive Virtual Reality. en. The Oxford Handbook of Interactive Audio (2014).
103. Ntoutsi, E. et al.: Bias in data-driven artificial intelligence systems-An introductory survey. en. WIREs Data Mining and Knowledge Discovery **10**, e1356 (2020).
104. Nyberg, D.: Computers, Customer Service Operatives and Cyborgs: Intraactions in Call Centres. en. Organization Studies **30**, 1181-1199 (2009).

105. Orlikowski, W. J.: The sociomateriality of organisational life: considering technology in management research. Cambridge Journal of Economics **34**, 125-141 (2010).
106. Osimo, S. A., Pizarro, R., Spanlang, B., Slater, M.: Conversations between self and self as Sigmund Freud-A virtual body ownership paradigm for self counselling. en. Scientific Reports **5**, 13899 (2015).
107. Computational Interaction (eds Oulasvirta, A., Kristensson, P. O., Bi, X., Howes, A.) (Oxford University Press, Oxford, New York, 2018).
108. Pai, D. K.: Multisensory Interaction: Real and Virtual en. in Robotics Research. The Eleventh International Symposium (eds Dario, P., Chatila, R.) (Springer, Berlin, Heidelberg, 2005), 489-498.
109. Parisi, G. I., Kemker, R., Part, J. L., Kanan, C., Wermter, S.: Continual lifelong learning with neural networks: A review. en. Neural Networks **113**, 54-71 (2019).
110. Paul, S.: Binaural Recording Technology: A Historical Review and Possible Future Developments. Acta Acustica united with Acustica **95**, 767-788 (2009).
111. Pinho, M. S., Bowman, D. A., Freitas, C. M.: Cooperative object manipulation in immersive virtual environments: framework and techniques in Proceedings of the ACM symposium on Virtual reality software and technology (Association for Computing Machinery, New York, NY, USA, 2002), 171-178.
112. Polotti, P., Rocchesso, D., Editors, D. R.: Sound to Sense , Sense to Sound A State of the Art in Sound and Music Computing (eds Polotti, P., Rocchesso, D.) (Logos Verlag Berlin, 2008).
113. Prepeliță, S. T., Gómez Bolaños, J., Geronazzo, M., Mehra, R., Savioja, L.: Pinna-related transfer functions and lossless wave equation using finitedifference methods: Verification and asymptotic solution. The Journal of the Acoustical Society of America **146**, 3629-3645 (2019).
114. Prepelit,?, S. T., Gómez Bolaños, J., Geronazzo, M., Mehra, R., Savioja, L.: Pinna-related transfer functions and lossless wave equation using finitedifference methods:Validation with measurements. The Journal of theAcoustical Society of America **147**, 3631-3645 (2020).
115. Ramstead, M. J., Kirchhoff, M. D., Friston, K. J.: A tale of two densities: active inference is enactive inference. en. Adaptive Behavior **28**, 225-239 (2020).
116. Riecke, B. E., Väljamäe, A., Schulte-Pelkum, J.: Moving Sounds Enhance the Visually-induced Self-motion Illusion (Circular Vection) in Virtual Reality. ACM Trans. Appl. Percept. **6**, 7:1-7:27 (2009).
117. River, J., MacTavish, T.: Research through provocation: a structured prototyping tool using interaction attributes of time, space and information. The Design Journal **20**, S3996-S4008 (2017).
118. Rocchesso, D., Bresin, R., Fernstrom, M.: Sounding objects. IEEE MultiMedia **10**, 42-52 (2003).
119. Ronga, I. et al.: Seeming confines: Electrophysiological evidence of peripersonal space remapping following tool-use in humans. en. Cortex (2021).
120. Rose, T., Nam, C. S., Chen, K. B.: Immersion of virtual reality for rehabilitation - Review. en. Applied Ergonomics **69**, 153-161 (2018).
121. Sadeghian, S., Hassenzahl, M.: From Limitations to Superpowers: A Design Approach to Better Focus on the Possibilities of Virtual Reality to Augment Human Capabilities in Designing Interactive Systems Conference 2021 (Association for Computing Machinery, New York, NY, USA, 2021), 180-189.
122. Sankaran, N., Hillis, J., Zannoli, M., Mehra, R.: Perceptual thresholds of spatial audio update latency in virtual auditory and audiovisual environments. The Journal of the Acoustical Society of America **140**, 3008-3008 (2016).
123. Sapontzis, S. F.: A Note on Merleau-Ponty's "Ambiguity". Philosophy and Phenomenological Research **38**, 538-543 (1978).
124. Sauzéon, H. et al.: The use of virtual reality for episodic memory assessment: effects of active navigation. eng. Experimental Psychology **59**, 99-108 (2011).
125. Schoeffler, M., Herre, J.: About the different types of listeners for rating the overall listening experience in In Proc. of ICMC|SMC|2014 (Athens, 2014), 886-892.

126. Schultze, U.: The Avatar as Sociomaterial Entanglement: A Performative Perspective on Identity, Agency and World-Making in Virtual Worlds. ICIS 2011 Proceedings (2011).
127. Serafin, S., Erkut, C.,Kojs, J., Nilsson,N. C.,Nordahl, R.: VirtualReality Musical Instruments: State of the Art, Design Principles, and Future Directions. Computer Music Journal **40**, 22-40 (2016).
128. Serafin, S., Geronazzo, M., Nilsson, N. C., Erkut, C., Nordahl, R.: Sonic interactions in virtual reality: state of the art, current challenges and future directions. IEEE Computer Graphics and Applications **38**, 31-43 (2018).
129. Serafin, S. et al.: Reflections from five years of Sonic Interactions in Virtual Environments workshops. Journal of New Music Research **49**, 24-34 (2020).
130. Serino, A.: Peripersonal space (PPS) as a multisensory interface between the individual and the environment, defining the space of the self. Neuroscience & Biobehavioral Reviews **99**, 138-159 (2019).
131. Shilling, R. D., Shinn-Cunningham, B. in Handbook of virtual environments: Design, implementation, and applications 65-92 (Lawrence Erlbaum Associates Publishers, Mahwah, NJ, US, 2002).
132. Shinn-Cunningham, B. G., Best, V.: Selective Attention in Normal and Impaired Hearing. Trends in Amplification **12**, 283-299 (2008).
133. Skarbez, R., Polys, N. F., Ogle, J. T., North, C., Bowman, D. A.: Immersive Analytics: Theory and Research Agenda. English. Frontiers in Robotics and AI **6** (2019).
134. Skarbez, R., Smith, M., Whitton, M. C.: Revisiting Milgram and Kishino's Reality-Virtuality Continuum. Frontiers in Virtual Reality **2**, 27 (2021).
135. Slater, M.: Place illusion and plausibility can lead to realistic behaviour in immersive virtual environments. Philosophical Transactions of the Royal Society B: Biological Sciences **364**, 3549-3557 (2009).
136. Slater, M., Brogni, A., Steed, A.: Physiological Responses to Breaks in Presence: A Pilot Study. en. Presence 2003: The 6th annual international workshop on presence **157**, 4 (2003).
137. Slater, M., Wilbur, S.: A Framework for Immersive Virtual Environments (FIVE): Speculations on the Role of Presence in Virtual Environments. en. Presence: Teleoperators and Virtual Environments **6**, 603-616 (1997).
138. Stevenson, R. A., James, T. W.: Affective auditory stimuli: Characterization of the International Affective Digitized Sounds (IADS) by discrete emotional categories. Behavior Research Methods **40**, 315-321 (2008).
139. Stitt, P., Picinali, L., Katz, B. F. G.: Auditory Accommodation to Poorly Matched Non-Individual Spectral Localization Cues Through Active Learning. En. Scientific Reports **9**, 1063 (2019).
140. Stockburger, A.: The game environment from an auditory perspective in Proc. Level Up: Digital Games Research Conference (eds Copier, M., Raessens, J.) (Utrecht, 2003).
141. Suchman, L.: Human/Machine Reconsidered. Cognitive Studies: Bulletin of the Japanese Cognitive Science Society **5**, 1_5-1_13 (1998).
142. Sugimoto, M., Hosoi, K., Hashizume, H.: Caretta: a system for supporting face-to-face collaboration by integrating personal and shared spaces in Proceedings of the SIGCHI Conference on Human Factors in Computing Systems (Association for Computing Machinery, New York, NY, USA, 2004), 41-48.
143. Tarde, G.: Monadology and Sociology Illustrated edition. English. Trans. By Lorenc, T. (re.press, 2012).
144. Teneggi, C., Canzoneri, E., di Pellegrino, G., Serino, A.: Social Modulation of Peripersonal Space Boundaries. Current Biology **23**, 406-411 (2013).
145. Tsingos, N., Gallo, E., Drettakis, G.: Perceptual audio rendering of complex virtual environments. ACM Transactions on Graphics **23**, 249-258 (2004).
146. Udesen, J., Piechowiak, T., Gran, F.: The Effect of Vision on Psychoacoustic Testing with Headphone-Based Virtual Sound. Journal of the Audio Engineering Society **63**, 552-561 (2015).

147. Välimäki, V., Parker, J. D., Savioja, L., Smith, J. O., Abel, J. S.: Fifty Years of Artificial Reverberation. IEEE Transactions on Audio, Speech, and Language Processing **20**, 1421-1448 (2012).
148. Varela, F., Thompson, E., Rosch, E.: The Embodied Mind (MIT Press, Cambridge, MA, 1991).
149. Verbeek, P.-P.: Cyborg intentionality: Rethinking the phenomenology of human-technology relations. Phenomenology and the Cognitive Sciences **7**, 387-395 (2008).
150. Verbeek, P.-P.: Beyond interaction: a short introduction to mediation theory. Interactions **22**, 26-31 (2015).
151. Vindenes, J., Wasson, B.: A Postphenomenological Framework for Studying User Experience of Immersive Virtual Reality. Frontiers in Virtual Reality **2**, 40 (2021).
152. Von Berg, M., Steffens, J., Weinzierl, S., Müllensiefen, D.: Assessing room acoustic listening expertise. The Journal of the Acoustical Society of America **150**, 2539-2548 (2021).
153. Vorländer, M.: Virtual Acoustics. Archives of Acoustics **39** (2015).
154. Warren, W. H.: Direct Perception: The View from Here. Philosophical Topics **33**, 335-361 (2005).
155. Weibel, D., Wissmath, B., Mast, F.W.: Immersion in mediated environments: the role of personality traits. eng. Cyberpsychology, Behavior and Social Networking **13**, 251-256 (2010).
156. Witmer, B. G., Singer, M. J.: Measuring Presence in Virtual Environments: A Presence Questionnaire. Presence: Teleoperators and Virtual Environments **7**, 225-240 (1998).
157. Xiangyu Wang, P. S. D.: A user-centered taxonomy for specifying mixed reality systems for aec industry. ITcon Vol. **16**, 493-508 (2011).
158. Zacharov, N.: Sensory Evaluation of Sound en (CRC Press, 2019).
159. Zahorik, P., Jenison, R. L.: Presence as Being-in-the-World. Presence: Teleoperators and Virtual Environments **7**, 78-89 (1998).
160. Zonooz, B., Opstal, A. J.V.: Differential Adaptation in Azimuth and Elevation to Acute Monaural Spatial Hearing after Training with Visual Feedback. en. eNeuro **6** (2019).

# Part II
# Interactive and Immersive Audio

# Chapter 2
# Procedural Modeling of Interactive Sound Sources in Virtual Reality

Federico Avanzini

**Abstract** This chapter addresses the first building block of sonic interactions in virtual environments, i.e., the modeling and synthesis of sound sources. Our main focus is on procedural approaches, which strive to gain recognition in commercial applications and in the overall sound design workflow, firmly grounded in the use of samples and event-based logics. Special emphasis is placed on physics-based sound synthesis methods and their potential for improved interactivity. The chapter starts with a discussion of the categories, functions, and affordances of sounds that we listen to and interact with in real and virtual environments. We then address perceptual and cognitive aspects, with the aim of emphasizing the relevance of sound source modeling with respect to the senses of presence and embodiment of a user in a virtual environment. Next, procedural approaches are presented and compared to sample-based approaches, in terms of models, methods, and computational costs. Finally, we analyze the state of the art in current uses of these approaches for Virtual Reality applications.

## 2.1 Introduction

Takala and Hahn [86] were possibly the first scholars who proposed a sound rendering pipeline, in analogy with the image rendering pipeline, aimed at producing an overall "soundtrack" starting from a description of the objects in an audio-visual scene. Their pipeline included sound modeling and sound rendering stages, running in parallel with the image rendering pipeline. Figure 2.1 proposes an updated picture, which considers several aspects investigated by researchers throughout the last three decades and may represent a general pipeline for sound simulation in Virtual Reality (hereinafter, VR).

Much of recent and current research is concerned with aspects related to the "Propagation" and "Rendering" blocks represented in this figure, as well as the

---

F. Avanzini (✉)
Laboratory of Music Informatics, Department of Computer Science, University of Milano, Via G. Celoria 18, IT-20135 Milano, Italy
e-mail: federico.avanzini@di.unimi.it

© The Author(s) 2023
M. Geronazzo and S. Serafin (eds.), *Sonic Interactions in Virtual Environments*, Human—Computer Interaction Series, https://doi.org/10.1007/978-3-031-04021-4_2

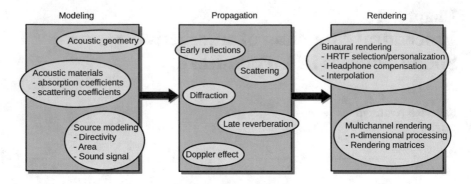

**Fig. 2.1** A general pipeline for sound simulation in Virtual Reality (figure based on [51])

geometrical and material properties of acoustic enclosures in the "Modeling" block. This chapter focuses instead on the remaining balloon of the "Modeling" block, the modeling of *sound sources*.

One obvious motivation for looking into sound source modeling is that all sounds occurring in a virtual (and in a real) environment originate from some sources, before propagating into the environment and finally reaching the listener. Secondly, many of the sonic interactions occurring in a virtual environments are interactions between the subject's avatar and sound sources. Here, our definition of *interactive* is analogous to the one given by Collins [20] for video-game audio: whereas adaptive audio generically refers to audio that reacts appropriately to events and changes occurring in the simulation, interactive audio refers to sound events occurring directly in reaction to avatar's gestures (ranging from pressing a button to walking or hitting objects in the virtual scene).

The current dominant paradigm in VR audio, largely based on sound samples[1] triggered by specific events generated by the avatar or the simulation, is minimally adaptive and interactive. This is the main motivation for looking into *procedural* approaches to sound generation.

## 2.2   What to Model

The first question that should be asked is as follows: what are the sound sources that need to be modeled in a virtual environment, and how can these be organized into a coherent and comprehensive taxonomy? Such a taxonomy would provide a useful tool to analyze in a systematic way the state of the art of the research in this field and possibly to spot research directions that are still under-explored.

---

[1] For the sake of clarity, in this chapter, we use the term "sample" in its commonly accepted meaning of pre-recorded/pre-processed sound excerpt, rather than that of a single value of a digital signal.

## 2.2.1   Diegetic Sounds

One first possible and often used distinction can be mutated from narrative theory. The term *diegesis* has been used in film theory to refer to the fictional world of the film story, and correspondingly the adjective *diegetic* refers to elements that are part of the depicted fictional world. By contrast, non-diegetic elements are those which should be considered non-existent in the fictional world.

As far as sound in particular is concerned, three main categories are traditionally used in films: speech and dialogue, sound effects, and music [80]. The first two categories comprise diegetic sounds, while music is a non-diegetic element having mostly an affective and emotional role, a distinction that may be related to the motto "Sound effects make it real, music makes you feel" [49].

Several taxonomies for sounds in video-games have been proposed and are typically based on similar categories [42]. These may be employed in the context of VR as well, with the additional caveat that VR applications only partly overlap with video-games. In particular, VR, and immersive VR specifically, may be defined as "a medium in which people respond with their whole bodies, treating what they perceive as real" [77]. In light of this definition, in this chapter, we focus on diegetic sounds, those that "make it real": in other words, those that contribute most to the overall sense of the presence of a user within a virtual environment, which we will discuss in Sect. 2.3.

An interesting example of a taxonomy for sound in games is provided by Stockburger [84], who considers five different types of sound objects. Non-diegetic elements include (i) music, but also (ii) interface sounds, which may sometimes be included into the diegetic part of the game environment; proper diegetic elements instead comprise the three categories of (iii) speech and dialogue, (iv) ambience (or "zone" sounds in Stockburger's definition), and (v) effects.

Speech and dialogue are very relevant components of a virtual environment; however, our focus in this chapter is on non-verbal sound. The distinction between ambience and effect sounds is mainly a perspectival one: the former are background sounds, connected to locations or zones (understood both as different spatial locations in an environment and different levels in a game) and having distinct auditory qualities; the latter are instead foreground sounds other than speech, that are cognitively linked to objects or events, and are therefore perceived as being produced by such objects and events. Sound-producing objects may be moving or static elements, may be directly interactable by the avatar or just synchronized to the visual simulation, or may be even outside the visual field of view.

Stockburger [84] proceeds in distinguishing effect subcategories, depending on the elements of the environment they are linked to. His classification is heavily tailored to games, but serves as an inspiration to further inspect and subdivide effect sounds. For the purpose of the present discussion, we only make a distinction between two subcategories: (i) effects linked to the avatar, and (ii) all remaining effects in the environment. Effects linked to the avatar are related to sounds produced by the avatar's movement or object manipulation: footsteps, swishing of an object cutting

**Fig. 2.2** Categories and
interactivity of diegetic
sounds in a virtual
environment

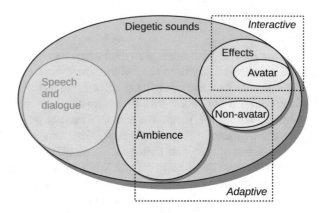

through the air, knocking on a wall, clothes, etc. They can also include sounds
produced by the avatar's own body, such as breathing or scratching. The remaining
effects in the environment may include non-verbal human sounds, sounds produced
by human activities, machine sounds, and so on. A visual summary is provided in
Fig. 2.2. The categories and subcategories identified here can be usefully mapped
into interactive and adaptive sound sources.

### 2.2.2  Everyday Sounds

An orthogonal approach with respect to the previous one amounts to characterizing
sound sources in terms of the physical mechanisms and events that are associated to
those sources.

Typical lists of audio assets for games or VR include, at the second level of classification (after the branch between ambience and sound effects), such categories as
footsteps, doors, wind and weather, and cars and engines, with varying degrees of
detail. These categories in fact refer to objects and events that are physically responsible for the corresponding sounds; however, such classifications follow common
practices rather than a standardized taxonomy. A more systematic categorization can
be found in the classic works by Gaver [33, 34], who proposed an "ecological" categorization of everyday sounds (the ecological approach to auditory perception will
be discussed in more detail in Sect. 2.3.2). Gaver derived a tentative map of everyday
sounds, which is shown in Fig. 2.3 and discussed in the remainder of this section.

At the highest level, Gaver's taxonomy considers three broad classes of sounds:
those involving vibrating solids, liquids, and aerodynamics in sound generation,
respectively. Sounds generated by solid objects have patterns of vibrations structured
by a number of physical attributes: those of the *interaction* that has produced the
vibration, those of the *material* of the vibrating objects, and those of the *geometry* and
configuration of the objects. Sounds involving liquids (e.g., dripping and splashing)
also depend on an initial deformation that is counter-acted by restoring forces in

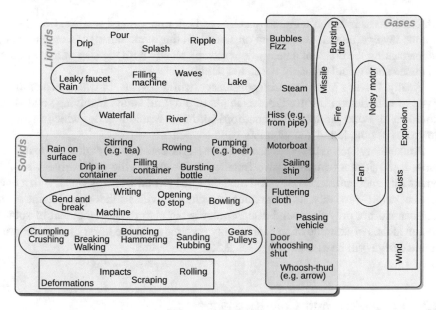

**Fig. 2.3** A taxonomy of everyday sounds that may be present in a virtual environment. Within each class (solids, liquids, and gases), rectangles, rounded rectangles, and ellipses represent basic, patterned, and compound sounds, respectively. Intersections between classes represent hybrid sounds. Figure based on the taxonomy of everyday sounds by Gaver [34, Fig. 7]

the material, but no audible sound is produced by the vibrations of the liquid and instead the resulting sounds are created by the resonant cavities (bubbles) that form and oscillate in the liquid. Aerodynamic sounds are caused by the direct modification of atmospheric pressure differences from some source, such as those created by an exploding balloon or by the noise of a fan, or even events in which such changes in pressure transmit energy to objects and set them into vibration (e.g., when wind passes through a wire).

At the next level, sounds are classified along layers of complexity, defined as follows. "Basic" sound-producing events are identified for solids, liquids, and gases: sounds made by vibrating solids may be caused by impacts, scraping, or other interactions; liquid sounds may be caused by discrete drips, or by more continuous splashing, rippling, or pouring events; and aerodynamic sounds may be made by discrete, sudden changes of pressure (explosions), or by more continuous introductions of pressure variations (gusts and wind). "Patterned" sounds are situated at a higher level of complexity, as they are produced through temporal patterning of basic events. As an example, walking, breaking, bouncing, and so on are all complex events involving patterns of simpler impacts. Similarly, crumpling or crushing are examples of patterned deformation sounds. "Compound" sounds occupy the third level of complexity and involve more than one type of basic and patterned events. An example may be provided by the sound of a door slam, which involves the squeak of scraping hinges and the impact of the door on its frame, or a complex activity such as writing, which involves irregular temporal patterns of both impacts and scrapes. Compound sounds involve mutual constraints on their building components: as an example, concatenating the creak of a heavy door closing slowly with the slap of a light door slammed shut would arguably not sound natural.

Finally, Gaver's taxonomy also considers "hybrid" events, in which two or three types of material are involved. An example of a hybrid sound involving solids and liquids is the one produced by raindrops hitting a window glass, which involves attributes of both liquid and vibrating solid sounds.

A taxonomy such as the one discussed here has at least two very attractive features. First, it provides a comprehensive framework for classifying any everyday sound potentially encountered in our world (and thus in a virtual world as well), with a fine level of detail. Secondly, its hierarchical structure provides a theoretical framework that can aid not only the sound design process but also the development of sound design tools. An example of an ecologically inspired software library for procedural sound design will be discussed in Sect. 2.5.3.

## 2.3 Perceptual and Cognitive Aspects

In this section, we critically review and discuss some relevant aspects related to the perception and cognition of sonic interactions and provide links between these aspects and central concepts of VR, such as the plausibility illusion, the place illusion, the sense of embodiment, and the sense of agency. Nordahl and Nillson [57] also consider how sound production and perception relate to plausibility illusion, place illusion, and the sense of body ownership, although from a somewhat different angle.

Our main claim is that interactive sound sources in a virtual environment contribute in particular to the plausibility illusion, the sense of agency, and the sense of body ownership. In addition, our analysis of perceptual and cognitive aspects provides requirements and guidelines for the development and the implementation of sound models.

### 2.3.1 Latency, Causality, and Multisensory Integration

In any interactive system, latency and its associated jitter have a major perceptual impact. High latency or jitter may impair the user's performance or, at least, provide a frustrating and tiring experience. Perceptually acceptable limits for latency and jitter in an interactive system should therefore be determined. However, such limits depend on several factors which are not easily disentangled.

Characterizing latency and jitter in the sound rendering pipeline can be restated as a problem of perceived synchronization between pairs of events [46], which in turn may be divided into three categories: (i) an external and an internal temporal pattern (such as those occurring in a collaborative activity, e.g., music playing, between two persons in a virtual environment); (ii) pairs of external events (which may or may not pertain to the same sensory modality, such as pairs of sounds or a visual flash and a sound); (iii) actions of the user and their effects (e.g., the pressing of a button and the corresponding feedback sound).

The latter case in particular is tightly connected to the definition of interactive sound adopted in this chapter. It is inherently a problem of multimodal synchronization, as it involves a form of extrinsic (auditory) feedback and a form of intrinsic (tactile, proprioceptive, and kinesthetic) feedback generated by the user's action [53]. The complex interaction occurring between these modalities influences their perceived synchronization (and thus the acceptable latency). High latencies can deteriorate the quality of the interaction, impair the performance on a given task, and even disrupt the perceived link of causality between the user's action and the resulting sonic outcome.

The task at hand also influences the acceptable latency. As an example, it has been traditionally accepted that music performance is a task requiring extremely low ($\leq$ 10 ms) latencies between the player's actions and the response of a digital musical instrument [99]. Similarly, it has been shown that even small amounts of jitter can be detrimental to the perceived quality of the interaction [41]. In this respect, music provides a good "worst case" and a lower bound for latency in other, non-musical tasks, where various studies suggest that higher latencies may be acceptable or even unperceivable [43, 93].

The type of interaction must be considered as well. Impulsive interactions (either musical, such as playing a drum, or non-musical, such as knocking on a door) are likely to require lower latencies than continuous ones (bowing a violin string, or accompanying a closing door). As an example, it has been shown that the continuous interaction involved in playing a theremin allows for relatively high (> 30 ms) latencies, despite this being a musical task [54]. Finally, cognitive aspects also play a role: humans create expectations for the latency between their actions and the resulting feedback, detect disturbances to such expectations, and compensate for them. A study on the latency in live musical sound monitoring [48] showed significant discrepancies between different instruments, suggesting that certain players (e.g., pianists) are more tolerant to latency as they are accustomed to the inherent mechanical latency of their instrument, while others (e.g., drummers) are less so.

We conclude this section with a hint at the second type of synchronization mentioned at the beginning, i.e., that between pairs of external (possibly multimodal) events. Humans achieve robust perception through both the combination and the integration of information from multiple sensory modalities: the former strategy refers to interactions between non-redundant and complementary sensory signals aimed at disambiguating the sensory estimate, while the latter describes interactions between redundant signals aimed at reducing the variance in the sensory estimate and increasing its reliability [28]. The temporal relationships between inputs from different senses play an important role in multisensory combination and integration, which can be realized only within a window of synchrony between different modalities (e.g., auditory and visual, or auditory and haptic feedbacks) where a single percept is produced. Many studies [19, 83, 96] report quantitative results about "integration windows" between modalities, which can be used as constraints for the synchronization of the sound simulation pipeline with the visual (and possibly the haptic) modality. For more details regarding these issues, please refer to Part IV in this book, and in particular to Ch. 10.


## 2.3.2   Everyday Listening and the Plausibility Illusion

Human listeners are extremely good at interpreting sounds in terms of the events that produced them. The patterns of mechanical or aeroacoustic vibrations generated by sound-producing events depend on (and thus carry information about) contact forces, duration of contact, time-variations of the interaction, sizes, shapes, materials, and textures of the involved objects. We are immersed in a landscape of everyday sounds since the day we are born, and we have learned to extract meaning from this continuous and omnidirectional flow of information.

Gaver [34] introduced the concept of *everyday listening*, as opposed to *musical listening*. When a listener hears a sound, she might concentrate on attributes like pitch, loudness, and timbre, or she might notice its masking effect on other sounds. These are examples of musical listening, meaning that the considered perceptual dimensions and attributes have to do with the sound itself, and are those used in the creation of music. On the other hand, the listener might concentrate on the characteristics of the sound source and possibly the surrounding environment. When hearing an approaching car, she might notice that the engine is powerful, that the car is approaching quickly from behind, or even that the road is a narrow alley with echoing walls on each side. This is an example of everyday listening.

The two perceptual processes associated to musical and everyday listening cannot be completely disentangled and may occur simultaneously. Still, the idea that in our everyday listening experience the physical characteristics of sound-producing objects can be linked to the corresponding acoustic features is a powerful one. The literature of ecological acoustics provides several quantitative results on such links. The underlying assumption is that the flow of acoustic energy reaching our ears, the *acoustic array*, contains specific patterns, or *invariants*, which the listener exploits to infer information about the environment and guide her action. These concepts and terminology originate in the framework of ecological perception, rooted in Gibson's works on visual perception in the 1950s [35, 55].[2]

Acoustic invariants associated to sound events may include several attributes of a vibrating solid, such as its size, shape, and density, as these attributes contribute differently to characteristics of the resulting sound such as pitch, spectrum, amplitude envelope, and so on. In patterned sounds (see Sect. 2.2.2), the relevant information is also carried by the timing of successive events: footstep sounds must occur within

---

[2] In this context, the label "ecological" is associated to two main concepts: first, perception is an achievement of animal-environment systems, not simply animals, or their brains; second, the main purpose of perception is to guide action, so a theory of perception cannot ignore what animals do.

a range of rates and regularities in order to be perceived as walking; the regularity in the temporal pattern of a bouncing sound provides information about the shape of the object (e.g., a sphere versus a cube).

The mapping between physical parameters and acoustic features is in general many-to-many. A single physical parameter can influence simultaneously many characteristics of the sound, and different physical parameters influence the same characteristics in different ways. As an example, changing the size of an object will scale the sound spectrum, i.e., will change the frequencies of the sound but not their pattern. On the other hand, changing the object's shape results in a change in both the frequencies and their relationships. Acoustic invariants are thus the result of these complex patterns of change. Surveys of classic studies in ecological acoustics and acoustic invariants have been provided in previous works [5, 36].

The above discussion provides a solid theoretical framework to reason on the importance of ecologically valid acoustic information in eliciting the qualia of *presence* [72] in an immersive VR system. Among the many definitions proposed in the literature, we follow Skarbez et al. [76] in defining presence broadly as "the perceived realness of a mediated or virtual experience". Slater et al. [77] introduced the concepts of plausibility illusion and place illusion, to refer to two distinct subjective internal feelings, both of which contribute to eliciting the sense of presence in a subject experiencing an immersive VR scenario. This conceptual model of presence is depicted in Fig. 2.4.[3]

In this section we are particularly interested in the plausibility illusion, i.e., the illusion that the scenario being depicted is actually occurring (we will discuss the place illusion in Sect. 2.3.3 next). This is determined by the overall credibility of a virtual environment in comparison with subjective expectations. Slater argued that an important component of the plausibility illusion is "for the virtual reality to provide correlations between external events not directly caused by the participant and his/her own sensations" [77]. Skarbez et al. [76] proposed the construct of coherence, an objective characteristic of a virtual scenario that gives rise to the plausibility illusion (see Fig. 2.4, right) and depends on the internal logical and behavioral consistency of the virtual experience, with respect to prior knowledge. Building on these definitions, we argue that sound will contribute to the plausibility illusion of a virtual scenario as long as coherence is ensured for the auditory modality, i.e., as long as sound carries relevant ecological information expected by the user's everyday listening experience.

It shall be noted that coherence makes no assumptions about the high fidelity of a virtual environment to the real world. Consequently, the plausibility illusion "does not require physical realism" [77]: several studies show that virtual characters or objects displayed with low visual fidelity in the virtual environment do not disrupt the illusion. With regard to the auditory domain, this observation may be related to the concept of cartoon sounds [69], i.e., simplified descriptions of sounding phenomena with exaggerated features. We argue that cartoon sounds do not disrupt the

---

[3] Skarbez et al. [76] consider a third component, the social presence illusion, which we do not address here.

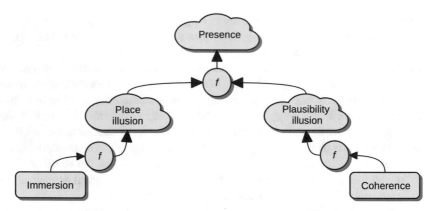

**Fig. 2.4** A conceptual model of presence: cloud boxes represent subjective internal feelings (qualia), circles represent functions affected by individual differences, and rounded rectangles represent objective characteristics of the virtual experience. Figure based on Skarbez [76, Fig. 2]

plausibility illusion as long as they still carry relevant ecological information. This is fundamentally the same principle exploited in the empirical science of Foley Art for creating ecologically plausible sound effects [2].

### 2.3.3 Active Perception, Place Illusion, Embodiment

The "enactive" approach to experience posits that it is not possible to disassociate perception and action schematically and that every kind of perception is intrinsically active and thoughtful. One of the most influential contributions in this direction is due to Varela et al. [94]. In the authors' conception, experience does not occur inside the perceiver, but rather it is enacted by the perceiver while exploring the environment. In this view, the subject of mental states is the embodied, environmentally situated perceiver. The term "embodied" highlights two main points: (i) perception depends upon the kinds of experience that are generated from specific motor capabilities, and (ii) these capabilities are themselves embedded in a biological, psychological, and cultural context. Sensory and motor processes are fundamentally inseparable, and perception consists in exercising an exploratory skill. As an example [58], the sensation of softness experienced when holding a sponge consists in being aware that one can exercise certain skills: one can press the sponge, and it will yield under the pressure. The experience of the softness of the sponge is characterized by a variety of such possible patterns of interaction. Sensorimotor dependencies, or contingencies, are the laws that describe these interactions. When a perceiver knows that he is exercising the sensorimotor contingencies associated with softness, then he is experiencing the sensation of softness.

Embodied theories of perception provide the ground for discussing further central concepts for VR, such as immersion, place illusion, sense of embodiment, and their relation to interactive sound. As depicted in Fig. 2.4 (left), immersion is an objective property of a VR system. Research has concentrated largely on characteristics such as latency, rendering frame rate, and tracking [22]. However, immersive systems can be also characterized in relation to the supported sensorimotor contingencies, which in turn define a set of valid actions that are perceptually meaningful (for instance, with a head-mounted display and head-tracking, it is possible to turn your head or bend forward producing changes in the rendered visual images). When a system supports sensorimotor contingencies that approximate those of physical reality, it can give rise to the place illusion, a specific subjective internal feeling which is the illusion of being located inside the rendered virtual environment, of "being there" [77]. Whereas the plausibility illusion is based on what a subject perceives in the virtual environment, the place illusion is based on how she is able to perceive it.

The great majority of studies addressing explicitly the effect of sound on the place illusion are concerned with spatial attributes: this is not entirely surprising, since many of these attributes are perceived by exercising specific motor actions (e.g., rotating the head to perceive the distance or the direction of a sound source or a reflecting surface). In this respect, directivity is possibly the only sound source attribute contributing to the place illusion, while other ecological attributes are more likely to contribute to the plausibility illusion only, as discussed in Sect. 2.3.2. In accordance with this picture, over the years, various authors [11, 38, 60] found that spatialized sound positively influences presence as being there when compared to no-sound or non-spatialized sound conditions, but does not affect the perceived realism of the environment. A comprehensive survey up to 2010 is provided by Larsson [47].

The sense of embodiment refers to yet another subjective internal feeling. Specifically, the sense of embodiment in an immersive virtual environment is concerned with the relationship between one's self and one's body, whereas the sense of presence refers to the relationship between one's self and the environment (and may occur even without the sensation of having a body). Kilteni et al. [45] provide a working definition of a sense of embodiment toward an artificial body, as the sense that emerges when that artificial body's properties are processed as if they were the properties of one's own biological body. Further, the authors associate it to three main components: (i) the sense of self-location, (ii) of body ownership, and (iii) of agency, the latter being investigated as an independent construct by other researchers [17].

The sense of self-location refers to one's spatial experience of being inside a body, rather than being inside a world (with or without a body), and is highly determined by the visuospatial perspective, proprioception, and vestibular signals, as well as tactile sensations at the border between our body and the environment. The sense of body ownership refers to one's self-attribution of an artificial body perceived as the source of the experienced sensations and emerges as a complex combination of afferent multisensory information and cognitive processes that may modulate the processing of sensory stimuli, as demonstrated by the well-known rubber hand illusion [13]. The sense of agency refers to the sense of having global motor control in relation to one's own body and has been proposed to result from a comparison between the predicted and the actual sensory consequences of one's actions [24]: when the two match by, for example, the presence of synchronous visuomotor correlations under active movement, one feels oneself to be the agent of those actions.

The above discussion suggests that interactive sounds occurring directly in reaction to the avatar's gestures in a virtual scenario, and coherently with the available sensorimotor contingencies, can positively affect the sense of agency in particular. One relevant example is provided by footsteps: several studies have addressed the issue of generating footstep sounds [14, 85, 95] however without assessing their specific relevance to the sense of agency. Other studies have shown that interactively generated sound can support haptic sensations, as in the case of impact sounds reinforcing or modulating the perceived hardness of an impulsive contact [6], or friction sounds affecting the perceived effort in dragging an object [4] (refer to Chap. 12 for other audio-haptic case studies). Yet, no attempt was made in these studies to specifically address the issue of agency.

Even less research seems to have been conducted on the effects of interactive sound on the sense of body ownership. Footsteps provide a relevant example also in this case, as the sound of steps can be related to the perceived weight of one's own body [85] or that of an avatar [74]. Sikström et al. [73] evaluated the role of self-produced sounds in participants' sensation of ownership of virtual wings in an immersive scenario. A related issue is that of the sound of one's own voice in a virtual environment [61].

## 2.4 Events Versus Processes

Having discussed the perceptual and cognitive aspects involved in interactive sound generation, we now jump back to the pipeline of Fig. 2.1 and look specifically at the "source modeling" box.

When creating sound sources in a virtual environment, approaches based on sample playback are still the most common ones [12], taking advantage of sound design techniques that have been refined through a long history, and being able to yield perfect realism, "at least for single sounds triggered only once" [21]. From a completely different perspective, procedural approaches defer the generation of sound signals until runtime, when information on sound-producing event is available and can be used to yield more interactive sonic results. This section discusses these two dichotomical approaches.

### 2.4.1 Event-Driven Approaches

Approaches based on sample playback follow an event-driven logics, in which a specific sound exists as a waveform stored in a file or a table in memory and is

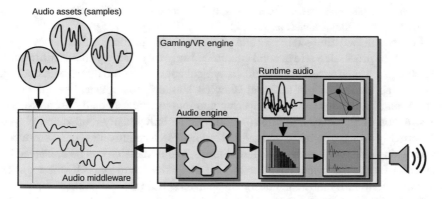

**Fig. 2.5** Event-driven logics for VR sound design using samples and audio middleware software

bound to some event occurring in the virtual world. Borrowing an example from Farnell [31]: if (moves(gate)) play(scrape.wav).

One immediate consequence of this is that the playback and the post-processing of samples are dissociated from the underlying physics engine and the graphical rendering engine. In the case of a sound played back once, the length of the sound is predetermined and thus any timing relationship between auditory and visual elements must also be predefined. In the case of a looped sound, the endpoint must be explicitly given, e.g., as a response to a subsequent event. More in general, the playback of sound is controlled by a finite and small set of states (such as in the case of an elevator that can be starting, moving, stopping, or stopped). Correspondingly, any event is bound to a sound "asset", or to some post-processing of that asset.

Current practices of sound design for VR are deeply and firmly rooted in such event-driven logics, depicted in Fig. 2.5. One clear example of this is provided by "audio middleware" software [12], which are tools that facilitate the work of the sound designer by reducing programming time and testing the sound design in real time along with the game engine. The most commonly adopted middleware solutions, such as FMOD Studio (Firelight Technologies)[4] and Wwise (Audiokinetic),[5] largely follow the traditional paradigm of DAWs (Digital Audio Workstations) and include GUIs for adding, controlling, and processing samples; linking them to objects, areas, and events of the virtual environment; and imposing rules for triggering and playback.

One of the main acknowledged limitations of samples is that they are static, and they are just single, atomic instances of events. The repetitiveness involved in multiple playbacks of the same sounds has the potential to disrupt many of the perceptual and cognitive effects discussed in Sect. 2.3, and even to lead to fatigue. Partial remedies to this problem include the use of multiple samples for the same event, as well as the

---

[4] https://www.fmod.com/.

[5] https://www.audiokinetic.com/products/wwise/.

use of various post-processing operations, the most common being modifications to pitch, time, dynamics, as well as sound layering and looping [75].

Well-established time-stretching and pitch-shifting algorithms exist; however, the quality of the processing is in general guaranteed only for relatively small shifting and stretching factors. Concerning dynamics, typical approaches are based on blending, cross-fading, and mixing of different samples, similarly to a musical sampler (and with similar limitations as well). Layering and looping are especially useful for the construction of ambiences: multiple sounds can be individually looped and played concurrently to create complex and layered ambiences. Repetitiveness can be reduced by assigning different lengths to different loops, and immersion can be enhanced by rendering individual layers at different virtual spatial locations. All this requires manual operations by the sound designer, such as splitting, cross-fading, and so on.

Further countermeasures to repetition and listener fatigue include the use of techniques based on randomization. These can be applied to many aspects of sound, including, but not limited to (i) pitch and amplitude variations, (ii) sample selection, (iii) sample concatenation, (iv) looping, and (v) location of sound sources. As an example, randomized sample selection amounts to performing randomizations of alternative samples associated to the same event, e.g., a collision: a different sample is played back at each occurrence of the event, mimicking the differences occurring due to slightly different contact points and velocities. In randomized concatenation, different samples are concatenated to build a composite sound in response to a repetitive sequence of events, such as in the case of footsteps, weapon sounds, and so on. Triggering different points with different probabilities can also be used to reduce the repetitiveness of looped layers in ambience sounds. The audio middleware solutions mentioned above typically implement several of these techniques.

Randomization techniques hint at another issue with samples, which is the need for very large amounts of data. Putting together a large sample library is a slow and labor-intensive process. Moreover, data need to be stored in memory, possibly in secondary storage, from which they then have to be prefetched before playback.

### 2.4.2 Procedural Approaches

Techniques based on the randomization of several sample-processing parameters, such as those discussed above, are sometimes loosely referred to as *procedural* in the sound design practice [75, Chap. 2]. Here, we favor a stricter definition. In Farnell's words [30], procedural audio is *"sound as a process, rather than sound as data"*. This definition shifts the focus onto the creation of audio assets, as opposed to the manipulation of existing ones.

Procedural audio is thus synthetic sound, is real time, and most importantly is created according to a set of programmatic rules and live input. This implies that procedurally generated sound is synthesized at runtime, when all the needed input

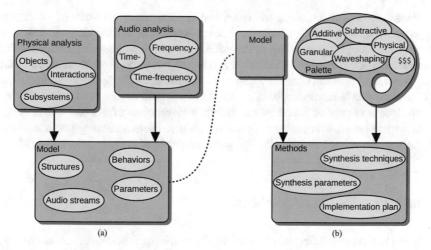

**Fig. 2.6** Procedural sound design: **a** model building, and **b** method analysis stages (figures loosely based on Farnell [30, Figs. 16.4–5])

and contextual information are available, whereas in a sample-based approach, most of the work is performed offline prior to execution, implying that "many decisions are made in advance and cast in stone" [31].

The stages involved in the process of procedural sound design may be loosely based on those of software life-cycle, including (i) requirements analysis, (ii) research and acquisition, (iii) model building, (iv) method analysis, (v) implementation, (vi) integration, (vii) test and iteration, and (viii) maintenance. Figure 2.6 provides a graphical summary of the two central stages, i.e., model building and method analysis.

Building a model (Fig. 2.6a) provides a simplification of the properties and behaviors of a real object, which starts from the analysis of sound data (including time- and/or frequency-domain analysis, extraction of relevant audio features, etc.), as well as a physical analysis of the involved sound-generating mechanisms, and results into a set of parametric controls and behaviors. The hierarchy of everyday sounds depicted in Fig. 2.3 provides a useful reference framework: the model at hand can be positioned inside this hierarchy. Moreover, following the discussion on everyday listening of Sect. 2.3.2, the choice of the model parametrization can be informed by the knowledge of relevant acoustic invariants carrying information about sound-generating objects and events.

The method analysis stage is where the most appropriate sound synthesis and processing techniques are chosen, starting from a palette of available ones, and based on the model at hand. Figure 2.6b shows a set of commonly employed sound synthesis techniques (in Sect. 2.4.3, we will explore physics-based techniques in particular). As a result of this stage, an implementation plan is produced that includes a set of techniques and corresponding low-level synthesis parameters, as well as the involved audio streams.

Based on this discussion, we can identify two main qualities of procedural approaches with respect to sample playback. The first one is their intrinsic adaptability and interactivity (according to the definitions given in Sect. 2.1), which derive from the deferring of sound generation at runtime based on programmatic rules and user input, and result in ever-changing sonic results in response to real-time control. The second one is flexibility, where a single procedural model can be parametrized to produce a variety of sound events within a given class of sounds: this contrasts with sample-based, event-driven approaches, where ever-increasing amounts of data and assets are needed in order to cope with the needs of complex virtual worlds.

### 2.4.3 Physics-Based Methods

Looking back at Fig. 2.6b, one of the available paints in the palette of sound synthesis techniques is that of physics-based methods.

The boundaries between what can be considered physical (or physics-based, or physics-informed) sound synthesis are somewhat blurry in the scientific literature. Here, we adopt the definition given by Smith [78] and refer to synthesis techniques where " [...] there is an explicit representation of the relevant physical state of the sound source. For example, a string physical model must offer the possibility of exciting the string at any point along its length. [...] All we need is Newton." The last claim refers to the idea that physical modeling always starts with a quantitative description of the sound sources based on Newtonian mechanics. Such description may be approximate and simplified to various extents, but the above definition provides an unambiguous—albeit broad—characterization in terms of physical state access. Resorting to a simple (yet historically relevant [68]) example, we can say that additive synthesis of bell sounds is not physics-based, as additive sinusoidal partials only describe the time-frequency characteristics of the sound signal without any reference to the physical state of the bell. On the other hand, modal synthesis [1] of the same bell, with modal oscillators tuned to the sound partials, is only apparently a similar approach: a linear combination of the modes can provide the displacement and the velocity at any point of the bell, and each modal shape defines to what extent an external force applied at a given point affects the corresponding mode.

The history of physics-based synthesis is rooted in studies on the acoustics of the vocal apparatus [44] and of musical instruments [39, 40], where numerical models were initially used for simulation rather than synthesis purposes. Current techniques are based on several alternative formulations and methods, including ordinary or partial differential equations, equivalent circuit representations, modal representations, finite-difference and finite-element schemes, and so on [78]. Comprehensive surveys of physical modeling approaches have been published [79, 89]. Although these deal with musical sound synthesis mostly, much of what has been learned in that domain can be applied to the physical modeling of any sounding object.

Although physics-based synthesis is sometimes made synonymous with procedural audio, Fig. 2.6b provides a clear picture of the relation between the two. In this perspective, "procedural audio is more than physical modeling," [31] and the latter can be seen as one of the tools at the disposal of the sound designer to reduce a sound to its behavioral realization. Combining physics-based approaches with knowledge of auditory perception and cognition often results in procedural models in which the physical description has been drastically simplified while retaining the ecological validity of sounds and the realism of the interactions, thus preserving the plausibility illusion of the resulting sonic world and the sense of agency of the subject (see related discussions in Sects. 2.3.2 and 2.3.3).

## 2.4.4   Computational Costs

Event-driven and procedural approaches must be analyzed also in terms of the involved computational requirements. In case of insufficient resources, excessive computational costs may introduce artifacts in the rendered sound or in alternative may require to increase the overall latency of the rendering up to a point where the perception of causality and multisensory integration are disrupted (see Sect. 2.3.1).

With reference to Fig. 2.1, it can be stated that one main computational bottleneck in the sound simulation rendering pipeline [51] is the "per sound source" cost. This relates in particular to the sound propagation stage (see Chap. 3), as reflections, scattering, occlusions, Doppler effects, and so on must be computed for each sound source involved in the simulation. But it also includes the source modeling stage, with particular reference to the generation of the sound source signals.

Sample playback has a fixed cost, irrespective of the sound being played. Moreover, the cost of playback is very small. However, samples must be loaded in memory before being played. As a consequence, when a sound is triggered, the playback may involve a prefetch phase where a soundbank is loaded from the secondary memory. Moreover, some management of polyphony must be set in place in order to prioritize the playback in case of several simultaneously active sounds. This can use policies similar to those employed in music synthesizers: typically, sounds falling below a certain amplitude threshold are dropped, leaving place for other sounds. The underlying assumption is that louder sounds mask softer ones, so that dropping the latter has no or minimal perceptual consequences. Although modern architectures allow for the simultaneous playback of hundreds of audio assets, generating complex soundscapes may exceed the amount of available channels.

On the other hand, procedural sound has variable costs, which depend on the complexity of the corresponding model and on the employed methods. This is particularly evident in the case of physics-based techniques: for large-scale, brute-force approaches, like higher dimensional finite-element or finite-difference methods, real time is still hard to achieve. On the other hand, techniques like modal synthesis can be implemented very efficiently, albeit at the cost of reduced flexibility of the models (e.g., interaction with sounding objects limited to single input-output), which in turn can have a detrimental effect on the plausibility illusion. Some non-physical methods are very cheap in terms of computational requirements, as in the case of subtractive synthesis for generating wind or fire sounds. Section 2.5.1 provides several examples of procedural methods for various classes of everyday sounds.

Although it is generally true that sample-based methods outperform procedural audio for small amounts of sounds, it has been noted [30] that this is not necessarily true in the limit of larger numbers: whereas the fixed cost of sample playback results in a computational complexity that is linear in the number of rendered sources, the availability of very cheap procedural models can produce the result that for high numbers of sources the situation reverses and procedural sound starts to outperform sample-based methods.

## 2.5   Procedural and Physics-Based Approaches in VR Audio

Given these premises, what is the current development of procedural and physics-based approaches in audio for VR? In this section, we show that, despite a substantial amount of research, these approaches are still struggling to gain popularity in real-world products and practices.

### 2.5.1   Methods

Far from providing a comprehensive survey of previous literature in the field, which would go way beyond the scope of this chapter, this section aims at assessing to what extent the taxonomy of everyday sounds provided in Fig. 2.3 has been covered by existing procedural approaches. This exercise also serves as a testbed to verify the generality of that taxonomy. For a recent and broad survey, see Liu and Manocha [51].

Solid sounds are by far the most investigated category. For basic models, modal synthesis [1] is the dominant approach. There are several works investigating the use of modal methods for the procedural generation of contact sounds between solid objects, including the optimization of modal synthesis through specialized numerical schemes and/or perceptual criteria, as in the work by Raghuvanshi et al. [63]. Procedural models of surface textures have been proposed by several scholars [66, 91] and applied to scraping and rolling sounds [64]. Basic interaction forces (impact and sliding friction) can be modeled with a variety of approaches that range from qualitative approximations of temporal profiles of impulsive force magnitudes [92] to the physical simulation of stick-slip phenomena in friction forces [7].

At the next level of complexity, models of patterned solid sounds have also been widely studied. Stochastic models of crumpling phenomena have been proposed, with applications to cloth sound synthesis [3], crumpling paper sounds, or sounds produced by deformations of aggregate materials, such as sand, snow, or gravel [15]. The latter have also been used in the context of walking interactions [81] (see also Sect. 2.3.3) to simulate the sound of a footstep onto aggregate grounds. Breaking sounds have been modeled especially with the purpose of synchronizing animations of brittle fractures produced by a physics engine [59, 100].

The category of aerodynamic sounds is less studied. Within the basic level of complexity, the sound produced by wind includes those resulting from interaction with large static obstructions, aeolian tones, and cavity tones: these have been procedurally modeled with techniques ranging from computationally intensive fluid-dynamics simulations [26] to simple (yet efficient and effective) subtractive schemes using noisy sources and filters [30]. These can be straightforwardly employed to construct patterned and compound sonic events, including windy scenes, swinging objects, and so on [71]. Other basic aeroacoustic events include turbulences, most notably explosions, which are a key component of more complex sounds such as gunshots [37] and fire [18]. Yet another relevant patterned sonic event is that produced by combustion engines [10].

Liquid sounds appear to be the least addressed category. Basic procedural models include sounds produced by drops in a liquid [90] or by pouring a liquid [65], whereas patterned and compound sonic events have been more often simulated using concatenative approaches relying on the output of the graphical procedural simulation [98]. A relevant example of hybrid solid-liquid sounds is that of rain [50].

### 2.5.2   Optimizations

We have provided in Sect. 2.4.4 a general discussion on computational costs associated to procedural approaches, in comparison to sample-based methods. Since the former typically results in higher "per sound source" costs than the latter, various studies have proposed strategies for reducing the load of complex procedural audio scenes in virtual environments.

One attractive feature of procedural sound in terms of computational complexity is the possibility of dynamically adapting the level of detail (LOD) of the synthesized audio. The concept of LOD is a long-established one in computer graphics and encompasses various optimization techniques for decreasing the complexity of 3D object rendering [52]. The general goal of LOD techniques is to increase the rendering speed by reducing details while minimizing the perceived degradation of quality. Most commonly, the LOD is varied as a function of the distance from the camera, but other metrics can be used, including size, speed of motion, priority, and so on. Reducing the LOD may be achieved by simplifying the 3D object mesh, or by using impostors (i.e., replacing mesh-based with image-based rendering), and other approaches can be used to dynamically control the LOD of landscape rendering, crowd simulation, and so on.

Similar ideas may be applied to procedural sound, achieving further reductions of computational costs for complex sound scenes with respect to sample playback. However, very few studies explored the concept of LOD in the auditory domain, and there is not even a commonly accepted definition in the related literature: some scholars have coined the term Sound Level Of Detail (SLOD) [70], while others use

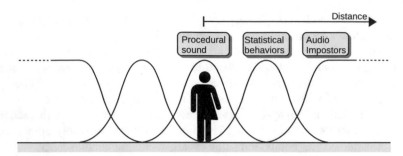

**Fig. 2.7** Example of dynamic LOAD based on the radial distance from the listener, where levels of details are associated to three overlapping proximity profiles. Figure partly based on Schwarz et al. [70, Fig. 3]

Level Of Audio Detail (LOAD) [27], both generically referring to varying sound resolution according to the required perceived precision. Here, we stick to the latter definition (LOAD), since this seems to be more frequently adopted in recent literature.

Strategies for dynamic LOAD can be partly derived from graphics. Simple approaches amount to fade out and turn off distant sounds based on radial distance or zoning. Depending on their distance, sound sources may be also clustered or activated according to some predefined behavior. Techniques based on impostors can be used as well: as an example, when rendering the sound of a crowd, individual sounds emitted by several characters can be replaced by a global sample-based ambience sound. However, one should be aware of the differences between visual and auditory perception and exploit the peculiarities of the latter to develop more advanced strategies for dynamic LOAD. Figure 2.7 depicts an example of a dynamic LOAD strategy based on radial distance, in which levels of details are associated to three overlapping proximity profiles around the listener (foreground, middle ground, and background): sounds in the foreground are rendered individually through procedural approaches; those that fall into the middle ground can be rendered through some simplifying approaches (clustering, grouping, and statistical behaviors); and finally, sounds in the background may be substituted by audio impostors such as audio files.

Pioneering work in this direction was carried out by Fouad et al. [32], although the authors did not explicitly refer to the concept of LOD. This work proposes a set of "perceptually based scheduling algorithms", that allows a scheduler to assign execution time to each sound in the scene minimizing some perceptually motivated error metric. In particular, sounds are prioritized depending on the listener's gaze, the loudness, and the age of the sound. Tsingos and coworkers [56, 88] proposed an approach to reduce the number of (sample-based) sound sources in a complex scenario, by combining perceptual culling and perceptual clustering. The culling stage removes perceptually inaudible sources based on a global masking model, while the clustering stage groups the remaining sound sources into a predefined number of clusters: as a result, a representative point source is constructed for each cluster and a set of equivalent source signals is generated. Schwarz et al. [70] proposed a design with three LOADs based on proximity and smooth transitions between proximity levels, very much like those depicted in Fig. 2.7: (i) foreground, i.e., individually driven sound events (e.g., individual raindrops on tree leaves); (ii) middle ground, i.e., group-driven sound events, at the point where individual events cannot be isolated and can be replaced by stochastical behaviors; (iii) background, i.e., sound sources that are further away and can be rendered by audio impostors such as audio files or dynamic mixing of groups of procedural impostors. More recently, Dall'Avanzi et al. [23] analyzed the effect on player's immersion in response to soundscapes with two applied LOADs. Two groups of participants played two different versions of the same game, and the player's immersion was measured through two questionnaires. However, results in this case showed no considerable difference between the two groups.

Other researchers proposed or evaluated LOAD techniques specifically tailored to certain synthesis methods. Raghuvanshi et al. [63] addressed modal synthesis and investigated various perceptually motivated techniques for improving the efficiency of the synthesis. These include a "quality scaling" technique that effectively controls the dynamic LOAD: briefly, in a scene involving many sounding objects, the number of modes assigned to individual objects scales with objects location from foreground to background, without significant losses in perceived quality. Durr et al. [27] evaluated through subjective tests various procedural models of sound sources with three applied LOADs. Specifically, three procedural models proposed by Farnell [30] (see also Sect. 2.5.1) were chosen for investigation: (i) fire sounds employ subtractive synthesis to generate and combine hissing, crackling, and lapping features; (ii) bubbles sounds use a form of additive synthesis with frequency- and amplitude-controlled sinusoidal components representing single bubbles; (iii) wind sounds are again produced using subtractive synthesis (amplitude-modulated noise and various filtering elements to represent different wind effects). A different approach to applying LOAD was implemented for each model. Correspondingly, listening tests provided different results for each model in terms of perceived quality at different LOADs.

The reader interested in further discussion about audio quality should also refer to Chap. 5.

### 2.5.3   Tools

In spite of all the valuable research results produced so far, there is still a lack of software tools that assist the sound designer in using procedural approaches.

Designers working with procedural audio use a variety of audio programming environments. Popular choices include (but are not limited to) Pure Data,[6] Max/MSP,[7] or CSound.[8] The first two in particular implement a common, dataflow-

---

[6] https://puredata.info/.

[7] https://cycling74.com/.

[8] https://csound.com/.

oriented paradigm [62] and use a visual patch language where "the diagram is the program": Farnell [31] argues that this paradigm is particularly suited for procedural audio as it has a natural congruence with the abstract model resulting from the design process. On the other hand, integrating these environments into the most widespread gaming/VR engines is not straightforward: at the time of writing, some active open-source projects include libpd [16], a C library that turns Pure Data into an embeddable audio synthesis library and provides wrappers for a range of languages, and Cabbage [97], a framework for developing audio plugins in Csound, including plugins for the FMOD middleware. Commercial gaming/VR engines typically provide limited functionalities to support procedural sound design, although some recent developments may hint at an ongoing change of perspective: as an example, the Blueprint visual scripting system within the Unreal Engine has been used for dataflow-oriented procedural audio programming, also using some native synthesis (subtractive, etc.) capabilities.

All of the tools mentioned above still require to work at a low level of abstraction, implying that the sound designer must have the technical skills needed to deal with low-level synthesis methods and parameters, and at the same time limiting productivity. There is a clear need for tools that allow the designer to work at higher levels of abstraction. One instructive example is provided by the Sound Design Toolkit (SDT), an open-source software package developed over several years [9, 25] which provides a set of sound models for the interactive generation of several acoustic phenomena. In its current embodiment, SDT is composed of a core C library exposing an API, plus a set of wrappers for Max and Pure Data, and a related collection of patches and help files. Interestingly, the collection is based on a hierarchical taxonomy of everyday sound events which follows very closely the one depicted in Fig. 2.3 and implements a rich subset of its items. The designer has access to both low-level parameters (e.g., the modal frequencies of a basic solid resonator) and to high-level ones (e.g., the initial height of a bouncing object).

Commercial products facilitating the designer's workflow are also far from abundant: Lesound[9] (formerly Audiogaming) sells a set of plugins for FMOD and Wwise that include procedural simulations of wind, rain, motor, and weather sounds, while for its part AudioKinetic (developer of Wwise) develops the soundseed plugin series, which include procedural generation of wind and whooshing sounds as well as impact sounds. Nemisindo[10] provides a web-based platform for real-time synthesis and manipulation of procedural audio, which stems from the FXive academic project [8], but no plugin-based integration with VR engines or audio middleware software is available at the time of writing.

A much-needed facilitating tool for the sound designer is one that automates part of the design process, allowing in particular for automatic tuning of the parameters of a procedural model starting from a target (e.g., recorded) sound. This would provide a means to recreate procedurally a desired sound and more in general to ease the design by providing a starting set of parameter values that can be further edited.

---

[9] https://lesound.io/.

[10] https://nemisindo.com.

In the context of modal synthesis, various authors have proposed automatic analysis approaches for determining modal parameters from a target signal (e.g., an impact sound). In this case, the parametrization of the model is relatively simple: every mode at a given position is fully characterized by a triplet of scalars representing its frequency, decay coefficient, and gain. This generalizes to an array of gains if multiple points on the object are considered, or to continuous modal shapes as functions of spatial coordinates on the object. Ren et al. [67] proposed a method that extracts perceptually salient features from audio examples and a parameter estimation algorithm searches for the best material parameters for modal synthesis. Based on this work, Sterling et al. [82] added a probabilistic model for the damping parameters in order to reduce the effect of external factors (object support, background noise, etc.) and non-linearities on the estimate of damping. Tiraboschi et al. [87] also presented an approach to the automatic estimation of modal parameters based on a target sound, which employs a spectral modeling algorithm to track energy envelopes of detected sinusoidal components and then performs linear regression to estimate the corresponding modal parameters.

While the case of solid objects and modal synthesis is a relatively simple one, the issue of automatic parameter estimation has been largely disregarded for other classes of sounds and models.

## 2.6  Conclusions

Our discussion in this chapter has hopefully shown that procedural approaches offer extensive possibilities for designing sonic interactions in virtual environments. And yet as of today the number of real-world applications and tools utilizing these approaches is very limited. In fact, not much has changed since ten or fifteen years ago, when other researchers observed a similar lack of interest from the industry [12, 29], with the same technical and cultural obstacles to adoption still in place. In a way recent technological developments have further favored the use of sample-based approaches: in particular, decreasing costs of RAM and secondary storage, as well as optimized strategies to manage caching and prefetching of sound assets, have made it possible to store ever larger amounts of data. This state of affairs mimics closely what happened in the music industry during the last three decades: physics-based techniques in particular have been around for a long time, but the higher sound quality and accuracy of samples are still preferred over the flexibility of physical models for the emulation of musical instruments.

Perhaps then the question is not whether procedural approaches can overcome sample-based audio, but when, i.e., under what specific circumstances. In this chapter, we have provided some elements, particularly links to a number of relevant perceptual and cognitive aspects, such as the plausibility and place illusions, the sense of embodiment, and the sense of agency. We argue that procedural audio can compete with samples in cases where either (i) very large amounts of data are needed to minimize repetition and support the plausibility illusion, or (ii) interactivity is needed beyond an event-driven logics, in order to provide tight synchronization and plausible variations with user actions, and to support her sense of agency and body ownership.

One example of the first circumstance is provided by wind sounds: good recordings of real wind effects are technically difficult to come by and long recordings are required to create convincing ambiences of windy scenes using looping, while on the other hand procedurally generated wind sounds achieve high levels of realism. It is therefore no surprise that the few commercially available tools for procedural sound all include wind (see Sect. 2.5.3) and have been successfully employed also in large productions.[11] While wind falls in the category of adaptive, rather than interactive sounds, two relevant examples for the second circumstance may be provided by footsteps and sliding friction (bike breaking, hinges squeaking, rubbing, etc.): beside requiring large amounts of data and randomization to avoid repetition, these sounds arise in response to complex and continuous motor actions by the user, which cannot be fully captured by an event-driven logics.

Future research and development should therefore focus on cases where procedural models can compete with samples, looking more deeply into the effects on the plausibility illusion, sense of agency, and sense of body ownership. From a more technical perspective, promising directions for future research include the development of dynamic LOAD techniques, as well as high-level authoring tools and automation.

**Acknowledgements** This chapter is partly based on the ideas and materials which I developed for my course "Sound in Interaction", held at the University of Milano for the MSc degree in Computer Science.

# References

1. Adrien, J.-M. in Representations of Musical Signals (eds De Poli, G., Piccialli, A., Roads, C.) 269-297 (MIT Press, Cambridge, MA, 1991).
2. Ament, V. T.: The Foley grail: The art of performing sound for film, games, and animation Second edition (CRC Press, New York, 2014).
3. An, S. S., James, D. L., Marschner, S.: Motion-driven Concatenative Synthesis of Cloth Sounds. ACM Trans. Graphics **31** (July 2012).
4. Avanzini, F., Rocchesso, D., Serafin, S.: Friction sounds for sensory substitution, in Proc. Int. Conf. Auditory Display (ICAD04) (Sidney, July 2004).
5. Avanzini, F. in Sound to Sense, Sense to Sound. A State of the Art in Sound and Music Computing (eds Rocchesso, D., Polotti, P.) 345–396 (Logos Verlag, Berlin, 2008).
6. Avanzini, F., Crosato, P. in Haptic and audio interaction design (eds Mc-Gookin, D., Brewster, S.) 24–35 (Lecture Notes in Computer Science 4129/2006, Springer Verlag, Berlin/Heidelberg, 2006).

[11] As an example, the procedural wind simulator by Lesound has been reportedly used for generating ambiences in Quentin Tarantino's Django Unchained, see http://lesound.io/product/audiowind-pro/.

7. Avanzini, F., Serafin, S., Rocchesso, D.: Interactive simulation of rigid body interaction with friction-induced sound generation. IEEE Trans. Speech Audio Process. **13**, 1073–1081 (2005).
8. Bahadoran, P., Benito, A., Vassallo, T., Reiss, J. D.: FXive: A web platform for procedural sound synthesis, in Proc. 144 Audio Engin. Soc. Conv. (Milano, 2018).
9. Baldan, S., Delle Monache, S., Rocchesso, D.: The sound design toolkit. SoftwareX **6**, 255–260 (2017).
10. Baldan, S., Lachambre, H., Delle Monache, S., Boussard, P.: Physically informed car engine sound synthesis for virtual and augmented environments, in Proc. IEEE Int. Workshop on Sonic Interactions for Virtual Environments (SIVE2015) (Arles, 2015), 21–26.
11. Bormann, K.: Presence and the utility of audio spatialization. Presence: Teleoperators and Virtual Environment **14**, 278–297 (2005).
12. Böttcher, N.: Current problems and future possibilities of procedural audio in computer games. Journal of Gaming & Virtual Worlds **5**, 215–234 (2013).
13. Botvinick, M., Cohen, J.: Rubber hands 'feel' touch that eyes see. Nature **391**, 756–756 (1998).
14. Bresin, R., Papetti, S., Civolani, M., Fontana, F.: Expressive sonification of footstep sounds, in Proc. Interactive Sonification Workshop (Stockholm, 2010), 51–54.
15. Bresin, R. et al.: Auditory feedback through continuous control of crumpling sound synthesis, in Proc. Workshop Sonic Interaction Design (CHI2008) (Firenze, 2008), 23–28.
16. Brinkmann, P., Wilcox, D., Kirshboim, T., Eakin, R., Alexander, R.: Libpd: Past, Present, and Future of Embedding Pure Data, in Proc. Pure Data Convention (New York, 2016).
17. Caspar, E. A., Cleeremans, A., Haggard, P.: The relationship between human agency and embodiment. Consciousness and cognition **33**, 226–236 (2015).
18. Chadwick, J. N., James, D. L.: Animating Fire with Sound. ACM Trans. Graphics **30** (2011).
19. Chen, L., Vroomen, J.: Intersensory binding across space and time: a tutorial review. Attention, Perception, & Psychophysics **75**, 790–811 (2013).
20. Collins, K. in Essays on Sound and Vision (eds Richardson, J., Hawkins, S.) 263–298 (Helsinki University Press, Helsinki, 2007).
21. Cook, P. R.: Real sound synthesis for interactive applications (CRC Press, 2002).
22. Cummings, J. J., Bailenson, J.N.: How immersive is enough? A meta-analysis of the effect of immersive technology on user presence. Media Psychology **19**, 272–309 (2016).
23. Dall'Avanzi, I., Yee-King, M.: Measuring the impact of level of detail for environmental soundscapes in digital games, in Proc. 146 Audio Engin. Soc. Conv. (London, 2019).
24. David, N., Newen, A., Vogeley, K.: The "sense of agency" and its underlying cognitive and neural mechanisms. Consciousness and cognition **17**, 523–534 (2008).
25. Delle Monache, S., Polotti, P., Rocchesso, D.: A toolkit for explorations in sonic interaction design, in Proc. Int. Conf. Audio Mostly (AM2010) (Piteå, 2010), 1–7.
26. Dobashi, Y.,Yamamoto, T., Nishita, T.: Real-time Rendering of Aerodynamic Sound using Sound Textures based on Computational Fluid Dynamics, in Proc. ACM SIGGRAPH 2003 (San Diego, 2003), 732–740.
27. Durr, G., Peixoto, L., Souza, M., Tanoue, R., Reiss, J. D.: Implementation and evaluation of dynamic level of audio detail, in Proc. 56th AES Int. Conf. Audio for Games (London, 2015).
28. Ernst, M. O., Bülthoff, H. H.: Merging the senses into a robust percept. TRENDS in Cognitive Sciences **8**, 162–169 (2004).
29. Farnell, A.: An introduction to procedural audio and its application in computer games (2007). URL http://obiwannabe.co.uk/html/papers/proc-audio/proc-audio.pdf. Accessed March 29, 2021.
30. Farnell, A.: Designing sound (MIT Press, 2010).
31. Farnell, A. in Game sound technology and player interaction: Concepts and developments (ed Grimshaw, M.) 313–339 (Information Science Reference, 2011).
32. Fouad, H., Hahn, J. K., Ballas, J. A.: Perceptually Based Scheduling Algorithms for Real-time Synthesis of Complex Sonic Environments, in Proc. Int. Conf. Auditory Display (ICAD97) (Palo Alto, 1997).

33. Gaver, W. W.: How do we hear in the world? Explorations of ecological acoustics. Ecological Psychology **5**, 285–313 (1993).
34. Gaver, W. W.: What in the world do we hear? An ecological approach to auditory event perception. Ecological Psychology **5**, 1–29 (1993).
35. Gibson, J. J.: The ecological approach to visual perception (Lawrence Erlbaum Associates, Mahwah, NJ, 1986).
36. Giordano, B., Avanzini, F. in Multisensory Softness (ed Luca, M. D.) 49–84 (Springer Verlag, London, 2014).
37. Hacıhabiboğlu, H. in Game Dynamics: Best Practices in Procedural and Dynamic Game Content Generation (eds Korn, O., Lee, N.) 47–69 (Springer International Publishing, Cham, 2017).
38. Hendrix, C., Barfield, W.: The Sense of Presence within Auditory Virtual Environments. Presence: Teleoperators and Virtual Environment **5**, 290–301 (1996).
39. Hiller, L., Ruiz, P.: Synthesizing Musical Sounds by Solving the Wave Equation for Vibrating Objects: Part I. J. Audio Eng. Soc. **19**, 462–470 (1971).
40. Hiller, L., Ruiz, P.: Synthesizing Musical Sounds by Solving the Wave Equation for Vibrating Objects: Part II. J. Audio Eng. Soc. **19**, 542–551 (1971).
41. Jack, R. H., Stockman, T., McPherson, A.: Effect of latency on performer interaction and subjective quality assessment of a digital musical instrument, in Proc. Int. Conf. Audio Mostly (AM'16) (Norrköping, 2016), 116–123.
42. Jørgensen, K. in Game sound technology and player interaction: Concepts and developments (ed Grimshaw, M.) 78–97 (Information Science Reference, 2011).
43. Kaaresoja, T., Brewster, S., Lantz, V.: Towards the temporally perfect virtual button: touch-feedback simultaneity and perceived quality in mobile touchscreen press interactions. ACM Trans. Applied Perception **11**, 1–25 (2014).
44. Kelly, J. L., Lochbaum, C. C.: Speech synthesis, in Proc. 4th Int. Congr. Acoustics (Copenhagen, 1962), 1–4.
45. Kilteni, K., Groten, R., Slater, M.: The sense of embodiment in virtual reality. Presence: Teleoperators and Virtual Environments **21**, 373–387 (2012).
46. Lago, N. P., Kon, F.: The quest for low latency, in Proc. Int. Computer Music Conf. (ICMC2004) (Miami, 2004).
47. Larsson, P., Väljamäe, A., Västfjäll, D., Tajadura-Jiménez, A., Kleiner, M. in The engineering of mixed reality systems (eds Dubois, E., Gray, P., Nigay, L.) 143–163 (Springer, 2010).
48. Lester, M., Boley, J.: The effects of latency on live sound monitoring, in Proc. 123 Audio Engin. Soc. Convention (New York, 2007).
49. Liljedahl, M. in Game sound technology and player interaction: Concepts and developments (ed Grimshaw, M.) 22–43 (Information Science Reference, 2011).
50. Liu, S., Cheng, H., Tong, Y.: Physically-Based Statistical Simulation of Rain Sound. ACM Trans. Graphics **38** (2019).
51. Liu, S., Manocha, D.: Sound Synthesis, Propagation, and Rendering: A Survey. arXiv preprint. 2020.
52. Luebke, D. et al.: Level of detail for 3D graphics (Morgan Kaufmann, 2003).
53. Magill, R. A., Anderson, D. I.: Motor learning and control: Concepts and applications. Eleventh edition (McGraw-Hill New York, 2017).
54. Mäki-Patola, T., Hämäläinen, P.: Latency tolerance for gesture controlled continuous sound instrument without tactile feedback, in Proc. Int. Computer Music Conf. (ICMC2004) (Miami, 2004).
55. Michaels, C. F., Carello, C.: Direct Perception (Prentice-Hall, Englewood Cliffs, NJ, 1981).
56. Moeck, T. et al.: Progressive perceptual audio rendering of complex scenes, in Proc. Symp. on Interactive 3D Graphics and Games (I3D'07) (Seattle, 2007), 189–196.
57. Nordahl, R., Nilsson, N. C. in The Oxford handbook of interactive audio (eds Collins, K., Kapralos, B., Tessler, H.) (Oxford University Press, 2014).
58. O'Regan, J. K., Noë, A.: A sensorimotor account of vision and visual consciousness. Behavioral and Brain Sciences **24**, 883–917 (2001).

59. Picard, C., Tsingos, N., Faure, F.: Retargetting Example Sounds to Interactive Physics-Driven Animations, in Proc. AES Conf. Audio in Games (London, 2009).
60. Poeschl, S., Wall, K., Doering, N.: Integration of spatial sound in immersive virtual environments an experimental study on effects of spatial sound on presence, in Proc. IEEE Conf. Virtual Reality (Orlando, 2013), 129–130.
61. Pörschmann, C.: One's own voice in auditory virtual environments. Acta Acustica un. w. Acustica **87**, 378–388 (2001).
62. Puckette, M.: Max at seventeen. Computer Music J. **26**, 31–43 (2002).
63. Raghuvanshi, N., Lin, M. C.: Physically Based Sound Synthesis for Large-Scale Virtual Environments. IEEE Computer Graphics and Applications **27**, 14–18 (2007).
64. Rath, M., Rocchesso, D.: Continuous sonic feedback from a rolling ball. IEEE MultiMedia **12**, 60–69 (2005).
65. Rath, M., Fontana, F. in The Sounding Object (eds Rocchesso, D., Fontana, F.) 173–204 (Mondo Estremo, Firenze, 2003).
66. Ren, Z., Yeh, H., Lin, M. C.: Synthesizing contact sounds between textured models, in Proc. IEEE Conf. Virtual Reality (Waltham, 2010), 139–146.
67. Ren, Z., Yeh, H., Lin, M. C.: Example-guided physically based modal sound synthesis. ACM Trans. on Graphics **32**, 1 (2013).
68. Risset, J.-C., Wessel, D. L. in The psychology of music (ed Deutsch, D.) Second edition, 113–169 (Elsevier, 1999).
69. Rocchesso, D., Bresin, R., Fernstrom, M.: Sounding objects. IEEE MultiMedia **10**, 42–52 (2003).
70. Schwarz, D., Cahen, R., Brument, F., Ding, H., Jacquemin, C.: Sound level of detail in interactive audiographic 3D scenes, in Proc. Int. Computer Music Conf. (ICMC2011) (Huddersfield, 2011), 312–315.
71. Selfridge, R., Moffat, D., Reiss, J. D.: Sound synthesis of objects swinging through air using physical models. Applied Sciences **7**, 1177 (2017).
72. Sheridan, T. B., Furness, T. A. (eds.): Premier Issue, Presence: Teleoperators and Virtual Environment, vol. 1 (1992).
73. Sikström, E., De Götzen, A., Serafin, S.: The role of sound in the sensation of ownership of a pair of virtual wings in immersive VR, in Proc. Int. Conf. Audio Mostly (AM'14) (Aalborg, 2014), 1–6.
74. Sikström, E., De Götzen, A., Serafin, S.: Self-characterstics and sound in immersive virtual reality - Estimating avatar weight from footstep sounds, in Proc. IEEE Conf. Virtual Reality (Arles, 2015), 283–284.
75. Sinclair, J.-L.: Principles of Game Audio and Sound Design: Sound Design and Audio Implementation for Interactive and Immersive Media (CRC Press, 2020).
76. Skarbez, R., Brooks Jr, F. P., Whitton, M. C.: A survey of presence and related concepts. ACM Computing Surveys **50**, 1–39 (2017).
77. Slater, M.: Place illusion and plausibility can lead to realistic behaviour in immersive virtual environments. Phil. Trans. R. Soc. B **364**, 3549–3557 (2009).
78. Smith, J. O.: Physical Audio Signal Processing. Online book. 2010. URL http://ccrma. stanford.edu/Ëœjos/pasp/. Accessed March 11, 2021.
79. Smith, J. O.: Virtual acoustic musical instruments: Review and update. J. New Music Res. **33**, 283–304 (2004).
80. Sonnenschein, D.: Sound design: The expressive power of music, voice, and sound effects in cinema (Michael Wiese Productions, 2001).
81. Human Walking in Virtual Environments: Perception, Technology, and Applications (eds Steinicke, F., Visell, Y., Campos, J., Lecuyer, A.) (Springer Verlag, New York, 2013).
82. Sterling, A., Rewkowski, N., Klatzky, R. L., Lin, M. C.: Audio-Material Reconstruction for Virtualized Reality Using a Probabilistic Damping Model. IEEE Trans. on Visualization and Comp. Graphics **25**, 1855–1864 (2019).
83. Stevenson, R. A. et al.: Identifying and quantifying multisensory integration: a tutorial review. Brain Topography **27**, 707–730 (2014).

84. Stockburger, A.: The game environment from an auditory perspective, in Proc. Level Up: Digital Games Research Conference (eds Copier, M., Raessens, J.) (Utrecht, 2003).
85. Tajadura-Jiménez, A. et al.: As light as your footsteps: altering walking sounds to change perceived body weight, emotional state and gait, in Proc. ACM Conf. on Human Factors in Computing Systems (Seoul, 2015), 2943–2952.
86. Takala, T., Hahn, J.: Sound Rendering. Computer Graphics **26**, 211–220 (1992).
87. Tiraboschi, M., Avanzini, F., Ntalampiras, S.: Spectral Analysis for Modal Parameters Linear Estimate, in Proc. Int. Conf. Sound and Music Computing (SMC2020) (Torino, 2020), 276–283.
88. Tsingos, N., Gallo, E., Drettakis, G.: Perceptual audio rendering of complex virtual environments. ACM Trans. on Graphics (TOG) **23**, 249–258 (2004).
89. Välimäki, V., Pakarinen, J., Erkut, C., Karjalainen, M.: Discrete-time modelling of musical instruments. Rep. Prog. Phys. **69**, 1–78 (2006).
90. Van den Doel, K.: Physically based models for liquid sounds. ACM Trans. Applied Perception **2**, 534–546 (2005).
91. Van den Doel, K., Kry, P. G., Pai, D. K.: FoleyAutomatic: Physically-based Sound Effects for Interactive Simulation and Animation, in Proc. ACM SIGGRAPH 2001 (Los Angeles, 2001), 537–544.
92. Van den Doel, K., Pai, D. K. in Audio Anecdotes (ed Greenebaum, K.) (AK Peters, Natick, MA, 2004).
93. Van Vugt, F. T., Tillmann, B.: Thresholds of auditory-motor coupling measured with a simple task in musicians and non-musicians: was the sound simultaneous to the key press? PLoS One **9**, e87176 (2014).
94. Varela, F., Thompson, E., Rosch, E.: The Embodied Mind (MIT Press, Cambridge, MA, 1991).
95. Visell, Y. et al.: Sound design and perception in walking interactions. Int. J. Human-Computer Studies **67**, 947–959 (2009).
96. Vroomen, J., Keetels, M.: Perception of intersensory synchrony: a tutorial review. Attention, Perception, & Psychophysics **72**, 871–884 (2010).
97. Walsh, R.: Audio plugin development with cabbage, in Proc. Linux Audio Conf. (Maynooth, 2011), 47–53.
98. Wang, K., Liu, S.: Example-based synthesis for sound of ocean waves caused by bubble dynamics. Comput. Anim. and Virtual Worlds **29**, e1835 (2018).
99. Wessel, D.,Wright, M.: Problems and prospects for intimate musical control of computers. Computer Music J. **26**, 11–22 (2002).
100. Zheng, C., James, D. L.: Rigid-body fracture sound with precomputed soundbanks. ACM Trans. Graphics **29** (2010).

# Chapter 3
# Interactive and Immersive Auralization

Nikunj Raghuvanshi and Hannes Gamper

**Abstract** Real-time auralization is essential in virtual reality (VR), gaming, and architecture to enable an immersive audio-visual experience. The audio rendering must be congruent with visual feedback and respond with minimal delay to interactive events and user motion. The wave nature of sound poses critical challenges for plausible and immersive rendering and leads to enormous computational costs. These costs have only increased as virtual scenes have progressed away from enclosures toward complex, city-scale scenes that mix indoor and outdoor areas. However, hard real-time constraints must be obeyed while supporting numerous dynamic sound sources, frequently within a tightly limited computational budget. In this chapter, we provide a general overview of VR auralization systems and approaches that allow them to meet such stringent requirements. We focus on the mathematical foundation, perceptual considerations, and application-specific design requirements of practical systems today, and the future challenges that remain.

## 3.1 Introduction

Audition and vision are unique among our senses: they perceive propagating waves. As a result, they bring us detailed information not only of our immediate surroundings but of the world much beyond as well. Imagine talking to a friend in a cafe, the door is open, and outside is a bustling city intersection. While touch and smell give a detailed sense of our immediate surroundings, sight and sound tell us we are conversing with a friend, surrounded by other people in the cafe, immersed in a city, its sounds streaming in through the door. Virtual reality ultimately aims to re-create this sense of presence and immersion in a virtual environment, enabling a vast array of applications for society, ranging from entertainment to architecture and social interaction without the constraints of distance.

N. Raghuvanshi (✉) · H. Gamper
Microsoft Research, Redmond, USA
e-mail: nikunjr@microsoft.com

H. Gamper
e-mail: hannes.gamper@microsoft.com

© The Author(s) 2023
M. Geronazzo and S. Serafin (eds.), *Sonic Interactions in Virtual Environments*,
Human—Computer Interaction Series, https://doi.org/10.1007/978-3-031-04021-4_3

**Rendering.** To reproduce the audio-visual experience given in the example above, one requires a dynamic, digital 3D simulation of the world describing how *both* light and sound would be radiated, propagated, and perceived by an observer immersed in the computed virtual fields of light and sound. The world model usually takes the form of a 3D geometric description composed of triangulated meshes and surface materials. Sources of light and sound are specified with their 3D positions and radiative properties, including their directivity and the energy emitted within the perceivable frequency range. Given this information as input, special algorithms produce dynamic audio-visual signals that are displayed to the user via screens and speaker arrays or stereoscopic head-mounted displays and near-to-ear speakers or headphones. This is the overall process of *rendering*, whose two components are *visualization* and *auralization* (or visual- and audio-rendering).

Rendering has been a central problem in both the graphics and audio communities for decades. While the initial thrust for graphics came from computer-aided design applications, within audio, room acoustic auralization of planned auditoria and concert halls was a central driving force. The technical challenge with rendering is that modeling propagation in complex worlds is immensely compute-intensive. A naïve implementation of classical physical laws governing optics and acoustics is found to be many orders of magnitude slower than required (elaborated in Sect. 3.2.1). Furthermore, the exponential increase in compute power governed by Moore's law has begun to stall in the last decade due to fundamental physical limits [97]. These two facts together mean that modeling propagation quickly enough for practical use requires research into specialized system architectures and simulation algorithms.

**Perception and Interactivity.** A common theme in rendering research is that quantitative accuracy as required in engineering applications is not the primary goal. Rather, perception plays the central role: one must find ways to compute those aspects of physical phenomena that inform our sensory system. Consequently, initial graphics research in the 1970s focused on visible-surface determination [54] to convey spatial relations and object silhouettes, while initial room acoustics research focused on reverberation time [60] to convey presence in a room and indicate its size. With that foundation, subsequent research has been devoted toward increasing the amount of detail to reach "perceptually authentic" audio-visual rendering: one that is indistinguishable from an audio-visual capture of a real scene. Research has focused on the coupled problems of increasing our knowledge of psycho-physics, and designing fast techniques that leverage this knowledge to reduce computation while providing the means to test new psycho-physical hypotheses.

The interactivity of virtual reality and games adds an additional dimension of difficulty. In linear media such as movies, the sequence of events is fixed, and computation times of hours or days for pre-rendered digital content can be acceptable, with human assistance provided as necessary. However, interactive applications cannot be pre-rendered in this way, as the user actions are not known in advance. Instead, the computer must perform *real-time rendering*: as events unfold based on user input, the system must model how the scene would look and sound from moment to moment as the user moves and interacts with the virtual world. It must do so with minimal latency of about 10–100 ms, depending on the application. Audio introduces the additional challenge of a *hard* real-time deadline. While a visual frame rendered slightly late is not ideal but perhaps acceptable, audio lags may result in silent gaps in the output. Such signal discontinuities annoy the user and break immersion and presence. Therefore, auralization systems in VR tend to prioritize computational efficiency and perceptual plausibility while building toward perceptual authenticity from that starting point.

**Goal.** The purpose of this chapter is to present the fundamental concepts and design principles of modern real-time auralization systems, with an emphasis on recent developments in virtual reality and gaming applications. We do not aim for an exhaustive treatment of the theory and methods in the field. For such a treatment, we refer the reader to Vorländer's treatise on the subject [102].

**Organization.** We begin by outlining the computational challenges and the resulting architectural design choices of real-time auralization systems in Sect. 3.2. This architecture is then formalized via the Bidirectional Impulse Response (BIR), Head-Related Transfer Functions (HRTFs), and rendering equation in Sect. 3.3. In Sect. 3.4, we summarize relevant psycho-acoustic phenomena in complex VR scenes and elaborate on how one must balance a believable rendering with real-time constraints among other system design factors in Sect. 3.5. We then discuss in Sect. 3.6 how the formalism, perception, and design constraints come together into the deterministic-statistical decomposition of the BIR, a powerful idea employed by most auralization systems. Section 3.7 provides a brief overview of the two common approaches to acoustical simulation: geometric and wave-based methods. In Sect. 3.8, we discuss some example systems in use today in more depth, to illustrate how they balance the various constraints informing their design decisions, followed by the conclusion in Sect. 3.9.

## 3.2 Architecture of Real-time Auralization Systems

In this section, we discuss the specific physical aspects of sound that make it computationally difficult to model, which motivates a modular, efficient system architecture.

### 3.2.1 Computational Cost

To understand the specific modeling concerns of auralization, it helps to juxtapose with light simulation in games and VR applications. In particular

- **Speed:** The propagation speed of sound is low enough that we perceive its various transient aspects such as initial reflections and reverberation, which carry distinct perceptible information, while light propagation can be treated as instantaneous;

- **Phase:** Everyday sounds are often coherent or harmonic signals whose phase must be treated carefully throughout the auralization pipeline to avoid audible distortions such as signal discontinuities, whereas natural light sources tend to be incoherent;
- **Wavelength:** Audible sound wavelengths are comparable to the size of architectural and human features (cm to m) which makes wave diffraction ubiquitous. Unlike visuals, audible sound is not limited by line of sight.

Given the unique characteristics of sound propagation outlined above, auralization must begin with a fundamental treatment of sound as a transient, coherent wave phenomenon, while lighting can assume a much simpler geometric formulation of ray propagation for computing a stochastic, steady-state solution [57]. Auralization must carefully approximate the relevant physical mechanisms underlying the vibration of objects, propagation in air, and scattering by the listener's body. All these mechanisms require modeling highly oscillatory wave fields that must be sufficiently sampled in space and time, giving rise to the tremendous computational expense of brute-force simulation.

Assume some physical domain of interest with diameter $\mathcal{D}$, the highest frequency of interest $\nu_{max}$ and speed of propagation $c$. The smallest propagating wavelength of interest is $c/\nu_{max}$. Thus, the total degrees of freedom in the space-time volume of interest are $N_{dof} = (2\mathcal{D}\nu_{max}/c)^4$. The factor of two is due to the Nyquist limit which enforces two degrees of freedom per oscillation. As an example, for full audible bandwidth simulation of sound propagation up to $\nu_{max} = 20,000$ Hz in a scene that is $\mathcal{D} = 100$ m across, with $c = 340$ m/s in air: $N_{dof} = 1.9 \times 10^{16}$. For an update interval of 60 ms to meet latency requirements for interactive listener head orientation updates [22], one would thus need a computational rate of over 100 PetaFLOPS. By comparison, a typical game or VR application will allocate a single CPU core for audio with a computational rate in the range of tens of GigaFLOPS, which is too slow by a factor of at least one million. This gap motivates research in the area.

## 3.2.2 Modular Design

Since pioneering work in the 1990s such as DIVA [86, 96], most real-time auralization systems follow a modular architecture shown in Fig. 3.1. This architecture results in a flexible implementation and significant reduction of computational complexity, without substantially impacting simulation accuracy in cases of practical interest.

Rather than simulating the global scene as a single system which might be prohibitively expensive (see Sect. 3.2.1), the problem is divided into three components in a causal chain without feedback:

- **Production:** Sound is first produced at the source due to vibration, which, combined with local self-scattering, results in a direction-dependent radiated source signal;

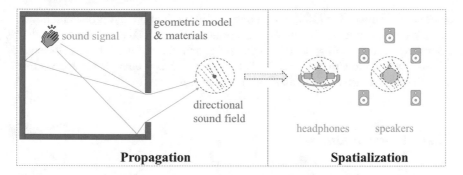

**Fig. 3.1** Modular architecture of real-time auralization systems. The propagation of sound emitted from each source is simulated within the 3D environment to compute a directional sound field immersing the listener. This field is given to the spatializer component that computes appropriate transducer signals for headphone or speaker playback

- **Propagation:** The radiated sound diffracts, scatters, and reflects in the scene to result in a direction-dependent sound field at the listener location;
- **Spatialization:** The sound field is heard by the listener. The spatialization component computes transducer signals for playback, taking the listener's head orientation into account. In the case of using headphones, this implies accounting for scattering due to the listener's head and shoulders, as described by the head-related transfer function (HRTF).

Our focus in this chapter will be on the latter two components; sound production techniques such as physical-modeling synthesis are covered in Chap. 2. Here, we assume a source modeled as a (monophonic) radiated signal combined with a direction-dependent radiation pattern.

This separation of the auralization problem into different components is key for efficient computation. Firstly, the perceptual characteristics of all three components may be studied separately and then approximated with tailored numerical methods. Secondly, since the final rendering is composed of these separate models, they can be flexibly modified at runtime. For instance, a source's sound and directivity pattern may be updated, or the listener orientation may change, without expensive re-computation of global sound propagation. Section 3.3 will formalize this idea.

**Limitations.** This architecture is not a good fit for cases with strong near-field interaction. For instance, if the listener's head is close to a wall, there can be non-negligible multiple scattering, so the feedback between propagation and spatialization cannot be ignored. This can be an important scenario in VR [69]. Similarly, if one plays a trumpet with its bell very close to a surface, the resonant modes and radiated sound will be modified, much like placing a mute, which is a case where there is feedback between all three components outlined above. Thus, numerical simulations for musical acoustics tend to be quite challenging. The interested reader can consult Bilbao's text on the subject [12] and more recent overview [14]. In the computer graphics community, the work in [104] also shows sound production and propagation modeled directly without the separability assumption, with special emphasis on handling dynamic geometry, for application in computer animation. Such simulations tend to be off-line, but modern graphics cards have become fast enough for approximate modeling of interactive 2D wind instruments in real-time [6].

### 3.2.3  Propagation

The propagation component takes the locations of a source and listener in the scene to predict the scene's acoustic response, modeling salient effects such as diffracted occlusion, initial reflections, and reverberation. Combined with source sounds and radiation patterns, it outputs a directional sound field to the listener. Propagation is usually the most compute-intensive portion of an auralization pipeline, motivating many techniques and systems, which we will discuss in Sects. 3.7 and 3.8. The methods have two assumptions in common.

**Linearity.** For most auralization applications, it is safe to assume that sound amplitudes remain low enough to obey ideal linear propagation, modeled by the scalar wave equation. As a result, the sound field at the listener location is a linear summation of contributions from all sound sources. There are some cases in games and VR when the assumption of linearity may be violated, for instance with explosions or brass instruments. In most such cases, the non-linear behavior is restricted to the vicinity of the event and may be treated via a first-order perturbative approximation which amounts to linear propagation with a locally varying sound speed [4, 27].

**Quasi-static scene configuration.** Interactive scenes are dynamic, but most propagation methods assume that the problem may be treated as quasi-static. At some fixed update rate, such as a visual frame, they take a static snapshot of the scene shape as well as the locations of the source and listener within it. Then propagation is modeled assuming a linear, time-invariant system for the duration of the visual frame. The computed response for each sound source is smoothly interpolated over frames to ensure a dynamic rendering free of artifacts to the listener.

Fast-moving sources need to be treated with additional care as direct interpolation of acoustic responses can become error-prone [80]. An important related aspect is the Doppler Shift on first arrival, a salient, audible effect. It may be approximated in the source model by modifying the radiated signal based on source and listener velocities, or by interpolating the propagation delay of the initial sound. Another case violating the quasi-static assumption are aero-acoustic sounds radiated from fast object motion through the air. These can be approximated within the source model with Lighthill's acoustic analogy [53], with subsequent linear propagation for real-time rendering [30, 31].

## 3.2.4  *Spatialization*

In a virtual reality scenario, the target of the audio rendering engine is typically a listener located within the virtual scene experiencing the virtual acoustic environment with both ears. For this experience to feel plausible or natural, sound should be rendered to the user's ears as if they were actually present in the virtual scene. The architecture in Fig. 3.1 neglects the effect of the listener on global sound propagation. The *spatialization* system (shown to the right in the figure) inserts the listener virtually into the scene and requires additional processing. A properly spatialized virtual sound source should be perceived by the listener as emanating from a given location. In the simplest case of free-field propagation, a sound source can be positioned virtually by convolving the source signal with a pair of filters (also known as *head-related transfer functions* (HRTFs)). This results in two ear input signals that can be presented directly to the listener over headphones. For a more complex virtual scene containing multiple sound sources as well as their acoustic interactions with the virtual environment, spatialization entails encoding appropriate localization cues to the sound field at the listener's ear entrances. Common approaches include spherical-harmonics based rendering ("Ambisonics") [42, 67] as well as object-based rendering [17].

**HRTFs.** If the sound is played back to the listener via headphones, this implies simulating the filtering that sound undergoes in a real sound field as it enters the ear entrances, due to reflections and scattering from the listener's torso, head, and pinnae. A convenient way to describe this filtering behavior is via the HRTFs. The HRTFs are a function of the direction of arrival and contain the localization cues that the human auditory system decodes to determine the direction of an incoming wavefront. HRTFs for a particular listener are usually constructed via measurements in an anechoic chamber [40], though recent efforts exist to derive HRTFs for a listener on the fly without an anechoic chamber [50, 61], by adapting or *personalizing* existing HRTF databases using anthropometric features [15, 38, 41, 89, 106], or by capturing image or depth data to model the HRTFs numerically [20, 58, 65]. For a review of HRTF personalization techniques, refer to Chap. 4 and see [48]. The HRTFs can be tabulated as two spherical functions $H^{\{l,r\}}(s, t)$ that encapsulate the angle-dependent acoustic transfer in the free field to the left and right ears. The set of incident angles $s$ contained in the HRTF dataset is typically dictated by the HRTF measurement setup [5, 39]. The process of applying HRTFs to a virtual source signal to encode localization cues is referred to as *binaural spatialization*.

Spatialization for loudspeaker arrays is also possible, commonly performed using channel-based methods such as Vector Base Amplitude Panning [72] or Ambisonics [42]. It is also possible to physically reproduce the virtual directional sound field using Wave Field Synthesis [2] with large loudspeaker arrays. For the rest of this chapter, we will focus on binaural spatialization, although most of the discussion can be easily adapted to loudspeaker reproduction as discussed in Chap. 5.

**Spherical-harmonics based rendering.** Various methods exist to spatialize acoustic scenes. A convenient description of directional fields is via spherical harmonics (SHs) or Ambisonics [43]. Given a SH representation of a scene, binaural ear input signals can be obtained directly via filtering with a SH representation of the listener's HRTFs [29]. However, encoding complex acoustic scenes to SHs of sufficiently high order while minimizing audible artifacts can be challenging [10, 11, 19, 51]. The openly available Resonance Audio [47] system follows this approach.

**Object-based rendering.** In this chapter, we will follow the direct parameterization over time and angle of arrival which is also common in practice, such as the illustrative auralization system we discuss in Sect. 3.8.4. The system directly outputs signals and directions, suitable for spatialization by applying appropriate HRTF pairs. The description of the acoustic propagation problem from a source to the listener in terms of a directional sound field as presented in Sect. 3.3.4 results in a convenient interface between the propagation model and the spatialization engine.

This provides three major advantages. Firstly, it enables a modular system design that treats propagation modeling and (real-time) spatialization as separate problems that are solved by independent sub-systems. This separation in turn allows improving and optimizing the sub-systems individually and can lead to significant computational cost savings. Secondly, a description of a sound field enveloping the listener in terms of time and angle of arrival is equivalent to an object-based representation, which is a well-established input format for existing spatialization software, thus allowing the system designer to build easily on existing spatialization systems. Finally, psycho-acoustic research on perceptual limits of human spatial hearing, such as just-noticeable-differences, are expressed as a function of time and angle of arrival (Sect. 3.4). Knowledge of these perceptual limits can be exploited for further computational savings.

## 3.3   Mathematical Model

Auralization may be formalized as a linear, time-invariant process as follows. Assume a quasi-static state of the world at the current visual frame. To auralize a sound source, consider its current *pose* (position and orientation) to determine its directional sound radiation and then model propagation and spatialization as a feed-forward chain of linear filters. Those filters in turn depend on the current world shape and listener pose, respectively.

**Notation.** For the remainder of this chapter, for any quantity $(\star)$ referring to the listener, we use prime $(\star')$ to denote a corresponding quantity referring to the source. In particular, $x$ is listener location and $x'$ source location. Temporal convolution is denoted by $*$.

### 3.3.1  The Green's Function

With the linearity and time-invariance assumptions, along with the absence of mean flow or wind, the Navier-Stokes equations simplify to the scalar wave equation that models propagating longitudinal pressure deviations from quiescent atmospheric pressure [70]:

$$\left[(1/c^2)\,\partial_t^2 - \nabla_x^2\right] p\left(t, x, x'\right) = \delta\left(t\right)\delta\left(x - x'\right), \tag{3.1}$$

where $c = 340$ m/s is the speed of sound, $\nabla_x^2$ the 3D Laplacian operator ranging over $x$. The solution is performed on some 3D domain provided by the scene's shape, with appropriate boundary conditions to model the frequency-dependent absorptivity of physical materials.

Sound propagation is induced by a pulsed excitation at time $t = 0$ and source location $x'$ with $\delta(\cdot)$ denoting the Dirac delta function. The solution $p(t, x, x')$ is Green's function that fully describes the scene's global wave transport, including diffraction and scattering. The principle of acoustic reciprocity ensures that source and listener positions are interchangeable [70]:

$$p(t, x, x') = p(t, x', x). \tag{3.2}$$

For treating general scenes, a numerical solver must be employed to discretely sample Green's function in space and time. This includes accurate wave-based methods that directly solve for the time-evolving field on a grid, or fast geometric methods that employ the high-frequency Eikonal approximation. We will discuss solution methods in Sect. 3.7.

In principle, Green's function has complete information [3], including directionality, which can be extracted via spatio-temporal convolution of $p(t, x, x')$ with volumetric source and listener distributions that can model arbitrary radiation patterns [13] and listener directivity [91]. But such an approach is too expensive for real-time evaluation on large scenes, requiring temporal convolution and spatial quadrature over sub-wavelength grids that need to be repeated when either the source or listener moves. Geometric techniques cannot follow such an approach at all, as they do not model wave phase.

This is where modularity (Sect. 3.2.2) becomes indispensable: the source and listener are not directly included within the propagation simulation, but are instead incorporated via tabulated directivity functions that result from their local radiation and scattering characteristics. Below, we formulate the propagation component of this modular approach, beginning with the simplest case of an isotropic source and listener, building up to a fully bidirectional representation that can be combined with arbitrary source and listener directivity during rendering.

### 3.3.2   Impulse Response

Consider an isotropic (omni-directional) sound source located at $x'$ that is emitting a coherent pressure signal $q'(t)$. The resulting pressure signal at listener location $x$ can be computed using a temporal convolution:

$$q(t; x, x') = q'(t) \ast p(t; x, x'). \tag{3.3}$$

Here, $p(t; x, x')$ is obtained by evaluating Green's function between the listener and source locations $(x, x')$. We denote this evaluation by putting them after semi-colon $p(t; x, x')$ to signify they are held constant, yielding a function of time alone. This function is the (monoaural) impulse response capturing the various acoustic path delays and amplitudes from the source to the listener via the scene. The vibrational aspects of how the source event generated the sound $q'(t)$ are abstracted away— it may be synthesized at runtime, or read out from a pre-recorded file and freely substituted.

### 3.3.3   Directional Impulse Response

The *directional* impulse response $d(t, s; x, x')$ [32] generalizes the impulse response $p(t; x, x')$ to include direction of arrival, $s$. Intuitively, it is the signal obtained by the listener if they were to point an ideal directional microphone in direction $s$ when the source at $x'$ emits an isotropic impulse.

   Given a directional impulse response, spatialization for the listener can be performed to reproduce the directional listening experience via

$$q^{\{l,r\}}(t; x, x') = q'(t) \ast \int_{\mathcal{S}^2} d\left(t, s; x, x'\right) \ast H^{\{l,r\}}\left(\mathcal{R}^{-1}(s), t\right) ds, \tag{3.4}$$

where $H^{\{l,r\}}(s, t)$ are the left and right HRTFs of the listener as discussed in Sect. 3.2.4, $\mathcal{R}$ is a rotation matrix mapping from head to world coordinate system, and $s \in \mathcal{S}^2$ represents the space of incident spherical directions forming the integration domain. Note the advantage of separating propagation (directional impulse response) from spatialization (HRTF application). The expensive simulation necessary for solving (3.1) can ignore the listener's body entirely, which is inserted later taking its dynamic rotation $\mathcal{R}$ into account, via separately tabulated HRTFs as in (3.4).

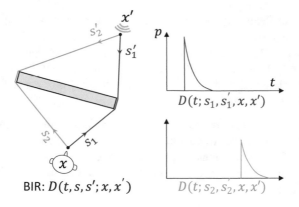

**Fig. 3.2** Bidirectional impulse response (BIR). An impulse radiates from source position $x'$, propagates through a scene, and arrives via two paths in this simple case at listener position $x$. The paths radiate in directions $s_1'$ and $s_2'$ and arrive from directions $s_1$ and $s_2$, respectively, with delays based on the respective path lengths. The bidirectional impulse response (BIR) denoted by $D(t, s, s'; x, x')$ contains this time-dependent directional information. Evaluating for specific radiant and incoming directions isolates arrivals, as shown on the right. (figure adapted from [26])

### 3.3.4   Bidirectional Impulse Response (BIR) and Rendering Equation

The above still leaves out direction-dependent radiation at the source. A complete description of auralization for localized sound sources can be achieved by the natural extension to the bidirectional impulse response (BIR) [26]; an 11-dimensional function of the wave field, $D(t, s, s'; x, x')$, illustrated in Fig. 3.2. Analogous to the HRTF, the source's radiation pattern is tabulated in a source directivity function (SDF), $S(s', t)$, such that its radiated signal in any direction $s'$ is given by $q'(t) * S(t; s')$. We can now write the (binaural) rendering equation:

$$q^{\{l,r\}}(t; x, x') = q'(t) *$$
$$\iint D\left(t, s, s'; x, x'\right) * S\left(\mathcal{R}'^{-1}(s'), t\right) * H^{\{l,r\}}\left(\mathcal{R}^{-1}(s), t\right) \, ds \, ds',$$

(3.5)

where $\mathcal{R}$ is a rotation matrix mapping from the listener's head to the world coordinate system, $\mathcal{R}'$ maps rotation from the source to the world coordinate system, and the double integral varies over the space of both incident and emitted directions $s, s' \in \mathcal{S}^2$. A similar formulation can be obtained for speaker-based rendering by using, for instance, VBAP speaker panning weights [72] instead of HRTFs.

The BIR is convolved with the source's and listener's free-field directional responses $S$ and $H^{\{l,r\}}$, respectively, while accounting for their rotation since $(s, s')$

are in world coordinates, to capture modification due to directional radiation and reception. The integral repeats this for all combinations of $(s, s')$, yielding the net binaural response. This is finally convolved with the emitted signal $q'(t)$ to obtain a binaural output that should be delivered to the entrances of the listener's ear canals. Finally, if multiple sound sources are present, this process is repeated for each source and the results are summed.

**Bidirectional decomposition and reciprocity.** The bidirectional impulse response generalizes the more restrictive notions of impulse response in (3.4) and (3.3), illustrated in Fig. 3.2. The directional impulse response can be obtained by integrating over all radiating directions $s'$ and yields directional effects to the listener for an omnidirectional source:

$$d(t, s; x, x') \equiv \int_{S^2} D(t, s, s'; x, x') \, ds'. \tag{3.6}$$

Similarly, a subsequent integration over directions to the listener, $s$, yields back the monoaural impulse response, $p(t; x, x')$.

The BIR admits direct geometric interpretation. With source and listener located at $(x', x)$, respectively, consider any pair of radiated and arrival directions $(s', s)$. In general, multiple paths connect these pairs, $(x', s') \rightsquigarrow (x, s)$, with corresponding delays and amplitudes, all of which are captured by $D(t, s, s'; x, x')$. Figure 3.2 illustrates a simple case. The BIR is thus a fully reciprocal description of sound propagation within an arbitrary scene. Interchanging source and listener, all propagation paths reverse:

$$D(t, s, s'; x, x') = D(t, s', s; x', x). \tag{3.7}$$

This reciprocal symmetry mirrors that for the underlying wave field, $p(t; x, x') = p(t; x', x)$ and requires a full bidirectional description. In particular, the directional impulse response is non-reciprocal.

## 3.3.5   Band-limitation and the Diffraction Limit

It is important to remember that the bidirectional impulse response is a mathematically convenient intermediate representation only, and cannot be realized physically. The only physically observed quantity is the final rendered audio, $q^{\{l,r\}}(t; x, x')$. In particular, the BIR representation allows unlimited resolution in time and direction. The source signal, $q'(t)$, is temporally band-limited for typical sounds, due to aggressive absorption in solid media and air as frequency increases. Similarly, auditory perception is limited to 20 kHz. Band-limitation holds for directional resolution as well because of the *diffraction limit* [16] which places a fundamental restriction on the angular resolution achievable with a spatially finite radiator or receiver.

For a propagating wavelength $\lambda$, the diffraction-limited angular resolution scales as $\mathcal{D}/\lambda$, where $\mathcal{D}$ is the diameter of an enclosing sphere, such as around a radiating object, or the listener's head and shoulders in the case of HRTFs [105]. Therefore, all the convolutions and spherical quadratures in (3.5) may be performed on a discretization with sufficient sub-wavelength resolution at the highest frequency of interest. Alternatively, it is common to perform time convolutions in frequency domain via the Fast Fourier Transform (FFT) for efficiency. Similarly, spherical harmonics (SH) form an orthonormal linear basis over the sphere and can be used to accelerate the spherical quadrature of function product to an inner product of spherical harmonic (SH) coefficients. An end-to-end auralization system using this approach was shown in [63].

## 3.4 Structure and Perception of the Bidirectional Impulse Response (BIR)

To explain how the theory outlined above can be put into practice, we will first review the physical and perceptual structure of the BIR, followed by a discussion of how auralization systems approximate in various ways.

### 3.4.1 Physical Structure

The structure of a typical (bidirectional) impulse response may be understood in three phases in time, as illustrated in Fig. 3.3. First, the emitted sound must propagate via the shortest path, potentially diffracting around obstruction edges to reach the listener after some onset delay. This is the initial (or "direct") sound. The initial sound is followed by early reflections due to scattering and reflection from scene geometry. As sound continues to scatter multiple times from the scene, the temporal arrival

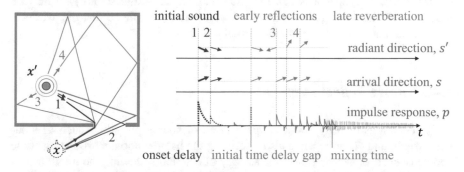

**Fig. 3.3** Structure of the bidirectional impulse response (figure adapted from [26])

density of reflections increases, while the energy of an individual arrival decreases due to absorption at material boundaries and in the air. Over time, with sufficient scattering, the response approaches decaying Gaussian noise, which is referred to as late reverberation. The transition from early reflections to late reverberation is demarcated by the *mixing time* [1, 98].

As we discuss next, each of these phases has a distinct contribution to the overall spatial perception of a sound. These properties of the human auditory perception play a key role in informing how one might approximate the rendering equation (3.5) within limited computational resources, while still retaining an immersive auditory experience. A more detailed review of perception of room acoustics can be found in [37] and [60]. All observations and terms below can be found in these references, unless otherwise noted.

### 3.4.2 Initial ("Direct") Sound

Our perception strongly relies on the initial sound to localize sound sources, a phenomenon called the *precedence effect* [62]. Referring to Fig. 3.3, if there is a secondary arrival that is roughly within 1 ms of the initial sound, we perceive a direction intermediate between the two arrival directions, termed *summing localization*, representing the temporal resolution of spatial hearing. Beyond this 1 ms time window, our perceptual system exerts a strongly non-linear suppression effect, so people do not confuse the direction of strong reflections with the true heading of the sound. Sometimes called the *Haas effect*, a later arrival may need to be as much as 10 dB louder than the initial sound to affect the perceived direction significantly. Note that this is not to say that the later arrival is not perceived at all, only that its effect is not to substantially change the localized direction.

Consider the case shown in Fig. 3.3, and assume the walls do not substantially transmit sound. The sound shown inside the room would be localized by the listener outside as arriving from the direction of the doorway, rather than the line of sight. Such cues are a natural part of how we navigate to visually occluded events in everyday life. The upshot is that in virtual reality, the initial sound path may be multiply-diffracted and must be modeled with particular care so that the user gets localization cues consistent with the virtual world.

### 3.4.3 Early Reflections

Early reflections directly affect the perception of source properties such as loudness, width, and distance while also informing the listener about surrounding scene geometry such as nearby reflectors. A copy of a sound following the initial arrival is perceptually fused up until a delay called the *echo threshold*, beyond which it is perceived as a separate auditory event. The echo threshold varies between 10 ms for impulsive sounds, through 50 ms for speech to 80 ms for orchestral music [62, Table 1].

The impact of the loudness of early reflections is important in two ways. Firstly, the perception of source distance is known to correlate with the energy ratio between initial sound and remaining response (whose energy mostly comes from early reflections), called the direct-to-reverberant ratio (DRR) [92]. This is often also called the "wet ratio" by audio designers. Secondly, how well one can understand and localize sounds depends on the ratio of the energy of direct sound and early reflection in the first 50 ms to the rest of the response, as measured by *clarity* ($C_{50}$).

The directional distribution of reflections conveys important detail about the size and shape of the local environment around the listener and source. The ratio of reflected energy arriving horizontally and perpendicular to the initial sound is called *lateral energy fraction* and contributes to the perception of spaciousness and affects the *apparent source width*. Further, in VR, strong individual reflections from surfaces close to the listener provide an important proximity cue [69].

Thus, an auralization system must model strong initial reflections as well as the aggregate energy and directionality of later reflections up to the first 80 ms to ensure important cues about the sound source and environment are conveyed.

### 3.4.4 Late Reverberation

The reverberation time, $T_{60}$, is the time taken by the reverberant energy to decay by 60 dB. Since the reverberation contains numerous, lengthy paths through the scene, it provides a sense of the overall scene, such as its size. The $T_{60}$ is frequency-dependent; the relative decay rate across various frequencies informs the listener about the acoustic materials in a scene and atmospheric absorption.

The aggregate directional properties of reverberation affect *listener envelopment* which is the perception of being present in a room and immersed in its reverberant field (see Chap. 11 and Sect. 11.4.3 for further discussions on related topics). In virtual reality, one may often be present *outside* a room containing sounds and any implausible envelopment becomes especially distracting. For instance, consider the situation in Fig. 3.3—rendering an enveloping room reverberation for the listener will sound wrong, since the expectation would be low envelopment.

## 3.5 System Design Considerations for VR Auralization

Many types of real-time auralization systems exist today that approximate the rendering equation (3.5), and in particular, how to evaluate the scene's sound propagation (i.e., the BIR, $D(t, s, s'; x, x')$) which is typically the most compute-intensive portion. They gain efficiency by making approximations based on the intended application, with a knowledge of the limits of auditory perception.

### 3.5.1 Room Auralization

The roots of auralization research lie in the area of computational modeling of room acoustics, an active area of research with developments dating back at least 50 years [7, 60]. The main objective of these computer models has been to aid in the architectural design of enclosures, such as offices, classrooms, and concert halls. The predictions of these models can then be used by acousticians to propose architectural design changes or acoustic treatments to improve the reverberant properties of a particular room or hall, such as speech intelligibility in a classroom. This requires models that simulate the room's first reflections and reverberation with perceptual authenticity. The direct path in such applications can often be computed analytically since the line of sight is rarely blocked. We direct the reader to Gade's book chapter [37] on the subject of room acoustics for an excellent summary of the requirements, metrics, and methods in the field from the viewpoint of concert hall design.

While initially the computer models could only produce quantitative estimates of room acoustic parameters, with increasing compute power, real-time auralization systems were proposed near the beginning of the millennium [86]. As we will discuss in more detail shortly, geometric methods are standard in the area today because they are especially well-suited for modeling a single enclosure where visual occlusion between sounds and listener is not dominant. This holds very well in any hall designed for speech or music. Room auralization is available today in commercial packages such as ODEON [82] and CATT [28].

### 3.5.2 VR Auralization

The concerns of real-time VR auralization are quite distinct along a number of dimensions, which result from going from individual room to a scene that can span entire city blocks with numerous indoor and outdoor areas. This results in a unique set of considerations that we enumerate below, for two reasons. Firstly, they provide a framing for understanding current research in the area and the trade-offs current systems make, which we will discuss in the following sections. Secondly, we hope that the concise listing of practical problems motivates new research in the area, as no system today can meet all these criteria.

1. **Real time within limited computation.** A VR application's auralization component can usually only use a single or a few CPU cores for audio simulation at runtime, since resources must be shared with simulating other aspects of the world, such as rigid-body collisions, character animation, and AI path plan-

ning. In contrast, owing to the application, in room acoustic auralization one can consume a majority of the resources of a computer including the parallel compute power of modern graphics cards. With power-efficient mobile processors integrated into phones and standalone head-mounted displays, the pressure to minimize computation has only increased.

2. **Scene complexity and non line of sight.** Room acoustics theory often starts by assuming a single connected space such as a concert hall that has lines of sight from the stage to all listener locations. This allows for a powerful simplification of the sound field as an analytically computable direct sound combined with a diffuse reverberant field. Modern VR systems for building and game acoustics consider the much broader class of all scenes such as a building floor with many rooms, or a street canyon with buildings that may be entered. These are complex scenes not just in the sense of surface detail but also in that the air volume is topologically complex, with many concavities. As a result, non line of sight cases are common. For instance, hearing sounds in the same room with plausible reverberation can be as important as *not* hearing sounds inside another room, or hearing sounds from unseen sources diffracted around a corner or door.

3. **Perception.** Physical accuracy is important to VR auralization not as a goal in itself but rather in so far as it impacts sensory immersion. This opens opportunities for fast approximations, and deeply informs practical systems that scale their errors based on the acuity of the human auditory system. This observation underlies the deterministic-statistical decomposition discussed in the next section. Further, in many applications such as games, plausibility can be sufficient as a starting point, while for instance in auralizing building acoustics one might need perceptual authenticity.

4. **Dynamic sounds.** VR auralization must often support dynamic sound sources that can translate and rotate. The rendering must respond with low latency and without distracting artifacts, even for fast source motion. This adds significant complexity to a minimum-viable practical system. However, in architectural acoustic systems, static sound sources can be a feasible starting point.

5. **Dynamic geometry.** In many applications, the scene geometry can be changed interactively. This may be while designing a virtual space, in which case an acoustical system for static scenes may re-compute on the updated geometry; depending on the system this can take seconds to hours. The more challenging case is when the geometry is changing in real time. The change might be "locally dynamic", such as opening a door or moving an obstruction. Since such changes are localized in an otherwise static scene, many systems are able to model such effects. Lastly, the scene may be "globally dynamic", where there might be unpredictable global changes, such as when a game player creates a building in Minecraft or Fortnite and expects to hear the audio rendering adapt to it in real time—while this has the most practical utility it is also the most challenging case.

6. **Robustness.** VR requires high robustness given unpredictable user inputs. This means the severity and frequency of large outlying errors may matter more than average error. For instance, as the listener moves quickly through a scene

through multiple rooms, the variation in reverberation and diffracted occlusion must stay smooth reliably. This is a tightly restrictive constraint: a technique that has large outlying errors may not be viable in immersive VR regardless of its average error. As an example, an implausible error in calculating occlusion with only 0.1% probability for an experience running at 30 frames per second means distracting the user every 33 s on average. This deteriorates to 3.3 s with 10 sound sources and so on.

7. **Scalability.** The system should ideally expose compute-quality trade-offs along two axes. Firstly, VR scenes can contain hundreds to thousands of dynamic sound sources, and it is desirable if the signal processing can scale from high-quality rendering of a few sound sources to lower quality (but still plausible) rendering for numerous sound sources. Secondly, the acoustical simulation should also allow methods for reducing quality gracefully as scene size increases. For instance, high-quality propagation modeling of a conference room, up to a rough simulating of a city.

8. **Automation.** For VR applications, it is preferable to avoid any per-scene manual work, such as geometric scene simplification. Game scenes in particular can span over kilometers with multiple buildings designed iteratively during the production process. This makes manual simplification a major hurdle for practical usage. The auralization system must ideally directly ingest complex scenes with millions of polygons, and perform any necessary simplification while minimizing any human expertise or input, unlike in room auralization.

9. **Artistic direction.** VR often requires the final rendering to be controlled by a sound designer. For instance, the reverberation and diffracted occlusion on important dialogue might be reduced to boost speech intelligibility in a game. Or one might want to re-map the dynamic range of the audio rendering with the limits of the audio reproduction system or user comfort in mind. A viable system must provide methods that allow such design intent to be expressed and influence the auralization process appropriately.

## 3.6   Rendering the BIR: the Deterministic-Statistical Decomposition

A powerful technique employed by most real-time auralization systems is to decompose the BIR as a sum of a deterministic and statistical component. This is deeply informed by acoustical perception (Sect. 3.4) and is key to enabling the computational trade-offs VR auralization must contend with, as described in the prior section. The initial sound and strong early reflections, such as sound heard via a portal or echoes heard from nearby large surfaces, are treated deterministically: that is, simulated and rendered in physical detail, and updated in real time based on the dynamic source and listener pose and scene geometry. Weak early reflections and late reverberation are represented only statistically, ignoring the precise details of each of the amplitudes and delays of thousands of arrivals or more, which are perceived in aggregate.

To formalize, the BIR is decomposed as

$$D(t, s, s'; x, x') = D_d(t, s, s'; x, x') + D_s(t, s, s'; x, x'). \qquad (3.8)$$

Referring to Fig. 3.3, the initial sound and early reflection spikes deemed perceptually salient can be included accurately in $D_d$. The residual is $D_s$, which is usually modeled as noise characterized by its perceptually relevant statistical properties.

Substituting into the rendering equation (3.5) and observing linearity, we have

$$q^{\{l,r\}}(t; x, x') = \sum_{\{d,s\}} q'(t) * \iint D_{\{d,s\}} * S\left(\mathcal{R}'^{-1}(s'), t\right) * H^{\{l,r\}}\left(\mathcal{R}^{-1}(s), t\right) ds \, ds',$$
$$(3.9)$$

so that the input mono signal, $q'(t)$, is split off as input into separate filtering processes for the two components, whose binaural outputs are summed. This is a fairly standard architecture followed by both research and commercial systems, as the two components may be approximated independently with perception and the particular application in mind. For the remainder of this section, we will assume the BIR components have been computed and focus on the signal processing for rendering. The next section will discuss how this decomposition informs the design of acoustic simulation methods.

### 3.6.1 Deterministic Component, $D_d$

The deterministic component, $D_d$, is typically represented as a set of $n_d$ peaks:

$$D_d(t, s, s'; x, x') \approx \sum_{i=0}^{n_d-1} a_i(t) * \delta(t - \tau_i) \, \delta(s' - s_i') \, \delta(s - s_i). \qquad (3.10)$$

Each term represents an echo of the emitted impulse that arrives at the listener position after a delay of $\tau_i$ from world direction $s_i$, having been previously radiated from the source in world direction $s_i'$ at time $t = 0$. The amplitude filter $a_i(t)$ captures transport effects along the path from edge diffraction, scattering, and frequency-dependent transmission/reflection from scene geometry. Note that the amplitude filter is causal, i.e., $a_i(t) = 0$ for $t < 0$, and by convention $\tau_{i+1} > \tau_i$. The parameter $n_d$ is key for trading between rendering quality and computational resources. It is usual to at least treat the initial sound path deterministically (i.e., $n_d \geq 1$) because of its high importance for localization due to the Precedence Effect. Audio engines will usually designate this ($i = 0$) as the "dry" path with separate design controls due to its perceptual importance.

Substituting from (3.10) into Eq. (3.9), we get

$$q_d^{\{l,r\}}(t) = \sum_{i=0}^{n_d-1} q'(t) \, * \, \delta(t - \tau_i) * a_i(t) * S\left(\mathcal{R}'^{-1}(s_i'), t\right) * H^{\{l,r\}}\left(\mathcal{R}^{-1}(s_i), t\right).$$

(3.11)

Thus, each path's processing is a linear filter chain whose binaural output is summed to render the deterministic component to the listener. Reading the equation from left to right: for each path, take the monophonic source signal and input it to a delay line. Read the delay line at (fractional) delay $\tau_i$ and filter the output based on amplitude filter $a_i$, then filter it based on the source's radiation pattern. The lookup via $\mathcal{R}'^{-1}(s_i')$ signifies that one must rotate the radiant direction of the path from world space to the local coordinate system of the source's spherical radiation pattern data.

Finally, the last factor makes concrete the modularity shown in Fig. 3.1: the resulting monophonic signal from this prior processing is sent to the spatializer module as arriving from direction $\mathcal{R}^{-1}(s_i)$ relative to the listener. One is free to substitute any spatializer to separately trade off quality and speed of spatialization versus other costs and priorities for the system. One could even use multiple spatialization techniques, such as high-quality spatialization for the initial path, and lower fidelity for reflections. In a software implementation, the spatializer often acts as a sink for monophonic signals, processing each, mixing their outputs, and sending them to a low-level audio engine for transmission to transducers, thus performing the summation in (3.11) as well.

Similar to the choice of spatializer, the details of all other filtering operations are highly flexible. For the amplitude filter $a_i$, the simplest realization is to multiply by a scalar for average magnitude over frequencies, thus representing arrivals with idealized Dirac spikes. But for the initial sound filter $a_0$, even in a minimalistic setting it is common to apply a low-pass filter to capture the audible muffling of visually occluded sounds. A more accurate implementation accounting for frequency-dependent boundary impedance could use equalization filters in octave bands. For source directivity, it is common to measure and store radiation patterns as third-octave or octave-band data tabulated over the sphere of directions while ignoring phase. Convolution can then be realized via modern fast graphic equalizer algorithms that employ recursive time-domain filters [68].

The commutative and associative properties of convolution are a powerful tool to optimize signal processing. The ordering of filters in (3.11) has been chosen to illustrate this. The delay is applied in the very first operation. This makes it so that we only need one single-write-multiple-read delay line shared across all paths. The signal $q'(t)$ is written as input, and each path reads out at delay $\tau_i$. This is a commonly used optimization. Further, one may then use the associative property to group the factors: $a_i(t) * S\left(\mathcal{R}'^{-1}(s_i'), t\right)$. If both are implemented, say, using an octave-band graphic equalizer, then the per-band amplitudes can be multiplied first and provided to a single instance of the equalizer—a nearly two-fold reduction in equalization compute. These optimizations illustrate the importance of linearity and modularity in the efficient implementation of auralization systems.

## 3.6.2   Statistical Component, $D_s$

The central concept for rendering the statistical component, $D_s$, is to use an analysis-synthesis approach [56]. The analysis phase does lossy perceptual coding of the statistical component of the BIR, $D_s$, to compute $\bar{D}_s$ as the energy envelope of the response summing over time, frequency, and direction. We use the over-bar notation $\bar{f}(\bar{y})$ to indicate that $y$ is sub-sampled, and $f$'s corresponding energy is appropriately summed at each sample of $\bar{y}$ without loss via some windowing. For instance, if $p(t)$ is an impulse response, $\bar{p}(\bar{t})$ indicates the corresponding *echogram*, which is the histogram of $p^2(t)$ sampled at some time-bin centers, $\bar{t}$. This notation is introduced to indicate the reduction in the sampling rate of $y$, and loss of fine structure information in $f$ at its original sampling rate, such as phase.

**Parametric reverberation.** During real-time rendering, the description captured in $\bar{D}_s$ can be synthesized using fast *parametric reverberation* techniques: the "parameters" being statistical properties that determine $\bar{D}_s$, as we will discuss. The key advantage is that since the fine structure of the response in time, frequency, and direction is left unspecified, one has vast freedom in choosing efficient techniques. These techniques often rely on recursive time-domain filtering which can potentially make the CPU cost far smaller than applying a few seconds long filter via frequency-domain convolution. The research problem is to make the artificial reverberation sound natural. Among other concerns, the produced reverberation must have realistically high temporal echo density and sound colorless, not introducing perceivable spectral or temporal modulations that cannot be controlled. For further reading, we point readers to the extensive survey in [99]. In the following, we focus on how one might characterize $\bar{D}_s$.

**Energy Decay Relief (EDR).** The EDR [56] is a central concept for statistical encoding of acoustical responses. Consider a monoaural impulse response, $p(t)$. The EDR, $\bar{p}(\bar{t}, \bar{\omega})$, is computed by performing short-time Fourier analysis on $p(t)$ to compute how its energy spectral density integrated over perceptual frequency bands with centers $\bar{\omega}$ varies over time-bin centers $\bar{t}$. It can be visualized as a spectrogram. Frequency dependence results from materials of the boundary (e.g., wood tends to be more absorbent at high frequencies compared to concrete) and atmospheric absorption. Frequency band centers are typically spaced by octaves for real-time auralization, and time bins typically have a width of around 10 ms.

The reduced sampling rate makes the EDR, $\bar{p}$, already quite compact compared to $p$, which is a highly oscillatory noisy signal at audio sample rates. Further, the EDR is smooth in time: it exhibits slow variation during early reflections (especially if the strong peaks have been separated out already into $D_d$) followed by monotonic decay during late reverberation. This opens up many avenues for a low-dimensional description with a few parameters. For instance, for a single enclosure, the EDR in each frequency band may be well-approximated by an exponential decay, resulting in a compact description for the late reverberation parameterized by the initial energy, $\bar{p}_0$, and 60-dB decay time, $T_{60}$ in each frequency band:

$$\bar{p}(\bar{t}, \bar{\omega}) \approx \bar{p}_0(\bar{\omega}) 10^{-6\bar{t}/T_{60}(\bar{\omega})}. \tag{3.12}$$

Apart from substantial further compression, the great advantage of such a parametric description is that it is easy to interpret, allowing artistic direction. Reverberation plugins will typically provide $\bar{p}_0$ as a combination of a broadband "wet gain" and a graphic equalizer, as well as the decay times, $T_{60}(\bar{\omega})$ over frequency bands. For interactive auralization, the artist can exert aesthetic control by the simple means of modifying the reverberation parameters produced from acoustic simulation. For instance, when the player enters a narrow tunnel in VR, footsteps might get a realistic initial power ($\bar{p}_0$) to convey the constricted space, yet speech might have the wet gain reduced to increase the clarity ($C_{50}$) and improve the intelligibility of dialogue.

**Bidirectional EDR.** For an enclosure where conditions approach ideal diffuse reverberation, the EDR can be a sufficient description. Parametric reverberators will typically ensure that the same EDR is realized at both the ears but that the fine structure is mutually decorrelated, so that the reverberation is perceived by the listener as outside their head. However, in VR applications it becomes important to model the directionality inherent in reverberation because it can become strongly anisotropic. For instance, a visually occluded sound in another room heard through a door will be temporally diffuse, but directionally localized towards the door.

The concept of EDR can be extended naturally to the *bidirectional* EDR, $\bar{D}_s(\bar{t}, \bar{\omega}, \bar{s}, \bar{s}'; x, x')$, which adds dependence on direction for both source and listener. It can be constructed and interpreted as follows. Consider a source located at $x'$ that radiates a Dirac impulse in a beam centered around directional bin center $\bar{s}'$. After propagating through the scene, it is received by the listener at location $x$, who beamforms in the direction $\bar{s}$ and then computes the EDR on the received time-dependent signal. The bidirectional EDR thus captures the frequency-dependent energy decay for all direction-bin pairs $\{\bar{s}, \bar{s}'\}$.

Invoking the exponential decay model, the bidirectional EDR may be approximated as

$$\bar{D}_s(\bar{t}, \bar{\omega}, \bar{s}, \bar{s}'; x, x') \approx \bar{p}_0(\bar{\omega}, \bar{s}, \bar{s}'; x, x') 10^{-6\bar{t}/T_{60}(\bar{\omega}, \bar{s}, \bar{s}'; x, x')}. \tag{3.13}$$

Due to the curse of dimensionality, simulating and rendering the bidirectional EDR can get quite costly despite the simplifications. In practice, one must choose the sampling resolution of all the parameters judiciously depending on the application. An extreme case of this is when we sum over the entire range of a parameter, effectively removing it as a dimension.

Let's consider one example that illustrates the kind of trade-offs offered by statistical modeling in balancing rendering quality and computational complexity. One may profitably compute the $T_{60}$ for energy summed over all listener directions $s$, and source directions $s'$, which amounts to computing the monophonic EDR to derive the reverberation time. In that case, one obtains a simplified hybrid approximation:

$$\bar{\bar{D}}_s(\bar{t}, \bar{\omega}, \bar{s}, \bar{s}'; x, x') \approx \bar{p}_0(\bar{\omega}, \bar{s}, \bar{s}'; x, x') 10^{-6\bar{t}/T_{60}(\bar{\omega}; x, x')}. \tag{3.14}$$

The first factor still captures strong anisotropy in reverberant energy, such as reverberation heard by a listener as streaming from a portal, or reverberant power being higher when a human speaker faces a close by reverberant chamber rather than away. In fact, $\bar{p}_0(\bar{\omega}, \bar{s}, \bar{s}'; x, x')$ can be understood as a multiple-input-multiple-output (MIMO) frequency-dependent transfer matrix for incoherent energy between a source and receiver for directional channels sampled via $s'$ and $s$, respectively. The approximation lies in the second factor—directionally varying decay times for a single sound source are not modeled, which may be quite subtle to perceive in many cases.

## 3.7 Computing the BIR

Acoustic simulation is the key computationally expensive task in modern auralization systems due to the high complexity of today's virtual scenes. In particular, at every visual frame, for all source and listener pairs with locations $(x, x')$, the system must compute the BIR $D(t, s, s'; x, x')$, which may then be applied on each source's audio as discussed in the prior section. There are two distinct ways the problem may be approached: geometric and wave-based methods. In this section, we will discuss the fundamental ideas behind these techniques.

### 3.7.1 Geometric Acoustics (GA)

Geometric methods approximate sound propagation via the zero-wavelength (infinite frequency) asymptotic limit of the wave equation (3.1). Borrowing terminology from fluid mechanics, this yields a Lagrangian approach, where packets of energy are tracked explicitly through the scene as they travel along rays and repeatedly scatter into multiple packets in all directions each time they hit the scene boundary. The key strength of geometric methods is speed and flexibility: compared to a full-bandwidth wave simulation, tracing rays can be much cheaper, and it is much easier to incorporate physical phenomena and construct the BIR, assembled by explicitly constructing paths connecting source to listener. Today, these methods are standard in the area of room auralization.

Their key challenge falls into two categories. Firstly, one must efficiently search for paths connecting source to listener via complex scenes. Searching costs computation. Doing too little can under-sample the response, causing audible jumps in the rendering. Secondly, diffraction at audible wavelengths must be considered explicitly (since it is not present by default) to ensure plausibility. Both must be incorporated while balancing smooth rendering for moving sources and listener against the CPU cost of geometric analysis inherent in path search.

Below, we briefly elaborate on the general design of GA systems and practical implications for VR auralization, and refer the reader to Savioja and Svensson's excellent survey on the recent developments in GA techniques [87].

**Simplified geometry.** Due to the zero-wavelength approximation, geometric methods remain sensitive to geometric detail indefinitely below audible wavelengths. For instance, if one directly used a visual mesh for GA simulation, a coffee mug can create a strong audible echo if the source and listener are connected by a specular reflection path hitting the cup. Such specular glints are observed for light, but not sound with its much longer wavelength. So, it becomes important to build an equivalent simplified acoustical model of the scene which captures only large facets, combined with coefficients that summarize scattering due to diffraction. For instance, the seating area in a concert hall might be replaced with an enclosing box with an equivalent scattering coefficient. This process requires the user to have a degree of acoustical expertise, and inaccuracies can result without carefully specified geometry and boundary data [21]. However, for VR auralization, automation is highly desirable, with some recent work along these lines [88].

**Deterministic-statistical decomposition.** Geometric methods directly incorporate the deterministic-statistical decomposition in the simulation process to reduce CPU burden. In particular, the two components $D_d$ and $D_s$ are typically computed and rendered separately and then mixed in the final rendering to balance quality and speed.

GA methods perform a deterministic path search only up to a certain number of bounces on the scene boundary, called the *reflection order*. This is a key parameter for GA systems because it has a sensitive impact on both performance and rendering quality, varying by system and application. Typically, the user can specify this parameter, which then implicitly determines the number of deterministic peaks rendered, $n_d$, in (3.10). To accelerate path search, early methods [86] proposed using the image source method [7], which is well-suited for single enclosures but scales exponentially with reflection order and does not account for edge diffraction.

Following work on beam tracing, [36] showed that in multi-room scenes, precomputing a beam-tree data structure can at once control the exponential scaling and also incorporate edge diffraction which is crucial for plausibility in such densely occluded scenes. The system introduced precomputation as a powerful technique for reducing runtime acoustics computation, which most modern systems employ at least to some degree.

A key general concept employed in the beam tracing work in [36] is the *room-portal decomposition*: an indoor scene with many rooms is approximately decomposed into a set of Simplicial convex shapes that represent room volume, connected by flat portals representing doors. This is a frequently used method in GA systems, as it allows efficient deterministic path search on the discrete graph formed by rooms as nodes and portals as connecting edges. However, room-portal decomposition does not generalize to outdoor or mixed scenes, which is a key limitation that recent research is focusing on to allow fast deterministic search of high-order diffraction paths [34, 88].

Techniques developed for light transport in the computer graphics community are a great fit for computing the statistical component owing to its phase incoherence. Many methods are possible, such as those based on radiosity [8, 93]. Stochastic path tracing is a standard method in both graphics and acoustics communities today, used originally by DIVA [86] and in modern systems like RAVEN [90]. More recent improvements use bidirectional path tracing [24], which directly exploits the bidirectional reciprocity principle (3.7) to accelerate computation.

GA methods cannot construct the fine structure of the reverberant portion of the response, but as we discussed in Sect. 3.6.2, it is often sufficient to build the bidirectional energy decay relief, $\bar{D}_s(\bar{t}, \bar{\omega}, \bar{s}, \bar{s}'; x, x')$, or some lower dimensional approximation ignoring directionality. With path tracing techniques, this is directly accomplished by accumulating into a histogram indexed on all the function parameters— each path represents an energy packet that accumulates into its corresponding histogram bin. The key parameter trading quality and cost is the number of paths sampled so that the energy value in each histogram bin is sufficiently converged.

With simplified scenes admitting a room-portal decomposition one can expect robust convergence, or even use approximations that avoid path tracing altogether [94], but for path tracing in complex VR scenes, the required number of paths for a converged histogram can vary significantly based on source and listener locations, $\{x, x'\}$. For instance, if they are connected only through a few narrow apertures in the scene, it can be hard to find connecting paths despite extensive random searching. There is precedence for such issues in computer graphics as well [101], representing a frontier for new research with systematic convergence studies, as initiated in [24].

### 3.7.2   Wave Acoustics (WA)

Wave acoustic methods take an Eulerian approach: space time is discretized onto a fictitious background, such as a uniform discrete grid, and then one updates pressure amplitude in each cell at each time-step. Paths are not constructed explicitly, so as energy scatters in various directions from scene surfaces, the amount of information tracked does not change. Thus, arbitrary combinations of diffraction and scattering are naturally captured by wave methods. By running a simulation with a source located at $x'$, a discrete approximation of Green's function $p(t, x; x')$ is directly produced by running a volumetric simulation for a sufficient duration. The BIR $D(t; s, s', x, x')$ may then be computed via accurate plane-wave decomposition in a volume centered at the source and listener location [2, 91] or via the much faster approximation using instantaneous flux density [26], first applied to audio coding in [74].

**Numerical solvers.** The main challenge of wave methods is their computational cost. Since wave solvers directly resolve the detailed wave field by discretizing space and time, their cost scales as the fourth power of the maximum simulated frequency and third power of the scene diameter, due to Nyquist criteria as outlined in Sect. 3.2.1. This made them outright infeasible for most practical uses until the last decade, apart from low-frequency modal simulations up to a few hundred Hertz. However, they have seen a resurgence of interest over the last decade, with many kinds of solvers being actively researched today for auralization, such as spectral methods [52, 77], finite difference methods [49, 85], and the finite element method [71, 103]. Alongside the progress in numerical methods, the increased computational power of CPUs and graphics processors, as well as the availability of increased RAM, now allows simulations of practical cases of interest, such as concert halls, up to mid-frequencies (1 kHz and beyond). This is still short of complete audible bandwidth, and it is common to use approximate extrapolation beyond the band-limit frequency. The compute times remain suitable only for off-line computation, ranging in a few hours. The availability of commodity cloud computation has further aided the wider applicability of wave methods despite the cost.

**Precomputation and static scenes.** The idea of precomputation has been central to the increasing application of wave methods in VR auralization. Real-time auralization with wave methods was first shown to be viable for complex scenes in [80]. The method performs multiple simulations off-line and the resulting (monophonic) impulse responses are encoded and stored in a file. At runtime, this file is loaded, and the sampled acoustical data are spatially interpolated for a dynamic source and listener which informs spatialization of the source audio. This overall architecture is followed by most wave-based auralization methods.

The disadvantage of precomputation is that it is limited to static scenes. However, it has the great benefit that the fidelity of acoustical simulation becomes decoupled from runtime CPU usage. One may perform a detailed simulation directly on complex scene geometry ensuring robust results at runtime. These trade-offs are highly analogous to "light baking" which is a common feature of game engines today: expensive global illumination is simulated beforehand on static scenes to ensure fast runtime rendering. Similar to developments in lighting, one can conceivably incorporate local dynamism such as additional occlusion from portals [76] or moving objects [84] in the future.

**Parametric encoding.** The key research challenge introduced by precomputation is that the BIR field $D(t, s, s', x, x')$ is 11-dimensional and highly oscillatory. Capturing it in detail can easily take an impractical amount of storage. Spatial audio coding methods such as DirAC [73, 74] demonstrate a path forward, in that they extract and render perceptual properties from directional audio recordings rather than trying to re-create the physical sound field. This in turn is similar in spirit to audio coding methods such as MP3 where precise waveform reconstruction is eschewed in favor of controllable trade-offs between perceived quality and compressed size.

These observations have motivated a new thread of auralization research on wave-based parametric methods [26, 78, 79] that combine precomputed wave acoustics with compact, perceptual coding of the resulting BIR fields. Such methods are practical enough today to be employed in many gaming applications. The deterministic-statistical decomposition plays a crucial role in this encoding stage, as we will elaborate in Sect. 3.8.4 when we discuss [26] in more detail.

**Physical encoding.** In a parallel thread, there has been work on methods that directly approximate and convolve the complete BIR without involving perceptual coding.

The equivalent source method was proposed in [63, 64], at the expense of restricting to scenes that are a sparse set of exterior-scattering building facades. More recent methods for high-quality building auralization have been developed, which sample and interpolate BIRs for dynamic rendering [55]. The advantage is that no inherent assumptions are made about the perception or the structure of the BIR, but in turn, such systems tend to be more expensive and current technology is limited to static sound sources.

## 3.8  Auralization Systems

In this section, we will discuss a few illustrative example systems in more detail. We emphasize that this should not be interpreted as a representative survey. Instead, our aim is to illustrate how the design of practical systems can vary widely depending on the intended application, chosen algorithms, and in particular how systems choose to prioritize a subset of the design constraints (Sect. 3.5). Most of these systems are available for download and experimentation.

### 3.8.1  Room Acoustics for Virtual Environments (RAVEN)

RAVEN [90] is a research system built from the ground up aiming for perceptually authentic and real-time auralization in VR. The computational budget is thus on the high side, such as all the resources of a single or few networked computers. This is in line with the intended application: for an acoustician evaluating a planned design, it is more important to hear a result with reliable predictive value, and the precise amount of computation does not matter as long as it is real time. RAVEN is a great example of the archetypal decisions involved in the end-to-end design of modern real-time geometric systems.

A key assumption in the system is that the scene is a typical building floor. Many decisions and efficiencies flow naturally. Chiefly, one can employ the room-portal decomposition as discussed in Sect. 3.7.1. Local scene dynamism is also allowed by the system, such as opening or closing doors, with limited precomputation on the scene geometry. However, like most geometric acoustic systems, the scene geometry has to be manually simplified with acoustical expertise to achieve the simplified cells required by rooms and portals. Flexible signal processing that can include artistic design need not be considered, since the application is physical prediction.

RAVEN models diffraction on both the deterministic and statistical components of the BIR. The former uses the image source method, with reflection orders up to 3 for real-time evaluation. Edge sources are introduced to account for diffraction paths that, e.g., first undergo a bounce from a flat surface and then diffract around a portal edge. Capturing such effects is especially important for smooth results on dynamic source and listener motion, which RAVEN carefully models.

The statistical component uses stochastic ray tracing with improved convergence using the "diffuse rain" technique [90]. To model diffraction for reverberation, a probabilistic scheme is used [95] that deflects rays that pass close enough to scene edges. Since the precise reconstruction of the reverberant characteristics is of central importance in architectural acoustics, RAVEN models the complete bidirectional energy decay relief, as illustrated in [90, Fig. 5.19].

### 3.8.2   Wwise Spatial Audio

Audiokinetic's Wwise [9] is a commonly employed audio engine in video games, alongside many other audio design applications. Wwise provides both geometric acoustical simulation and HRTF spatialization using either object-based or spherical-harmonic processing (Sect. 3.2.4). The system stands in illustrative contrast to RAVEN, showing how different application needs can deeply shape technical choices of auralization systems. A detailed description of ideas and motivation can be found in the series of white papers [23].

Gaming applications require very low CPU utilization (fraction of a single core) without requiring physical accuracy. But one needs to approximate carefully. The rendering must stay perceptually believable, such as smooth acoustic changes on fast source motion or visual occlusion. Minimizing precomputation is desirable for reducing artist iteration times. Finally, the ability of artists to interpret the acoustic simulation and design the rendered output is paramount.

To meet these goals, Wwise also starts with a deterministic-statistical decomposition. Like most geometric systems, the user must provide a simplified audio geometry for the scene, which is the bulk of the work. Once this is done, the system responds interactively without precomputation. The initial sound is derived based on an explicit path search on simplified geometry at runtime, with reflections modeled via image sources up to some user-controlled reflection order (usually ~3 for efficiency).

Importantly, rather than estimating diffraction losses based on physical approximations such as the Uniform Theory of Diffraction [59] that cost CPU, the system exposes an abstract "diffraction coefficient" that varies smoothly as the sound source, and corresponding image sources transition between visual occlusion and visibility. This ameliorates the key perceptual deficit of audible loudness jumps that result when diffraction is ignored. The audio designer can draw a function in the user interface to map the diffraction coefficient to loudness attenuation. This design underlines how practical systems balance CPU cost, plausible rendering, and artistic control. Note how just reducing accuracy to gain CPU is not the path taken: instead, one must carefully understand which physical behaviors must be preserved to not violate our (stringent) sensory expectations, such as that sound fields rarely show a sudden audible variation on small movement in everyday life.

For modeling the statistical component, the system avoids costly stochastic ray tracing in favor of reverberation flow modeled on a room-portal decomposition of the simplified scene. The design is in the vein of [94], with diffuse energy flow on a graph composed of rooms as nodes and portals as edges. However, in keeping with the primary goal of audio design, the user is free to choose or parametrically design individual filters for each room, while the system ensures that the net result correctly accumulates reverberation and spatializes it as streaming to the listener from (potentially) multiple portals. Again, plausibility, performance, and design are prioritized over adherence to accuracy, keeping in mind the primary use case of scalable rendering for games and VR.

### 3.8.3  Steam Audio and Resonance Audio

Steam Audio [100] and Resonance Audio [46] are geometric acoustics systems also designed for gaming and VR applications with similar considerations as Wwise Spatial Audio. They both offer HRTF spatialization combined with geometric acoustics modeling; however, diffraction is ignored. A distinctive aspect of Steam Audio is the capability to precompute room reverberation filters (i.e., the statistical component) directly from scene geometry without requiring any simplification, auralized dynamically based on listener location. Resonance Audio on the other hand primarily focuses on highly efficient spatialization [47] that scales down to mobile devices for numerous sources, using up to third-order spherical harmonics. In fact, Resonance Audio can be used as a plugin within the Wwise audio engine to perform spatialization, illustrating the utility of the modular design of auralization systems (Sect. 3.2).

### 3.8.4  Project Acoustics (PA)

We now consider a wave-based system, Project Acoustics [66], which has shown practical viability for gaming [81] and VR [45] experiences recently. We summarize its key design ideas here; technical details can be found in [26, 78, 79]. As is typical for wave acoustics systems (Sect. 3.7.2), costly simulation is performed in a pre-computation stage, shown on the left of Fig. 3.4. Many simulations are performed in parallel that collectively sample and compress the entire BIR field $D(t, s, s', x, x')$ into an acoustic dataset. With today's commodity cloud computing resources, complete game scenes may be processed in less than an hour.

The bidirectional reciprocity principle (3.7) plays an important role. The listener location, $x$, is typically restricted in motion to head height above the ground, thus varying in two dimensions rather than three, such as the floors of a building. Potential listener locations are sampled in the lowered dimension adapting to local geometry [25]. Note that source locations, $x'$, may still vary in three dimensions. Then, a series of 3D wave simulations are performed with each potential *listener* location

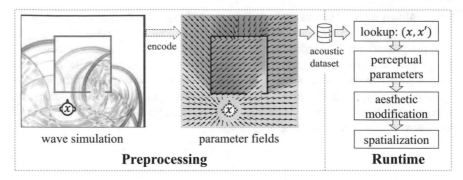

**Fig. 3.4** High-level architecture of Project Acoustics' wave-based parametric auralization

acting as *source* during simulation. The reduction in BIR field dimension by one yields an order-of-magnitude reduction in data size.

Project Acoustics' main idea is to employ lossy perceptual encoding on the BIR field to bring it within practical storage budgets of a few hundred MB. The deterministic-statistical decomposition is employed at this stage. The initial arrival time and direction are encoded explicitly to ensure the correct localization of the sound, and the rest of the response is encoded statistically (i.e., $n_d = 1$ referring to Sect. 3.6.1). An example simulation snapshot is shown in Fig. 3.4 with the corresponding initial path encoding visualized on the right. Color shows frequency-averaged loudness, and arrows show the localized direction at the listener location, x, with the source location $x'$ varying over the image. For instance, any source inside the room would be localized by the listener as arriving from the door, so the arrows inside the room consistently point in the door-to-listener direction. The perceptual parameters vary smoothly over space, mirroring our everyday experience, allowing further compression via entropy coding [78].

The statistical component simplifies (3.14) further to average over all simulated frequencies, approximating the bidirectional energy decay relief as

$$\bar{\bar{D}}_s(\bar{t}, \bar{\omega}, \bar{s}, \bar{s}'; x, x') \approx \bar{p}_0(\bar{s}, \bar{s}'; x, x') 10^{-6\bar{t}/T_60(x,x')}.$$

The directions $\{\bar{s}, \bar{s}'\}$ sample the six signed Cartesian directions, thus discretizing $\bar{p}_0$ to a $6 \times 6$ "reflections transfer" matrix that compactly approximates directional reverberation, alongside a single $T_{60}$ value across direction and frequency. Visualizations of the reflections transfer matrix can be found in [26] that illustrate how it captures anisotropic effects like directional reverberation from portals or nearby reverberant chambers.

One can observe that this encoding is quite simplified and can be expected to only plausibly reproduce the simulated BIR field. The choices result from the system's goal: capturing key geometry-dependent audio cues within a compact storage budget—too large a size simply obviates practical use. For instance, one could encode much more detailed information such as numerous ($n_d \sim 20-50$) individual reflection peaks [80] but that is far too costly, in turn motivating recent research on how one might trade between number of encoded peaks ($n_d$) and perceived authenticity [18].

Generally speaking, precomputed systems shift the trade-off from quality-versus-CPU as with runtime propagation simulation to quality-versus-storage (Sects. 3.8.1 and 3.8.2). This holds regardless of whether the precomputation is geometric (Steam Audio) or wave-based (Project Acoustics). Precomputation can introduce limitations such as slower artist turnaround times and static scenes, but in return significantly lowers the barrier to viability whenever the available CPU is severely restricted, which is the case for gaming applications or untethered VR platforms.

Wave simulation forces precomputation in today's systems due to its high computational cost, but its advantage compared to geometric methods is that complex visual scene geometry is processed directly, without requiring any manual simplification. Further, arbitrary order of diffraction around detailed geometry in general scenes (trees, buildings, chairs, etc.) is modeled, which avoids the risk of not sampling a salient path. In sum, one pays a high, fixed precomputation cost largely insensitive to scene complexity, and if that is feasible, obtains robust results directly from visual geometry with a low CPU cost.

As discussed in Sect. 3.6.2, parametric approaches enable intuitive controls for sound designers, which is of crucial importance in gaming applications, as we also saw in the design of the Wwise Spatial Audio system. In the case of PA, the parameters are looked up at each source-listener location pair at runtime (right of Fig. 3.4), and it becomes possible for the artist to specify dynamic aesthetic *modifications* of the physically-based baseline produced by simulation [44]. The sounds and modified acoustic parameters can then be sent to any efficient parametric reverberation and spatialization sub-system for rendering the binaural output.

## 3.9  Summary and Outlook

Creating an immersive and interactive sonic experience for virtual reality applications requires auralizing complex 3D scenes robustly and within tight real-time constraints. To meet these requirements, real-time systems follow a modular approach of dividing the problem into sound production, propagation, and spatialization. These can be mathematically formulated via the source directivity function, bidirectional impulse responses (BIR), and head-related transfer functions (HRTFs), respectively, leading to a general framework. Human auditory perception of acoustic responses deeply informs most systems, motivating optimizations such as the deterministic-statistical decomposition of the BIR.

We discussed many design considerations that inform the design of practical systems. We illustrated with a few auralization systems how the application requirements shape design choices, ranging from perceptual authenticity in architectural acoustics, to game engines where believability, audio design, and CPU usage take central priority. With more development, one can hope for auralization systems in the future that are capable of scaling their quality-compute trade-offs to span all applications of VR auralization. Such a convergent evolution would be in line with current trends in visual rendering where off-line photo-realistic rendering techniques and real-time game techniques are becoming increasingly unified [33].

Looking to the future, real-time auralization faces two major research challenges: scalability and scene dynamics. Game and VR scenes are trending toward completely open worlds where entire cities are modeled at once, spanning tens of kilometers, with numerous sound sources, where very few assumptions can be made about the scene's geometry or complexity. Similar considerations hold for engineering prediction of outdoor acoustics, such as noise levels in a city. We need real-time techniques that can scale to such challenging scenarios within CPU budgets, perhaps by analogy with level-of-detail techniques used in graphics. Scene dynamism is a related challenge. Many current game engines allow the users to make global changes to immersive 3D worlds in real time. Dynamic techniques are required that can model, for instance, the diffraction loss around a just-created wall within tolerable latency. Progress in this direction has only just begun [35, 75, 83, 84].

The open challenge for the future is to build real-time auralization systems that can gracefully scale from plausible to accurate audio rendering for complex, dynamic, city-scale scenes depending on available computational resources. There is much to be done, and many undiscovered, foundational ideas remain.

# References

1. Abel, J. S., Huang, P.: A Simple, Robust Measure of Reverberation Echo Density in Audio Engineering Society Convention 121 (2006).
2. Ahrens, J.: Analytic Methods of Sound Field Synthesis (T-Labs Series in Telecommunication Services) Two thousand, twelfth (Springer, 2014).
3. Ajdler, T., Sbaiz, L.,Vetterli, M.: The Plenacoustic Function and Its Sampling. Signal Processing, IEEE Transactions on **54**, 3790–3804 (2006).
4. Albert, D. G., Liu, L.: The Effect of Buildings on Acoustic Pulse Propagation in an Urban Environment. The Journal of the Acoustical Society of America **127**, 1335–1346 (2010).
5. Algazi, V. R., Duda, R. O., Thompson, D. M., Avendano, C.: The cipic hrtf database in Proceedings of the 2001 IEEE Workshop on the Applications of Signal Processing to Audio and Acoustics (Cat. No. 01TH8575) (2001), 99–102.
6. Allen, A., Raghuvanshi, N.: Aerophones in Flatland: Interactive Wave Simulation of Wind Instruments. ACM Trans. Graph. **34** (2015).
7. Allen, J. B., Berkley, D. A.: Image Method for Efficiently Simulating Small- Room Acoustics. J. Acoust. Soc. Am **65**, 943–950 (1979).
8. Antani, L., Chandak, A., Taylor, M., Manocha, D.: Direct-to-Indirect Acoustic Radiance Transfer. IEEE Transactions on Visualization and Computer Graphics **18**, 261–269 (2012).
9. AudioKinetic Inc.: Wwise https://www.audiokinetic.com/products/wwise/. 2018.
10. Avni, A. et al.: Spatial perception of sound fields recorded by spherical microphone arrays with varying spatial resolution. The Journal of the Acoustical Society of America **133**, 2711–2721 (2013).

11. Ben-Hur, Z., Brinkmann, F., Sheaffer, J., Weinzierl, S., Rafaely, B.: Spectral equalization in binaural signals represented by order-truncated spherical harmonics. The Journal of the Acoustical Society of America **141**, 4087–4096 (2017).

12. Bilbao, S.: Numerical Sound Synthesis: Finite Difference Schemes and Simulation in Musical Acoustics First (Wiley, 2009).

13. Bilbao, S., Hamilton, B.: Directional Sources in Wave-Based Acoustic Simulation. IEEE/ACM Transactions on Audio, Speech, and Language Processing **27**, 415–428 (2019).

14. Bilbao, S. et al.: Physical Modeling, Algorithms, and Sound Synthesis: The NESS Project. Computer Music Journal **43**, 15–30 (2020).

15. Bilinski, P., Ahrens, J., Thomas, M. R., Tashev, I. J., Platt, J. C.: HRTF magnitude synthesis via sparse representation of anthropometric features in 2014 IEEE International Conference on Acoustics, Speech and Signal Processing (ICASSP) (2014), 4468–4472.

16. Born, M., Wolf, E.: Principles of Optics: 60th Anniversary Edition 7th edition. English (Cambridge University Press, Cambridge, 2019).

17. Breebaart, J. et al.: Spatial Audio Object Coding (SAOC) - The Upcoming MPEG Standard on Parametric Object Based Audio Coding English. In (Audio Engineering Society, 2008).

18. Brinkmann, F., Gamper, H., Raghuvanshi, N., Tashev, I.: Towards Encoding Perceptually Salient Early Reflections for Parametric Spatial Audio Rendering English. in Audio Engineering Society Convention 148 (Audio Engineering Society, 2020).

19. Brinkmann, F., Weinzierl, S.: Comparison of Head-Related Transfer Functions Pre-Processing Techniques for Spherical Harmonics Decomposition. English (2018).

20. Brinkmann, F. et al.: A Cross-Evaluated Database of Measured and Simulated HRTFs Including 3D Head Meshes, Anthropometric Features, and Headphone Impulse Responses. en. Journal of the Audio Engineering Society **67**, 705–718 (2019).

21. Brinkmann, F. et al.: A Round Robin on Room Acoustical Simulation and Auralization. J. Acoustical Soc. of Am. (2019).

22. Brungart, D. S., Kordik, A. J., Simpson, B. D.: Effects of Headtracker Latency in Virtual Audio Displays. en. J. Audio Eng. Soc. **54**, 13 (2006).

23. Buffoni, L.-X.: A Wwise Approach to Spatial Audio (Blog Series) https://blog.audiokinetic.com/a-wwise-approach-to-spatial-audiopart-1/. 2020.

24. Cao, C., Ren, Z., Schissler, C., Manocha, D., Zhou, K.: Interactive Sound Propagation with Bidirectional Path Tracing. ACM Transactions on Graphics (TOG) **35**, 180 (2016).

25. Chaitanya, C. R. A., Snyder, J. M., Godin, K., Nowrouzezahrai, D., Raghuvanshi, N.: Adaptive Sampling for Sound Propagation. IEEE Trans. on Vis. Comp. Graphics **25**, 1846–1854 (2019).

26. Chaitanya, C. R. A. et al.: Directional Sources and Listeners in Interactive Sound Propagation Using Reciprocal Wave Field Coding. ACM Transactions on Graphics (SIGGRAPH 2020) **39** (2020).

27. Cooper, C. M., Abel, J. S.: Digital Simulation of "Brassiness" and Amplitude- Dependent Propagation Speed in Wind Instruments in Proc. 13th Int. Conf. on Digital Audio Effects (DAFx-10) (2010), 1–6.

28. Dalenbäck, B.-I.: CATT-Acoustic Software https://www.catt.se/.2021.

29. Davis, L. S. et al.: High Order Spatial Audio Capture and Its Binaural Head-Tracked Playback Over Headphones with HRTF Cues English. In Audio Engineering Society Convention 119 (Audio Engineering Society, 2005).

30. Dobashi, Y., Yamamoto, T., Nishita, T.: Real-Time Rendering of Aerodynamic Sound Using Sound Textures Based on Computational Fluid Dynamics. ACM Trans. Graph. **22**, 732–740 (2003).

31. Dobashi, Y., Yamamoto, T., Nishita, T.: Synthesizing Sound from Turbulent Field Using Sound Textures for Interactive Fluid Simulation. Computer Graphics Forum (Proc. EUROGRAPHICS 2004) **23**, 539–546 (2004).

32. Embrechts, J.-J.: Review on the Applications of Directional Impulse Responses in Room Acoustics in Actes Du CFA 2016 (2016).

33. Epic Games: Unreal Engine 5 Documentation https://docs.unrealengine.com/5.0/en-US/RenderingFeatures/Lumen/. 2020.

34. Erraji, A., Stienen, J., Vorländer, M.: The Image Edge Model. en. Acta Acustica **5**, 17 (2021).
35. Fan, Z., Vineet, V., Gamper, H., Raghuvanshi, N.: Fast Acoustic Scattering Using Convolutional Neural Networks in ICASSP 2020 - 2020 IEEE International Conference on Acoustics, Speech and Signal Processing (ICASSP) (2020), 171–175.
36. Funkhouser, T. et al.: A Beam Tracing Method for Interactive Architectural Acoustics. The Journal of the Acoustical Society of America **115**, 739–756 (2004).
37. Gade, A. in Springer Handbook of Acoustics (ed Rossing, T.) Two thousand, seventh. Chap. 9 (Springer, 2007).
38. Gamper, H., Johnston, D., Tashev, I. J.: Interaural time delay personalisation using incomplete head scans in 2017 IEEE International Conference on Acoustics, Speech and Signal Processing (ICASSP) (2017), 461–465.
39. Gardner, B., Martin, K., et al.: HRFT Measurements of a KEMAR Dummyhead Microphone (Vision and Modeling Group, Media Laboratory, Massachusetts Institute of Technology, 1994).
40. Gardner, W. G., Martin, K. D.: HRTF measurements of a KEMAR. The Journal of the Acoustical Society of America **97**, 3907–3908 (1995).
41. Geronazzo, M., Spagnol, S., Bedin, A.,Avanzini, F.: Enhancing vertical localization with image-guided selection of non-individual head-related transfer functions in 2014 IEEE International Conference on Acoustics, Speech and Signal Processing (ICASSP) (2014), 4463–4467.
42. Gerzon, M. A.: Ambisonics in Multichannel Broadcasting and Video. J. Audio Eng. Soc. **33**, 859–871 (1985).
43. Gerzon, M. A.: Periphony: With-Height Sound Reproduction. J. Audio Eng. Soc **21**, 2–10 (1973).
44. Godin, K., Gamper, H., Raghuvanshi, N.: Aesthetic Modification of Room Impulse Responses for Interactive Auralization in AES International Conference on Immersive and Interactive Audio (Audio Engineering Society, 2019).
45. Godin, K. W., Rohrer, R., Snyder, J., Raghuvanshi, N.: Wave Acoustics in a Mixed Reality Shell in AES Conf. on Audio for Virt. and Augmented Reality (AVAR) (2018).
46. Google Inc.: Resonance Audio https://developers.google.com/resonance-audio/. 2018.
47. Gorzel, M. et al.: Efficient Encoding and Decoding of Binaural Sound with Resonance Audio in AES International Conference on Immersive and Interactive Audio (2019).
48. Guezenoc, C., Seguier, R.: HRTF individualization: A survey. arXiv preprint arXiv:2003.06183 (2020).
49. Hamilton, B., Bilbao, S.: FDTD Methods for 3-D RoomAcoustics Simulation With High-Order Accuracy in Space and Time. IEEE/ACM Transactions on Audio, Speech, and Language Processing **25** (2017).
50. He, J., Ranjan, R., Gan, W.-S.: Fast continuous HRTF acquisition with unconstrained movements of human subjects in 2016 IEEE International Conference on Acoustics, Speech and Signal Processing (ICASSP) (2016), 321–325.
51. Hold, C., Gamper, H., Pulkki, V., Raghuvanshi, N., Tashev, I.: Improving Binaural Ambisonics Decoding by Spherical Harmonics Domain Tapering and Coloration Compensation in Proc. IEEE International Conference on Acoustics, Speech, and Signal Processing (ICASSP) (2019).
52. Hornikx, M., Forssén, J.: Modelling of Sound Propagation to Three- Dimensional Urban Courtyards Using the Extended Fourier PSTD Method. Applied Acoustics **72**, 665–676 (2011).
53. Howe, M. S.: Theory of Vortex Sound 1st edition. English (Cambridge University Press, New York, 2002).
54. Hughes, J. et al.: Computer Graphics: Principles and Practice 3rd edition. English (Addison-Wesley Professional, Upper Saddle River, New Jersey, 2013).
55. Jörgensson, F. K. P.: Wave-Based Virtual Acoustics English. PhD thesis (Technical University of Denmark, 2020).

56. Jot, J.-M.: An Analysis/Synthesis Approach to Real-Time Artificial Reverberation in [Proceedings] ICASSP-92: 1992 IEEE International Conference on Acoustics, Speech, and Signal Processing **2** (1992), 221–224.
57. Kajiya, J. T.: The Rendering Equation in Proceedings of the 13th Annual Conference on Computer Graphics and Interactive Techniques **20** (ACM, New York, NY, USA, 1986), 143–150.
58. Katz, B. F.: Boundary element method calculation of individual head-related transfer function. I. Rigid model calculation. The Journal of the Acoustical Society of America **110**, 2440–2448 (2001).
59. Kouyoumjian, R., Pathak, P.: A Uniform Geometrical Theory of Diffraction for an Edge in a Perfectly Conducting Surface. Proceedings of the IEEE **62**, 1448–1461 (1974).
60. Kuttruff, H.: Room Acoustics Fourth (Taylor & Francis, 2000).
61. Li, S., Tobbala, A., Peissig, J.: Towards Mobile 3D HRTF Measurement English. in (Audio Engineering Society, 2020).
62. Litovsky, R. Y., Colburn, S. H., Yost, W. A., Guzman, S. J.: The Precedence Effect. The Journal of the Acoustical Society of America **106**, 1633–1654 (1999).
63. Mehra, R., Antani, L., Kim, S., Manocha, D.: Source and Listener Directivity for Interactive Wave-Based Sound Propagation. IEEE Transactions on Visualization and Computer Graphics **20**, 495–503 (2014).
64. Mehra, R. et al.: Wave-Based Sound Propagation in Large Open Scenes Using an Equivalent Source Formulation. ACM Trans. Graph. **32** (2013).
65. Meshram, A. et al.: P-HRTF: Efficient personalized HRTF computation for high-fidelity spatial sound in 2014 IEEE International Symposium on Mixed and Augmented Reality (ISMAR) (2014), 53–61.
66. Microsoft Corp.: Project Acoustics https://aka.ms/acoustics. 2018.
67. Noisternig, M., Sontacchi, A., Musil, T., Hóldrich, R.: A 3D ambisonic based binaural sound reproduction system in Audio Engineering Society Conference: 24th International Conference: Multichannel Audio, The New Reality (2003).
68. Oliver, R. J., Jot, J.-M.: Efficient Multi-Band DigitalAudio Graphic Equalizer with Accurate Frequency Response Control in Audio Engineering Society Convention 139 (2015).
69. Paasonen, J., Karapetyan, A., Plogsties, J., Pulkki, V.: Proximity of Surfaces - Acoustic and Perceptual Effects. J. Audio Eng. Soc **65**, 997–1004 (2017).
70. Pierce, A. D.: Acoustics: An Introduction to Its Physical Principles and Applications (Acoustical Society of America, 1989).
71. Pind, F. et al.: Time Domain Room Acoustic Simulations Using the Spectral Element Method. The Journal of the Acoustical Society of America **145**, 3299–3310 (2019).
72. Pulkki, V.: Virtual Sound Source Positioning Using Vector Base Amplitude Panning. English. Journal of the Audio Engineering Society **45**, 456–466 (1997).
73. Pulkki, V.: Spatial Sound Reproduction with Directional Audio Coding. J. Audio Eng. Soc. (2007).
74. Pulkki, V., Merimaa, J.: Spatial ImpulseResponseRendering II:Reproduction of Diffuse Sound and Listening Tests. J. Aud. Eng. Soc. **54**, 3–20 (2006).
75. Pulkki, V., Svensson, U. P.: Machine-Learning-Based Estimation and Rendering of Scattering in Virtual Reality. J. Acoust. Soc. Am. **145**, 2664–2676 (2019).
76. Raghuvanshi, N.: Dynamic Portal Occlusion for Precomputed Interactive Sound Propagation. arXiv:2107.11548 [cs, eess] (2021).
77. Raghuvanshi, N., Narain, R., Lin, M. C.: Efficient and Accurate Sound Propagation Using Adaptive Rectangular Decomposition. IEEE Transactions on Visualization and Computer Graphics **15**, 789–801 (2009).
78. Raghuvanshi, N., Snyder, J.: ParametricWave Field Coding for Precomputed Sound Propagation. ACM Transactions on Graphics (TOG) - Proceedings of ACM SIGGRAPH 2014 **33** (2014).
79. Raghuvanshi, N., Snyder, J.: Parametric Directional Coding for Precomputed Sound Propagation. ACM Trans. Graph. (2018).

80. Raghuvanshi, N., Snyder, J., Mehra, R., Lin, M. C., Govindaraju, N. K.: PrecomputedWave Simulation for Real-Time Sound Propagation of Dynamic Sources in Complex Scenes. ACM Transactions on Graphics **29** (2010).
81. Raghuvanshi, N., Tennant, J., Snyder, J.: Triton: Practical Pre-Computed Sound Propagation for Games and Virtual Reality. The Journal of the Acoustical Society of America **141**, 3455–3455 (2017).
82. Rindel, J. H., Christensen, C. L.: The Use of Colors, Animations and Auralizations in Room Acoustics in Internoise 2013 (2013).
83. Rosen, M., Godin, K. W., Raghuvanshi, N.: Interactive Sound Propagation for Dynamic Scenes Using 2D Wave Simulation. en. Computer Graphics Forum **39**, 39–46 (2020).
84. Rungta, A., Schissler, C.,Rewkowski,N., Mehra, R., Manocha, D.: Diffraction Kernels for Interactive Sound Propagation in Dynamic Environments. IEEE Transactions on Visualization and Computer Graphics **24**, 1613–1622 (2018).
85. Savioja, L.: Real-Time 3D Finite-Difference Time-Domain Simulation of Mid-Frequency Room Acoustics in 13th International Conference on Digital Audio Effects (2010).
86. Savioja, L., Huaniemi, J., Lokki, T.,Vaananen, R.: Creating InteractiveVirtual Acoustic Environments. J. Audio Eng. Soc. (1999).
87. Savioja, L., Svensson, U. P.: Overview of Geometrical Room Acoustic Modeling Techniques. The Journal of the Acoustical Society of America **138**, 708–730 (2015).
88. Schissler, C., Mehra, R., Manocha, D.: High-Order Diffraction and Diffuse Reflections for Interactive Sound Propagation in Large Environments. ACM Transactions on Graphics (TOG) **33**, 39 (2014).
89. Schonstein, D., Katz, B. F.: HRTF selection for binaural synthesis from a database using morphological parameters in International Congress on Acoustics (ICA) (2010).
90. Schröder, D.: Physically Based Real-Time Auralization of Interactive Virtual Environments (Logos Verlag, 2011).
91. Sheaffer, J., Van Walstijn, M., Rafaely, B., Kowalczyk, K.: Binaural Reproduction of Finite Difference Simulations Using Spherical Array Processing. IEEE/ACM Trans. Audio, Speech and Lang. Proc. **23**, 2125–2135 (2015).
92. Shinn-Cunningham, B. G.: Distance cues for virtual auditory space in Proceedings of the IEEE-PCM **2000** (2000), 227–230.
93. Siltanen, S., Lokki, T., Kiminki, S., Savioja, L.: The Room Acoustic Rendering Equation. J. Acoust. Soc. Am. (2007).
94. Stavrakis, E., Tsingos, N., Calamia, P.: Topological Sound Propagation with Reverberation Graphs. Acta Acustica/Acustica - the Journal of the European Acoustics Association (EAA) (2008).
95. Stephenson, U. M., Svensson, U. P.: An Improved Energetic Approach to Diffraction Based on theUncertainty Principle in 19th Int. Cong. onAcoustics (ICA) (2007).
96. Takala, T., Hahn, J.: Sound Rendering. SIGGRAPH Comput. Graph. **26**, 211–220 (1992).
97. Theis, T. N., Wong, H.-S. P.: The end of Moore's law: A new beginning for information technology. Computing in Science & Engineering **19**, 41–50 (2017).
98. Tukuljac, H. P. et al.: A Sparsity Measure for Echo Density Growth in General Environments in ICASSP 2019 - 2019 IEEE International Conference on Acoustics, Speech and Signal Processing (ICASSP) (2019), 1–5.
99. Valimaki, V., Parker, J. D., Savioja, L., Smith, J. O., Abel, J. S.: Fifty Years of Artificial Reverberation. IEEE Transactions on Audio, Speech, and Language Processing **20**, 1421–1448 (2012).
100. Valve Corporation: Steam Audio ().
101. Veach, E., Guibas, L. J.: Metropolis Light Transport in Proceedings of the 24th Annual Conference on Computer Graphics and Interactive Techniques (ACM Press/Addison-Wesley Publishing Co., USA, 1997), 65–76.
102. Vorländer, M.: Auralization: Fundamentals of Acoustics, Modelling, Simulation, Algorithms andAcousticVirtualReality (RWTHedition) First (Springer, 2007).

103. Wang, H., Sihar, I., Pagán Muñoz, R., Hornikx, M.: Room Acoustics Modelling in the Time-Domain with the Nodal Discontinuous Galerkin Method. The Journal of the Acoustical Society of America **145**, 2650–2663 (2019).
104. Wang, J.-H., Qu, A., Langlois, T. R., James, D. L.: Toward Wave-based Sound Synthesis for Computer Animation. ACM Trans. Graph. **37**, 109:1–109:16 (2018).
105. Zhang, W., Abhayapala, T. D., Kennedy, R. A., Duraiswami, R.: Insights into Head-Related Transfer Function: Spatial Dimensionality and Continuous Representation. The Journal of the Acoustical Society of America **127**, 2347–2357 (2010).
106. Zotkin, D., Hwang, J., Duraiswaini, R., Davis, L. S.: HRTF personalization using anthropometric measurements in 2003 IEEE Workshop on Applications of Signal Processing to Audio and Acoustics (IEEE Cat. No. 03TH8684) (2003), 157–160.

# Chapter 4
# System-to-User and User-to-System Adaptations in Binaural Audio

**Lorenzo Picinali and Brian F. G. Katz**

**Abstract** This chapter concerns concepts of adaption in a binaural audio context (i.e. headphone-based three-dimensional audio rendering and associated spatial hearing aspects), considering first the adaptation of the rendering system to the acoustic and perceptual properties of the user, and second the adaptation of the user to the rendering quality of the system. We start with an overview of the basic mechanisms of human sound source localisation, introducing expressions such as localisation cues and interaural differences, and the concept of the Head-Related Transfer Function (HRTF), which is the basis of most 3D spatialisation systems in VR. The chapter then moves to more complex concepts and processes, such as HRTF selection (system-to-user adaptation) and HRTF accommodation (user-to-system adaptation). State-of-the-art HRTF modelling and selection methods are presented, looking at various approaches and at how these have been evaluated. Similarly, the process of HRTF accommodation is detailed, with a case study employed as an example. Finally, the potential of these two approaches are discussed, considering their combined use in a practical context, as well as introducing a few open challenges for future research.

## 4.1 Introduction

Binaural technology is the solution for sound spatialisation which is the closest to real-life listening. It attempts to mimic the entirety of acoustic cues associated with the human localisation of sounds, reproducing the corresponding acoustic pressure signal at the entrance of the two ear canals of the listener (binaural literally means "related to two ears"). These two signals should be a complete and sufficient representation of the sound scene, since they are the only information that the auditory system requires in

L. Picinali (✉)
Imperial College London, South Kensington Campus, London SW7 2AZ, UK
e-mail: l.picinali@imperial.ac.uk

B. F. G. Katz
Sorbonne Université, CNRS, UMR 7190, Institut Jean Le Rond d'Alembert,
Lutheries - Acoustique - Musique, Paris, France
e-mail: brian.katz@sorbonne-universite.fr

© The Author(s) 2023                                                                                     115
M. Geronazzo and S. Serafin (eds.), *Sonic Interactions in Virtual Environments*,
Human—Computer Interaction Series, https://doi.org/10.1007/978-3-031-04021-4_4

order to identify the 3D location of a sound source. Thus, binaural rendering of spatial information is fundamentally based on the production (either through recording or synthesis) of localisation cues that are the consequence of the incident sound upon the listener's torso, head, and ears on the way to the ear canal, and subsequently to the eardrums. These cues are, namely, the ITD (interaural time difference), the ILD (interaural level difference) and spectral cues [48, 68]. Their combined effects are represented by the Head-Related Transfer Function (HRTF), which characterises the spectro-temporal filtering of a locus of source positions around a given head.[1]

### 4.1.1  Localisation Cues and Their Individual Nature

The ILD and ITD as a function of source position are determined principally by the size and shape of the head, as well as the position of the ears on the two sides. In order to better understand these localisation cues, Fig. 4.1 shows how ITD and ILD vary as a function of both distance (1.5–10 m) and azimuth. This comparison highlights potential effects of ITD/ILD mismatch, especially if they occur near the interaural axis where they can affect distance perception. The results were obtained by Boundary Element Method (BEM) simulation of the HRTF using the open-source mesh2hrtf software [110, 111]. The mesh employed was obtained from an MRI scan of a Neumann dummy recording head (model KU-100), previously used in HRTF computation [32] and measurement [4] comparisons. These cues vary as a function of frequency. For this example, the ITD was calculated using the *Threshold lp −30 dB* method (for a summary of various ITD estimation methods see [50]), which detects the first onset using a −30 dB relative threshold on a 3 kHz low-pass filtered version of the HRIR, as this has been shown to be the most perceptually relevant method for ITD estimation among 32 different estimation methods and variants [7, 50]. The ILD was calculated as the difference of left and right HRIR RMS values, after applying a 3kHz high-pass filter. The use of low-pass and high-pass filters for the two different acoustic cues is based on previous studies showing the frequency dependence of the different auditory cues [101], with ITD being dominated by low-frequency content (with interpretation of phase information being inconclusive for frequencies smaller than head dimensions) and ILD varying more significantly with high-frequency content (where the wavelength is less than the dimensions of the head). The application of a 2–3 kHz filter can be used to generally separate the contributions of the pinnae in the HRIR [50]. One can observe that ITD varies little over the simulated distance range, while becoming more vague and ambiguous near the

---

[1] We use the term *HRTF* to indicate the set of filters, each representing a pair of transfer functions from a point source in space at a given distance around a given head to the left and right ear, normalised by the transfer function with the body absent. The plural, *HRTFs*, therefore, represents a collection of more than one HRTF, typically for different heads or test conditions. The head-related impulse response or *HRIR* is the time domain transform of the HRTF.

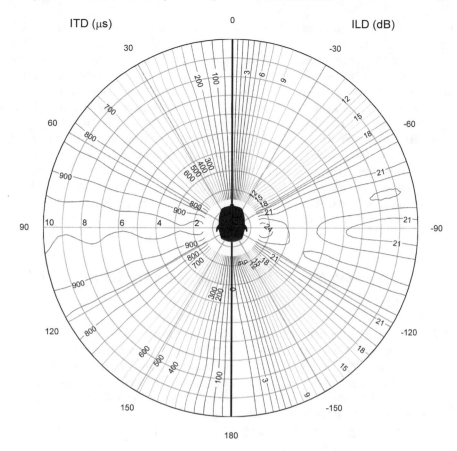

**Fig. 4.1** Isocontours for ITD (left) and ILD (right) as a function of azimuth (in degrees) and radial distance (from 1.5 to 10 m) obtained via numerical simulation of the HRTF of a dummy head (not shown to scale). ITD (3 kHz low-pass Head-Related Impulse Response—HRIR, *Threshold*, −30 dB first onset method) 50 μs contours. ILD (3 kHz high-pass HRIR, RMS difference) 1 dB contours (from [48])

interaural axis. In contrast, the ILD varies with distance in the same interaural axis range of 70°–110°.

Other physical interactions between the sound wave and the torso, head, and pinnae (the external parts of the ear) introduce a range of spectral cues (principally through series of peaks and notches) which can be used to judge whether a sound source is e.g. above or below, to the front or rear of the listener, while ITD and ILD remain relatively unchanged. Considering the various morphological regions of the pinnae, as indicated later in Sect. 4.2.1—Fig. 4.2a, each of these is potentially related to specific characteristic of the HRTF filters. As such, individual morphological variations will result in different HRTFs. When reproducing binaural audio, it has been experimentally demonstrated that using an HRTF that does not match the one of the listener has a detrimental effect on the accuracy and realism of virtual sound perception. For example, it has been noted that listeners are able to localise virtual sounds that have been spatialized using their own HRTFs with a similar accuracy to free field listening, though some studies have shown poorer elevation judgements and increased front-back confusions [67], which may be due to the idealised ane-choic nature of HRTFs and the importance of slight head movements and associated dynamic cues [37, 102]. These errors can significantly increase when using someone else's HRTF [99]. Furthermore, using non-individual HRTFs (see Sect. 4.1.2) has been shown to affect various perceptual attributes when considering complex scenes, in addition to those associated with source localisation: i.e. Coloration, Externalisa-tion, Immersion, Realism and Relief/Depth [87]. In this chapter, the primary focus is on localisation as the perceptual evaluation metric. Chapter 5 introduces and dis-cusses other relevant metrics.

## 4.1.2 Minimising HRTF Mismatch Between the System and the Listener

Various means have been investigated to minimise erroneous or conflicting binaural acoustic localisation cues relative to the natural cues delivered to the auditory sys-tem and, as such, improve the quality of the resulting binaural rendering. Majority of research has focused on improving the similarity between the rendering sys-tems' localisation cues and those of the individual listener. This is generally termed "individualisation" or "individualised" binaural rendering. To clarify questions of nomenclature, we propose the following terms:

- *individual* to identify the HRTF of the user;
- *individualised* or *personalised* to indicated an HRTF modified or selected to best accommodate the user;
- *non-individual* or *non-individualised* to indicate an HRTF that has not been tailored to the user and
- *dummy head* or so-called *generic* HRTF sets are specific instances of non-individual HRTFs, often designed with the goal of representing a certain pool of subjects.

While not exhaustive, a general overview of individualisation methods is discussed here.

### Binaural Recordings and Synthesis

The first and most direct method to create an individual rendering is to perform the recording with binaural microphones placed in the ear canal of the listener. This is however, in most cases, an impractical solution. The second still rather direct method is to measure the HRTF of an individual for a collection of spatial positions and to then use this individual HRTF to produce an individual binaural synthesis rendering through convolution of the sound source with the relevant incident direction HRTF [14, 105]. While this is the most common method employed to date, it is generally limited to those with the facilities and equipment to carry out such measurements [4].

The general pros and cons between binaural recordings and binaural synthesis merit mention. While individual binaural recordings provide arguably the most accurate 3D audio capture/reproduction method, they require the sonic environment and the individual to be situated accordingly. For any reasonable production, this would resemble a theatrical piece being performed around the individual in a first person context. The recording would capture the acoustic detail of the soundscape, including reflections from various surfaces, diffraction and scattering effects. However, the head orientation of the individual would be encoded into the recording, imposed on the listener at playback. If presented to another individual, the issues of HRTF mismatch are introduced, degrading the spatial audio quality to an unknown degree for each individual. In laboratory conditions, this method suffers additional difficulty, as the individual takes part in the recording, making the presentation of unfamiliar material difficult. In contrast, binaural synthesis allows for the scripting, manipulation and mixing of 3D scenarios without the intended listener present. With real-time synthesis, head tracking can be incorporated allowing freedom of movement by the individual, a basic requirement for VR applications. HRTF mismatch is alleviated through the use of individual HRTFs. However, the quality of the production is affected by the level of detail in the acoustic simulation of the environment, including elements such as source and surface properties. Highly complex scenes and acoustic environments can require significant computational resources (the interested reader can refer to Chap. 3 for further details on this topic). Spatial synthesis using HRTF data is also affected by the measurement conditions of the employed HRTF, predominantly the measurement distance. If sound sources are to be rendered at various distances, this requires either multiple HRTF datasets, or deformation of the individual HRTF data to approximate such changes in distance. Further discussion of these details is beyond the scope of this chapter. In continuing, the focus will be limited to questions concerning the individual nature of the HRTF as integrated into an auditory VR environment through binaural synthesis.

**Introduction to System-to-User and User-to-System adaptation**

A variety of alternative methods exist in order to improve the match between the HRTF used for the rendering and the specific HRTF of the listener. It is the aim of this chapter to present an overview of those approaches that have been evaluated and validated through experimental research. In order to map the various methods and at the same time simplify the narrative and facilitate the reading, the text has been organised in two separate sections. Section 4.2 presents research which looks at matching the rendering system to the specific listener (system-to-user adaptation), thus aiming to provide every individual with the best HRTF possible. Section 4.3 looks at the problem from a diametrically opposite point of view, introducing studies where the listener is trained in order to adapt to the rendering system (user-to-system adaptation), therefore aiming at improving the performance of a specific individual when using non-individual HRTFs.

While a rather extensive number of studies exist on the topic of system-to-user adaptation, a more limited amount of research has been carried out focusing on user-to-system adaptation. For this reason, while Sect. 4.2 is presented as an extensive review of several research projects, Sect. 4.3, after an initial overview, then dives more in depth into one specific study carried out by this chapter's authors, giving details of the methodology and briefly discussing the results. Section 4.5 concludes by presenting a brief overview of open challenges on this topic.

## 4.2  System-to-User Adaptation: HRTF Synthesis and Selection

Two main approaches exist for obtaining individual (or at least personalised) HRTFs without having to measure them acoustically. The first one focuses on numerical simulations, therefore using mathematical methods to generate an HRTF for a given individual from 3D models of the head, torso, and pinnae. Techniques such as the Boundary Element Method (BEM), Finite Element Method (FEM), and Finite Difference Time Domain (FDTD) method which are commonly employed in diffraction, scattering, and resonance problems allow one to calculate the HRTF of a given individual based on precise geometrical data (e.g. coming from a 3D scan of the head and pinnae), which have been used for this purpose since the late 1990s, and have shown increased uptake and success in the past years thanks to technological advancements in domains such as high-performance computing and high-resolution 3D scanning. An example of such a resulting 3D mesh from a Neumann KU-100 dummy head can be seen in Fig. 4.2b. The second one relies on using HRTFs from available datasets, either transforming them in order to provide a better fit for a given listener or selecting a best fit considering, for example, preference or performance, e.g. using a sound localisation task or signal metric. Due to the relative independence between the ITD and the Spectral Cues, the HRTF can be decomposed and different elements addressed by different methods, e.g. an ITD structural model can be used with best fit selected Spectra Cues [22, 78].

As can be expected, each of these approaches comes with specific challenges. Moreover, the success in employing one or the other depends significantly on factors such as the available data (quantity and quality), the time constraints in order to run the tests and the calculations, and the context for which the rendering is needed (i.e. the requirements in terms of quality, interactivity, etc.). An overview of the various techniques and related challenges, including solutions found through state-of-the art research studies, is presented in the following sections.

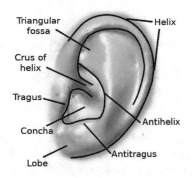

(a) Diagram of the pinna with anthropometric labels.

(b) Mesh of Neumann KU-100 dummy head fitted with a parametric pinna model.

**Fig. 4.2**   Pinna morphology nomenclature and example BEM mesh (from [91])

### 4.2.1  HRTF Modelling

Various attempts have been made to investigate the function of the pinna, linking HRTFs to its morphology as well as that of the head and torso. Early work by Teranishi and Shaw [93] looked at creating a physical model of the pinnae and analysing the various excitation modes generated by a nearby point source. The model, based on very simple geometries, showed responses similar to those of real data, and represented one of the first steps towards better understanding the spatially varying acoustic role of the pinna. Similar work was done by Batteau [12], who created a mathematical representation of the acoustical transformation performed by the pinna and produced the first mathematically described theory of sound source localisation based on a reflection-diffraction model. These studies were the baseline of research carried out 30 and more years later, when the available computational power allowed to create more complex models, and to validate those by comparing them with experimental measures (e.g. [58]). Further modelling work was carried out looking at simplified models and approximations. Notable examples are those of Genuit [26] based on a structural simplification model of the pinnae, Algazi and colleagues [1] based on an approximation of the head and the torso using ellipsoidal and spherical models, and Spagnol and colleagues [89] looking at ray-tracing analysis of pinna reflection patterns. It is relevant to note that many of the early studies focused on models for understanding the various phenomena and principles involved, rather than models for binaural audio rendering. For these early studies, much of the research on spatial perception was carried out independently from acoustical/morphological studies regarding the details of the pinnae.

## Structural Modelling

One of the first experiments using these techniques applied to HRTFs (including pinnae) was carried out by Katz [49, 51, 52]. This work focused on using BEM to calculate HRTFs by modifying various aspects of the geometrical models, for example, eliminating the pinna, changing the size and shape of the head, and accounting for hair acoustic impedance. Results from numerical simulations were then compared with experimental measures, validating the technique and improving our understanding of the role of the pinnae in modifying the incoming sound in a direction-dependent manner. Similar work was carried out in the same period by Kahana [44, 46]. Such simulations were initially limited, due to computational resources, to an upper frequency of 6 kHz, then extended to 10 and 20 kHz in later studies [32, 45]. Even in these cases the validation was performed comparing the numerical model results with experimental measurements showing a good match between the two, also in light of the variances observed between different HRTF measurement systems for the same individual [4, 47]. The computational complexity of these numerical methods was a major limitation in the early years of using this technique for generating HRTFs. Various optimisation techniques are being proposed [35, 55, 70], allowing significantly faster computation times with reasonable processing resources (i.e. no longer needing super computers). This led to the development of easy-to-use and open-source tools for the numerical calculation of HRTFs. A notable example is mesh2hrtf [110], a software package centred on a BEM solver, as well as tools for the pre-processing of geometry data, generation of evaluation grids and post-processing of calculation results. It is essential here to consider a major challenge to be tackled when approaching HRTF synthesis from geometrical models, which is the acquisition and processing of the 3D models from which the HRTFs are computed. Evaluations of various 3D scanning methods, specifically looking at capturing the geometry of the pinnae, have been carried out [44, 69, 80].

Numerical simulations also brought significant benefits with regard to repeatability, replicability and reproducibility. A comparison of different numerical tools for simulating an HRTF from scan data by Greff and Katz [32] (here employing the high-resolution scan of a Neumann KU-100 shown in Fig. 4.2b) showed little variance. In contrast, a similar comparison of acoustical HRTF measurements using the same head at different laboratories [4] showed significant variations between resulting HRTFs. Another significant advantage of numerically modelling HRTFs rather than measuring them is that with physical measurements on human subjects it is difficult or impossible to isolate the influence of different morphological characteristics on the actual HRTF filters.

## Morphological Relationships

Exploring and modelling the relationship between geometrical features and filter characteristics is indeed a very important step for advancing our understanding of the spatial hearing processes. Research in this area was strongly advanced with the distribution of the CIPIC HRTF database [2], which included associated morpho-

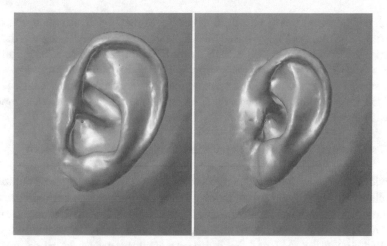

**Fig. 4.3** Two pinna created with the parametric model developed in [91]

logical parameter data for most subjects. This effort was followed with the LISTEN HRTF database [98], providing similar data. Benefiting from the power of numerical simulation and controlled geometrical models, Katz and Stitt [91] investigated the effect of morphological changes by varying specific morphological parameters, an extension of the CIPIC set of morphological parameters to provide more unique solutions. In order to do this, they created a Parametric Pinna Model (PPM) and with BEM they investigated the sensitivity of the HRTF to specific morphological alterations. Examples of pinnae created using this PPM can be seen in Fig. 4.3. Evaluations included the use of auditory models [88] to identify those morphological changes most likely to affect spatial hearing perception. In line with previous studies, morphological features near to the rear of the helix were found to have little influence on HRTF objective metrics, while the dimension of the concha had a much more relevant impact, both looking at the directional and diffuse HRTF spectral components. [2] Other relevant findings include the importance of the region around the triangular fossa, which is often not considered when looking at HRTF personalisation, and the fact that the relief (or depth, directions parallel to the interaural axis) parameters were found to be at least as important as side-facing parameters, which are more frequently cited in morphological/HRTF studies.

Such interest in binaural audio, combined with major advancements in terms of available technologies, has encouraged the publication of large datasets of BEM-generated HRTFs and correspondent high-accuracy 3D geometrical models. An example is the Sydney York Morphological and Acoustic Recordings of Ears (SYMARE) database [42], which was then followed by other examples of either head-related or more reduced complexity pinnae-related datasets [18, 34]. The availability

---

[2] The diffuse field component is the spatial average of the HRTF. When removed from the HRTF, the result is a diffuse field equalised *directional transfer function* (DTF) [64].

of such large datasets opened the door to the use of machine learning approaches to tackle the issue of morphology-based HRTF personalisation. An example is the work by Grijalva and colleagues [33], where a non-linear dimensionality reduction technique is used to decompose and reconstruct the HRTF for individualisation, focusing on elements which vary the most between positions and across individuals. Results may offer improved performance over linear methods, such as principal component analysis (e.g. [81]).

### HRTFs, Binaural Models and Perceptual Evaluations

It is evident that since the 1990s a large amount of work has been carried out looking at synthesising HRTFs and better understanding the relationship between these and morphological features of the pinnae, head and torso. Nevertheless, it must be reiterated that very few of the reviewed studies have included perceptual evaluations on the modelled HRTFs [18, 56], and that in no case such subject-based validations were extensive enough to fully support the use of synthesised HRTFs instead of measured ones. It is therefore clear that significant research is still needed in order to develop and validate models that can describe, classify and ultimately generate individual HRTFs from a reduced set of parameters.

While numerical assessments can be very useful when trying to better explain experimental results, they cannot be the only way to explore and validate the quality of the rendering choices. Binaural models (e.g. [88]) could become an invaluable tool to help overcome such limitations, as they offer a computational simulation of binaural auditory processing and, in certain cases, also allow to predict listeners' responses to binaural signals. Using them, it is possible to rapidly perform comprehensive evaluations that would be too time-consuming to implement as actual auditory experiments (e.g. [17]).

An example of this approach can be found in [29], where an anthropometry-based mismatch function between HRTF pairs, looking at the relationship between pinna geometry and localisation cues, was used to select an optimal HRTF for a given individual, specifically looking at vertical localisation. The outcome of the selection was then evaluated using an auditory model which computed a mapping between HRTF spectra and perceived spatial locations. While this study outlined that the best fitting HRTF selected with the proposed method was predicted to yield a significantly improved vertical localisation when compared to a selected generic HRTF, it must be reiterated that the reliability of perceptual models is still to be thoroughly validated, and potential biases can be identified and dealt with only through actual perceptual evaluations. Another similar application of binaural models has been recently published, focusing on the comparison between different Ambisonics-based binaural rendering methods [25]. The very large number of independent variables (e.g. each method was tested with Ambisonics orders from 1 to 44), as well as the complexity of the interactions between such variables, would make it very challenging to run perceptual evaluations with subjects. This study showed not only that models' predictions were consistent with previous perceptual data, but also contributed to validate the models' ability to predict user responses to binaural signals.

It is likely that models will never be able to provide 100% accurate assessments near to the zone of perfect reproduction, in part due to the difficulties in modelling processes such as cognitive loading and procedural/perceptual learning. However, it is reasonable to expect them to provide broadly correct predictions for larger errors. This means that they could be particularly useful when prototyping rendering algorithms and designing HRTF personalisation experiments, in order to rapidly reduce the number of conditions and variables which are subsequently assessed through real subject-based perceptual evaluations.

Artificial intelligence and machine learning should play an important role in such future research, looking at improving both HRTF synthesis and selection processes, as well as perceptual models accuracy and reliability.

## 4.2.2 HRTF Selection

A different approach for obtaining individual (or at least personalised) HRTFs without having to acoustically measure them is to rely on available HRTF databases, either transforming/tuning the transfer function according to certain subjective criteria, or designing a process for selecting the best fitting HRTF for a given subject. Regarding the first option, as mentioned at the beginning of this section, it is generally known that frequency-independent ITDs from a given HRTF can be modified and personalised according to e.g. the head circumference of a given listener [9]. Such a technique is implemented in a few binaural spatialisers [22, 78]. However, the personalisation of other HRTF features, such as monoaural and interaural Spectral Cues, presents more significant challenges. Early works in this direction looked at improving vertical localisation by scaling the HRTF in frequency [64, 65]. Other "simpler" approaches to tuning were found to be effective, for example, by manually modifying frequency and phase for every HRTF direction, for the left and right ears independently [86]. Hwang and colleagues [40] carried out a principal component analysis on the CIPIC HRTFs and used the output components to develop a customisation method based on subjective tuning of a generalised HRTF. Such customisation allowed listeners to perform significantly better in vertical perception and front-back discrimination tasks. The same approach was used to modify and personalise a KEMAR HRTF, resulting also in this case in significantly improved vertical localisation abilities [84].

### HRTF Selection Methods

Methods for selecting a best fit HRTF based on subjective criteria can be grouped into two general categories: physical measurement-based matching and perceptual selection. The first pertains to selecting an HRTF from an existing set based on morphological measurements or sparse acoustical measurements. Of importance is the determination of the relevant morphological features, as they pertain to spatial hearing and HRTF-related cues, as examined by [91]. Zotkin and colleagues [112] looked at a selection strategy based on matching certain anthrophometric pinnae parameters of the specific subject with those of HRTFs within a dataset, while providing associated low-frequency information using a "head-and-torso" model. Comparison between a non-personalised HRTF and the selected HRTF via this method showed heightened localisation accuracy and improved subjective perception of the virtual auditory scene when using the latter. A similar approach was used by [81], where advanced statistical methods were employed to create a subset of morphological parameters, which were then employed for predicting what might be the subject's preferred HRTF based on measurement matching. HRTFs selected using this method performed better than randomly selected ones. An alternate selection perspective was proposed in [30], where a reflection model was applied to the picture of the pinnae of the subject, facilitating the extraction of relevant anthropometric parameters which were then used for selecting one or more HRTFs from an existing database. This selection method resulted in a significant improvement in elevation localisation performances, as well as an enhancement of the perceived externalisation of the simulated sources. The relationship between features of the pinna shape and HRTF notches, focusing specifically on elevation perception, was successfully used in [27] for selecting a best fitting HRTF from pinna images. Interestingly, studies on Spectral Cues have suggested the importance of notches over peaks in the HRTF [31]. Another work from Geronazzo and colleagues [28] introduced a rather original approach by developing the *Mixed Structural Modelling* (MSM), a framework for HRTF individualisation which combines structural modelling and HRTF selection. The level of flexibility of this solution, which allows to mix modelled and recorded components (therefore HRTF selection and synthesis), is particularly promising when looking at the HRTF personalisation process.

**HRTF Evaluation**

It must be highlighted that whether selection is based on measured or perceptual data, the evaluation of said method is necessarily perceptual as the final application is a human-centred experience. With this in mind, a fundamental yet unanswered question is: "What determines the suitability of an HRTF for a given subject?" [48]. When establishing whether an HRTF is a good fit, should one look at how precisely sound sources can be localised using that HRTF (direct approaches), or should other subjective metrics (e.g. realism, spatial quality or overall preference) be employed [87]? In employing perceptual selection, the choice of protocol becomes more critical. In addition, as was observed with acoustical measurements, the repeatability of the measurement apparatus (here the response of human subjects) must be examined and taken into account. As an example, past studies using binaural audio rendering for applications other than spatial hearing research (e.g. [74]) relied on simple perceptually based HRTF selection procedures which, at a later stage, resulted in being less repeatable than originally thought [6]. Without extensive training as seen in some of the principal earlier studies, the reliability of naive listeners (those situations which are also more representative of applied uses of binaural audio rather than studies on fundamental auditory processing) must be taken into account. Early studies on HRTF selection through ratings [53, 74] assumed innate reliability in quality judgements.

**Fig. 4.4** Trajectory graphic description reference for HRTF quality ratings: horizontal (left) and median (right) plane trajectories indicating the start/stop position and trajectory direction (● --→) (from [92])

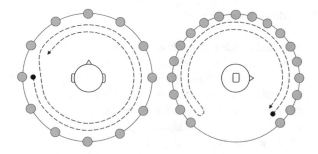

More recently, studies have shown that such reliability cannot be assumed, but must be evaluated, with some listeners being highly repeatable while others are not [6].

It can be assumed that different HRTFs will, for a given subject, result in different performances in a sound source localisation task. From this we can infer that an optimal HRTF could be selected looking at such performances, for example, using metrics such as localisation errors and front-back and up-down confusion rates (see Sect. 4.3.2 for metric definitions). This assumption has been the baseline of several studies where an HRTF selection procedure was designed and evaluated based on localisation performances [41, 83, 96]. Such methods previously required specialised hardware, though current consumer Virtual Reality (VR) devices, thanks to their increasingly higher performance in terms of tracking capabilities (e.g. [43]), can now be employed for rendering and reporting the perceived direction of the sound source. However, these methods still remain rather time-consuming, as a large number of positions across the whole sphere should be evaluated in order to obtain reliable results.

Alternatively, HRTF selection can be the result of subjective evaluations based on indirect quality judgement approaches. Several research works have looked at asking listeners to rate HRTFs based on the perceived quality of some descriptive attributes, from the overall impression [106] to how well the auditory presentation matched specifically described locations or movements of the virtual source [53, 83, 85] (e.g. Fig. 4.4). Several methods have been introduced for ultimately being able to select one or more best performing HRTFs; these include ranking [83], rating on scales [6, 53, 82], multiple selection-elimination rounds [97] and pairwise comparisons [85, 106]. In general, there seems to be an agreement on the fact that expert assessors (as defined by [107]) perform significantly better (i.e. in a more reliable and repeatable manner) if compared with initiated assessors [6, 54]. To gain further insight into indirect method results, some work has been carried out to develop global perceptual distance metrics with the aim to describe both HRTF and listener similarities [8]. In addition to proposing and evaluating a set of perceptual metrics, this work encourages further research into novel experiment design which could help in minimising the need for data normalisation and, more importantly, outlines the need for further investigations on the stability of these perceptual experiments/evaluations, specifically looking at repeatability and training.

**Methods Comparison**

Few studies have examined the similarity between direct (i.e. localisation performances) and indirect HRTF selection methods. Using an immersive VR reporting system for the localisation test, results from [108] indicated a significant and positive mean correlation between HRTF selection based on localisation performance and HRTF ranking/selection based on quality judgement; the best HRTF selected according to one method had significantly better rating according to metrics in the other method. In contrast, using a gestalt reporting method through the use of an avatar representation of the listener's head, results from [54] showed no significant correlations. A number of protocol differences exist between these two studies, including the type of tasks used for both methods, the user interface (see [10, 11] regarding localisation reporting method effects), the stimuli signals, as well as the metrics evaluated in the quality judgement task.

## 4.3   User-to-System Adaptation: HRTF Accommodation

The previous section examined HRTF selection and individualisation methods in the signal domain. While such methods aim to provide every individual user with the best HRTF possible, such approaches are not always available in all conditions. However, evidence is increasingly available showing that the adult brain is adaptable to environmental changes. It has been demonstrated that this adaptability (or plasticity) regarding spatial auditory processing can lead to a reduction in localisation error over time in the case when a listener's normal localisation cues are significantly modified.

It has been established that one can adapt to modified HRTFs over time, with ear moulds inserted in the pinnae [19, 38, 94, 95], or with non-individual HRTFs through binaural rendering [73, 77, 90, 92, 99, 109]. Studies have shown that one can adapt to distorted HRTFs, e.g. in [60] where participants suffering from hearing loss learned to use HRTFs whose spectrum had been warped to move audio cues back into frequency bands they could perceive. HRTF learning is not only possible, but lasting in time [62, 92, 109]: users have been shown to retain performance improvements up to 4 months after training [109]. Given enough time, participants using non-individual HRTFs may achieve localisation performance on par with participants using their own individual HRTFs [73, 77, 92].

This concept has been successfully used to improve user localisation performance within virtual auditory environments when using non-individual HRTFs. Readers are referred to [61, 104] for more general reviews on the broader topic of HRTF learning.

## 4.3.1   Training Protocol Parameters

Learning methods explored in previous studies are often based on a localisation task. This type of learning is referred to as *explicit* learning [61], as opposed to *implicit* learning where the training task does not immediately focus participant attention on localisation cues [73, 92]. Performance-wise, there is no evidence to suggest either type is better than the other. Implicit learning gives more leeway for task design *gamification*. The technique is more and more applied to the design of HRTF learning methods [39, 73, 90, 92], and while its impact on HRTF learning rates remains uncertain [90], its benefit for learning, in general, is, however, well established [36]. On the other hand, explicit learning more readily produces training protocols where participants are *consciously* focusing on the learning process [63], potentially helping with the unconscious re-adjustment of auditory spatial mapping.

As much as the nature of the task, providing feedback can play an important role during learning. VR technologies are more and more relied upon to increase feedback density in the hope of increasing HRTF learning rates (in Chap. 10, the interested reader can find further insights on multisensory feedback in VR). While results encourage the use of a visual virtual environment [60], it has been reported that proprioceptive feedback alone can be used to improve learning rates [16, 73]. Direct comparison of experimental results suggests that active learning with direct feedback is more efficient (i.e. leads to faster improvement) than passive learning from sound exposure [61]. There is also a growing consensus on the use of adaptive (i.e. head-tracked) binaural rendering during training to improve learning rates [19], despite the generalised use of static head-locked localisation tasks to assess performance evolution [61]. It is not trivial to ascertain whether the benefit of head-tracked rendering comes from continuous situated feedback improving audio cue recalibration, or from unbalanced comparison, as static head-locked rendering creates user frustration and results in less sound exposure [90]).

Studies on the training stimulus indicate that learning extends to more than the signals used during learning [39, 90]. This result is likely dependent on specific characteristics of the stimuli and how these relate to auditory localisation mechanisms, i.e. whether they present the transient energy and broad frequency content necessary for auditory spatial discrimination [24, 57, 72].

There is no clear cut result on optimum training session duration and scheduling. Training session duration reported in previous studies ranges from $\approx$8 min [66] to $\approx$2h [60]. Comparative analysis argues in favour of several short training sessions over long ones [61]. Training session spread is also widely distributed in the literature, ranging from all sessions in one day [57] versus one every week or every other week [92]. Where results suggest spreading training over time benefits learning (all in 1 day versus spread over 7 days) [57] outcomes from [73, 92] indicate that weekly sessions and daily sessions result in the same overall performance improvement (for equal total training duration). There is some example of latent learning (improvement between sessions) in the literature [66], naturally encouraging the spread of training sessions. Regardless of duration and spread, studies have shown that learning saturation occurs after a while. In [59], most of the training effect took place within the first 400 trials ($\approx$160 min), a result comparable to that reported by [20] where saturation was reached after 252 to 324 trials.

One of the critical questions not fully answered to date is the role of the HRTF fit in the training process or how similar the training HRTF is to the actual HRTF of the individual. It would appear that a certain degree of affinity between a participant and the training HRTF facilitates learning [73, 92]. In contrast, lack of adaptation can occur if the HRTF to be learned is too different from one's own HRTF. This is evidenced by mixed adaptation results in studies where ill-suited HRTF matches were tested.

## 4.3.2 HRTF Accommodation Example

We present here as an example HRTF learning study by Stitt et al. [92], which examined the effect of adaptation to non-individual HRTFs. This study was chosen for this example as it provides a controlled study over a significant number of training sessions. As a "*worst-case*" real-world scenario, perceptually worst-rated non-individual HRTFs were chosen by each subject to allow for maximum potential for improvement, another factor of interest in its design. This study is part of a series of studies on the subject of user-to-system adaptation, providing continuity of comparisons [15, 73, 77]. The methodology consisted of a training game and a localisation test to evaluate performance carried out over 10 sessions. Subjects using non-individual HRTFs (group **W10**) were tested alongside control subjects using their own individual measured HRTFs (group **C10**).

Prior to any training, subjects were assigned non-individual HRTFs based on quality judgements of rendered sound object trajectories for 7 HRTF sets, taken as "*perceptually orthogonal*" [53]. These trajectories, shown in Fig. 4.4, were presented to subjects as a reference. Following the results of [8], which examined the reliability and repeatability of HRTF judgements by naive and experienced subjects, this rating task was performed three times, leading to a total of six ratings per subject, counting the two trajectories, with the overall judgement rating taken as the overall mean. The lowest rated HRTF for each subject was then used as that subject's *worst*-match HRTF. This method is an improvement over alternate methods which are either uncontrolled (e.g. a single HRTF used by all listeners) or limited in the extent of relative spectral changes presented to subjects when compared to their individual HRTFs.

The training procedure for the 10 sessions was devised as a simple game with a searching task in which the listener had to find a target at a hidden position in some direction ($\theta$, $\phi$), ignoring radial distance. Subjects searched for the hidden target by moving the motion-tracked hand-held object around their head (see concept in Fig. 4.5). For the duration of the search, alternating pink/white noise (50–20000 Hz) with an overall level of approximately 55 dBA measured at the ear was presented to the listener, positioned at the location of the tracked hand-held object relative to the

**Fig. 4.5** Training game
concept design

subject's head. This provided a link between the proprioceptively known position of the subject's own hand and spatial cues in the binaural rendering. The alternation *rate* of the pink/white noise bursts increased with increasing angular proximity to the target direction using a Geiger counter metaphor [71, 79]. Once the subject reached the intended target direction, a success sound would play, spatialised at the target's location. The training game lasted 12 min and subjects were instructed to find as many targets as possible in the time available. Sessions 1–4 occurred at 1-week interval, while the remaining sessions occurred at 2-week interval.

It should be emphasised that no auditory localisation on the part of the subject was actually required to accomplish this task, only tempo judgements of the alternation *rate* of the pink/white noise bursts and proprioceptive knowledge of one's hand position. HRTF adaptation was therefore an implicit result of game play, but not the task of the game as far as the participant was aware. This task was designed to facilitate learning with source positions outside of the visual field of view, as well as to function for individuals with visual impairments.

**Performance Evaluation Metrics**

The HRTF accommodation was evaluated via localisation tests. Subjects were presented a brief burst of noise (to limit the influence of any possible head movement during playback) and would subsequently point in the perceived direction of the sound using the hand-held object. No feedback was given to subjects regarding the target position. The noise burst consisted of a train of three, 40ms Gaussian broadband noise pulses (20000 Hz) with 2 ms raised cosine window applied at onset and offset and 30ms of silence between each burst [73]. There were 25 target directions with 5 repetitions of each target, resulting in the tested sphere including a full 360° of azimuth, and −40–90° of elevation.

Two types of metrics were used to analyse localisation errors: *angular* and *confusion* metrics. The interaural coordinate system defines a lateral and polar angle Fig. 4.6a. The lateral angle is the angle between the interaural axis and the line between the

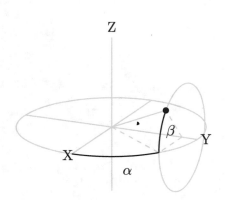

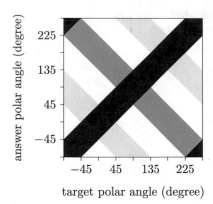

target polar angle (degree)

(a) Interaural coordinate systems. Interaural lateral angle $\alpha$ defined in [-90:90], polar angle $\beta$ in [-90:270]. Lateral angle is shifted by 90° compared to original definition [67]. Listeners facing $X$ with their left ear pointing towards $Y$.

(b) Definition of the 4 different cone-of-confusion response classification zones: ■ *Precision*, ■ *Front-Back*, ▨ *Up-Down*, □ *Combined*(from [108]).

**Fig. 4.6** Interaural polar coordinate system and associated polar angle cone-of-confusion zone definitions

origin and the source. The lateral angle approaches cones-of-confusion along which the interaural cues (ITD and ILD) are approximately equal. A cone-of-confusion is defined by the contour around the listener for a given ITD or ILD (see Fig. 4.1). For ITD, these contours can be generally represented by a hyperbolic function, where the difference in arrival time to the two ears is constant and the vertex is on the interaural axis, between the two ears. The intersection of the ITD and ILD cones-of-confusion for a given stimulus prescribes a closed curve (approaching a circle). The ITD and ILD are insufficient to resolve the localisation ambiguity, requiring further information, such as from Spectral Cues or head movements. The polar angle is the angle between the horizontal plane and a perpendicular line from the interaural axis to the point, such that the polar angle prescribes the source location on the cone-of-confusion. The polar angle is primarily linked with the monaural, Spectral Cues in the HRTF. This independence of binaural and Spectral Cues makes the interaural coordinate system a natural choice when looking at localisation performance. If the perceived ILD, ITD and Spectral Cues of a given source do not adequately coincide with the expectations of the auditory system for a single point in space, uncertainty in localisation response ensues. The most commonly referenced uncertainties are polar angle confusions.

Polar angle confusions are classified using a traditional segmentation of the cone-of-confusion [73, 92], revised in [108]. The classification results in three potential confusion types, front-back, up-down and combined, with a fourth type corresponding to precision errors, represented schematically in Fig. 4.6b. The *precision* category designates any response close enough to the real target so as not to be associated to

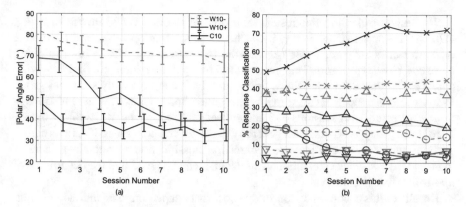

**Fig. 4.7** Result analysis by subgroup. **a** Mean absolute polar angle error and 95% confidence intervals for groups **W10+**, **W10–** and **C10** across sessions 1–10. **b** Response classification analysis: Mean classification of results for group **W10** by type (*precision* (×), *front-back* error (○), *up-down* error (▽) and *combined* error (△)) for groups **W10+** (—, 3 subjects) and **W10–** (- -, 5 subjects) over sessions 1–10 (from [92])

the other confusion types. In short, responses classified under *precision* are for those within ±45° of the target angle, *front-back* classified errors are responses reflected in the frontal plane, and those classified *up-down* are for those reflected in the transverse plane. Any responses that fall outside of these regions are classified as *combined* type errors.

### Performance Evaluation Results

Results examined the evolution of polar angle error and confusion rates. As a measure of accommodation, the *rate of improvement* was defined as the gradient of the linear regression of polar angle error. The rates of improvement for the 8 subjects spanned values of 0.5° to 4.6°/session over sessions 5–10 (as results for initial sessions have been shown to be influenced by procedural learning effects [59]). In contrast, results for the control group over the same sessions spanned 0° to 2.2°/session. A clustering analysis of the test group relative to the control group, **C10**, separated those whose rate of improvement exceeded that of the control group (subgroup **W10+**) and the remaining subjects (**W10–**) who did not. This second group failed to exhibit clear HRTF adaptation results over and above that of the control group whose improvement can be considered primarily as procedural learning.

The polar errors are shown in Fig. 4.7a for groups **W10+**, **W10–** and **C10**. Group **W10+** approached a similar level of absolute performance to **C10**. This demonstrates that these subjects were able to adapt well to their *worst*-rated HRTF to a level approaching subjects using their individually measured one. It also shows clearly that, despite continuous training, some subjects (**W10–**) exhibited little or no improvement beyond the procedural learning seen in **C10**.

The response classification results for groups **W10+** and **W10–** are shown in Fig. 4.7b. At the outset of the study, it can be observed that *up-down* and *front-back* type error rates are comparable between the two subgroups, with **W10–** exhibiting more *combined* type errors. This metric could be a potential indicator for identifying poor HRTF adaptation conditions. Subsequently, it can be clearly seen that group **W10+** exhibits a steady increase in *precision* classified responses, with reductions in *front-back* errors over sessions 3–5 and subsequent reductions in *combined* errors. In contrast, group **W10–** exhibits generally consistent response classifications across sessions, with only small increases in *precision* classification mirrored by a decreasing trend in *front-back* errors. For all subjects, it can be noted that the occurrence of *up-down* errors is quite rare.

Results of this accommodation study show that adaptation to an individual's perceptually worst-rated HRTF can continue as long as training is provided, though the rate of improvement decreases after a certain amount of training. A subgroup achieving localisation performance levels approaching the control group with individual HRTFs. These performance levels were comparable to those observed in [73] with identical test protocol, where subjects performed only three training sessions using their perceptually *best rated* HRTF.

## 4.4  Discussion

It is clear that, while various methods and tools are available for selecting a best fit HRTF for a given listener, there is no established evaluation protocol to determine how well these methods work and compare with each other. While some work is advancing in proposing common methodologies and metrics [75], the lack of established methods raises some very relevant questions about the feasibility of a unique HRTF selection task which performs reliably and independently from factors such as the listeners expertise, the signals employed, the user interface, the context where the tests are carried out and, more in general, the task for which the final quality is judged. It seems evident that any major leap forward in this field is limited until two primary issues are addressed: (1) the establishment of pertinent metrics to perceptually assess HRTFs and (2) the relationship between these metrics and specific characteristics of the signal domain HRTF filters.

The use of HRTF adaptation, in examining the results of this and previous studies, has been shown to be a viable option to improve spatial audio rendering, at least with regard to localisation. The level of adaptation achievable is related to the initial suitability (perceptual similarity) between the system HRTF and the user's individual HRTF, with more suitable HRTFs showing more rapid adaptation. No significant effect has been found regarding the specific training intervals, though spreading out sessions is better than multiple sessions on the same day. The adaptation method could be integrated into a stand-alone game application, or as part of device setup and personalization configurations, typical of most VR devices to some degree. The major limitation, once the training HRTF is chosen, is the need for repeated training

**Fig. 4.8** Example active HRTF learning training game. Training setup: (top-left) participant in the experiment room, (bottom-left) third person view of the training platform, (right) participant viewpoint during the training (from [77])

sessions, and this must be made clear to users so that they do not expect ideal results from the start.

The combination of user-to-system and system-to-user adaptation is a promising solution. While user-to-system adaptation appears limited by the initial training HRTF employed, system-to-user adaptation methods provide various means of providing, if not a perfect individual HRTF, a reasonable near approximation. As such, selection of a *pretty-good* HRTF match followed by user training could be a viable real-world solution.

An example of such a tailored HRTF training has been tested in [77]. In this work, as compared to the previous mentioned study in Sect. 4.3.2, the subject was aware of the goal of the training, with specific HRTF-based localisation difficulties presented with increasing difficulty (see Fig. 4.8). In addition, a best match HRTF condition was employed using an interactive exploration method, rather than the general ranking described in Sect. 4.2.2 and a worst-case selection scenario. Results indicated that the proposed training program led to improved learning rates compared to that of previous studies. A further addition of this study was the inclusion of a simulated room acoustic response, moving from the typical anechoic conditions of previous studies to a more natural acoustic for the user. Results showed that the addition of the room acoustics improved HRTF adaptation rate across sessions.

## 4.5 Conclusions and Future Directions

While binaural audio and spatial hearing have been studied for over 100 years, major advancements in these fields have occurred in the last two to three decades, possibly thanks to progress in real-time computing technologies. It has been extensively shown that everyone perceives spatial sound differently thanks to the particular shape of their ears, head and torso. For this reason, either high-quality simulations need to be uniquely tailored to each individual listener, or the listener needs to adapt to the configuration (i.e. the HRTF on offer) of the rendering system, or again some combination of both using individualised HRTFs. This chapter has provided an overview of research aimed at systematically exploring, assessing and validating various aspects of these two approaches. But while there is a good level of agreement on certain notions and principles, e.g. that using non-individual HRTFs can result in impaired localisation performance which can however be improved through perceptual training, there are still open challenges in need of further investigation.

A rather general but very important question that has yet to be addressed is how we can measure whether a simulated immersive audio experience is suitable and of sufficient quality for a given individual. Previous work has established a certain level of standardisation for assessing general audio quality (e.g. related to telecommunication and audio compression algorithms), but equivalent work has yet to be carried out in the field of immersive audio. Objective and subjective metrics for assessing HRTF similarity have been explored and evaluated in the past [5], and recently published research suggests that additional metrics might exist, e.g. looking at speech understanding performance [21] or machine learning artificial localization tests [3, 13]. Nevertheless, extensive research is still needed in order to understand and model low-level psychophysical (sensory) as well as high-level psychological (cognitive) spatial hearing perception.

Factors other than choices related to binaural audio processing could also have an impact on the overall perception of the rendered scenes. The fact that high-quality, albeit non-interactive, immersive audio rendering can be achieved through recordings done with a simple binaural microphone, which by definition do not account for individualised HRTFs, can be considered an example of the major complexity and dimensionality of the problem. Matters such as the choice of audio content, the context of the rendered scene, as well as the experience of the listener (e.g. whether they have previously participated in immersive audio assessments) have been shown to be relevant when assessing the perceived quality of the immersive audio rendering [6, 54]. Such a discussion found a natural continuation in Chap. 5.

Looking more in depth at the need to quantify the individually perceived quality of the rendering, the understanding of the perceptual weighting of morphological factors contributing to spatial hearing becomes an essential target to be achieved. Data-based machine learning approaches may be a useful tool when tackling this, as well as challenges related to user-to-system adaptation. Examples include allowing a certain level of customisation of the training by individually and adaptively varying the difficulty of the challenge, maximising learning and at the same time avoiding an overload of sensory and cognitive capabilities. Further explorations on spatial hearing adaptation shall focus on exploring the transferability of the acquired training between different hearing skills (e.g. [100]) and examining to what extent spatial auditory training performed in VR is transferable to real-life tasks.

Another very relevant yet still under-explored area of research is employing cognitive and psycho-physiological measurements when trying to assess both the quality of rendered spatial hearing cues and the cognitive effort during HRTF training. In the first case, measures related with behavioural performance, as well as electroencephalographic markers of selective attention, could be used to assess the suitability of immersive rendering choices [23], possibly opening the path towards passive perceptual-based HRTF selection. In the second case, similar metrics, with the addition of other measures of listening effort such as pupil dilation [103], could be employed for customising spatial hearing training routines, maximising outcomes while maintaining engagement and feasibility of the proposed tasks.

**Final Thoughts**

While most studies have focused on laboratory conditions to isolate specific perception elements, recent context-relevant studies have begun to examine the impact of spatial audio quality on task accomplishment. For example, [76] compared performance in a first-person-shooter VR game context with different HRTF conditions. Results showed performance for extreme elevation target positions was affected by the quality of HRTF matching. In addition, a subgroup of participants showed higher sensitivity to HRTF choice than others. At the same time, low-level sensory perception is only one of the dimensions where immersive audio simulations can have a significant impact. In order to significantly advance our understanding of the impact of HRTF personalisation in virtually rendered scenes and tasks, research needs to move beyond the evaluation of individual immersive audio tasks and metrics (e.g. sound localisation and/or perceived quality of the rendering), moving towards the evaluation of full experiences. The impact of immersive audio beyond perceptual metrics such as localisation, externalisation and immersion [87] is an as yet unexplored area of research, specifically when related with social interaction, entering the behavioural and cognitive realms.

In the past, several studies have been published in which auditory-based AR/VR interactions were created and evaluated without considering HRTF choice or using HRTF personalisation approaches that had not previously been appropriately validated from a perceptual point of view, or again ignoring the effects of HRTF accommodation, or blaming them in order to justify unexpected results. Considering our current knowledge and experience in immersive audio research, we are keen to recommend carrying out some level of personalisation of the spatial rendering when performing studies which involve auditory-based or multimodal interactions in AR/VR. As a baseline, ITDs can easily be customised to match the head circumference of the specific listener (as mentioned above, this function is already implemented in a few spatialisers, such as [22, 78]). Furthermore, HRTF selection routines, both perceptual and morphology based, could be very beneficial if carried out before the experiment, albeit it is important for the repeatability of such choices to be assessed with the specific subject (i.e. repeating the selection several times in order to verify the consistency across the trials, and possibly discard subjects/methods which do not show a sufficient level of repeatability). Regarding the use of synthesised HRTFs, until these are validated through extensive perceptual studies our advice is to use measured ones, possibly coming from the same dataset in order to avoid measurement-based differences.

In addition to these recommendations, it is important to emphasize that the future of immersive audio research will need to include studies focusing on different contexts (e.g. AR/VR interactions, virtual museum explorations and virtual assistant avatars), exploring the impact (and need) of HRTF personalisation on complex tasks such as interpersonal exchanges and distance learning in VR. Furthermore, in order to ensure a sufficient level of standardisation and consistently advance the achievements of research in this area, it seems evident that a concerted and coordinated effort across disciplines and research groups is highly desirable.

**Acknowledgements** Preparation of the chapter was made possible by support from SONICOM (www.sonicom.eu), a project that has received funding from the European Union's Horizon 2020 research and innovation program under grant agreement No. 101017743.

# References

1. Algazi, V. R., Duda, R. O., Duraiswami, R., Gumerov, N. A., Tang, Z.: Approximating the head-related transfer function using simple geometric models of the head and torso. J Acoust Soc Am **112**, 2053–2064 (2002).
2. Algazi, V. R., Duda, R. O., Thompson, D. M., Avendano, C.: The cipic hrtf database in Proceedings of the 2001 IEEE Workshop on the Applications of Signal Processing to Audio and Acoustics (Cat. No. 01TH8575) (2001), 99–102.
3. Ananthabhotla, I., Ithapu, V. K., Brimijoin, W. O.: A framework for designing head-related transfer function distance metrics that capture localization perception. JASA Express Letters **1**, 044401:1–6 (2021).
4. Andreopoulou, A., Begault, D. R., Katz, B. F.: Inter-Laboratory Round Robin HRTF Measurement Comparison. IEEE J Selected Topics in Signal Processing **9**, 895–906 (2015).
5. Andreopoulou, A., Katz, B. F. G.: On the use of subjective HRTF evaluations for creating global perceptual similarity metrics of assessors and assessees in Intl Conf on Auditory Display (2015), 13–20.
6. Andreopoulou, A., Katz, B. F. G.: Investigation on Subjective HRTF Rating Repeatability in Audio Eng Soc Conv **140** (Paris, June 2016), 9597:1–10.
7. Andreopoulou, A., Katz, B. F.: Identification of perceptually relevant methods of inter-aural time difference estimation. J Acoust Soc Am **142**, 588–598 (2017).
8. Andreopoulou, A., Katz, B. F.: Subjective HRTF evaluations for obtaining global similarity metrics of assessors and assessees. Journal on Multimodal User Interfaces **10**, 259–271 (2016).
9. Aussal, M., Alouges, F., Katz, B. F.: ITD Interpolation and Personalization for Binaural Synthesis Using Spherical Harmonics in Audio Eng Soc UK Conf (York, UK, Mar. 2012), 04:01–10.
10. Bahu, H.: Localisation auditive en contexte de synthèse binaurale nonindividuelle PhD thesis (Université Pierre et Marie Curie-Paris VI, 2016).
11. Bahu, H., Carpentier, T., Noisternig, M.,Warusfel, O.: Comparison of different egocentric pointing methods for 3D sound localization experiments. Acta Acust **102**, 107–118 (2016).
12. Batteau, D. W.: The role of the pinna in human localization. Proceedings of the Royal Society of London. Series B. Biological Sciences **168**, 158–180 (1967).
13. Baumgartner, R., Majdak, P., Laback, B.: Modeling sound-source localization in sagittal planes for human listeners. J Acoust Soc Am **136**, 791–802 (2014).
14. Begault, D. R.: 3-D Sound for Virtual Reality and Multimedia (Academic Press, Cambridge, 1994).

15. Blum, A., Katz, B., Warusfel, O.: Eliciting adaptation to non-individual HRTF spectral cues with multi-modal training in 7ème Cong de la Soc Française d'Acoustique et 30ème congrès de la Soc Allemande d'Acoustique (CFA/DAGA) (Strasbourg, 2004), 1225–1226.
16. Bouchara, T., Bara, T.-G., Weiss, P.-L., Guilbert, A.: Influence of vision on short-termsound localization training with non-individualized HRTF in EAA Spatial Audio Signal Processing Symp (2019), 55–60.
17. Brinkmann, F., Weinzierl, S.: Comparison of Head-Related Transfer Functions Pre-Processing Techniques for Spherical Harmonics Decomposition English. in (Audio Engineering Society, Aug. 2018).
18. Brinkmann, F. et al.: A cross-evaluated database of measured and simulated HRTFs including 3D head meshes, anthropometric features, and headphone impulse responses. J Audio Eng Soc **67**, 705–718 (2019).
19. Carlile, S., Balachandar, K., Kelly, H.: Accommodating to new ears: the effects of sensory and sensory-motor feedback. J Acous Soc America **135**, 2002–2011 (2014).
20. Carlile, S., Leong, P., Hyams, S.: The nature and distribution of errors in sound localization by human listeners. Hearing Research **114**, 179–196 (1997).
21. Cuevas-Rodriguez, M., Gonzalez-Toledo, D., Reyes-Lecuona, A., Picinali, L.: Impact of non-individualised head related transfer functions on speechin- noise performances within a synthesised virtual environment. The JAcoust Soc Am **149**, 2573–2586 (2021).
22. Cuevas-Rodríguez, M. et al.: 3D Tune-In Toolkit: An open-source library for real-time binaural spatialisation. PloS one **14**, e0211899 (2019).
23. Deng, Y., Choi, I., Shinn-Cunningham, B., Baumgartner, R.: Impoverished auditory cues limit engagement of brain networks controlling spatial selective attention. NeuroImage **202**, 116151 (2019).
24. Dramas, F., Katz, B., Jouffrais, C.: Auditory-guided reaching movements in the peripersonal frontal space in Acoustics'08. 9e Congrèès Français d'Acoustique of the SFA. **123** (Acoustical Society of America, 2008), 3723.
25. Engel, I., Goodman, D. F. M., Picinali, L.: Assessing HRTF preprocessing methods for Ambisonics rendering through perceptual models. en. Acta Acustica **6**, 4 (2022).
26. Genuit, K.: A model for the description of outer-ear transmission characteristics PhD thesis (Rhenish-Westphalian Technical University, Düsseldorf, 1984), 220.
27. Geronazzo, M., Peruch, E., Prandoni, F.,Avanzini, F.: Applying a single-notch metric to image-guided head-related transfer function selection for improved vertical localization. Journal of the Audio Engineering Society **67**, 414–428 (2019).
28. Geronazzo, M., Spagnol, S., Avanzini, F.: Mixed structural modeling of headrelated transfer functions for customized binaural audio delivery in 2013 18th International Conference on Digital Signal Processing (DSP) (2013), 1–8.
29. Geronazzo, M., Spagnol, S., Avanzini, F.: Do we need individual head-related transfer functions for vertical localization? The case study of a spectral notch distance metric. IEEE/ACM Transactions on Audio, Speech, and Language Processing **26**, 1247–1260 (2018).
30. Geronazzo, M., Spagnol, S., Bedin, A.,Avanzini, F.: Enhancing vertical localization with image-guided selection of non-individual head-related transfer functions in 2014 IEEE International Conference on Acoustics, Speech and Signal Processing (ICASSP) (2014), 4463–4467.
31. Greff, R., Katz, B.: Perceptual evaluation of HRTF notches versus peaks for vertical localisation in Intl Cong on Acoustics **19** (Madrid, Spain, 2007), 1–6.
32. Greff, R., Katz, B.: Round Robin comparison of HRTF simulation results : preliminary results. in Audio Eng Soc Conv **123** (New York, USA, 2007), 1–5.
33. Grijalva, F., Martini, L., Florencio, D., Goldenstein, S.: A manifold learning approach for personalizing HRTFs from anthropometric features. IEEE/ACM Transactions on Audio, Speech, and Language Processing **24**, 559–570 (2016).
34. Guezenoc, C., Seguier, R.: A wide dataset of ear shapes and pinna-related transfer functions generated by random ear drawings. J Acoust Soc Am **147**, 4087–4096 (2020).
35. Gumerov, N. A., O'Donovan, A. E., Duraiswami, R., Zotkin, D. N.: Computation of the head-related transfer function via the fast multipole accelerated boundary element method and its spherical harmonic representation. JAcoust Soc Am **127**, 370–386 (2010).

36. Hamari, J., Koivisto, J., Sarsa, H.: Does gamification work? A literature review of empirical studies on gamification in Intl Conf on System Sciences (2014), 3025–3034.
37. Hendrickx, E. et al.: Influence of head tracking on the externalization of speech stimuli for non-individualized binaural synthesis. J Acoust Soc Am **141**, 2011–2023 (2017).
38. Hofman, P. M., Van Riswick, J. G., Van Opstal, A. J.: Relearning sound localization with new ears. Nature Neuroscience **1**, 417–421 (1998).
39. Honda, A. et al.: Transfer effects on sound localization performances from playing a virtual three-dimensional auditory game. Applied Acoustics **68**, 885–896 (2007).
40. Hwang, S., Park, Y., Park, Y.-s.: Modeling and customization of head-related impulse responses based on general basis functions in time domain. Acta Acustica united with Acustica **94**, 965–980 (2008).
41. Iwaya,Y.: Individualization of head-related transfer functions with tournamentstyle listening test: Listening with other's ears. Acoustical Science & Technology **27**, 340–343 (2006).
42. Jin, C. T. et al.: Creating the Sydney York morphological and acoustic recordings of ears database. IEEE Transactions on Multimedia **16**, 37–46 (2013).
43. Jost, T. A., Nelson, B., Rylander, J.: Quantitative analysis of the Oculus Rift S in controlled movement. Disability and Rehabilitation: Assistive Technology, 1–5 (2019).
44. Kahana, Y.: Numerical modelling of the head-related transfer function PhD thesis (University of Southampton, 2000).
45. Kahana, Y., Nelson, P. A.: Boundary element simulations of the transfer function of human heads and baffled pinnae using accurate geometric models. Journal of Sound and Vibration **300**, 552–579 (2007).
46. Kahana, Y., Nelson, P. A., Petyt, M., Choi, S.: Boundary element simulation of HRTFs and sound fields produced by virtual acoustic imaging systems in Audio Engineering Society Convention 105 (1998).
47. Katz, B., Begault, D.: Round robin comparison of HRTF measurement systems : preliminary results. in Intl Cong on Acoustics **19** (Madrid, Spain, 2007), 1–6.
48. Katz, B., Nicol, R. in Sensory Evaluation of Sound (ed Zacharov, N.) 349–388 (CRC Press, Boca Raton, 2019).
49. Katz, B. F. G.: Measurement and Calculation of Individual Head-Related Transfer Functions Using a Boundary Element Model Including the Measurement and Effect of Skin and Hair Impedance PhD thesis (The Pennsylvania State University, 1998).
50. Katz, B. F. G., Noisternig, M.: A comparative study of interaural time delay estimation methods. J Acoust Soc Am **135**, 3530–3540 (2014).
51. Katz, B. F.: Boundary element method calculation of individual head-related transfer function. I. Rigid model calculation. J Acoust Soc Am **110**, 2440–2448 (2001).
52. Katz, B. F.: Boundary element method calculation of individual head-related transfer function. II. Impedance effects and comparisons to real measurements. J Acoust Soc Am **110**, 2449–2455 (2001).
53. Katz, B. F., Parseihian, G.: Perceptually based head-related transfer function database optimization. J Acoust Soc Am **131**, EL99–EL105 (2012).
54. Kim, C., Lim, V., Picinali, L.: Investigation Into Consistency of Subjective and Objective Perceptual Selection of Non-individual Head-Related Transfer Functions. J Audio Eng Soc **68**, 819–831 (2020).
55. Kreuzer, W., Majdak, P., Chen, Z.: Fast multipole boundary element method to calculate head-related transfer functions for a wide frequency range. J Acoust Soc Am **126**, 1280–1290 (2009).
56. Kreuzer, W., Majdak, P., Haider, A.: A boundary element model to calculate HRTFs. Comparison between calculated and measured data in Proceedings of the NAG-DAGA International Conference 2009 (2009), 196–199.
57. Kumpik, D. P., Kacelnik, O., King, A. J.: Adaptive reweighting of auditory localization cues in response to chronic unilateral earplugging in humans. J of Neuroscience **30**, 4883–4894 (2010).
58. Lopez-Poveda, E. A., Meddis, R.: A physical model of sound diffraction and reflections in the human concha. J Acoust Soc Am **100**, 3248–3259 (1996).

59. Majdak, P., Goupell, M. J., Laback, B.: 3-D localization of virtual sound sources: Effects of visual environment, pointing method, and training. Attention, Perception, & Psychophysics **72**, 454–469 (2010).
60. Majdak, P., Walder, T., Laback, B.: Effect of long-term training on sound localization performance with spectrally warped and band-limited head-related transfer functions. J Acous Soc America **134**, 2148–2159 (2013).
61. Mendonça, C.: A review on auditory space adaptations to altered head-related cues. Frontiers in Neuroscience **8**, 219:1–14 (2014).
62. Mendonça, C., Campos, G., Dias, P., Santos, J. A.: Learning auditory space: Generalization and long-term effects. PloS One **8**, 1–14 (2013).
63. Mendonça, C. et al.: On the improvement of localization accuracy with nonindividualized HRTF-based sounds. J Audio Eng Soc **60**, 821–830 (2012).
64. Middlebrooks, J. C.: Individual differences in external-ear transfer functions reduced by scaling in frequency. J Acoust Soc Am **106**, 1480–1492 (1999).
65. Middlebrooks, J. C., Macpherson, E. A., Onsan, Z. A.: Psychophysical customization of directional transfer functions for virtual sound localization. J Acoust Soc Am **108**, 3088–3091 (2000).
66. Molloy, K., Moore, D. R., Sohoglu, E., Amitay, S.: Less is more: latent learning is maximized by shorter training sessions in auditory perceptual learning. PloS One **7**, 1–13 (2012).
67. Morimoto, M., Aokata, H.: Localization cues of sound sources in the upper hemisphere. J Acous Soc Japan **5**, 165–173 (1984).
68. Nicol, R.: Binaural Technology 77 (Audio Engineering Society, New York 2010).
69. Ospina, F. R., Emerit, M., Katz, B. F.: The 3D morphological database for spatial hearing research of the BiLi project in Proc. of Meetings on Acoustics **23** (Pittsburg, May 2015), 1–17.
70. Otani, M., Ise, S.: Fast calculation system specialized for head-related transfer function based on boundary element method. J Acoust Soc Am **119**, 2589–2598 (2006).
71. Parseihian, G., Katz, B., Conan, S.: Sound effect metaphors for near field distance sonification in Intl Conf on Auditory Display (Atlanta, June 2012), 6–13.
72. Parseihian, G., Katz, B. F. G.: Morphocons: A New Sonification Concept Based on Morphological Earcons. J Audio Eng Soc **60**, 409–418 (2012).
73. Parseihian, G., Katz, B. F. G.: Rapid head-related transfer function adaptation using a virtual auditory environment. J Acous Soc America **131**, 2948–2957 (2012).
74. Picinali, L., Afonso, A., Denis, M., Katz, B. F.: Exploration of architectural spaces by blind people using auditory virtual reality for the construction of spatial knowledge. International Journal of Human-Computer Studies **72**, 393–407 (2014).
75. Poirier-Quinot, D., Stitt, P., Katz, B. in Advances in Fundamental and Applied Research on Spatial Audio (eds Katz, B., Majdak, P.) (InTech, 2022).
76. Poirier-Quinot, D., Katz, B. F.: Assessing the impact of Head-Related Transfer Function individualization on task performance: Case of a virtual reality shooter game. J. Audio Eng. Soc **68**, 248–260 (2020).
77. Poirier-Quinot, D., Katz, B. F.: On the improvement of accommodation to non-individual HRTFs via VR active learning and inclusion of a 3D room response. Acta Acustica **5**, 1–17 (2021).
78. Poirier-Quinot, D., Katz, B. F.: The Anaglyph binaural audio engine in Audio Engineering Society Convention 144 (2018).
79. Poirier-Quinot, D., Parseihian, G., Katz, B. F.: Comparative study on the effect of Parameter Mapping Sonification on perceived instabilities, efficiency, and accuracy in real-time interactive exploration of noisy data streams. Displays **47**, 2–11 (2016).
80. Reichinger, A., Majdak, P., Sablatnig, R., Maierhofer, S.: Evaluation of methods for optical 3-D scanning of human pinnas in 2013 International Conference on 3D Vision-3DV 2013 (2013), 390–397.
81. Schonstein, D., Katz, B. F.: HRTF selection for binaural synthesis from a database using morphological parameters in International Congress on Acoustics (ICA) (2010).

82. Schönstein, D., Katz, B. F.: Variability in perceptual evaluation of HRTFs. Journal of the Audio Engineering Society **60**, 783–793 (2012).
83. Seeber, B. U., Fastl, H.: Subjective selection of non-individual head-related transfer functions in Proceedings of the 2003 Intl Conf on Auditory Display (ICAD) (2003), 259–262.
84. Shin, K. H., Park, Y.: Enhanced vertical perception through head-related impulse response customization based on pinna response tuning in the median plane. IEICE Transactions on Fundamentals of Electronics, Communications and Computer Sciences **91**, 345–356 (2008).
85. Shukla, R., Stewart, R., Roginska, A., Sandler, M.: User selection of optimal HRTF sets via holistic comparative evaluation in the Audio Engineering Society Conference on Audio for Virtual and Augmented Reality (AVAR) 2018 (Audio Engineering Society, Redmond, WA, USA, 2018).
86. Silzle, A.: Selection and tuning of HRTFs in Audio Eng Soc Conv 112 (2002), 1–14.
87. Simon, L., Zacharov, N., Katz, B. F. G.: Perceptual attributes for the comparison of Head-Related Transfer Functions. J Acous Soc America **140**, 3623–3632 (Nov. 2016).
88. Søndergaard, P., Majdak, P. in The Technology of Binaural Listening (ed Blauert, J.) 33–56 (Springer, Berlin, Heidelberg, 2013).
89. Spagnol, S., Geronazzo, M., Avanzini, F.: On the relation between pinna reflection patterns and head-related transfer function features. IEEE transactions on audio, speech, and language processing **21**, 508–519 (2012).
90. Steadman, M. A., Kim, C., Lestang, J.-H., Goodman, D. F., Picinali, L.: Short-term effects of sound localization training in virtual reality. Scientific Reports **9**, 1–17 (2019).
91. Stitt, P., Katz, B. F.: Sensitivity analysis of pinna morphology on head-related transfer functions simulated via a parametric pinna model. J Acoust Soc Am **149**, 2559–2572 (2021).
92. Stitt, P., Picinali, L., Katz, B. F. G.: Auditory Accommodation to poorly MatchedNon-Individual spectral Localization Cues throughActive Learning. Scientific Reports **9**, 1063:1–14 (2019).
93. Teranishi, R., Shaw, E. A.: External-Ear Acoustic Models with Simple Geometry. J Acoust Soc Am **44**, 257–263 (1968).
94. Trapeau, R., Aubrais, V., Schönwiesner, M.: Fast and persistent adaptation to new spectral cues for sound localization suggests a many-to-one mapping mechanism. J Acous Soc America **140**, 879–890 (2016).
95. Van Wanrooij, M. M., Van Opstal, A. J.: Relearning sound localization with a new ear. J of Neuroscience **25**, 5413–5424 (2005).
96. Voong, T. M., Oehler, M.: Tournament Formats as Method for Determining Best-fitting HRTF Profiles for Individuals wearing Bone Conduction Headphones in Proceedings of the 23rd International Congress on Acoustics : integrating 4th EAA Euroregio 2019 : 9–13 September 2019 in Aachen, Germany (eds Ochmann, M., Vorländer, M., Fels, J.) (Berlin, Germany, Sept. 9, 2019), 4841–4847.
97. Wan, Y., Zare, A., McMullen, K.: Evaluating the consistency of subjectively selected head-related transfer functions (HRTFs) over time in Audio Engineering Society Conference: 55th International Conference: Spatial Audio (2014).
98. Warusfel, O.: IRCAM Listen HRTF database http://recherche.ircam.fr/equipes/salles/listen. 2003.
99. Wenzel, E. M., Arruda, M., Kistler, D. J.,Wightman, F. L.: Localization using nonindividualized head-related transfer functions. J Acous Soc America **94**, 111–123 (1993).
100. Whitton, J. P., Hancock, K. E., Shannon, J. M., Polley, D. B.: Audiomotor perceptual training enhances speech intelligibility in background noise. Current Biology **27**, 3237–3247 (2017).
101. Wightman, F. L., Kistler, D. J.: The dominant role of low-frequency interaural time differences in sound localization. J Acoust SocAm **91**, 1648–1661 (Mar. 1992).
102. Wightman, F. L., Kistler, D. J.: Resolution of front-back ambiguity in spatial hearing by listener and source movement. J Acoust Soc Am **105**, 2841–2853 (1999).
103. Winn, M. B., Wendt, D., Koelewijn, T., Kuchinsky, S. E.: Best practices and advice for using pupillometry to measure listening effort: An introduction for those who want to get started. Trends in hearing **22**, 1–32 (2018).

104. Wright, B. A., Zhang, Y.: A review of learning with normal and altered sound-localization cues in human adults. Intl J of Audiology **45**, 92–98 (2006).
105. Xie, B.: Head-Related Transfer Functions and Virtual Auditory Display 2nd ed. (J. Ross Publishing, Plantation, FL, USA, 2013).
106. Yairi, S., Iwaya,Y.,Yôiti, S.: Individualization feature of head-related transfer functions based on subjective evaluation in 14th Intl Conf onAuditory Display (Paris, 2008).
107. Zacharov, N., Lorho, G.: What are the requirements of a listening panel for evaluating spatial audio quality? in Proc. Int.Workshop on Spatial Audio and Sensory Evaluation Techniques (2006).
108. Zagala, F., Noisternig, M., Katz, B. F.: Comparison of direct and indirect perceptual head-related transfer function selection methods. J Acoust Soc Am **147**, 3376–3389 (2020).
109. Zahorik, P., Bangayan, P., Sundareswaran, V.,Wang, K., Tam, C.: Perceptual recalibration in human sound localization: Learning to remediate front-back reversals. J Acous Soc America **120**, 343–359 (2006).
110. Ziegelwanger, H., Kreuzer, W., Majdak, P.: Mesh2HRTF: An open-source software package for the numerical calculation of head-related transfer functions in 22nd International Congress on Sound and Vibration (2015).
111. Ziegelwanger, H., Majdak, P., Kreuzer,W.: Numerical calculation of listenerspecific head-related transfer functions and sound localization: Microphone model and mesh discretization. J Acoust Soc Am **138**, 208–222 (2015).
112. Zotkin, D., Hwang, J., Duraiswaini, R., Davis, L. S.: HRTF personalization using anthropometric measurements in 2003 IEEEWorkshop on Applications of Signal Processing to Audio and Acoustics (IEEE Cat. No. 03TH8684) (2003), 157–160.

# Chapter 5
# Audio Quality Assessment for Virtual Reality

**Fabian Brinkmann and Stefan Weinzierl**

**Abstract** A variety of methods for audio quality evaluation are available ranging
from classic psychoacoustic methods like alternative forced-choice tests to more
recent approaches such as quality taxonomies and plausibility. This chapter introduces methods that are deemed to be relevant for audio evaluation in virtual and
augmented reality. It details in how far these methods can directly be used for testing
in virtual reality or have to be adapted with respect to specific aspects. In addition,
it highlights new areas, for example, quality of experience and presence that arise
from audiovisual interactions and the mediation of virtual reality. After briefly introducing 3D audio reproduction approaches for virtual reality, the quality that these
approaches can achieve is discussed along with the aspects that influence the quality.
The concluding section elaborates on current challenges and hot topics in the field of
audio quality evaluation and audio reproduction for virtual reality. To bridge the gap
between theory and practice useful resources, software and hardware for 3D audio
production and research are pointed out.

## 5.1 Introduction

Over the past years, an increasing number of virtual and augmented reality (VR/AR)
applications emerged due to the advent of mobile devices such as smartphones and
head-mounted displays. Audio plays an important role within these applications that
is by far not restricted to conveying semantic information, for example, through
dialogues or warning sounds. Beyond that, audio holds information about the spaciousness of a scene including the location of sound sources and the reverberance
or size of a virtual environment. In this way, audio can be regarded as a channel

F. Brinkmann (✉) · S. Weinzierl
Audio Communication Group, Technical University of Berlin, Einsteinufer 17, 10587 Berlin,
Germany
e-mail: fabian.brinkmann@tu-berlin.de

S. Weinzierl
e-mail: stefan.weinzierl@tu-berlin.de

© The Author(s) 2023
M. Geronazzo and S. Serafin (eds.), *Sonic Interactions in Virtual Environments*,
Human—Computer Interaction Series, https://doi.org/10.1007/978-3-031-04021-4_5

to provide semantic information and spatial information and improve the sense of presence and immersion at the same time. Due to the key role of audio in VR/AR, this chapter gives an overview of methods for audio quality assessment in Sect. 5.2, followed by a brief introduction of audio reproduction techniques for VR/AR in Sect. 5.3. Readers who are familiar with audio reproduction techniques might skip Sect. 5.3 and directly continue with Sect. 5.4 that gives an overview of the quality of existing audio reproduction systems.

## 5.2 Perceptual Qualities and Their Measurement

Methods and systems for generating virtual and augmented environments can be understood as a special case of (interactive) audio reproduction systems. Thus, in principle, all procedures for the perceptual evaluation of audio systems can also be used for the evaluation of VR systems [6]. These include the procedures for the evaluation of "Basic Audio Quality", which are standardized in various ITU recommendations and focus on the technical system properties and signal processing, as well as approaches with a wider focus on the listening situation and the presented audio content, taking into account the "Overall Listening Experience". In addition, a number of measures have recently been proposed to more specifically determine the extent to which technologies for virtual and augmented environments live up to their claim of providing a convincing equivalent to physical acoustic reality. Finally, in addition to these holistic measures for evaluating VR and AR, there are a number of (VR-specific and VR-nonspecific) quality inventories that can be used to perform a differential diagnosis of VR systems, highlighting the individual strengths and weaknesses of the system and drawing conclusions for the targeted improvement.

### 5.2.1 Generic Measures

#### 5.2.1.1 Basic Audio Quality

Since the mid-1990s, the Radiocommunication Sector of the International Telecommunication Union (ITU-R) has developed a series of recommendations for the "Subjective assessment of sound quality". The series includes an overview of the areas of application of the recommendations with instructions for the selection of the appropriate standard [35] as well as an overview of "general methods" which are applied slightly differently in the different standards [36]. They contain instructions for experimental design, selection of the listening panel, test paradigms and scales, reproduction devices, and listening conditions up to the statistical treatment of collected data. Originally, these recommendations were mainly used for the perceptual evaluation of audio codecs, but later, they were also used for the evaluation of multi-channel reproduction systems and 3D audio techniques. The central construct to be

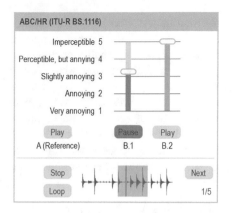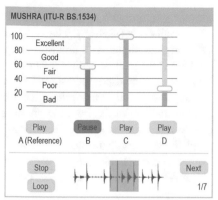

**Fig. 5.1** User interfaces for ABC/HR and MUSHRA tests. Active conditions are indicated by orange buttons; loop range and current playback position by orange boxes and lines. The ABC/HR interface shows only one condition but versions with multiple conditions per rating screen are also possible. If multiple conditions are displayed on a single screen, an additional button to sort the conditions according to the current ratings might help subjects to establish more reliable ratings (CC-BY, Fabian Brinkmann)

evaluated by all ITU procedures is "Basic Audio Quality" (BAQ). It can be evaluated either by direct scaling or by rating the "impairment" relative to an explicit or implicit reference and caused by deficits of the transmission system such as a low-bitrate audio codec or by limitations of the spatial reproduction. By definition BAQ includes "all aspects of the sound quality being assessed", such as "timbre, transparency, stereophonic imaging, spatial presentation, reverberance, echoes, harmonic distortions, quantisation noise, pops, clicks and background noise" [36, p. 7], In studies of impairment, listeners are asked "to judge any and all detected differences between the reference and the object" [34, p. 7]. In this case, the evaluation of BAQ thus corresponds to a rating of general "similarity" or "difference".

The most popular standards for BAQ are (cf. Fig. 5.1)

- ITU-R BS. 1116-3:2016 (Methods for the subjective assessment of small impairments in audio systems) [34]. Listeners are asked to rate the difference between an audio stimulus and a given reference stimulus using a continuous scale with five labels ("Imperceptible"/"Perceptible, but not annoying"/"Slightly annoying"/ "Annoying"/"Very annoying") used as "anchors". Participants are presented with three stimuli (A, B, C). A is the reference, and B and C are rated, with one of the two stimuli again being the hidden reference (double-blind triple-stimulus with hidden reference).
- ITU-R BS.1534 (Method for the subjective assessment of intermediate quality level of audio systems) [37]. Unlike ITU-R BS. 1116-3, it is a multi-stimulus test where direct comparisons between the different stimuli are possible. Quality is rated on a continuous scale with five labels ("Excellent"/"Good"/"Fair"/"Poor"/ "Bad"). Participants are presented with a reference, no more than nine stimuli

under test, and two anchor signals (MUlti-Stimulus test with Hidden Reference and Anchor, MUSHRA). The standard anchors are a low-pass filtered version of the original signal with a cut-off frequency of 3.5 kHz (low-quality anchor) and 7 kHz (mid-quality anchor). Alternatively or additionally, further non-standard anchors can be used; they should resemble the character of the systems' artifacts being tested and indicate how the systems under test compares to well-known audio quality levels. Possible anchors in the context of spatial audio might be conventional mono/stereo recordings or non-individual signals. Since listeners can directly compare the signals under test with the reference and among each other, more reliable ratings can be expected in situations where stimuli differ significantly from the reference, but only slightly from each other.

Although BAQ is the standard attribute to be tested in both ITU recommendations, other attributes are suggested to test more specific aspects of audio systems such as spatial and timbral qualities. ITU-R BS.1284-2 contains a list of main attributes and sub-attributes, from which one can choose those suitable for a particular test [36, Attachment 1]. In this respect, both recommendations are often used only as an experimental paradigm, but applied to qualities other than BAQ, e.g., those developed in various taxonomies on the properties of VR systems (see Sect. 5.2.2.4).

A number of issues were raised addressing specific aspects of the ITU recommendations [55]. One pertains to the scale labels being multidimensional, which could distort the ratings. This can be avoided by using clearly unidimensional labels at both ends, e.g., "imperceptible"/"very perceptible" for ABC/HR or "good"/"bad" for MUSHRA and additional unlabeled lines for orientation. Another issue points out that data from MUSHRA tests often violate assumptions for conducting an Analysis of Variance (ANOVA), the most common means for statistical analysis of the results. This can be considered by using general linear models for the analysis, that are more flexible than ANOVA and pose less requirements on the input data [33].

### 5.2.1.2  Overall Listening Experience

The construct of "Overall Listening Experience" (OLE) [70] was derived from the concept of "Quality of Experience", which in the context of quality management describes "the degree of delight or annoyance of the user of an application or service" [11], considering not only the technical performance of a system but also the expectations and personality and current state of the user as influencing factors. In contrast to listening tests according to the ITU recommendations, the musical content is thus explicitly part of the judgment that listeners make about the OLE.

A measurement of the OLE can be a useful alternative or supplement to purely system-related evaluations insofar as, for example, the difference between different playback systems for music may very well be audible in a direct comparison, but hardly relevant for everyday music consumption, also in comparison to the liking of the music played. In this respect, an evaluation according to ITU may possibly convey a false picture of the general relevance of technical functions. This becomes

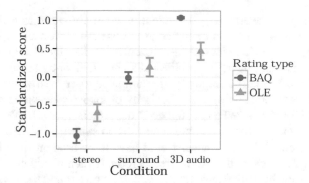

**Fig. 5.2** Results of a listening test (z-standardized scores) of Basic Audio Quality (BAQ) and Overall Listening Experience (OLE) for three different spatial audio systems (2.0 stereo, 5.0 surround,
22.2 sound referred to as "3D Audio"). BAQ ratings were given according to ITU-R BS.1534 relative to the "3D audio" condition as an explicit reference, whereas OLE ratings were given without
a reference stimulus [71, p. 84]

evident, for example, in a direct comparison between BAQ and OLE ratings of spatial
audio systems, where the differences between BAQ ratings are generally larger than
between OLE ratings. In a listening test, both BAQ ratings according to ITU-R BS.
1534 with explicit reference and OLE ratings ("Please rate for each audio excerpt
how much you enjoyed listening to it") without explicit reference were collected for
three different spatial audio systems (2.0 stereo, 5.0 surround, 22.2 surround [71]).
While the difference between 2.0 and 5.0 was equally visible in BAQ and OLE, the
difference between 5.0 and 22.2 was clearly audible in a direct comparison (BAQ),
but did obviously not result in a significant increase in listening pleasure (OLE,
Fig. 5.2).

## 5.2.2   VR/AR-Specifc Measures

### 5.2.2.1   Authenticity

A simulation that is indistinguishable from the physical sound field it is intended to
simulate could be termed authentic. The term could be used in a physical sense; then
it would aim at the identity of sound fields, be it the identity of sound pressures in the
ear canal (binaural technology) or the identity of sound fields in an extended spatial
area (sound field synthesis). Since no technical system is currently able to guarantee
such an identity, and since such a physical identity may also not be required for the
users of VR/AR systems, the term authenticity is mostly used in the psychological
sense. In this sense, it denotes a simulation that is perceptually indistinguishable
from the corresponding real sound field [8].

The challenge in determining perceptual authenticity is not to let the presence of a simulation or the physical reference in the listening test become recognizable solely through the environment of the presentation, i.e., by wearing headphones as opposed to listening freely in the physical sound field, or by listening in a studio environment that does not correspond to the simulated space even purely visually. For this reason, a determination of the authenticity of loudspeaker-based systems such as Wave Field Synthesis (WFS) or Higher-Order Ambisonics (HOA) can hardly be carried out in practice, because even if one were to suppress the visual impression by means of a blindfold, the listener would have to be brought from the playback room of the synthesis into the real reference room, which would no longer allow a direct comparison due to the temporal delay. Setting up a sound field synthesis in the corresponding physical room, on the other hand, would be prohibited, since the room acoustics of the physical room would influence the sound field of the loudspeaker synthesis.

A determination of authenticity is simpler for binaural technology systems. By using open headphones that are largely transparent to the external sound field and whose influence can possibly be compensated by an equalization filter, a direct comparison can be made by switching back and forth between a physical sound source and its binaural simulation [8]. The influence of the headphones on the external sound field can be further minimized by using extra-aural headphones suspended a few centimeters in front of the ear [18]. Such an influence can also come from other VR devices such as head-mounted displays that are close to the ear canal [27]. An example of a listening test setup is shown in Fig. 5.3.

As a paradigm for the listening test, classical procedures such as ABX with explicit reference [12, 44] or forced-choice procedures (N-AFC) with non-explicit reference [21] can be used, which have proven suitable for detecting small differences between two stimuli. It should be noted that, especially in the case of minor differences, the presentation mode can have a great influence on the recognition rate, such as the fact whether the two stimuli (simulation and reference) can be heard by the test

**Fig. 5.3** Listening test setup for testing authenticity and plausibility. For seamless switching between audio from the loudspeakers and their binaural simulation, the subject is wearing extra-aural headphones that minimize distortions of exterior sound fields. The head position of the subject is tracked by an electromagnetic sensor pair mounted on the top of the chair and headphones. See also Sect. 5.4.1.1 (CC-BY, Fabian Brinkmann)

**Fig. 5.4** User interfaces for testing authenticity with an ABX test (also termed 2-interval/2-alternative forced choice, 2i/2AFC) test and testing plausibility with a yes/no paradigm. Responses/active conditions are indicated by orange buttons; loop range and current playback position by orange boxes and lines. In case of the test for plausibility, the audio starts automatically and can only be heard once (CC-BY, Fabian Brinkmann)

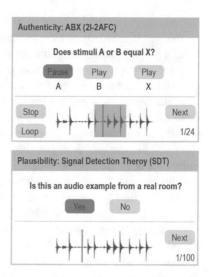

participants only once or as often as desired [8, p. 1793 f]. An example of a user interface is given in Fig. 5.4.

Binaural representations can also be used to make comparisons of physical sound fields and simulations based on loudspeaker arrays [85]. For this purpose, the measured or numerically simulated sound field of a loudspeaker array at a given listening position can be presented in the listening test as a binaural synthesis, thus avoiding the problems described above when comparing physical and loudspeaker-simulated sound fields. It should be noted, however, in this case, the simulation (binaural synthesis) of a simulation (sound field synthesis) becomes audible, so it may be difficult to separate the artifacts of the two methods.

#### 5.2.2.2 Plausibility

While the authenticity of virtual environments can be determined by the (physical or perceptual) identity of physical and simulated sound fields, plausibility has been proposed as a measure of the extent to which a simulation is "in agreement with the listener's expectation towards a corresponding real event" [47]. Plausibility thus does not address the comparison with an external, presented reference, but the consideration against the background of an inner reference that reflects the credibility of the simulation, based on the listener's experience and expectations of the internal structure of acoustic scenes or environments. The operationalization of this construct thus does not require a comparative evaluation, but a yes–no decision.

By analyzing such yes–no decisions with the statistical framework of signal detection theory (SDT, [84]), one can separate the response bias, i.e., a general, subjective tendency to consider stimuli as "real" or "simulated", from the actual impairments of the simulation. Signal detection theory is originally a method for determining threshold values. For example, the absolute hearing threshold of sounds can be determined by the statistical analysis of a 2x2 contingency table in which two correct answers (sound present and heard, sound absent and not heard, i.e., hits and correct rejections) and two incorrect answers (sound present and not heard, sound absent and heard, i.e., misses and false alarms) occur. By contrasting these response frequencies, the response bias, i.e., a general tendency to mark sounds as "heard," can be separated from actual recognition performance. The latter is represented by the sensitivity $d'$ which can be converted to a corresponding 2AFC detection rate. A number of at least 100 yes–no decisions per subject is considered necessary for obtaining stable individual SDT parameters [40].

This approach can be applied to the evaluation of virtual realities, in that the artifacts caused by deficits in the simulation take on the role of a stimulus to be discovered, and listeners are asked to identify the environment as "simulated" if they notice them. The prerequisite for such an experiment is, however, that—similar to an experiment on "authenticity"—one can present both physically "real" and simulated sound fields without the nature of the stimulus already being recognizable on the basis of the experimental environment, for example, by providing a visual representation of the physical sound source also in the simulated case, or by conducting the experiment with closed or blindfolded eyes.

### 5.2.2.3  Sense of Presence and Immersion

A central function of VR systems is to create a "sense of presence", i.e., the feeling of being or acting in a place, even when one is physically situated in another location and the sensory input is known to be technically mediated. The concept of presence, also called "telepresence" in older literature in reference to teleoperation systems used to manipulate remote physical objects [58], has given rise to its own research direction and community in the form of presence research, which is organized in societies such as the International Society for Presence Research (ISPR) and conferences such as the biennial PRESENCE conference.[1]

To measure the degree of presence, different questionnaires have been developed. For an overview see [72]. The instrument of Whitmer and Singer [87], one of the most widely used questionnaires, contains 28 questions such as "How much were you able to control events?", "How responsive was the environment to actions that you initiated (or performed)?", "How natural did your interactions with the environment seem?", or "How completely were all of your senses engaged?". Analyzing the response patterns in these questionnaires, different dimensions such as "Involvement", "Sensory fidelity", "Adaptation/immersion", and "Interface quality" have emerged in factor analytic studies [86].

Other approaches to measuring presence include behavioral measurements. If one assumes that presence is given if the reactions to a virtual environment correspond to the behavior in physical environments, then for example, the swaying caused by

---

[1] https://ispr.info (last access 2022/06/17).

a moving visual scene or ducking in response to a flying object can be used as an indicator for the degree of presence [19]. As a prerequisite for such realistic behavior, Slater considers two aspects: The sensation of being in a real place ("place illusion") and the illusion that the scenario being depicted is actually occurring ("plausibility illusion") [75]. Note, however, that "plausibility" is used here, in comparison with the understanding used in Sect. 5.2.2.2, in a narrower sense with a slightly different meaning.

A similar idea is behind the use of psychophysiological measures. If the normal physiological response of a person to a particular situation is replicated in a VR environment, this can be considered as an indicator of presence. Although physiological parameters have been used to measure various functions and applications of VR systems [28], they have also been used to measure presence in several studies. Depending on the scenario presented, the Electroencephalogram (EEG) [5], heart rate (HR) [14], or skin conductance and heart rate variability [13] were shown to be indicators of different degrees of presence. The exact correlations, however, seem to depend very much on the scenario presented in each case, and in any case, comparative values from a corresponding real-life stimulus are required to calibrate the measurement. Also breaks in presence (BIPs), i.e., moments where the users become aware of the mediatedness of the VR experience due to shortcomings of the system becoming suddenly obvious seem to be associated with physiological responses [76].

In general, these approaches seem to be limited to situations in which physiological reactions are sufficiently pronounced, such as anger, fear, or stress [54], whereas reactions are less pronounced when the person is predominantly an observer of a scene that has little emotional impact. This may be the reason why manipulations to the level of presence in these studies were almost exclusively realized through changes to the visual display and user interaction, while physiological parameters were hardly used to evaluate the degree of presence in *acoustic* virtual environments.

The sense of presence, long used as a measure for evaluating VR and AR systems alone, has recently gained increasing attention as a general neuropsychological phenomenon evolving from biological as well as cultural factors [68]. From the perspective of evolutionary psychology, the sense of presence has evolved not to distinguish between real and virtual conditions, but to distinguish the external world from phenomena attributable to one's own body and mind. On such a theoretical basis, it seems consequent that for achieving a high presence not only the sensory plausibility and the naturalness of the interaction but also the meaning and relevance of the scene for the respective user is essential. The degree of presence in a virtual scene will remain limited if the content is irrelevant to the respective user [66].

Related to the sense of presence, but less consistently used, is the concept of "immersion". In some literature, it is treated as an objective property of VR and AR systems [77]. According to this technical understanding, a 5-channel system is considered more "immersive" than a two-channel system, simply because it is able to present a wider range of sound incidence directions to the listener. In other works, however, immersion is treated as psychological construct, i.e., a human response to a technical system [87], shifting the meaning of "immersion" closer to the concept of presence [74]. Finally, in many works, especially in the field of audio, it remains unclear whether the reasoning about immersion is on a technical or psychological level. Chapter 11 discusses more in depth the aforementioned issue focusing on audiovisual experiences.

### 5.2.2.4  Attributes and Taxonomies

With properties such as authenticity, plausibility, or the sense of presence, a global assessment of VR systems is intended. In order to obtain indications of the strengths and weaknesses of these systems and to draw appropriate conclusions for improvement, however, a differential diagnosis is required that separately assesses different qualities of the respective systems. To distinguish these perceptual qualities from technical parameters of the system that may have an influence on them, the former is also referred to as "Quality features" and the latter as "Quality elements" in the Context of Product-Sound Quality [38].

For this purpose, different taxonomies for the qualities of virtual acoustic environments, 3D audio or spatial audio systems have been developed. Some of these are based on earlier collections of attributes for sound quality and spatial audio quality [42] which were clustered in sound families using semantic analyses such as free categorization or multidimensional scaling (MDS) [43]. Pedersen and Zacharov (2015) [62] developed a sound wheel to present such a lexicon for reproduced sound.[2] The wheel format has a longer tradition in the domain of food quality and sensory evaluation [60] as a structured and hierarchical form of a lexicon of different sensory characteristics. The selection of the items and the structure of the wheel in [62] are based on empirical methods such as hierarchical cluster analysis and measures for discrimination, reliability, and inter-rater agreement of the individual items.

While the taxonomies mentioned above were developed for spatial audio systems and product categories such as headphones, loudspeakers, multi-channel sound in general, others were generated with a stronger focus on virtual acoustic environments. Developed by qualitative methods such as expert surveys (DELPHI method [73]) and expert focus groups [48], they contain between 7 [73] and 48 attributes [48], from which those relevant to the specific experiment can be selected. Examples of a VR/AR specific taxonomy and a rating interface are shown in Figs. 5.5 and 5.6.

## 5.2.3  VR/AR-Specific User Interfaces, Test Procedures, and Toolkits

While the quality measures introduced so far can theoretically be directly transferred for testing in VR and AR, there are specific features that should be addressed: The

---

[2] Currently maintained under https://forcetechnology.com/en/articles/gated-content-senselab-sound-wheel (last access 2022/06/17).

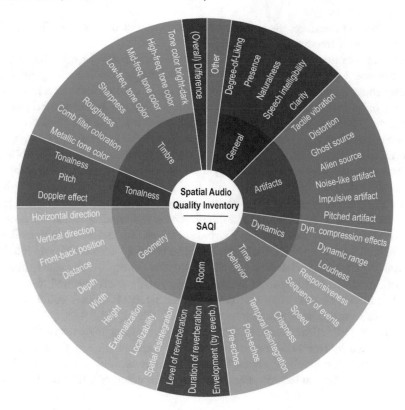

**Fig. 5.5** SAQI wheel for the evaluation of virtual acoustic environments, structured into informal categories (inner ring) and attributes (outer ring). For definitions and sound examples refer to depositonce.tu-berlin.de/handle/11303/157.2 (CC-BY, Fabian Brinkmann)

**Fig. 5.6** User interface for conducting a SAQI test. The interface is similar to that of a MUSHRA test shown in Fig. 5.1 with the difference that the current quality to be rated is given together with the possibility to show its definition (info button) and that the rating scale can also be bipolar. In any case, zero ratings indicated no perceivable difference (CC-BY, Fabian Brinkmann)

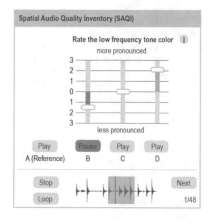

test method and interface, the technical administration of the test, and the effect of added degrees of freedom on the subjects.

First, most of the test methods and user interfaces were developed to be accessed on a computer with a mouse as a pointing and clicking device. The rating procedure and the elements on the user interface might thus not be optimal for testing in VR/AR. This might be less relevant for simple paradigms such as ABX or yes/no tests but can certainly become an issue for rating the quality of multiple test conditions.

Two approaches were suggested to account for this. Völker et al. [81] suggested a modified MUSHRA to simplify the rating interface and make it easier to establish an order between test conditions, especially if many test conditions are to be compared against the reference and each other (cf. Fig. 5.7). The idea is to unify playback and rating by making use of drag and drop actions, where the playback is triggered when the subject drags a button corresponding to a test condition, and the rating is achieved by dropping the button on a two-dimensional scale. Ratings obtained with the modified interface were comparable to those obtained with the classic interface in terms of test–retest reliability and discrimination ability. At the same time, the modified interface was preferred by the subjects, and subjects needed less time to complete the rating task. Note that the Drag and Drop MUSHRA could be easily adapted for testing quality taxonomies introduced in Sect. 5.2.2.4.

A VR/AR-tailored approach to further simplify the rating procedure and interface was suggested by Rummukainen et al. [67]. They designed a simple and easy-to-operate interface, where the subject eliminates the conditions one after another in the order from worst to best (cf. Fig. 5.8). The elimination constitutes a rank order

**Fig. 5.7** Interface of the Drag and Drop MUSHRA after [81]. The currently playing condition is indicated by the orange button; the loop range and playback position by the orange box and line (CC-BY, Fabian Brinkmann)

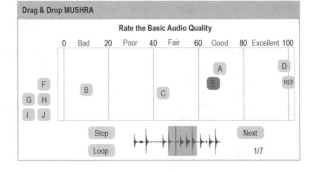

**Fig. 5.8** Interface of the elimination task after [67]. The currently playing condition is indicated by the orange button (CC-BY, Fabian Brinkmann)

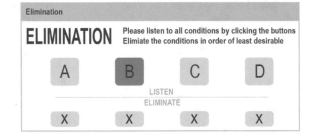

between the stimuli from which interval scaled values—similar to Basic Audio Quality ratings—were obtained by fitting Plackett–Luce models to the ranking vectors. As with the Drag and Drop MUSHRA, the elimination task could be adapted for testing against a reference and using taxonomies.

Classic tests of Basic Audio Quality are most often conducted for (static) audio-only conditions and a variety of software solutions is available to conduct such tests [6, Sect. 9.2.3]. In contrast, tests in VR/AR require the experimental control of complex audiovisual scenes. In addition, the display of rating interfaces might affect the Quality of Experience (QoE) of interactive environments due to their potentially negative effect on the perceived presence [65]. An emerging tool to account for these aspects of AR/VR is the Quality of Experience Evaluation Tool (Q.ExE) currently developed by Raake et al. [65].

A third VR/AR-specific aspect is the possibility of freely exploring an audiovisual scene in six degrees of freedom (6DoF). Introducing 6DoF clearly affects the rating behavior of subjects [67] and might thus be considered problematic at first glance. An unrestricted 6DoF exploration is, however, the most realistic test condition. While this might introduce additional variance in the results, it might also be argued that results are more comprehensive and reflect more aspects of the audiovisual scene due to free exploration. Whether or not the exploration should be restricted will thus ultimately depend on the aim of an investigation.

## 5.3  Audio Reproduction Techniques

Two fundamentally different paradigms can be distinguished in audio reproduction for VR/AR that can be illustrated with the help of Fig. 5.9. The picture shows a simple sound field of a point source being reflected by an infinite wall.

The first paradigm is to reproduce the entire sound field in a controlled zone, which has two advantages. First, multiple listeners can freely explore the sound field at the same time, and second, the reproduction is already individual as every listener naturally perceives the sound through their own ears. However, there are three disadvantages. First, reproducing the entire sound field requires tens or hundreds of loudspeakers depending on the reproduction algorithm and the size of the listening area. Second, it requires an acoustically treated environment to avoid detrimental effects due to reflections from the reproduction room itself. Third, it is often challenging to achieve a correct reproduction covering the entire hearing range from approximately 20 Hz to 20 kHz. In the following, this reproduction paradigm will be referred to as *sound field synthesis* (SFS).

The second paradigm is to only reproduce the sound field at the listeners' ears. The three advantages of this approach are that it can be realized with a single pair of headphones or loudspeakers, that at least headphone-based reproduction does not pose any demands on the reproduction room, and that a broad frequency range can be correctly reproduced. In turn, two disadvantages arise. First, the position and head orientation of the listeners must be tracked to enable a free exploration of the

**Fig. 5.9** Sound field of a point source reflected by an infinite wall. The direct and reflected sound fields are shown as red and blue circles and the direct and reflected sound paths to the listener as red and blue dashed lines. The image of the head in gray denotes the listening position. (CC-BY, Fabian Brinkmann)

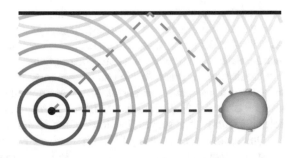

sound field. Second, the individualization of the ear signals is challenging. Often, the reproduced signals stem from a dummy head, which can cause artifacts such as coloration and increased localization errors in case the ears, head, and torso of the listener differ from the dummy head. This reproduction paradigm will be referred to as *binaural synthesis* in the following.

It is interesting to see that the advantages and disadvantages of the two paradigms are exactly contrary thus generating a strong bond between the application and reproduction paradigm, whereas binaural synthesis is the apparent option for any application on mobile devices, sound field synthesis is appealing for public or open spaces such as artistic performances and public address systems. The next sections will introduce the two paradigms in more detail. We focus on technical aspects but start with brief theoretical introductions to foster a better understanding of the subject as a whole.

### 5.3.1 Sound Field Analysis and Synthesis

The idea behind sound field analysis and synthesis (SFA/SFS) is to reproduce a desired sound field within a defined listening area using a loudspeaker array. The example in Fig. 5.10 shows this for the simple case of a plane wave traveling in the normal direction of a linear array.

Two fundamentally different SFA/SFS approaches can be distinguished. *Physically motivated* algorithms aim at capturing and reproducing sound fields physically correct, while *perceptually motivated* methods aim at capturing and synthesizing sound field properties that are deemed to be of high perceptual relevance.

#### 5.3.1.1 Sound Field Acquisition and Analysis

Sound field synthesis requires a sound field that should be reproduced and there are two options for its acquisition: through measurement or simulation. Measured sound fields can have a high degree of realism and can, for example, be used for broadcasting concerts, while simulated sound fields offer more flexibility in the

**Fig. 5.10** Sound field synthesis of a plane wave traveling from bottom to top (red fat lines) by a linear point source array (blue points and blue thin semi-circles) flush-mounted into a sound hard wall (gray line) (CC-BY, Fabian Brinkmann)

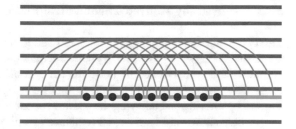

design of the auditory scene and are thus often used in game audio engines (please refer to Chap. 3 for an introduction to interactive auralization). The description and evaluation of sound field simulation techniques is beyond the scope of the article and the interested reader is kindly referred to related review articles [10, 79].

Sound fields are usually measured through microphone arrays, i.e., spatially distributed microphones that are in most cases positioned on the surface of a rigid or imaginary sphere. They can be used to directly record sound scenes such as concerts. In some cases, however, a direct recording will be limiting as it does not allow to change the audio content once the recording is finished. This can be realized if so-called spatial room impulse responses (SRIRs) are measured, i.e., impulse responses that describe the sound propagation between sound sources and each microphone of the array.

A common method for physically motivated SFA is the plane wave decomposition (PWD), which applies Fourier Transforms with respect to time and space to the acquired sound field [64, Chap. 2]. It derives a spatially continuous description of the analyzed sound field containing information on the times and directions of arriving plane wave. If the analyzing array has sufficiently many microphones, PWD can yield a physically correct and complete description of the sound field.

Popular approaches for perceptually motivates SFA are spatial impulse response rendering (SIRR), directional audio coding (DirAC), and the spatial decomposition method (SDM) [64, 78, Chaps. 4–6]. These approaches use a time–frequency analysis to extract the direction of arrival and in case of SIRR and DirAC also the residual diffuseness for each time–frequency slot. The intention of this is to extract these information from signals recorded with only a few microphones—typically between 4 and 16—and reproduce the signals with an increased resolution using methods introduced in the following sections. SIRR and SDM only work with SRIRs, while PWD and DirAC also work with direct recordings. While SDM uses a broadband frequency analysis and extremely short time windows, the remaining methods use perceptually motivated time and frequency resolutions. SDM is able to extract a single prominent reflection per time window while the PWD and higher order realizations of SIRR and DirAC can detect multiple reflections in each time–frequency slot.

### 5.3.1.2    Physically Motivated Sound Field Reproduction

The two methods for physically motivated sound field reproduction are wave field synthesis (WFS, works with linear, planar, rectangular, and cubic loudspeaker arrays) and near-field compensated higher order Ambisonics (NFC-HOA, works with circular and spherical arrays) [1]. Both methods can reproduce plane waves and point sources by filtering and delaying the sounds for each loudspeaker in the array. In the simple case shown in Fig. 5.10, all loudspeakers play identical signals. Because of their high computational demand, WFS and NFC-HOA are rarely used with measured sound fields that consist of hundreds of sources/waves. One possible approach is to use only a few point sources for the direct sound and early reflections, and a small number of plane waves for the reverberation.

### 5.3.1.3    Perceptually Motivated Sound Field Reproduction

The most common methods for perceptually motivated sound field reproduction are vector-based amplitude panning (VBAP), multiple direction amplitude panning (MDAP), and Ambisonics panning, which aim at reproducing point-like sources [89, Chaps. 1, 3, and 4]. VBAP is extensions of stereo panning to arbitrary loudspeaker array geometries. It uses one to three speakers that are closest to the position of the virtual source to create a phantom source. MDAP creates a discrete ring of phantom sources—each realized using VBAP—around the position of the virtual source to achieve that the perceived source width becomes almost independent from the position of the virtual source. Ambisonics panning could be thought of as a beamformer that uses all loudspeakers of the array simultaneously to excite circular or spherical sound field modes. In this case, the position of the virtual source is given by the position of the beam. Similar to MDAP, Ambisonics yields virtual sources with an almost position-independent perceived width. In all cases, the degree to which the width of the sources can be controlled increases with the number of loudspeakers.

In many applications, these methods are used as a means to reproduce sound fields that were analyzed using SIRR, SDM, and DirAC. Two reasons for this are their computational efficiency and the fact that they are relatively robust against irregular loudspeaker arrays (non-spherical, missing speakers), which are advantages over physically motivated approaches. VBAP and MDAP are robust to irregular arrays by design (they do not pose any demands on the array geometry). This is not generally true for Ambisonics panning, however, the state-of-the-art All-Round Ambisoncs Decoder (AllRAD, [89, Sect. 4.9.6]), which combines VBAP and Ambisonics panning, can well handle irregular arrays.

## 5.3.2  Binaural Synthesis

The fundamental theorem of binaural technology is that recording and reproducing the sound pressure signals at a listener's ears will evoke the same auditory perception as if the listener was exposed to the actual sound field. This is because all acoustic cues that the human auditory system exploits for spatial hearing are contained in the ear signals. These cues are interaural time and level differences (ITD, ILD), spectral cues (SC), and environmental cues. ITD and ILD stem from the spatial separation of the ears and the acoustic shadow of the head and make it possible to perceive the position of a source in the lateral dimension (left/right). Spectral cues originate from direction-dependent filtering of the outer ear and enable us to perceive the source position in the polar dimension (up/down). The most prominent environmental cue might be reverberation from which information about the source distance and the size of a room can be extracted. For more information please refer to Blauert [7] and to Chap. 4 of this volume.

An example of a binaural processing pipeline with headphone reproduction is shown in Fig. 5.11. The processed binaural signals are stored or directly streamed to the listener whereby the signals are selected and/or processed according to the current position and head orientation of the listener. In any case, a physically correct simulation requires compensating the recording and reproduction equipment (loudspeakers, microphones, headphones) to assure an unaltered reproduction of the binaural signals. These compensation filters are usually separated for signal acquisition and reproduction to maximize the flexibility of the pipeline. For the same reason, anechoic or dry audio content is often convoluted with acquired binaural impulse responses, which makes it possible to change the audio content, without changing the stored binaural signals. The next sections detail the blocks of the introduced reproduction pipeline one by one.

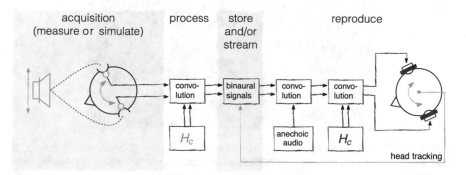

**Fig. 5.11** Example of a headphone-based pipeline for binaural synthesis. Dashed lines indicate acoustic signals; black lines indicate digital signals; gray lines indicate movements in 6DoF. $H_c$ denote compensation filters for the recording (yellow) and reproduction equipment (red, CC-BY, Fabian Brinkmann)

### 5.3.2.1 Signal Acquisition and Processing

The most basic technique is to directly record sound events—for example a concert—with a dummy head, i.e., a replica of a human head (and torso) that is equipped with microphones at the positions of the ear channel entrance or inside artificial ear channels. This requires a straightforward compensation of the recording microphones by means of an inverse filter, whereas the sources are considered to be a part of the scene and thus remain uncompensated. This approach is, however, very inflexible because the position and orientation of the listener and sources can not be changed during reproduction. It is thus more common to measure or simulate spherical sets of head-related impulse responses (HRIRs) that describe the sound propagation between a free-field sound source and the listeners ears (cf. [88, Chaps. 2 and 4] and Fig. 5.12). In this case, the sound source has to be compensated as well. The gain in flexibility stems from the possibility to use anechoic or dry audio content and select the HRIR according to the current source and head position of the listener. While HRIRs are not often directly used because anechoic listening conditions are unrealistic for most applications, they are essential for room acoustic simulations [80]. Acoustic simulations can be used to obtain binaural room impulse responses (BRIRs) that describe the sound propagation between a sound source in a reverberant environment and the listeners ears. BRIRs can also be measured, thereby increasing the degree of realism at the cost of increasing the effort to measure BRIRs for multiple positions and orientations of the listener to enable listener movements during playback.

**Fig. 5.12** HRIR measurement system at the Technical University of Berlin with details of the position procedure using cross line lasers. During the measurement, the subjects are wearing in-ear microphones, are sitting on the chair in the center of the loudspeaker array, and are continuously rotated to measure a full spherical HRIR data set. In addition, the wire frames on the floor are covered with absorbing material (CC-BY, Fabian Brinkmann)

### 5.3.2.2   Head Tracking

Tracking the head position of the listener is required for dynamic binaural reproduction, i.e., a reproduction that accounts for movements of the listener by providing binaural signals according to the angle and distance between the source and the listener's head. While it will be sufficient for some applications to only track the head orientation, the general VR/AR case requires six degrees of freedom (6DoF, i.e., translation and rotation in x, y, and z).

In general, two tracking approaches exist. Relative tracking systems track the position of the listener with respect to a potentially unknown starting point, while absolute tracking systems establish a world coordinate system within which the absolute position of the listener is tracked. Relative systems usually use inertial measurement units (IMU) to derive the listener position from combined sensing of a gyroscope, an accelerometer, and possibly a magnetometer. Absolute systems can use optical tracking by deriving the listener position from images of a single or multiple (infrared) cameras, or GPS data.

Artifact-free rendering requires a tracking precision of 1° and 1 cm [32, 46], and a total system latency of about 50 ms [45]. Note that a significantly lower latency of about 15 ms is required for rendering visual stimuli in AR applications [39]. A challenge for relative tracking systems is to control long-term drift of the IMU unit, while visual occlusion is problematic for optical absolute tracking systems.

### 5.3.2.3   Reproduction with Headphones

Headphone reproduction requires a compensation of the headphone transfer function (HpTF) by means of an inverse filter to deliver the binaural signals to the listener's ear without introducing additional coloration. However, the design of the inverse filter is not straightforward. Two aspects are problematic. First, the HpTF considerably varies across listeners and headphone models, which may require the use of listener and model-specific compensation filters depending on the demands of the application. Second, the low-frequency response and the center frequency and depth of high-frequency notches in the HpTF strongly depend on the fit of the headphone and may considerably change if the listener re-positions the headphones (cf. Fig. 5.13). To account for the variance, the average HpTF can be used to design the inverse filter, and the filter gain at low and high frequencies can be restricted using regularized inversion [24, 46]. Once calculated, the static headphone filter can be applied to the binaural signals by means of convolution.

In addition to this static convolution, a dynamic convolution is often required to render the current HRIR or BRIR. Since real-time audio processing works on blocks of audio, this is simply achieved by using the current HRIR as long as the listener does not move. If the listener moves, the past and current HRIR are both convolved simultaneously and a cross fade with the length of one audio block is applied between the two [82].

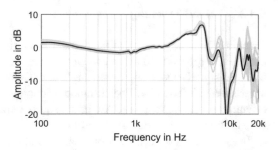

**Fig. 5.13** Headphone transfer functions of subject 6 from the HUTUBS HRTF database for the left ear of a Sennheiser HD650 headphone [9]. Gray lines show the effect of re-positioning. Black lines show the averaged HpTF (CC-BY, Fabian Brinkmann)

#### 5.3.2.4   Reproduction with Loudspeakers

While delivering binaural signals through headphones is the most obvious solution due to the one-to-one correspondence between the two ears and two speakers of the headphone, two approaches for transaural reproduction using loudspeakers are also available.

The first approach uses only two loudspeakers. In analogy to headphone reproduction, there is a one-to-one correspondence between the ear signals and speakers, and the filter for the left loudspeaker compensates for the transfer function between the speaker and the left ear. In contrast to headphone reproduction, however, this requires an additional filter for cross-talk cancellation (CTC) between the right speaker and the left ear (the filters for the right ear work accordingly). This requires an iterative design of the compensation filters for all possible positions of the head with respect to the loudspeakers and thus a dynamic convolution already for the compensation filters [51]. Optionally, more loudspeakers can be used to optimize the system for different listening positions or frequency ranges.

The second approach uses linear or circular loudspeaker arrays. Here, the idea is to shoot two narrow audio beams in the direction of the listener's ears. Because the beams concentrate most of their energy towards the listener's ears, a high separation between the left and right ear beams can be achieved depending on the array geometry [20]. In this case, a one-to-one correspondence is established between the two beams and the ears, and cross-talk compensation is not required if the beams are sufficiently narrow. In this case, a dynamic convolution is required to update the beamformers according to the listener's position.

### 5.3.3   Binaural Reproduction of Synthesized Sound Fields

It is worth to note that SFS approaches can be combined with binaural reproduction, either by virtualizing the loudspeaker array with an array of HRIRs or through binaural processing stages that build upon the sound field analysis (c.f., [2], [64, Sect. 6.4.2] and [89, Sect. 4.11]). This makes binaural reproduction the prime framework for rendering spatial audio in AR/VR and SFS a versatile tool within the framework: First, SFS makes it possible to efficiently render binaural signals for arbitrary head orientations from a single SRIR (might require pre-processing to achieve a reasonable quality as detailed in Sect. 5.4.3). Second, SFS makes it possible to include listener movements (translation)—to a limited extent—and thus enables rendering with 6DoF. The realization of 6DoF rendering depends on the sound field representation, which strongly differs across SFS approaches. However, the general idea agrees in many cases. Head rotations can be realized by an inverse rotation of the sound field. For perceptually motivated SFS methods, translation can be realized by manipulating the directions and times of arrival that were obtained through SFA according to the listener's movements (e.g., [41]). The possibility of realizing translation with physically motivated SFS approaches and measured sound fields is, however, rather limited as this would require arrays with hundreds if not thousands of microphones.

## 5.4 System Performance

This section details the quality that can be achieved with the different reproduction paradigms, starting with binaural synthesis. This is the most common approach, and in case it is used in combination with SFS, it also limits the maximally achievable quality of the SFS.

### 5.4.1 Binaural Synthesis

The authenticity and plausibility of a reproduction system are without a doubt the most integral and comprehensive quality measures and are thus discussed first. However, it is also important to shed light on the relevance of individual components in the reproduction pipeline. While there are many small pieces that contribute to the overall quality, the most relevant might be the individualization of binaural signals, head tracking, and audiovisual stimulation, which are discussed separately.

#### 5.4.1.1 Authenticity and Plausibility

Headphone-based individual dynamic binaural synthesis can be authentic if reverberant environments and real-life signals, such as speech, are simulated. For this typical use case, 66% of the subjects in Brinkmann et al. [8] could not hear any differences between a real loudspeaker and its binaural simulation (cf. Fig. 5.14, bottom). However, differences such as coloration become audible if simulating anechoic environments or artificial noise signals. Remaining differences stem from accumulated measurement errors in the range of 1 dB mostly related to the positioning of the subject and the in-ear microphones during the experiment (cf. Fig. 5.3, top). Clearly, these differences can be detected more easily with steady broadband signals such as noise. The effect of reverberance might be twofold. First, the reverberation might be able to mask audible coloration in the direct sound, and second, reverberant parts of the BRIR might be less prone to coloration artifacts because measurement errors could cancel across reflections arriving from multiple directions.

Loudspeaker-based individual binaural synthesis by means of CTC can be authentic in anechoic reproduction rooms [59]. However, the quality drastically decreases if the CTC system is set up in reverberant environments, thus limiting the usability of this approach. The decrease in quality is caused by undesired reflections from the reproduction room that can not be compensated in practice due to uncertainties in the exact position of the listener [69].

Non-individual dynamic binaural synthesis is not authentic but can be plausible, i.e., matching the listeners expectation towards the acoustic environment. This means that differences between a real sound field and a non-individual simulation are audible in a direct comparison, but they are not large enough for the simulation to be detected

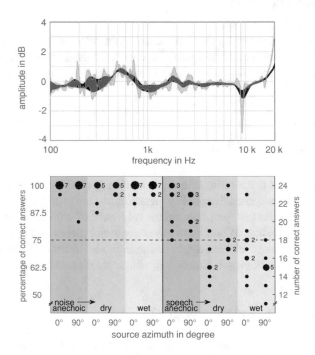

**Fig. 5.14** Results of the test for authenticity. Top: Range of differences between the sound field of the real and virtual frontal loudspeakers across head-above-torso orientations. Data was measured at the blocked ear channel entrance and is shown as 12th (light blue) and 3rd octave (dark blue) smoothed magnitude spectra. Bottom: 2-Alternative Forced Choice detection rates for all participants, two audio contents, source positions in front (0°) and to the left (90°), and three different acoustical environments (cf. Fig. 5.3). The size of the dots and the numbers next to them indicates how many participants scored identical results. Results on or above the dashed line are significantly above chance, indicating that differences between simulated and real sound fields were reliably audible. 50% correct answers denotes guessing (CC-BY, Fabian Brinkmann)

as such in an indirect comparison. Although the plausibility was only shown for headphone base reproduction of reverberant environments [47, 63], it is reasonable to assume that this also holds the simulation of anechoic environments and loudspeaker based reproduction in anechoic environments. Remaining differences between real sound fields and binaural simulations are discussed in the following section.

An example setup for testing authenticity and plausibility is shown in Fig. 5.14. It is important to note that authentic simulations can only be achieved under carefully controlled laboratory conditions. Otherwise, the placement of the headphones will already introduce audible artifacts that would be hard to control in any consumer application [61]. It can, however, be assumed that such artifacts are irrelevant for the vast majority of VR/AR applications, where plausibility is a sufficient quality criterion.

### 5.4.1.2 Effect of Individualization

Binaural signals (binaural recordings, HRIRs, BRIRs) are highly individual, i.e., they differ across listeners due to different shapes of the listeners' ears, heads, and bodies. As a consequence, listening to non-individual binaural signals decreases the audio quality and can be thought of as listening through someone else's ears. While the decrease in quality could already be seen in the integral measures authenticity and plausibility, this section will look at differences in more detail.

The most discussed degradation caused by non-individual signals is increased uncertainty in source localization [57]. Using individual head-related transfer functions (HRTFs, the frequency domain HRIRs), median route mean squared localization errors are approximately 27° for the polar angle, which denotes the up/down source position, and 15° for the lateral angle, which denotes the left/right position. Quadrant errors, which are a measure for front–back and up–down confusions (and mixtures thereof), occur in only 4% of the cases. A drastic increase of the quadrant error by a factor of 5 to about 20% and the polar error by a factor of 1.5 to about 40° can be observed if using non-individual signals. Because source localization in the polar dimension relies on high-frequency cues in the binaural signal, the increased errors can be attributed to differences in ear shapes, which have the strongest influence on binaural signals at high frequencies. The lateral error increases by only 2°. In this case, the auditory system exploits interaural cues (ITD, ILD) for localization, which stems from the overall head shape. The fact that head shapes differ less between listeners than ear shapes explains the relatively small changes in this case.

Whereas localization might be one of the most important properties of audio in virtual acoustic realities, it is by far not the only aspect that degrades due to non-individual signals. An extensive qualitative analysis is shown in Fig. 5.15. The results were obtained with pulsed pink noise as audio content in a direct comparison between a frontal loudspeaker- and headphone-based dynamic binaural syntheses using the setup shown in Fig. 5.3. Apart from qualities related to the scene geometry (localization, externalization, etc.), considerable degradations can also be observed for aspects related to the tone color. In sum, this also lead to a larger overall difference

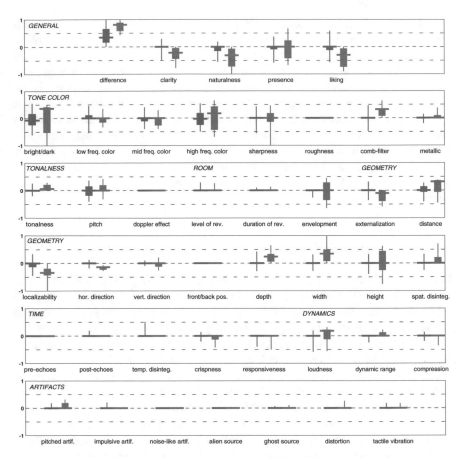

**Fig. 5.15** Perceived differences between a real sound field and the individual (blue, left) and non-individual (red, right) dynamic binaural simulation thereof. Results are pooled across an anechoic, dry, and wet acoustic environment. The horizontal lines show the medians, the boxes the interquartile ranges, and the vertical lines the minimum and maximum perceived differences. Scale labels were omitted for clarity and can be found in [48] (CC-BY, Fabian Brinkmann)

and subjects rated the non-individual simulation to be less natural and clear than its individual counterpart. As a result, the individual simulation was generally preferred (attribute *liking*), however, the presence was not affected. Because the similarity between the individual BRIRs and the non-individual BRIRs used in the test depends on the listener, the results for non-individual synthesis have considerably higher variance (indicated by the interquartile ranges).

Differences for individual binaural synthesis are small compared to non-individual synthesis. In this case, noteworthy differences only remain for the tone color. These differences stem from measurement uncertainties that arise mostly due to positioning inaccuracies of the subjects and in-ear microphones. As mentioned above, these differences become inaudible if using speech signals instead of pulsed noise.

Individualization is not only important for HRIRs and BRIRs but also for the headphone compensation (HpC). The examples above either used fully individual (individual HRIRs/BRIRs and HpC) or fully non-individual (non-individual HRIRs/BRIRs and HpC) simulations. Combinations of these cases were investigated by Engel et al. [15] and Gupta et al. [26]. As expected, fully individual simulations always have the highest quality, and considerable degradations can be observed if using individual signals with a non-individual HpC. If an individual HpC is not feasible, differences between individual and non-individual signals were only significant for the source direction but not for the perceived distance, coloration, and overall similarity. In any case, at least a non-individual HpC should be used because differences are the largest for simulations without HpC.

Many individualization approaches are available that mitigate the detrimental effects of non-individual signals to a certain degree [25]. However, they demand additional action from the listener to obtain individual or individualized signals. It is thus worth noting—and discussed in the next sections—that head tracking and visual stimulation are two means to mitigate some effects that do not require actions from the listener.

### 5.4.1.3    Effect of Head Tracking

Without head tracking, the auditory scene will move if the listeners move their head, which is a very unnatural behavior for most VR/AR applications. Head-tracked dynamic simulations in which the auditory scene remains stable during head movements have thus become the standard. Besides the general improvement of the sense of presence and immersion, this has at least two more benefits.

First, localization errors for non-individual signals decrease if head tracking is enabled [52]. While the lateral localization errors remain largely unaffected, front–back confusion completely disappears if the listeners rotate their head by 32° or more to the left or right. This can be explained by movement-induced dynamic changes in the binaural signals. As listeners move their head to the left, the left ear moves away from the source if it is in front, and the right ear moves towards it. Because this behavior would be exactly reversed for a source behind the listener, the auditory system is able to resolve the front–back confusion through the head motion. Up–down confusion can be resolved in analogy through head nodding to the left or right. Additionally, the elevation error decreases by a third for head rotations of 64° to the left or right. This can be explained by the fact that dynamic changes in the binaural signals are largest for a frontal source and almost disappear for a source above and below the listener.

The second benefit pertains to the externalization of non-individual virtual sources [31]. While sources to the side are well externalized even with non-individual signals, sources to the front and rear were often reported to be perceived as being inside the head. The most likely reason for this is that signals for sources close to the median plane are similar for the left and right ears. In contrast, the ear signals differ in time and level for sources to the side. These differences stem from the spatial separation of the ears and the acoustic shadow of the head and might provide the auditory system with evidence of the presence of an external source. If listeners perform large head rotations to the left and right, dynamic binaural cues are induced and the externalization of frontal and rear sources significantly increases.

Despite the positive effects of head tracking, it has to be kept in mind that listeners will not always perform large head movements just because they can. The actual benefit might thus often be smaller than reported above. However, dynamic cues that are similar to those of head movements can also be induced by a moving source, which was shown to have a similarly positive effect on externalization [30]. An effect of source movements for localization has not yet been extensively investigated. For the case of distance localization, it was already shown that active self-motion is more efficient than passive self-motion and source motion [22].

### 5.4.1.4 Effect of Visual Stimulation

Because VR/AR applications usually provide congruent audiovisual signals, it is worth to consider the effect of visual stimulation on the audio quality. Interestingly—and in contrast to head tracking—visual stimulation can have positive and negative effects.

The possibly most important positive aspect is the ventriloquism effect, which describes the phenomenon that a fused audiovisual event is perceived at the location of the visual stimuli even if the position of the auditory event deviates from that of the visual event. Median thresholds below which fusion appears are approximately 15° in the horizontal plane and 45° in the median plane if presenting a realistic stereoscopic 3D video of a talker [29]. Comparing this to localization errors reported in Sect. 5.4.1.2, it can be hypothesized that localization errors will drastically decrease if not completely disappear even for non-individual binaural synthesis due to audiovisual fusion and the ventriloquism effect if a source is visible and in the field of view. It has to be kept in mind, however, that the degree of realism of the visual stimulation—termed *compellingness* in [29]—affects the strength of the ventriloquism effect. Thus, fusion thresholds can decrease for less realistic visual stimulation.

Quality degrading effects can occur if the (expected) acoustics of the visually presented room does not match the acoustics of the auditorily presented room—an effect termed *room divergence*. This effect is especially relevant for AR applications where listeners can naturally explore real audiovisual environments to which artificial auditory or audiovisual events are added. However, room divergence can also appear in VR applications for example due to badly parameterized room acoustic simulations. Room divergence is not extensively researched up to date, but it was already shown that it can affect distance perception and externalization [23, 83]. While degradations with respect to these qualities might as well be mitigated by the ventriloquism effect [56], the room divergence might also affect higher level qualities such as plausibility and presence.

## 5.4.2   Sound Field Synthesis

The discussion of SFA/SFS is limited to perceptually motivated approaches because they are predominantly used in VR/AR applications. In-depth evaluations of physically motivated approaches were, for example, conducted by Wierstorf [85] and Erbes [17].

### 5.4.2.1   Vector-Based and Ambisonics Panning

The most important quality factor for loudspeaker-based reproduction approaches is the number of loudspeakers $L$. In case of Ambisonics, there is a strict dependency between $L$ and the achievable spatial resolution, which is determined by the so-called Ambisonics order $N \lesssim (L + 1)^2$. Intuitively, the spatial resolution increases with increasing Ambisonics order. For the amplitude panning methods, the fluctuation of the perceived source width across source positions (VBAP) and the minimally achievable source width that is independent of the source position (MDAP) increase with $L$.

Both approaches—vector-based and Ambisonics panning—have distinct disadvantages at very low orders $N \lesssim 2$, i.e., for arrays consisting of only about four to nine loudspeakers. In this case, Ambisonics and MDAP have a rather limited spatial resolution and Ambisonics additionally exhibits a dull sound color. For VBAP, on the other hand, the source width heavily depends on the position of the virtual source. Using state-of-the-art Ambisonics decoders, the differences between the approaches decrease at orders $N \gtrsim 3$, i.e., for arrays consisting of 16 loudspeakers or more. For such arrays, all methods are able to produce virtual sources whose width and loudness are independent of the source position. For an in-depth discussion of these properties the interested reader is referred to Zotter and Frank [89, Chaps. 1 and 3] and Pulkki et al. [64, Chap. 5].

### 5.4.2.2   SIRR, SDM, and DirAC

Different versions of SIRR and DirAC have been proposed over the past years. The two most advanced versions are the so-called Virtual Microphone DirAC, which improved the rendering of diffuse sound field components over the original DirAC version, and higher order DirAC/SIRR, which make it possible to estimate more than one directional component for each time frame to improve the rendering of challenging acoustic scenes [53, 64, Chaps. 5 and 6]. For an array consisting of 16 loudspeakers that are set up in acoustically treated environments (anechoic or very dry), SIRR and DirAC can achieve a high audio quality of about 80–90% on a MUSHRA-like rating scale (cf. Sect. 5.2.1.1). Best results are obtained for idealized microphone array signals, i.e., if the SIRR/DirAC input signals are synthetically

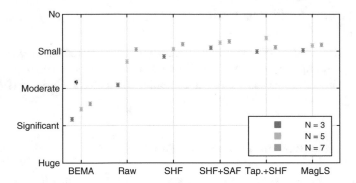

**Fig. 5.16** Perceived differences between a reference and order limited binaural renderings of microphone array recordings. For details refer to [49] (CC-BY, Tim Lübeck)

generated instead of recorded with a real microphone. Using a real microphone array decreased the audio quality by about 10% on average.

Similar audio qualities were obtained for SDM [78] and binaural SDM [2]. The latter study showed that binaural SDM has a *plausibility score* similar to sound fields emitted by real loudspeakers. Although the plausibility score differs from the definition of plausibility in Sect. 5.2.2.2, it is reasonable to assume that SDM—and also SIRR and DirAC—can be plausible, however, not authentic.

So far, perceptual evaluations were conducted in acoustically treated listening rooms and it is plausible to expect that the quality decreases with an increasing degree of reverberation in the listening environment. Moreover, a comprehensive comparative evaluation of SIRR and SDM is missing to date and existing studies sometimes used test conditions that might have favored one approach over the others.

SIRR, SDM, and DirAC might be the most common, but by far, not the only methods for perceptually motivated SFS. Broader overviews are, for example, given by Pulkki et al. [64, Chap. 4] and Zotter and Frank [89, Sect. 5.8].

### 5.4.3 Binaural Reproduction of Synthesized Sound Fields

As mentioned before, SFS approaches can be reproduced via headphones if virtualizing the loudspeaker array with a set of HRTFs. The virtualization is uncritical if the number of virtual loudspeakers can be freely selected, which often is the case for SIRR, SDM, and DirAC. The situation is more difficult, however, for Ambisonics signals which are typically order limited to $1 \lesssim N \lesssim 7$. The challenge in this case is to derive an Ambisonics version of the HRTF data set with the same order restriction. Without specifically tailored algorithms, an order of $N \approx 35$ is required for an authentic Ambisonics representation of HRTFs and simply restricting the order causes clearly audible artifacts [3].

A variety of methods have been proposed to mitigate these artifacts. This comprises a global spectral equalization with or without windowing (tapering) of the spherical harmonics coefficients or a separate treatment of the HRTF phase by means of (frequency-dependent) time alignment or finding an optimal phase that reduces errors in the HRTF magnitude [3, 89, Sect. 4.11]. A comparative study of these algorithms was conducted by Lübeck et al. [49]. As shown in Fig. 5.16, the differences between a reference and binaural renderings are small already for $N = 3$, at least for the best algorithms.

Another benefit of headphone reproduction is that different reproduction techniques can be combined to fine-tune the trade-off between perceptual quality and computational efficiency. One possible solution is to use HRTFs with a high spatial resolution for direct sound rendering (high computational cost, high quality) combined with Ambisonics-based rendering of reverberant components (cost and quality adjustable by means of the SH order) [16]. This exploits the fact, that the spatial resolution of the auditory system is higher for the direct sound than for reverberant components [50].

## 5.5  Conclusion

Section 5.2 gave an overview of existing quality measures for evaluating 3D audio content and it became apparent that the underlying concepts can also be used to assess audio quality in audiovisual virtual reality. Good suggestions were made to adapt the application of these measures for AR/VR by simplifying the associated rating interfaces and/or adapting methods for the statistical analysis. Open questions in this field mainly seem to relate to the higher level constructs of QoE and presence. It will be interesting to see how these can be measured with less intrusive user interfaces or—in the best case—with indirect physiological or psychological measures. If such methods would be established, it would also be possible to further investigate how far these higher level constructs are affected by specific aspects of audio quality.

Sections 5.3 and 5.4 introduced selected approaches for generating 3D audio for AR/VR and reviewed their quality. The current best practice of using non-individual binaural synthesis with compensated headphones for audio reproduction can generate plausible simulations and can significantly benefit from additional information provided by 3D visual content. Recent advances in signal processing fostered the combination of SFS and binaural reproduction. This improved the efficiency—a key factor for enabling 3D audio rendering in mobile applications—without introducing significant quality degradations. One current hot topic in the combination of SFS and binaural reproduction is clearly 6DoF rendering. Many algorithms were suggested for this, however, their development and even more so their perceptual evaluation are still under investigation in the majority of cases. The interested reader may have a look at recent articles as a starting point for discovering this field (e.g., [4, 41]). A second hot topic is the individualization of binaural technology. The effects of individualization were discussed and it was shown that this makes it possible to create simulations that are perceptually identical to a real sound field. Approaches for individualization were, however, not detailed and the interested reader is referred to the overview of Guezenoc and Renaud [25].

From the user perspective, it is worth to note that an increasing pool of software and hardware is available for 3D audio reproduction.[3] State-of-the-art audio processing and reproduction methods are available as plug-ins that can easily be integrated into the production workflow as well as in toolboxes that can be used for further research and product development. This is complemented by VR/AR-ready hardware such as microphone arrays as well as head-mounted displays and headphones with build-in head trackers.

# References

1. Ahrens, J.: Analytic methods of sound field synthesis 1st Edition (eds Möller, S., Küpper, A., Raake, A.) (Springer, Heidelberg, Germany, 2012).
2. Amengual Garí, S. V., Arend, J. M., Calamia, P. T., Robinson, P. W.: Optimizations of the Spatial Decomposition Method for Binaural Reproduction. J. Audio Eng. Soc. **68**, 959–976 (Dec. 2020).
3. Arend, J. M., Brinkmann, F., Pörschmann, C.: Assessing Spherical Harmonics Interpolation of Time-Aligned Head-Related Transfer Functions. J. Audio Eng. Soc. **69**, 104–117 (Feb. 2021).
4. Arend, J. M., Garí, S. V. A., Schissler, C., Klein, F., Robinson, P. W.: Six- Degrees-of-Freedom Parametric SpatialAudio Based on One MonauralRoom Impulse Response. Journal of the Audio Engineering Society **69**, 557–575 (July 2021).
5. Athif, M. et al.: Using Biosignals for Objective Measurement of Presence in Virtual Reality Environments in 2020 42nd Annual International Conference of the IEEE Engineering in Medicine & Biology Society (EMBC) (2020), 3035–3039.
6. Bech, S. N. Z.: Perceptual audio evaluation. Theroy, method and application (John Wiley & Sons, West Sussex, England, 2006).
7. Blauert, J.: Spatial Hearing. The psychophysics of human sound localization Revised (MIT Press, Cambridge, Massachusetts, 1997).
8. Brinkmann, F., Lindau, A., Weinzierl, S.: On the authenticity of individual dynamic binaural synthesis. J.Acoust. Soc. Am. **142**, 1784–1795 (Oct. 2017).
9. Brinkmann, F. et al.: A cross-evaluated database of measured and simulated HRTFs including 3D head meshes, anthropometric features, and headphone impulse responses. J. Audio Eng. Soc. **67**, 705–718 (Sept. 2019).
10. Brinkmann, F. et al.: A round robin on room acoustical simulation and auralization. J. Acoust. Soc. Am. **145**, 2746–2760 (Apr. 2019).
11. Brunnström, K. et al.: Qualinet white paper on definitions of quality of experience in 5th Qualinet meeting (Novi Sad, Serbia, 2013).
12. Burstein, H.: Approximation formulas for error risk and sample size in abx testing. Journal of the Audio Engineering Society **36**, 879–883 (1988).

---

[3] A list of available tools can, for example, be found at https://www.audio-technology.info/ under the *Resources* section of the *Binaural Technology* chapter (last access 2022/06/17).

13. Deniaud, C., Honnet, V., Jeanne, B., Mestre, D.: An investigation into physiological responses in driving simulators: An objective measurement of presence in 2015 Science and Information Conference (SAI) (2015), 739–748.
14. Dey, A., Phoon, J., Saha, S., Dobbins, C., Billinghurst, M.: Neurophysiological Effects of Presence in Calm Virtual Environments in 2020 IEEE Conference on Virtual Reality and 3D User Interfaces Abstracts and Workshops (VRW) (2020), 744–745.
15. Engel, I., Alon, D. L., Robinson, P. W., Mehra, R.: The Effect of Generic Headphone Compensation on Binaural Renderings in AES International Conference on Immersive and Interactive Audio (Audio Engineering Society, York, UK, Mar. 2019).
16. Engel, I., Henry, C., Amengual Garí, S. V., Robinson, P. W., Picinali, L.: Perceptual implications of different Ambisonics-based methods for binaural reverberation. J. Acoust. Soc. Am. **149**, 895–910 (Feb. 2021).
17. Erbes, V.: Wave field synthesis in a listening room Doctoral Thesis (University of Rostock, Rostock, Germany, Aug. 2020).
18. Erbes, V., Schultz, F., Lindau, A., Weinzierl, S.: An extraaural headphone system for optimized binaural reproduction in Fortschritte der Akustik -DAGA 2012 (Darmstadt, Germany, Mar. 2012), 313–314.
19. Freeman, J., Avons, S. E., Meddis, R., Pearson, D. E., IJsselsteijn, W.: Using behavioral realism to estimate presence: A study of the utility of postural responses to motion stimuli. Presence: Teleoperators&Virtual Environments **9**, 149–164 (2000).
20. Gálvez, M. F. S., Menzies, D., Fazi, F. M.: Dynamic Audio Reproduction with Linear Loudspeaker Arrays. J. Audio Eng. Soc. **67**, 190–200 (Apr. 2019).
21. Gelfand, S. A.: Hearing: An introduction to psychological and physiological acoustics (CRC Press, 2017).
22. Genzel, D., Schutte, M., Brimijoin, W. O., MacNeilage, P. R., Wiegrebe, L.: Psychophysical evidence for auditory motion parallax. Proceedings of the National Academy of Sciences of the United States of America **115**, 4264–4269 (Apr. 2018).
23. Gil-Carvajal, J. C., Cubick, J., Santurette, S., Dau, T.: Spatial Hearing with Incongruent Visual or Auditory Room Cues. Scientific Reports **6**, 37342 EP (Nov. 2016).
24. Gomez-Bolaños, J., Mäkivirta, A., Pulkki, V.: Automatic regularization parameter for headphone transfer function inversion. J. Audio Eng. Soc. **64**, 752–761 (Oct. 2016).
25. Guezenoc, C., Séguier, R.: HRTF Individualization: A Survey in 145th AES Convention (New York, NY, USA, Oct. 2018), Paper 10129.
26. Gupta, R., Ranjan, R., He, J., Gan, W.-S.: Study on differences between individualized and non-indiviudalized hear-thorough equalization for natural augmented listening. In: AES Conf. on Headphone Technology, San Francisco, CA, USA (Aug. 2019).
27. Gupta, R., Ranjan, R., He, J., Woon-Seng, G.: Investigation of effect of VR/AR headgear on Head related transfer functions for natural listening in Audio Engineering Society Conference: 2018 AES International Conference on Audio for Virtual and Augmented Reality (2018).
28. Halbig, A., Latoschik, M. E.: A Systematic Review of Physiological Measurements, Factors, Methods, and Applications in Virtual Reality. Frontiers in Virtual Reality **2**, 89 (2021).
29. Hendrickx, E., Paquier, M., Koehl, V., Palacino, J.: Ventriloquism effect with sound stimuli varying in both azimuth and elevation. J. Acoust. Soc. Am. **138**, 3686–3697 (2015).
30. Hendrickx, E. et al.: Improvement of Externalization by Listener and Source Movement Using a "Binauralized" Microphone Array. J. Audio Eng. Soc. **65**, 589–599 (July 2017).
31. Hendrickx, E. et al.: Influence of head tracking on the externalization of speech stimuli for non-individualized binaural synthesis. J. Acoust. Soc. Am. **141**, 2011–2023 (Mar. 2017).
32. Hiekkanen, T., Mäkivirta, A., Karjalainen, M.: Virtualized listening tests for loudspeakers. J. Audio Eng. Soc. **57**, 237–251 (2009).
33. Hox, J. J.: Multilevel Analysis. Techniques and Apllications Second (ed Marcoulides, G. A.) (Routledge, New York, Hove, 2010).
34. ITU-R BS.1116-3: Methods for the subjective assessment of small impairments in audio systems (ITU, Geneva, Switzerland, 2015).

35. ITU-R BS.1283-2: Guidance for the selection of the most appropriate ITU-R Recommendation(s) for subjective assessment of sound quality (ITU, Geneva, Switzerland, 2019).
36. ITU-R BS.1284-2: General methods for the subjective assessment of sound quality (ITU, Geneva, Switzerland, 2019).
37. ITU-R BS.1534-3: Methods for the subjective assessment of intermediate quality level of audio systems (ITU, Geneva, Switzerland, 2015).
38. Jekosch, U.: Basic Concepts and Terms of. acta acustica united with Acustica **90**, 999–1006 (2004).
39. Jerald, J., Whitton, M.: Relating Scene-Motion Thresholds to Latency Thresholds for Head-Mounted Displays in 2009 IEEE Virtual Reality Conference (Mar. 2009), 211–218.
40. Kadlec, H.: Statistical properties of $d'$ and $\beta$ estimates of signal detection theory. Psychological Methods **4**, 22 (1999).
41. Kentgens, M., Jax, P.: Comparison of Methods for Plausible Sound Field Translation in Fortschritte der Akustik - DAGA 2021 (Vienna, Austria, Aug. 2021), 302–305.
42. Le Bagousse, S., Colomes, C., Paquier, M.: State of the art on subjective assessment of spatial sound quality inAudio Engineering Society Conference: 38th International Conference: Sound Quality Evaluation (2010).
43. Le Bagousse, S., Paquier, M., Colomes, C.: Families of sound attributes for assessment of spatial audio in 129th AES Convention (2010), Convention-Paper.
44. Leventhal, L.: Type 1 and type 2 errors in the statistical analysis of listening tests. Journal of the Audio Engineering Society **34**, 437–453 (1986).
45. Lindau, A.: The perception of system latency in dynamic binaural synthesis in NAG/DAGA 2009, International Conference on Acoustics (Rotterdam, Netherland, 2009), 1063–1066.
46. Lindau, A., Weinzierl, S.: On the spatial resolution of virtual acoustic environments for head movements on horizontal, vertical and lateral direction in EAA Symposium on Auralization (Espoo, Finland, June 2009).
47. Lindau, A., Weinzierl, S.: Assessing the plausibility of virtual acoustic environments. Acta Acust. united Ac. **98**, 804–810 (Sept. 2012).
48. Lindau, A. et al.: A Spatial Audio Quality Inventory (SAQI). Acta Acust. united Ac. **100**, 984–994 (Sept. 2014).
49. Lübeck, T., Helmholz, H., Arend, J. M., Pörschmann, C., Ahrens, J.: Perceptual Evaluation of Mitigation Approaches of Impairments due to Spatial Undersampling in Binaural Rendering of Spherical Microphone Array Data. J. Audio Eng. Soc. **68**, 428–440 (June 2020).
50. Lübeck, T., Pörschmann, C., Arend, J. M.: Perception of direct sound, early reflections, andreverberation in auralizations of sparsely measuredbinaural room impulse responses in AES Int. Conf. Audio for Virtual and Augmented Reality (AVAR) (Aug. 2020).
51. Majdak, P., Masiero, B., Fels, J.: Sound localization in individualized and non-individualized crosstalk cancellation systems. J. Acoust. Soc. Am. **133**, 2055–2068 (Apr. 2013).
52. McAnally, K. I., Martin, R. L.: Sound localization with head movement: implications for 3-d audio displays. Frontiers in Neuroscience **8**, 210 (2014).
53. McCormack, L., Pulkki, V., Politis, A., Scheuregger, O., Marschall, M.: Higher-Order Spatial Impulse Response Rendering: Investigating the Perceived Effects of Spherical Order, Dedicated Diffuse Rendering, and Frequency Resolution. J. Audio Eng. Soc. **68**, 338–354 (May 2020).
54. Meehan, M., Insko, B., Whitton, M., Brooks Jr, F. P.: Physiological measures of presence in stressful virtual environments. Acm transactions on graphics (tog) **21**, 645–652 (2002).
55. Mendonça, C., Delikaris-Manias, S.: Statistical Tests with MUSHRA Data in 144th AES Convention (Milan, Italy, May 2018), Paper 10006.
56. Mendonça, C., Mandelli, P., Pulkki, V.: Modeling the perception of audiovisual distance: Bayesian causal inference and other models. PLoS ONE **11**, e0165391 (2016).
57. Middlebrooks, J. C.: Virtual localization improved by scaling nonindividualized external-ear transfer functions in frequency. J. Acoust. Soc. Am. **106**, 1493–1510 (Sept. 1999).
58. Minsky, M.: Telepresence. Omni, 45–51 (1980).
59. Moore, A. H., Tew, A. I., Nicol, R.: An initial validation of individualised crosstalk cancellation filters for binaural perceptual experiments. J. Audio Eng. Soc. **58**, 36–45 (Jan. 2010).

60. Noble, A. C. et al.: Modification of a standardized system of wine aroma terminology. American journal of Enology and Viticulture **38**, 143–146 (1987).
61. Paquier, M., Koehl, V.: Discriminability of the placement of supra-aural and circumaural headphones. Applied Accoustics **93**, 130–139 (2015).
62. Pedersen, T. H., Zacharov, N.: The development of a sound wheel for reproduced sound in Audio Engineering Society Convention 138 (2015).
63. Pike, C., Melchior, F.,Tew,T.: Assessing the plausibility of non-individualised dynamic binaural synthesis in a small room in AES 55th International Conference (Helsinki, Finland, 2014).
64. Parametric time-frequency domain spatial audio First (eds Pulkki, V., Delikaris-Manias, S., Politis, A.) (Wiley, Hoboken, NJ, USA, 2018).
65. Raake, A., Rummukainen, O. S., Habets, E. A. P., Robotham, T., Singla, A.: QoEvaVE - QoE Evaluation of Interactive Virtual Environments with Audiovisual Scenes in Fortschritte der Akustik - DAGA 2021 (Vienna, Austria, Aug. 2021), 1332–1335.
66. Riva, G., Waterworth, J. A., Waterworth, E. L.: The layers of presence: a bio-cultural approach to understanding presence in natural and mediated environments. CyberPsychology & Behavior **7**, 402–416 (2004).
67. Rummukainen, O. et al.: Audio Quality evaluation in virtual reality: Multiple stimulus ranking with behaviour tracking in AES Int. Conf. on Audio for Virtual and Augmented Reality (AVAR) (Redmond, USA, Aug. 2018).
68. Sanchez-Vives, M. V., Slater, M.: From presence to consciousness through virtual reality. Nature Reviews Neuroscience **6**, 332–339 (2005).
69. Schlenstedt, G., Brinkmann, F., Pelzer, S., Weinzierl, S.: Perceptual evaluation of transaural binaural synthesis under consideration of the playback room [German: Perzeptive Evaluation transauraler Binauralsynthese unter Berücksichtigung des Wiedergaberaums] in Fortschritte der Akustik - DAGA 2016 (Aachen, Germany, Mar. 2016), 561–564.
70. Schoeffler, M., Herre, J.: About the different types of listeners for rating the overall listening experience in Proceedings of the ICMC|SMC (Athens, Greece, 2014), 886–892.
71. Schoeffler, M., Silzle, A., Herre, J.: Evaluation of spatial/3D audio: Basic audio quality versus quality of experience. IEEE Journal of Selected Topics in Signal Processing **11**, 75–88 (2016).
72. Schwind, V., Knierim, P., Haas, N., Henze, N.: Using presence questionnaires in virtual reality in Proceedings of the 2019 CHI conference on human factors in computing systems (2019), 1–12.
73. Silzle, A.: Quality taxonomies for auditory virtual environments in Audio Engineering Society Convention 122 (2007).
74. Slater, M.: Measuring presence: A response to the Witmer and Singer presence questionnaire. Presence **8**, 560–565 (1999).
75. Slater, M.: Place illusion and plausibility can lead to realistic behaviour in immersive virtual environments. Phil. Trans. R. Soc. B **364**, 3549–3557 (2009).
76. Slater, M., Brogni, A., Steed, A.: Physiological responses to breaks in presence: A pilot study in Presence 2003: The 6th annual international workshop on presence **157** (2003).
77. Slater, M., Wilbur, S.: A framework for immersive virtual environments (FIVE): Speculations on the role of presence in virtual environments. Presence: Teleoperators & Virtual Environments **6**, 603–616 (1997).
78. Tervo, S., Pätynen, J., Kuusinen, A., Lokki, T.: Spatial decomposition method for room impulse responses. J. Audio Eng. Soc. **61**, 17–28 (Jan. 2013).
79. Välimäki,V., Parker, J., Savioja, L., Smith, J. O.,Abel, J.: More Than 50Years of Artificial-Reverberation in 60th Int. AES Conf.DREAMS(Dereverberation and Reverberation of Audio, Music, and Speech) (Leuven, Belgium, Feb. 2016).
80. Välimäki, V., Parker, J. D., Savioja, L., Smith, J. O., Abel, J. S.: Fifty Years of Artificial Reverberation. IEEE Transactions on Audio, Speech, and Language Processing **20**, 1421–1448 (July 2012).
81. Völker, C., Bisitz, T., Huber, R., Kollmeier, B., Ernst, S. M. A.: Modifications of the MUlti stimulus test with Hidden Reference and Anchor (MUSHRA) for use in audiology. Int. J. Audiology (2016).

82. Wefers, F.: Partitioned convolution algorithms for real-time auralization PhD thesis (RWTH Aachen University, Aachen, Germany, Sept. 2014).
83. Werner, S., Klein, F., Mayenfels, T., Brandenburg, K.: Asummary on acoustic room divergence and its effect on externalization of auditory events in 8th Int. Conf. Quality of Multimedia Experience (QoMEX) (Lisbon, Portugal, June 2016).
84. Wickens, T. D.: Elementary Signal Detection Theory (Oxford University Press, Oxford et al., 2002).
85. Wierstorf, H.: Perceptual assessment of sound field synthesis Doctoral Thesis (Technical University of Berlin, Berlin, Germany, Sept. 2014).
86. Witmer, B. G., Jerome, C. J., Singer, M. J.: The factor structure of the presence questionnaire. Presence: Teleoperators & Virtual Environments **14**, 298–312 (2005).
87. Witmer, B. G., Singer, M. J.: Measuring presence in virtual environments: A presence questionnaire. Presence **7**, 225–240 (1998).
88. Xie, B.: Head-related transfer function and virtual auditory display Second (J. Ross Publishing, Plantation, FL, USA, 2013).
89. Zotter, F., Frank, M.: Ambisonics. A practical 3D audio theroy for recording, studio production, sound reinforcement, and virtual reality (Springer Open, Cham, Switzerland, 2019).

# Part III
# Sonic Interactions

# Chapter 6
# Spatial Design Considerations for Interactive Audio in Virtual Reality

Thomas Deacon and Mathieu Barthet

**Abstract** Space is a fundamental feature of virtual reality (VR) systems, and more generally, human experience. Space is a place where we can produce and transform ideas and act to create meaning. It is also an information container. When working with sound and space interactions, making VR systems becomes a fundamentally interdisciplinary endeavour. To support the design of future systems, designers need an understanding of spatial design decisions that impact audio practitioners' processes and communication. This chapter proposes a typology of VR interactive audio systems, focusing on their function and the role of space in their design. Spatial categories are proposed to be able to analyse the role of space within existing interactive audio VR products. Based on the spatial design considerations explored in this chapter, a series of implications for design are offered that future research can exploit.

## 6.1 Introduction

Technologies like virtual reality (VR) offer many ways of using space that could benefit creative audio production and immersive experience applications. Using VRs affordances for embodied interaction and spatial user interfaces, new forms of spatial expression can be explored. Running parallel to VR research efforts in sonic interaction in virtual environments(SIVE), much of sonic practice exists as applied design, either as music making tools [110], experiential products [106], or games [102]. Commercial work is influenced by academia, but it is also based on broader professional constituencies and practices not related to sound and music interaction design.

T. Deacon (✉)
Media and Arts Technology CDT, Queen Mary University of London, London, United Kingdom

M. Barthet
Centre for Digital Music, Queen Mary University of London, London, United Kingdom
e-mail: m.barthet@qmul.ac.uk

© The Author(s) 2023

M. Geronazzo and S. Serafin (eds.), *Sonic Interactions in Virtual Environments*,
Human—Computer Interaction Series, https://doi.org/10.1007/978-3-031-04021-4_6

Much of VR design practice is communicated as professional dialogues, such as platform or technology best practice guides [120, 121], or reviews of "lessons-learned" in industrial settings [105, 122]. Within these professional dialogues, previous research, new technological capabilities, and commercial user research are collected together to inform communities on how to best support users and task domains. For the field of SIVE, and sound and music Computing(SMC) more broadly, there is still work to be done to bridge commercial practice and academic endeavours. Despite recent works [6, 77], there is a paucity of design recommendations and analysis regarding how to build spaces, interfaces, and spatial interactions with sound. For the potential of VR to be unlocked as a creative medium, multi and interdisciplinary work must be undertaken to bring together the disciplines that touch on space, interaction, and sound.

Studying how people make immersive tools, in commercial and academic settings, requires a means of framing how spatial design decisions impact users. This brings up two problems, what role do commercial artefacts have in broadening research understanding, and how is relevant knowledge generated from such products? Objects, prototypes, and artefacts create a context for forming new understanding [46]. By analysing an artefact design, research can discover (recover and invent) requirements to create technological propositions related to domain-specific concerns [82]. This is because an artefact collects designers judgements about specific design spaces [33], for instance how to solve interaction problems, and what aspects are of priority to users at different points in an activity. However, this means we cannot recover the needs of design by direct questioning the users alone. A broader research picture is needed, one that integrates action with tools, users, and reflection on devices. So, to develop an understanding for future design interventions, research should gather diverse data to understand the existing practice and perceived professional constituencies.[1]

Section 6.2 sets out the problem of space in more detail, highlighting important contributions to the design of VR sound and music interaction systems. Section 6.2 also describes the suitability of typologies to spatial analysis for this research. Following on from this, Sect. 6.3.1 outlines the approach taken to the design review and typology, indicating how relevant work was identified, selected, and coded. Section 6.3 sets out a typology of interactive audio systems in VR, and presents case studies of spatial design in the field. Section 6.5 looks across analyses and offers ways to understand the design space of VR for SMC. Based on findings and reflections, Sect. 6.6 proposes actionable design outcomes for further research, then Sect. 6.7 draws the work to a close.

---

[1] Prototypes are any representation of a design idea, regardless of medium, and an artefact is a product or interactive system created for a design intervention/experiment [46].

## 6.2   Background

### 6.2.1   Terminology

This chapter analyses the spatial design of interactive audio systems (IAS) in VR. IAS refers to any sound and music computing system that involves human interaction that can modify the state of the sound or music system, however, we do not review information-only auditory displays or audio-rendering technologies. While both auditory displays and rendering technologies do include interactivity in their operation, this chapter is interested in the use of interactive sound as the primary function in the VR application, rather than when sound is used as an information medium or renderer of spatial sounds without interactive feedback beyond head rotation. No doubt there are significant overlaps in theory and application, that would be valuable to explore, but trying to address all aspects in one chapter requires a different focus.

The following research areas pertain to spatial interaction with user interfaces (UI)s:

- Spatial user interface (SUI): Human-computer interaction (HCI) with 3D or 2D UI that is operated through spatial interaction, graphically or otherwise [59].
- Three-dimensional user interface (3DUI): A UI that involves 3D interaction [16].
- Distributed user interface (DUI): UIs that are distributed across devices, users, or spatial access points [89].

There are also many terms to describe virtual spaces used for sound and music; in particular, this research is concerned with immersive VR technology, following the definition provided in [6]:

- Virtual—to be a virtual reality, the reality must be simulated (e.g. computer-generated).
- Immersive—to be a virtual reality, the reality must give its users the sensation of being surrounded by a world.
- Interactive—to be a virtual reality, the reality must allow its users to affect the reality in some meaningful way.

The term VR can refer to the hardware systems for delivering immersive experiences and to refer to the immersive experiences themselves. Hardware systems can include commercial head-mounted display (HMD) technology, such as Oculus or HTC Vive, through to complex stereographic projection-based Cave Automatic Virtual Environment (CAVEs) [12]. The key thing is that in these immersive environments the visual system and interaction capacities are mediated through technological means. In the case of social virtual reality (SVR), described in Chap. 8 of this volume, communication layers (speech, posture, and gesture) may or may not be mediated through technological means, for instance co-located users may share a virtual world via

HMD but speech communication is unmediated. Or remote SVR users' communication could be completely mediated by avatar representations and voice over internet protocol (VoIP) technology.

## 6.2.2 Standing on the Shoulders of Giants, but Which Ones?!

SMC and SIVE are linked to the larger research field of HCI, so it is common practice to adopt HCI research findings on how best to design systems. Below, Sect. 6.2.2.1 describes two examples of how interaction methods are used in the design of VR for IAS. But as research in VR for SMC has developed, researchers have needed to define and collect design principles specific to sound and music in VR, this work is reviewed in Sect. 6.2.2.2.

### 6.2.2.1 Adapting Existing VR HCI Frameworks to Audio System Design

To establish a dialogue around spatial considerations, there is a need to adopt findings from other VR HCI disciplines. But as with the adoption of HCI evaluation frameworks within new interfaces for musical expression (NIME) [78, 91, 98], critical understanding of the target domain (SMC) needs to be established [70, 81]. For instance, making expressive systems for musical creation or sonic experiences has different design requirements than usability engineering [42], or demonstrations of interaction techniques [8]. This is not to say that usability engineering is not important, but rather the goal of design and evaluation needs to expand to include sonic aesthetic qualities for audio-first spatial scenarios.

**Selection and Manipulation Techniques**

Object selection and manipulation is fundamental to VR environments where users perform spatial tasks [52]. At a basic level, there are two main categories that describe 3D interaction for VR: Direct and indirect interaction techniques [5]. Object manip-

(a) Direct Interaction                    (b) Indirect Interaction

**Fig. 6.1** Selection and manipulation mechanics in VR

ulation examples of direct and indirect techniques can be seen in Fig. 6.1. Direct interaction refers to having 'virtual hands'; similar to touching and grabbing objects in the real world. A benefit of direct interaction is that control maps virtual tasks identically with real tasks, resulting in more natural interaction [5]. Indirect interaction refers to virtual pointing; like using a laser pointer (ray-casting) that can pickup and drop objects in space. Indirect interaction lets users select objects beyond their area of reach and require relatively less physical movement. Overcoming the physical constraints of the real world provides substantial benefits for the design of virtual spaces, as the arrangement of elements can expand beyond body-scaled interaction. Across both direct and indirect mechanics, interaction should be rapid, accurate, error proof, easy to understand and control, and aim for low levels of fatigue [5]. Depending on how they are designed, both direct and indirect interactions enable spatial transformations of objects, including rotation, scaling, and translation.

In adapting this research to sound and music interfaces, we must ask how techniques impact musical processes and practices. For example, [13] describes the tradeoffs designers make when picking different control systems for virtual reality music instrument (VRMIs). Work that has received less attention in SMC includes how to design for some of the unique properties of VR media. The affordances of VR expand into non-real interaction, so there is a fuzzy middle ground between direct and indirect interaction. For instance, the Go-Go technique enlarges a user's limbs to be able to 'touch' distal objects [74]. In broader VR research, techniques like the Go-Go are described under the term homuncular flexibility [93]; the ability to augment proprioceptive perception of action capacity in VR, adapting interaction to include novel bodies that have extra appendages or appendages capable of atypical movements. An example of this type of research into IAS can be found in [27], where magical indirect interaction was implemented to have audio control objects float towards the user based on pinch actions (via Leap Motion sensor attached to the HMD).

**User Interface Elements**

Reviewing 3DUI for immersive music production interfaces, [11] proposes three categories of representation for sound processes and parameters: Virtual sensors like buttons and sliders, dynamic/reactive widgets, spatial structures; Fig. 6.2 provides examples. These different representation categories provide a set of design templates for audio production SUIs. For instance, fine-grained individual parameter control may be better suited to sensor devices with precise control relationships. Whereas, if spatio-visual feedback is required about an audio process being applied, a dynamic widget is a suitable device to explore. Spatial structures can be used to represent sequencers and relationships between parameters; as Sect. 6.4 indicates later, several VR audio systems use these to represent either modular synthesis units or whole musical sequencers.

### 6.2.2.2  Audio-Specific Design Frameworks

Design for IASs in VR is a developing field, surfacing the potential for new forms of sound and music experience [20]. But the opportunities and constraints of VR require critical analysis. For instance, embodied interfaces may offer benefits in productivity and creative expression [62], but we still do not know if the same effects are gathered by embodied interfaces in VR. Alongside this gap, there are gaps in design understanding, with only a few design frameworks addressing how to create VR interfaces and interactions for sound and music [6, 11, 77]. Across these works, a deep level of design analysis around the fundamentals of perception, technology, and action is prevalent. But, in terms of design knowledge to aid designers conceptualising space, and the construction of audio interactions and experiences in it, information is limited. Below is a review of the spatial aspects implicated in the design guidelines of existing VR music system research.

Reviewing VRMI case studies, Serafin *et al.* outline nine principles to guide design, focusing on immersive visualisation from performers' viewpoint [77]. Design principles support design focus on levels of abstraction, immersion, and imagination. Their review of works features many examples of hybrid virtual-physical systems and also highlights that VRMI are well suited to multi-process instruments given SUI affordances. Regarding system design their principles offer robust advice for musical performance but there is a lack of detail on how to go about designing different types of spaces and interactions. For instance, within the principles, an emphasis is put on making experiences social, but no guidance is provided on the design or evaluation of social experience in VR. However, aspects of the case studies do draw attention to spatial factors such as menu design can 'cloud' the performance space; in large interfaces, the mixture of control device and interface design means arm movements

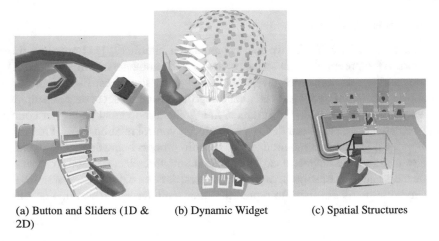

(a) Button and Sliders (1D & 2D)          (b) Dynamic Widget          (c) Spatial Structures

**Fig. 6.2** Types of spatial UI for sound processes. Images from Leap motion VR UI design sprint, reproduced with permission from owner, Ultraleap limited

and travel distances can be tiring; and the inclusion of physical control systems supports natural, body-based interaction.

Addressing *Artful Design* for VR sound interaction, Atherton and Wang describe a series of design lenses with subordinate principles using case study analysis [6]. Their work focuses on the idea of creating totally immersive sonic VR. A central concept of their work is the difference between designing for *doing* as distinct from *being* in VR: *"doing is taking action with a purpose; intentionally acting to achieve an intended outcome. In contrast, we define being as the manner in which we inhabit the world around us"* [6]. Expanding on [77]'s suggestion to exploit the 'magical' opportunities of VR, Atherton and Wang highlight that designers should experiment with *virtual physics*, *scale and user perspective*, and *time*, however, these seem to be general principles for VR interaction rather than sound-specific opportunities. Within their discussions spatial concepts emerge, for instance, designers can phase levels interactivity to create different spaces for action in a scene. An actionable design idea relating to this is to guide gaze attention throughout a space related to narrative elements; want people to stop doing and slow down, just put something in the sky above them, as it is not an ideal place to work or interact. Atherton and Wang highlight that designers need to determine different languages of interaction. Design concepts should move beyond functional language towards things that map well to sonic expressions, e.g. instead of physical descriptors like speed of movement and gravity on an object, an interaction language would be *intensity* and *weight and weightlessness*. For Atherton and Wang, play, and particularly social play, is a synthesis of *doing* and *being*, as it is both an activity and a state. Designers can support play by:

1. the lowering users' inhibitions and encouraging them to play;
2. engaging users in diverse movement;
3. allowing users to be silly;
4. making opportunities for discovery in virtual space.

Related to play and interaction, on the social level, designers should provide sub-spaces within larger worlds and engineer collective interaction scenarios.

### 6.2.3 Typologies and Spatial Analysis

A typology is a classification of individual units within a set of categories that are useful for a particular purpose. Typologies support the evaluation of a number of different indicators in an integrated manner, based on the identification of relevant links or themes. Within architecture, design typologies are a common method of spatio-visual analysis [24, 72]. The teaching of architectural systems uses an ordered set of types to define areas of interlocking design [22], for instance, in Fig. 6.3 the concept of form is described using a series of types and representative examples.

But typologies can also represent 'spatial qualities' regarding interaction, see Fig. 6.4 where different creative spaces (meeting rooms, maker spaces) can possess positive and negative attributes for certain activities (socially inviting or separating, playful or serious) [84]. It is this interpretive layer within a set of similar objects that makes typologies a valuable analysis method. We can step out from just the formal representation of space and shape and ask, how does this form or behaviour impact human needs and experience.

Compared to a systematic literature review, a design typology includes references to artefacts regardless of whether it has received formal user evaluation or received previous research analysis. The reasoning is that much of the work happening in the VR music field is happening outside academia, so rather than reflecting design parameters only within previous academic dialogues, design understanding should also be based on practice.

Compared to a taxonomy, typology is preferred for this work, as the separation of types is non-hierarchical and potentially multi-faceted. Classification is done according to structural features, common characteristics, or other forms of patterns across instances. Within a typology, there is no implicit or explicit hierarchy connecting different research artefacts and products in VR. Also depending on the granularity of the type suggested, a single artefact may exist within two types simultaneously. Using typologies, themes of significance can be traced across systems, these patterns may describe best practices, observe patterns in interaction, explain good designs, or capture experience or insight so that other people can reuse these solutions.

## 6.3 Design Analysis

### 6.3.1 Methodology

As a formal process the typology was built upon identification, selection, and coding of audio-visual virtual spaces.

*Identification*: Literature gathering was achieved by parsing VR examples from the Musical XR literature dataset. Practice and product examples were gathered across the first author's thesis research period using search engines, internet forums, interviews, and social media [25].[2]

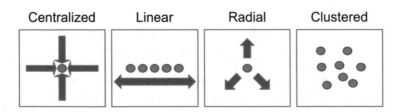

**Fig. 6.3** Example of a spatial typology of form within architecture, adapted from [22]

---

[2] https://github.com/lucaturchet/Musical_XR_publication_database.

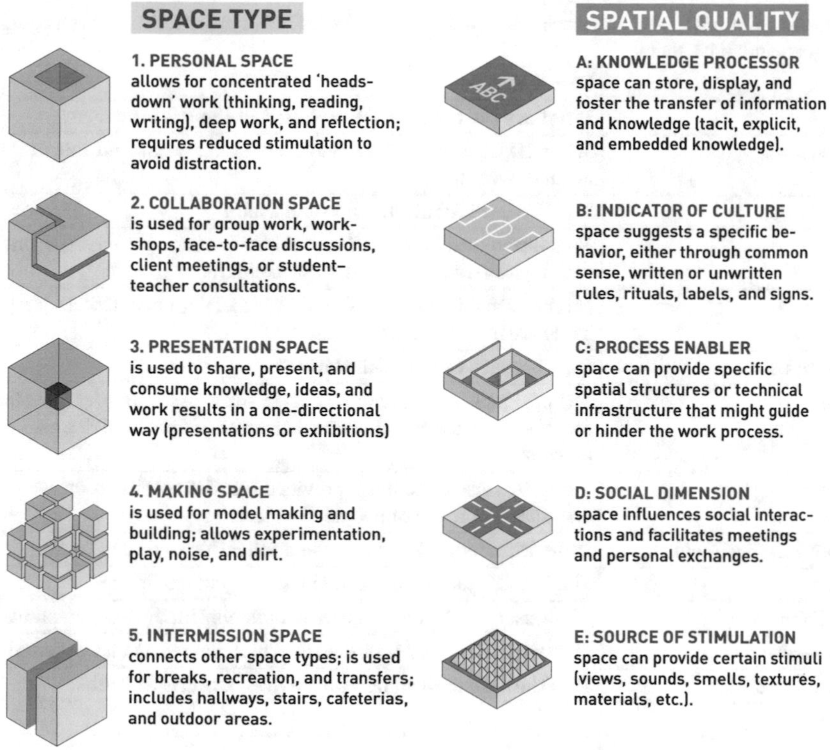

**SPACE TYPE**

**1. PERSONAL SPACE**
allows for concentrated 'heads-down' work (thinking, reading, writing), deep work, and reflection; requires reduced stimulation to avoid distraction.

**2. COLLABORATION SPACE**
is used for group work, work-shops, face-to-face discussions, client meetings, or student–teacher consultations.

**3. PRESENTATION SPACE**
is used to share, present, and consume knowledge, ideas, and work results in a one-directional way (presentations or exhibitions)

**4. MAKING SPACE**
is used for model making and building; allows experimentation, play, noise, and dirt.

**5. INTERMISSION SPACE**
connects other space types; is used for breaks, recreation, and transfers; includes hallways, stairs, cafeterias, and outdoor areas.

**SPATIAL QUALITY**

**A: KNOWLEDGE PROCESSOR**
space can store, display, and foster the transfer of information and knowledge (tacit, explicit, and embedded knowledge).

**B: INDICATOR OF CULTURE**
space suggests a specific be-havior, either through common sense, written or unwritten rules, rituals, labels, and signs.

**C: PROCESS ENABLER**
space can provide specific spatial structures or technical infrastructure that might guide or hinder the work process.

**D: SOCIAL DIMENSION**
space influences social interac-tions and facilitates meetings and personal exchanges.

**E: SOURCE OF STIMULATION**
space can provide certain stimuli (views, sounds, smells, textures, materials, etc.).

**Fig. 6.4** Example of a spatial typology within design, taken from [84]. Reprinted from design studies, 56, Thoring *et al.*, creative environments for design education and practice: A typology of creative spaces, 54–83, Copyright (2018), with permission from Elsevier and Katja Thoring

*Selection*: Findings were assessed for relevance to the analysis. Cases were included on the basis of the following criteria; (1) Is the system based on immersive VR technology via an HMD? (2) Is the primary function or design intention of the artefact related to sound or music?

*Coding*: A form of deductive and inductive thematic coding was undertaken, based upon thematic analysis [17]. An inductive approach involves allowing the data to determine your themes, whereas a deductive approach involves coming to the data with some preconceived themes you expect to find reflected there, based on theory or existing knowledge. For this research, the deductive element was the setting of top-level coding categories (UI, Space Use, Social Engagement, Skill Level, Interactions) that probe how a VR IAS was constructed, the questions used are available in Table 6.1. The inductive coding reflects themes within the deductive categories based on the interface designs. Coding sources would involve: Use of the VR system where possible; review online video sources; analysis of images; and review of documentation and published literature. In each activity, notes and open-coding were undertaken on system design using qualitative data analysis software.

**Table 6.1** Coding system developed for typology. Bold codes indicate deductive code categories, italics are inductive themes

| Code | Description |
| --- | --- |
| **UI** | **What are the types of UI exploited in the VR interface?** |
| *Screen-like* | 3D or 2D UI is used in VR that behaves like a standard screen menu or workspace |
| *3D Objects* | 3D UI is used for information and action |
| *None* | No conventional UI or SUI is provided to users, such as an open world terrain or an external musical controller |
| *Physical* | No functional UI or SUI offered inside is VE, but external hardware musical controller used |
| **Space Use** | **How is space used in this device?** |
| *Sonic* | The positions of people or objects in space has an impact on sound processing, space as a functional element of the sound design process |
| *Visual* | Interactive visual feedback provided based on positions or orientation in space of people or objects |
| **Social Engagement** | **What number of users was the application designed to support?** |
| *Solo* | Single user spaces with no intelligent-agent interaction |
| *Collaborative* | Multi-user or single/multi user with intelligent-agent interactions |
| *Collective* | Massive multiplayer environments, both human and agent-based |
| **Skill Level** | **Was the system designed for novices, experts or both?** |
| *Novice* | |
| *Expert* | |
| *NA* | No formal user study conducted |
| **Interactions** | **What is the flow of action and the related system response?** |
| *Sonic-Visual* | Coupling between sound and visual features, where sound changes visual features |
| *Visual-sonic* | Coupling between visual and auditory information, where the visual information changessound properties |
| *Sonic-sonic* | Audio input used to control system features that relate to sound |

After this, the deductive sweep was undertaken where the sources, open-codings and notes were reviewed in the context of each deductive category, and this resulted in the inductive themes that can be found in Table 6.1.

## *6.3.2 Typology of Virtual Reality Interactive Audio Systems*

Here a typology of VR IASs is proposed, delineating how different systems overall function and the use of space in their design. The referencing of work in this section differentiates between commercial products and academic publications, using two different reference sections for clarity. The typology is split into two broad categories within which VR products and research are discussed:

1. Type of Experience/Application—here we collate instances of products and research by their function as a sound and music system in VR.
2. Role of Space—in this phase we look across the different types of systems to suggest how the design of space can be categorised.

### 6.3.2.1  Type of Experience

Most implementations of interactive VR sound and music systems fall into one or several of the categories in the subsequent list. Many cited products have no formal user testing results available.

- **Audio-Visual Performance Environment**: Audience-oriented systems for playback or live performance of compositions with audio-visual interactions [14, 51, 101, 109]. For audience-oriented systems, interactivity is related to being part of a social group of spectators, rather than being able to interact sonically.
- **Augmented Virtuality (AV)**: A VR HMD acts as a visual output modality alongside physical controllers or smart objects, creating a AV system [34, 43, 100]. This descriptor excludes augmented reality (AR) technologies, such as HoloLens, as the visual overlay effect is considered different to the total re-representation of visual stimuli that occur in VR [99].
- **Collaborative**: Some form of collaborative interaction occurs in the VR audio system (human or agent-based). The interaction must be to directly make sound/music together [12, 25, 51, 63, 103, 110, 119], rather than more presentational systems like an audience cohabiting with performers in a virtual shared space; denoted by the *Audio-Visual Performance Environments* category. Examples and design considerations are described in Sect. 6.4.
- **Conductor**: Controlling audio-visual playback characteristics of pre-existing composition [51, 117].
- **Control Surface**: VR as a visual and interactive element to manipulate an existing digital audio workstation (DAWs) functionality, e.g., Reaper [104].
- **Generative Music System**: Partial or total algorithmic music composition, where the sound is experienced in VR space, and/or controlled by spatial interaction in VR [57, 116].
- **Learning Interface**: VR systems to support the learning of music, either as performance tutoring, theory, or general concepts in music such as genre [48].
- **Music Game**: Systems where gameplay is oriented around the player's interactions with a musical score or individual songs. A good example is Beat Sabre [102], the highest selling VR game of all time at the time of publication.
- **Narrative and Soundscape**: Pieces that integrate interactive audio in virtual reality [85, 116].
- **Physics Interaction**: Physics-based sonic interaction systems [27, 106].

- **Sandbox**[3]: Designed like visual programming languages for digital sound synthesis—such as Pure Data, Max/MSP, and VCVRack—these VR sandboxes use patching together of modules to create sound. [112–114]
- **Sequencer**: Drum and music sequencers in VR. As sequencing is a common thing in many musical applications, this category refers to interfaces that are either just a sequencer or use sequencing somewhere within their interaction design [27, 63, 103, 110, 112, 119].
- **Spatial Audio Controller**: Mixer style control of spatial audio characteristics of sources and effects [9, 25, 27, 43, 69, 90, 104].
- **Sounding Object**: Virtual object manipulation with parametric sound output [67, 68].
- **Scientific Instrument**: VR systems designed to test an audio or interaction tool/feature, a good example is a VR-based binaural spatialisation evaluation system [35, 73].
- **VR DAW**: Virtual audio environment, multi-process 3D interfaces for creation and manipulation of audio. Important feature is the recording of either audio or performance data from real-time interaction. Interface abstraction and control metaphors may differ significantly to conventional desktop DAWs [12, 27, 88, 103, 110, 119].
- **VRMI**: Virtual modelling and representations of existing acoustic instruments or synthesis methods [9, 12, 19, 31, 34, 51, 56, 61, 66, 68, 71, 80, 110, 114, 118].

**Overlaps and Contrasts**

Due to the broad design scopes of some systems, an artefact can appear in multiple categories, or exist in a space between two categories. For instance, [51] is in *Audio-Visual Performance Environments*, *Collaborative*, *Conductor*, and *VRMI*. While [12] is a technically a *VR DAW*, the audio and interaction design concept is highly idiosyncratic, so it becomes closer to a *VRMI*. The following statements intend to clarify any issues regarding overlaps in terminology.

- *Sounding Objects vs. Physics Interaction*: Both types refer to physics-based interactions, sounding objects are when the mesh structures of objects are the source of sound generation/control (e.g. scanned synthesis of an elastic mesh), whereas physics interactions include collision-based interactions for sound generation or use of physics systems to control single or multiple audio features (e.g. parameters or spatialisation). The interested reader might refer to Chap. 2 for more details on these topics.
- *VRMI vs. Sandbox*: While both can refer to synthesis methods, sandboxes are specifically modular construction environments, whereas synthesis methods in VRMIs would be a closed form of synthesiser e.g. playing a DX7 emulator in virtual reality.

---

[3] Category name and description sourced from [4].

#### 6.3.2.2   Role of Space

Many of the systems outlined above offer novel interaction methods coupled with 3D visualisation. Looking at how space is used in VR music and audio systems provides a different way to group research and design contributions. For simplicity, the following categories are presented as discrete areas, but dimensions would also be suitable (i.e. systems could belong to several categories, see [15, 39] for examples of dimension-based classification for digital musical instrument (DMI)).

**Space as a holder of elements for musical input/sonic control**   The most dominant form of spatial design is to use space as a container for interactive elements that either produce sound or control sound in some way. Within this category, key differences are whether menu-based SUI is used [103], or more object-based 3DUI is exploited [12]; this is discussed further in the next section. Other works include: [19, 27, 31, 56, 61, 63, 66–69, 71, 88, 100]. [104, 109, 110, 112–114, 118]

**Space as a medium of sonic experience**   In these sorts of systems, space is woven into every aspect of user experience or system design. For instance, in [9], the sonic operation of the VR system makes no sense if users do not engage in collaborative spatial behaviours [9]. In this category, the relationship of spatial interaction to system feedback can be predominantly passive, like a recorded soundscape [85], or fully interactive, like an audio-visual arts piece that maps spatial input to output modalities [90]. In some cases, visual space may only be a supporting medium for a spatial sonic experience [85]. It is worth noting that **spatial audio controllers** are not instantly considered as part of this category. As **spatial audio controllers** deal with controlling and manipulating elements, they are considered to be part of the *Space as a holder of elements for musical input/sonic control* category. Rather, this category holds experiences where spatiality is more intrinsically involved in the interaction between elements and user experience, whereas in a controller system it is a functional relationship. Other works include: [43, 57, 80, 106].

**Space as a visual resource to enhance musical performance**   In this category, space is primarily used for its visual and spatial representation opportunities rather than as a direct control system or as an intrinsic part of the sonic experience derived from the system. Designers use space as an extra layer to a music performance or system, for example, this can be to:

1. Present performers' with enhanced visual feedback related to their Playing of a musical instrument [34];
2. Provide a space for an audience to contribute to a collective experience of musical performance [14]; or
3. Use space as a place for an audience to convene for a music performance in VR [101, 109].

## 6.4  Spatial Design Analysis Case Studies

The state of the art in VR audio production and immersive musical experiences include single-user and collaborative approaches. In the following case studies, the spatial and social design decisions are discussed; noting that each of the systems serves different purposes as musical experiences. Our motivation is to further detail design typology categories, by understanding and comparing the decisions VR designers make. Reviews are broken into four areas: *single user systems*, *collaborative systems*, *collective systems*, and *spatial audio production systems*. The reason we focus on these previous areas, only within immersive music and interactive sound production, is so that design comparisons and implications can have some level of shared context. We chose the field of immersive music as a point of shared interest between academia and industry. But it would be valuable to probe design decisions comparatively between broader fields of SIVE design, for instance, auditory display and sound production systems; however, this would be a different contribution.

### 6.4.1  Single-User Systems

Figure 6.5 shows the *music room* [118], an *instrument space* containing multiple VRMIs that are designed to be played with the VR controllers, following a DAW-like workflow of perform and record, then arrange and edit. Instruments include a drum-kit, laser harp, pedal steel guitar and a chord harp. The spatial setup mimics a

**Fig. 6.5** Single-user VR spatial design considerations A—*music room* instrument space, with drum kit instrument being used and the recording panel UI visible, displaying previously recorded data

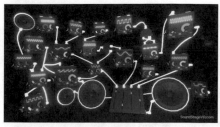 

(a) SoundStage VR for HTC Vive. Sound control devices float in space and are connected by wires, emulating a modular synthesis workflow.

(b) A Mux composition, highlighting the complexity of the workspace.

 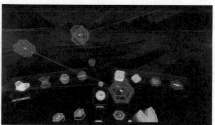

(c) LyraVR user editing a 3D parameter cube widget surrounded by other interface elements, highlighting the spatial complexity of node-edge musical structures.

(d) LyraVR: view of 3DUI elements that float in fixed space.

**Fig. 6.6** Single-user VR spatial design considerations B—sandboxes, node-edge structures and modular systems

conventional studio. In Fig. 6.5 we can see spatial 2D graphical user interface (GUIs) presenting recorded information and menu function, while 3DUI objects are used to represent instruments, and a 360 photograph of a real studio provides the visual backdrop. A design decision of the space was to situate all instruments in a circle around the user, presumably to be able to play all the VRMIs in a small physical space. Two areas are utilised for the UI, *action space* and *display space*. The action space is for the VRMIs, and the display space, further away from the user, provides a conventional GUI. To be able to interact with the distant GUI, laser pointers are used.

*Sound Stage* [114] (Fig. 6.6a) and *Mux* [113] are modular instrument building *Sandboxes* in VR. Users can define their own systems to perform music through those systems. Both are multi-process VRMIs designed for room-scale interaction. In these systems, a user surrounds themselves with modules and reactive widgets, and 'patches' them up using VR controllers. While stimulating and highly interactive, the resulting virtual spaces can be complex and messy spatial arrangements (author's opinion); Fig. 6.6a shows an example of a sound system made with Mux, highlighting the spatial-visual complexity. One possible reason arrangements become complex is because spatial organisation is arbitrary and user-defined. A novel spatial feature is that speaker scale controls source loudness, and this turns a slider or number UI into a 3DUI interaction process.

The *LyraVR* [112] and *Drops* [106] are two examples of *Sandbox* systems that build the temporal behaviour of the composition using spatial relationships. Figure 6.6b and c show *LyraVR* a musical 'playground' where users build music sequences in space to create audio-visual compositions. The node-based sequencer allows the creation of units in free space. Although aimed at single users, such interaction and playback method would be scalable to collaborative systems. *Drops* is a VR 'rhythm garden', where a user creates musical patterns using the interaction of objects and simulated gravity. The system requires setting up of object nodes ('eggs') that releases 'marbles' that make a sound when they strike other surfaces—the size and release frequency of marbles can be manipulated by the user. By adding more surfaces and modifying planes of movement for marbles, the musical composition is built using a 'physical' design process. In *LyraVR*, *Mux*, and *Sound Stage*, users interact with sound elements via spatial node-edge structures, and this gains a level of immediacy for musical changes at the cost of vision-spatial complexity. But the embodied control of temporal musical behaviour via the arbitrary positioning 3DUI does create an experimental creative process driven by interaction in space.

### 6.4.2 Collaborative Systems

*Block Rocking Beats* [103], *LeMo* [63], and *Polyadic* [25] are collaborative music making (CMM) *Sequencers* . However, the systems have different approaches to spatial design for collaborative interaction. Both *LeMo* and *Polyadic* are the only collaborative systems in this review that have undergone formal user studies [25, 63, 64].

*Block Rocking Beats*, Fig. 6.7a and b, enables avatar-based (head and hands only) remote collaborative music production in a virtual sound studio for up to three people. The space is modelled like a futuristic studio, adapting a conventional layout of production equipment areas and multiple screens. The environment provides a sequencer interface for each user while project information is displayed on a single large screen within the environment, and this provides some level of shared visual information. Additionally, reactive systems alter environment appearance in sync with music created. As a spatial layout, users' positions are fixed in the space, a few meters from each other in a semi-circle facing the front screen. The layout limits the capacity to view each other's workspaces and may inhibit forms of mutual monitoring. Regarding avatar design, the character's design is highly stylised, and the 'hand' representation is designed like a tapered wand. The taper is designed to enlarge the usable sequencer area, as when buttons are designed at a normal scale the size of the controller would hit multiple buttons.

The *LeMo* allows two co-located users avatar-based CMM in VR, using a variety of sequencer instruments [63–65]. Depending on experimental condition, different

(a) *Block Rocking Beats* collaborative composition environment, two users pictured working in their own areas.

(b) *Block Rocking Beats*, view of single user display area.

 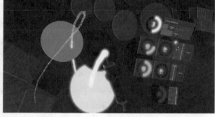

(c) *EXA* collaborative composition environment. Freely configurable space for multiple people to musically perform and sequence sounds.

(d) *EXA* collaborative composition environment. View of a user inputting information with an instrument context window open to the side.

(e) *LeMo* collaborative composition environment [75–77]. Freely configurable space for multiple people to sequence sounds. Transparent SUI used to sequence the sounds, sequencers can be minimised into 'bubbles' to rearrange space.

(f) *Polyadic* collaborative drum sequencer [28]

**Fig. 6.7**  Collaborative VR music production interfaces

spatial features would be activated, such as private workspace areas and spatially reactive loudness. Studies of *LeMo* evaluated visual and sonic workspace design, based on the concept of public and private territory, developing design implications for SVR; for detailed findings please consult Chap. 8 of this volume. Barring the experimental findings, as a spatial design, compared to *Block Rocking Beats* and *Polyadic*, *LeMo* allows users to move and rotate their workspaces to accommodate social interaction around the task of music making, commonly using face-to-face or side-by-side arrangements (see Fig. 6.7e). A novel design feature of note is that SUI sequencers can be minimised into 'bubbles' to rearrange space. As these sounds are spatially located, the bubble acts as both a UI and an audio object. Additionally, the inclusion of 3D drawing as a communication medium enables a variety of annotation behaviours. Like *Block Rocking Beats* and *Polyadic*, avatar design was rudimentary offering a head with gaze direction, however, the use of Leap Motion as the input device enables more detailed hand representations. These were used for functional input and social communication, e.g. waving and pointing.

*Polyadic* enables collaborative composition of drum loops to accompany backing tracks for two co-located participants [25]. The system is designed to be instantiated in two user interface media, VR and Desktop. The design motivation of *Polyadic* was to compare VR and Desktop media concerning usability, creativity support, and collaboration. In order to create a fair comparison of media, constraints were imposed on the design of both media types. This limited the design of features to only use control methods that could work equally across both conditions, namely a standard step sequencer with per step volume and timing control. In the VR condition, the environment uses fixed placement of 3DUI sequencers made up of virtual sensor buttons and sliders, see Fig. 6.7f. Low fidelity avatars were utilised to allow rudimentary social cues. Avatars used a sphere head with 'sunglasses' to indicate gaze direction and two smaller spheres to indicate hands, enabling simple spatial referencing. Additionally, each user's workspace and interface actions were replicated within the other users' environment, enabling referencing and looking at what the other is doing.

*EXA* [110], Fig. 6.7d, is a collaborative *Instrument Space* where multiple users can compose, record, and perform music using instruments of their own design. *EXA* differs from the previous examples as users input musical sequence information in real time using drum-like instruments, rather than pressing sequencer buttons. Once sequences are made they can be edited using menus and button presses. Similar to *LeMo*, EXA allows users to freely organise their workspace in line with collaborative needs. Also, the custom design of VRMIs introduces idiosyncratic uses of space in order to perform each VRMIs. Like others, *EXA* utilises simple head and hands avatars.

### 6.4.3  Collective Systems

The following reviews are special cases, social VR platforms designed for musical experiences, pictured in Fig. 6.8. As predominantly music visualisations in VR, there is limited sonic interactivity for users. So the focus is on how these spaces act as collective social experiences in VR. For broader discussion of music visualisation in XR, see [92]. While not sound production platforms in themselves, the experience of a collective engagement in VR, related to audio-visual performance, is an area of immersive entertainment where new production tools and design experience are required.

*The WaveVR* [101], Fig. 6.8a, is a cross-platform social VR experience, like going to a 'gig' in VR. Artists can use it to make audio-visual experiences for audiences across the world. As a virtual space, the shared focus of a stage is used for most performances, but the virtual space is reconfigured for each 'gig'; similar to different theatre performances all taking place on the same stage. In one instance, music toy spaces were designed for the audience to interact with musical compositions, these took the form of objects that change the level of audio effects based on spatial position or touch interaction. As the objects cannot all be controlled by one person, this creates a collective 'remix' of the content [111]. For further reviews of some individual 'gigs' in *The WaveVR* see [6].

*Volta* is an immersive experience creation and broadcasting system [108]. Performances are rendered in VR using artists' existing tools and workflows, such as parameter mapping a DAW to drive visual feedback systems. In addition to the VR performance, a mixed reality (MR) experience is also broadcast to streaming platforms like Youtube and Twitch. Volta differs to *The WaveVR* in its production method for the artist. In *The WaveVR* developing a performance environment can take a development team months to build, and a significant cost. *Volta* cuts down production time by integrating existing tools with spatial experience design templates (e.g. particle systems), into a streamlined production process for real-time virtual performance environments. [4]

### 6.4.4  Spatial Audio Production Systems

In the following review of spatial audio production systems in VR, all systems use binaural spatial sound presented over headphones (Chaps. 3 and 4 provide an effective introduction to such audio technology). It is possible for some of the systems (*DearVR Spatial Connect, ObjectsVR*) to be used with speaker arrays but the design implications of this are not considered in this review.

Addressing spatial audio production, both the *Invoke* [25] & *DearVR Spatial Connect* [104] systems allow users to record motion in VR to control sound objects.

---

[4] The first author supported the design of early prototypes of Volta XR, interested readers can review the design development at https://thefuturehappened.org/Volta.

(a) The WaveVR's space for an audience to spectate the audio-visual experience.

(b) Volta XR's spatial creation workflow, picturing an audience space in development.

**Fig. 6.8** Collective music experience spaces in VR

The main functional difference between the systems is that *DearVR Spatial Connect* uses a DAW to host the audio session with the VR system acting as a control layer for spatial and FX automation, while *Invoke* is a self-contained collaborative spatial audio mixing system. The systems also differ in their design approach to space and sonic interaction.

Figure 6.9a shows *Invoke*, a collaborative system that focuses on expressive spatial audio production using voice as an input method. The system utilises a mixture of direct and indirect spatial interaction to record spatial-sonic relationships. A *Voice Drawing* feature allows for the specification of spatio-temporal sonic behaviour in a

(a) Invoke spatial audio controller. Image is of a user manipulating audio trajectory points.

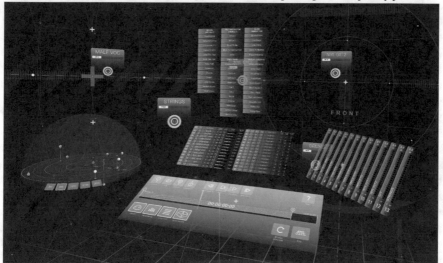

(b) DearVR Spatial Connect system with all interface modules active and five sources positioned in space.

**Fig. 6.9**   VR spatial audio production systems

continuous multimodal interaction. Voice input is recorded as loudness automation, while a drawn trajectory controls the location of the spatialised audio over time. Using an automated process the trajectory is segmented in a bézier curve with multiple control points for further collaborative manipulation. The UI design uses a mixture of 3DUI (audio objects, trajectories) and semi-transparent 'screens-in-space' (hand menus, world-space menus). Spatially, users can navigate the virtual space using teleport functionality, all menus travel with the user when they teleport. *Invoke* is the only system in this review to implement more detailed avatar design, each user is represented by a body, head and arms, utilising additional sensors on each user to provide accurate body-to-avatar positioning. This enabled detailed forms of social interaction and spatial awareness [25].

Figure 6.9b shows *DearVR Spatial Connect*, a professional spatial audio production application. The system uses indirect interaction method to control objects in space; a laser pointer controls position while the VR controller thumb-stick controls distance from the centre. The design of the surrounding space adds no features beyond the interface panels and 3DUI (e.g. sound sources), as users commonly project a 360 video into the production space. Also, the user is 'pinned' to the centre of the space, again in line with the rendering perspective of spatial audio for 360 video. One issue of the central design is a lack of perspective on multiple objects that may be distant from the centre. Also, fatigue and motion noise (distant object 'wobble' more spatially) impact control of objects at a distance (dependent on input device design and user-based ergonomic factors like strength and motor control) [5]. Comparing this to *Invoke*, which does not constrain users to the central listening position when mixing audio objects, users can freely teleport around to gain different sonic and visual/interaction perspectives. This is important as the spatio-temporal mixing of sound creates a complex field of trajectories and sound objects [25].[5]

*ObjectsVR* is a system for expressive interaction with spatial sound objects. The system provides spatio-temporal interaction with electronic music using 3D geometric shapes and a series of novel interaction mappings, examples can be seen in Fig. 6.10. User hand control is provided via a Leap Motion, and the experience is rendered using a HMD. As a spatial audio control system, object positions were a mixture of direct manipulation and 'magical' physics-based interaction. Users could pick up and throw sounds around the space, but an orbiting mechanic meant that sound objects would always move back within grabbing distance. A novel spatial feature of this environment was the use of contextual UI when users grabbed certain objects. When a user grabbed objects that had 3D mappings, a 3D grid of points would appear to provide relative positioning guidance. When released the grid fades away. System design and evaluation investigate users' natural exploration and probes the formation of understanding needed to interact creatively in VR, full details of the evaluation can be found in [27]. [6]

---

[5] The first author participated in formal beta testing of the DearVR Spatial Connect product.

[6] *ObjectsVR* was a single-user system designed and tested by the first author during a research internship at a VR experience design firm.

(a) User experimenting with Audio-Visual Feedback used to indicate an error of inserting the wrong type of item into a holder

(b) User utilising magnetic grabbing technique to grab object at a distance. Object controls drum track sound effects

(c) User exploring a bass cube transferring it between both hands

**Fig. 6.10**  ObjectsVR interface user interaction examples

## 6.5  Discussion and Implications

### 6.5.1  Spatial Design Considerations

Consolidating the reviews of products and research, a series of design parameters emerge.

**Complexity of spatial representation**

Based on the analysis of *Sandbox* systems (Mux and Sound Stage), it is suggested that an unrestricted patching metaphor may be too visually complex for applications like collaborative audio production in VR. Also, systems that build the timing of compositions in space, *LyraVR & Drops*, suffer from spatial-visual complexity issues. Similar to visual programming languages [36], when all points of state-change are presented in one space (a low level of abstraction), the information becomes diffuse, and errors may become more frequent. Also, when space is used for functional relationships, like musical time, visual design cannot bracket the visual complexity without the design of abstractions. Related to these issues, the impacts of these design features is unknown for collaborative systems. Future research could design systems to observe spatial organisation patterns undertaken by users to make sense of, and work with arrangements.

**Screens-in-space and workspace zones**

For certain information (selection menus, settings, note sequences), systems use either conventional 2D information presentation in a floating screen (*Music Room, Block Rocking Beats, EXA, DearVR Spatial Connect*), or attempt to redesign information using forms of 3DUI (*Lyra, Mux*). Also, as described in the *Music Room* analysis, space can be delineated into different action or information presentation spaces. The decision to locate functionality in screens or more novel 3DUI is an important one for collaborative systems, as each different method offers different access points and levels of shared visual information for collaboration. For instance, in *LeMo*, each SUI could be minimised into a bubble for easy arrangement and organisation. A temptation of VR design could be to embody all interaction in 'physical' 3DUI, such as novel interaction widgets or spatially multiplexed 3DUI (see Fig. 6.2). But this could result in added spatio-visual complexity like in *Sandbox* systems, to deal with this there would be a need for contextual interaction layers (e.g. when I put a cube here its different from when I put it there), or function navigation using button combinations on controllers (VR 3D modelling software do this [107]). Another impact of using entirely 3DUI is that it could limit the amount of shared visual information, as arrangements of 'physical' objects naturally obscure each other. However, 3DUI may provide more access points to embodied collaboration.

### Level of acoustic spatial freedom

Related to spatial audio the ability to move from the centre position is a key design decision that needs to be made, especially for collaborative audio production software. For single-user apps, being able to manipulate arrangements, away from the sweet spot is of value. For collaborative apps, multiple users located at the sweet spot would severely impact normal social interaction.

### Workspace organisation

For workspace organisation, it should be considered whether fixed or movable UI is preferred for certain audio production tasks. For instance *LeMo*, *EXA*, and *Invoke* each utilised methods for users to reorganise the SUI, while artefacts like *Block Rocking Beats* and *Polyadic* did not.

### Control, Play and Expression

Designers should consider how playful they make spatial audio experiences, or whether specific control and sound automation is the design target. For instance, in the *ObjectsVR* system spatial audio objects had 'magical' interaction, contrasting this, *DearVR Spatial Connect* emulates DAW automation. What is missing here is more examples of user experience in mixed systems, and environments to playfully explore spatial sound interactions with levels of direct control and serendipity. Related to making experience of control more expressive, integrating different modalities provides opportunities to expand on the DAW control paradigm, such as in *Invoke*.

### Egocentric spatial design

Related to the previous two features, some systems (e.g. *Mux, Music Room*) tend towards egocentric spatial patterns, with devices and elements situated around the user, oriented to one spatial viewpoint. While making sense for an individual application, these forms of design decisions need to be carefully considered in collaborative systems.

### Avatar Design

An issue of importance to collaborative systems is avatar design and the spatial behaviours that they enable. For instance, inside *LeMo*, the use of the Leap Motion compared to standard VR controllers enabled more detailed forms of hand gesturing. Within HCI work has already begun to evaluate avatars based on the constraints of commercial VR [53]. What this area should focus on is moving beyond the so-called *Minimalist Immersion* in VR using only simplistic avatar design. Within *Invoke*, the avatar design utilised a more detailed body representation, offering beneficial characteristics for social space awareness, as users can interpret gaze and body orientations along with hand gestures. This highlights an important area of further research for collaborative and collective systems, where there should be detailed evaluations of the avatar designs' impact music production activities.[7]

## 6.5.2  Role of Space and Interaction

Comparing the separation of the *Role of Space* with previous research on the *space of interaction* [75], similarities emerge. River and MacTavish analyse space, time and information concepts within HCI across a series of paradigms [75]:

- Media Spaces [86]—media types
- Windows, icons, menus, pointer (WIMP) [47]—user space management
- Tangible user interface (TUI) [44]—space-body-thing interaction
- Reality-based interaction (RBI) [49]—emerging embodied interaction styles
- Information spaces [10]—interaction trajectories and navigation of information
- Proxemic interactions [37]—social spatial relationships

The key spatial dimensions that emerge are:

**Dimension 1**   *Media and Space Management ↔ Meaning through interaction*
**Dimension 2**   *Personal and physical ↔ Social and behavioural*

Dimension 1 describes the difference between conventional GUI design (e.g. WIMP) versus approaches using space and the embodiment of technology (e.g. RBI). Dimension 1 relates to the previous analysis on the *Role of Space* (Sect. 6.3.2.2):

- Space as a holder of elements for musical input/sonic control
- Space as a medium of sonic experience
- Space as a visual resource to enhance musical performance

Dimension 2 highlights how space influences personal and social interactions. This is because information is distributed across technologies and is also embedded into contextual spaces, from immediate personal space through to social groups and larger collective social interaction spaces. Looking at these ideas together, a framework of research emerges for VR IAS spatial design. The functional uses of space in VR IAS relates to traditional understanding in the design of media types, user space management, and TUI. While *space as a medium of sonic experience* can benefit from

---

[7] Preprint available at https://hal.archives-ouvertes.fr/hal-03099274.

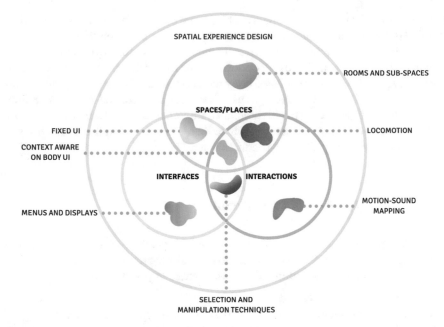

SPATIAL EXPERIENCE DESIGN

ROOMS AND SUB-SPACES

SPACES/PLACES

FIXED UI

CONTEXT AWARE
ON BODY UI

LOCOMOTION

INTERFACES          INTERACTIONS

MENUS AND DISPLAYS

MOTION-SOUND
MAPPING

SELECTION AND
MANIPULATION TECHNIQUES

**Fig. 6.11** Spatial experience design in VR IAS Venn diagram

research in the areas of RBI, and information spaces. Finally, proxemic interaction can inform things like social spaces for musical enhancement. But this doesn't go far enough. What needs to be included in space for interactive audio is an understanding of architectural space. This is because VR designers must make important decisions regarding space as an element of user experience. Regarding social aspects, as highlighted earlier in Fig. 6.4 [84], we can design space for functions, activities and for their spatial quality. We must design spaces for intimate individual action, shareable group interaction, and visibility and safety in large collective action spaces. Acoustically the sorts of choices we make here matter too. For example, using simple voice chat algorithms could make voice intelligibility poor and yield something similar to 'zoom fatigue' [7]. Instead, we can utilise spatially aware audio communications to deliver intelligible audio for each user in an area of space [60], a commercial approach to this already exists that can handle hundreds of listener-sources across a space [115].

We suggest that spaces need elevated priority in our VR design and evaluation practices. To support this process, we suggest three top-level spatial categories that need to be addressed through interdisciplinary design work: *spaces/places, interfaces, interactions*. Visualised in Fig. 6.11, some of the elements discussed in this chapter are positioned within the different design spaces; for instance, VR selection and manipulation techniques sit between *interfaces* and *interactions*. For brevity, only the category of *spaces/places* is discussed in detail below, as previous research within *interfaces* and *interactions* is already well documented in this chapter and other

research [6, 12, 77]. The categories scaffold future design by drawing together topics, theories, and previous art. Addressing elements that overlap with *spaces/places*
in Fig. 6.11, we can use the Venn structure to ask new questions about the interaction
of spaces in feature design. For instance, context-aware on body UI refers to the idea
that if we have more specific spaces for interaction we can also tune the needs of UI
to be relevant to that moment in space and time. The notion of putting it on our body,
like a virtual smart watch, means that this design element is part of both *interfaces*,
*interactions*, and *spaces/places*. Implicit in such simple categories is the equalising
of spaces as a design concern alongside more thoroughly investigated work like spatial interfaces and spatial interaction. Fully describing such a framework is out-with
the capacity of this chapter; instead, it is offered as a proposition for the research
field to further explore together.

### 6.5.2.1  Spaces/Places

Spaces are the architectural layouts and areas that form features of a virtual environment used for sound and music activities in VR. An example of a space can be
seen in Fig. 6.12. In that figure a central production area is enclosed in a grid/cage
structure, bounding it off from the wider spatial setting of floating 'sand-dunes' and
night sky. But what does it mean to design for experience within space, and how
does this related to an IAS? Borrowing from human geography and architecture [22,
87], some spatial concepts to consider are:

1. Boundaries;
2. Form and space;
3. Organisations and arrangements;
4. Circulation (i.e. movement through space);
5. Proportion and scale;
6. Principles and metaphors (e.g. Symmetry, Hierarchy, Rhythm).

Places are spaces with fixed or emergent social meaning [32]. We can aim to
design the spatial qualities of spaces, for instance, the typology of [84] in Fig. 6.4,
gives designers ways to conceptualise creative spaces. We can ask, what is the space
type (e.g. personal or collaborative), and what is the intended spatial quality (e.g.
knowledge processor or process enabler)? Then we can ask, within those boundaries, what are other spatial characteristics i.e. comfort, sound, sight, spaciousness,
movement, aliveness/animus?

As architecture, human geography, and interior design are such deep disciplines,
interdisciplinary work needs to be done here to produce a dialogue around the design
of space for sonic and musical expression. One area of mutual influence to consider is
the design of immersive installations that involve technology to alter user experience.
VR can learn from techniques and theories in this area [3], as well as be used to
prototype systems for physical installation.

**Fig. 6.12** Example of a VR IAS space, *invoke* artefact's spatial audio composition area

## 6.6 Research Directions and Opportunities

### 6.6.1 Embodied Motion Design

Echoing the design principles within Atherton and Wang's work [6], motion, embodiment and play are important design spaces to explore. However, human motion and spatial analysis is not a new discipline for computing and technology, with special research groups such as the International Conference on Movement and Computing (MOCO) and the ACM SIGGRAPH Conference on Motion, Interaction and Games (MIG). Within these existing dialogues, the role of embodiment is a central topic of design [83] (see Chap. 7 for further details). What would differ in virtual spaces is a form of synthesis, or symbiosis, between visual and proprioceptive embodiments. The plural is intentional, as virtual environments may introduce the idea that embodiment is not a fixed state, with avatars and motion feedback being augmented by the virtual setting. A research problem in this area is determining appropriate vocabularies for low-level and high-level motion so that systems of motion analysis and mapping can be utilised in an informed way. But the difficulty in VR IAS is systems will often need to utilise data from only the headset and controllers, where many previous approaches have been developed using high-resolution motion capture data [29]. Also, motion design is not just a single person experience. Take for instance dancing in a crowd. Research into virtual *togetherness* through joint embodied action is a rich direction for collaborative and collective systems to explore [40].

## 6.6.2   Designing for Collaborative Sound and Music in Virtual Reality

There is a paucity of design and evaluation frameworks addressing social experiences in sound and music VR. While work is ongoing in this area. For instance, Men and Bryan-Kinns' chapter in this volume (Chap. 8), to address the gap in design knowledge for VR, design perspectives from other embodied CMM and HCI research provide valid considerations for the design of SVR. The following integration of research from other fields intends to offer SMC actionable research directions to support collaboration in VR.

**Adapting Tangible User Interface Research**
An area of potential influence on spatial design for social VR is to look at how TUIs are designed to support spatial collaboration. For example, [65]'s research on CMM in VR shows similar results to co-located CMM using TUIs [96], regarding the design of public and private workspaces. When designing TUIs for co-located CMM, spatial orientation and configuration are important design areas. The *Hitmachine* is a tangible music-making tool for children, focused on creating and understanding collective interaction experiences [38]. To understand interactions with devices like the *Hitmachine*, there is a need to design social interactions and technology together. For designers, this means specifying and evaluating how people *distribute attention*, *share attention*, *dialogue*, and engage in *collective action*. To analyse designs in context, spatial formations of peoples' positions and orientations can be analysed to understand different constructions of social play in CMM [38]. Observations of social engagement around *Hitmachine* found that the configuration of space (people, furniture, and music interfaces) altered the level of social interaction. Also, regarding the design of space in VR, research findings from VR CMM resemble the results from the *Hitmachine* analysis [64]: How spatial encounters are set up for music interaction impact social interaction. So, to design collective interaction spaces, how basic spatial partitions are implemented matters.

Another TUI design principle of relevance is to provide multiple access points to a collaborative task [45, 76]. This means devising multiple spatial ways for different users to act on the same object, creating a form of DUI. Research suggests that the more access points participants have to a collaborative task improves how equitable participation is [76]. Increasing the tangibility is also said to improve participation. This is because users can complement what each other are doing in spatial tasks, using space as an organiser of the shared activity [76]. Adapting tangibility to VR means designing the affordances of objects appropriately to allow collective spatial interaction, while keeping in mind that we can move beyond some of the constraints embedded in physical reality. A good example of this is in VR *Sandboxes*. In physical reality, physics governs layout patterns of blocks whereas in VR elements can be placed in any part of 3D space. This in turn impacts the design of modules how users connect them [6]. But as mentioned previously, idiosyncratic design patterns within *Sandboxes* may need additional support for collaboration, and this is where previous TUI work could be integrated [97].

Collectively, these similarities suggest that as a form of spatial collaboration, VR CMM can benefit from other non-VR research findings regarding spatial interaction to design systems. But, directly importing collaborative design concepts from other media should be done carefully, and thoroughly evaluated for any differences in results across media (see [25] for a media comparison study focusing on this).

**Designing for Embodiment in Collaboration**
Embodied spatial input and avatar representation are key features of VR for supporting intimacy [54], awareness and coordination [41], and control [1]. Spatial media, such as VR, has the capacity for visual and spatial abstraction of UI, something needed for the complex requirements of expert music production [28]. The following examples highlight some specific opportunities to support spatial collaboration.

**Augmented Object Interaction**    The affordances of embodied interaction in SUI offer possibilities to transform how joint action on complex digital objects can occur [1, 2, 8, 21, 55].

**Awareness Support**    Embodied control and spatial representation in VR can ameliorate mutual understanding issues in shared workspaces compared to other media [79]; support informal awareness to co-ordinate actions given shared visual information [30]; provide pointer mechanisms that support referencing of content and environmental objects [23, 94, 95]; allow for the recording of embodied motion, as a form of embodied memory within an environment [58, 63]; provide novel mechanisms for the division of labour and workspace organisation [64].

**Spatial Problems**    Space is a powerful organiser of human memory and can change how we solve problems [18, 50], and VR, compared to WIMP systems, is suggested to alter problem-solving strategy in spatial tasks [50].

These considerations have in common an influence on the interaction space in collaboration. This suggests that the collaborative process in sound and music production could be improved by designing support for augmented interaction and awareness. For example, in a common studio environment, usually, a shared screen (or set of screens), a keyboard and mouse, mixing desk with dedicated audio outboards, are the tools in the hands of audio producers. In contrast, in an embodied VR interface, the possible interaction space can centre around collaborative spaces where functionality is engineered to support mutual access and modification, adapting levels of visibility and position based on collaborative needs.

## 6.6.3   Spatial Audio Production for Immersive Entertainment

VR provides an ostensibly promising environment for spatial audio production, it is an example of professional workflow that could benefit from further research into interaction methods in VR. The spatial nature of the technology, and action in it, could support problem issues encountered when making audio compositions in space (e.g. transformation of spatial reference frames between self and audience)

[25, 26]. Regarding the previous analysis, a highly significant research area would be the management of complexity in the information design of spatial representation. The impact of these improvements would be felt within fields such as immersive entertainment, where spatial audio technologies allow the engineering of sound-scapes that represent real or imagined sonic worlds, using the location of sounds in space as a critical component of audience experience. In particular, there is an under-explored research opportunity in VR to enable more collaborative practice for spatial audio production. This addresses a need in professional audio production communities that look to make content for immersive entertainment.[8]

## 6.7   Conclusion

Much of how we design VR is based on borrowed design principles. We import ideas from other disciplines and hope they 'fit'. But to capitalise on any opportunities for enhanced expression and new forms of sonic entertainment presented by VR, we must set out how we design, what that involves, and what that excludes. Given such a broad focus embedded in the concept of space, the first goal of any schematic representation of design types and guidelines is to find suitable descriptors to collect the features relevant to domains of research. For researchers, this means setting out the design rationale behind systems clearly, so that over time we can understand the emerging practice and propose novel directions. This research offered the beginning of this process for the design of IAS for VR, setting out the different functional types both research and commercial interests pursue while reflecting on the way space is implicated in their design. This provides a framework for spatial design, highlighting a set of actionable areas for future design research. From our perspective, a key missing piece is guidance about how to design spatial social experiences in VR for engagement with sound and music. We need to define the transitions between individual, collaborative and collective interaction when it comes to audio interaction. A stepping stone in this gap is more research into avatar design for SIVE, as to start assessing spatial transitions in social activity we need to understand virtual embodiment as the vessel that affords basic social communication beyond speech. Looking forward, we should begin to think about what it means to be an immersive application designer that is audio-first. Realising that practice will need to integrate concepts from acoustics, architecture, phenomenology, HCI and SMC, this calls us to think about transdisciplinary pedagogical models to support development in the field.

---

[8] Narrative and physical experiences that engage an audience member in a fictional world, for instance immersive VR theatre production.

# References

1. Aguerreche, L., Duval, T., Lécuyer, A.: Comparison of Three Interactive Techniques for Collaborative Manipulation of Objects in Virtual Reality in CGI (Computer Graphics International) (Singapore, 2010).
2. Aguerreche, L., Duval, T., Lécuyer, A.: Reconfigurable Tangible Devices for 3D Virtual Object Manipulation by Single or Multiple Users. Proceedings of the 17th ACM Symposium on Virtual Reality Software and Technology, 227–230 (2010).
3. Akpan, I., Marshall, P., Bird, J., Harrison, D.: Exploring the effects of space and place on engagement with an interactive installation in ACM Conference on Human Factors in Computing Systems (CHI) (ACM Press, New York, New York, USA, Apr. 2013), 2213.
4. Andersson, N., Erkut, C., Serafin, S.: Immersive Audio Programming in a Virtual Reality Sandbox English. in Audio Engineering Society Conference:2019 AES International Conference on Immersive and Interactive Audio (Audio Engineering Society, Mar. 2019).
5. Argelaguet, F., Andujar, C.: A survey of 3D object selection techniques for virtual environments. Computers and Graphics (Pergamon) **37**, 121–136 (2013).
6. Atherton, J., Wang, G.: Doing vs. Being: A philosophy of design for artful VR. Journal of New Music Research **49**, 35–59 (2020).
7. Bailenson, J.N.: Nonverbal Overload:ATheoretical Argument for the Causes of Zoom Fatigue. Technology, Mind, and Behavior 2 (Feb. 23, 2021).
8. Baron, N.: CollaborativeConstraint : UI for Collaborative 3D Manipulation Operations in IEEE Symposium on 3D User Interfaces (2016), 269–270.
9. Barrass, S., Barrass, T.: Musical creativity in collaborative virtual environments. Virtual Reality **10**, 149–157 (2006).
10. Benyon, D., Höök, K., Nigay, L.: Spaces of Interaction in Proceedings of the 2010 ACM-BCS Visions of Computer Science Conference (BCS Learning & Development Ltd., Swindon, GBR, Apr. 2010), 1–7.
11. Berthaut, F.: 3D interaction techniques for musical expression. Journal of New Music Research **49**, 60–72 (2020).
12. Berthaut, F., Desainte-Catherine, M., Hachet, M.: DRILE: an immersive environment for hierarchical live-looping in Proceedings of the International Conference on New Interfaces for Musical Expression (NIME) (2010), 192–197.
13. Berthaut, F., Hachety, M., Desainte-Catherine, M.: Piivert: Percussion-based interaction for immersive virtual environments. IEEE Symposium on 3D User Interfaces (3DUI), 15–18 (2010).
14. Berthaut, F., Martinez, D., Hachet, M.: Reflets : Combining and Revealing Spaces for Musical Performances. Proceedings of the International Conference on New Interfaces for Musical Expression, 116–120 (2015).
15. Birnbaum, D., Fiebrink, R., Malloch, J.,Wanderley, M. M.: Towards a dimension space for musical devices in Proceedings of the International Conference on New Interfaces for Musical Expression (NIME) (2005), 192–195.
16. Bowman, D. a. et al.: New Directions in 3D User Interfaces. International Journal **5**, 3–14 (2006).
17. Braun, V., Clarke, V.: Using thematic analysis in psychology. Qualitative research in psychology **3**, 77–101 (2006).
18. Burgess,N.: Spatial memory: how egocentric and allocentric combine. Trends in Cognitive Sciences **10**, 551–557 (2006).
19. Cabral, M. et al.: Crosscale: A 3D virtual musical instrument interface in 2015 IEEE Symposium on 3D User Interfaces (3DUI) (Mar. 2015), 199–200.
20. Çamcı, A., Hamilton, R.: Audio-first VR: New perspectives on musical experiences in virtual environments. Journal of New Music Research **49**, 1–7 (2020).
21. Chénéchal, M. L., Lacoche, J.: When the Giant meets the Ant An Asymmetric Approach for Collaborative and Concurrent Object Manipulation in a Multi-Scale Environment. IEEE Symposium on 3D User Interfaces, 277–278 (2016).

22. Ching, F. D. K.: Architecture: Form, Space, & Order Fourth edition (Wiley, Hoboken, New Jersey, 2015).
23. Cockburn, A., Quinn, P., Gutwin, C., Ramos, G., Looser, J.: Air pointing: Design and evaluation of spatial target acquisition with and without visual feedback. International Journal of Human-Computer Studies **69**, 401–414 (2011).
24. Colquhoun, A.: Typology and Design Method. Perspecta, 71–74 (1969).
25. Deacon, T.: Shaping Sounds in Space: Exploring the Design of Collaborative Virtual Reality Audio Production Tools PhD thesis (Queen Mary University of London, 2020).
26. Deacon, T., Bryan-Kinns, N., Healey, P. G., Barthet, M.: Shaping sounds: The role of gesture in collaborative spatial music composition in Creativity and Cognition (ACM, San Diego, 2019), 121–132.
27. Deacon, T., Stockman, T., Barthet, M. in Bridging People and Sound: 12th International Symposium, CMMR 2016, São Paulo, Brazil, July 5–8, 2016, Revised Selected Papers (eds Aramaki, M., Kronland-Martinet, R., Ystad, S.) vol 10525, 192–216 (Springer International Publishing, Cham, 2017).
28. Duignan, M., Noble, J., Biddle, R.: Abstraction and Activity in Computer- Mediated Music Production. Computer Music Journal **34**, 22–33 (2010).
29. Durupinar, F., Kapadia, M., Deutsch, S., Neff, M., Badler, N. I.: PERFORM: Perceptual Approach for Adding OCEAN Personality to Human Motion Using Laban Movement Analysis. ACM Transactions on Graphics **36**, 6:1–6:16 (Oct. 2016).
30. Ens, B. et al.: Revisiting collaboration through mixed reality: The evolution of groupware. Computer Supported Cooperative Work **131**, 81–98 (2019).
31. Fillwalk, J.: ChromaChord : A Virtual Musical Instrument in 2015 IEEE Symposium on 3D User Interfaces, 3DUI 2015 - Proceedings (2015), 201–202.
32. Gardair, C., Healey, P. G. T., Welton, M.: Performing places. Proceedings of the 8th ACM conference on Creativity and cognition - C&C '11, 51 (2011).
33. Gaver, W. W.: What Should We Expect From Research Through Design? In ACM Conference on Human Factors in Computing Systems (CHI) (2012), 937–946.
34. Gelineck, S., Böttcher, N., Martinussen, L., Serafin, S.: Virtual Reality Instruments capable of changing Dimensions in Real-time in Enactive (2005).
35. Geronazzo, M. et al.: The Impact of an Accurate Vertical Localization with HRTFs on Short Explorations of ImmersiveVirtual Reality Scenarios in 2018 IEEE International Symposium on Mixed and Augmented Reality (ISMAR) (Oct. 2018), 90–97.
36. Green, T. R. G., Petre, M.: Usability Analysis of Visual Programming Environments: A 'Cognitive Dimensions' Framework. Journal of Visual Languages and Computing **7**, 131–174 (1996).
37. Greenberg, S., Marquardt, N., Ballendat, T., Diaz-Marino, R., Wang, M.: Proxemic Interactions: The New Ubicomp? Interactions **18**, 42–50 (Jan. 2011).
38. Grønbæk, J. E. et al.: Designing for Children's Collective Music Making: How Spatial Orientation and Configuration Matter in Nordic Conference on Human-Computer Interaction (NordiCHI) (2016), 23–27.
39. Hattwick, I., Wanderley, M. M.: A Dimension Space for Evaluating Collaborative Musical Performance Systems in Proceedings of the International Conference on New Interfaces for Musical Expression (NIME) (2012), 429–432.
40. Himberg, T., Laroche, J., Bigé, R., Buchkowski, M., Bachrach, A.: Coordinated Interpersonal Behaviour in Collective Dance Improvisation: The Aesthetics of Kinaesthetic Togetherness. en. Behavioral Sciences 8, 23 (Feb. 2018).
41. Hindmarsh, J., Fraser, M., Heath, C., Benford, S., Greenhalgh, C.: Object focused interaction in collaborative virtual environments. ACM Transactions on Computer-Human Interaction **7**, 477–509 (2000).
42. Hix, D., Gabbard, J. L. in Handbook of Virtual Environments chap. 28 (2014).
43. Honigman, C.: The Third Room : A 3D Virtual Music Paradigm in Proceedings of the International Conference onNewInterfaces for Musical Expression (NIME) (2011).

44. Hornecker, E., Buur, J.: Getting a grip on tangible interaction in ACM Conference on Human Factors in Computing Systems (CHI) (2006), 437.
45. Hornecker, E., Marshall, P., Rogers, Y.: From Entry and Access - How Shareability Comes About in Designing pleasurable products and interfaces (2007).
46. Houde, S., Hill, C.: What do prototypes prototype? Handbook of Human Computer Interaction, 1–16 (1997).
47. Hutchings, D. R., Stasko, J.: Revisiting Display Space Management: Understanding Current Practice to Inform next-Generation Design in Proceedings of Graphics Interface 2004 (Canadian Human-Computer Communications Society, Waterloo, CAN, May 2004), 127–134.
48. Innocenti, E. D. et al.: Mobile Virtual Reality for Musical Genre Learning in Primary Education. en. Computers & Education **139**, 102–117 (Oct. 2019).
49. Jacob, R. et al.: Reality-based interaction: a framework for post-WIMP interfaces in ACM Conference on Human Factors in Computing Systems (CHI) (2008), 201–210.
50. Jin, Y., Lee, S.: Designing in virtual reality: a comparison of problem-solving styles between desktop and VR environments. Digital Creativity 6268 (2019).
51. Jung, B., Hwang, J., Lee, S., Kim, G. J., Kim, H.: Incorporating Co-Presence in Distributed-Virtual Music Environment in Proceedings of the ACM Symposium on Virtual Reality Software and Technology (Association for Computing Machinery, New York, NY, USA, Oct. 2000), 206–211.
52. Jung, J. et al.: A Review on Interaction Techniques in Virtual Environments. Proceedings of the 2014 International Conference on Industrial Engineering and Operations Management, 1582–1590 (2014).
53. Kolesnichenko, A., McVeigh-Schultz, J., Isbister, K.: Understanding Emerging Design Practices for Avatar Systems in the Commercial Social VR Ecology in Proceedings of the 2019 on Designing Interactive Systems Conference (Association for Computing Machinery, New York, NY, USA, June 2019), 241–252.
54. Kolkmeier, J., Vroon, J., Heylen, D.: Interacting with virtual agents in shared space: Single and joint effects of gaze and proxemics. Lecture Notes in Computer Science (including subseries Lecture Notes in Artificial Intelligence and Lecture Notes in Bioinformatics) **10011 LNAI**, 1–14 (2016).
55. Lages, W.: Ray, Camera, Action ! A Technique for Collaborative 3D Manipulation. IEEE Symposium on 3D User Interfaces, 277–278 (2016).
56. Lages, W., Nabiyouni, M., Tibau, J., Bowman, D. A.: Interval Player: Designing a virtual musical instrument using in-air gestures in 2015 IEEE Symposium on 3D User Interfaces, 3DUI 2015 - Proceedings (2015), 203–204.
57. Le Groux, S., Manzolli, J., Verschure, P. F. J.: VR-RoBoser: Real-Time Adaptive Sonification of Virtual Environments Based on Avatar Behavior in Proceedings of the International Conference on New Interfaces for Musical Expression (NIME) (2007).
58. Lilija, K., Pohl, H., Hornbæk, K.: Manipulation Who Put That There? Temporal Navigation of Spatial Recordings by Direct Manipulation in CHI Conference on Human Factors in Computing Systems (Association for Computing Machinery, 2020).
59. Lubos, P., Bruder, G., Ariza, O., Steinicke, F.: Touching the Sphere: Leveraging Joint-Centered Kinespheres for Spatial User Interaction. Proceedings of the ACM Symposium on Spatial User Interaction (SUI'16), 13–22 (2016).
60. Lugasi, M., Rafaely, B.: Speech Enhancement Using Masking for Binaural Reproduction of Ambisonics Signals. IEEE/ACM Transactions on Audio, Speech, and Language Processing **28**, 1767–1777 (2020).
61. Mäki-patola, T., Laitinen, J., Kanerva, A., Takala, T.: Experiments with virtual reality instruments in Proceedings of the International Conference on New Interfaces for Musical Expression (NIME) (2005), 11–16.
62. Melchior, F., Pike, C., Brooks, M., Grace, S.: Sound Source Control in Spatial Audio Systems in Audio Engineering Society Convention (Rome, Italy, 2013).
63. Men, L., Bryan-Kinns, N.: LeMo: Supporting Collaborative Music Making in Virtual Reality. IEEE 4TH VR Workshop SIVE (2018).

64. Men, L., Bryan-Kinns, N.: LeMo: Exploring virtual space for collaborative creativity in Creativity and Cognition (ACM, San Diego, USA, June 2019), 71–82.
65. Men, L., Bryan-Kinns, N., Bryce, L.: Designing spaces to support collaborative creativity in shared virtual environments. PeerJ Computer Science **5**, e229 (2019).
66. Moore, A. G., Howell, M. J., Stiles, A. W., Herrera, N. S., McMahan, R. P.: Wedge: A musical interface for building and playing composition-appropriate immersive environments in 2015 IEEE Symposium on 3D User Interfaces (3DUI) (Mar. 2015), 205–206.
67. Mulder, A., Fels, S. S., Mase, K.: Mapping virtual object manipulation to sound variation. IPSJ Sig Notes **97**, 63–68 (1997).
68. Mulder, A., Fels, S. S., Mase, K.: Design of Virtual 3D Instruments for Musical Interaction. Graphics Interface, 76–83 (1999).
69. Naef, M., Collicott, D.: A VR Interface for Collaborative 3D Audio Performance in Proceedings of the International Conference on New Interfaces for Musical Expression (NIME) (2006).
70. O'Modhrain, S.: A Framework for the Evaluation of Digital Musical Instruments. en. Computer Music Journal **35**, 28–42 (Mar. 2011).
71. Palumbo, M., Zonta, A.,Wakefield, G.: Modular reality: Analogues of patching in immersive space. Journal of New Music Research **49**, 8–23 (2020).
72. Plowright, P. D.: Revealing Architectural Design: Methods, Frameworks and Tools (Routledge, 2014).
73. Poirier-Quinot, D., Katz, B.: Assessing the Impact of Head-Related Transfer Function Individualization on Task Performance: Case of a Virtual Reality Shooter Game. en. Journal of the Audio Engineering Society **68**, 248–260 (May 2020).
74. Poupyrev, I., Billinghurst, M., Weghorst, S., Ichikawa, T.: The Go-Go Interaction Technique: Non-Linear Mapping for Direct Manipulation in VR. Proc. UIST '96 (ACM Symposium on User Interface Software and Technology), 79–80 (1996).
75. River, J., MacTavish, T.: Research through Provocation: A Structured Prototyping Tool Using Interaction Attributes of Time, Space and Information. The Design Journal **20**, S3996–S4008 (July 2017).
76. Rogers, Y., Lim, Y.-k., Hazlewood,W. R., Marshall, P.: Equal Opportunities: Do Shareable Interfaces Promote More Group Participation Than Single User Displays? Human-Computer Interaction **24**, 79–116 (2009).
77. Serafin, S., Erkut, C.,Kojs, J., Nilsson,N. C.,Nordahl, R.: VirtualReality Musical Instruments: State of the Art, Design Principles, and Future Directions. Computer Music Journal **40**, 22–40 (2016).
78. El-shimy, D., Cooperstock, J. R.: User-Driven Techniques for the Design and Evaluation of New Musical Interfaces. Computer Music journal **39**, 28–46 (2015).
79. Smith, H. J., Neff, M.: Communication Behavior in Embodied Virtual Reality in ACM Conference on Human Factors in Computing Systems (CHI) (2018).
80. Snook, K. et al.: Concordia: A musical XR instrument for playing the solar system. Journal of New Music Research **49**, 88–103 (2020).
81. Stowell, D., Robertson, A., Bryan-Kinns, N., Plumbley, M. D.: Evaluation of live human-computer music-making: Quantitative and qualitative approaches. International Journal of Human-Computer Studies **67**, 960–975 (2009).
82. Suchman, L., Trigg, R., Blomberg, J.: Working artefacts: ethnomethods of the prototype. The British Journal of Sociology **53**, 163–179 (2002).
83. Svanæs, D.: Interaction Design for and with the Lived Body : Some Implications of Merleau-Ponty ' s Phenomenology. ACM Transactions on Computer-Human Interaction **20**, 1–30 (2013).
84. Thoring, K., Desmet, P., Badke-Schaub, P.: Creative Environments for Design Education and Practice: A Typology of Creative Spaces. en. Design Studies **56**, 54–83 (May 2018).
85. Trommer, M.: Points Further North: An acoustemological cartography of non-place. Journal of New Music Research **49**, 73–87 (2020).

86. Trumbo, J.: The Spatial Environment in Multimedia Design: Physical, Conceptual, Perceptual, and Behavioral Aspects of Design Space. Design Issues **13**, 19–28 (1997).
87. Tuan, Y.-F.: Space and Place: The Perspective of Experience. **4**, 513 (1978).
88. Valbom, L., Marcos, A.: Wave: Sound and music in an immersive environment. Computers & Graphics **29**, 871–881 (2005).
89. Vanderdonckt, J.: Distributed user interfaces: how to distribute user interface elements across users, platforms, and environments. Proc. of XI Interacción, 20–32 (2010).
90. Wakefield, G., Smith, W.: Cosm : a Toolkit for Composing Immersive Audio- Visual Worlds of Agency and Autonomy in Proceedings of the International Computer Music Conference (ICMC) (2011).
91. Wanderley, M. M., Orio, N.: Evaluation of Input Devices for Musical Expression : Borrowing Tools from HCI. Computer Music Journal **26**, 62–76 (2002).
92. Weinel, J. in Technology, Design and the Arts-Opportunities and Challenges 209–227 (Springer, Cham, 2020).
93. Won, A. S., Bailenson, J. N., Lanier, J. in Emerging Trends in the Social and Behavioral Sciences 1–16 (2015).
94. Wong, N., Gutwin, C.: Where are you pointing? Proceedings of the 28th international conference on Human factors in computing systems - CHI '10, 1029 (2010).
95. Wong, N., Gutwin, C.: Support for Deictic Pointing in CVEs : Still Fragmented after All These years? in Computer Supported Cooperative Work (2014), 1377–1387.
96. Xambó, A., Laney, R., Dobbyn, C., Jordá, S. P.: Multi-touch interaction principles for collaborative real-time music activities: towards a pattern language. Proc. of ICMC'11, 403–406 (2011).
97. Xambó, A. et al.: Exploring Social Interaction With a Tangible Music Interface. Interacting with Computers 28 (2016).
98. Young, G., Murphy, D.: HCI Models for Digital Musical Instruments: Methodologies for Rigorous Testing of Digital Musical Instruments. International Symposium on Computer Music Multidisciplinary Research (CMMR) (2015).
99. Zhou, F., Dun, H. B. L., Billinghurst, M.: Trends in augmented reality tracking, interaction and display: A review of ten years of ISMAR. Proceedings - 7th IEEE International Symposium on Mixed and Augmented Reality 2008, ISMAR 2008, 193–202 (2008).
100. Zielasko, D. et al.: Cirque des Bouteilles : The Art of Blowing on Bottles in 2015 IEEE Symposium on 3D User Interfaces, 3DUI 2015 - Proceedings (2015), 209–210.

## Products and Grey Literature

101. Arrigo, A., Lemke, A.: Wave http://wavexr.com/. Austin, TX, USA, 2016.
102. Beat Saber - VR Rhythm Game Beat Games. 2019.
103. Block Rocking Beats http://blockrockingbeats.com/. 2016.
104. DearVR Spatial Connect https://www.dearvr.com/products/dearvrspatial-connect. Düsseldorf, Germany, 2018.
105. Designing For Virtual Reality en. https://www.ustwo.com/blog/designing-for-virtual-reality/. 2015.
106. Drops https://drops.garden/. 2018.
107. Gravity Sketch https://www.gravitysketch.com/. Aug. 2017.
108. Kane, A.: Volta https://volta-xr.com/. 2021.
109. Kane, A.: Volta https://www.voltaaudio.com. London, UK, 2019.
110. Kinstner, Z.: EXA: The Infinite Instrument https://store.steampowered.com/app/606920/EXA_The_Infinite_Instrument/. Grand Rapids, Michigan, USA, 2017.
111. Lee, J., Strangeloop: The Lune Rouge Experience The WaveVR. 2017.

112. LyraVR http://lyravr.com/. 2018.
113. Mux https://store.steampowered.com/app/673970/MuX/ http://playmux.com/. 2017.
114. Olson, L., Havok, R., Ozil, G., Fish, R.: Soundstage VR https://github.com/googlearchive/
     soundstagevr. 2017.
115. Spatial Audio API https://www.highfidelity.com/. 2021.
116. The Garden https://www.biomecollective.com/the-garden. Dundee, UK, 2019.
117. The Last Maestro https://www.maestrogames.com/. 2021.
118. The Music Room http://www.musicroomvr.com/. 2016.
119. Tranzient https://www.aliveintech.com. 2019.
120. Virtual    Reality    Best    Practices    en-US.    https://docs.unrealengine.com/en-US/
     SharingAndReleasing/XRDevelopment/VR/DevelopVR/ContentSetup/index.html.
121. VR Best Practice https://learn.unity.com/tutorial/vr-bestpractice. 2017.
122. VR Design : Best Practices en-US. http://blog.dsky.co/2015/07/30/vr-design-best-practices/.
     July 2015.

# Chapter 7
# Embodied and Sonic Interactions in Virtual Environments: Tactics and Exemplars

**Sophus Bénéé Olsen, Emil Rosenlund Høeg, and Cumhur Erkut**

**Abstract** As the next generation of active video games (AVG) and virtual reality (VR) systems enter people's lives, designers may wrongly aim for an experience decoupled from bodies. However, both AVG and VR clearly afford opportunities to bring experiences, technologies, and users' physical and experiential bodies together, and to study and teach these open-ended relationships of enaction and meaning-making in the framework of embodied interaction. Without such a framework, an aesthetic pleasure, lasting satisfaction, and enjoyment would be impossible to achieve in designing sonic interactions in virtual environments (SIVE). In this chapter, we introduce this framework and focus on design exemplars that come from a soma design ideation workshop and balance rehabilitation. Within the field of physiotherapy, developing new conceptual interventions, with a more patient-centered approach, is still scarce but has huge potential for overcoming some of the challenges facing health care. We indicate how the tactics such as making space, subtle guidance, defamiliarization, and intimate correspondence have informed the exemplars, both in the workshop and also in our ongoing physiotherapy case. Implications for these tactics and design strategies for our design, as well as for general practitioners of SIVE are outlined.

S. B. Olsen · E. R. Høeg · C. Erkut (✉)
Multisensory Experience Lab, Aalborg University Copenhagen, Copenhagen, Denmark
e-mail: cer@create.aau.dk

S. B. Olsen
e-mail: sbol13@student.aau.dk

E. R. Høeg
e-mail: erh@create.aau.dk

M. Geronazzo and S. Serafin (eds.), *Sonic Interactions in Virtual Environments*,
Human—Computer Interaction Series, https://doi.org/10.1007/978-3-031-04021-4_7

219

## 7.1  Introduction

> I felt that there was an opportunity to create a new design discipline, dedicated to creating
> imaginative and attractive solutions in a virtual world, where one could design behaviors,
> animations, and sounds as well as shapes. This would be the equivalent of industrial design
> but in software rather than three-dimensional objects. Like industrial design, the discipline
> would start from the needs and desires of the people who use a product or service, and
> strive to create designs that would give aesthetic pleasure as well as lasting satisfaction and
> enjoyment [17].

Thus spoke the IDEO founder Bill Moggridge in his book Designing Interactions (2007), on inventing the term "interaction design". The field Sonic Interaction Design was initially concerned with the aesthetic pleasure, lasting satisfaction, and enjoyment [24], but more recently the research focus in sonic interaction in virtual environments (SIVE) has shifted towards the sound spatialization tools and techniques. We posit that uniting sound and movement can bring back the desired qualities of sonic interaction to SIVE.

When we reviewed the interaction styles and metaphors in the past SIVE papers [24], we noticed how movement was mentioned as an integral part of sonic interaction, and we identified three broad categories of sonic interaction in those papers (1) object-focused, (2) direct mapping, and (3) movement-focused [10]. Twenty-six papers mentioned the term '*movement*' in the SIVE corpus (119 times total). Yet, no paper in the corpus gave a processual account on how these sound-movement interactions are actually designed. In other words, the coupling between movement and sound is treated as a black-box in SIVE papers, and the design dimensions such as aesthetic pleasure, lasting satisfaction, and enjoyment are not considered.

This is why we propose the general approach and particular elements of soma design for designing interaction in virtual environments. Soma design is a design process where designers aim for an improved sensory appreciation through their lived, sentient, subjective, purposive bodies—both improving their own design skills and sensitivities, but also aiming to deliver designs to end-users [12, 27]. Soma design aims to provide aesthetic pleasure, a lasting satisfaction, and enjoyment to a wide range of users, also in virtual environments. This aim pertains to the hardest living conditions, including but not limited to, aging, frailty, and physical pain.

This chapter focuses on encounters between soma design and movement-focused sonic interaction. By providing selected soma design concepts, design exemplars, and tactics, we hope to better articulate the need for movement-sound-interaction relations. To do this, we focus on the subtlest manifestation of these relations: the act of balance. We start with five soma design concepts we find most related to balance, and review three soma design exemplars using these concepts. We then put our considerations into an ongoing physiotherapy case study, which is being conducted in collaboration with an outpatient rehabilitation center in Frederiksberg, Denmark. We finally outline the implications of soma design in our next design phase, as well as on sonic interaction design practitioners in general. The structure of this chapter follows this narrative.

## 7.2  Soma Design

Philosophically, soma design is based on Shusterman's project somaesthetics, which is defined as the "critical, meliorative study of the experience and use of one's body as a locus of sensory-aesthetic appreciation (aesthesis) and creative self-fashioning" [25]. Somaesthetics has been adapted as a theoretical foundation for explaining the aesthetic experience of interaction early on, but Höök has *translated* also the practical aspects of somaesthetics into the design disciplines [12, 27].

In 2017, the last author of the current chapter organized a soma design workshop with the leading proponents of the approach, design professionals, and about a dozen researches. Our focus was the movement, sound, and light design on an actual bridge, connecting two buildings in our campus.[1] We have learned how to pay close attention to our bodies and first-person experiences while walking forwards and backwards, dancing, and crawling on the bridge (see Fig. 7.1), as well as during collective movement and reflective sessions. We also noted how this pragmatic approach differs from more cognitively rooted approaches in sound design [18] by putting movement in the forefront, and keeping the attention on the entire body or its parts at all times. In the following, we iterate the reflections towards experiential virtual environments, by visualizing the concepts in Fig. 7.2, as a seed for future multisensory world-making sessions in extended realities.

The **Inscription Bridge** considers how people use different parts of their bodies dominantly while leaving traces on the bridge. The traces will be initiated by light and spatialized ambient sound, but will be "carved" on the bridge by its curvature, and body parts. The curvature is,

> felt with your balance, how it changes your walking up or down. Which part of the body (people) use will change the experience, in a different way every time.

Smoothed carving and particle rolling sounds could complete the act of inscription.

The rationale of the second concept, **Bridge to Heaven** was to make people more aware of their surrounding outside of the bridge. In order to build such an awareness, the designers decided to create a dangerous zone at the bridge width, and envisioned to remove the side walls in a virtual environment. They wanted people to feel the danger and tension while passing through an open bridge without any fence. In designers' words

> "An everyday zone and then enter the danger zone as we call it Heaven." "Totally open bridge no fence nothing . . . . In order to be safe, you have to be aware of the surrounding!" "Tension and relief and tension. . ."

This design concept replaces an interior soundscape with an exterior one, and sonifies the danger zone with buzzing, supernatural, electric-like warning sounds. At the Heaven side, there will be a localized, granulated, and evolving major-seventh chord played by strings and a harp.

---

[1] See http://soma-rhythms-2017.weebly.com.

**Fig. 7.1** Soma workshop process

**Fig. 7.2** Soma workshop outcomes. **a** Inscription bridge (left), **b** Bridge to Heaven (middle), and **c** Awe and wonder bridge (right)

The third concept, the **Awe and Wonder Bridge** concentrated on the ceiling. This is a design concept that will be sensible only if people slow down and explore the bridge. They will experience a night sky full of stars on the ceiling, and use it as a canvas to create their own painting. In designers' words:

> "We decided to put the emphasis on the ceiling because not to disturb people who don't want to get involved like people who just walk there, drink coffee..." "If you just walk slowly and then stop, that might be a start. Because the ceiling is your canvas, you are an artist, and you friends are artists as well..." "You move, you participate as you slow down... You create your painting!"

This concept clearly took inspiration from Petros Vrellis' interactive rendering of Van Gogh's painting *Starry Night*[2] and affords a similar, granular soundscape with localized, high-pitch star tines.

We hope the workshop process and ideation outcomes provide insight into the soma design space, and its relevance for sonic interactions in virtual environments. More recently, in a series of investigations, Plant *et al.* used soma design in tandem with critical incident technique for ideation and interactive machine learning for computation [22]. Sensory misalignment in virtual environments has informed the work of Tennent and colleagues [28]. At the same time, the teaching space of soma design has been more widely disseminated [29, 30], and applied to VR [7]. We are now able to try out and exchange soma design practices in wide range of domains [10], including virtual and augmented realities. Therefore we are in a good position to extend the multimodal listening design framework introduced in [26] towards bodily interaction through soma design.

A brief description of some characteristics encompassed by soma design can be outlined as follows: *subtle guidance* (directing focus and attention, for example towards a part of the body, without grabbing attention), *making space* (slowing down time, disrupting habitual routines and literal secluded areas), *intimate correspondence* (synchronized feedback loops) and *articulate experience* (provide opportunities to articulate the felt bodily experience). An important grounding in these methodologies is the concept of perspectives. Also, the act of defamiliarization shapes these characteristics. Defamiliarization, also known as estrangement [31] is a tactic to unbalance an established relationship between a movement, interaction, or sound (e.g., acousmatic listening) for generating novel design ideas [14].

## 7.2.1   Defamiliarization: Making Strange

A key aspect of the design approach outlined in [14], and elaborated further in [31] is the concept of "Making Strange". It aims to change certain aspects of a familiar activity until automated behavior acquired through habitual practice or experience (ingrained somatic habits) is broken, and a reflection on the inner processes is initiated within our bodies. The phases of defamiliarization may be grouped into four discrete

---

[2] http://artof01.com/vrellis/works/starry_night.html.

steps [31]: *disrupt*, *destabilize*, *emerge*, and *embody*. In our bridge workshop, we have defamiliarized our everyday experience of passing the bridge by dancing and crawling on it, for example.

Postural stability, also more popularly referred to as balance, could be another example for making strange. It is something we all do every day when walking, running, sitting, and standing. To really understand what is involved in our balancing habits, we need to *disrupt* them. But engaging in arbitrary disruption might not destabilize the core of what we are searching for. Since we usually do not get sonic feedback from our balancing activities (except maybe from external auditory stimuli such as a creaking floor, or audible sounds from our joints in acute conditions), sound may provide the disruption needed. Within physiotherapy, both static and dynamic balance exercises, are often embedded in many therapy programs specifically targeting elderly, since postural instability generally increases with age [21]. The imbalance may be caused by an inability to integrate somatosensory, vestibular, or visual information [20]. Ideally, the participants will take on and understand what a sonification of balance might entail, through a first person intellectual, visceral, and somatic engagement. For an exemplar on balance and its relation to soma design and sensory misalignment in virtual reality using vibratory haptics, please see [28].

## 7.2.2 Perspectives

Soma design distinguishes between three perspective modes, namely the first, second, and third-person perspectives [12, 27]. The third-person perspective conceptualizes an observatory approach to design, encompassing routine methods in interaction design such as observing, interviewing, and user testing. The second person is important in user-centered or participatory design. Soma design puts forth the case of designing from a first-person perspective instead.

The first-person approach is represented by the designer actively engaging her physical body with the artifact under consideration during every part of the design process. In other words, this perspective evolves around *being* the user and attempting to experience what they will inevitably experience. Participatory design approaches are not neglected in this scenario. Höök argues that in order to make a meaningful design artifact, the designer has to take an active part in the participation aspect, not merely rely on observations. This creates a stronger coupling between the intended design idea (mental map) and how it is perceived by its end-users.

A related concept was also used in [14], distinguishing between the mover, observer, and machine perspectives. The mover perspective is very similar to the first-person perspective. It ensures that designers generate first-hand experiences about the activity being developed, which remain closely linked to the felt, lived experience of the potential user. The observer represents the idea of subjective evaluation through inspection of data, for example, video analysis or motion capture. The observer perspective is a loop meant to improve the desired movement through performance and subsequent inspection. Any application that uses movement as the primary source of interaction must process and make sense of the inputs. Hence, this perspective is about mapping movement captured or recorded by some sensing technologies into meaningful representations and/or feedback for the observer and mover. The machines currently only capture movement with considerable loss, in space, time, or range. Understanding these limitations is crucial in human-computer interaction.[3] Loke and colleagues provide convincing examples of how these three perspectives can be combined in design holistically [14].

## 7.3 Soma Design Exemplars for Balance

### 7.3.1 Balance Rehabilitation

The ability to maintain balance is fundamental for an individual's capabilities to move and function independently. Since postural instability declines with age, it puts older adults at an increased risk of falling, which can result in severe injuries. Therefore, balance training is often a well-integrated part of rehabilitation programs to improve balance and self-efficacy in activities of daily living (ADL) [20]. According to [2] balance loss usually occurs in a situation where attention is diverted; therefore, many interventions seek to embed physical activities that increase body awareness and kinesthetic awareness, including but not limited to dance-based training, aerobic, and tai chi, to increase balance and reduce falls [13]. However, the training has to be repeated procedurally to promote motor learning, causing many patients to lose interest and motivation [4]. Both AVG and VR systems have been deployed to increase enjoyment and exercise adherence. Most often such systems rely on visual, audio-visual, and/or vibrotactile feedback. However, balance deficiencies are compensated by both visual or podal dependences, and (static) balance rehabilitation often includes exercises that utilize both visual cues (open eyes) and without (closed eyes) [15]. In fact, previous research suggests that balance therapy using visual deprivation is more effective than when using vision as well, which indicates that vision can become a compensatory coping strategy for balance deficiencies [3]. Yet, augmented systems rarely rely solely on auditory feedback, meaning that such systems likely delimit the user from training other sensory-motor modalities which are critical to postural stability [5]. For this reason, it is highly necessary to explore how SIVE, focused on auditory feedback only during closed-eyes balance tasks, can be used to support balance training.

---

[3] Readers interested in the machine perspective are referred to the MOCO provocation at https://provocations.online/whatescapescomputation/.

## 7.3.2 SWAY

SWAY is a prototype that seeks to encourage exploration of postural stance and stability through somaesthetic experiences [1]. On a high level, SWAY conceptualizes a dedicated space. Users within this space are tracked (observed) by a Kinect depth camera, which serves as the only means of capturing interactions with the system. From the pose (skeleton) acquired through the Kinect software, the authors extract an estimate of the center of mass (COM) relative to a fixed origin. Fluctuations of the COM in the XZ-axes are used to control two feedback mechanisms. The first element is a mechanical plate resembling a square bowl, which contains a set of marbles. This element is, within the SWAY space, placed in front of the user. The element delivers both visual and aural feedback. Micro-movements (fluctuations in the COM) tilt the plate, which in turn makes the marbles move. In the words of the authors *"...audio feedback from the marbles on the wooden platform, creates a soothing soundscape that could be compared to the sound of rolling waves"* [1, p. 471]. The second element is a wooden platform placed at the user's feet. Two loudspeakers underneath the plate propagate vibrations through the material, serving as a haptic feedback. The amplitude of the vibration signal is panned across the two speakers depending on the current offset of the COM. As a result of the combined modalities experienced through these elements, SWAY embraces many of the somaesthetic appreciation design concepts [11]. Its innate physicality relates it to *making space*. The quality of *subtle guidance* towards posture is achieved through the soundscape arising from the rolling marbles and the haptic vibrations. SWAY especially seeks to embrace the quality of *intimate correspondence*, with the feedback serving as an amplifying mirror of the bodily micro-movements.

## 7.3.3 Snap-Snap T-Shirt

Snap-Snap is a wearable garment embedded with a matrix of magnets spread out at even intervals across the back [16]. Through rich haptic feedback, Snap-Snap gives information about the posture of the back. Intended for people suffering from repetitive strain injury, Snap-Snap seeks to create acute awareness of posture through playful and somaesthetic experience. The design process of Snap-Snap is an exemplar of utilizing the different perspectives as laid out by soma design. Working primarily from a first-person perspective, the designer molds the intentions of the garment to fit the perceptions of the co-designer. The co-designer, in turn, provides feedback on their reflections and felt experiences during a three-stage design process. In addition, it serves as a good example of the mover-observer perspectives. Switching between the designer being the mover, then becoming the observer during trials by the co-designer, and vice versa. The result of this design process is that Snap-Snap became an excellent example both in terms of using the *subtle guidance* and *intimate correspondence* qualities of soma design. The strength of the haptic feedback was gradually corrected over the course of the design process, to provide just enough attention towards current posture of the back. The close coupling between muscle contraction/movement in the back and the haptic vibrations unifies in a feedback loop. The final design of Snap-Snap can be linked to the "Making Strange" principle as well. The final placements of the magnets within the garment require its user to move in uncustomary ways to activate the haptic feedback around certain parts of the back. This, in effect, was observed to cause the wearer to move more.

### 7.3.4 Slow Floor

Another prototype closely related to balance and estrangement is slowing down walking significantly, as done for example in Butoh dancing, and providing sonic feedback on the quality of the micro-movements [8, 9]. The authors collected phenomenological accounts of participants walking in relationship to the feedback provided by auditory displays. A program of case studies working directly with 13 movers from dance and somatic practices in "slow walking" evaluations combined with pilot design interventions in exhibition contexts informed the iterative and reflective cycles in this research. These case studies reveal themes around the first person felt qualities, the variant and exploratory nature of movement, and the rhythmic patterning that all result from the pressure-mediated auditory display. The final case study derives morphologies and features of micro-movement efforts as variant or invariant to movement intention, thus exploring the felt, first-person perspective in relation to high-level pressure data resolution.

## 7.4 Work in Progress: Balance Rehabilitation

Given the outline of the design strategy and three design exemplars, we will briefly explain how this relates to sonic interaction in virtual environments. A movement-based interaction consists of finely nuanced coordination between cognitive effort and bodily function, and does not entirely concentrate on the objects in the environment, but on the body itself. In that state, sound could be strategically used to maintain attention. Therefore, we kept the idea and the sound model of a rolling ball [23], but removed its tangible interface. Next, we provide a case study on how we tackle this nuanced movement-based sonic interaction in balance rehabilitation.

We made two visits to a Frederiksberg outpatient rehabilitation center and conducted semi-structured interviews with the primary contact therapists. These interviews helped us to determine the target group and their needs. Sessions at the rehab center in this context consist of a heterogeneous group of people of varying ages and diagnoses. Unique sessions for treatment of certain illnesses are available. However, the therapists would use a classification of their patient teams as those being "bad" and those being "good". The bad teams are patients who are severely physically indisposed. The good teams are those who are recovering from minor inhibitions. Independent of unique illness, age, and severity of physical inhibition, therapists would reuse certain exercise programs and schemes.

In addition to interviews, ethnographic observations were also carried out over three physical therapy sessions at the outpatient center. These observations served two purposes: **(1)** gather further insight on the potential target group, and **(2)** generate an understanding of everyday sessions to determine which type of technological intervention best fit into daily routines. During these observations, informal interviews were also carried out with both the present therapist and her patients. When asked whether the therapist could see herself using a technological artifact during her sessions, she was generally positive. She expressed that such a thing could be weaved into her program, or in some cases replace another exercise. However, she pointed out that if the technology was too difficult to handle (e.g., too complicated to understand or too unpractical to maneuver) she would be hesitant to use it.

A couple of the patients were asked to reflect on their exercises. One patient explained, that his view towards an exercise was dependent on the challenge it presented. He explained that it was a self-reinforcing effect, whether he enjoyed it or not. If the exercise was too difficult or too exhausting, he would gradually come to dislike it. A group of patients explained that it was largely dependent on their mood on the given day, and what they perceived themselves to be able to do physically.

## 7.4.1 System Architecture

Based on these observations, a virtual prototype based on SWAY was constructed, see Fig. 7.3. The primary software running the prototype is a macOS program developed in Unity3D using the C# programming language. The program development has been realized through object-oriented programming (OOP) principles and has been constructed in a modular fashion. The complete architecture can be divided into five distinct areas:

1. **Audio Module**: The audio module taps into Unity's built-in audio pipeline. It contains the main classes that handle all audio processing.
2. **OSCulator application**: An OSCulator application is responsible for communicating with a Wii Balance Board (WBB) through a connected Bluetooth port. Sensor data from the board is parsed and further broadcast through open sound control (OSC).
3. **Balance Board Module**: The WBB module is in charge of receiving the OSC messages from OSCulator, and interpreting sensor data from the board. It also contains the main classes handling physics and game logic.
4. **Interaction Module**: The interaction module is the bridge between the WBB module and the audio module. It interprets user actions from the WBB module and supplies excitation signals to the audio module.

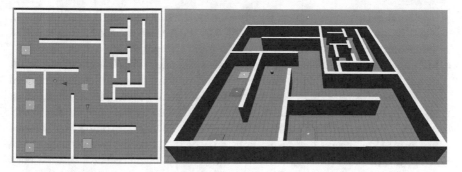

**Fig. 7.3** Perspectives of the virtual environment (which is invisible to the users) developed on unity

5. **Python Web App**: The Python web app is a simple WebAPI that is in charge of heavy-duty matrix operations.

Consider the following scenario. A rehabilitation patient steps onto the WBB, puts on a pair of headphones, and closes his/her eyes. By distributing weight across its four sensors, the **WBB module** controls a 3D object in a virtual environment invisible to the user, see e.g., Fig. 7.3. A physics simulation in turn makes the object move, and its kinematic properties are used to generate excitation signals which are used by the **audio module** to generate feedback to the patient. While this auditory feedback is generated by physical model of a rolling ball, and therefore inherently object-focused, can we turn the attention back to the body and movement by employing soma design elements?

### 7.4.2 Soma Design Elements

The design of the prototype can so far be brought together by describing how the different aspects relate to creating somaesthethic experiences. Let us break down how the different elements of the experience correspond to certain qualities of soma design:

- *Making Space* has been approached by several design elements. The prototype is meant to be experienced with eyes closed. This should, in theory, force the sensory system to weight the vestibular and somatosensory systems higher [12]. By placing oneself on the WBB combined with the closing of eyes, transfers your mind and body into a dedicated *space*, both mentally and physically. The interspersed moment of standstill slows the down time and provides an opportunity for reflection.
- *Intimate Correspondence* has been approached through the feedback loops arising due to the mapping strategy. This is connected to the aural feedback, which is provided by an invisible object controlled by physics. Properties of physics such as

inertia extend the movement of the virtual object when attempting to do standstill, which in turn extends the aural feedback. This evokes a correctional movement in the mover, which results in a feedback loop until a total standstill is achieved.

- **Subtle Guidance** is achieved design of the aural feedback. The audio is a result of a feedback chain starting from the mover, moving through the machine, and the effects of a physics system controlling a virtual object. Hence, there is an argument for making the audio be physically inspired as well. Recall the SWAY project [1], which created a rich soundscape through marbles rolling on a wooden platform. Drawing on this inspiration, investigations on the audio design were aimed towards real-time synthesis of rolling and bouncing objects. This has been established by modal synthesis, as is customary in sound source modeling (see Chap. 2 for guidance on this topic). The other components of SIVE, namely (1) sound propagation modeling and (2) sound receiver modeling [24] remain to be implemented in our prototype.

### 7.4.3 Initial Observations

To evaluate the sound-source modeling of prototype, a small study was conducted. The participants we designed with consisted of four patients (*mean age = 71, SD = 8*); three males and one female. Three of the four patients were recovering from chemotherapy and one was having general balance issues. Three of the patients had never used technology in a rehabilitation context, while one had used it 4–5 times. To gather further insight on the felt bodily experiences, the first author encouraged participants to "think aloud" (as per the think-aloud method, e.g. [19]), or to "articulate experience" (e.g. [11]).

### 7.4.4 Test Procedure

The test was conducted on April 14, 2021 at the outpatient rehabilitation center in Frederiksberg, Denmark, during an actual therapy session. The prototype was allowed to take the place of an exercise, and be incorporated in a routine therapy session (see Fig. 7.4). Before commencing the test, the participants read, understood and signed a consent form. The whole evaluation procedure took approximately one hour. Each participant was allotted 15 min, whereas approximately 10 min were spent trying the prototype and another 5 min to filling in the rating scales. Before trying the prototype, each participant was informed about the general purpose of the test. They were asked to equip the headphones and step onto the balance board. The board was placed behind a chair which the participant could use for support (see Fig. 7.4). From this point, the application would be run, and the participant was told to close his or her eyes and just explore the space available by distributing weight across the balance board. During this time, they were encouraged to report on their general

**Fig. 7.4** Test setup at the rehabilitation center

thoughts. After a while, or if the tester recognized that the participant was stuck, they were allowed to open their eyes and try the application with visual feedback from the otherwise "invisible" virtual environment. After having tried the prototype, they were asked to fill out the evaluation surveys.

### 7.4.5  Observations

The first participant (male, age 80) was hesitant to try the prototype at the outset. After he was convinced to try it by the present therapist, he struggled to understand the concept. While observing the virtual interface, the author noticed that he was unable to get the virtual object moving at all, which in turn resulted in little to no feedback. During the whole 10 min, even when allowed visual stimuli, he was unable to navigate around. Admittedly, he was frail and had a hard time even standing up without frontal support. Hence, he could not create enough force for pressure sensors in the WBB to recognize his attempts.

The second participant (male, age 74) did better. Even though he was similarly in need of support, he managed to navigate around the virtual environment with his eyes closed, hence producing a feedback. When visual stimuli was allowed, he was able to complete several obstacles and manage to score a point.

The third participant (male, age 58) simply did not comprehend the interaction. When asked to elaborate, he explained that he could not perceive what the goal was. Again, similar to participant one, he was a bit hesitant to give into the experience, and declined to have his eyes closed. He could maneuver around fine, but chose to use the support anyways.

The fourth and final participant (female, age 74) was surprisingly positive. Of the four participants, she was the most able and/or agile, but still chose to use the provided support. She was able to navigate around using only sound, and even managed to explore an obstacle, which unfortunately she could not escape. After allowing her visual stimuli, she considerably improved, both in terms of game progression and participation factor. Struggling from existing balance problems, she was used to doing various rehabilitation exercises, and explained that she had a hard time pushing herself to maintain them. She explained, in contrast, that she could see herself using the prototype often. However, she expressed that she really did not care about any of the aural elements and that they did not affect her in any way. However, just using the primitive interface to the virtual environment, she could keep going for a long time.

These observations indicate that we need to work harder to design meaningful soma-based physical rehabilitation experiences. We also need to complete the entire sound design chain, as well as incorporate other modalities. In addition, opening yourself towards somaesthetic experiences and bodily reflections requires a certain internal will to do so. Similar notions were observed in SWAY, whose users had a hard time reflecting on their felt experiences. As such, one would agree with [12], that creating designs which quietly cater towards enabling such reflection is rather hard to achieve.

## 7.5   Conclusions and Future Work

This chapter highlighted three themes of soma design that can be useful for designing sonic interaction in virtual environments: Making space, intimate correspondence, and subtle guidance. These elements should be trained by the designers first, then introduced to users. The first ideation workshop describes how they are trained by the designers, and the therapy case study illustrates how they are introduced to the users.

- **Making Space**: Allow your users to be on a dedicated physical or virtual *space,* slow down time, and facilitate inner sensorial tuning and reflection.
- **Intimate Correspondence:** Facilitate and embrace the feedback loops.
- **Subtle Guidance:** Externalize attention subtly, and try to keep it on movement as much as possible.

Perspectives and defamiliarization should frame all these elements. We invite sound designers to try soma-based approaches and reflect on their design sessions regularly and actively. One way of doing this is using body maps before and after the design sessions. We regret this was not the case in the case studies reported here, but we will include them in the future.

Body maps are simple sketches of body contour, used to recognize, visualize, and reflect on all three elements of soma design outlined above. Besides its ubiquitous use in soma design, body mapping currently informs research projects with populations marginalized by disability, mental health status, and other vulnerable identities [6], enabling diverse technologies such as wearables, virtual reality, and web-based technologies. The approach can also have a significant impact on sound design, from externalization of sound sources to participatory sense-making in dynamic soundscapes. We plan to implement the three bridges of the ideation workshop in VR, together with the body maps and soma sound design principles.

Finally, the therapeutic applications of soma-based sound design should be further developed. While somaesthetics has rich relation to therapeutic movement correction through defamiliarization, soma design is yet to embrace this direction with technological interventions. We hope to contribute to this line of research by re-implementing the ideas and soma-based methods in exemplars such as the Slow Floor and using body maps as a reflection tool in our own research.

**Acknowledgements** The authors wish to thank the workshop co-organizer Sofia Dahl, instructors, and the participants. Special thanks to Aycan Yilmaz who coded the workshop videos and prepared the outcome illustrations in Fig. 1.2. during her Erasmus+ student exchange period. We also thank the Frederiksberg outpatient rehabilitation center therapists and patients.

# References

1. Asplund, S., Jonsson, M.: SWAY - Designing for Balance and Posture Awareness in Proc. Intl. Conf. Tangible, Embedded, and Embodied Interaction (TEI) (2018), 470–475.
2. Beauchet, O. et al.: Stops walking when talking: a predictor of falls in older adults? European journal of neurology **16**, 786–795 (2009).
3. Bonan, I. V. et al.: Reliance on visual information after stroke. Part II: Effectiveness of a balance rehabilitation program with visual cue deprivation after stroke: a randomized controlled trial. Archives of physical medicine and rehabilitation **85**, 274–278 (2004).
4. Burke, J. W. et al.: Optimising engagement for stroke rehabilitation using serious games. The Visual Computer **25**, 1085–1099 (2009).
5. Cimino, V. et al.: Objective evaluation of Nintendo Wii Fit Plus balance program training on postural stability in Multiple Sclerosis patients: a pilot study. International Journal of Rehabilitation Research **43**, 199–205 (2020).
6. Dew, A., Collings, S., Senior, K., Smith, L.: Applying Body Mapping In Research (Routledge, London, UK, 2020).
7. Erkut, C., Dahl, S.: Incorporating Virtual Reality with Experiential Somaesthetics in an Embodied Interaction Course. Journal of Somaesthetics **4**, 25–39 (2019).

8. Feltham, F., Loke, L.: Felt Sense through Auditory Display: A Design Case Study into Sound for Somatic Awareness whileWalking in Proc. ACM Conf. Creativity and Cognition (2017), 287–298.

9. Feltham, F., Loke, L., van den Hoven, E., Hannam, J., Bongers, B.: The slow floor: increasing creative agency while walking on an interactive surface in Intl. Conf. Tangible, Embedded and Embodied Interaction (Feb. 2014).

10. Gillies, M.: Understanding the Role of Interactive Machine Learning in Movement Interaction Design. ACM Transactions on Computer-Human Interaction **26**, 1–34 (2019).

11. Höök, K., Jonsson, M. P., Ståhl, A., Mercurio, J. in Proceedings of the 2016 CHI Conference on Human Factors in Computing Systems 3131–3142 (Association for Computing Machinery, New York, NY, USA, 2016).

12. Höök, K. et al.: Embracing First-Person Perspectives in Soma-Based Design. Informatics **5**, 8 (Mar. 2018).

13. Lange, B. S. et al.: The potential of virtual reality and gaming to assist successful aging with disability. Physical Medicine and Rehabilitation Clinics **21**, 339–356 (2010).

14. Loke, L., Robertson, T.: Moving and making strange. English. ACM Transactions on Computer-Human Interaction (TOCHI **20**, 1–25 (Mar. 2013).

15. Melzer, I., Oddsson, L. I.: Improving balance control and self-reported lower extremity function in community-dwelling older adults: a randomized control trial. Clinical rehabilitation **27**, 195–206 (2013).

16. Mironcika, S., Hupfeld, A., Frens, J., Asjes, J., Wensveen, S.: Snap-snap T-shirt: posture awareness through playful and somaesthetic experience in Proceedings of the Fourteenth International Conference on Tangible, Embedded, and Embodied Interaction (2020), 799–809.

17. Moggridge, B.: Designing Interactions (MIT Press, Oct. 2007).

18. Monache, S. D. et al.: Embodied Sound Design. International Journal of Human-Computer Studies **118**, 47–59 (2018).

19. Nielsen, J., Clemmensen, T., Yssing, C.: Getting access to what goes on in people's heads? Reflections on the think-aloud technique in Proceedings of the second Nordic conference on Human-computer interaction (2002), 101–110.

20. O'Sullivan, S. B., Schmitz, T. J., Fulk, G.: Physical rehabilitation (FA Davis, 2019).

21. Osoba, M. Y., Rao, A. K., Agrawal, S. K., Lalwani, A. K.: Balance and gait in the elderly: A contemporary review. Laryngoscope Investigative Otolaryngology **4**, 143–153 (2019).

22. Plant, N. et al.: Interactive Machine Learning for Embodied Interaction Design: A tool and methodology in Proc. Intl. Conf. Tangible, Embedded, and Embodied Interaction (TEI) (2021), 1–5.

23. Rath, M., Rocchesso, D.: Continuous Sonic Feedback From a Rolling Ball. IEEE Multimedia **12**, 60–69 (2005).

24. Serafin, S., Geronazzo, M., Erkut, C., Nilsson, N. C., Nordahl, R.: Sonic Interactions in Virtual Reality. IEEE Computer Graphics and Applications **38**, 31–43 (2018).

25. Shusterman, R.: Thinking through the Body: Essays in Somaesthetics (Cambridge University Press, Cambridge, UK, 2012).

26. Summers, C., Lympouridis, V., Erkut, C.: Sonic interaction design for virtual and augmented reality environments in Sonic Interactions for Virtual Environments (SIVE), 2015 IEEE 2nd VR Workshop (IEEE, 2015), 1–6.

27. Svanæs, D.: Designing with the Body: Interview with Kristina Höök on Somaesthetics and Design. J. Somaesthetics **4**, 79–95 (2019).

28. Tennent, P. et al.: Soma Design and Sensory Misalignment in Proceedings of the 2020 CHI Conference on Human Factors in Computing Systems (Apr. 2020), nil.

29. Tsaknaki, V. et al.: Teaching Soma Design in Proc. Designing Interactive Systems Conf. (DIS) (2019), 1237–1249.

30. Waern, A. et al.: Moving Embodied Design Education Online: Experiences from a Course in Embodied Interaction during the COVID-19 Pandemic in Extended Abstracts of the 2021 CHI Conference on Human Factors in Computing Systems (May 2021), nil.

31. Wilde, D., Vallgårda, A. a.: Embodied Design Ideation Methods: Analysing the Power of Estrangement in Conf. Human Factors in Computing Systems (CHI) (Denver, CO, USA, 2017), 5158–5170.

# Chapter 8
# Supporting Sonic Interaction in Creative, Shared Virtual Environments

**Liang Men and Nick Bryan-Kinns**

**Abstract** This chapter examines user experience design for collaborative music making in shared virtual environments (SVEs). Whilst SVEs have been extensively researched for many application domains including education, entertainment, work and training, there is limited research on the creative aspects. This results in many unanswered design questions such as how to design the user experience without being detrimental to the creative output, and how to design spatial configurations to support both individual creativity and collaboration. Here, we explore multi-modal approaches to supporting creativity in collaborative music making in SVEs. We outline an SVE, LeMo, which allows two people to create music collaboratively. We then present two studies; the first explores how free-form visual 3D annotations instead of spoken communication can support collaborative composition processes and human–human interaction. Five classes of use of annotation were identified in the study, three of which are particularly relevant to the future design of sonic interactions in virtual environments. The second study used a modified version of LeMo to test the support for a creative collaboration of two different spatial audio settings, which according to the results, changed participants' behaviour and affected their collaboration. Finally, design implications for the auditory design of SVEs focusing on supporting creative collaboration are given.

L. Men (✉)
Liverpool John Moores University, Liverpool, United Kingdom
e-mail: l.men@ljmu.ac.uk

N. Bryan-Kinns
Queen Mary University of London, London, United Kingdom
e-mail: n.bryan-kinns@qmul.ac.uk

© The Author(s) 2023
M. Geronazzo and S. Serafin (eds.), *Sonic Interactions in Virtual Environments*,
Human—Computer Interaction Series, https://doi.org/10.1007/978-3-031-04021-4_8

## 8.1    Introduction

Music has long been produced in social and collaborative ways [16, 67], being inherently multi-modal, music making includes not only the produced sound itself but
also other presentations such as body posture[25], physical activation of the instrument [7], and written symbols and sketches [40, 66] to manage the joint creation and
production of music. Many of these modalities such as body position are promoted by
the physical proximity of musicians. Immersive virtual environments (VEs) provide
a great opportunity to mimic these multi-modal experiences and to explore radical
sonic interaction design spaces for collaborative music making (CMM) [17, 70],
such as telepresence for networked performance and composition. Indeed, whilst
many screen-based collaborative systems treat users as outsiders looking in [3], VEs
offer an opportunity to truly immerse people into interactions. Compared to traditional media, VEs may provide a greater sense of community and more intuitive
interactions [68], and offer new forms of human–computer interaction [36] and interpersonal interaction [34]. Furthermore, VEs have some unique advantages over other
media to simulate multi-modal senses and enable people to interact in a natural way
that is similar to the real world.

   However, although VEs have become a hot topic and have been researched in depth
and the potential of multi-user immersive virtual reality to promote social activities
has been well established (see AlterspaceVR,[1] Venues from Oculus[2]), little attention
is paid to interpersonal interactions in creativity, which includes collaborative sonic
interactions, e.g. CMM. This raises many open research questions on how to design
user experiences in VEs to support collaborative sonic interactions, such as CMM.
In this chapter we will explore two design features of SVEs, trying to understand
their roles in supporting collaborative sonic interaction: i) visual annotation and ii)
acoustic attenuation.

   We will start by reviewing the related work in related areas. Then two studies will
be presented, with each exploring one of the two features. Finally, the findings of
the two studies will be compared and implications for supporting collaborative sonic
interaction in SVEs will be proposed.

## 8.2    Shared Virtual Environments

The term VE can be traced back to the early 1990s [12], and it emerged as a competitive term to virtual reality (VR). Both are usually equally used to refer to the
world created entirely by computer simulation [32]. In the mid-1990s, the development of network technology made it possible to connect many users in the same
VE, prompting the shared virtual environments (SVEs) [53]. In addition to "SVEs",
other similar terms being used include multi-user virtual environments, multi-user

---

[1] AltSpaceVR: https://altvr.com.

[2] Venues: https://www.oculus.com/experiences/quest/3002729676463989/

virtual reality [18], collaborative virtual environments (CVEs) [75] and social virtual reality (SVR) [19]. To stay consistent, we will herein use the term SVEs to refer to VE systems in which users experience other participants as being mutually present in the same environment and can interact inter-personally [53]. Whilst single-person VEs concern how to create detailed (visual) simulations, the design of SVEs usually prioritises enabling collaboration between users [41]. By providing a natural medium for three-dimensional collaborative work [6] and allowing multiple people to interact with each other, SVEs are considered emerging tools for a variety of purposes, including community activities [31], online education [51], distributed work and training [42], and gaming and entertainment [45, 47]. Despite this, there is little research in the field of supporting collaborative creativity (such as CMMs), which presents the necessity to explore the design space to support the rich forms of interpersonal interaction inherent in CMMs, and leaves many open questions: whether collaborative creativity in SVEs follows a similar pattern with real-world collaborative creativity or not; how to design the virtual environments support creative collaboration is also unclear, see [2]. For further discussions on these issues, refer also to Chap. 6.

## 8.2.1  Embodiment in Collaborative Virtual Environments

Our bodies provide continuous and immediate information about our presence, activity, attention, availability, mood, status, location, identity, capabilities and many other factors to ourselves and others, hence using body language explicitly to facilitate communication is recommended [3]. Questions have been voiced in regard to embodiment, including the impact of embodiment on users' social communication and behaviour [68], how the avatars' appearances and behaviours impact users' sense of presence [20, 38, 57, 64] and co-presence [48, 59]. Research suggests that the embodiment plays an important role in conveying presence, location and identity [3, 4], all of which are crucial to the success of collaboration [16, 21]. Social interactions in the real world and in virtual environments are regulated by the same social norms [73]. An appropriate use of embodiment can enhance the sense of telepresence [43], the sense of social presence (the feeling that others are present with the user in the mediated environment) [3, 43] and promote the sense of community [52]. Having embodiment is also beneficial to achieve a better sense of co-worker's locations, actions, intention and construction of workspace awareness, see [24]. The embodiment can also create a strong sense of identification, which is essential in collaboration since it is a fundamental component in creating workspace awareness [24], and it can influence collaboration both positively and negatively in group work situations [21]. Mutually engaging interactions can be significantly increased with proper awareness of the identity of others[16], and in VEs, to a large extent, the identification is shaped by the embodiment. As a result, embodiment decisions are critical and can influence the quality and scope of collaboration in VR [68]. The avatar might be as basic as a T-shape with eyes to indicate orientation and viewing direction, or as sophisticated as a full 3D body scan of the user [58].

## 8.2.2 Collaborative Music Making

As previously discussed, music making, as a collaborative activity that relies on common goals, understanding and good interpersonal communication, has long been a key form of collaborative creativity (cf. [16, 67]). Although music making tools for multiple users have become more and more popular with the aid of digital technologies, this field remains fairly unexplored [29]. In 2003, Blaine and Fels [8] explored the design criteria of CMM systems and pointed out the main features including the media used, player interaction, learning curve of systems, physical interfaces and so on. In the same year, inspired by Rodden's Classification Space for collaborative software [49], otherwise known as groupware, Barbosa developed the Networked Music Systems Classification Space [1], which classifies CMM systems in terms of the time dimension (synchronous/asynchronous) and space dimension (remote/co-located). Examples based on tangible user interfaces include reacTable, where multiple users can construct and play the instrument by moving the tangible objects on the table [29], and Jam-O-Drum [9], which enables participants to join collaborative, musical improvisation. The Music Room provides a room-scale experience, allowing people without music expertise to compose original music inside an interactive space [39]. Sync'n'Move enables two users to explore a multi-channel pre-recorded music piece and users can generate an audio content by synchronising their movements using mobile phones as a collaborative interface. Another phone-based system is Daisyphone [13], which provides shared editing of short musical loops. Other examples include BilliArT [11], which offers a co-located music-making experience, and Ocarina [69], which provides a distributed experience. Though many CMMs have been developed, most of them rely on users to be in a relatively fixed position, e.g. in front of a computer [72]. Potentially, the head tracking and spatialised audio provided by VEs can be applied to break this chain and free users. However, this research area is little explored, especially for the collaborative aspect.

## 8.3 LeMo: An SVE Supporting CMM

To build a basis for exploring CMM in SVEs, we created Let's Move (LeMo[3]), which enables two users to manipulate virtual music interfaces together in an SVE to create a music loop, see Fig. 8.1. LeMo was programmed in Unity, and models and textures were made in Cinema 4D and Adobe Photoshop, respectively. The run-

---

[3] More information is available at:
https://sites.google.com/view/liangmen/projects/LeMo

**Fig. 8.1** LeMos enable two players to work together on a music loop in VR  (reproduced from [36] and [34])

time environment includes two HTC Vive headsets (each with one Leap Motion mounted, see Fig. 8.1c) and two PCs connected and synchronised via a LAN cable. LeMo currently has two major versions: LeMo I and LeMo II (together referred to as LeMos). Both LeMos have three key elements:

- Music interface—For producing music. As shown in Fig. 8.2, the *matrix* interface contains a grid of grids/dots. Each row represents the same pitch, forming an octave from bottom to top, see Fig. 8.2. Users can edit notes by tapping the grids/dots. A vertical play-head repeatedly moves from left to right playing corresponding activated notes. In this way, each interface generates a music loop.
- Avatars—Each user has an avatar, including a head and both hands, check Fig. 8.1. Avatars are synchronised with users' real movements in real time, including position and rotation of heads, as well as gestures. So users can not only see their own embodiment but also their collaborator's.
- A virtual space in which users co-present. LeMos provide visual aids for collaboration by synchronising the virtual environment (virtual space and music interfaces) and avatars across a network, providing participants the sense of being in the same virtual environment and manipulating the same set of interfaces.

LeMo I and II have three major differences, which are mainly because LeMo II was built later on the basis of LeMo I, and thus provides more and possibly better functionalities. These differences are:

- Size of interface matrix of LeMo I is 8*7 while that for LeMo II is 16*8. So participants can create an 8-beat loop in LeMo I and can create 16-beat loops in LeMo II, see Fig. 8.2.

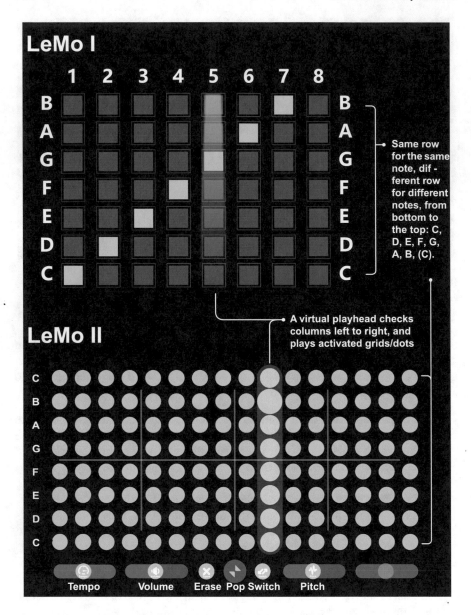

**Fig. 8.2** The interfaces of LeMo I and LeMo II

**Fig. 8.3** **a** The gesture to generate a new interface; **b** *Matrix* (opened interface) and *sphere* (packed interface), double-click the pop button to switch in between (reproduced from [34])

- While LeMo I only provides one stationary music interface, LeMo II allows users to generate, remove, position and edit up to eight virtual music interfaces. Music interfaces in LeMo II have two modes: *sphere* and *matrix* (Fig. 8.3b), with *sphere* mainly for storage and positioning, and *matrix* for music editing. Users can generate *sphere*s with pinch and stretch gesture, see Fig. 8.3a. The *sphere* and the *matrix* form can be switched in between using the pop button at the central bottom of the interface, see Fig. 8.3b. Users can have up to eight music interfaces at the same time,[4] which means they can have eight music loops at the maximum at the same time.
- Compared with LeMo I, LeMo II allows users to control more music features; users can now use sliders to control tempo, volume and pitch, and use "erase" button and "switch" button to erase or switch among four different instruments, including piano, drum, marimba and guitar, see bottom part of Figs. 8.2 and 8.3b.

## 8.4 Study I—Visual Approach: 3D Annotation

Writing and sketching are often used in collaboration to exchange ideas, acting as a memory aid, conveying approval, ideas, doubts and so on. In the CMM systems Daisyphone and Daisyfield in [14], people are given a shared annotation mechanism, which enables collaborators to draw lines that are publicly visible. This has been suggested as an advantage to music making. Taking inspiration from this, the goal of this study is to explore how similar visual cues (e.g. 3D annotations) might impact the creative collaboration when it comes to VR setting. We are interested in exploring how this capability may be used in an SVE to allow collaborative sonic interactions (CMM in this case).

To explore this, LeMo I enables users to draw 3D lines (annotations) by pinching their thumb and index finger together and moving their hands, see left part of Fig. 8.4. These 3D lines are shared and visible to both collaborators, and can therefore potentially be used for communication. To avoid clutter or confusion, users can flip both

---

[4] We limit the number to 8 to achieve a proper frame rate.

before highlighting                                    after highlighting

**Fig. 8.4** All annotations in subsequent figures have been emphasised by darkening the background and brightening the annotation lines to enhance their legibility outside of VR (from [33])

hands downward to discard all the 3D lines. Users can add or discard lines at any time as they wish.

### 8.4.1 Participants and Procedure

Thirty-two participants (16 pairs) were recruited via group emails at the authors' university and the authors' social media for this study.[5] Of the participants, 25% had not used VR before, 37.5% of them had tried it only once, nearly a third (28.5%) of them played 2–5 times and nearly 10% played VR frequently. Only two rated themselves as music experts, with the majority rating themselves as novices in musical field. Twelve pairs of participants were familiar with their study partner prior to the study. It took each pair of participants roughly 1 h to finish the experiment, participants received no compensation.

After reading and signing informed consent forms, each pair of participants first received a tutorial on how to use LeMo I and then undertook a task-free trial of LeMo I for 5 min, during which they could change music notes and make annotations, helping them get familiar with LeMo. After that, each pair undertook four sessions of composing music, each lasting 5 min. They were asked to create a music loop that sounds nice to them together. Note only two of these sessions were set for this study, in which participants could make annotations. Participants' annotations were recorded and are highlighted for better readability—see an example in Fig. 8.4. The study ended with a semi-structured interview (around 5 min). Although participants are physically co-located during the experiment, we purposefully did not support nor allow spoken communication. This is because the creative content is in the sound domain and we are interested in how to design systems which foreground the creative uses of sound whilst using complementary modalities to manage the creative process.

---

[5] The Queen Mary Research Ethics Committee granted ethical approval to carry out the study within its facilities (Ethical Application Ref: QMREC1592).

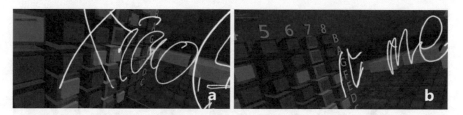

**Fig. 8.5** Presence annotation: *"XiaoB"* (**a**) and *"it me"* (**b**), from [33]

## 8.4.2   Annotation Categories

Seventy-eight annotations were post-hoc identified and categorised by the researchers according to the annotations for Mutual Engagement classification scheme (referred to as aME classification) in distributed music making: presence, making it happen, quality, social and localisation [14]. We use aME classification scheme as a starting point for understanding the use of annotations in LeMo I. The following subsections report on the kinds of annotations participants used when making music together in LeMo I, and later sections reflect on these annotations and the utility of the aME classification scheme for SVEs.

### 8.4.2.1   Presence

The concept of presence has been defined and interpreted in different ways, e.g. [26, 62, 63, 71]. Presence is a subjective experience [26, 61] which can greatly affect collaboration [22, 50]—having knowledge of oneself and those we are working with is important in collaboration. An earlier study found many participants in distributed music making used annotations as a way to express and query presence, helping participants know about each other's existence [14]. In this study only two users used annotations to convey presence. One wrote *"XiaoB"* (the participant's name) and the other wrote *'it me"* to tell the collaborators their presence and identity, see Fig. 8.5. The reason that much fewer people used annotations to convey presence could be that the avatars provided a sense of presence and identity not available in the original Daisy studies in [14]. Avatars intuitively show the collaborators where they are, what they are doing and where they are looking. Another reason might be because the collaborators were co-located and that they had previously met in the real world before entering the virtual realm.

### 8.4.2.2   Making It Happen

Annotations were also used to support the process of collaborative music making in four ways explored below:

**Fig. 8.6** Turn taking annotations: *"You go ahead"* (**a**); *"you make"* (**b**); *"I make"* written in Chinese (**c**); *"you do"*(**d**)  (reproduced from [33])

- *Turn Taking:* Although LeMo I allows simultaneous editing of the shared musical loop, at some points participants took turns to contribute the musical notes and used annotations to manage the process. As shown in Fig. 8.6, participants wrote *"Let me"* or *"you do"* to switch who had the active role. By doing so, the active person could either require or give away full control of the music interface until they agree to a turn change—note that there was no explicit ownership control of the musical interface, so in these cases participants were self-managing their access to the shared musical loop.
- *Composition Thoughts:* Some annotations emerged that were expressing composition ideas at different levels, covering the highest level—music style, the medium level—patterns formed of notes, and the most specific level- single notes. By drawing lines aligning with possible notes on the grid, Fig. 8.7b, c, d, e sketch out participants' composition ideas. These are more specific communication compared with annotations revealing musical ideas (e.g. *"Chinese style?"* in Fig. 8.7a). These annotations were usually drawn before activating the corresponding buttons to make and share a plan, possibly so that the partner could help to construct the sequence of notes. Occasionally, these compositional sketches were drawn afterwards (e.g. Fig. 8.7e) and were used to demonstrate a musical idea. In both cases, this kind of annotation may have helped participants to better formulate and understand the collaborative music plan/idea. More directed use of annotations in composition is illustrated in Fig. 8.7f where the participant made three dot markers near the column reference system (B, G and D specifically), asking the partner to make notes in these three columns, which resulted in the partner adding these notes to the shared musical loop. A similar case is shown in 7 h, in which the partner was asked to make notes in rows C, E and G. Participants also directly wrote the reference to ask partners to change specific notes, see Fig. 8.7 h, i, j, k.
- *Area and Position Arrangement:* Annotations were also used to divide the working area and to manage participants' work focus in the VE. Fig. 8.8a shows an example in which participants drew a horizontal line to divide the music interface into two parts, each for one participant. The pair was composed within their own working

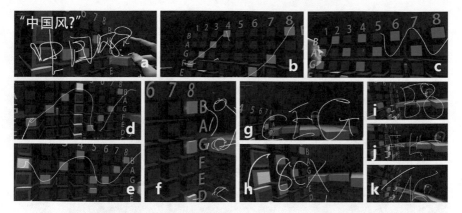

**Fig. 8.7**  *"Chinese style?"* written in Chinese (**a**); Patterns formed of notes (**b, c, d, e**); Note markers (**f**); References of notes (**g, h, i, j, k**) (from [33])

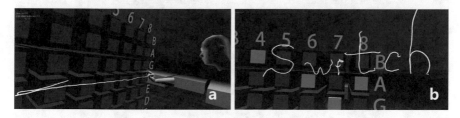

**Fig. 8.8**  Annotations for working area arrangement (from [33])

area after the line was drawn, and later on, a word *"Switch"* was written to ask to switch positions (i.e. to swap from top to bottom and vice versa), see Fig. 8.8b. These annotations may have contributed to participants' working areas and space management.

- *Confusion Expressions:* Participants used annotation to write *"what"* or to draw a question mark to presumably express confusion about their partners' activities given that such annotations were made directly after their partners changed notes, drew, wrote or made gestures. Fig. 8.10 illustrates typical indicators of confusion.

### 8.4.2.3  Quality

When creating the music loop, reflecting and exchanging the ideas of the quality of the piece is crucial to smooth the cooperation and ensure a final output with good quality. In LeMo I, participants used annotations to express and exchange their judgments of the quality. These annotations are usually short words or simple shapes, either positive (e.g. *"OK"*, *"Nice"*, *"Cool"*, *"Good"* and heart shape) or negative (e.g. *"No"*), as illustrated in Fig. 8.9. Some of the confusion expressions such as *"?"* were probably indicators of queries of quality, not just queries about

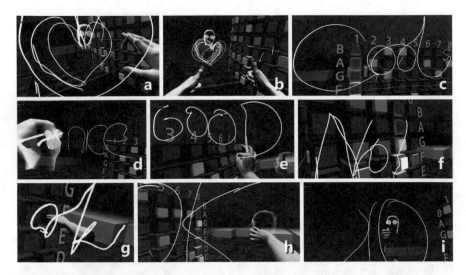

**Fig. 8.9** Quality Annotations (from [33])

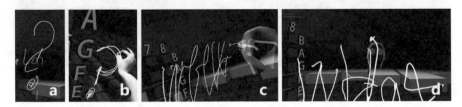

**Fig. 8.10** Confusion annotations (from [33])

the process. It is also interesting to note that positive words may convey different meanings when temporal relationships change. For example, a *"yes"* written shortly after a note addition means the writer's satisfaction with the addition while an *"OK"* write much later with a certain addition has fewer relation with the addition and means more satisfaction about the whole piece. These emerging annotation-based judgments help collaborators exchange feelings about the piece being made, reduce the idea variation and strengthen the cooperation on the activity.

### 8.4.2.4  Social

Beyond music making and process management, annotations were also used for non-task-related purposes, as illustrated in Figs. 8.11 and 8.12. As shown in Fig. 8.12, one participant started detailed steps of a social drawing activity, their partner then saw this and joined in with the drawing activity and they finished the drawing together. It is interesting to note that in total five human doodles appeared, two of which were drawn collaboratively. The possible reasons for its frequent emergence could be that

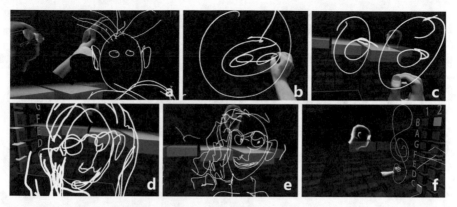

**Fig. 8.11** Annotations for social purposes (from [33])

| Participant C started with eyes and mouth | Participant D drew the face contour | C wrote D's name "Gabana" | D drew a culry arrow, pointing to D's name, and added hair |

**Fig. 8.12** Annotations for social purposes (reproduced from [33])

participants were inspired unknowingly by the kinetic avatar or people just naturally love to draw faces. Although social annotations did not contribute to the music directly, making these lighthearted drawings, as a social interaction, contributes to a close relationship between the collaborators.

### 8.4.2.5  Localisation

Bryan-Kinns [14] identified the frequent use of annotation as a localisation cue (mainly by drawing arrows), but in LeMo I we only found one similar case, in which the participant drew an arrow, and from the review of the interaction successfully obtained their partner's attention, as illustrated in Fig. 8.13. However, in this case the arrow may have been more to attract attention to the activity rather than to highlight a specific part of the joint creation. The reason that annotations are not used for localisation in LeMo I could be that participants could simply draw each other's attention to a certain location by waving their hands and then pointing to that location.

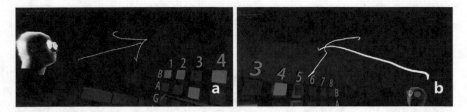

**Fig. 8.13** A participant drew an arrow (**a**), and this successfully drew their partner's attention to the intended area (**b**) (from [33])

### 8.4.3 Interviews

Post-task interviews with participants revealed more reflective insights into the use of the annotations. The interviews were transcribed (around 5,000 words) and a thematic analysis was undertaken, see more information about thematic analysis in [10, 74]. The thematic analysis started with a reading through of the transcript, then an inductive analysis of the data was performed, and relevant patterns were collapsed into codes. Next, these codes were combined into overarching themes, which were then reviewed and adjusted until they were appropriate for the codes. In total, 41 codes and 4 overarching themes emerged from the thematic analysis. Two themes were directly related to annotation: (i) annotation's usefulness, and (ii) annotation's problems.

Many participants described that they had a positive feeling when they could write something to support their communication. They reported annotations were used to make "signs and symbols" to support composition, or to "create drawing together [...] like a physical warm up". Participants also reported that annotations exceeded vocal communication in some ways, "with the lines, [they] could just circle the notes to say that was [note] G and go back to [note] C, from that perspective, drawing was more effective". Many participants reported that they successfully understood each other's intentions via the annotations, e.g. one participant drew a line and "used the line to affect the partner", guiding their partner to move notes to lower positions, the partner fully understood and reported they "did the changes". Other examples mentioned are showing satisfaction by "writing an OK" or using "Hi" for greetings.

Meanwhile, writing and reading in 3D space were reported by participants to be quite different from the real world and these differences caused inconveniences and problems. For instance, the 3D nature of the annotations reduced their readability, it only "makes sense to [them] from [their] perspective[s], because it was 3D". For ease of identifying the annotations, "[they] need to stand where the person wrote it stood". Furthermore, making annotations was reported as being time-consuming, and "when [they] finish[ed] it, it [did] not make sense" anymore. Also, the low accuracy of movement tracking led to annotations being drawn at quite a large size, which then led to a limitation of "how much [they] [could] write". Finally, participants reported that it was hard to notice each others' annotation activities, a participant "waved hands to [their partner], but [the partner] did not see", the participant "had to wave hands [closer], directly in front of [the partner]" to draw their attention to the annotations so as to get the annotations read. This was probably due to the narrower field of view (FOV) in VR *vs* real life as the FOV is about 100 horizontal degrees with HTC Vive *vs* about 200 degrees binocular FOV in real life, see [28, 30].

## 8.4.4  Reflection of Study I

Similar to Bryan-Kinns' findings [14], most of the annotations that emerged in the use of LeMo I fall into three types: making it happen, quality and social. However, unlike the aME classification, presence and localisation appear to be well managed through avatar interaction. This similarity suggests that 3D annotations can function similarly in an immersive collaborative music-making system as they can in a 2D non-immersive CMM system. However, much fewer annotations are used to convey presence compared with the findings of Bryan-Kinns [14] which may be because avatars already support this well, or it may also have been due to the physical col-location of participants with LeMo I compared to the Daisy* studies which were distributed remotely. The length of the musical loop in LeMo I is 8 beats, whereas in the Daisy* studies the length was 48 beats which may have affected the kinds of annotation produced as the LeMo I loop was simpler and required less temporal organisation. Regardless of these issues, the use of aME to classify annotations in a study of CMM indicates that the annotation classification scheme applies to media beyond the Daisy* systems it was previously used to evaluate [14].

For sonic interaction design of VEs, the findings of this exploratory study indicate that 3D graphical annotations of a virtual environment can support a music making as a tool for communication where the co-produced sound is prioritised over other modalities—CMM in our case. We specifically prevented conversation during the creative process to allow us to explore how to support collaboration without interrupting or interfering with the music being created by collaborators. The step sequencer used in LeMo I was intentionally simple to allow initial exploration of the role of annotations without conflating this with the complexity of an interface. For richer and more complex sonic creation and exploration in VR, we suggest that annotations could usefully support communication about the process, quality and also social aspects of interaction without compromising the joint product being produced. It may facilitate a foregrounding of the creative sound product to such an extent that the sounds created are able to use the full width of the sound domain at the exclusion of all other parts of the human–human interaction necessary for collaboration.

Whilst the annotations of LeMo I supported co-creation of music, they did generate some issues. More specifically, making annotations and viewing them were reported to be very different from real life, daily experiences. Participants needed to get used to controlling strokes by pinching and releasing fingers. Besides, compared with writing or drawing with a real pen, the LeMo I has a less accuracy in supporting these. To increase the readability of written contents and sketches, participants tended to write or draw in a bigger size, which resulted in a limitation of how much they could write/draw. But on the positive side, the larger size made it possible to write and draw together, which expanded the range of annotating action, making it less personal but more social-friendly and more accommodating to multiple people. Another unexpected problem found in this study was that 3D annotations can, of course, be viewed from many angles, so written text is often reversed for a participant's collaborator, especially if they write in the space between themselves. This clearly decreases the readability of the annotations. Some participants wrote in reverse to try to compensate for this issue, see an example shown in Fig. 8.9h and i. Future development of the use of annotations in VR would need to explore how this mirroring issue could be addressed.

## 8.5 Study II—Audio Approach: Augmented Acoustic Attenuation

Sound attenuates as a result of diminishing intensity when travelling through a medium. Acoustic attenuation is one of the primary cues for sound localisation of distance; it enables humans to use their innate spatial abilities to retrieve and localise information and to aid performance, see [5]. Whilst augmenting the acoustic attenuation of a real medium (e.g. the air) is difficult, this can be easily done in VEs with the aid of audio simulation (refer to Chap. 3 for modularity in the auralisation). Research has begun to investigate the impacts of spatialised sounds on user experience in VR, see [27]. However, little research explores how the spatialisation of sound may affect or aid collaboration in a VR context. Considering sound is both the primary medium and the final output of the creative task [34], by affecting sound, different settings of acoustic attenuation can possibly affect the collaboration differently. With the ability to modify the simulated acoustic attenuation in an immersive virtual environment, we can possibly create sonic privacy by augmenting acoustic attenuation, and then use sonic privacy as personal space to support individual creativity in CMM. Supporting individual creativity is important as it contributes to the group creativity [37, 44, 46, 60].

### 8.5.1 Hypotheses

Research has suggested users should be allowed to work individually in their personal spaces at their own pace, cooperatively work together in the shared space and smoothly transition between both of the spaces during collaboration [23, 56, 65]. In a previous study [34], following this implication, we built three different spatial configurations (public space only, public space + publicly visible personal space, public space + publicly invisible personal space), and tested different impacts of these spatial configurations on collaborative music making in SVEs. The results show adding personal space to be helpful in supporting collaborative music making in SVE, since it provides a chance to explore individual ideas, and provides higher efficiency in making notes. However, several negative impacts also showed up along with the addition of personal space, e.g. longer average distance between participants, reduced group territory and group edits [34]. We believe this might due to: (i) the separated stationary locations of the personal spaces forced users to leave each other to access, causing a longer distance between participants and less collaboration; (ii) the rigid boundary between public space and personal space made users more isolated, resulting in a higher sense of isolation. Thus allowing users to access personal space without leaving each other far away might eliminate these disadvantages.

To make the shift between personal and public spaces more fluid, inspired by the implication that the separation between public and personal workspace should be gradual rather than too rigid [23], the attenuation feature can possibly be applied to form a gradual personal space, enabling a fluid transition between personal space and public space. This is because sound is both the primary medium of collaborative tasks and the final work of CMM [33], thus by manipulating acoustic attenuation, we can produce sonic privacy. Thus H1 was developed.

**H1**: Attenuation can play a similar role to personal space with rigid form in CMM in SVE, providing collaborators a personal space and supporting individual creativity during the collaboration.

Additionally, an acoustic attenuation, rather than a personal space with rigid separation from public space, enables a gradual shift between personal and public workspace, which may possibly increase the fluidity of the experience and support collaboration better, cf. [23]. Thus we developed H2.

**H2**: Acoustic attenuation provides a fluid transition (no hard borders nor rigid forms) between personal and public spaces, which introduces less negative impacts on collaboration compared with personal space with rigid form in [34].

### 8.5.2  Independent Variable

Spatial configuration is an independent variable in this experiment. Two spatial configurations were designed as the independent variable levels, as shown in Fig. 8.14, including the following:

- Condition 1: **Pub**lic space only (referred to as $C_{pub}$): where players can generate, remove or manipulate music interfaces, and have equal access to all of the space and the music interfaces. As no personal space is provided, a shift between public and personal space does not exist, i.e. users cannot shift to personal space.
- Condition 2: Public space + **Aug**mented Attenuation Personal Space (referred to as $C_{aug}$). In addition to $C_{pub}$), the sound attenuation is augmented. The volume of audio drops much faster, creating a sonic privacy, which can be seen as a personal

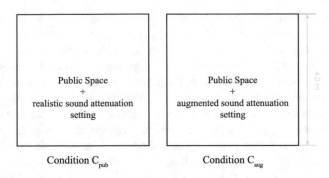

**Fig. 8.14** Top view of the two experimental condition settings

space. As the volume changes gradually with the changes of distance, the shift between personal space and public space is gradual.

### 8.5.3 Dependent Variables

To identify how users use the space and the effect of adding augmented sound attenuation as personal space, dependent variables were developed. The Igroup Presence Questionnaire (IPQ) was used to inform the design of questions about sense of collaborator's presence [54]. The IPQ measures the sense of presence using one general measurement—sense of being there, plus three sub-scales covering spatial presence, involvement and experience realism. Questions about output quality, communication and contribution were adapted from the Mutual Engagement Questionnaire (MEQ) [15]. The MEQ is formed of two parts: (i) participant ratings of the quality of the musical outcome and their interaction with musical interface; (ii) participant choices between different conditions when being provided a series of statements covering the music quality, enjoyment, involvement and frustration. The rest of the questions were designed to question people's preference for conditions. The questionnaire included measures on:

- *Presence*: (i) Sense of self-presence, (ii) sense of co-worker's presence and (iii) sense of collaborator's activities.
- *Communication*: quality of communication, which may vary as the visibility of spaces can possibly affect the embodiment and nonverbal communication.
- *Content assessment*: the satisfaction of the final music created reflects the quality of collaboration, cf. [15, 16].
- *Preference*: preference of the conditions, to see if users have subjective preferences towards the settings.
- *Contribution*: (i) the feeling of self's contribution; (ii) the feeling of others' contribution.

**Table 8.1**  Results of Post-Session Questionnaire and the results of Wilcoxon Rank-Sum Test (two-tailed)[a]

| Questions (Measure) | $C_{pub}$ | | $C_{aug}$ | | $C_{pub}$ *vs* $C_{aug}$ | |
|---|---|---|---|---|---|---|
| | M | SD | M | SD | p | W |
| PSQ1 (support for creativity)—I think the space setting in this session was extremely helpful for creativity | 8.55 | 1.44 | 8.77 | 1.34 | 0.5695 | 259 |
| PSQ2 (support for creativity)—I feel like the space setting in this session was extremely helpful to support the development of my own ideas | 7.82 | 1.92 | 8.35 | 1.50 | 0.5211 | 255.5 |
| PSQ3 (preference)—I enjoyed the space setting of this virtual world very much | 8.27 | 1.61 | 8.65 | 1.60 | 0.2622 | 233 |
| PSQ4 (sense of collaborator's presence)—I always had strong feeling that my collaborator was there, collaborating with me together, all the time | 8.91 | 0.92 | 8.54 | 1.68 | 0.7961 | 298.5 |
| PSQ5 (content assessments)—How satisfied are you with the final piece of loop music you two created in this session | 8.64 | 1.09 | 8.50 | 1.36 | 0.7644 | 300.5 |
| PSQ6 (communication quality)—How would you rate the quality of communication between you and your collaborator during the session | 8.68 | 1.09 | 8.50 | 1.36 | 0.7644 | 300.5 |
| PSQ7 (sense of collaborator's activity)—I had a clear sense what my collaborator was doing | 8.73 | 1.20 | 7.96 | 1.54 | 0.08094 | 368.5 |
| PSQ8 (amount of contribution)—The amount of your contribution to the joint piece of music is | 8.41 | 1.44 | 8.15 | 1.46 | 0.4776 | 320 |
| PSQ9 (amount of contribution)—The amount of your collaborator's contribution to the joint piece of music is | 8.18 | 1.26 | 8.23 | 1.39 | 0.8486 | 276.5 |
| PSQ10 (quality of contribution)—What do you think of the quality of your contribution to the joint piece of music is | 8.05 | 1.70 | 7.81 | 1.41 | 0.319 | 333.5 |
| PSQ11 (quality of contribution)—What do you think of the quality of your collaborator's contribution to the joint piece of music is | 7.73 | 1.52 | 8.19 | 1.20 | 0.3496 | 241.5 |

[a] Note: statistics in this table are calculated based on the data collected from third and fourth session to better counterbalance the learning effect

These measures are grouped into a Post-Session Questionnaire (PSQ, see items in Table 8.1).

### 8.5.4  Participants and Procedure

Fifty-two participants (26 pairs) were recruited through group emails at the authors' university for this study.[6] Each participant was compensated 10 GBP for their time (roughly 1 h). Participants' rating of musical theory knowledge is 3.92 (SD = 2.50) on a 10-point Likert scale, where higher values indicate increased knowledge; 24

---

[6] The Queen Mary Research Ethics Committee granted ethical approval to carry out the study within its facilities (Ethical Application Ref: QMREC2005).

participants play one or more instruments, and the remaining 28 do not. Twenty participants had tried VR 2–5 times before, 20 had only tried once and the remaining 12 had no VR experience previously. Thirty-seven participants knew their collaborators very well prior to the experiment; three met their collaborators several times, and the remaining 12 did not know their collaborators at all prior to the experiment.

The experiment started with participants reading the information form and signing the consent form. Then they first received an explanation of the music interface of LeMo II (see Fig. 8.2), with all of the interaction gestures supported in LeMo II demonstrated by an experimenter. Next, a trial (roughly 5–15 min) session was carried out, where participants could try all of the possible interactions. The trial ended once participants were confident enough of all available interactions. The length of time of the tutorial session was flexible to ensure participants with diverse musical knowledge could grasp LeMo II. Participants were then asked to have four sessions of collaboratively composing music that was mutually satisfying and compliments an animation loop. Two of these sessions were set for this study; each covered a condition ($C_{pub}/C_{aug}$), and the sequence of conditions was fully randomised to counterbalance the learning effect. We set each session as 7 min because based on our pilot study and a previous study [33], we found 7–8 min were sufficient for the task. In total, four visual, silent animation loops were introduced to trigger participants' creativity; each to be played in one experimental session on four virtual screens surrounding the virtual stage. These clips were played in an independently randomised sequence to counterbalance impacts on the study. Each session ended with a Post-Session Questionnaire (PSQ, see Table 8.1). After all the four sessions finished, a short interview was carried out.

## 8.5.5 Results

Wilcoxon Rank-Sum tests were run to compare the ratings of $C_{pub}$ with $C_{aug}$ collected by PSQ, see results in Table 8.1. No significant effect was found between $C_{aug}$ and $C_{pub}$. Post-task interviews revealed more reflective insights. Around 41,000 words of audio recorded interview responses were transcribed and a thematic analysis of the transcription was undertaken (more details about the thematic analysis in Sect. 8.4.3). As shown in Fig. 8.15, in total, 439 coded segments, 15 codes and 3 overarching themes emerged from the thematic analysis: (i) learning effects; (ii) preferences, advantages and disadvantages of conditions; and (iii) advantages, disadvantages of LeMo II and suggestions for improvements. Next, we will only cover the former two themes as the final one is not directly related to the scope of this chapter.

### 8.5.5.1 Learning Effects

Members of 18 groups mentioned the effect of the session sequence. Specifically, 43 coded segments contributed by 27 participants were related to learning effects. For

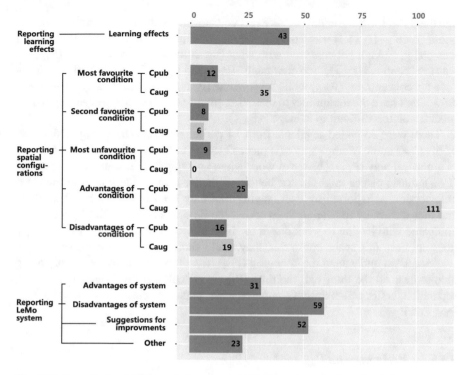

**Fig. 8.15** Ingredients of all the coded segments of the interview; number of coded segments are shown in the bars

example, Participant 15A (participant A in group 15, referred to as $P_{15A}$) reported the sequence is an "important factor". The first session was felt to be hard as they were "just being introduced to [the system and they were] still adjusting" to it ($P_{5A}$), trying to "[figure] out how the system was working" ($P_{16A}$), as they "were progressing into latter sessions, [they] felt easier to communicate and use gestures to manipulate the sound, being able to collaborate more, more used to the system" ($P_{5B}$), these changes led to a higher level of satisfaction and more enjoyment in later conditions. To better counterbalance the impact of sequence, Table 8.1 only includes data collected from the latter two sessions (note: as aforementioned, there were four sessions that were randomly sequenced, and two of which were related to this study).

### 8.5.5.2   $C_{pub}$—Simple but can be Chaotic

With no personal space, participants had to hear all the interfaces throughout the session. In total, 16 coded segments are about the disadvantages of $C_{pub}$; some exemplars are: "a bit troubling"—$P_{11B}$,[7] "music always very loud"—$P_{9A}$, "it was global music,

---

[7] $P_{11B}$ refers to participant B in group 11, similarly, $P_{9A}$ indicates participant A in group 9.

and there was someone annoying"—P$_{2A}$, "you are not going to say anything" to avoid being "rude"—(P$_{2A}$). It was easier if there is something helpful "to perceive what I was doing, and not get confused with what [the collaborator] was doing" (P$_{15B}$), it was too "chaotic" (P$_{20A}$), "too confusing" (P$_{22A}$ and P$_{22B}$), "annoying" (P$_{25B}$). They "can not concentrate" (P$_{25B}$) while "everything [is] open and quite noisy" (P$_{26B}$), and they "don't have the tranquillity to operating [their] sounds or the everything's come mixed, which is difficult to manage" (P$_{22A}$).

There were 25 coded segments from 14 participants reporting the positive side of the C$_{pub}$; some examples are: (i) pieces created in "personal space" might clash in a musical way (P$_{1A}$), "better to work when knowing how it sounds all together" (P$_{17B}$), music pieces might match better; (ii) better for providing help to the other collaborator, as reported by P4A, saying that they needed someone to lead them and thus the ability to hear all the work all the time was helpful; (iii) "space wise", compared with having to work closer to "hear the sound well" (P$_{12A}$) in C$_{aug}$, C$_{pub}$ does not have this space constraint, they could chose to work "anywhere" (P$_{24A}$); iv) "easier" to understand the condition (P$_{6B}$), fewer confusions when simply being able to hear all the things all the time (P$_{13A}$); v) "collaborative wise" (P$_{13A}$), less separation, better collaboration compared with "personal space" was provided (P$_{3B}$, P$_{18A}$ and P$_{18B}$).

### 8.5.5.3   Preference on C$_{aug}$

There were 35 coded segments contributed by 24 participants favouring condition C$_{aug}$, higher than 12 segments contributed by 11 participants for C$_{pub}$. There are 111 coded segments contributed by 33 participants from 25 groups reporting the advantages of this condition, much higher than the number of segments reporting other conditions' advantages. These reports reveal some insights behind the popularity of C$_{aug}$. C$_{aug}$'s advantages reported by participants can be grouped into 4 groups:

- *Higher team cohesiveness and lower sense of separation.* Participants reported that, without the rigid personal space, they had to "work with the other person" (P$_{6A}$). With no rigid personal space, C$_{aug}$'s "forces [them] to collaborate more the most because [they] had to stay very close to compose music " (P$_{9B}$).

- *An appropriate environment for creativity, more consistency and convenience.* As described by participants, it was "a middle point between personal space and no personal space" (P$_{6A}$), without even triggering something, "[they] could decide in a continuous way if [they] were able to listen to the other sound sources or not", and "to what extent [they] want to isolate [themselves]" (P$_{16A}$). Compared with having to hear all sounds in C$_{pub}$, this provided them a "less stressing" (P$_{4A}$) context, and they can selectively move away to avoid "getting interrupted with the other" (P$_{5B}$) and overlapping music. Being able to still "hear a bit of it in the background but not completely" (P$_{20A}$) was reported good as this kept them "up to date" (P$_{9A}$) and helped them to "tailor what [the participant] was making" (P$_{22B}$) to match the co-created music and to make something new and see if it "fit with"

($P_{20A}$) the old. $C_{aug}$ provided them with "a little bit of personal space" although not a quite a "defined thing" ($P_{6A}$), which provided the possibility "to work on something individually" but also being able to "share work quite easily" ($P_{20A}$).

- *Easier to identify sounds.* Participants reported it was easier to "locate the source of the sound" ($P_{16A}$) and "perceive what [they were] doing" ($P_{15B}$), which helped them "understand instruments better" ($P_{7B}$) and "not get confused" ($P_{15B}$);
- *More real.* Interestingly, instead of $C_{pub}$, which simulates the real-world sound attenuation, $C_{aug}$ was reported to be "real". "If you want to hear something, you just come closer, like in the real world" ($P_{11B}$ and $P_{11B}$), "it was good like we were feeling like the real-time experience ($P_{26B}$)".

It should also be noted that, along with these reports about advantage, there are 19 segments reporting $C_{aug}$'s limitations, including: (i) a preference "to hear all the instruments all the time" in $C_{pub}$ ($P_{26B}$), (ii) $C_{aug}$ might lead to "another type of compositions" and "influence the piece" ($P_{16B}$) and (iii) without being able to hear all sounds led to a feeling of separation ($P_{18A}$).

## 8.5.6  Discussion

The issues from having no personal space are clear. Especially for the music-making task in this study, participants reported that without personal space, the auditory background could be messy to develop own ideas, and their creativity required a quieter and more controllable environment, which could be provided by personal space. Providing such an environment is crucial considering individual creativity is an important part of the collaborative creativity. Having personal space was reported to be "an added advantage" because it promoted their own creativity, which can then be combined and contributed to the joint piece. This matches the findings in [34], that providing personal spaces is helpful as it provides a chance to explore individual ideas freely, which then added an interesting dynamic to the collaborative work. However, adding personal space indeed brought a few impacts, next we discuss the impacts of using acoustic attenuation as personal space and its characteristics.

### 8.5.6.1  Impacts of Adding Acoustic Attenuation as Personal Space

As mentioned above, in the previous study [34], we found the addition of personal space located on the opposite side of the public space led to a shrunken size of group territory, fewer group note edits, a larger size of personal territory, more personal note edits, a larger average distance between collaborators and fewer times of paying attention to collaborator. We argued that these negative impacts are mainly due to the personal spaces distributed on the opposite side of the group space resulting in a larger distance between participants. So we proposed personal space with different features (e.g. gradual boundary—$C_{aug}$) might reduce these negative effects. In many ways, $C_{aug}$ is quite similar to $C_{pub}$, e.g. both do not have a visual boundary for spaces, so not surprisingly, no significant differences were found in most of the statistical measures, see Table 8.1, and most previously identified disadvantages brought by adding rigid personal spaces have been successfully eliminated; more detailed results are available in [35]. By making the personal space invisible and gradual, the isolation and difficulty of coordinating that introduced by the additional personal space was minimised. For example, in the interview, participants reported $C_{aug}$ provided a proper level of group work as working context, making easier to create new that matches the old.

### 8.5.6.2 Providing Personal Space with Fluid Boundary

Although no significant differences were found in PSQ2, see Table 8.1, which questioned the support each condition gave to individual creativity, $C_{aug}$ has a higher mean rating. The thematic analysis revealed more insights. $C_{aug}$ provides both "an appropriate background" with which participants felt "less stressed" and were able to "tailor" the individual composing to match the co-work, and a space personal enough to "work on something individually". No major differences were found between $C_{pub}$ and $C_{aug}$ in PSQ, indicating $C_{aug}$ provides a very mild solution, with limited impacts on people's collaborative behaviour introduced, whilst still providing sufficient support for individual creativity during collaboration, thus H1 is validated.

Compared with natural attenuation in $C_{pub}$, $C_{aug}$'s augmented sound attenuation setting forced or prompted people to work more closely in order to hear each other's work, as reported by some participants. Compared with adding personal space with visible rigid boundary, by enabling participants to "decide in a continuous way" ($P_{16A}$) if they want to hear other's work, an invisible gradual boundary in $C_{aug}$ led to less separation, and higher consistency between personal and public space. H2 is therefore supported. This finding also echos the implication proposed in [23] that there should be many gradations between personal and public space to enable people fluidly shift in between. Popularity—the code "advantage of $C_{aug}$" has 111 coded segments, and the code "most favourite—$C_{aug}$" has 35 coded segments, both are greater than what $C_{pub}$ gets. All indicate $C_{aug}$ is the most popular condition. The popularity is also partially verified by that $C_{aug}$ has the highest mean in preference measure (PSQ3 in Table 8.1). We believe the reasons behind this popularity are mainly due to its unique advantages, which as reported by participants, include: (i) an appropriate environment for creativity, (ii) easier to identify sounds and (iii) perceived as more "real" (although it should be noted that $C_{pub}$ is more similar to real-world audio attenuation). These features of $C_{aug}$ made it provide better support for collaborative creativity and therefore led to its popularity.

**Table 8.2** Comparison between the two routes

|  | 3D Annotation | Augmented Attenuation |
|---|---|---|
| Modality | Visual | Auditory |
| Type of interaction | Explicit interaction—active drawing | Implicit interaction—passive body movement |
| Supports for collaboration | Supporting communication between users | Supporting development of individual creativity |
| Characteristic | No influence introduced on audio channel, users hear roughly the same audio[a] | Influence introduced on audio and composition, users do not hear the same audio |
| Applications | Wider range of application, not restricted to audio tasks, audio tasks requiring precise audio output, or users with hearing/speech impairment | Application restricted to auditory tasks with no requirement for precise audio outputs |

[a]Strictly speaking, what users hear still slightly differs unless the realistic spatialisation of audio is disabled

## 8.6 General Discussion

The two studies have explored 3D annotation and augmented acoustic attenuation's role in CMM. This section compares the two approaches against each other, seeking the potential differences and finding out the usage scenarios. The comparison results are summarised in Table 8.2.

### 8.6.1 Modality and Interaction Type

3D annotation is a visual approach, while augmented attenuation is an audio approach. This fundamental difference led to their unique advantages and disadvantages, which then determine their scope of usage scenarios. Specifically, the visual approach can fully avoid influencing the audio channel, leaving that modality purely for composers to hear the project they are working on. While on the contrary, the audio approach imposes unavoidable effects on how the audio sounds, as the privacy is produced by augmenting the acoustic attenuation of the medium of the sound.

Unlike 3D annotation, which requires explicit interaction to make 3D lines, the augmented attenuation in Study II only relies on users' passive listening and active physical locating in space. Explicit interaction is consciously deciding to interact, e.g. clicking a button. It is what we normally think about when we're interacting with a computer [55]. Compared with explicit interaction, implicit interaction does not require users to perform conscious actions; the interaction is mainly the movement (e.g. head movement and eye movement) of the user. As a result, the 3D annotation introduced a higher learning cost.

### 8.6.2   Key Support for Collaboration

The 3D annotation helps people to warm up at the beginning, supports the non-vocal communication and provides help for collaborators to understand each other's attention. In other words, it supports the social aspects of the collaboration by intensifying the links between collaborators. While the augmented attenuation gives collaborators the choice to be separated, hence provides support for individual creation. With this flexibility, users have the choice to develop their own work and to switch fluidly between working on own and teamwork.

### 8.6.3   Characteristic and Application

3D annotation completely avoids impacts on the auditory channel. This supportive measure suits where the sonic output comes with stringent requirements, and users must be able to hear exactly the same final output during their working. Its application is not limited to sonic task because it provides support to communication, which is required by many collaborative tasks in SVEs. In contrast, the augmented attenuation has a narrower application range. It provides better support for individual activity, with still enough context of group work and the cost of hearing (slightly) differed output, making it only appropriate to audio related-tasks with no rigid requirements, e.g. people are improvising music for fun.

These two supportive features do not necessarily contradict each other, and could be applied simultaneously. To manage the simultaneous use, a manipulation system might be needed. For example, the transparency of the visual 3D annotation and the degree of augmentation of attenuation can be adjusted to modify their impacts (visibility/audibility), fitting collaborators' needs during different stages of the collaborative composing. When only one feature is needed, the other can be adjusted to zero, wiping out its impacts entirely.

## 8.7   Conclusions and Future Work

In this chapter, two different approaches to support collaborative sonic interaction in SVEs have been presented, one exploited visual modality and the other exploited audio modality. The results of both studies have been presented and reflected upon. A comparison between the two approaches has been made. Next, following the findings and discussion above, we propose six implications for supporting collaborative sonic interaction in SVEs, e.g. CMM.

1. Adding a system that supports 3D annotation may be considered to aid collaborator's communication, especially if co-produced sound has to be prioritised over other modalities to avoid any impacts.

2. For audio-related tasks in SVEs, adding personal space should be considered, as it provides sonic privacy and essential support for the development of individual creativity, which forms a key part of the collaborative creativity. This is especially essential when the output of the task is vulnerable (e.g. audio), and co-workers need a space where they can think of own ideas and develop own work.

3. For audio-related tasks (e.g. collaborative music making), manipulating acoustic attenuation as personal space can be an effective way to allow users to shift between personal and public working space continuously by adjusting their relative distance. With light-weight form, it introduces mild impacts compared with the prominent negative impacts introduced by rigid personal space [34].

4. The level of privacy can be adjusted by manipulating the level of augmentation. For instance, in $C_{aug}$ of Study II, participants adjusted their distance between themselves and collaborators to achieve different levels of being personal (herein referred to as "personalness"). Instead of changing positions, adjusting the sound attenuation rate with distance can impact the level of "personalness" and therefore producing a varied level of personalness. Potentially, adding a method allowing users to adjust the level might be useful so users can shift between having a "very personal and isolated" space and a "very public" space.

5. Augmented attenuation can be exploited for creative audio privacy, which can be then used to promote individual creativity during the collaboration. However, augmented attenuation introduces differences in what collaborators hear, making it only applicable to contexts with no rigid requirements on audio outputs.

6. We suggest that augmented attenuation and 3D annotation could be applied together or chosen with a flexible switch so that users can choose the feature fitting their needs during different stages of the collaborative composition.

Future works concern an exploration of how multi-modal approaches can be applied simultaneously, and designing and applying tools based on other modalities to support collaborative sonic interaction in SVEs, such as visual modality. For each modality, it could be interesting to test how that sensory cue can be augmented/depressed to adjust the level of its influence.

**Acknowledgements**  This work is partially supported by EPSRC and AHRC Centre for Doctoral Training in Media and Arts Technology (EP/ L01632X/1). We would also like to thank Ms Louise Bryce and Ms Danqi Zhao for their help in proofreading this chapter.

# References

1. Barbosa, Á.: Displaced soundscapes: A survey of network systems for music and sonic art creation. Leonardo Music Journal **13**, 53–59 (2003).
2. Basdogan, C., Ho, C.-H., Srinivasan, M. A., Slater, M.: An experimental study on the role of touch in shared virtual environments. ACM Transactions on Computer-Human Interaction (TOCHI) **7**, 443–460 (2000).

3. Benford, S., Bowers, J., Fahlén, L. E., Greenhalgh, C., Snowdon, D.: User embodiment in collaborative virtual environments in Proceedings of the SIGCHI conference on Human factors in computing systems (1995), 242–249.
4. Benford, S., Greenhalgh, C., Rodden, T., Pycock, J.: Collaborative virtual environments. Communications of the ACM **44**, 79–85 (2001).
5. Billinghurst, M., Kato, H.: Collaborative augmented reality. Communications of the ACM **45**, 64–70 (2002).
6. Billinghurst, M., Poupyrev, I., Kato, H., May, R.: Mixing realities in shared space: An augmented reality interface for collaborative computing in Multimedia and Expo, 2000. ICME 2000. 2000 IEEE International Conference on **3** (2000), 1641–1644.
7. Bin, S. A., Bryan-Kinns, N., McPherson, A., et al.: Hands where we can see them! investigating the impact of gesture size on audience perception. International Computer Music Conference (2017).
8. Blaine, T., Fels, S.: Contexts of collaborative musical experiences in Proceedings of the 2003 conference on New interfaces for musical expression (2003), 129–134.
9. Blaine, T., Perkis, T.: The Jam-O-Drum Interactive Music System: A Study in Interaction Design in Proceedings of the 3rd Conference on Designing Interactive Systems: Processes, Practices, Methods, and Techniques (Association for Computing Machinery, New York City, New York, USA, 2000), 165–173.
10. Braun, V., Clarke, V.: Using thematic analysis in psychology. Qualitative research in psychology **3**, 77–101 (2006).
11. Bressan, F., Vets, T., Leman, M.: A multimodal interactive installation for collaborative music making: From preservation to enhanced user design in Proceedings of the European Society for Cognitive Sciences Of Music (ESCOM) Conference, Ghent University (2017), 23–26.
12. Brooks Jr, F. et al.: Research directions in virtual environments. Computer Graphics **26**, 153 (1992).
13. Bryan-Kinns, N.: Daisyphone: the design and impact of a novel environment for remote group music improvisation in Proceedings of the 5th conference on Designing interactive systems: processes, practices, methods, and techniques (2004), 135–144.
14. Bryan-Kinns, N.: Annotating distributed scores for mutual engagement in daisyphone and beyond. Leonardo Music Journal **21**, 51–55 (2011).
15. Bryan-Kinns, N.: Mutual engagement and collocation with shared representations. International Journal of Human-Computer Studies **71**, 76–90 (2013).
16. Bryan-Kinns, N., Hamilton, F.: Identifying mutual engagement. Behaviour & Information Technology **31**, 101–125 (2012).
17. Bryan-Kinns, N., Healey, P. G.: Decay in collaborative music making in Proceedings of the 2006 conference on new interfaces for musical expression (2006), 114–117.
18. Carlsson, C., Hagsand, O.: DIVE A multi-user virtual reality system in Proceedings of IEEE Virtual Reality Annual International Symposium (1993), 394–400.
19. De Simone, F. et al.: Watching Videos Together in Social Virtual Reality: An Experimental Study on User's QoE in 2019 IEEE Conference on Virtual Reality and 3D User Interfaces (VR) (2019), 890–891.
20. Draper, J. V., Kaber, D. B., Usher, J. M.: Telepresence. Human Factors **40**, 354–375 (1998).
21. Ellemers, N., Rink, F. in Social Identification in Groups 1–41 (Emerald Group Publishing Limited, 2005).
22. Frécon, E., Greenhalgh, C., Stenius, M.: The DiveBone-an application-level network architecture for Internet-based CVEs in Proceedings of the ACM symposium on Virtual reality software and technology (1999), 58–65.
23. Greenberg, S., Boyle, M., LaBerge, J.: PDAs and shared public displays: Making personal information public, and public information personal. Personal Technologies **3**, 54–64 (1999).
24. Gutwin, C., Greenberg, S. in Team cognition: Understanding the Factors that Drive Process and Performance (eds Salas, E., Fiore, S. M.) 177–201 (Washington, DC, US: American Psychological Association, 2004).

25. Healey, P. G., Leach, J., Bryan-Kinns, N.: Inter-play: Understanding group music improvisation as a form of everyday interaction. Proceedings of Less is More-Simple Computing in an Age of Complexity (2005).
26. Heeter, C.: Being there: The subjective experience of presence. Presence: Teleoperators & Virtual Environments 1, 262–271 (1992).
27. Hendrix, C., Barfield, W.: The sense of presence within auditory virtual environments. Presence: Teleoperators & Virtual Environments 5, 290–301 (1996).
28. Hunt, C.: Field of view face-off: Rift vs Vive vs Gear VR vs PSVR https://www.vrheads.com/field-view-faceoff-rift-vs-vive-vsgear-vr-vs-psvr.
29. Jordá, S.: On stage: the reactable and other musical tangibles go real. Int. J. Arts Technol. 1, 268–287 (2008).
30. Lab, R. L.: Field of View for Virtual Reality Headsets Explained https://vr-lens-lab.com/field-of-view-for-virtual-reality-headsets/.
31. Lea, R., Honda, Y., Matsuda, K.: Virtual society: Collaboration in 3D spaces on the Internet. Computer Supported CooperativeWork (CSCW) 6, 227–250 (1997).
32. Luciani, A. in Enaction and enactive interfaces : a handbook of terms 299–300 (Enactive Systems Book, 2007).
33. Men, L., Bryan-Kinns, N.: LeMo: Supporting Collaborative Music Making in Virtual Reality in 2018 IEEE 4th VR Workshop on Sonic Interactions for Virtual Environments (SIVE) (2018), 1–6.
34. Men, L., Bryan-Kinns, N.: LeMo: Exploring Virtual Space for Collaborative Creativity in Proceedings of ACM conference on Creativity and cognition 2019 (2019).
35. Men, L., Bryan-Kinns, N., Bryce, L.: Designing spaces to support collaborative creativity in shared virtual environments. PeerJ Computer Science 5, e229 (2019).
36. Men, L., Bryan-Kinns, N., Hassard, A. S., Ma, Z.: The impact of transitions on user experience in virtual reality in Virtual Reality (VR), 2017 IEEE (2017), 285–286.
37. Men, L., Zhao, D.: Designing Privacy for Collaborative Music Making in Virtual Reality in Proceedings of the 16th International Conference on Audio Mostly (Trento, Italy, 2021).
38. Minsky, M.: Telepresence. Omni, 45–51 (1980).
39. Morreale, F., Angeli, A. D., O'Modhrain, S.: Musical Interface Design: An Experience-oriented Framework in Proceedings of the International Conference on New Interfaces for Musical Expression (NIME) (2014), 467–472.
40. Nabavian, S., Bryan-Kinns, N.: Analysing group creativity: A distributed cognitive study of joint music composition. Proc. of Cognitive Science, 1856–1861 (2006).
41. Nassiri, N., Powell, N., Moore, D.: Human interactions and personal space in collaborative virtual environments. Virtual reality 14, 229–240 (2010).
42. Nedel, L. et al.: Using Immersive Virtual Reality to Reduce Work Accidents in Developing Countries. IEEE Computer Graphics and Applications 36, 36–46 (2016).
43. Nowak, K. L., Biocca, F.: The effect of the agency and anthropomorphism on users' sense of telepresence, copresence, and social presence in virtual environments. Presence: Teleoperators & Virtual Environments 12, 481–494 (2003).
44. Ochse, R., Ochse, R.: Before the gates of excellence: The determinants of creative genius (CUP Archive, 1990).
45. Oculus: Toybox Demo for Oculus Touch https://www.youtube.com/watch?v=iFEMiyGMa58.
46. Pirola-Merlo, A., Mann, L.: The relationship between individual creativity and team creativity: Aggregating across people and time. Journal of Organizational behavior 25, 235–257 (2004).
47. Plante, C.: A PlayStation VR demo made me cry from laughing https://www.theverge.com/2016/3/16/11246334/playstation-virtualreality-social-vr-demo.
48. Rice, R. E.: Media appropriateness: Using social presence theory to compare traditional and new organizational media. Human Communication Research 19, 451–484 (1993).
49. Rodden, T.: A survey of CSCW systems. Interacting with computers 3, 319–353 (1991).
50. Romano, D. M., Brna, P., Self, J. A.: Collaborative decision-making and presence in shared dynamic virtual environments in Proceedings of the Workshop on Presence in SharedVirtual Environments.BTLabs, Martlesham Heath (1998).

51. Roussos, M. et al.: NICE: combining constructionism, narrative and collaboration in a virtual learning environment. Computer Graphics-New York- Association for Computing Machinery **31**, 62–63 (1997).
52. Rovai, A. P.: Building sense of community at a distance. The International Review of Research in Open and Distributed Learning **3** (2002).
53. Schroeder, R.: The social life of avatars: Presence and interaction in shared virtual environments (Springer Science & Business Media, 2012).
54. Schubert, T., Friedmann, F., Regenbrecht, H.: The experience of presence: Factor analytic insights. Presence: Teleoperators & Virtual Environments **10**, 266–281 (2001).
55. Serim, B., Jacucci, G.: Explicating" Implicit Interaction": An Examination of the Concept and Challenges for Research in Proceedings of the 2019 CHI Conference on Human Factors in Computing Systems (2019), 417.
56. Shen, C., Everitt, K., Ryall, K.: UbiTable: Impromptu face-to-face collaboration on horizontal interactive surfaces in International Conference on Ubiquitous Computing (2003), 281–288.
57. Sheridan, T. B.: Musings on telepresence and virtual presence. Presence: Teleoperators & Virtual Environments **1**, 120–126 (1992).
58. Sherman, W. R., Craig, A. B.: Understanding Virtual reality: Interface, Application, and Design (Morgan Kaufmann, 2018).
59. Short, J., Williams, E., Christie, B.: The social psychology of telecommunications. The Social Psychology of Telecommunications (1976).
60. Simonton, D. K.: Creative productivity: A predictive and explanatory model of career trajectories and landmarks. Psychological review **104**, 66 (1997).
61. Slater, M., Usoh, M., Steed, A.: Depth of Presence in Virtual Environments. Presence **3**, 130–144 (1994).
62. Slater, M.: Place illusion and plausibility can lead to realistic behaviour in immersive virtual environments. Phil. Trans. R. Soc. B **364**, 3549–3557 (2009).
63. Slater, M., Wilbur, S.: A framework for immersive virtual environments (FIVE): Speculations on the role of presence in virtual environments. Presence: Teleoperators & Virtual Environments **6**, 603–616 (1997).
64. Steuer, J.: Defining virtual reality: Dimensions determining telepresence. Journal of Communication **42**, 73–93 (1992).
65. Sugimoto, M., Hosoi, K., Hashizume, H.: Caretta: a system for supporting face-to-face collaboration by integrating personal and shared spaces in Proceedings of the SIGCHI conference on Human factors in computing systems (2004), 41–48.
66. Thiebaut, J.-B., Healey, P. G., Bryan-Kinns, N.: Drawing Electroacoustic Music. in ICMC (2008).
67. Titon, J. T., Slobin, M.: The music-culture as a world of music. Worlds of music: an introduction to the music of the world's peoples. New York: Schirmer Books (1996).
68. Wallace, P., Maryott, J.: The impact of avatar self-representation on collaboration in virtual worlds. Innovate: Journal of Online Education **5**, 3 (2009).
69. Wang, G.: Designing Smule's Ocarina: The iPhone's Magic Flute. in NIME (2009), 303–307.
70. Weinberg, G.: Interconnected musical networks-bringing expression and thoughtfulness to collaborative music making in Massachusetts Institute of Technology Media Laboratory (2003).
71. Witmer, B. G., Singer, M. J.: Measuring presence in virtual environments: A presence questionnaire. Presence **7**, 225–240 (1998).
72. Wozniewski, M., Bouillot, N., Settel, Z., Cooperstock, J. R.: Large-Scale Mobile Audio Environments for Collaborative Musical Interaction. in NIME (2008), 13–18.
73. Yee, N., Bailenson, J. N., Urbanek, M., Chang, F., Merget, D.: The unbearable likeness of being digital: the persistence of nonverbal social norms in online virtual environments. CyberPsychology & Behavior **10**, 115–121 (2007).
74. Yin, R. K.: Case study research and applications: Design and methods (Sage publications, 2017).
75. Zhang, X., Furnas, G. W.: The effectiveness of multiscale collaboration in virtual environments in CHI'03 Extended Abstracts on Human Factors in Computing Systems (2003), 790–791.

# Chapter 9
# Spatial Audio Mixing in Virtual Reality

Anders Riddershom Bargum, Oddur Ingi Kristjánsson, Péter Babó,
Rasmus Eske Waage Nielsen, Simon Rostami Mosen, and Stefania Serafin

**Abstract** The development of Virtual Reality (VR) systems and multimodal simulations presents possibilities in spatial-music mixing, be it in virtual spaces, for ensembles and orchestral compositions or for surround sound in film and music. Traditionally, user interfaces for mixing music have employed the channel-strip metaphor for controlling volume, panning and other audio effects that are aspects that also have grown into the culture of mixing music spatially. Simulated rooms and two-dimensional panning systems are simply implemented on computer screens to facilitate the placement of sound sources within space. In this chapter, we present design aspects for mixing in VR, investigating already existing virtual music mixing products and creating a framework from which a virtual spatial-music mixing tool can be implemented. Finally, the tool will be tested against a similar computer version to examine whether or not the sensory benefits and palpable spatial proportions of a VE can improve the process of mixing 3D sound.

## 9.1 Introduction

Mixing is the activity of placing and levelling sounds. When a sound source in the real world is placed spatially, the sound source's distance and direction is digitally managed in the process of mixing and thereafter perceived through different cues. This is done on a mixing console, being the primary interface for mixing 2D music; the console includes additional parameters to manipulate the general relationship between the sound sources. The parameters are amongst other things panning, volume, and equalisation, on each track. The mixing console is divided into functional sections, which constitute different metaphors [10]. As an example, each track has a channel strip, used as the main way to adjust the volume. The volume parameter

A. Riddershom Bargum · O. Ingi Kristjánsson · P. Babó · R. Eske Waage Nielsen ·
S. Rostami Mosen · S. Serafin (✉)
Department of Architecture, Design, and Media Technology, Aalborg University Copenhagen,
Copenhagen, Denmark
e-mail: sts@create.aau.dk

M. Geronazzo and S. Serafin (eds.), *Sonic Interactions in Virtual Environments*,
Human—Computer Interaction Series, https://doi.org/10.1007/978-3-031-04021-4_9

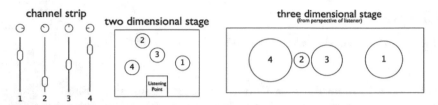

**Fig. 9.1**  Channel strip versus stage metaphor. *Hand Motion-Controlled Audio Mixing Interface* [23]

(also called a fader), is often built on a slide potentiometer and is seen as a universal metaphor for amplitude [3]. Simultaneously the pan potentiometer represents the track's placement and spatial position of a source in a stereo mix. Here, the pan potentiometer maps the left and right position of a knob to the left and right location of a sound. In general, the mixing console can be seen as a metaphor on its own and it has brought with it visually rich interfaces and representations of controls via graphical faders and knobs [15]. A mixing console can be divided into two main categories:

- Analog mixing console: it deploys a one-to-one mapping where every slider, knob and button has a dedicated function [10]. It is widely used and is known to be fast and intuitive.
- Digital mixing console: it reduces the design of the analog mixer by introducing sub-menus and layers, breaking the one-to-one mapping. It is still built on the channel-strip metaphor but enables a smaller interface as a user can scroll through the tracks. It thus allows for much more possibilities but demands more effort from the user, while it also might be harder to learn and control in a live situation [10].

The general channel-strip metaphor has furthermore been the standard way of implementing a mixing interface in different Digital Audio Workstations (DAWs).

Contrary to a mixer based on the channel-strip metaphor, either physical or digital, the stage metaphor/paradigm is a popular way of representing sound sources in a stereo field. In the stage metaphor, the level and stereo position (and possibly other parameters) are modified using the position of a movable icon on a 2D or 3D image of a stage [7] as seen in Fig. 9.1. This metaphor was first proposed by Gibson, who called it a 'virtual mixer' [12]. Even though the stage metaphor mostly uses one-to-one mapping in terms of volume and panning, it also incorporates one-to-many mappings, as the position of each sphere as an example can affect both the volume but also filtering and reverb in relation to the distance as mentioned earlier [7].

Both mixing metaphors come with drawbacks usability-wise. Firstly, it is obvious that when using several tracks on the original channel-strip mixing console, it can be hard to visualise and get an overview of the different tracks—all tracks that are panned to the left will as an example not necessarily be controlled by the faders and pan potentiometers on the left side of the mixer. This is easier in the stage metaphor, where each source is graphically visualised in a 3D space. However, the stage metaphor suffers from organisational consequences as all tracks are scattered around the virtual room. With the channel-strip metaphor, each audio channel is always located in the same place, which makes it easy to find and control [10].

As mentioned by Gibson, the way humans perceive sound, besides physical sound waves and directional cues, is by imagining sounds between two speakers [12]. 'Imaging' works as a substitute of actually seeing the source that produces the sound [12]. Mixing engineers use both sound pressure as a perceptional tool when mixing, but also imagination, as it allows the engineer to create a wide range of dynamics [12], through the likes of asymmetric panning or uneven volume relationships, when visually placing sound sources 'between' the speakers [12]. Especially here the stage metaphor and the general visual representation thereof serves as a helping tool and underlines the importance and usefulness of VR in such a connection.

## 9.2  Audio-Visual Interaction

Vision is an important element in sound localization. As stated by Yantis and Abrams [28] and extensively discussed in Chap. 10, when conflicting information about sound localisation is given to both the auditory and visual system, the visual information dominates the perception. This effect, called *ventriloquism effect*, makes the person perceive the sound coming from the location determined by the visual system.

There are, however, three factors that can bias the visually perceived location [24]:

- The visual and auditory events must be close in time. Ideally, the visual event should happen before the auditory event.
- The events should be plausibly linked. In other words, the sound must be something that could have come from the visual source.
- The visual and auditory events must be plausibly close together in space. An example of this is if the sound is played through headphones, but the visual source is located behind the wall, you are likely to perceive the sound coming from the headphones and not the visual source.

In a study by Tabry, et al. [26] subjects were asked to localise a sound source by either pointing in the direction with their head or hand. There were two conditions: one where they were blindfolded, one where they were not. The results showed that the subjects were able to better localise sound on the horizontal axis than the vertical. Moreover, the subjects localised the sound more accurately when not blindfolded. This supports Abrams and Yantis' statement that humans, in some way, rely on both visual and auditory stimuli when it comes to sound localisation.

Furthermore, it was stated by Tabry, et al. that the results suggest a greater dependence on visual cues for orienting one's head towards a specific location in space than for orienting one's arm [26]. It can be argued that this fact supports the use of VR when mixing spatial audio as it gives the user visual feedback of the sound localisation.

## 9.3 Designing Computer Music in VR

While there has been a lot of investigation in the world of designing VR for computer music, especially within the field of Virtual Music Instruments (VMI) and New Interfaces for Musical Expression (NIME) [16], little focus has been on graphically representing mixing, mastering and audio effects processing. With VR defined as an immersive artificial environment experienced through technologically simulated sensory stimuli [25], there is no doubt that this, combined with VR's inclusion of multidimensional spaces and free rotation/movement, enables the possibility of visually placing, moving and mixing sound sources in a 3D space. Concerning VMIs, Perry Cook states that copying an instrument is dumb, leveraging expert technique is smart [6]. This principle is, in particular, relevant to interfaces in VR as its visual qualities and lack of physical limitations can be used as a tool and paired with external applications like DAW or real-world speaker systems. The following section will focus on the aspects that might facilitate this and outline important guidelines for designing a VE for sound synthesis and mixing. The most important principles will include technological considerations such as latency and cybersickness, interaction types and possibilities, modelling sound in a physical space, as well as the overall graphical representation of the system.

### 9.3.1 Technology

There are multiple aspects to consider when designing virtual spaces and applications in VR in general, such as ensuring smooth interactivity through minimum latency as well as by preventing cybersickness. In a real-world modelling ideal it is preferable with a latency of 15 ms or less, when moving a head or object to see a new and corrected view of the scene. However, a lot of the head mounted displays (HMDs) only achieve a latency of 30 ms [21]. Getting as close as possible to the latency limits is important as synchronisation between the arrival of stimuli in different modalities is known to influence the perceptual binding that occurs in response to an event producing multimodal stimulation [17]. As individual senses in a virtual world still are not represented independently, synchronised audiovisual feedback is not only important as it serves as a response to a user's actions, it also creates a bridge between an activity and its given sound [17]. In 1998, Miner and Claudel [19] investigated the sensitivity of delay of auditory stimulus in multimedia applications. According to their analysis, requirements for sound-synthesis simulation of environmental effects like reverberation, Doppler Shift, and the generation of 3D sounds are at least 66 ms. It is thus clear that high latency when manipulating sound in a virtual 3D space will affect both the user experience and the overall perception of sound. Latency is as earlier mentioned believed to increase cybersickness, which also is affected by aspects such as display flicker and wrong calibrations. To prevent cybersickness, especially in an environment dealing with movement and placement of virtual objects, one-to-one mapping between virtual and real translations/rotations is advisable, as the vestibular system, in particular, is sensitive to such motion [25].

## 9.3.2   Interaction

Considering the interaction in a VR system, categories within the field of both user-orientation and user experience have to be examined. To fulfil good interaction in computer music interfaces, the musician, computer scientist, and designer Ge Wang suggests that the system amongst other things should [27]:

1.  Be real-time if possible.
2.  Design sound and graphics in tandem and seek salient mappings.
3.  Hide technology and focus on substance.
4.  Introduce arbitrary constraints.

In general, this means that interaction with sound sources should be easy, quick, streamlined and noticeable and that virtual objects need to match location and motion of auditory objects. Simultaneously, the user should not be confronted with technology or implementation, to increase excitement and interest. Another thing that will support the user's interest, but also immersion and virtuosity, is feedback. Various studies state that especially haptic and tactile feedback allows a user to develop musical skills and understanding of controls [25]. Inclusion of external controls that allow for touch or vibrational feedback thus could be beneficial. Gelineck et al. investigated this by comparing the stage metaphor (iPad App visualising a stage) to the channel-strip metaphor (normal faders and panning) when completing a stereo mix [11]. While they concluded that there was no significant difference in terms of performance, the iPad application was user experience-wise preferred for its intuitiveness, enjoyability and its ability to reveal the spaciousness of the mix [11]. They, however, outline a side effect of representing the mix visually, with the fact being that it might take away focus from listening. It thus is important to find the right balance of the graphical representation and haptic/tactile feedback, in order to keep the focus on the main aspects: mixing and listening to sound.

Using the strengths of VR will possibly improve this interaction. As mentioned by Serafin et al. it is believed that virtual reality shows the greatest potential when facilitating experiences that cannot be encountered in the real world [25]. This leads to the principle of considering natural and magical interaction in the system. The principle suggests that combining natural interaction (normal feedback to real-world movements) with magical interaction (interaction that is not limited by real-world constraint as flying and teleporting) will open up for new and non-traditional interaction possibilities for already realised interfaces [25].

### 9.3.3 Sound in Space

Looking at the space in which the sound will be virtually presented, VR has several possibilities as introduced in Chaps. 1 and 6. Sound itself will in different physical spaces be shaped by the room's spectral characteristics and modified by room properties such as size, material, and shape. One can choose different methods when employing the models of spatialisation to the virtual rooms adjustment of the sound. Robert Hamilton distinguishes between two main models: the user-centric perspective and the space-centric perspective [14]. In the user-centric perspective, the sound will be manipulated from a first-person point of view, where sounds in the virtual world will correspond to a real-world-based model of hearing: they will be placed in a general aural spectrum known from the everyday, with corresponding depth cues implemented through filtering and delay. This can be done by tracking the coordinate distance between event locations and the user's in-game avatar [14]. The space-centric perspective, on the other hand, shifts the focus to the sound itself correlated between the virtual and physical world. In this model, sounds are no longer contextualised based on their proximity and relationship to a given user [14]. Instead, they are processed in relation to both the virtual and physical world, meaning the placement in each environment (as an example a spatialised speaker system) will affect it. This allows for multiple users and a communal experience [14]. In relation to the user-centric perspective, Gödde et al. [13], with a focus on the cinematic narration in VR, describe two possible 'user-centric' roles: a passive role, where the viewer is only an observer with no connection to the scene [13]—here the experience is more laid back and requires lower involvement resulting in focus on narration and the environment, and an active role where the viewer is part of the scene [13]—here the experience is involving resulting in a higher potential of presence that however might take focus away from narration and environment [13].

Besides handling the geometrical aspects of a virtual room, such as a sound source's spectral position and distance from the listener, it is also necessary to include a simulation of the acoustics of the given room. This will ensure a VR application that realistically represents the perception of sound. As stated by Falch et al. incorporating room simulation in binaural sound reproduction systems is important to improve localization capabilities as well as out of head localizations [30], which undoubtedly indicates the importance of acoustics when replicating binaural sound.

## 9.3.4  Graphical Interface

In relation to the graphical and visual representation of objects and environment in a 3D world, Wang proposes four aesthetic principles [27]:

1. Simplify: Identify core elements, trim the rest
2. Animate, create smoothness, imply motion: it is not just about how things look, but how they move
3. Be whimsical, organic: glow, flow, pulsate, breathe: imbue visual elements with personality
4. Aesthetic: have one; never be satisfied with 'functional'.

Since it is known that spatial audio approaches tend to facilitate interaction that is intuitive and familiar, the above principles are important as they can further enhance this. Especially the characteristics of simple and organic elements, as well as animating smooth motion of objects, will increase the user experience. This can as an example be done through the addition of shader programs as they aim to make virtual objects similar to their real counterpart, as shape, behaviour and appearance [18]. Shader programs are mainly used for the adjustment of a scene's illumination, post-processing or special effects [18], and the two most known shader types are Vertex shaders: the process that performs the transformations of vertices and texture coordinates from object space to window space, and, fragment shaders: A pixel shader that takes care of how the pixels between the vertices look [22].

Besides the principles of Wang, Gale et al. furthermore suggest that one especially should avoid visual clutter, meaning too many objects potentially overlapping and/or occluding each other on the screen [29]. As a part of object cluster and general control, Serafin et al. state that it additionally can be enhanced by visually representing the player's body [25]. People cannot see their own body in VR and this can be overcome by generating a visual substitution of a person's real body seen from first-person perspective. This will create a visual illusion and result in a 'virtual body ownership', which allows users to get the necessary presence that successful feedback requires [25]. However, different visual representations of the body will create different interaction expectations. A realistic representation of hands has as an example proven to create a more natural interaction experience than the given system allowed [2]. Thus the appearance of the virtual representation and the expectations it produces is important to consider.

## 9.4  Existing Mixing Interfaces

Different programs that have been created and used for mixing audio for 3D will be examined in this section. The focus will be on the implementation, design, and usability of the systems. Furthermore, features and standards of the existing programs will be examined in order to find inspiration and reach a state-of-the-art level for this project's product.

'Auro Technologies'[1] is a company that aims to create the next generation audio standard by becoming the leader in state-of-the-art sound. They offer a product that can be used in the game and film industries as well as for mobile and automotive industries . This is made possible with AAX plugins, which allow the user to mix for a 11.1 system where the approach is to treat different elevation angles as layers, 'lower', 'height', and 'top'. Through algorithms, the audio is backward compatible with 5.1 and 7.1 systems.

The plugin offers an overview of where each speaker is located in a 3D space as well as displaying modifiable parameters, such as depth of reverb, bass and treble equaliser, and volume of the sound.

While mixing, each individual audio track in the session has a relevant plugin inserted. These plugins include 'Auro-Panner', 'Auro Bus', 'Auro-Mixing Engine', and the 'Auro-return'. The Auro-3D system is thus comprised of several plugins which, furthermore, requires a processor called 'A3DHost' to be running in the background while working with Auro plugins, as well as 'Auro-Dmix Control' in order to down-mix the bounce to a specific format.

Objectively, the approach of Auro-3D can be problematic as it may require a significant number of plugins to be running at the same time in a large project, which will affect the processing power. A powerful computer is therefore needed for it to be used with low latency. Simultaneously, one might argue that it is troublesome and counter-intuitive to individually place several plugins on each audio channel. An additional downside to this product is that it only works with Pro Tools, and only on Mac computers , which can eliminate a large number of potential users.

However, the product is still used heavily in the industry , and has won multiple awards.[2] Especially the design of it is important to have in mind when it comes to the product of this project. Even though it requires multiple plugins on each individual audio channel, the plugins have a clear user interface that highlights affordances and uses signifiers and feedback to give the user an understanding of what can be adjusted and modified. An example is the effects controls. Firstly, they are designed to look like knobs with labels above them to signify what each knob controls.[3] Additionally, there is feedback in the middle of the knobs to show which value they are set to, which furthermore is highlighted with lights around them to show where on the rotation axis they are set. This light also visualises in which range the knobs work and their boundaries in both directions. Some sliders control the volume of both the sound source and the amount of the reverb, which is a common way to control volume when working with audio. Even though the interface is not in 3D, it can be seen that Wang's aesthetic principles (Sect. 9.3.4) are relevant. Only essential settings for the volume and reverb are visible and modifiable (simplification), the sliders have value

---

[1] https://www.auro-3d.com.

[2] https://www.auro-3d.com/about-us/mission/.

[3] Knobs are commonly used on audio-related products and mixers.

feedback and the knobs have both value and light feedback (animation), which gives the interface and its controls a simple design that is easy to get an overview of.

Another product, although not commercialised, was made by Wakefield and Gale [9]. Their product was created in a research on how to solve perceptional problems in the 3D stage paradigm/metaphor when it comes to mixing audio. When more audio tracks are added, the visualisation can soon become cluttered, which causes problems in relation to depth perception that will be limited, leading to difficult interaction [9]. Furthermore, they wanted to minimise the risk of 'gorilla arm', which is a term referred to when users keep their arm elevated for a long period of time [5, 9]. Wakefield and Gale created an environment in VR for mixing audio. The system allows multiple options for adjusting each audio signal. There are send-effects control, filters, equaliser, volume, and pan parameters. All this is controlled with one controller. According to their studies, the VR mixing interface may have helped with depth perception of the audio. However, it did not improve clutter and object occlusion [9]. It may be reasonable to think that the UI of the program has affected those problems. Only one audio track is in the environment but the effect controls fill out almost the whole screen. So, even though the necessary parameters are present and no mentioning from participants of them being problematic, the displaying and arrangement of them might be something to keep in mind when designing the UI for the product of this project. With Wang's aesthetic principles in mind, it is clear that the interface is neither simplified nor aesthetic.

Dear Reality is a German company which specialises in creating 'ultimate tools for immersive 3D audio production'.[4] They offer multiple products under the name 'dearVR' for game engines, controllers, and DAWs. The 'dearVR Pro' product offers full 360° manipulation of sound with built-in acoustics and reflections controls

## 9.5   Target Group

Since this project aims to develop an aid for mixing spatial audio in VR, the user is expected to have previous experience in mixing audio but not necessarily spatially. This will allow the user to be aware of the given possibilities that a product facilitating spatial mixing gives (panning, volume change in depth, filtering as a result of elevation), but still explore the product as an entity. The product thus can be targeted at different groups ranging from game developers wanting to quickly sketch an audio-based atmosphere for their in-game environment, to music composers mixing spatialised audio for surround sound or VR applications and experimental musicians wanting to explore the use of 3D sound.

Since VR offers sensory feedback and spatial proportions differently to a desktop application, and since it is known that programs using the stage metaphor are intuitive (see Sect. 9.3.2), an everyday use of the end product could target composers and producers, that eventually might need a quick and easy assisting tool for the audio

---

[4] https://www.dearvr.com.

spatialisation process, be it music for film, sound design or audio for games. With this scenario in mind, the target group, therefore, covers both hobby producers, semi-professional producers as well as professional mixing engineers and composers, etc.—as long as they are familiar with mixing. To further understand the needs of a producer or composer mixing music for spatial media, an expert interview was conducted. An extensive questionnaire was sent to audio engineer Gestur Sveinsson, from the recording studio 'Studio Syrland' in Reykjavik, in order to get his opinions on necessities when mixing audio spatially. Having worked with surround sound for both cinema and music, Sveinsson notes the importance of having touchscreen mixing tools that allow him to quickly and intuitively translate his idea into reality. He furthermore adds that a visualisation tool for audio placement indeed would make sense as long as it is based on the idea of analog faders and panning knobs. In relation to his personal workflow, Sveinsson states that he visually sees the angles of the sound sources on a screen and arranges the mix without having to turn his head towards the angles that a given sound is coming from. Nonetheless, he thinks that a face tracking system would be useful and especially from a consumer point of view, it could make the experience 'hyper-realistic'. In relation to his personal preferences, he rates the aesthetics and design as well as the intuitiveness, and thus the time it takes to do a mixing task, as very important aspects in a mixing device, whereas the precision of it comes secondary.

With this knowledge in mind, the virtual mixing tool thus will be implemented using the research information above to target composers or producers that can use the mix both quickly, intuitively and precisely.

## 9.6   Conceptual Overview

The user is placed in a 3D VR environment where different tracks from Ableton Live are represented as spherical sound sources in space with belonging labels. A ray is cast from the user's controllers to signify which sound source one interacts with. If the ray is positioned on a sound source, the controller will respond with vibration to signify contact between the ray and a sound source. After selecting a sound source, the user can now move it in space. Data on position, distance, and angles will be passed into Max by Cycling 74 where the auditory placement in space will happen. This will result in the visual locations, as well as the auditory locations of the objects to match, and give an audiovisual experience in space as well as create a tool for users to visually place and mix different sound sources spatially.

## 9.7   Virtual Environment

To keep the centre of attention on the sound source's spatial proportions, the environmental setting will consist of very few props being a stage and virtual objects linked to audio tracks. It has been decided to design and model a stage-like environment

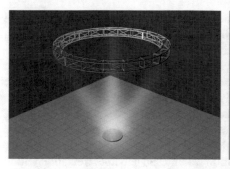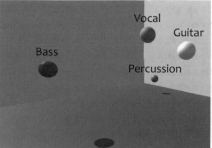

**Fig. 9.2** Sketch of the design in its initial stage

as the main aspect of the surroundings, as this might elicit the stage metaphor and the virtual mixer as explained by Gibson in the analysis. This will allow the user to manually place objects in space with respect to a realistic and intuitive behaviour of the sound sources in the scene, like changing size according to distance or lighting up when pressed. Design-wise, it has been decided to develop an environment where the user is centralised in the scene on a slightly elevated cylindrical surface, to emphasis its role as a mixer/positional conductor. A circular truss will be positioned above the user (Sect. 9.7.1) to further highlight the 'stage' look. An illustration of both the initial design of the stage, truss as well as sound sources depicted as spheres is shown in Fig. 9.2.

To focus on the 'substance' principle, the scene will consist of: (i) A simple yet aesthetic environment to focus on the importance of the mixing task. (ii) The different objects' relations to the localisation of sound. (iii) Picturing spheres around a stage, to use the benefits of the stage metaphor like 'intuitiveness, enjoyability and its ability to reveal the spaciousness of the mix', as earlier stated by Gelineck et. Al (Sect. 9.3.2). To keep an aesthetically pleasing, yet simple design that guides the user's attention to the mixing task rather than the visuals, it has been decided to avoid scenes with myriad different elements such as concert halls and theatre stages, as this might take focus away from listening. To further enhance the feeling of spaciousness within the environment, it has been decided to use a 'grid-like' structure on walls, floors and ceilings. This is, as seen in the state-of-the-art section (Sect. 9.4), a widely used technique to display and give the user a sense of dimensions and will automatically create spatial constraints as it outlines the boundaries of the room, giving possible distance limits in relation to sound source placement. These constraints are furthermore supported by the truss, which represents the outer boundary of object placement—the user cannot place sound sources outside of the truss area.

An aspect that is widely used especially within cinematic VR, also called 360° videos, is the use of cues to guide the user's attention, as the user can freely rotate its head and thus choose the field-of-view (FoV) [20]. Whereas these cues normally focus on storytelling and narration, cues like implicit diegetic cues are also applicable within this exact environment. Implicit diegetic cues are factors like objects or props within the scene that implicitly guide the user to do something [20]. This is, as an example, seen in the truss acting as an environmental constraint as mentioned above—the truss is a barrier signifying the limitation of object placement and thus forcing the user to re-orientate. The sound sources themselves are furthermore important implicit diegetic cues as they give the user a sense of their placement and space when the user has to redirect attention. The sound sources act between being onscreen and off-screen diegetic cues according to when they are present within the FoV [4]. As the spheres serve as spatial guidance, both their look, sound, and feel are of high importance when it comes to attention leading and general orientation within the environment. In relation to this, it has, as an example, been chosen to make the different sound sources light up when hovered over by the user, as this gives the user a better overview of the mix, as well as avoiding confusion by changing colour when something is 'soloed'—the act of isolating a sound.

As mentioned, these cues simply affect the FoV and thus also the 'user-centric perspective' that manipulates the sound from a first-person point of view and contextualises it to the position of the user. The placement of the camera, which also serves as the perspective of the user, therefore has to match the general viewing position. This will be done in Unity using the camera as the viewpoint. For the vertices and fragments of objects and shaders, the 'user-centric perspective' will be handled using the 'object to clip' node, which transforms a position in object/local space to the camera's clip space.

### 9.7.1  Rendering and Lighting

The 'Lightweight Rendering Pipeline' (LWRP) in Unity will be applied to render the scene and its light. Since the Oculus Quest used is dependent on its hardware, the LWRP will be optimal as it targets a broad range of mobile platforms, VR and games with limited real-time light capabilities.[5] By making a few trade-offs in relation to lighting and shadows, like fewer draw calls, the LWRP optimises the real-time performance of the system thus allowing for uncomplicated real-time processing and salient functional mappings, which was mentioned as important design requirements.

In relation to the lighting within the scene, general directional lighting is used to illuminate the environment. The lighting was chosen to be coloured to add to the atmosphere within the scene. Coloured lights were simultaneously used as decoration within the scene, where bars in red and blue represent LED strips. The emission of white rings on the walls and in the surface additionally adds light to the scene and through global illumination, surface reflections were simulated. To enhance the 'stage aesthetics' even further, coloured fog was included, as fog is usually experienced within concert experiences.

---

[5] https://docs.unity3d.com/Packages/com.unity.render-pipelines.lightweight@4.0/manual/index.html.

## 9.7.2   Interaction

The VR system contains three main interaction types and their respective feedback, including visual and auditory feedback, which is a combination that reinforces a user's given action, meaning that the user both sees and hears the results of the actions made. The different interactions and their feedback, as pictured in the conceptual overview above can be explained as:

- Touch/haptic interaction: the selection and manipulation of the different sound objects will constitute the haptic interaction. Here the user is allowed to touch/ select, by pressing a button and move, by moving its arm, the different objects.
- Visual feedback: an object will light up corresponding to it being clicked/ selected, and move corresponding to the user's force and arm movement. The visuals are thus designed with a focus on natural mapping as the sound sources, with respect to their auditory perception, are placed where they would be placed in a real-world situation.
- Auditory feedback: the panning and the volume of the chosen sound source will change accordingly to the placement of the object both on the horizontal axis (azimuth) and depth (distance).
- Tactile feedback: vibration will happen when the user hovers over an object to signify its allowance of being selected. This is to help the user find and aim at the desired object.

To sum up, it can be said that the visual feedback of the haptic interaction facilitates the stage metaphor and virtual mixer analogy, as sound sources are positioned in space relative to the user, whereas the auditory feedback facilitates the binaural synthesis and combine the interplay of visual and auditory cues used in human perception. The tactile feedback, on the other hand, constitutes increased usability of the product and the potential of the user to, within the environment, gain skills and understanding of the different controls. Additionally, it acts as a substitute of the mixing console, which as earlier mentioned also is a tangible controller. How the user scrolls through the audio tracks, and visually as well as auditory pans and levels them, is now an integrated part of the VE, rather then the mixing console.

## 9.7.3   Shaders and Visual Appearance

In Fig. 9.4, the visual appearance of the final environment is shown. This design was reached from aesthetic and stylistic ideas received from different scenarios seen in the mood-board below. Inspired by the 'stage metaphor', spheres were used as sound sources, instead of objects picturing the actual instrument/object the sound source is coming from. This was done to avoid unrealistic representations of the sound sources, which potentially could create user aversion and additionally introduce latency problems for the Oculus Quest. The spheres were furthermore chosen as

**Fig. 9.3** Inspirational mood-board for visual appearance and colours

the main audio representation as they could constitute an abstract feeling to the very artistic subject that music and mixing is, as well as being used in products such as the dearVR (Fig. 9.3).

As seen in the mood-board, the colours blue and red, as well as the effect of lasers serve as a big inspiration for the look of both the environment and the shaders.

### 9.7.4  Audio Design

For the audio, head related impulse responses (HRIR) from MIT were used.[6] The pack includes IRs ranging from −40° to +90° on the vertical axis where each elevation had their own IR for the azimuth (5 degrees between each IR). Each IR was measured at a distance of 1.4 m. As this pack consists of 710 different IRs, the computation would both be heavy and complicated and, therefore, it was decided to evaluate whether it was needed to implement the IRs for elevation, as humans have perceptual difficulties placing audio on the vertical axis.

#### 9.7.4.1  Can We Remove Auditory Elevation Cues?

A total of 14 participants were gathered for the evaluation, which was set up at Aalborg University in Copenhagen. The participants were informed of the research question *'Do you feel like the sound is matching the position of the object?'* before the test started and asked to answer either 'yes' or 'no', with the option to hear the

---

[6] https://sound.media.mit.edu/resources/KEMAR.html.

sound again, if needed. Additionally, they were encouraged to focus on a sphere centred in the middle of the screen, but they were allowed to look around.

The threshold of accuracy was set to 80% for scenes with no elevation, and 50% for scenes with elevation. There was no audio manipulation (volume change, filtering) for the elevation. The results showed that 91.4% of the participants felt that the audio matched the position of the object with 0° elevation and 95.2% felt the audio matched the object's position when it was elevated.

The results from this evaluation show that having visual cues for the audio source made the audience interpret the sound to originate from the visible object. Even though no audio manipulation took place regarding elevation, overwhelming majority perceived the audio to be elevated. Therefore, it was decided to not implement the HRIRs for the elevation, and instead, sound design-wise only relies on azimuth and distance cues.

Even though no audio manipulation was implemented for this particular test, it is important to implement acoustics manipulation relevant to the environment. This relates both to volume change based on distance (Inverse-square law) and reverberation based on the dimensions of the room. Both reverb and low-pass filtering will, therefore, be added to change timbral properties and give the sound an applicable aspect of room acoustics. The properties will be applied based on subjective sound-aesthetics and not by using physical models.

### 9.7.5   Summarising Design

Conclusively, to keep the attention of the user focused on the sound sources location, the VR will consist of very few props consisting of a stage and virtual sound sources. The stage metaphor, as well as a grid shader for walls and floor, is used to reveal the spaciousness of the mix as well as the VR. Other shaders, such as a fresnel effect, are used to signify user action as well as provide aesthetic value. Using theory from cinematic VR, sound sources can be considered on- and off-screen diegetic cues, guiding the user's attention, while the view facilitates an active user-centric perspective. To optimise the performance of the system the rendering pipeline 'LWRP' is used, while it also was decided to keep the lighting of the scene relatively simple. A combination of haptic, visuals, auditory and tactile feedback is used to enhance usability. Spheres were chosen to represent sound sources to constitute an abstract aspect of audio mixing and imaging as explained by Gibson. Based on the conducted evaluation of perception of elevation, showing that an overwhelming majority perceived auditory elevation based on visual feedback only, it was decided to only implement HRIRs for azimuth. Simple acoustics manipulation will furthermore be applied to simulate distance of sound sources. An illustration of the final environment, including colours, shaders and lighting can be seen in Fig. 9.4.

**Fig. 9.4** Final design of the environment

## 9.8 Implementation

The implementation of the interactive VR environment and its inclusion of dynamic binaural synthesis consists of different steps and programs:

1. Firstly, a combination of the Oculus Quest system and the game engine Unity will be used to create a 3D environment that allows the user to manipulate and position objects within a virtual space. Support for VR in Unity will be imported through asset store items, in this case, Oculus Integration is used.[7]
2. Secondly, object coordinates, angles and user head rotation, will be implemented and retrieved based on different scripts. This will be sent through Open Sound Control (OSC) to Max via User Datagram Protocol (UDP) connection. An additional Unity asset store item called 'OSC simpl' is here used.[8]
3. Finally, Max and its live integration with Ableton Live will execute real-time sound rendering and binaural synthesis, through a convolution process of different HRIRs related to the respective sound object angles.
4. The communication between Unity and Max will furthermore be emphasised, as the track/audio names from Ableton Live will be displayed as part of the sound sources in the VR environment. This will additionally be implemented through OSC communication.

UDP is a connectionless communication protocol used across the Internet, especially for time-sensitive transmissions and is considered a quick communication protocol, as it allows data transfers before the receiving party agrees to the commu-

---

[7] https://assetstore.unity.com/packages/tools/integration/oculus-integration-82022.

[8] https://assetstore.unity.com/packages/tools/input-management/osc-simpl-53710.

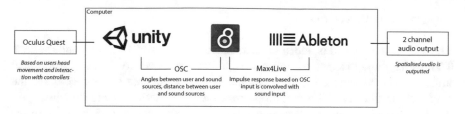

**Fig. 9.5** Illustration of the system

nication.[9] OSC is, likewise, a protocol especially for networking sound synthesisers and computers. It uses UDP to transfer data within local subnets and is thus an obvious protocol for UDP communication. An overview of the different stages, systems and software used can be seen in Fig. 9.5:

The process of representing real-time audio spatialisation is done using a range of scripts developed to ultimately pass the necessary information from Unity to Max to create a spatialised mix.

### Convolution

The convolution of the incoming signal and the signal of the different HRIRs is done in the frequency domain using the `pfft ~` object. The `pfft~` object essentially is a processing manager that splits the FFT process into smaller tasks, each taking care of their own FFT process.

### Distance Simulation

While it earlier was confirmed that humans have a hard time distinguishing between elevations of sound, especially being accompanied by a visual object, the simulation of distance is easy to perceive and important both in relation to the display and localisation of sounds. In this project, it has been decided to use the Inverse-square law to simulate distance. In relation to the difference of sound in each ear, due to the acoustic shadow of the head, this project only takes the interaural time difference (ITD) and sound intensity in space into consideration. The frequency dissimilarity and the ITD at longer distances (the ITD is covered through the HRIRs at closer distances) are thus not considered. This has been decided due to the fact that spectral cues at shorter distances (10 m) are insignificant and that sound has to travel more than 100 m for frequencies around 4kHz to be attenuated 7 dB [1].

---

[9] https://www.howtogeek.com/190014/htg-explains-what-is-the-difference-between-tcp-and-udp/.

**Integration With Ableton**

The Max patch created is added to each audio track in Ableton as an audio effect. The azimuth and distance for left and right ear are shown to the user. Additional information is visualised for the user such as the *wet* amount of the reverb and the cutoff of the filter used. From a drop-down menu, the user can choose which port this track should listen to. This ensures that the same patch can be used for all the tracks and only the port has to be changed. Additionally, the IRs are read in and when loaded, they are automatically applied to all active patches in the Ableton project.

## 9.9  Creating the Computer Version

As earlier mentioned, a computer version was created for comparison purposes with the VR version. It has been decided to compare the VR version to its 'computer screen' counterpart, as this will put the possible advantages of the VR version in focus and thus not be influenced by aspects such as look or controls. The computer version of the final product was created to be as similar to the VR version as possible, however, there are some key differences when it comes to how the interaction is carried out. A ray is cast to wherever the mouse cursor is placed in the scene. When holding right-click, camera rotation is enabled, and the camera rotates based on mouse movement to imitate the camera interaction of the VR version. The 'track' object is 'grabbed' by hovering the mouse cursor over an object and holding left-click, whereafter it is possible to move and place the grabbed object by using the keyboard keys 'W-A-S-D'. A combination of left- and right-click makes the grabbed object follow the camera rotation.

The environment in the scene uses the same exact objects, coordinates and other visual aspects to eliminate any bias against or towards any of the two versions in this aspect. However, there are some small differences, because of different hardware, like display colours and refresh rate.

## 9.10  Evaluation

The following evaluation presents the setting, procedure and results of both the final focus group interview and mixing task evaluation. The mixing task evaluation uses a t-test to investigate the relationship of precision and time used between a VR version of the program and computer screen version. This is done to examine whether or not the benefits of VR and its sensory inclusion, can be seen as an overall improvement when mixing spatial audio. The computer screen version thus acts as the control condition representing similar interaction, affordances and sensory stimuli that can be found when placing audio spatially on a computer screen. However, it is important to note, that it is not a specific resemblance of already existing products.

For the t-tests, the following two hypotheses are further evaluated:

- **H0**—The mixes made by the participants in the VR version have no difference or less relative precision to the reference mix, than the mixes made in the computer version.
- **H1**—The participants in the VR version, used less time on recreating the reference mix, compared to the computer version.


## 9.11  Setting and Procedure

Both the focus group interview and part of the mixing task evaluation took place at Aalborg University Copenhagen. The other part of the mixing test took place in an apartment in Nørrebro due to convenience of test participants. Twelve students and a professor from the 'Music Production Bachelor' of the 'Rhythmic Conservatory of Copenhagen' attended the focus group interview, whereas 24 participants with different musical backgrounds and mixing experience, took part in the mixing task evaluation.

The *focus group interview* was carried out after the 'Danish Sound Network' event 'Behind The Scenes' on the 2nd of December 2019, where each participant had tried the VR mixing program for at least 5 min, including instructions. During the trial, the participants were instructed to try out and notice different aspects such as free rotation, elevation, auditory feedback and visual appearance. After the possibility of giving individual oral feedback, a focus group interview was conducted. Here each participant had the possibility of discussing and evaluating different topics selected by the conductor, with each other. The focus group interview was carried out in informal surroundings and lasted for 55 min.

The *mixing task evaluation* was carried out over three days, from the 9th to 11th of December 2019. The evaluation took place in a separated room, where each participant tried both the VR version and the computer screen version of the program, in randomised order to avoid an experience bias. Both time and precision for each participant were computed. It is important to note that the precision of the participant mix in relation to the reference mix, is measured in units (in unity called metres). While the amplitude of sound normally decays logarithmically, the distance between sound sources close to the participant is of higher significance than sound sources farther away. Half a unit is, as an example, visually experienced as a bigger distance near the participant than for objects in the distance. The measure of precision should thus be seen as a relative unit of measurement and not a counterpart to objects in the real world.

The participants were clearly instructed that their only task was to recreate the given audio mix in each version and that they had an unlimited amount of time until they felt satisfied with the mix. In both cases, clear instructions and a poster showing the different controls were offered. The participants had time to familiarise themselves in each environment before they proceeded to the mixing task. The Oculus Quest VR-headset and a Macbook Pro were used for the VR and computer screen versions, respectively. The audio was routed from a separate computer through a pair of wireless AIAIAI TMA-2 headphones. The mixing task sessions lasted between 25–45 min for each participant, depending on the amount of time used on each mix.

## 9.12  Participants

Before the participants of the mixing task evaluation started, they were asked to answer a few questions regarding their musical/production/mixing background. These questions were used to ensure that the participants, and therefore the data gathered, matched the pre-defined target group; hobby producers, semi-professional producers, professional mixing engineers and composers (Sect. 9.5).

It could be seen that the majority of the participants had a lot of mixing experience, where 54.2% had 3+ years of experience, and of them, 41.7% had 5+ years of experience. The rest, 45.8% had 1–2 years of experience in mixing music. The same percentage was seen regarding their experience in mixing spatial audio (binaural, surround, ambisonic). The majority (54.2%) did not have any experience, whereas 45.8% had experience. Lastly, a question regarding whether or not the participants had tried VR before, was asked, where the majority had tried it before (83.3%).

## 9.13  Results

This section will focus on presenting the results from the evaluation. The section will be divided into three different sub-sections: Focus group interview (conducted with students from Rhythmic Conservatory of Copenhagen) and the mixing task evaluation including a post-evaluation survey.

### 9.13.1  Focus Group Interview

As mentioned, the first part of the evaluation consisted of a focus group interview. Below different quotes, opinions and summaries divided into themes and main topics are outlined, as discussed in the focus group interview. See appendix C for full interview transcription.

**Efficiency**

- 'I consider time. If it takes more or less time to do in VR. I don't know'.

- 'I could imaging that you would get done faster with some things. It seems very effective'.

The participants were asked about their initial thoughts regarding VR as a mixing tool and were all concerned of how efficient it potentially could be. Some participants felt that VR might be used as a quick sketching tool and compared it to a big brush painting on a canvas. Besides the concept of this project, it could be used as a more creative tool, rather than something one would use for precision.

**Environment**

- 'It could potentially set an atmosphere'.
- '... when I mix it is definitely something visual happening in front of me, I see the elements in front of me. It is not necessarily that I see the orchestra in front of me—it is much more abstract. A sprinkle over here, the sub-frequencies being another shape'.

It was stated that the virtual room could set a mood for the production by having different abstract elements. One participant pointed out that if the room should set a mood, it should be in a visually abstract way and not by looking realistic as this was the way he mixed mentally. It was furthermore stated that the decision of keeping the environment relatively neutral made sense in order not to influence the mix in an undesired direction and that the visuals used were pleasant and made sense in a mixing situation.

**Spatial Sound Algorithm**

- 'I found it slightly under-dimensioned so when you panned things to the side it was not as much as you would imagine. Front and back made sense well. When I panned something this much to the right I would also expect to hear it more to the right'.

One participant described the panning as being 'under-dimensioned', but in general the participants found the spatial algorithm satisfying. A few participants noticed the exclusion of elevation, whereas most participants felt the match between sound and source movement realistic.

**Features**

- 'It could also be used to do automation in a mix. ... You would have a much bigger area to draw on. I think that would be extremely useful'.
- '... they (objects) could have different shapes depending on if it is a string instrument or a wind instrument, or drums, or vocals'.
- 'Shouldn't the other button be mute?'
- 'I think it is necessary to know that there is activity on the track'.
- 'Put a number on the dB, like a gain volume'.

Multiple participants described how they could imagine using this tool to create automation. Having different visual representations of the different sound sources was also confirmed by several participants as well as having a visual representation of sound activity on each track as a VU-metre on mixers.

**Precision**

- 'In a DAW [it would be most precise]'.
- 'But also hard to say, when we only tried this a bit'.

There was a general consensus that a DAW was expected to be more precise than the implemented VR program. It was pointed out by one of the participants that it is hard to say when they have not spent more time using the VR program, but in general, the program, together with the binaural algorithm was experienced as something quick rather than precise. All participants agreed that the program gave enough information to make a judicious mix, but the concept made it hard to fiddle and go into small detail.

**Concept**

- '... I still think it suddenly is more about my experience mixing it instead of making an experience for others. And those two things can of course play well together, but I think I can install myself in a studio environment which helps me to get a good experience without a VR-headset'.
- '... it feels a bit more like you are going to play a game. In some parts of the process it might be a positive thing, I mean also more for composition'.
- 'I cannot accept that I have not decided what it is this movement does. ... I do not have any emotional connection to this'.
- 'I think as the program is right now it might work even better for people who do not have experience making music and have to learn to visualise music in an extremely intuitive way'.

A participant pointed out that he found the prototype to be useless for him since it was designed for spatial mixing and not directly suitable for exporting a stereo mix. He pointed out that the prototype seemed to be designed for the producer to have a good experience instead of the final listener to have a good experience. It was mentioned by one participant that the application would be more relevant to use if it at least included the functions of a large format console channel strip, for each audio track.

**Comfort in VR**

- 'I felt a bit sick. When I took of the glasses I felt really dizzy, but I think it is something you maybe have to get used to'.
- '(In the environment I could spend) 5–10 min or something like that'

One participant explained how he felt dizzy after using the prototype, while another participant imagined that he could not spend more than 5–10 min in VR. It was furthermore discussed by several participants whether switching between headset and screen was better than staying in VR. Both ideas were supported by other participants.

**Table 9.1** Mean and Std Deviation of Precision and Time across the two experimental conditions

|  | Precision (Unity units) | | Time (s) | |
|---|---|---|---|---|
|  | Screen | VR | Screen | VR |
| Mean | 35.74 | 35.60 | 558.38 | 448.04 |
| Std. dev. | 12.64 | 12.48 | 325.21 | 248.17 |

## 9.13.2 Mixing Task

Besides the focus group interview, the final evaluation consisted of a mixing task in two different versions. The means, standard deviations as well as histograms of the collected data for both time (in seconds) and sums of relative precision compared to the reference mix (in Unity units), are shown (Table 9.1).

The level of measurement of this evaluation is ratio data and since the study is using a within-group design, homogeneity of variance can be assumed without testing this. To test if the data is normally distributed an Anderson-Darling test is used on each data set for both precision and time.

For precision data, the results of the Anderson-Darling tests confirmed that the null hypothesis 'the data are normally distributed' should not be rejected, outputting p-values for screen version and VR version, respectively, $p = 0.4381$ and $p = 0.0693$.

For time data, the results of the Anderson-Darling tests showed that the null hypothesis 'the data are normally distributed' should be rejected, outputting p-values for screen version and VR version respectively, $p = 0.0005$ and $p = 0.0422$, meaning that the data is *not* normally distributed. The differences of the samples were also seen in the standard error, which is a measure of the sample reflects the population, in this case, 66.3 and 50.5, respectively. Additionally, the correlation coefficients describing the relationship between accuracy and time spent with the mixing task indicate no significant correlation, neither in VR ($r = -0.3$) nor in the PC version ($r = -0.2$).

Since only the data from the precision test is normally distributed and thereby fulfils all assumptions for parametric tests, t-tests will be used only on the precision data. The t-test does not reject the null hypothesis 'The mixes made by the participants in the VR version has no difference or less relative precision to the reference mix, compared to the computer version' with 95% confidence. A high p-value, ($p = 0.9531$) simultaneously shows that no significant differences between means are found.

It was mentioned by multiple test participants, that they had a significantly harder time spatially positioning the 'choir' track (a track in the pre-made mix) in the VR version, compared to the other tracks (discussed in Sect. 9.14). If the position of the 'choir' track is left out in the data sets, the t-test rejects the null hypothesis 'The mixes made by the participants in the VR version has no difference or less relative precision to the reference mix, compared to the computer version' with a 95% confidence level. It furthermore has a low p-value ($p = 0.0015$), meaning that

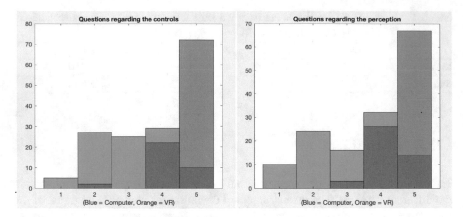

**Fig. 9.6** Results from the two different categories of questions. Left: Questions for the controls. Right: Questions for the perception

**Table 9.2** The means of the answers for each category and medium

|          | Controls | Perception |
|----------|----------|------------|
| Overall  | 3.917    | 3.917      |
| VR       | 4.708    | 4.667      |
| Computer | 3.125    | 3.167      |

a significant difference between means is found and that there is a small possibility that the difference between the groups happened by chance alone. Moreover, the effect size of the t-test result was calculated to be 0.16, which is a small effect.

As mentioned at the start of this section, a post-evaluation survey was carried out where the participants were asked to answer questions related to the two evaluated platforms. The results can be seen in Fig. 9.6, where all items addressing the same aspect have been added together. This was possible as the categories showed a Cronbach's alpha value of 0.81, meaning there is a good internal consistency, and thus reliability, within the answers [8]. Additionally, the mean of the answers, both overall for each category and separately for each medium is shown in Table 9.2.

## 9.14 General Discussion

The following section will discuss the results outlined in the result chapter above. It will examine the outcome of the t-tests and debate the opinions of the focus group interview.

## Precision and Effect of 'Choir' Track

As mentioned in Sect. 9.13.2, the results from the evaluation fail to reject the null hypothesis that the VR version has no difference or less precision compared to the computer version. Even though the mean of accuracy is **0.14** units lower in the VR version, the difference is so little that no conclusion can be made. However, it was seen that especially one audio track seemed to cause problems in the VR version, the 'choir' track. The mean of the accuracy of the 'choir' track in the computer version was **1.86** while being **9.95** in the VR version, a difference of **8.09**, even though the audio track being identical. There are a few things to consider why that may be the case.

In the computer version, the position of the 'choir' track in the reference mix was very close to the initial position of the visible 'choir' track, while in the VR version the 'choir' track was positioned behind the user and with greater distance. However, that can be said about some of the other audio tracks as well. Another explanation could be that the 'choir' track, even though being converted to mono, had different amplitude changes for each voice and the recording included a natural reverb. This could have made it difficult to perceive at what distance as well as angle the source was placed in the scene. Some participants mentioned this, saying they felt the choir track was in stereo which hindered them from correctly placing the audio track. They simultaneously added that it was hard to navigate as the track faded in and out, making it difficult to know whether or not it was playing. By removing the choir track from both scenes the mean accuracy of the computer version goes from **35.74** to **33.88** while the VR average goes from **35.60** to **25.63**. Furthermore, the removal of the choir from both versions results in the rejection of the null hypothesis with a 95% confidence as mentioned in Sect. 9.13.2. One might, therefore, consider the fact that the VR version statistically can be seen as being significantly more precise than the computer version.

## Efficiency

Another evaluated topic was whether the VR version was more efficient than the computer version. As mentioned in Sect. 9.13.2, the average time spent in VR was just under 2 min less than in the computer version. For the computer version furthermore, two outliers both spent just under 25 min. The time these outliners spent in the computer version does, however, not result in more accuracy as both were above the mean, **44.92** and **37.80**, respectively. However, even though it seemed that the participants on average were quicker in the VR version, there was no possibility of proving this statistically, as the data did not meet all of the parametric assumptions.

Looking at Fig. 9.6, its content might support the indication that VR, in this case, can be considered a quicker tool. Here it can be seen that the VR version scores significantly higher in regards to the controls and thus seemed more intuitive. Specifically, two questions stand out. Firstly, the question *'I felt comfortable using the controls in the computer version'* resulted in a completely split opinion as can be seen in Fig. 9.7.

**Fig. 9.7** Top: Question from post questionnaire regarding the comfortableness of the controllers in the computer version. Bottom: Question regarding the ease of placing sound sources in the computer version

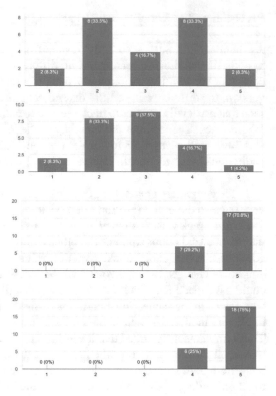

**Fig. 9.8** Top: Question regarding comfortableness of the VR controllers. Bottom: Question regarding the ease of placing sound sources in VR

Secondly, when asked *'In the computer version, the controls made it easy to place the visual sound sources (spheres) where I wanted them'* the majority were either neutral or felt the controls made it difficult, as shown on Fig. 9.7.

Since the participants struggled with placing the sound sources at the desired position, combined with finding the controls uncomfortable, it might have resulted in them taking longer time replicating the reference mix. Therefore, it cannot be concluded that VR is more efficient, however, the concept of the VR version hints towards a more instinctive way of working. The same questions for the VR versions resulted in *slightly agree* or *agree*, as shown in the figure (Fig. 9.8).

Another important aspect to consider for the time data is why it did not meet the parametric assumption of normality. The data of the time spent in the different versions by the participants simply was not symmetrically distributed around the mean in each version. In both scenarios, outliers were experienced and especially the VR version included widely spread data. These conclusions are supported by the standard deviation of each data set being **325.21** and **248.17** s respectively. The mean in each data set is thus not a good representative measure of the participants and looking at the standard error being **66.3** and **50.5** s for each distribution, it additionally is seen that the sample mean does not represent the population specifically well. Therefore, there could have been a missing correlation in the time spent by the participants and one might discuss whether the participants were enough alike to be considered a unified sample group/population. The experience in VR does not show any warning signs as almost everyone (83.3%) had tried it before. The questions then lie in whether or not mixing experience, as well as experience with and without spatial audio, could have affected the efficiency of the participants, creating a gap between their results. However, nothing supports this as 3 of the 5 outliers of time spent in VR had 5+ years of experience mixing music, which also was seen in 1 out of the 2 outliers in the computer version. Therefore, the whole test setup and the way that time is measured have to be reconsidered.

**Focus Group Interview**

Looking at the qualitative data from the focus group interview two main findings are clear: 1. The participants saw the product as a quick sketching tool to test ideas and outline mixes, rather than a tool to control precision and finer spatial details within the sound, and 2. The participants were overall positive about the interaction with the product and its visual appearance, sensory benefits and intuitive controls, which were generally well-received.

In relation to the first finding, several participants stated, just like the expert in the target group section, that time and intuitiveness, in general, was an important aspect for them in a mixing tool/device, and that the program indeed seemed to facilitate this. A participant expressed, amongst other things, that he 'could imagine that you would get done faster with some things', and that the program seemed 'very effective'. Furthermore, participants agreed that the VR program definitely could be used as a quick sketching tool for swift ideas and testing of audio placement in a given space. This could, amongst other things, have been a result of the intuitive way of placing sound sources as well as the quick dynamic sound feedback and the possibility to link it up with Ableton Live. However, it could also have been due to the simplicity of the environment and the fact that only fundamental controls, pre-made audio effects and interaction possibilities were included, giving it a 'to the bone' concept. Besides allowing positioning of sound sources (panning and volume), the program simply did not offer state-of-the-art possibilities such as the potential to manipulate the sound in finer detail, thus forcing the participant to use more time in the environment. This was moreover seen in the 'features' discussion of the interview, where participants emphasised a need for interactive dB scales, mute buttons and the possibility to 'do automation in a mix'. It is, therefore, clear that the opinion of the participants in the focus group interview, is somehow contradictory to the actual findings of the mixing task, which failed to show a significant time difference between the two conditions/programs. To understand this missing relationship, the post-evaluation survey as discussed above has to be taken into consideration. Besides the fact that the participants were overall satisfied with the interaction, it was clear in the opinion on the mixing task, that both the controls and the sensory feedback of the VR version made the experience easier, as well as more comfortable compared to the experience of spatially mixing audio on a computer screen. An aspect that, therefore, might have influenced the focus group participants' opinion on efficiency, could have been the general user experience—even though no statistical evidence showed that the participants were quicker in the VR program compared to the computer version. Using VR simply seemed like an intuitive and instinctive way of placing sound sources spatially, as it utilises both visual and auditory perceptional topics known from the everyday.

Contrary to the time data, there actually was a significant difference in the precision of the mixes in the two environments, which as mentioned to some extent conflicts with the thoughts of the focus group. It is important to note that the difference is statistically evident without the 'Choir' track, but there is no doubt that it does not match the expectations of the focus group, who did not experience the program as something specifically precise. When compared to the framework of a DAW, there was a general consensus that the environment made it hard to be exact, and few participants even saw this as a result of the under-dimensioned mappings distance- and angle-wise. This was, as an example, expressed in the quote 'I found it slightly under-dimensioned so when you panned things to the side it was not as much as you would imagine'. This may be the result of having $5°$ interval between IRs on the azimuth but could also just be the effect of the binaural HRIRs as they represent how sounds are naturally perceived instead of allowing for absolute panning.

The focus group had different opinions on the visual appearance of the environment, though the majority agreed that the neutrality of it was beneficial. Besides some participants mentioning that having the room aesthetics change relative to the mood of the music being mixed, the visualisation of the audio in the process of mixing was experienced to be subjective. Therefore, having pre-defined visuals and scenery might be more disadvantageous than beneficial. However, few participants mentioned that if the appearance should change, it should be unrealistic, abstract visuals since if it was too realistic it would be distracting.

As mentioned above, there were a few features lacking in the program. Firstly, colour coding tracks according to instruments, as well as making different shapes depending on instruments lacked. Secondly, participants uttered that having feedback or audio-reactive shaders on the spheres representing the tracks would help the user to understand when a track has sound on it. Suggestions for this were either a VU-metre for each audio track (as mentioned above) or having the spheres change shape relative to the sounds they represent, using frequency or timbre to manipulate vertices. Additionally, the focus group agreed that adding more tracks in the VR environment would introduce clutter problems. As they only worked with five tracks, having more potentially could eliminate the benefits of VR compared to PC. Related to this, amongst other things it was stated: 'When we tried it here it was very manageable with five tracks, but if you have 67 tracks as we talked about, it might hinder you more than it helps'. A suggestion for this was being able to group tracks, 'Things could also be grouped visually, then you could press "show all" or see this group or this part [like in layers]. In that way, you could visually mute something'—as found in digital mixing consoles mentioned in the analysis.

In relation to the concept, some participants struggled to grasp the core idea behind the product, spatial mixing. The fact that the mix changed relative to head movement confused many participants and hindered them in understanding the possibilities and functionality of it. As one participant said, 'I often ended up looking one way and then imagining that I mixed in stereo [...] this just made me feel that everything was in-precise'. Other mentioned that due to the lack of exporting it so the user could perceive it the same way, the product would be of no use, '...also the thing where the sound picture changes when you move. It is fun by itself but if it has to work in real life you have a dimension included that you do not have in the end'. The fact that they, in some way, did not seem to understand the thought process behind the product, could have resulted in them preferring to work in DAWs with traditional controls, which they were more comfortable with and, therefore, believe VR to be less accurate.

While it is apparent that recreating a mix in the VR version in some instances and for some instruments, was more precise than doing it in the computer version, the results of the evaluation show no statistical evidence that it was more efficient for the participants to work in the VR version compared to the computer version. These findings contradict the opinions of the focus group interview of experts within the field of music production, who experienced the VR program as a quick sketching tool for ideas and a spatial overview. The following discussion will debate these results, and look further into the design of the test and the fulfilment of the requirements made for this product and project.

Starting off by looking at the time data and the fact that the VR version was not more efficient than the computer version, it is important to consider the test setup and the way the researchers used time as a measurable variable. In the different test conditions, time was used as a dependent variable influenced by the independent variable being the two versions of the program. However, time simultaneously was of secondary importance, as the participants were told to recreate the mix until their satisfactory (until they thought they were precise enough). The amount of time used, and thus efficiency, was therefore not an explicit part of the mixing task and its validity as a measure, therefore, is debatable. Time was omitted from the task introduction as it was seen as a potential confounding variable of the precision measure, forcing the participants to slack on the mix recreation in order to get a quick time. Thus, it was hoped for time to represent the natural efficiency, however, the researchers did not reflect on the potential bias that could be within this, while designing the test—participants could as an example have had different visions about time, maybe they were busy or, contradictory, immersed using more time. Thus, in order for time to have been a valid measure, it might be argued that two tasks for each version should have been carried out: one with precision as seen in this evaluation, and one with time where the participants were asked to recreate the mix to their satisfaction as quickly as possible. This would have given efficiency a more prominent role and possibly made it a valid and streamlined measure.

Another aspect that could have been changed about the test setup was the methodology used. It initially was decided to use a one-way Repeated Measures ANOVA, with three conditions allowing the researchers to exclude the role of the controls in the test. Whereas the evaluation now only has the possibility to give indications about the role of the controls, the ANOVA test could have completely ruled this out, since a middle variable combing the two version was used for extra guarantee. Conclusions cannot, in fact, be made of the Likert scale in this post-evaluation, only indications can be drawn, and therefore the scale's relevance to the test as well as the connection to the opinions of the target group interview should be considered carefully.

The opinions of the focus group and whether or not these, in general, are representative, is additionally an aspect that should be discussed. It was, as a starting point, decided to only use participants in each evaluation process that were experienced with mixing sound in one way or another. It was seen that both participants in the focus group interview (counting music production students), as well as people in the mixing task (including 'Sound and Music Computing' students, tonmeister and sound engineer students as well as professional and hobby producers), fulfilled these requirements. Even though the two sample groups might have had different visions, they represent the target group and it is thus assumed that results and opinions can be compared. However, the target group definition might in the first place have been wrong. As mentioned by the focus group participants, who only saw the product as an easy and quick sketching tool, its intuitiveness could be beneficial for beginners, who might not care about fine detail nor the lack stereo features. It could thus have been interesting to see the feedback and mixing task results of potential music production newcomers with less experience, to see if the sensory benefits and intuitive interaction of VR, would make even more sense in a beginner situation.

Additional aspect mentioned by the focus group was difficulties grasping the idea of mixing binaural audio. Multiple participants discussed how the fact that the audio mix changed relative to the head movement made it difficult to understand how the final mix would sound like. Especially the fact that if the mix was exported, they could not ensure that the end-user would hear it in the same way the mixing engineer intended. This was largely due to the fact that many of the focus group participants were locked on the idea of stereo mixing. The lack of a clear 'centre' position was new to them, as they are used to mixing in a fixed position in front of two speakers. With that said, the focus group agreed with the fact that the product enabled the user to very quickly and efficiently place sound at its correct position in the 3D space, possibly more quickly than with a computer. A possible application of the product was, as mentioned by one participant, placing audio sources at a correct position when working with movie sound. However, the lack of tools available, such as EQ, the possibility of choosing their own reverb, etc. would hinder them with mixing and, therefore, the product would be more suitable as an audio placement tool rather than mixing tool. Therefore, it is worth considering whether mixing music binaurally is suitable for current platforms and perhaps the focus of the test should have been on placing audio sources in a 'correct' position relative to the visuals when investigating accuracy. Additionally, an aspect that was not taken into consideration during the implementation of this project was the FoV. It is plausible that having a different FoV, be it bigger or smaller, could have affected the impression of the IRs. In other words, had the FoV been bigger, angles such as 90° or 270° may have mismatched the audio and visuals. The same can be said with a smaller FoV. This may have been a reason a member of the focus group felt the spatial algorithm to be under-dimensioned as he stated 'When you panned things to the side it was not as much as you would imagine [...] When I panned something this much to the right I would also expect to hear it more to the right'. Even though no other comments were made regarding the 'spatialness' of the sound, this is worth keeping in mind and it, looking back, could have been beneficial to make initial tests investigating the right relationship between the FoV and the sound.

With regard to the final evaluation, some technical problems were experienced. The main problem happening when the user soloed an audio track. Almost every participant (some more than once during the test) encountered a problem where the audio track's shader indicated that the track was soloed when in fact it was not. It is believed that this was caused by interference in the OSC (UDP) transmission between the computer running Unity and the one running Ableton Live. The problem took place when a track was soloed in Unity, which triggered the corresponding track to be soloed in Ableton Live. When the track was then un-soloed in Unity which updated the shader, the track stayed soloed in Ableton which caused confusion for the participant. This problem was something that was experienced during initial testing of the program and a specific trigger was created in order for the evaluator to quickly change/repair the state of the audio track in Ableton Live. This problem was almost non-existent in the VR version and could, therefore, have been a thing that affected the time measure. No initial test of controls and interaction was conducted before the final evaluation, whereas the VR version and controls had been tested with the focus group. The controls for the computer were thus purely decided by the project group, which may have resulted in non-intuitive controls and interaction, as was backed up by the post-evaluation survey. An initial evaluation or pilot test of the computer controls should have been conducted to ensure a more fair comparison.

In relation to the technical aspects, it also is worth discussing whether or not the HMD used for this project was the correct choice. The Oculus Quest was the chosen HMD due to it being wireless and thus consumer-relevant, providing the highest screen resolution, as well as having a satisfactory refresh rate. However, since it has the hardware built into the headset, the computational power is limited. Therefore, the whole Unity project had to be specifically optimised for the Quest and the complexity of the scene reduced. This may have come at a price of limited features, reactive shaders and objects. Having VU metres for each audio track or having the shape of the spheres change relative to the sounds they represent, may have made it easier for the user to distinguish which tracks were active. More or improved lighting may as well have improved the aesthetics of the environment as a whole, which could have been possible with another HMD such as the HTC Vive that solely relies on the power of a computer running the program. Using a different HMD could thus have optimised the VR program as well as the overall appeal and desired features of the focus group participants might have been fulfilled. However, wireless capabilities, ease of use and accessibility would, in this case, have been lost.

## 9.15   Conclusion

Based on an investigation of VR and spatial audio, it has been concluded that VR both has the sensory and interactive benefits to potentially enhance the experience of visually positioning sound sources in space. Its intuitive controls, sense of depth and user-including advantages are from research shown as instinctive behaviours and, from that standing point, this project examined whether or not aforementioned values could improve the process of spatial audio mixing, which nowadays mostly is carried out using 2D plugins on a computer screen. On this basis, a design framework for VR covering both interaction, binaural audio, perceptional cues, and graphical principles was built and an application was implemented to allow a user to visually mix real-time audio, retrieved from the DAW Ableton Live, using dynamic binaural synthesis. Each component and control of both the visual and the auditory system was carefully chosen based on requirements targeting both the benefits and necessities of pairing visuals and sound and in order to answer the final problem statement of the project, the VE was evaluated against its 'computer screen' counterpart.

Defined as measurable improvements by the projects researchers, the two main aspects 'efficiency' and 'precision', were evaluated in two different conditions: one evaluation using a focus group interview with experts examining the opinions, perceptions and feelings about the VE, and one evaluation consisting of a mixing task that quantitatively measured time and precision differences between the VR and the computer version. The evaluations were carried out over four days at Aalborg University Copenhagen, and 13 and 24 participants took part in each evaluation respectively.

The results of the evaluations showed ambiguous tendencies. The focus group participants were in general positively minded towards the program and saw it as a quick sketching tool due to its intuitiveness, controls and apparent sensory feedback, rather than a tool for finer detail and precision manoeuvring. These opinions were, however, not possible to prove in the mixing task test. Firstly, the data of time measurements did not meet the parametric assumption of normality, therefore it could not be tested through a t-test. Secondly, when comparing the means of the precision scores (average distance from reference mix) the t-test proved, that when removing the 'Choir' track—a track that caused problems for all participants—the VR version was more precise than the computer version with a 95% confidence. The evaluations thus indicate that even though the VR was not perceived as a precise tool, its sensory benefits and interaction possibilities, whose qualities both sample groups were in agreement about, are general improvements to the ones found on a computer. However, all conclusions should be taken with care, as especially the setup of the mixing task evaluation should have been reconsidered. A whole new test should, as an example, have been carried out to get efficiency as a valid measure and it simultaneously is important to note that the findings from the mixing task evaluation regarding the VE, can only be seen in the light of its 'computer screen' counterpart.

# References

1. Adler, D.: Virtual audio-three-dimensional audio in virtual environments (Swedish Institute of Computer Science, 1996).
2. Argelaguet, F., Hoyet, L., Trico, N., Lécuyer, A.: The Role of Interaction in Virtual Embodiment: Effects of the Virtual Hand Representation in (Mar. 2016).
3. Bongers, B.: Physical Interfaces in the Electronic Arts Interaction Theory and Interfacing Techniques for Real-time Performance. Trends in Gestural Control of Music **2000**, 41–70 (2000).
4. Bordwell, D., Thompson, K.: Film Art an Introduction (1986).
5. Boring, S., Jurmu, M., Butz, A.: Scroll, tilt or move it: using mobile phones to continuously control pointers on large public displays in Proceedings of the 21st Annual Conference of the Australian Computer-Human Interaction Special Interest Group: Design: Open 24/7 (2009), 161–168.
6. Cook, P. in A NIME Reader: Fifteen Years of New Interfaces for Musical Expression (eds Jensenius, A. R., Lyons, M. J.) 1–13 (Springer International Publishing, Cham, 2017).
7. De Man, B., Jillings, N., Stables, R.: Comparing Stage Metaphor Interfaces As A Controller For Stereo Position and Level in (Sept. 2018).
8. Field, A., Hole, G.: How to Design and Report Experiments (SAGE Publications, 2002).
9. Gale, W., Wakefield, J.: Investigating the use of virtual reality to solve the underlying problems with the 3D stage paradigm.
10. Gelineck, S., Büchert, M., Andersen, J.: Towards a more flexible and creative music mixing interface in (Apr. 2013), 733–738.
11. Gelineck, S., Korsgaard, D., Büchert, M.: Stage- vs. Channel-strip Metaphor: Comparing Performance when Adjusting Volume and Panning of a Single Channel in a Stereo Mix English. in Proceedings of the International Conference on New Interfaces for Musical Expression (NIME 2015) (ed Berdahl, E.) (Louisiana State University, June 2015), 343–346.
12. Gibson, D., Petersen, G.: The Art of Mixing: A Visual Guide to Recording, Engineering, and Production (MixBooks, 1997).
13. Gödde, M., Gabler, F., Siegmund, D., Braun, A.: Cinematic Narration in VR - Rethinking Film Conventions for 360 Degrees in (June 2018), 184–201.
14. Hamilton, R.: Building Interactive Networked Musical Environments Using q3osc in (Feb. 2009).
15. Holland, S., Mudd, T., Wilkie-Mckenna, K., McPherson, A., Wanderley, M. M.: New Directions in Music and Human-Computer Interaction 1st (Springer Publishing Company, Incorporated, 2019).
16. Jensenius, A. R., Lyons, M. J.: A NIME Reader: Fifteen Years of New Interfaces for Musical Expression (Springer, 2017).
17. Kohlrausch, A., van de Par, S.: Auditory-visual interaction: from fundamental research in cognitive psychology to (possible) applications in Human Vision and Electronic Imaging IV (eds Rogowitz, B. E., Pappas, T. N.) 3644 (SPIE, 1999), 34–44.
18. Machado, L., Moura, I.: Shader Integration in a Virtual Reality Framework in (May 2013).
19. Miner, N., Caudell, T.: Computational Requirements and Synchronization Issues for Virtual Acoustic Displays. Presence: Teleoper. Virtual Environ. **7**, 396–409 (Aug. 1998).
20. Nielsen, L. T. et al.: Missing the Point: An Exploration of How to Guide Users' Attention During Cinematic Virtual Reality in Proceedings of the 22Nd ACM Conference on Virtual Reality Software and Technology (ACM, Munich, Germany, 2016), 229–232.
21. Orland, K.: How fast does "virtual reality" have to be to look like "actual reality"? en. 2013.
22. Pursel, E.: Synthetic Vision: Visual Perception for Computer Generated Forces Using the Programmable Graphics Pipeline (Jan. 2004).
23. Ratcliffe, J.: Hand and Finger Motion-Controlled Audio Mixing Interface in NIME (2014).

24. Recanzone, G. H., Sutter, M. L.: The biological basis of audition. Annu. Rev. Psychol. **59**, 119–142 (2008).
25. Serafin, S., Erkut, C., Kojs, J., Nilsson, N., Nordahl, R.: Virtual Reality Musical Instruments: State of the Art, Design Principles, and Future Directions. English. Computer Music Journal **40**, 22–40 (2016).
26. Tabry,V., Zatorre, R. J.,Voss, P.: The influence of vision on sound localization abilities in both the horizontal and vertical planes. Frontiers in psychology **4**, 932 (2013).
27. Wang, X., Tokarchuk, L., Cuadrado, F., Poslad, S.: Adaptive Identification of Hashtags for Real-time Event Data Collection, 1–23.
28. Yantis, S., Richard, A. A.: Sensation and Perception (Worth Publishers, New York, NY, 2014).
29. Ye, J., Campbell, R., Page, T., Badni, K.: An investigation into the implementation of virtual reality technologies in support of conceptual design. Design Studies **27**, 77–97 (2006).
30. Zölzer, U.: DAFX: Digital Audio Effects (Wiley, 2011).

# Part IV
# Sonic Experiences

# Chapter 10
# Audio in Multisensory Interactions: From Experiments to Experiences

Stefania Serafin

**Abstract** In the real and virtual world, we usually experience sounds in combination with at least an additional modality, such as vision, touch or proprioception. Understanding how sound enhances, substitutes or modifies the way we perceive and interact with the world is an important element when designing interactive multimodal experiences. In this chapter, we present an overview of sound in a multimodal context, ranging from basic experiments in multimodal perception to more advanced interactive experiences in virtual reality.

## 10.1 Introduction

This book examines the role of sound in virtual environments (VEs). However, most of our interactions with both the physical and virtual worlds appear through a combination of different sensory modalities. Auditory feedback is often the consequence of an action produced by touch and is presented in the form of a combination of auditory, haptic and visual feedback. Let us consider for example the simple action of walking: The auditory feedback is given by the sound produced by the shoes interacting with the floor, the visual feedback is the surrounding environment, and the haptic feedback is the feeling of the surface one is stepping on. It is important that these different sensory modalities are perceived in synchronization, in order to experience a coherent action.

Since sound can be perceived from all directions, it is ideal for providing information when the eyes are otherwise occupied. This could be a situation where someone's visual attention should be entirely devoted to a specific task such as driving or a surgeon operating on a patient [46]. Another notable property of the human auditory system is its sensitivity to the temporal aspects of sound [3]. In many instances, response times for auditory stimuli are faster than those for visual stimuli [55]. Furthermore, given the higher temporal resolution of the auditory system compared to

S. Serafin (✉)
Department of Architecture, Design, and Media Technology, Aalborg University Copenhagen, Copenhagen, Denmark
e-mail: sts@create.aau.dk

M. Geronazzo and S. Serafin (eds.), *Sonic Interactions in Virtual Environments*, Human—Computer Interaction Series, https://doi.org/10.1007/978-3-031-04021-4_10

the visual system, people can resolve subtle temporal dynamics in sounds more readily than in visual stimuli; thus the rendering of data into sound may manifest periodic or other temporal information that is not easily perceivable in visualizations [17]. Moreover, the ears are capable of decomposing complex auditory scenes [3] and selectively attending to certain sources, as seen, for example, in the cocktail party problem [7]. Audition, then, may be the most appropriate modality for simple and intuitive (see [9, 37]) information display when data have complex patterns, express meaningful changes in time, or require immediate action.

In this chapter, an overview is presented of how knowledge of human perception and cognition can be helpful in the design of multimodal systems where interactive sonic feedback plays an important role. Table 10.1 presents a typology of different kinds of cross- modal interactions, adapted from [2].

Sonic feedback can interact with visual or haptic feedback in different ways. As an example, cross-modal mapping represents the situation where one or more dimensions of a sound are mapped to visual or haptic feedback: A beeping sound combined with a flashing light. In cross-modal mapping, there is no specific interaction between the two modalities, but simply a function that connects some parameters of one modality to the parameters of another.

**Table 10.1** Typology of different kinds of cross-modal interactions

| Cross-modal interaction | Description | Example |
| --- | --- | --- |
| Amodal mapping | Use of VEs or other representational system to map abstract or amodal information (e.g., time, amount, etc.) to some continuous or discrete sensory cue | The use of colour mapping and relative size in graphics and scientific visualization (e.g., colour, size, depth, etc.) |
| Cross-modal mapping | Use of a VE to map one or more dimensions of a sensory stimulus to another sensory channel | An oscilloscope |
| Intersensory biases | Stimuli from two or more sensory channels may represent discrepant/conflicting information | Ventriloquism effect [24] |
| Cross-modal enhancement | Stimuli from one sensory channel enhance or alter the perceptual interpretation of stimulation from another sensory channel | Increased perceived visual fidelity of display as a result of increased auditory fidelity |
| Cross-modal transfers or illusions | Stimulation in one sensory channel leads to the illusion of stimulation in another sensory channel | Synesthesia |

Intersensory biases become important where audition and a second modality provide conflicting cues. In the following section, several examples of intersensory biases will be provided. In most of these situations, the user tries to perceptually integrate the conflicting information. This conflict might lead to a bias towards a stronger modality. One classic example is the ventriloquism effect [24], which illustrates the dominance of visual over auditory information when spatially discrepant audio and visual cues are experienced as co-localized at the location of the visual cue.

The name clearly derives from the ventriloquists, who are able to give the impression that the speaking voice is originated from the dummy they are holding, as opposed as from the person herself. This effect is commonly used in cinemas and home theatres where, although the sound physically originates at the speakers, it appears as if coming from the moving images on screen. The ventriloquist effect occurs because the visual estimates of location are typically more accurate than the auditory estimates of location, and therefore the overall perception of location is largely determined by vision. This phenomenon is also known as visual capture [64]. Another classic example is the Colavita effect [8]. In the original experiment, Colavita presented participants with an auditory (tone) or visual (light) stimulus, to which they were instructed to respond by pressing the tone key or light key respectively. When presented with bimodal stimuli, the visual dominance effect refers to the phenomenon where participants respond more often to the visual component.

Vision is indeed the dominant sense in many circumstances. On one hand, visual dominance over hearing and other sensory modalities has been frequently demonstrated (e.g., [45]), and a neural basis has been posited for visual dominance in processing audiovisual objects (e.g., [48]). Cross-modal enhancement refers to stimuli from one sensory channel enhancing or altering the perceptual interpretation of stimuli from another sensory channel. As an example, three studies presented in [57] show how high-quality auditory displays coupled with high-quality visual displays increase the quality perception of the visual displays relative to the evaluation of the visual display alone. Moreover, the same study shows how low-quality auditory displays coupled with high-quality visual displays decrease the perception of quality of the auditory displays relative to the evaluation of the auditory display alone. These studies were performed by manipulating the pixel resolution of the visual display and Gaussian white noise level, and by manipulating the sampling frequency of the auditory display and Gaussian white noise level. These findings strongly suggest that the quality of realism in an audiovisual display must be a function of both auditory and visual display fidelities and their interactions. Cross-modal enhancements can occur even when extra-modal input does not provide information directly meaningful for the task. An early study by Stein asked subjects to rate the intensity of a beam of light. Their findings showed that the test subjects believed the light to be brighter when it was accompanied by a brief, broadband auditory stimulus than when it was presented alone. The auditory stimulus produced more enhancement for lower visual intensities, regardless of the relative location of the auditory cue source.

Cross-modal transfers or illusions are situations where stimulation in one sensory channel leads to the illusion of stimulation in another sensory channel. An example of this is synesthesia, which in the audio-visual domain is expressed as the ability to see a colour while hearing a sound. When considering inter-sensory discrepancies, Welch and Warren propose a modality appropriateness hypothesis [64] that suggests that various sensory modalities are differentially well-suited to the perception of different events. Generally, it is supposed that vision is more appropriate for the perception of spatial location than audition, with touch sited somewhere in between. Audition is most appropriate for the perception of temporally structured events. Touch is more appropriate than audition for the perception of texture, where vision and touch may be about equally appropriate for the perception of textures. The appropriateness is a consequence of the different temporal and spatial resolution of the auditory, haptic and visual systems. Moreover, especially when it is combined with touch stimulation, sound increases the sense of immersion [63].

Apart from the way that the different senses can interact, the auditory channel also presents some advantages when compared to other modalities. For example, humans have a complete sphere of receptivity around the head, while visual feedback has a limited spatial region in terms of field-of-view and field-of-regard. Because auditory information is primarily temporal, the temporal resolution of the auditory system is more precise. We can discriminate between a single click and a pair of clicks when the gap is only a few tens of microseconds [30]. Perception of temporal changes in the visual modality is much poorer, and the fastest visible flicker rate in normal conditions is about 40–50 Hz [4]. In multi-sensory interaction, therefore, audio tends to elicit the shortest response time [33].

In contrast, the maximum spatial resolution (contrast sensitivity) of the human eye is approximately 1/30 degrees, a much finer resolution than that of the auditory system, which is approximately 1 degree. Humans are sensitive to sounds arriving from anywhere within the environment whereas the visual field is limited to the frontal hemisphere, with good resolution limited specifically to the foveal region. Therefore, while the spatial resolution of the auditory modality is cruder, it can serve as a cue to events occurring outside the visual field-of-view.

In the rest of this chapter, we provide an overview of the interaction between audition and vision and between audition and touch, together with guidelines on how such knowledge can be used in the design of interactive sonic systems. By understanding how we naturally interact in a world where several sensorial stimuli are provided, we can apply this understanding to the design of sonic interactive systems. Research on multisensory perception and cognition can provide us with important guidelines on how to design virtual environments where interactive sound plays an important role. Through technical advancements such as mobile technologies and 3D interfaces, it has become possible to design systems that have similar natural multimodal properties as the physical world. These future interfaces understand human multimodal communication and can actively anticipate and act in line with human capabilities and limitations. A large challenge for the near future is the development of such natural multimodal interfaces, something that requires the active participation of industry, technology, and the human sciences.

## 10.2   Audio-Visual Interactions

Research into multimodal interaction between audition and other modalities has primarily focused on the interaction between audition and vision. This choice is naturally due to the fact that audition and vision are the most dominant modalities in the human perceptual system [29]. A well-known multimodal phenomenon is the McGurk effect [38]. The McGurk effect is an example of how vision alters speech perception; for instance, the sound "ba" is perceived as "da" when viewed with the lip movements for "ga". Notice that in this case, the percept is different from both the visual and auditory stimuli, so this is an example of intersensory bias, as described in the previous section.

The different experiments described until now show a dominance of vision over audition, when conflicting cues are provided. However, this is not always the case. As an example, in [53, 54], a visual illusion induced by sound is described. When a single visual flash is accompanied by multiple auditory beeps, the single flash is perceived as multiple flashes. These results were obtained by flashing a uniform white disk for a variable number of times, 50 milliseconds apart, on a black background. Flashes were accompanied by a variable number of beeps, each spaced 57 milliseconds apart. Observers were asked to judge how many visual flashes were presented on each trial. The trials were randomized and each stimulus combination was run five times on eight naive observers. Surprisingly, observers consistently and incorrectly reported seeing multiple flashes whenever a single flash was accompanied by more than one beep [53]. This experiment is known as sound-induced flash illusion. A follow-up experiment investigated whether the illusory flashes could be perceived independently at different spatial locations [26]. Two bars were displayed at two locations, creating an apparent motion. All subjects reported that an illusory bar was perceived with the second beep at a location between the real bars. This is analogous to the cutaneous rabbit perceptual illusion, where trains of successive cutaneous pulses delivered at a few widely separated locations produce sensations at many in-between points [19]. As a matter of fact, perception of time, wherein auditory estimates are typically more accurate, is dominated by hearing.

Another experiment explored whether two objects appear to bounce of each other or simply cross, if observers hear a beep when the objects could be in contact. In this particular case, a desktop computer displayed two identical objects moving towards each others. The display was ambiguous to provide two different interpretations after the objects met: They could either bounce off each other or cross. Since collisions usually produce a characteristic impact sound, introducing such sound when objects met promoted the perception of bouncing versus crossing. This experiment is usually known as motion-bounce illusion [51]. In a subsequent study, Sekuler and Sekuler found that any transient sound temporally aligned with the would-be collision increased the likelihood of a bounce percept [50]. This includes a pause, a flash of light on the screen, or a sudden disappearance of the discs. Auditory dominance has also been found in other examples with respect to time-based abilities such as precise temporal processing [47], temporal localization [5], and estimation of time durations [43]. Lipscomb and Kendall [34] provide another example of auditory dominance in a multimedia context (film). These researchers found that variation in participant semantic differential ratings was influenced more by the musical component than by the visual element. Particularly interesting in its implications for processing multisensory experiences is [22] pointing to the disappearance of visual dominance when a visual signal is presented simultaneously with an auditory and haptic signal (i.e., as a tri-sensory combination). The authors concluded that while vision can dominate both the auditory and the haptic sensory modalities, this is limited to bi-sensory combinations in which the visual signal is combined with another single stimulus.

More recent investigations examined the role of ecological auditory feedback in affecting multimodal perception of visual content. As an example, in a study presented in [15], the combined perceptual effect of visual and auditory information on the perception of a moving object's trajectory was investigated. Inspired by the experimental paradigm presented in [27], the visual stimuli consisted of a perspective rendering of a ball moving in a three-dimensional box. Each video was paired with one of three sound conditions: Silence, the sound of a ball rolling, or the sound of a ball hitting the ground. It was found that the sound condition influenced whether observers were more likely to perceive the ball as rolling back in depth on the floor of the box or jumping in the frontal plane.

Another interesting study related to the role of auditory cues in the perception of visual stimuli is the one presented in [60]. Two psychophysical studies were conducted to test whether visual sensitivity to point-light depictions of human gait reflects the action specific co-occurrence of visual and auditory cues typically produced by walking people. To perform the experiment, visual walking patterns were captured using a motion capture system, and a between-subject experimental procedure was adopted. Specifically, subjects were randomly exposed to one of the three experimental conditions: No sound, footstep sounds, or a pure tone at 1000 Hz, which represented a control case. Visual sensitivity to coherent human gait was measured by asking subjects if they could detect a person walking or not. Such sensitivity was greatest in the presence of temporally coincident and action-consistent sounds, in this case, the sound of footsteps. Visual sensitivity to human gait with coincident sounds that were not action-consistent, in this case the pure tone, was significantly lower and did not significantly differ from visual sensitivity to gaits presented without sound.

As an additional interaction between audition and vision, sound can help the user search for an object within a cluttered, continuously changing environment. It has been shown that a simple auditory pip drastically decreases search times for a synchronized visual object that is normally very difficult to find. This is known as the pip and pop effect [62]. Visual feedback can also affect several aspects of a musical performance, although in this chapter affective and emotional aspects of a musical performance are not considered. As an example, Schutz and Lipscomb report an audio-visual illusion in which an expert musician's gestures affect the perceived duration of a note without changing its acoustic length [49]. To demonstrate this, they recorded a world-renowned marimba player performing single notes on a marimba using long and short gestures. They paired both types of sounds with both types of gestures, resulting in a combination of natural (i.e., congruent gesture-note pairs) and hybrid (i.e., incongruent gesture-note pairs) stimuli. They informed participants that some auditory and visual components had been mismatched, and asked them to judge tone duration based on the auditory component alone. Despite these instructions, the participants' duration ratings were strongly influenced by visual gesture information. As a matter of fact, notes were rated as longer when paired with long gestures than when paired with short gestures. These results are somehow puzzling, since they contradict the view that judgments of tone duration are relatively immune from visual influence [64], that is, in temporal tasks visual influence on audition is negligible. However, the results are not based on information quality, but rather on perceived causality, given that visual influence in this paradigm is dependent on the presence of an ecologically plausible audiovisual relationship.

Indeed, it is also possible to consider the characteristics of vision and audition to predict which modality will prevail when conflicting information is provided. In this direction, [31] introduced the notion of auditory and visual objects. They describe the different characteristics of audition and vision, claiming that a primary source of information for vision is a surface, while a secondary source of information is the location and colour of sources. On the other hand, a primary source of information for audition is a source and a secondary source of information is a surface.

In [16], a theory is suggested on how our brain merges the different sources of information coming from the different modalities, specifically audition, vision, and touch. The first is what is called sensory combination, which means the maximization of information delivered from the different sensory modalities. The second strategy is called sensory integration, which means the reduction of variance in the sensory estimate to increase its reliability. Sensory combination describes interactions between sensory signals that are not redundant. By contrast, sensory integration describes interactions between redundant signals. Ernst and coworkers [16] describe the integration of sensory information as a bottom-up process.

The modality precision, also called modality appropriateness hypothesis, by [64], is often cited when trying to explain which modality dominates under what circumstances. This hypothesis states that discrepancies are always resolved in favour of the more precise or more appropriate modality. In spatial tasks, for example, the visual modality usually dominates, because it is the most precise at determining spatial information. However, according to [16], this terminology is misleading because it is not the modality itself or the stimulus that dominates. Rather, the dominance is determined by the estimate and how reliably it can be derived within a specific modality from a given stimulus.

A major design dilemma involves the extent to which audio interfaces should maintain the conventions of visual interfaces [40]. Indeed, most attempts at auditory display seek to emulate or translate elements of visual interfaces to the auditory modality. While retrofitting visual interfaces with sound can offer some consistencies across modalities, the constraints of this approach may hinder the design of auditory interfaces. While visual objects exist primarily in space, auditory stimuli occur in time. A more appropriate approach to auditory interface design, therefore, may require designers to focus more strictly on auditory capabilities. Such interfaces may present the items and objects of the interface in a fast, linear fashion over time rather than attempting to provide auditory versions of the spatial relationships found in visual interfaces.

## 10.3 Embodied Interactions

The experiments described until now assume a passive observer, in the sense that a subject is exposed to a fixed sequence of audiovisual stimuli and is asked to report on the resulting perceptual experience. When a subject is interacting with the stimuli provided, a tight sensory motor coupling is enabled, that is an important characteristic of embodied perception. According to embodiment theory, a person and the environment form a pair in which the two parts are coupled and determine each other. The term *embodied* highlights two points: First, cognition depends upon the kinds of experience that are generated from specific sensorimotor capacities. Second, these individual sensorimotor capacities are themselves embedded in a biological, psychological, and cultural context [14].

The notion of embodied interaction is based on the view that meanings are present in the actions that people engage in while interacting with objects, with other people, and with the environment in general. Embodied interfaces try to exploit the phenomenological attitude of looking at the direct experience, and let the meanings and structures emerge as experienced phenomena. Embodiment is not a property of artefacts but rather a property of how actions are performed with or through the artefacts.

The central role of our body in perception, cognition and interaction, has been previously addressed by philosophers (e.g., [39]), psychologists (e.g., [41]) and neuroscientists (e.g., [10]). A rather recent approach to the understanding of the design process, especially in its early stages, has been to focus on the role of multimodality and the contribution of non-verbal channels as key means of communication, kinaesthetic thinking, and more generally of doing design [59]. Audio-haptic interactions, described in the following section, also require a continuous action-feedback loop between a person and the environment, an important characteristic of embodied perception. Another approach, called embodied sound design, proposes to place the bodily experience (i.e., communication of sonic concepts through vocal and gestural imitations) at the centre of the sound creation process [12].

The role of the body in HCI has overall recently gained more attention, and interested readers can refer to the book by Hook [23] and to Chap. 7 in this volume.

## 10.4   Audio-Haptic Interactions

Although the investigation of audio-haptic interactions has not received as much attention as audiovisual interactions, it is certainly an interesting field of research, especially considering the tight connections existing between the sense of touch and audition. As a matter of fact, both audition and touch are sensitive to the very same kind of physical property, that is, mechanical pressure in the form of oscillations. The tight correlation between the information content (oscillatory patterns) being conveyed in the two senses can potentially support interactions of an integrative nature at a variety of levels along the sensory pathways. Auditory cues are normally elicited when one touches everyday objects, and these sounds often convey useful informational regarding the nature of the objects [18]. The feeling of skin dryness or moistness that arises when we rub our hands against each other is subjectively referred to the friction forces at the epidermis. Yet, it has been demonstrated that acoustic information also participates in this bodily sensation, because altering the sound arising from the hand rubbing action changes our sensation of dryness or moistness at the skin. This phenomenon is known as the parchment-skin illusion [25].

The parchment-skin illusion is an example of how interactive auditory feedback can affect subjects' haptic sensation. Specifically, in the experiment demonstrating the rubber-skin illusion, subjects were asked to sit with a microphone close to their hands, and then to rub their hands against each other. The sound of hands rubbing was captured by a microphone; they were then manipulated in real time, and played back through headphones. The sound was modified by attenuating the overall amplitude and by amplifying the high frequencies. Subjects were asked to rate the haptic sensation in their palms as a function of the different auditory cues provided, in a scale ranging from very moist to very dry. Results show that the provided auditory feedback significantly affected the perception of the skin's dryness. This study was extended in [20], by using a more rigorous psychophysical testing procedure. Results reported a similar increase in smooth-dry scale correlated to changes in auditory feedback, but not in the roughness judgments per se. However, both studies provide convincing empirical evidence demonstrating the modulatory effect of auditory cues on people's haptic perception of a variety of different surfaces. A similar experiment was performed combining auditory cues with haptic cues at the tongue. Specifically, subjects were asked to chew on potato chips, and the sound produced was again captured and manipulated in real time. Results show that the perception of potato chips' crispness was affected by the auditory feedback provided [56]. A surprising audio-haptic bodily illusion that demonstrates human observers rapidly update their assumptions about the material qualities of their body is the marble hand illusion [52]. By repeatedly gently hitting participants' hand while progressively replacing the natural sound of the hammer against the skin with the sound of a hammer hitting a piece of marble, it was possible to induce an illusory misperception of the material properties of the hand. After 5 min, the hand started feeling stiffer, heavier, harder, less sensitive, and unnatural, and showed enhanced galvanic skin response to threatening stimuli. This bodily illusion demonstrates that the experience of the material of our body can be quickly updated through multisensory integration. Another interesting example where sounds again affect body perception is shown in [58]. Here, the illusion is applied to footstep sounds. By digitally varying sounds produced by walking, it is possible to vary one's perception of weight.

Lately, artificial cues are appearing in audiohaptic interfaces, allowing us to carefully control the variations to the provided feedback and the resulting perceived effects on exposed subjects [13, 42, 61]. Artificial auditory cues have also been used in the context of sensory substitution, for artificial sensibility at the hands using hearing as a replacement for loss of sensation [35]. In this particular study, microphones placed at the fingertips captured and amplified the friction sound obtained when rubbing hard surfaces.

In [28], a nice investigation on the interaction between auditory and haptic cues in the near space is presented. The authors show an interesting illusion of how sounds delivered through headphones, presented near to the head induces an haptic experience. The left ear of a dummy head was stroked with a paintbrush and the sound was recorded. The sound was then presented to the participants who felt a tickling sensation when the sound was presented near to the head, but not when it was presented distant from the head.

Another kind of dynamic sonic objecthood is that obtained through data physicalization, which is the 3D rendering of a dataset in the form of a solid physical object. Although there is a long history of physicalization, this area of research has become increasingly interesting through the facilitation of 3D printing technology. Physicalizations allow the user to hold and manipulate a dataset in their hands, providing an embodied experience that allows rich naturalistic and intuitive interactions such as multi-finger touch, tapping, pressing, squeezing, scraping, and rotating [36].

Physical manipulation produces acoustic effects that are influenced by the material properties, shape, forces, modes of interaction and events over time. The idea that sound could be a way to augment data physicalization has been explored through acoustic sonifications in which the 3D printed dataset is super-imposed on the form of a sounding object, such as a bell or a singing bowl [1]. Since acoustic vibrations are strongly influenced by 3D form, the sound that is produced is influenced by the dataset that is used to shape the sounding object. On a similar vein, the design of musical instruments has also inspired the design of new interfaces for human-computer interaction. As stated by Jaron Lanier, musical instruments are the best user interfaces (see [1]), and we can learn to design new interfaces by looking at musical instruments. An example is the work of [32], where structural elements along the speaker-microphone pathway characteristically alter the acoustic output. Moreover, Chap. 12 proposes several case studies in the context of musical haptics.

In designing multimodal environments, several elements need to be taken into consideration. However, technology imposes some limitations, especially when the ultimate goal is to simulate systems that react in realtime. This issue is nicely addressed by Pai, who describes a tradeoff between accuracy and responsiveness, a crucial difference between models for science and models for interaction (see [44]). Specifically, computations about the physical world are always approximations. In general, it is possible to improve accuracy by constructing more detailed models and performing more precise measurements, but this increased accuracy comes at the cost of latency, i.e., the elapsed time before an answer is obtained. For multisensory models, it is also essential to ensure synchronization of time between different sensory modalities [44]. groups all of these temporal considerations, such as latency and synchronization, into a single category called responsiveness. The question then becomes how to balance accuracy and responsiveness. The choice between accuracy and responsiveness depends also on the final goal of the multimodal system design. Often, scientists are more concerned with accuracy, so responsiveness is only a soft constraint based on available resources. On the other hand, for interaction designers, responsiveness is an essential parameter that must be satisfied.

## 10.5   Conclusions

This chapter has provided an overview of several experiments whose goals were to achieve a better understanding of how the human auditory system is connected to visual and haptic channels. A better understanding of multimodal perception can have several applications. As an example, systems based on sensory substitution help people lacking a certain sensorial modality by replacing it with another sensorial modality. Moreover, cross-modal enhancement allows reduced stimuli in one sensorial modality to be augmented by a stronger stimulation in another modality.

Contemporary advances in hardware and software technology allow us to experiment in several ways with technologies for multimodal interaction design, building for example, haptic illusions with equipment available in a typical hardware store [21] or easily experimenting with sketching and rapid prototyping [6, 11]. These advances in technology create several possibilities for discovering novel cross-modal illusions and interactions between the senses, especially when a collaboration between cognitive psychologists and interaction designers is facilitated. A research challenge is not only to understand how humans process information coming from different senses, but also how information in a multimodal system should be distributed to different modalities in order to obtain the best user experience.

As an example, in a multi-modal system such as a system for controlling an haptic display, seeing a visual display and listening to interactive auditory display, it is important to determine which synchronicities are more important. At one extreme, a completely disjointed distribution of information over several modalities can offer the highest bandwidth, but the user may be confused in connecting the modalities and one modality might mask another and distract the user by focusing attention on events that might not be important. At the other extreme, a completely redundant distribution of information is known to increase the cognitive load and is not guaranteed to increase user performance.

Beyond the research on multimodal stimuli processing, studies are needed on the processing of multimodal stimuli that are connected via interaction. We would expect that the human brain and sensory system have been optimized to cope with a certain mixture of redundant information, and that information displays are better the more they follow this natural distribution. Overall, the more we achieve a better understanding of the ways humans interact with the everyday world, the more we can obtain inspiration for the design of effective natural multimodal interfaces.

# References

1. Barrass, S.: Diagnosing blood pressure with Acoustic Sonification singing bowls. International Journal of Human-Computer Studies **85**, 68–71 (2016).
2. Biocca, F., Kim, J., Choi, Y.: Visual touch in virtual environments: An exploratory study of presence, multimodal interfaces, and cross-modal sensory illusions. Presence: Teleoperators & Virtual Environments **10**, 247–265 (2001).
3. Bregman, A. S.: Auditory scene analysis: The perceptual organization of sound (MIT press, 1994).
4. Bruce, V., Green, P. R., Georgeson, M. A.: Visual perception: Physiology, psychology, & ecology (Psychology Press, 2003).
5. Burr, D., Banks, M. S., Morrone, M. C.: Auditory dominance over vision in the perception of interval duration. Experimental Brain Research **198**, 49 (2009).
6. Buxton, B.: Sketching user experiences: getting the design right and the right design (Morgan kaufmann, 2010).
7. Cherry, E. C.: Some experiments on the recognition of speech, with one and with two ears. The Journal of the acoustical society of America **25**, 975–979 (1953).
8. Colavita, F. B.: Human sensory dominance. Perception & Psychophysics **16**, 409–412 (1974).
9. Connell, B. R.: The principles of universal design, version 2.0. http://www.design.ncsu.edu/cud/univ/design/princ/overview.htm (1997).
10. Damasio, A. R.: Descartes' error (Random House, 2006).
11. Delle Monache, S., Polotti, P., Rocchesso, D.: A toolkit for explorations in sonic interaction design in Proc. Int. Conf. Audio Mostly (AM2010) (Piteå, 2010), 1–7.
12. Delle Monache, S. et al.: Embodied sound design. International Journal of Human-Computer Studies **118**, 47–59 (2018).
13. DiFilippo, D., Pai, D. K.: The AHI: An audio and haptic interface for contact interactions in Proceedings of the 13th annual ACM symposium on User interface software and technology (2000), 149–158.
14. Dourish, P.: Where the action is: the foundations of embodied interaction (MIT press, 2004).
15. Ecker, A. J., Heller, L. M.: Auditory Visual Interactions in the Perception of a Ball's Path. Perception **34**, 59–75 (2005).
16. Ernst, M. O., Bülthoff, H. H.: Merging the senses into a robust percept. Trends in cognitive sciences **8**, 162–169 (2004).
17. Flowers, J. H., Buhman, D. C., Turnage, K. D.: Data sonification from the desktop: Should sound be part of standard data analysis software? ACM Transactions on Applied Perception (TAP) **2**, 467–472 (2005).
18. Gaver,W.: What in the world do we hear?: An ecological approach to auditory event perception. Ecological Psychology **5**, 1–29 (1993).
19. Geldard, F. A., Sherrick, C. E.: The cutaneous" rabbit": A perceptual illusion. Science **178**, 178–179 (1972).
20. Guest, S., Catmur, C., Lloyd, D., Spence, C.: Audiotactile interactions in roughness perception. Experimental Brain Research **146**, 161–171 (2002).
21. Hayward, V.: A brief taxonomy of tactile illusions and demonstrations that can be done in a hardware store. Brain research bulletin **75**, 742–752 (2008).
22. Hecht, D., Reiner, M.: Sensory dominance in combinations of audio, visual and haptic stimuli. Experimental brain research **193**, 307–314 (2009).

23. Höök, K.: Designing with the body: Somaesthetic interaction design (MIT Press, 2018).
24. Jack, C. E., Thurlow,W. R.: Effects of degree of visual association and angle of displacement on the ?ventriloquism? effect. Perceptual and motor skills **37**, 967–979 (1973).
25. Jousmäki, V., Hari, R.: Parchment-skin illusion: sound-biased touch. Current biology **8**, R190–R191 (1998).
26. Kamitani, Y., Shimojo, S.: Sound-induced visual ?rabbit? Journal of vision **1**, 478–478 (2001).
27. Kersten, D., Mamassian, P., Knill, D. C.: Moving cast shadows induce apparent motion in depth. Perception **26**, 171–192 (1997).
28. Kitagawa, N., Zampini, M., Spence, C.: Audiotactile interactions in near and far space. Experimental Brain Research **166**, 528–537 (2005).
29. Kohlrausch, A., van de Par, S.: Auditory-visual interaction: from fundamental research in cognitive psychology to (possible) applications in Human Vision and Electronic Imaging IV **3644** (1999), 34–44.
30. Krumbholz, K., Patterson, R., Seither-Preisler, A., Lammertmann, C., Lütkenhöner, B.: Neuromagnetic evidence for a pitch processing center in Heschl?s gyrus. Cerebral Cortex **13**, 765–772 (2003).
31. Kubovy, M., Van Valkenburg, D.: Auditory and visual objects. Cognition **80**, 97–126 (2001).
32. Laput, G., Brockmeyer, E., Hudson, S. E., Harrison, C.: Acoustruments: Passive, acoustically-driven, interactive controls for handheld devices in Proceedings of the 33rd Annual ACM Conference on Human Factors in Computing Systems (2015), 2161–2170.
33. Li, T., Wang, D., Peng, C., Yu, C., Zhang, Y.: Speed-accuracy tradeoff of fingertip force control with visual/audio/haptic feedback. International Journal of Human-Computer Studies **110**, 33–44 (2018).
34. Lipscomb, S. D., Kendall, R. A.: Perceptual judgement of the relationship between musical and visual components in film. Psychomusicology: A Journal of Research in Music Cognition **13**, 60 (1994).
35. Lundborg, G., Rosén, B., Lindberg, S.: Hearing as substitution for sensation: a new principle for artificial sensibility. The Journal of hand surgery **24**, 219–224 (1999).
36. Lupton, D.: Feeling your data: Touch and making sense of personal digital data. New Media & Society **19**, 1599–1614 (2017).
37. Mcguire, J. M., Scott, S. S., Shaw, S. F.: Universal design and its applications in educational environments. Remedial and special education **27**, 166–175 (2006).
38. McGurk, H., MacDonald, J.: Hearing lips and seeing voices. Nature **264**, 746 (1976).
39. Merleau-Ponty, M.: Phenomenology of perception Routledge. UK.[France, 1945] (1962).
40. Mynatt, E. D., Edwards, W. K.: Mapping GUIs to auditory interfaces in Proceedings of the 5th annual ACM symposium on User interface software and technology (1992), 61–70.
41. Niedenthal, P. M., Barsalou, L. W., Winkielman, P., Krauth-Gruber, S., Ric, F.: Embodiment in attitudes, social perception, and emotion. Personality and social psychology review **9**, 184–211 (2005).
42. Nordahl, R. et al.: Preliminary experiment combining virtual reality haptic shoes and audio synthesis in International Conference on Human Haptic Sensing and Touch Enabled Computer Applications (2010), 123–129.
43. Ortega, L., Guzman-Martinez, E., Grabowecky, M., Suzuki, S.: Auditory dominance in time perception. Journal of Vision **9**, 1086–1086 (2009).
44. Pai, D. K.: Multisensory interaction: Real and virtual in Robotics Research. The Eleventh International Symposium (2005), 489–498.
45. Posner, M. I., Nissen, M. J., Klein, R. M.: Visual dominance: an informationprocessing account of its origins and significance. Psychological review **83**, 157 (1976).
46. Recarte, M. A., Nunes, L. M.: Mental workload while driving: effects on visual search, discrimination, and decision making. Journal of experimental psychology: Applied **9**, 119 (2003).
47. Repp, B. H., Penel, A.: Auditory dominance in temporal processing: new evidence from synchronization with simultaneous visual and auditory sequences. Journal of Experimental Psychology: Human Perception and Performance **28**, 1085 (2002).

48. Schmid, C., Büchel, C., Rose, M.: The neural basis of visual dominance in the context of audio-visual object processing. NeuroImage **55**, 304–311 (2011).
49. Schutz, M., Lipscomb, S.: Hearing gestures, seeing music: Vision influences perceived tone duration. Perception **36**, 888–897 (2007).
50. Sekuler, A. B., Sekuler, R.: Collisions between moving visual targets: what controls alternative ways of seeing an ambiguous display? Perception **28**, 415–432 (1999).
51. Sekuler, R.: Sound alters visual motion perception. Nature **385**, 308 (1997).
52. Senna, I., Maravita, A., Bolognini,N., Parise,C.V.: The marble-hand illusion. PloS one **9** (2014).
53. Shams, L., Kamitani, Y., Shimojo, S.: Illusions: What you see is what you hear. Nature **408**, 788 (2000).
54. Shams, L., Kamitani, Y., Shimojo, S.: Visual illusion induced by sound. Cognitive Brain Research **14**, 147–152 (2002).
55. Spence, C., Driver, J.: Audiovisual links in exogenous covert spatial orienting. Perception & psychophysics **59**, 1–22 (1997).
56. Spence, C., Zampini, M.: Auditory contributions to multisensory product perception. Acta Acustica united with Acustica **92**, 1009–1025 (2006).
57. Storms, R. L., Zyda, M. J.: Interactions in perceived quality of auditoryvisual displays. Presence: Teleoperators & Virtual Environments **9**, 557–580 (2000).
58. Tajadura-Jiménez, A. et al.: As light as your footsteps: altering walking sounds to change perceived body weight, emotional state and gait in Proc. ACM Conf. on Human Factors in Computing Systems (Seoul, Apr. 2015), 2943–2952.
59. Tholander, J., Karlgren, K., Ramberg, R., Sökjer, P.: Where all the interaction is: sketching in interaction design as an embodied practice in Proceedings of the 7th ACM conference on Designing interactive systems (2008), 445–454.
60. Thomas, J. P., Shiffrar, M.: I can see you better if I can hear you coming: Action-consistent sounds facilitate the visual detection of human gait. Journal of vision **10**, 14–14 (2010).
61. Van den Doel, K., Pai, D. K.: The sounds of physical shapes. Presence **7**, 382–395 (1998).
62. Van der Burg, E., Olivers, C. N., Bronkhorst, A. W., Theeuwes, J.: Pip and pop: nonspatial auditory signals improve spatial visual search. Journal of Experimental Psychology: Human Perception and Performance **34**, 1053 (2008).
63. Vi, C. T., Ablart, D., Gatti, E., Velasco, C., Obrist, M.: Not just seeing, but also feeling art: Mid-air haptic experiences integrated in a multisensory art exhibition. International Journal of Human-Computer Studies **108**, 1–14 (2017).
64. Welch, R. B., Warren, D. H.: Immediate perceptual response to intersensory discrepancy. Psychological bulletin **88**, 638 (1980).

# Chapter 11
# Immersion in Audiovisual Experiences

Sarvesh R. Agrawal and Søren Bech

**Abstract** Understanding the concept of immersion and its influencing factors is critical for enabling engaging audiovisual experiences. However, a lack of definitional consensus and suitable methods for assessing immersion hinder research on the subject. This chapter discusses the idea of immersion based on a non-exhaustive literature review of the topic and presents an adaptable definition of immersion that is not limited to virtual reality applications. Additionally, an exploratory experimental paradigm for measuring immersion in audiovisual experiences is described. The description of immersion and the experimental framework presented in this chapter are a starting point for resolving the difference in opinion and developing novel methods to thoroughly explore the concept of immersion respectively.

## 11.1 Introduction

Audiovisual technology has advanced drastically over the last decade. Spatial audio in conjunction with advanced visual technologies such as enhanced color reproduction and greater dynamic range is witnessing wide scale adoption for domestic audiovisual applications (e.g., gaming, entertainment, broadcast). In addition to the technological progress, the emergence of virtual reality (VR) and augmented reality (AR) is swiftly changing the paradigm for domestic audiovisual experiences.

S. R. Agrawal (✉) · S. Bech
Bang & Olufsen, Bang & Olufsen Allé 1, Struer, Denmark 7600
e-mail: sraj@bang-olufsen.dk

S. Bech
e-mail: sbe@bang-olufsen.dk

S. R. Agrawal
Technical University of Denmark, Department of Photonics Engineering, Lyngby, Denmark 2800

S. Bech
Department of Electronic Systems, Aalborg University, Aalborg, Denmark 9220

M. Geronazzo and S. Serafin (eds.), *Sonic Interactions in Virtual Environments*,
Human—Computer Interaction Series, https://doi.org/10.1007/978-3-031-04021-4_11

The vocabulary for describing new audiovisual experiences unlocked by these technologies has evolved as well. Immersion has emerged as the predominant term for describing audiovisual experiences. Nevertheless, the concept of immersion is poorly understood. Immersion is studied in a variety of different field such as film [52, 55, 68], video games [1, 8, 31, 53, 58], virtual reality [24, 41, 46, 51], and music [4, 14]. It is used to describe a large array of experiences that contributes to the ambiguity surrounding the term. Immersion is often considered synonymous to presence and envelopment which further dilutes the concept. A lack of definitional consensus and the interchangeable use with terms such as presence have reduced immersion to an "excessively vague, all inclusive concept" [39]. A formal definition of immersion is a prerequisite for communicating the idea effectively and conducting research on the topic. Thus, the first half of this chapter attempts to formalize the meaning immersion by proposing a definition that has been synthesized from a non-exhaustive literature review of the subject. A wide perspective has been adopted for the proposed definition such that it can be easily adapted for different applications as well as interactive and non-interactive activities.

As technologists, we are interested in enabling experiences with a greater degree of immersion on the premise that more immersive experiences are preferable. This can be achieved by developing a deeper understanding of the various factors that influence immersion and subsequently harnessing their capabilities for delivering more immersive experiences. However, the fundamental challenge in investigating immersion is a lack of methodologies for measuring immersion. To this end, an exploratory study was conducted for quantifying immersion in audiovisual experiences as a first step. The experimental framework detailed in the latter half of this chapter can form the basis for developing experimental paradigms aimed at investigating the impact of immersion's influencing factors.

## 11.2  Conceptualizations of Immersion

Immersion is a complex subject that can have a different meaning depending on the context and the field of study. While the origin of immersion's conceptualization is unknown, it is agreed that it is a metaphorical term derived from the physical experience of being surrounded by a completely different medium. Murray [43] has provided the following description of immersion:

> Immersion is a metaphorical term derived from the physical experience of being submerged in water. We seek the same feeling from a psychologically immersive experience that we do from a plunge in the ocean or swimming pool: the sensation of being surrounded by a completely other reality, as different as water is from air, that takes over all of our attention, our whole perceptual apparatus ([43], p. 99).

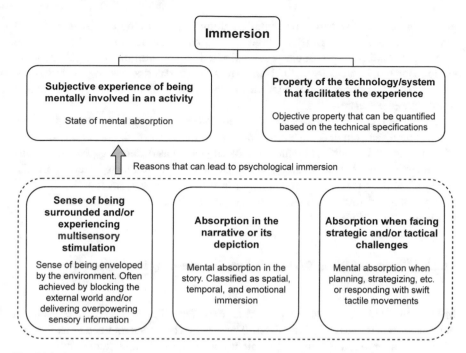

**Fig. 11.1** Structure of the proposed literature review. Adapted from [3]

The analogy of "experience of swimming underwater" has been open to interpretation as some researchers have approached the topic from a physical perspective (i.e., being surrounded by a different reality) while others view it from a psychological viewpoint (i.e., similar to the metaphorical derivation described by Murray [43] where attention is a factor). The descriptions of immersion appearing in literature can be largely classified into two perspectives: immersion as a psychological experience and immersion as an objective property of the system or the technology that facilitates the experience. A brief introduction to these perspectives and a visual summary of the literature review in this chapter is provided by Fig. 11.1.

## 11.2.1  Psychological Perspective

The psychological perspective on immersion states that immersion is the psychological state of the individual when they are mentally involved in an activity [37]. It argues that attention is at the heart of immersion and de-emphasizes the role of the system or the technology that mediates the experience.[1] Instead, significance is

---

[1] This is different from the concept of presence which is heavily influenced by the capabilities of the system/technology. Presence is the illusion of being in an environment other than the physical environment around the user in mediated experiences. Please refer to Sect. 11.4.1 for a brief discussion on the distinction between presence and immersion.

placed on the narrative and its presentation along with the individual participating in the experience. The idea of psychological immersion can be illustrated through the example of reading books. Books provide limited sensory stimulation to the reader in comparison to multisensory audiovisual experiences; nevertheless, the narrative content presented by books and its relevance to the reader can lead to a psychologically immersive experience.

The three recognized reasons that can lead to psychological immersion are the sense of being surrounded, absorption in the narrative or its depiction, and absorption when facing challenges. While these are often viewed as different types/dimensions of immersion, we believe that conclusive evidence is required to determine if the experiences they lead to are fundamentally different to warrant the classification of psychological immersion. An overview of the three reasons is presented in the following subsections.

### 11.2.1.1 Sense of Being Surrounded or Experiencing Multisensory Stimulation

Immersion[2] is often viewed as a perceptual experience that is directly dependent on the capabilities of the rendering system. The sense of being surrounded or experiencing multisensory stimulation is a prevalent conceptualization of immersion. Biocca and Delaney [7] dubbed this *perceptual immersion*: the extent of submersion of the user's perceptual system in the environment. It is believed that perceptual immersion can be measured objectively by "counting the number of the user's senses that are provided with input and the degree to which inputs from the physical environment are shut out" [36]. McMahan [39] stated that perceptual immersion can be achieved by blocking the external world and constraining the user's perception to the presented stimulus.

The role of sensory information in immersive gaming experiences was recognized by Ermi and Mäyrä [16] for the development of a gameplay experience model (sensory, challenge-based, and imaginative immersion model or SCI model). The authors called it *sensory immersion*: an overpowering of the sensory information from the real environment through large screens and powerful sounds to focus the user entirely on the stimulus. In their study on presence, Witmer and Singer [70] made the distinction between immersion and involvement such that the former is the subjective experience of being enveloped in an interactive environment and the latter is a psychological state which results from directing attention to the stimulus.

It may appear that what many researchers call perceptual or sensory immersion is a completely different perspective on immersion compared to psychological immersion. Nevertheless, it is instead a facilitator for psychological immersion since overpowering sensory information or blocking the stimuli from the immediate environ-

---

[2] This section was originally published in [3].

ment does not guarantee psychological immersion but can prevent "an exogenous shift of attention" [45] away from the activity; consequently, leading to psychological immersion. The current attempts to create supposed immersive audiovisual experiences are based on this idea of eliciting psychological immersion. It is assumed that augmenting the sensory information (e.g., in spatial audio reproduction) and/or attempting to reduce the inputs from the physical environment (e.g., virtual reality) will lead to the users focusing on the stimulus and experiencing psychological immersion.

### 11.2.1.2 Absorption in the Narrative or its Depiction

The role of the narrative is considered to be an important dimension of the immersive experience. Mental absorption in the story or the mediated world is the definition of being immersed on a diegetic level. Adam and Rollings [1] called it *narrative immersion*: "the feeling of being inside a story, completely involved and accepting the world and events of the story as real." A similar description has been provided by Thon [45]: "narrative immersion refers to the player's shift of attention to the unfolding of the story of the game and the characters therein as well as to the construction of a situation model representing not only the various characters and narrative events, but also the fictional game world as a whole." The idea of narrative immersion has been echoed in the context of video games under *imaginative immersion* [16] and as *fictional immersion* [5] for all narrative forms.

It has been suggested that an exciting story and interesting characters are prerequisites for experiencing narrative immersion [1]. Ryan [57] classified the causes that lead to narrative immersion as temporal, spatial, and emotional immersion. *Temporal immersion* is experienced when one is curious to known how the story unfolds. *Spatial immersion* refers to the experience of having a sense of space and enjoyment in exploration. Lastly, *emotional immersion* occurs when one is emotionally invested in the story and/or emotionally attached to the characters. It can also be observed when the narrative elements remind the individual of emotionally relevant instances or characters.

### 11.2.1.3 Absorption When Facing Challenges

The idea of being absorbed when facing challenges stems from the work conducted on immersion in gaming experiences. Absorption in the activity due to challenges occurs when a balance is achieved between ability and the perceived challenge [16]. These challenges can be mental challenges or sensorimotor challenges. Ermi and Mäyrä [16] believed that the challenges encountered will often be a combination of mental and sensorimotor challenges to a certain extent. Thus, the individuals must have attentional surplus to face the challenges simultaneously or the overlap between the challenges must be brief to avoid attentional overload [44]. The nature of the challenge was used to distinguish challenge-based immersion as strategic and tactical immersion by Adam and Rollings [1]. *Strategic immersion* is experienced when one is preoccupied strategizing and making choices mentally to conquer the task on hand. *Tactical immersion* refers to the state of mental absorption when one is fully concentrated on the activity that has a stream of demands for swift tactile movements (e.g., when playing action-packed video games).

Challenge in the current view refers to active hurdles encountered in participatory activities. Arsenault [5] argued that challenges are not required to experience immersion and suggested to substitute challenge-based immersion with *systematic immersion*: immersion in the activity where one accepts the mechanics (e.g., rules, physical movement, etc.) of the mediated experience instead of the mechanics from the unmediated reality. The idea of systematic immersion can be applied to non-participatory activities[3] such as a screening of a fictional film where one readily accepts the existence of magic and flying sea mammals, for instance.

## 11.2.2 Physical Perspective

A substantial portion of the work on immersion has been performed in the context of media consumption for interactive applications (e.g., video games, virtual environments). This has supposedly led to the notion of immersion being an objective property of the system or the technology that facilitates the experience. In Slater and Wilbur's [60] words, "Immersion is a description of a technology, and describes the extent to which the computer displays are capable of delivering an inclusive, extensive, surrounding and vivid illusion of reality to the senses of a human participant." In this regard, immersion is seen as the capability of the system/technology to support the different modalities, deliver sensory information, and provide interaction capabilities. Slater rejects the idea of immersion being a subjective experience. Instead, he views immersion as an objective property of the system that consists of reproduction fidelity of the different modalities, isolation from the physical world, and behavioral fidelity among others [62]. These properties of the "immersive system" can lead to different subjective experience of place and plausibility illusion according to him [62].[4]

It is important to state that approaching immersion as an objective property fails to consider the perceptual limits, context, and individual factors such as mood, preference, expertise, and expectations. It has been established that an improvement in the technical specifications of the system does not necessarily lead to a proportional perceptual change (evident by non-linear psychophysical curves). Limiting immersion to the physical domain removes the sensory and cognitive filters that play an active

---

[3] Non-participatory activities are activities where the user's actions cannot modify the outcome of the activity. Reading a book or watching a movie are examples of non-participatory activities. Contrarily, playing a video game where the user's inputs can have an impact on the storyline they experience (e.g., Grand Theft Auto 5) is an example of a participatory activity.

[4] Slater's description of place illusion is synonymous to the idea of physical presence as stated by him in [63].

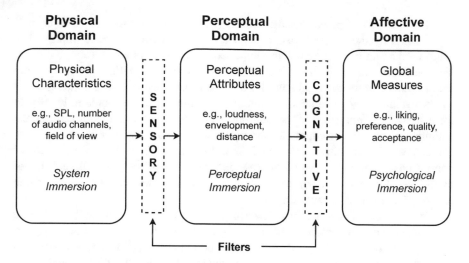

**Fig. 11.2** Filter model and the suggested terms for referring to the perspectives on immersion in the different domains

part in determining the overall experience. It has been appropriately suggested that the term *system immersion* [61] should be used when referring to this perspective on immersion.

The ideas of immersion being an objective property and perceptual or sensory immersion are closely related. An improvement in the technical specifications of the system such as an increase in the number of loudspeakers can increase the sensory information leading to psychological immersion as explained in Sect. 11.2.1.1. This can give the impression that it is the system or the sensory information that leads to psychological immersion. While the system is a factor that can influence immersion, it is not the only factor as the physical perspective suggests.

## 11.3 Immersion: A Cognitive Concept

It[5] is clear from the preceding section that we must organize the usage of the term *immersion* to communicate the intended ideas and conduct research on the subject. We use the *filter model* [6, 33] to differentiate and categorize the ideas conveyed by the common term. The model (depicted in Fig. 11.2) has been used for sensory analysis in food science, sound and image quality evaluations, and to study the spatial characteristic of sound among others [6].

The model starts with the *physical domain* which houses a physical stimulus (e.g., a music signal played by a loudspeaker). The stimulus is characterized by the physical measurements of the audio frequency content, spatial audio channels,

---

[5] Part of this section has been copied from [3] upon receiving the publisher's approval.

etc. The stimulus is perceived after passing through the sensory filter when it is transformed by the sensory system (e.g., auditory system) to neural energy. The result is an auditory event which is comprised of attributes of sound (e.g., loudness, envelopment). The elicitation of the attributes and their strength depends upon the characteristics of the physical stimulus and the sensory system. The auditory event can be evaluated by perceptual measurements in the perceptual domain. Finally, to form an overall impression of the auditory event, the perception passes through the cognitive filter which accounts for emotional state, expertise, expectations, mood, context, etc. The cognitive factors and the individual attributes from the perceptual domain contribute to the overall impression which requires an integrative frame of mind. These affective or hedonic measurements include assessment of quality, degree of liking, annoyance, acceptance, etc.

The filter model is simple yet powerful as it allows us to evaluate the influence of physical parameters of the system and signal on affective measurements by linking the two domains through the perceptual domain. The primary ideas conveyed by the use of the term *immersion* can be categorized using the filter model. First, we have Slater's idea of immersion as being an objective property of the technology/system. Slater [62] has stated that "Let's reserve the term 'immersion' to stand simply for what the technology delivers from an objective point of view. The more that a system delivers displays (in all sensory modalities) and tracking that preserves fidelity in relation to their equivalent real-world sensory modalities, the more that it is 'immersive'." Slater [61] has suggested the term *system immersion* to denote his understanding of immersion which is in the physical domain. Second, immersion is used to refer to the sense of being surrounded by a stimulus (see Sect. 11.2.1.1). This is the perception of the stimulus and thus exists in the perceptual domain. We recommend that the term *perceptual immersion* should be used when referring to the feeling of being surrounded. The goal with surrounding the user with a stimulus is often done with the hope of eliciting psychological immersion as both perceptual attributes and cognitive factors contribute to affective measurements as explained in the preceding paragraph. Finally, the idea of *psychological immersion* (see Sect. 11.2.1) or involvement/absorption in the activity can be explained in the cognitive domain. The user (their personal characteristics) plays an important role in the experience of psychological immersion but the perceptual attributes (e.g., envelopment, naturalness) can influence psychological immersion.

Our motivation for studying immersion is to identify the influencing factors so that they may be tuned to enhance experiences. The role of the individual is of utmost importance since experiences are, by their very nature, subjective. Thus, it is important to consider the holistic experience instead of focusing on individual parts that contribute to the experience. Assessment of audiovisual experiences has been historically driven from a bottom-up approach beginning from the technical specifications of the system that facilitates the experience. However, improvements in the technical capabilities of the system may not always lead to a perceptual difference (e.g., when the improvements are smaller than the just noticeable difference or beyond the thresholds of the human sensory system), rendering them insignificant for the goal of improving experiences. Therefore, we advocate a top-down approach where the idea is first studied holistically (in the cognitive domain) and then empirical relationships are forged to the technical parameters of the system (physical domain).

We view immersion from a psychological perspective (similar to Sect. 11.2.1). For the remainder of this chapter, our usage of the term immersion refers to psychological immersion unless noted otherwise. Synthesizing from the descriptions of immersion appearing in literature, we propose the following definition of immersion that can be applied to a wide range of applications:

> **Immersion** is a phenomenon experienced by an individual when they are in a state of deep mental involvement in which their cognitive processes (with or without sensory stimulation) cause a shift in their attentional state such that one may experience disassociation from the awareness of the physical world.

We consider immersion to be a normal occurrence of focused attention (on the activity) during waking consciousness. During immersion, the mind is absorbed in the current motivated activity and conscious attention is focused on the features of the situation that are related to the achievement of the intended goal. Still, during most normal circumstances the mind can easily be disturbed by extrinsic factors (e.g., noise in the environment), intrinsic dynamic tendencies (e.g., unfinished tasks or obligations), and random noise. Unlike hallucinations and dreaming during sleep states, the mind is still attentive or watchful (to some degree) to the occurrences in the world and monitors the present state of the body when immersed in a construction built by intrinsic factors. When something of significance for the maintenance of the subject's life and well-being occurs, the perturbations may usually rather easily destabilize the current state, change the focus of attention, and propel the mind into another and more stable attractor of orientation and search for the nature of the disturbance. For detailed discussions of consciousness, the reader is referred to [15, 18, 20, 38, 50].

Involvement in the current view necessitates an interaction between the subject and the system not only in a physical sense (the completion of a series of actions and operations upon the system) but also in a psychological sense (the interaction between the subject's motives for the interaction with the system and the system's objective capabilities for the pursuit of the subject's motives). Based on the proposed definition, immersion is a mental state which is why sensory stimulation is not required to experience immersion (e.g., daydreaming can be an immersive experience).

It is imperative to consider all sensory modalities for determining immersion since the presented stimuli may stimulate only a few senses but we continue to receive input from all the senses that can influence immersion. Therefore, all factors that can either facilitate or disrupt immersion must be considered. It is unreasonable to merely examine the stimulus or the system to determine immersion. While the system and the content can affect immersion, they are not immersive independent of the human subject. The idea of immersive potential can add clarity to the above explanation.

**Immersive potential**: The potential of a system or content to elicit immersion.

For a given piece of content presented by a system which does not change, the immersive potential remains constant. It does not simply increase with the betterment of the system's technical specifications. Instead, it depends on its ability to elicit immersion. The immersive potential is barred by the human perceptual limits and the changes to a system must lead to a discernible perceptual change to alter its immersive potential.

In addition to the system and the content, immersion also depends on the state of the individual at the moment in time as well as their immersive tendency.

**Immersive tendency** [70]: An individual's predisposition to experience immersion.

The immersive tendency can be determined with the help of questionnaires [69, 70] to learn if certain individuals can get immersed relatively easily compared to others. It can be assumed to stay constant over the course of an experiment which is conducted within a short duration of time.[6]

The five factors that can influence immersion are (1) the system (physical properties of the reproduction system and the content), (2) narrative (content), (3) environment (physical environment around the individual and the contextual conditions), (4) individual factors (affective states, mood, preference, skills, previous knowledge, expertise, goals, motivation, etc.), and (5) interaction between the individual and the experience (significance of the content to the individual, acceptance of the task, alignment of goal and motivation). These are similar to those which affect the quality of experience (QoE) [54] since immersion is an experience that is dependent on an individual's cognitive state and preference for the content. Nonetheless, there is a noteworthy distinction between the concept of QoE and immersive experiences. This is explained in the following subsection.

## 11.3.1  Quality of Experience (QoE) and Immersion

The concept of quality of experience (QoE) was introduced in the field of telecommunication and multimedia services. It is the successor to quality of service experienced (QoSE) which is the successor to quality of service (QoS).[7] The progression from QoS to QoE has shifted the approach to quality from technology-centric to user-centric. It is important to note that this shift is consistent with the widespread acknowledgment that only the end users are capable of judging quality [49]. Although

---

[6] Immersive tendency can change over time due to training, learning, experience, changes in personality, etc. Since these factors do not normally vary within a short duration of time (e.g., over the course of a few days), these can be assumed to be constant for conducting experiments. Nevertheless, it is recommended to limit tests to a single session.

[7] A detailed discussion of the terms and their relationship to QoE is beyond the scope of this chapter. Please refer to [28, 49, 67] for an extensive review.

several definitions of QoE are in use, the following definition by Raake and Egger [49] (based on the definition proposed in the Qualinet white paper [47]) provides a complete and functional description of the concept:

**Quality of experience (QoE)** is the degree of delight or annoyance of a person whose experience involves an application, service, or system. It results from the person's evaluation of the fulfillment of his or her expectations and needs with respect to the utility and/or enjoyment in the light of the person's context, personality, and current state.

The act of experiencing does not constitute quality judgement [49]. Evaluating quality requires cognitive processes in addition to those engaged during the act of experiencing [49]. Please refer to [30, 48] for additional information on quality formation process. QoE is a two-step process comprising of experiencing and forming a quality judgement. This is a major point of distinction between immersion and QoE. Immersion is the state of being mentally absorbed in an experience whereas QoE is the evaluation of quality for any experience, immersive or not.

An immersive experience is an experience where immersion is elicited. The quality of such an experience may be determined by methodologies inspired by QoE evaluations. Thus, we place immersion on a level below QoE in the hierarchy. Immersion may be a factor that can influence QoE but the scientific evidence is yet to emerge.

## 11.4  Differentiating Immersion from Interchangeably Used Terms

The preceding section presented a detailed explanation of immersion that is synthesized from a non-exhaustive literature review. To establish the terminology and add clarity to the concept of immersion, a brief review of interchangeably used terms is presented in the following sub-subsections and the ideas are differentiated from immersion.

### 11.4.1  Presence

Presence has been an important research topic for technology mediated experiences. Initially, presence referred to the experience of perceiving the physical environment and did not entail the use of technology [64]. However, presence is used in a much broader sense today. It is generally understood as "a psychological state or subjective perception in which even though part or all of an individual's current experience is generated by and/or filtered through human-made technology, part or all of the individual's perception fails to accurately acknowledge the role of the technology in the experience" [17]. This definition refers to what is known as *physical presence* (also called place illusion). Presence is also classified as social presence (the experience of being together with others) and co-presence (being together in the same physical space). The discussion here is limited to physical presence since it is the one that is often confused with immersion.

Place illusion (physical presence) and plausibility illusion[8] are required for realistic behaviors in virtual environments [63]. Place illusion is a technology mediated illusion where the user has the feeling of being in a real space which is not the actual physical space they are in. Slater [62] views place illusion as a subjective response to system immersion. He explains that "if immersion [system immersion] is analogous to wavelength distribution in the description of color then "'presence' is analogous to the perception of color." In this sense, presence is a perceptual attribute that is directly influenced by the properties of the system. To extend this in the context of the filter model, liking or the quality of presence would represent the overall impression of the experience in the cognitive domain.

When explaining why people often report the sense of "being there" when engaging with systems possessing low system immersion, Slater hypothesized that the reported presence experiences were qualitatively different from those encountered due to objectively better systems (higher system immersion) [44]. He [63] asserted that presence due to superior systems is caused because of the exposure to the sensory stimuli while presence experienced due to relatively inferior systems requires focused attention and deliberate learning [63]. Slater [63] goes on to state that "[the feeling of presence due to low system immersion] it is not simply a function of how the perceptual system normally works, but is something that essentially needs to be learned, and may be regarded as more complex." This explanation is at odds with the psychophysics-based description he has provided using the analogy to color perception. Although it has been argued that cognition plays a role in determining presence [59], the sensory information delivered by the system is paramount [62]. Please refer to [44] for an overview of presence theories.

At this stage, it is important to distinguish between place illusion and our definition of immersion which was presented in Sect. 11.3. Foremost, immersion is mental absorption in the activity whereas presence is the feeling of being in an unmediated environment even when the contrary is true. It follows that immersion resides in the cognitive domain whereas descriptions of presence suggest that it is a perceptual attribute. Secondly, presence requires technologically mediated experiences whereas immersion can be experienced even without sensory stimulation from the system.

We follow Jennett et al.'s [31] notion that the two concepts are independent and a double dissociation exists between immersion and presence. For participatory activities, immersion can be experienced when playing abstract games such as Pac-Man on a mobile phone but it is unlikely that the user will feel that they are present in the game environment. Similarly, a high fidelity audiovisual reproduction of an uninteresting

---

[8] The illusion that the events in the virtual environment is actually happening even when you know that they are not [63].

movie in virtual reality can deliver the illusion of being in an alternate environment but will fail to deliver an immersive experience. Nonetheless, it is important to note that presence and immersion can coincide as is often the case for engaging virtual reality experiences, for example.

## 11.4.2   Flow

The concept of flow was developed in the 1960s through a series of studies conducted to understand why people pursue arduous and often dangerous activities in the absence of discernible extrinsic rewards [12]. Multiple definitions and descriptions of flow have been presented including, "the holistic sensation that people feel when they act with total involvement" [10]; "a subjective state that people report when they are completely involved in something to the point of forgetting time, fatigue, and everything else but the activity itself" [12]; and "the state in which people are so involved in an activity that nothing else seems to matter; the experience itself is so enjoyable that people will do it even at great cost, for the sheer sake of doing it" [11]. Csikszentmihalyi [12] identified eight components of flow: clear goals, direct and immediate feedback, altered sense of time, loss of self-consciousness, concentration, balance between ability and challenge, sense of control, and escape from everyday life. However, researchers have not yet established the conditions that must be fulfilled for an experience to qualify as flow [66].

There is an evident overlap between flow and immersion, but the two are not synonymous. Immersion is a graded experience [2, 8] whereas flow is an "all-or-nothing" experience [9]. Flow is an optimal experience that is always enjoyable whereas enjoyment is not mandatory for immersion, i.e., an individual can experience negative emotions when immersed but it will not qualify as a state of flow since it is not pleasant. Additionally, the concept of flow is limited to interactive activities because flow components such as clear goals and immediate feedback are not applicable to passive activities. It has been argued that immersion is a precursor to flow, but flow is not simply the highest degree of immersion [31]. For instance, a passive, unpleasant experience can be highly immersive but will fail to qualify as flow due to a lack of enjoyment and the interactive components that constitute flow.

## 11.4.3   Envelopment

Envelopment is an important topic in concert hall acoustics and spatial audio. It is classified as *listener envelopment* (sense of being surrounded by the reverberant sound field) [56] and *source-related envelopment* (envelopment by sounds placed around the listener) [19]. It is clear from the literature [33] that envelopment is strictly a perceptual attribute. However, it continues to be confused with immersion. There are two reasons that can explain the replaceable usage: (1) use of the common analogy:

"feeling of swimming underwater" to illustrate immersion as well as envelopment, and (2) approaching immersion as *perceptual immersion* (see Sect. 11.2.1.1) makes the two synonymous.

The predominant difference between envelopment and immersion is that the former is perceptual while the latter is affective since it is an integrative measure that accounts for cognitive factors. A double dissociation exists between immersion and envelopment. For example, monophonic reproduction in a non-reverberant environment will not elicit the feeling of envelopment but it can be immersive. Similarly, an accurate reproduction of a soundscape is unlikely to be immersive due to a lack of an engaging narrative but will be reported to be highly enveloping. Nevertheless, it should be noted that envelopment and immersion can coexist. Further, envelopment can lead to immersion in an experience since sense of being surrounded is one of the reasons that can lead to psychological immersion (see Fig. 11.1).

## 11.5  Subjective Assessment of Immersion: An Exploratory Study

Quantification of immersion is the immediate step following the theoretical conceptualization of the topic. Nevertheless, a lack of established experimental paradigms for the assessment of immersion is the greatest challenge in developing our understanding of the topic. A lack of a consensus on the idea of immersion, fragile nature of immersive experiences [43], and limited information about the factors and their influence on immersion add to the complexity of quantifying immersion. Methodologies for assessing immersion can be classified as subjective and objective measures.[9] An outline of these is presented below.

### 11.5.1  Subjective and Objective Measures

Subjective measurement paradigms ask the participants to reflect on their experience and form a conscious judgement. Questionnaires, focus groups, think aloud paradigms, and interviews are examples of subjective measures. These are conducted post-experience in order to avoid infringing on the experience. Thus, they are less susceptible to the emotional and physiological idiosyncrasies. Subjective measures are attractive as they are non-invasive and easy to interpret for the participants. They allow researchers to explore multiple facets of immersion (e.g., emotions, mental and physical awareness, liking, etc.) as the areas of interest can be multiple items on a questionnaire or be verbally questioned in an interview. Moreover, subjective

---

[9] Please refer to [3] for literature on subjective and objective measures. Additionally, Zhang [71] has provided a detailed discussion on the pros and cons of the measures.

measures are excellent for determining individual differences as the responses can be directly compared and analyzed.

The simplicity and effectiveness of subjective measures is appealing but the drawbacks must be considered to select suitable experimental paradigms. Foremost, the post-experience nature of these measures can lead to inaccurate recall and recency effect. These can be particularly problematic when longer stimuli are used for evaluations. The retrospective recall also restricts the evaluation of temporal variations in immersion. Finally, for subjective measures that are based on a set of predefined questions (e.g., questionnaires), there is a risk of failing to capture all the aspects of the immersive experience that are beyond the scope of the listed items.

In contrast to subjective measures, objective measures attempt to record the user's response without requiring conscious evaluation and correlate those responses to immersion and/or its attributes. Behavioral and physiological measures are the two types of objective methods used for assessing immersion. The former includes measures such as secondary task reaction time (STRT)[10] while the latter involves the use of biological sensors to measure physical response to the stimulus (e.g., electroencephalography, eye tracking, and electrodermal activity). These methods do not allow for the direct measurement of immersion. Instead, the recorded response is correlated to immersion or the suspected to be attributes of immersion.

The objective and non-intrusive aspect of objective measures yields an accurate, time-variant measurement of concept under evaluation. Since the deliberate judgement formation process is eliminated unlike subjective measures, the measurements are not influenced by the various biases associated with subjective evaluations. The single most important criticism of objective measures is the lack of established relationship(s) between immersion and what is measured. Hence, there is a risk of measuring an idea that may not be related to immersion or differently related than assumed. In addition to the lack of one-to-one mapping, physiological signals can be highly sensitive, require specialized equipment in controlled environments, and may need extensive data analysis procedures.

## 11.5.2  Research Questions

An experiment was conducted to develop and test a suitable methodology for assessing immersion as a necessary first step.[11] Answers to the following research questions were sought in the study:

---

[10] The premise for STRT is that our cognitive resources are limited. Thus, if resources are largely expended on the primary task, less resources will be available for the secondary task which will reflect in the efficiency with which the secondary task is performed. The level of immersion can hence be measured by the performance of the secondary task, i.e., when STRT performance is low, high level of immersion was experienced.

[11] The experiment is covered in detail in [2]. Here, only the key points are discussed.

**RQ1** How can immersion in an audiovisual experience be quantified through subjective testing?
**RQ2** Is immersion a binary (all-or-nothing) or graded experience?
**RQ3** What is the influence of immersive tendency on immersion ratings?

### 11.5.3 Experimental Strategy and Design

Subjective and objectives tests each have their advantages and disadvantages as discussed in Sect. 11.5.1. The fundamental issue with physiological measures is the lack of established links between what is measured and immersion. Thus, one cannot be certain if what is being measured is immersion or is related to immersion in a quantifiable way. Experimental designs that incorporate behavioral responses such as STRT are potential alternatives but have failed to yield conclusive results. The limitations with objective measures limit us to subjective assessment of immersion [40].

Subjective assessment of immersion has been predominantly conducted using questionnaires. However, since the questionnaires often have in excess of 25 items, administering them for each experience adds to the experimental time and the workload for the participants. Further, questionnaires fail to capture the unexpected aspects of immersion or those that are unaccounted for in the set of questions [71]. Jennett et al. [31] compared the results from a questionnaire to that of a single question on the immersion experienced by the participants. Their experiments revealed that "people can reliably reflect on their own immersion in a single question" when grading immersion on a categorical 10-point scale. This is an important finding as it implies that immersion experiments may be conducted as rating experiments. Since rating experiments are the norm for audiovisual assessment and participants are familiar with the general paradigm, it was decided to conduct the experiment as a rating experiment.

Before the experimental design could be developed, it was necessary to outline the theoretical implications on the experimental paradigm. First, the participants cannot be permitted to switch between stimuli for making comparative judgments as it will destroy the state of immersion [3]. Similarly, the evaluations must be made post-experience. Second, it is hypothesized that individuals require time to return to their base or initial state after an immersive experience. Distractor tasks can be incorporated to shift attention away from the experience between consecutive presentations. Third, the experiment must be completed in a single session since participants experience fatigue faster in non-participatory tasks [29] and time can alter individual factors such as mood. Finally, each participant should be limited to one instance of any stimulus due to limited information regarding the effect of repetition on immersion.

With the implications in mind, a pilot test was conducted as a randomized complete block design to aid with the selection of stimuli and to test the protocol. Six participants each graded the same set of 5 stimuli. The pilot test results suggested that the session should be limited to 75–80 min in order to avoid participant fatigue.

Since a large number of stimuli had to be tested (particularly for RQ2) and repetitions were prohibited, a balanced incomplete block (BIB) design was determined to be the most appropriate choice for the main study. A major drawback of a simple BIB design is that as the number of stimuli to evaluate increases, the number of participants required increases drastically (provided the number of evaluations each participant performs does not change). Thus, precision had to be traded to reduce the number of participants required for the experiment [35].

The simple BIB design was reduced to a BIB design with 21 blocks (participants) and 15 treatments (stimuli). Every participant evaluated a subset of 5 stimuli from the set of 15. The stimuli were allocated such that each pair of stimuli (e.g., A and F) would only appear together in two blocks (i.e., only two participants would get both A and F). In total, there were 7 instances of each of the 15 stimuli that yielded 105 total observations as 21 participants graded 5 stimuli each. The allocation of the stimuli to the different blocks is shown in Table 11.1.

**Table 11.1** Allocation of stimuli to the experimental blocks for the balanced incomplete block (BIB) design used in the study. Reproduced from [2]

| Block | Exp. 1 | Exp. 2 | Exp. 3 | Exp. 4 | Exp. 5 |
|---|---|---|---|---|---|
| 1 | D | J | M | N | O |
| 2 | A | B | H | I | M |
| 3 | A | C | E | F | O |
| 4 | C | E | G | H | L |
| 5 | B | D | E | J | K |
| 6 | B | C | D | G | O |
| 7 | F | G | K | M | O |
| 8 | C | F | I | J | M |
| 9 | A | D | G | L | M |
| 10 | A | C | J | K | L |
| 11 | C | D | H | I | K |
| 12 | B | F | G | H | J |
| 13 | H | J | L | N | O |
| 14 | D | E | F | I | L |
| 15 | B | F | K | L | N |
| 16 | A | G | I | K | N |
| 17 | A | B | I | L | O |
| 18 | B | C | E | M | N |
| 19 | E | G | I | J | N |
| 20 | A | D | F | H | N |
| 21 | E | H | K | M | O |

The pre-fix "s" used for representing the stimuli is dropped in this table for clarity.

## 11.5.4   Methods

### 11.5.4.1   Program Material

There are various implications for selecting the program material for assessing immersion (see [3]). Foremost, the relevance of the program material to the participant plays a role in determining immersion and can vary among participants. Thus, it should not be assumed that any given stimulus can immerse all participants. Additionally, since knowledge and expectations may change with every trial of a stimulus, an assessor may not experience immersion during repeated presentations of the same stimulus.

It is important to select audiovisual excerpts with lengths sufficient to elicit immersion. It has been recommended that stimuli that are at least 10 min long must be used [29], but there is limited information regarding the temporal nature of immersion. The recommendation is focused on participatory activities, and we suspect that the length of the stimulus can be lower and is dependent on the narrative. Thus, excerpts ranging from 4 to 12 min were selected for this study.

Given the lack of knowledge regarding the effect of familiarity on immersion, it is suggested that content that is unfamiliar and that does not require additional background information must be selected. However, this stipulation limits the amount of content that can be selected. Therefore, it was decided to provide the participants with a short synopsis (1–2 sentences) regarding the narrative before each presentation. These were constructed only to include any relevant information required to make sense of the story and did not disclose any additional information.

Finally, to select the technical specifications of the excerpts, an informal survey of the domestic media landscape suggested that ultra high-definition (UHD), high dynamic range (HDR) visuals and spatial audio are emerging for domestic consumption. These are being incorporated by broadcasters, streaming platforms, and movie studios alike. Thus, it was decided to use a 7.1.4 audio rendering system coupled with an UHD HDR enabled screen. The 7.1.4 audio reproduction system was chosen as it was revealed to be the most common spatial audio reproduction system beyond traditional surround sound for domestic applications.

Audiovisual excerpts of different lengths and narratives that can elicit spatial, emotional, and temporal immersion were chosen for the experiment. An active effort was made to select stimuli that were distributed across the immersion scale as the results are directly dependent on the stimuli. The selection was made based on the pilot experiment and comments received from the pilot test participants because the technical specifications could not be used to choose the excerpts. A list of the excerpts and the genres is presented in Table 11.2.

The fundamental challenge with selecting stimuli that has UHD HDR visuals coupled with spatial audio was a lack of freely available content. Hence, commercially available content with Dolby or DTS audio had to be used for this experiment. Fifteen audiovisual excerpts that fulfilled the above-stated conditions were selected. The resolution, native aspect ratio, and chroma sub-sampling were not changed for reproduction. The audiovisual signals were not processed at any stage.

**Table 11.2**   Audiovisual excerpts used in the experiment. Reproduced from [2]

| Excerpt | Content | Genre | Year | Timecode |
|---|---|---|---|---|
| Example | Earth: One Amazing Day | Nature | 2018 | 00:08:50 – 00:16:49 |
| sA | Mission: Impossible – Fallout | Action | 2018 | 01:12:31 – 01:16:09 |
| sB | Apocalypse Now – Final Cut | War/Drama | 2019 | 02:12:45 – 02:20:24 |
| sC | The Revenant | Adventure | 2016 | 01:53:09 – 01:58:24 |
| sD | Fantastic Beasts: CG [a] | Fantasy/Adventure | 2019 | 01:34:50 – 01:42:47 |
| sE | Dynasties: Lion | Nature | 2018 | 00:16:11 – 00:20:00 |
| sF | The Darkest Hour | War/Drama | 2018 | 00:41:09 – 00:48:00 |
| sG | Murder on the Orient Express | Mystery/Drama | 2018 | 00:00:53 – 00:08:31 |
| sH | Braveheart | War/Drama | 2018 | 00:22:05 – 00:28:36 |
| sI | Ad Astra | Sci-fi | 2020 | 01:15:23 – 01:21:17 |
| sJ | Earth: One Amazing Day | Nature | 2018 | 00:57:50 – 01:02:39 |
| sK | Spider-Man: Into the Spider-Verse | Animation/Action | 2019 | 00:02:32 – 00:13:42 |
| sL | The Revenant | Adventure | 2016 | 00:02:30 – 00:14:59 |
| sM | Sicario | Crime/Action | 2018 | 00:01:00 – 00:12:53 |
| sN | Earth: One Amazing Day | Nature | 2018 | 00:47:47 – 00:51:37 |
| sO | Earth: One Amazing Day | Nature | 2018 | 00:16:50 – 00:22:35 |

[a] Crimes of Grindelwald

Notes:
1. The year of release refers to the UK year of release on 4K Blu-ray.
2. Please refer to Table 5 in [2] for the corresponding narrative synopsis.

## 11.5.4.2   Reproduction Setup

The audiovisual excerpts were presented directly from the Blu-ray player to every participant due to legal limitations. An HDCP compliant video switcher and the Genelec loudspeaker manager (GLM) were used to control the video and the audio respectively. The complete audiovisual signal chain is depicted in Fig. 11.3.

A 7.1.4 audio rendering system was used for audio reproduction. The audio was decoded by the Marantz AV7704 and the decoded channels were mapped to the corresponding loudspeaker channels. A phantom reproduction of the center audio channel was used since it was not feasible to have a physical loudspeaker due to the screen. The Genelec loudspeakers were distributed on a hemisphere with a 2 m radius around the listening position. The placement of the loudspeakers was in accordance with Dolby guidelines [13].

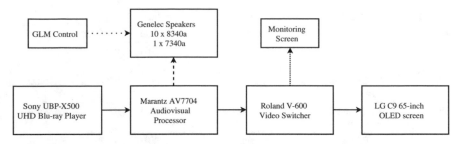

**Fig. 11.3** Audiovisual reproduction signal flow. The different line types refer to: HDMI 2.0 and HDCP 2.2 connection (——), analog audio feed over XLR (- - -), remote loudspeaker control over Ethernet (······), and HDMI 1.4 connection (········)

The loudspeakers were level calibrated and time aligned with respect to each other. To achieve approximately equal loudness among the stimuli, the level was varied such that the audio was equally loud at the listening position as determined by ear. All excerpts were auditioned by two experienced listeners to ensure that the stimuli were at comfortable loudness and that the audio was intelligible during the quieter segments.

A 65-inch LG C9 OLED screen was used to reproduce the visuals. The screen was centered with respect to the participants to obtain a zero degree viewing angle horizontally and vertically. It was placed at a distance of 2 m (same as the loudspeakers) following the design viewing distance in ITU-R BT.2022 recommendation [26]. To balance the judder of 24p video signal while exploiting the high dynamic range (HDR) capabilities of the screen, the screen brightness was lowered to nearly 120 nits and the environmental illuminance was less than 10 lux. The screen settings were tuned by two experienced viewers in part to get the chromaticity coordinates closer to the D65 value [27] and in part based on experience.

The audiovisual reproduction took place in an IEC 60268-13 [25] compliant listening room. All equipment except the screen and the loudspeakers were placed outside the room. The loudspeakers were hidden behind acoustical transparent curtains to limit visual influence.

### 11.5.4.3 Distractor Tasks

It was hypothesized that some time is required to return to the initial or base psychological state after an engaging experience. Presentation of stimuli in quick succession may lead to the preceding stimulus biasing the result of the following stimulus. In the absence of formal guidelines and conclusive evidence regarding the gap in time between presentation of stimuli, distractor tasks were incorporated in an attempt to shift attention away from the preceding stimulus by requiring active participation.

A 11 piece LEGO® unicorn puzzle (only instruction was to create a unicorn), an image for free interpretation,[12] a matchstick rearrangement puzzle, and a memory

---

[12] The participants were guided by asking them to note their impression of what was happening in the picture, what led to that impression, and what additional information could they collect.

(a) Matchstick puzzle      (b) Memory task      (c) Lego puzzle      (d) Image for interpretation

**Fig. 11.4** The four distractors tasks: **a** Matchstick rearrangement puzzle **b** Memory task ($7 \times 6$ tiles) **c** LEGO® puzzle **d** Image for free interpretation (obtained from the New York Times). All images reproduced from [2]

puzzle were the four distractor tasks. One task was chosen at random to be completed within four minutes between each successive presentation. The assessors were made aware of the correct solution for the matchstick and memory puzzle tasks before proceeding (Fig. 11.4).

### 11.5.4.4 Immersive Tendency Questionnaire

Questionnaires are the primary tool for gauging immersive tendency. Reduced version of widely used [23, 32, 34, 42] Witmer and Singer's [70] immersive tendency questionnaire (ITQ) was used for this study (see Table 11.3 for questionnaire items). Nonetheless, a few modifications were made to the existing questionnaire. The seven point categorical scale was substituted by the graphic line scale (also used for rating immersion) to obtain continuous data; middle word anchor from the categorical scale was dropped as it has been shown that scores can cluster around the verbal anchor [72]; and the terminal verbal anchors were modified to be perfect antonyms (similar modification was made in [23]). The order of questions was randomized for the participants. All assessors answered the ITQ.

### 11.5.4.5 Assessors

The participants were considered a blocking factor (see Sect. 11.5.3) in the experimental design. Twenty-one assessors (blend of experienced and inexperienced) were each assigned to a block at random. Audiovisual assessment expertise was not required since immersion is a cognitive concept. For this study, experienced

**Table 11.3** Witmer and Singer's [70] Immersive Tendency Questionnaire (ITQ). The items in the reduced version of the questionnaire and the corrected item-total correlations from the present study are shown below. Please refer to [2] for analysis of the questionnaire data. Taken from [2]

| | Question | Corrected item-total correlations[a] |
|---|---|---|
| A | Do you easily become deeply involved in movies or TV dramas? | 0.63 |
| B | Do you ever become so involved in a daydream that you are not aware of things happening around you? | 0.44 |
| C | Do you ever have dreams that are so real that you feel disoriented when you awake? | 0.34 |
| D | When watching sports, do you ever become so involved in the game that you react as if you were one of the players? | -0.12 |
| E | How good are you at blocking out external distractions when you are involved in something? | 0.00 |
| F | Have you ever remained apprehensive or fearful long after watching a scary movie? | 0.32 |
| G | Have you ever gotten scared by something happening on a TV show or in a movie? | 0.31 |
| H | Do you ever become so involved in a video game that it is as if you are inside the game rather than moving a joystick and watching the screen? | 0.65 |
| I | How often do you play arcade or video games? (OFTEN should be taken to mean every day or every two days, on average) | 0.41 |
| J | Have you ever gotten excited during a chase or fight scene on TV or in the movies? | 0.65 |
| K | How well do you concentrate on enjoyable activities? | 0.05 |
| L | Do you ever become so involved in a television program or book that people have problems getting your attention? | 0.26 |
| M | How mentally alert do you feel at the present time? | −0.33 |
| N | How physically fit do you feel today? | 0.17 |
| O | How frequently do you find yourself closely identifying with the characters in a story line? | 0.58 |
| P | When playing sports, do you become so involved in the game that you lose track of time? | 0.25 |
| Q | Do you ever become so involved in a movie that you are not aware of things happening around you? | 0.55 |
| R | Do you ever become so involved in doing something that you lose all track of time? | 0.68 |
| S | What kind of books do you read most frequently? Select one | |
| | Spy novels          Fantasies          Science Fiction | |
| | Adventure          Romance novels          Historical novels | |
| | Westerns          Mysteries          Other fiction | |
| | Biographies          Autobiographies          Other non-fiction | – |

[a] The corrected item-total correlations are Pearson product-moment correlations between the item and the sum of all items except the item it is being tested against. These numbers are from the current study.

assessor refers to participants who had experience participating in audiovisual tests, were under continuous weekly training and evaluation exercises, and participated in product development or research activities at Bang & Olufsen. Inexperienced assessors may have participated in audiovisual tests before but were not familiar with subjective evaluation, did not have formal training, and were not actively focused on the technical aspects of audiovisual products or experiences. In total, fifteen males and six females participated in the experiment. The mean age of the participants was 37.7 years (SD = 14.28). Auditory and visual acuity was self-reported by the participants.

## 11.5.5 Procedure

The experiment included two phases: rating part and administration of the immersive tendency questionnaire. Both were completed in a single session of approximately 90 min.

The participants were introduced to the experimental procedure and asked to confirm visual and auditory acuity before participating. The instructions were delivered verbally and in writing. For the rating phase, the participants were given the following description of immersion as stated in [2]:

*"Immersion, also known as deep mental involvement, can be described as being mentally lost (absorbed) in the experience. Immersion is encountered when the experience is involving and absorbs you mentally by capturing your attention. For example, immersion may be experienced when reading a book, playing video games, watching a movie, etc."*

The participants were asked to rate overall immersion on a graphic line scale. The motivation for the scale is found in sensory analysis. It is a 15 cm long line scale where the participants are instructed to insert an intersecting line to denote their perception. The distance from the left end of the scale is considered to be the score (e.g., 6.8 cm would equal to a rating of 6.8). The scale was chosen as it offers the participants infinite steps (in theory) to indicate the intensity of the idea under evaluation. The lack of numbers and verbal anchors (other than those near the endpoints) reduce the bias associated with them. The scale used for the test is shown in Fig. 11.5.

In addition to rating, familiarity with the content was documented by asking assessors to state if they had experienced the excerpts previously. An excerpt that

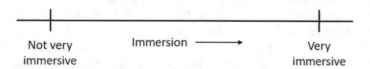

**Fig. 11.5** Graphic line scale for evaluating immersion. Same scale with different verbal anchors was used for the immersive tendency questionnaire (from [2])

could elicit immersion was shown before the test in an attempt to exemplify immersion. However, it was explicitly mentioned that it was only an attempt to illustrate immersion, should not be used as a reference, and may not lead to immersion for the participants. The participants were notified that there were no correct responses and that the use of the entire scale was not mandatory.

A synopsis was provided before each experience. A distractor task was chosen at random to be performed between successive presentation of excerpts. The immersive tendency questionnaire was administered at the end of the rating phase. The experiment was conducted as a pen-and-paper test and the data was collected withing three weeks.

## 11.5.6   Results

Ratings from both phases of the experiment were converted to scores between 0 and 15 (up to one decimal). The converted scores were used for analyzing the data.

### 11.5.6.1   Effect of Stimuli and Differences Between Stimuli Pairs

Data from the rating part of the experiment was analyzed using analysis of variance (ANOVA). Since the scale usage effects were confounded in the collected data and it was not feasible to account for and remove these effects, the estimated marginal means were used to estimating the effect [35]. A mixed effects model ANOVA with stimuli as a fixed factor and participants (blocks) as a random factor was used for analysis. The trials were independent of each other and the assumption of homogeneity of variances was upheld. The residuals were not statistically significantly dissimilar from the normal distribution, $W = 0.99, p = 0.710$ as per the Shapiro-Wilk test.

The ANOVA showed that the effect of the stimuli on immersion scores was significant, $F(14, 74.82) = 3.32, p < 0.001$. This proves that there were distinct differences between the pairs of stimuli and that the participants were able to distinguish between them. The blocking factor (participants) was not found to be statistically significant at $p > 0.05$. However, the effectiveness of the blocking factor is to control for the differences between the participants and cannot simply be judged by statistical significance . Due to a lack of repetitions, the interactions between stimuli and participants factors could not be investigated.

Pairwise comparisons were made between all pairs of stimuli on the basis of the estimated least square means. From the 105 pairs of stimuli, five were found to be statistically significant (Tukey's adjustment). These pairs are marked in Fig. 11.6 above the box plots. The results from the pairwise comparisons suggest that the stimuli fall in one of the three groups: where participants experienced high immersion (sB, sE, sL, and sM), low immersion (sA and sG), and moderate immersion (all remaining stimuli).

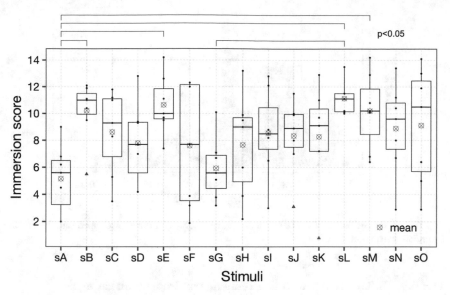

**Fig. 11.6** Visualization of the raw data (not adjusted for scale usage) from the rating phase of the experiment. The significant stimuli pairs as determined by the pairwise comparisons are shown above the box plots

### 11.5.6.2 Nature of Immersion: Binary or Graded?

The distribution of raw immersion scores can reveal whether immersion is a binary or a graded concept. When a large number of stimuli are evaluated, the scores should cluster toward the ends of the scale if immersion is a binary concept, i.e., the distribution of scores should be bimodal. Hartigan's dip test was used to determine if the distribution of immersion scores was unimodal or multimodal.

Hartigan's dip test is based on Hartigan's dip test statistics (HDS). This statistic is the maximum difference between the empirical distribution function (EDF) and the uniform distribution that minimizes the difference between the distributions. The uniform distribution is chosen as it is the least favorable unimodal distribution [21]. A large difference between the distributions leads to higher HDS value and signals movement away from unimodality. To compute the $p$-value, bootstrapped samples are generated and their dip test value is compared iteratively to the dip test value obtained from the empirical distribution. Please refer to [21, 22] for an in-depth explanation of the mathematical calculations. The distribution of the dip statistic values for the bootstrapped samples and the empirical distribution function is shown in Fig. 11.7.

The average $p$-value was 0.862 ($\sigma = 0.04$) for 100 calculations at 5% significance level. The null hypothesis that the distribution of data is unimodal could not be rejected. This result implies that immersion is a graded concept.

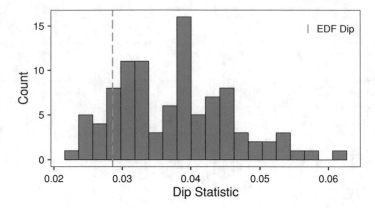

**Fig. 11.7** The distribution of the Hartigan dip statistic values for the bootstrapped samples and the empirical distribution function

### 11.5.6.3 Influence of Immersive Tendency on Immersion ratings

RQ3 was designed to study whether the susceptibility to become immersed in an experience has a direct influence on the immersion ratings. To this end, it was hypothesized that immersion ratings for any stimulus should increase with an increase in the ITQ total scores. Kendall's rank order correlation was chosen to investigate if a monotonic relationship existed between the immersion and ITQ total scores. The value of Kendall's $\tau$ ranges between $-1$ and $+1$ where $-1$ signifies complete disagreement and $+1$ points to a perfectly monotonic relationship. A value of 0 means that there is no monotonic relation between the two variables, but other relationships may exist.

The data and Kendall's rank order correlation coefficients are shown in Fig. 11.8. It was found that values for Kendall's $\tau$ were largely insignificant. Only 2 correlations (for stimuli sD and sJ) were found to be statistically significant. This result suggests that there is no direct influence of immersive tendency on immersion ratings. This inference is based on the critical assumption that the scale usage for the rating phase and the questionnaire items is identical and that immersive tendency is captured and reflected appropriately by the ITQ total score.

## 11.5.7 Discussion

There is a growing interest to study immersion for enhancing audiovisual experiences that have been enabled by technologies such as spatial audio and virtual reality. The primary challenge in investigating immersion is a lack of suitable methodologies for assessing immersion. In this study, we explored a rating experiment inspired

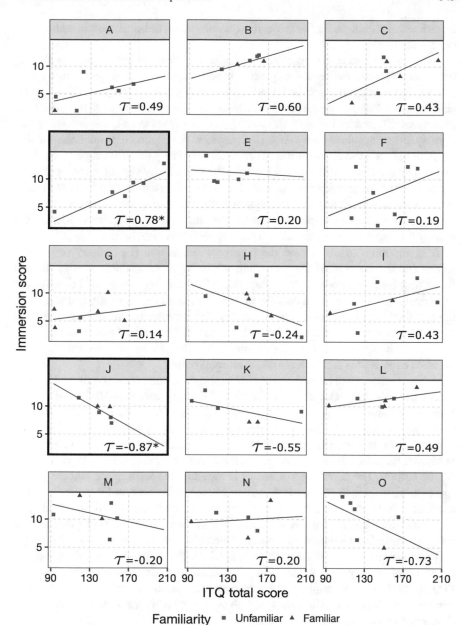

**Fig. 11.8** Kendall's rank order correlation between immersion scores and the immersive tendency questionnaire's total score. Kendall's $\tau$ was significant for stimuli D and J. Regression lines (in red) are plotted only to aid the reader. Participant's familiarity with the content is denoted by the shape of the data points. Adapted from [2]

experimental paradigm for the subjective quantification of immersion in audiovisual experiences.

In subjective testing, the instructions provided to the participants are critical since the assessors make deliberate judgments based on the provided descriptions. It is challenging to communicate the intended idea for cognitive concepts such as immersion due to a lack of standardized definitions and the inability to demonstrate the perceptual differences between stimuli. The results from the experiment show that participants were able to comprehend the provided description of immersion and distinguish between the different stimuli accordingly. The pairwise comparisons show that there were obvious differences between the statistically significant pairs of stimuli even when statistical power is limited. Additionally, the assessors did not report issues with understanding the description before or during the experiment. These results confirm that participants can reflect on the immersion they experience and convey it using a unidimensional scale as suggested by Jennett et al. [31].

It is important to understand the nature of immersion (i.e., binary or graded) to develop the conceptual understanding of the topic. Qualitative studies [8] and theoretical interpretations have conceptualized immersion as a graded concept but empirical tests have not been conducted. Results from Hartigan's dip test show that the distribution or immersion is not multimodal; hence suggesting that immersion is a graded concept. This is consistent with the conceptual understanding of the topic. Immersion being a graded concept implies that direct comparisons can be made between experiences and systems on an interval scale.

A direct influence of immersive tendency ratings on immersion scores could not be detected in this study. Only 2 out of the 15 correlations were found to be statistically significant. However, it is interesting to note that one of those correlations was negative, implying that individuals with higher degree of immersive tendencies found the stimulus to be less immersive. We are unable to explain this finding but believe that analyzing the contents of the excerpt and the comments provided by the participants can be helpful. The correlation of scores is based on the assumption that the participants use the scale in an identical manner for the rating task and the questionnaire exercise. Although this is a reasonable assumption, it has not been tested. Additionally, we assume that the equally weighted sum of scores from the ITQ questionnaire reflects immersive tendency accurately. Given the lack of internal consistency [2] and the unexplained theoretical grounds for including items on the questionnaire, the assumption may be violated. While it is difficult to draw conclusions about the ITQ due to the limited number of observations, the questionnaire must be examined, compared with other existing questionnaires, and/or new questionnaires should be developed to assess immersive tendency.

## 11.6 Summary and Future Work

The primary focus of this chapter has been to present the different perspectives on immersion and address the inconsistent and interchangeable usage of the term. The conceptualizations of immersion gathered from the literature are categorized and clarified using the filter model. We advocate for a top-down approach to study immersion and have synthesized a definition from the psychological standpoint. The definition presented below is intentionally broad and application agnostic to aid adaptability for different applications. Although it has been used for non-interactive application in this chapter, it is applicable to interactive activities as well.

> **Immersion** is a phenomenon experienced by an individual when they are in a state of deep mental involvement in which their cognitive processes (with or without sensory stimulation) cause a shift in their attentional state such that one may experience disassociation from the awareness of the physical world.

This definition was used as the foundation for drawing distinctions between immersion and commonly confused terms such as envelopment and presence. An exploratory experiment was performed by outlining the implications for the experimental paradigm and appraising the benefits and drawbacks of objective and subjective measures. A rating experiment inspired paradigm was chosen for evaluating immersion. The results for the experiment show that the participants were able to discriminate among stimuli even with limited statistical power. This is an important result as it demonstrates that the assessors were able to comprehend the task and reflect on the overall immersion in an experience. Another important result shows immersion is a graded concept which empirically confirms the theoretical conceptualizations of immersion.

The motivation to study and evaluate immersion is to improve the experience for the users ultimately. A key assumption in the quest to study immersion is that positive immersive experiences are preferred by users. It is critical to test this assumption before exploring the different avenues for future work. Efforts should focus on validating and optimizing the experimental paradigm presented in this in addition to overcoming the limitations of the current work stated above. Although the method was applied in the context of domestic audiovisual experiences, adapting the method for virtual and augmented reality applications can be beneficial for optimizing the general methodology. Future work should be focused on quantifying the influence of the physical characteristics of the audiovisual rendering systems on immersion. The results could then be used to improve experiences for the users. For example, determining the influence of audio spatialization can be helpful in designing appropriate sound systems for enabling immersive experiences. The filter model described in Sect. 11.3 is particularly useful for establishing relationships between the physical and the cognitive domains. Inspiration can be drawn from descriptive analysis techniques such as free elicitation [6] and open profiling of quality [65] to determine the key attributes of immersive experiences and acquire knowledge about the central ideas of immersion from the user's perspective.

**Acknowledgements** The authors would like to thank their collaborators for their contributions in [2, 3]. The Journal of the Audio Engineering Society is thanked for their cooperation and approval to reproduced material originally published in [2, 3]. This project has received funding from the European Union's Horizon 2020 research and innovation program under the Marie Skłodowska-Curie grant agreement No.765911.

# References

1. Adams, E., Rollings, A.: Fundamentals of Game Design (Prentice-Hall, Inc., Upper Saddle River, NJ, USA, 2006).
2. Agrawal, S., Bech, S., Bærentsen, K., De Moor, K., Forchhammer, S.: Method for Subjective Assessment of Immersion inAudiovisual Experiences. J.Audio Eng. Soc. **69**, 656–671 (2021).
3. Agrawal, S., Simon, A., Bech, S., Bærentsen, K., Forchhammer, S.: Defining Immersion: Literature Review and Implications for Research on Audiovisual Experiences. J. Audio Eng. Soc. **68**, 404–417 (2020).
4. Amatriain, X., Hollerer, T., Kuchera-Morin, J., Pope, S.: Immersive Audio and Music in the Allosphere in Int. Comp. Music Conf. (Aug. 2007).
5. Arsenault, D.: DarkWaters: Spotlight on Immersion in EUROSIS Game-On North America 2005 Conference (Ghent, Belgium, 2005).
6. Bech, S., Zacharov, N.: Perceptual Audio Evaluation. (Wiley, 2006).
7. Biocca, F., Delaney, B. in Communication in the Age of Virtual Reality (eds Biocca, F., Leavy, M.) (Lawrence Erlbaum Associates Inc, 1995).
8. Brown, E., Cairns, P.: A Grounded Investigation of Game Immersion in CHI '04 (Vienna, Austria, 2004), 1297–1300.
9. Cairns, P., Cox, A., Nordin, A. I. in Handbook of Digital Games (eds Angelides, M. C., Agius, H.) 337–361 (John Wiley & Sons, Ltd, 2014).
10. Csikszentmihalyi, M.: Beyond Boredom and Anxiety 36 (Jossey-Bass, San Francisco, 1977)
11. Csikszentmihalyi, M.: Flow: The Psychology of Optimal Experience 4 (Harper and Row, New York, 1990).
12. Csikszentmihalyi, M., Abuhamdeh, S., Nakamura, J. in Flow and the Foundations of Positive Psychology: The Collected Works of Mihaly Csikszentmihalyi 227–238 (Springer Netherlands, Dordrecht, 2014).
13. Dolby Atmos$^R$ Home Theater Installation Guidelines Guideline (Dolby Laboratories, San Francisco, Dec. 2018).
14. Dura, M. T.: The Phenomenology of the Music-listening Experience. Arts Educ. Policy Rev. **107**, 25–32 (2006).
15. Edelman Gerald & Tononi, G.: A universe of consciousness: How matter becomes imagination. (Basic Books, 2000).
16. Ermi, L., Mäyrä, F. in Worlds in play: International perspectives on digital games research (eds de Castell, S., Jenson, J.) 37–53 (Peter Lang Publishing, New York, NY, USA, 2005).
17. For Presence Research, I. S.: The Concept of Presence: Explication Statement 2000.
18. Freeman, W. J.: How Brains Make Up Their Minds. (Columbia University Press, 2001).
19. George, S., Zielinski, S., Rumsey, F., Bech, S.: Evaluating the Sensation of Envelopment Arising from 5-Channel Surround Sound Recordings in 124th Conv. Audio Eng. Soc. (May 2008).
20. Haken, H., Schiepek, G.: Synergetik in der Psychologie. Selbstorganisation verstehen und gestalten. (Hogrefe, 2010).
21. Hartigan, J. A., Hartigan, P. M.: The dip test of unimodality. Ann. Stat., 70–84 (1985).
22. Hartigan, P. M.: Algorithm AS 217: Computation of the Dip Statistic to Test for Unimodality. J R Stat Soc C-Appl **34**, 320–325 (1985).
23. Hou, J., Nam, Y., Peng, W., Lee, K.: Effects of screen size, viewing angle, and players' immersion tendencies on game experience. Comput. Hum. Behav. **28**, 617–623 (2012).
24. Hudson, S., Matson-Barkat, S., Pallamin, N., Jegou, G.: With or Without You? Interaction and Immersion in a Virtual Reality Experience. J. Bus. Res. **100**, 459–468 (2019).

25. IEC: Sound system equipment - Part 13: Listening tests on loudspeakers Standard 60268-13 (International Electrotechnical Commission, Geneva, Mar. 1998).
26. ITU-R: General viewing conditions for subjective assessment of quality of SDTV and HDTV television pictures on flat panel displays Recommendation BT. 2022 (International Telecommunication Union, Geneva, Aug. 2012).
27. ITU-R: Parameter values for ultra-high definition television systems for production and international programme exchange Recommendation BT. 2020-2 (International Telecommunication Union, Geneva, Oct. 2015).
28. ITU-T: Definitions of terms related to quality of service Recommendation E. 800 (International Telecommunication Union, Geneva, Sept. 2008).
29. ITU-T: Subjective evaluation methods for gaming quality Recommendation P. 809 (International Telecommunication Union, Geneva, June 2018).
30. Jekosch, U.: Voice and Speech Quality Perception. (Springer-Verlag Berlin Heidelberg, 2005).
31. Jennett, C. et al.: Measuring and Defining the Experience of Immersion in Games. Int. J. Hum. Comput. Stud. **66**, 641–661 (2008).
32. Jerome, C. J., Witmer, B. G. in Proceedings of the Human Factors and Ergonomics Society Annual Meeting **23**, 2613–2617 (2004).
33. Kaplanis, N., Bech, S., Jensen, S. H., van Waterschoot, T.: Perception of Reverberation in Small Rooms: A Literature Study in Audio Eng. Soc. Conf.: 55th Int. Conf.: Spatial Audio (Aug. 2014).
34. Kim, K. J., Park, E., Sundar, S. S., del Pobil, A. P.: The effects of immersive tendency and need to belong on human-robot interaction in 2012 7th ACM/IEEE International Conference on Human-Robot Interaction (HRI) (2012), 207–208.
35. Lawson, J.: Design and Analysis of Experiments with R. (Chapman and Hall/CRC, 2015).
36. Lombard, M., Ditton, T.: At the Heart of It All: The Concept of Presence. J. Comput.-Mediat. Commun. **3** (1997).
37. Lombard, M., Ditton, T. B., Weinstein, L.: Measuring Presence: The Temple Presence Inventory in Proc.12th Annu. Int.Workshop Presence (2009), 1–15.
38. Mateos, D. M., Wennberg, R., Guevara, R., Perez Velazquez, J. L.: Consciousness as a global property of brain dynamic activity. Phys. Rev. E 96 (Dec. 2017).
39. McMahan, A. in The Video Game Theory Reader (edsWolf, M., Bernard, P.) 67–86 (Routledge, London, 2003).
40. Moller, S., Schmidt, S., Zadtootaghaj, S.: New ITU-T Standards for Gaming QoE Evaluation and Management in 2018 Tenth International Conference on Quality of Multimedia Experience (QoMEX) (May 2018), 1–6.
41. Morie, J. F.: Virtual Reality, Immersion, and the Unforgettable Experience in Proc. SPIE 6055 (2006), 60551X.
42. Murray, C. D., Fox, J., Pettifer, S.: Absorption, dissociation, locus of control and presence in virtual reality. Comput. Hum. Behav.r **23**, 1347–1354 (2007).
43. Murray, J. H.: Hamlet on the Holodeck: The Future ofNarrative in Cyberspace (MIT press, 2017).
44. Nilsson, N. C., Nordahl, R., Serafin, S.: Immersion Revisited: A Review of Existing Definitions of Immersion and Their Relation to Different Theories of Presence. Hum. Technol. **12**, 108–134 (2016).
45. Noël, T. J. in Extending Experiences. Structure, Analysis and Design of Computer Game Player Experience (Lapland University Press, Rovaniemi, Finland, 2008).
46. Pausch, R., Proffitt, D., Williams, G.: Quantifying Immersion in Virtual Reality in Proc. of the 24th Annual Conference on Computer Graphics and Interactive Techniques (1997), 13–18.
47. Qualinet White Paper on Definitions of Quality of Experience (2012). tech. rep. (European Network on Quality of Experience in Multimedia Systems and Services (COST Action IC 1003), Mar. 2013).
48. Raake, A.: Speech Quality of VoIP: Assessment and Prediction. (Wiley, 2006).
49. Raake, A., Egger, S. in Quality of Experience: Advanced Concepts, Applications and Methods (eds Möller, S., Raake, A.) 11–33 (Springer International Publishing, Cham, 2014).

50. Raichle, M. E., Gusnard, D. A.: Intrinsic brain activity sets the stage for expression of motivated behavior. J. Comp. Neurol. **493**, 167–176 (2005).
51. Reaney, M.: Virtual Reality and the Theatre: Immersion in Virtual Worlds. Digital Creativity **10**, 183–188 (1999).
52. Recuber, T.: Immersion Cinema: The Rationalization and Reenchantment of Cinematic Space. Space Cult. **10**, 315–330 (2007).
53. Reichenbach, D. J. in Space, Time and the Limits of Human Understanding (edsWuppuluri, S., Ghirardi, G.) 503–512 (Springer International Publishing, Cham, Switzerland, 2017).
54. Reiter, U. et al. in Quality of Experience: Advanced Concepts, Applications and Methods (eds Möller, S., Raake, A.) 55–72 (Springer International Publishing, Cham, Switzerland, 2014).
55. Rooney, B., Benson, C., Hennessy, E.: The Apparent Reality of Movies and Emotional Arousal: A study using Physiological and Self-Report Measures. Poetics **40**, 405–422 (2012).
56. Rumsey, F.: Spatial Quality Evaluation for Reproduced Sound: Terminology, Meaning, and a Scene-Based Paradigm. J. Audio Eng. Soc. **50**, 651–666 (2002).
57. Ryan, M. L.: Narrative as Virtual Reality: Immersion and Interactivity in Literature and Electronic Media. (The Johns Hopkins University Press, Baltimore, MD, USA, 2003).
58. Sanders, T., Cairns, P. in Proc. 24th BCS Interact. Specialist Group Conf. 160–167 (Dundee, United Kingdom, 2010).
59. Schubert, T., Friedmann, F., Regenbrecht, H.: The Experience of Presence: Factor Analytic Insights. Presence **10**, 266–281 (2001).
60. Slater, M., Wilbur, S.: A Framework for Immersive Virtual Environments (FIVE): Speculations on the Role of Presence in Virtual Environments. Presence: Teleoperators & Virtual Environments **6** (1997).
61. Slater, M.: Measuring presence:Aresponse to theWitmer and Singer presence questionnaire. Presence **8**, 560–565 (1999).
62. Slater, M.: A note on presence terminology in Presence connect **3** (Jan. 2003).
63. Slater, M.: Place illusion and plausibility can lead to realistic behaviour in immersive virtual environments. Philos Trans R Soc Lond **364**, 3549–3557 (2009).
64. Steuer, J.: Defining Virtual Reality: Dimensions Determining Telepresence. J. Commun. **42**, 73–93 (1992).
65. Strohmeier, D., Jumisko-Pyykkö, S., Kunze, K.: Open Profiling of Quality: A Mixed Method Approach to Understanding Multimodal Quality Perception. Adv. Multim. **2010**, 658980:1–658980:28 (2010).
66. Swann, C., Keegan, R. J., Piggott, D., Crust, L.: A Systematic Review of the Experience, Occurrence, and Controllability of Flow States in Elite Sport. Psychol. Sport Exerc. **13**, 807–819 (2012).
67. Varela, M., Skorin-Kapov, L., Ebrahimi, T. in Quality of Experience: Advanced Concepts, Applications and Methods (eds Möller, S., Raake, A.) 85–96 (Springer International Publishing, Cham, 2014).
68. Visch, V. T.: The Emotional and Cognitive Effect of Immersion in Film Viewing. Cogn. Emot. **24**, 1439–1445 (2010).
69. Weibel, D.,Wissmath, B., Mast, F.W.: Immersion in Mediated Environments: The Role of Personality Traits. Cyberpsychology, Behavior, and Social Networking **13**, 251–256 (2010).
70. Witmer, B. G., Singer, M. J.: Measuring presence in virtual environments: A presence questionnaire. Presence **7**, 225–240 (1998).
71. Zhang, C.: The Why, What, and How of Immersive Experience. IEEE Access **8**, 90878–90888 (2020).
72. Zielinski, S., Rumsey, F., Bech, S.: On Some Biases Encountered in Modern Audio Quality Listening Tests-A Review. J. Audio Eng. Soc **56**, 427–451 (2008).

# Chapter 12
# Augmenting Sonic Experiences Through Haptic Feedback

Federico Fontana, Hanna Järveläinen, and Stefano Papetti

**Abstract** Sonic experiences are usually considered as the result of auditory feedback alone. From a psychological standpoint, however, this is true only when a listener is kept isolated from concurrent stimuli targeting the other senses. Such stimuli, in fact, may either interfere with the sonic experience if they distract the listener, or conversely enhance it if they convey sensations coherent with what is being heard. This chapter is concerned with haptic augmentations having effects on auditory perception, for example how different vibrotactile cues provided by an electronic musical instrument may affect its perceived sound quality or the playing experience. Results from different experiments are reviewed showing that the auditory and somatosensory channels together can produce constructive effects resulting in measurable perceptual enhancement. That may affect sonic dimensions ranging from basic auditory parameters, such as the perceived intensity of frequency components, up to more complex perceptions which contribute to forming our ecology of everyday or musical sounds.

F. Fontana (✉)
Department of Mathematics, Computer Science and Physics, University of Udine, via delle Scienze 206, Udine 33100, Italy
e-mail: federico.fontana@uniud.it

H. Järveläinen · S. Papetti
Institute for Computer Music and Sound Technology, Zurich University of the Arts, Pfingstweidstrasse 96, Zurich 8005, Switzerland
e-mail: hanna.jarvelainen@zhdk.ch

S. Papetti
e-mail: stefano.papetti@zhdk.ch

M. Geronazzo and S. Serafin (eds.), *Sonic Interactions in Virtual Environments*,
Human—Computer Interaction Series, https://doi.org/10.1007/978-3-031-04021-4_12

## 12.1   Introduction

During a sonic experience, humans give meaning to what is being listened to, based on their perception and cognition of the auditory scene. As other sensory channels normally convey stimuli in parallel to hearing, the human brain integrates a continuous flow of sensations while contextualizing the experience. If, on the one hand, vision, smell, and taste concur in describing an auditory scene, thanks to high-level connections involving our mental imagery [14], on the other hand, touch is often exposed to temporal patterns that exhibit a strong affinity with the acoustic signals hitting the eardrum with respect to their synchronism, amplitude, spectral content, and mutual localization. This similarity is evident, for instance, when a musician plays an instrument, and more in general whenever a human action generates an event producing sound as a (by-)product.

Our chapter is about whether the somatosensory feedback consequence of that action contributes to *augment* the sonic experience. Here, the term augmentation embraces all sorts of enrichment that a sonic experience would benefit from through the somatosensory channel, whether it makes a perceived sound stronger, clearer, more vivid, meaningful, pleasant, or ecologically valid. Such a variety of effects, affecting sound ranging from fundamental physical dimensions until its semantics, can be explained by the tight interactions that sound and vibration establish with one another, as soon as our brain associates them both with a unique event. Understanding such interactions and their effects is the main goal of scientists who investigate the psychophysics of auditory-tactile perception.

Perception psychologists were able to isolate the role of touch, especially during passive auditory tasks. Such tasks in fact lead to generally more robust design, control, and repeatability of the experiments. For this reason, the reference literature introducing this chapter deals mainly with passive touch. However, the most interesting sonic augmentations in an ecological or musical sense involve perception-action loops, in which the listener physically interacts with a sounding object. In the case of active exploration, or when a device reproduces tactile cues, the sense of touch conveys *haptic* feedback. Accordingly, our chapter will focus on effects reported by active listeners, as well as on sonic (either ecologic or musical) experiences resulting from passive tasks in the presence of various haptic interfaces.

### 12.1.1   Multisensory Processing of Touch and Audition

Multisensory processing—the convergence of information from various sensory channels—happens both in early cortical stages and in high-level structures. These processes can either enhance or depress response relative to the most robust unisensory information. This multisensory integration benefits feature integration, object processing, event detection, and decision-making especially when cues are weak or ambiguous [16, 54] (please refer also to Chap. 10 for a bigger picture on this topic). There is ample evidence of integration and interaction between the senses of hearing and touch. While somatosensory influence on higher auditory structures is well-known, evidence of low-level influence is more recent and increasing [30]. The cochlear nucleus in the brainstem responds to both somatosensory and auditory stimulation; this way somatosensory input may influence both sound lateralization and the suppression of self-generated sounds [10, 53]. The first cortical stages—previously thought to process unimodal sensory information—are now known to converge and sometimes process heteromodal information. The primary and the belt areas of the auditory cortex receive inputs from various low-level somatosensory areas, while fewer reports point to pathways from auditory to somatosensory areas. Higher-level multisensory areas that process auditory and somatosensory information include the *Superior temporal cortex* and the *Insular cortex* [15].

However, much of the multisensory integration that is necessary for the identification and localization of events takes place in the *Superior Colliculus* (SC), which is located in the midbrain: several subcortical and primary cortical areas project auditory, somatosensory, and visual information to this area. The neurons in the SC can respond differently to cross-modal stimuli than to either of the respective unimodal stimuli. Information is integrated according to a few general principles: spatially and temporally coherent stimuli produce maximal enhancement, and weaker stimuli produce a relatively greater enhancement (inverse effectiveness) [47].

Similar observations have been made on behavioral level: sounds and vibrations have been shown to interact constructively when congruent stimuli are delivered simultaneously [56, 57], with measurable auditory effects of somatosensory feedback [4, 36, 37, 39, 51, 52, 61]. Here congruence is defined depending on the experimental procedure: in general, it refers to conditions in which the multisensory stimulus shares common spatio-temporal as well as spectral features, as if it was originating from a unique source producing sounds and vibrations together. In parallel, simultaneity refers to a stimulus pair whose acoustic and vibratory components are rigorously constrained concerning their mutual synchronization: audio-tactile temporal resolution is superior to audio-visual or visuo-tactile combinations [20]. In this regard, it must be kept in mind that hearing and touch are both very sensitive to temporal delays, and detect especially low latency values relative to each other. By varying these values in the range 5–70 ms, Kaaresoja et al. have been able to change the perceived quality of virtual buttons during a clicking gesture [29]. More in general, mutual unsynchronization and/or delocalization of the acoustic and vibratory components leads to disparate effects that must be dealt with case by case [50], revealing the complexity of audio-tactile interactions. As this chapter focuses on haptic feedback, we will instead describe experiments where stimuli are simultaneous and co-localized.

Spatial collocation seems in fact somewhat less critical than temporal synchrony, judging by the presence of audio-tactile interactions and enhancement in many experiments where participants receive vibrotactile feedback through the hand and auditory stimuli through headphones [31]. Nevertheless, humans have good spatial discrimination ability between auditory and tactile stimuli: lateral angles of $\geq 5.3°$ were detected between electrotactile stimulation at the fingertip and sound source in an experiment by Altinsoy [2]. (To put this in context, auditory localization blur for the scraping sounds used as stimuli in the experiment was 3.9°.) Indeed, the seeming failure of some studies to demonstrate spatial modulations of audio-tactile interactions may be due to the fact that stimuli have been presented at hands or otherwise at some distance from the head; more recently, spatial modulation effects have indeed been observed especially in the space close to the head [31]. However, these phenomena are not thoroughly known yet; note that in the peripersonal space, even unimodal auditory localization differs from that at greater distances [6–8].

The psychophysical literature specifically dealing with the effects of touch on auditory perception is sparse, mostly focusing on intensity and pitch as primary objects of investigation. As opposed to the previously described constructive effect valid for multisensory cues of intensity, the interactions between auditory pitch and tactile frequency discrimination are more complex [5, 59]. In particular, tactile frequencies do not need simultaneity nor co-localization to affect pitch perception [62]. As part of their study on the audio-tactile pitch and loudness interactions, Yau et al. found separate mechanisms for tactile influence on loudness and pitch, with audio-tactile loudness perception depending more on the timing of the stimuli [60]. Anyhow, pitch is perceived much more accurately through the hearing system, hence touch in general plays no supportive role during the perception of frequency components in an audio-tactile signal. Still, tactile frequency discrimination ability has been ascertained [23, 55], with surprising accuracy in congenitally deaf individuals [35]. This evidence naturally leads to the question about musical sensations induced by touch, an issue which has fascinated several scientists [49] and, hence, occupies an important part of this chapter.

Some deaf musicians show an indisputable ability to "feel the vibrations" during music performance, not merely for entraining with other musicians [12, 22, 25, 26], but also for sharing melody and timbre with them. This ability seems to be the result of the long training *any* (i.e., including the normally able) good musician has accumulated with all senses on their instrument [34] during a continuous perception-action process. Such a training, hence, refines a multisensory acuity for the instrument quality, not limited to its sound [21, 58].

Non-musicians can also discriminate musical timbre and relative pitch intervals from vibrotactile cues, to some extent even without training [24, 49]. However, generalizing the above-mentioned higher-level phenomena to musically untrained individuals is not obvious [3]. Being inherently psychophysical, there is no reason to think that the summation of auditory and tactile cues of intensity would not apply to non-musicians. In parallel, musical training seems to facilitate more subtle audio-tactile synergies mediated by higher nervous system levels, such as those linking pitch and tactile frequency recognition [11, 33]. Amid these two facts, the possibility for touch to enable the detection in normal listeners of frequency components otherwise inaudible, due to masking or threshold effects, is yet to be systematically explored.

**Table 12.1**  Key characteristics of the experiments forming the chapter

| Experiment | Conditions | Input gesture | Haptic feedback | Audio feedback | Results |
|---|---|---|---|---|---|
| Ball bouncing on everyday materials [13] | Passive | Finger-pad contact | Recorded stimuli | Recorded stimuli | Audio-tactile summation leads to best identification |
| Reproduction of target pressing forces [27] | Interactive, musical | Finger pressing | Sine wave | Sine wave | Audio-tactile summation offers best performance |
| Perception of musical scales [48] | Passive, musical | Hand-instrument contact | Musical scale | Masking noise | Differences between scales are discriminated |
| Perception of plucked strings [44] | Interactive, musical | String plucking | Guitar string | Guitar string | Haptic feedback does not increase sound quality |
| Piano playing [18] | Interactive musical | Free playing | Piano vibration on and off | Piano | Natural vibrations alter perceived piano quality |
| Digital piano playing [19] | Interactive, musical | Free playing | Piano vibration, filtered noise | Piano | Vibrations alter perceived keyboard quality |
| Playing experience on a haptic surface for musical expression [41] | Interactive, musical | Free playing | None, sine wave, filtered audio, band-passed noise | Expressive/dull | Vibrations coherent with audio feedback improve perceived interface quality/playing experience |

## 12.1.2   Chapter Outline

In their respective interaction contexts and with different confidence levels, hence, the experiments chosen for this chapter share the general assumption that a sonic experience can be influenced by somatosensory cues. Some of them (e.g., [19, 48]) contributed to give form to the musical haptics research methodology and, hence, led to inevitably less robust conclusions. For this reason, they are certainly more suggestive than conclusive.

In an aim to orient the reader to the experiments which reflect his or her interests, Table 12.1 summarizes their key characteristics. Moreover, the table labels the experiments with gray tones classifying their dependence on specific elements. According to this classification, the first two experiments define an abstract context which is in principle applicable to multiple interaction contexts. The third and fourth experiments limit these contexts respectively to musical scales and plucked strings perception. The fifth and sixth ones further restrict the context respectively to acoustic and digital pianos. Finally, the seventh experiment specifically targets haptic versions of sound wave templates.

More in detail, the first experiment suggests a role of tactile frequency discrimination in enhancing the auditory perception of near-threshold frequency components; this role emerged during the audio-tactile identification of everyday materials from their response to a ball hitting them [13]. Next, we present an experiment conducted using an audio-tactile interface [40], showing that individuals performing a basic musical gesture such as finger pressing were able to reproduce previously learnt target forces more accurately if receiving contextual audio-tactile feedback instead of auditory or tactile feedback alone [27].

The third and fourth experiments link the aforementioned effects to musical experiences. As evidence of the power of the vibrotactile channel to deliver musical information, we first review a test in which Western and Indian musicians categorized and even identified music scales from both traditions by touching the surface of a harmonium [48]. Then, a robotic stringed instrument prototype called Keytar is described, in which the accurate haptic rendering of its virtual strings was significantly appreciated by users, however with no significant improvements for the perceived sound quality [44].

Conversely, a constructive effect was measured in pianists playing an acoustic piano whose natural vibrations could be switched on and off, thanks to peculiar engineering of the keyboard: in this case, the inclusion of vibrotactile feedback resulted in a measurable improvement of the instrument sound quality [18]. A similar effect was measured in musicians playing an actuated digital piano when this instrument reproduced vibrations recorded on a real piano [19].

Finally, using a force-sensitive haptic surface for musical expression which controlled a synthesizer, the effect of various vibration types on perceived quality attributes and the playing experience was assessed [41].

## 12.2 Ball Bouncing on Everyday Materials

Two experiments [13] studied the role of impact sounds and vibrations for the subjective classification of three flat objects, which were respectively made of wood, plastic, and metal—see Fig. 12.1.

The task consisted of feeling an actuated surface and listening through headphones to the recorded feedback of a ping-pong ball hitting such objects (Fig. 12.2, left), after they had been experienced during a training task (Fig. 12.2, right).

In Experiment 1, sounds and vibrations were recorded by keeping the objects in mechanical isolation. In Experiment 2, recordings were taken while the same objects stood on a table, causing their resonances to fade faster due to mechanical coupling with the support. Twenty-five subjects, aged between 23 and 61 years (M = 32.1, SD = 10.1), participated in Experiment 1, and twenty-seven (21–54 years old; M = 29.0, SD = 6.8) in Experiment 2. Eight subjects participated in both experiments. Roughly one-third of the participants were female. In terms of musical training, participants were not screened, and they reflect the general population average.

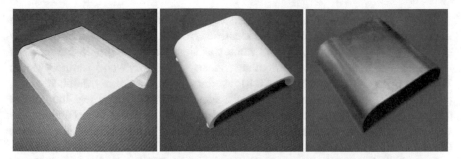

**Fig. 12.1**  Materials used in the experiment. Left: wood. Center: plastic. Right: metal

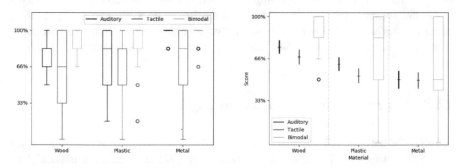

**Fig. 12.2**  Experimental tasks. Left: perceptual task. Right: training task

**Fig. 12.3**  Boxplot of and mean proportions correct with SE bars for all condition combinations. Left: Experiment 1. Right: Experiment 2

As a general result, in both experiments tactile identification was less accurate than auditory identification. In parallel, the *bimodal* (i.e., simultaneously auditory and tactile) identification ranked significantly better in both experiments, providing evidence of support from touch to auditory material identification (Fig. 12.3).

This conclusion was not contradicted by a control experiment, in which participants were asked to identify the materials from real bounces as during the training shown in Fig. 12.2, right.

Between Experiments 1 and 2, some interesting differences are observed between materials. In Experiment 1, metal was identified from auditory cues almost perfectly (difference between both plastic and wood was significant in multiple comparisons following a significant Friedman test: AuditoryWood-AuditoryMetal: $Z = 4.3$, Bonferroni-corrected $p < 0.01$; AuditoryPlastic-AuditoryMetal: $Z = 3.4$, $p < .01$). In contrast, in Experiment 2, the identification of metal was the poorest of the three materials. In a two-way repeated-measures ANOVA with Greenhouse-Geisser correction for insphericity, a significant main effect of Material was detected $(F(1.61,41.9) = 16.3, p \leq 0.001)$. The 95% confidence intervals of the three materials result in a partial overlap between Plastic (0.51–0.64) and Metal (0.42–0.57), whereas the 95% CI for Wood is entirely above their combined range (0.65–0.78). As the main difference between the stimuli in Experiments 1 and 2 was the length of the decay, it seems that the longer decay in Experiment 1 was an important identification cue, especially for metal.

Importantly for this chapter, the ability of our subjects to maximize their identification accuracy when using sounds and vibrations together suggests that audio-tactile summation may work in all individuals as soon as they have acquired a solid knowledge about a multisensory event belonging to the everyday experience, and not only if they have accumulated peculiar audio-tactile skills, e.g., by practicing for a long time with a musical instrument. This conclusion was reinforced by a further test, part of the same research, where *incongruent* bimodal stimuli were prepared by assembling sounds and vibrations reporting respectively on two different materials. This test in fact suggested that tactile feedback, in its limited possibility to convey timbre, became progressively more relevant as the auditory channel, in front of incongruent materials, left its leading role while remaining supportive of cross-modal perception.

## 12.3  Reproduction of Target Pressing Forces

An effect of haptic feedback on the control of finger-pressing force has been shown in the literature (e.g., [1, 28]). The present setup [27] approaches a musical task in that it measures memorized force targets in the presence of both auditory and vibrotactile feedback. The experiment was carried out by means of a tabletop device capable of measuring normal force while displaying vibrotactile feedback at its top panel (Fig. 12.4).

To simulate the haptic exchange taking place when playing acoustic or electroacoustic instruments—where musicians would learn the response of the instrument and would then perform by relying on kinesthetic memory [38]—participants first learned three target forces during a training phase, without additional feedback. Those targets were chosen empirically according to low, medium, and high pressing forces, within the data resolution of the interface (10-bit, corresponding to the 0–1023 range) and without anchoring them to corresponding values in Newton: the low target was set to 400, the medium one to 650, and the high target to 850. A double-sided window of 50 units was considered around each target as the acceptance range. The task was

**Fig. 12.4** The interface used in the experiment for recording finger-pressing force and providing vibrotactile feedback

then to reproduce such forces "out of memory" under four feedback conditions: no feedback (N), auditory only (A), vibrotactile only (T), and auditory and vibrotactile together (AT). When participants believed they had reached the asked target they had to press an "OK" button with their free hand, while maintaining the pressing force on the touch panel.

For the sake of simplicity, a sinusoidal signal was chosen for rendering both auditory and tactile feedback, whose amplitude varied proportionally to the applied pressing force—thus implementing a gesture mapping commonly found in musical practice. The maximum intensity of vibrotactile stimuli was empirically set to the highest level that could be reproduced without perceivable distortion. The frequency of the sine wave was set to 200 Hz so as to maximize the produced vibrotactile sensation [55].

The test followed a 2-factor within-subjects design, where each participant was tested under each combination of conditions (12). All combinations were repeated 10 times, resulting in 120 trials that were presented in randomized order. Fourteen people (average age 33) participated in the experiment: five of them were pianists, five other musicians, and four non-musicians.[1]

Data analysis[2] showed a significant main effect of feedback factor ($F(3,143) = 16$, $p < 0.0001$). The effect of target force level was not significant ($F(2,143) = 0.7$, $p = 0.52$); however, the interaction "feedback $\times$ target level" was significant ($F(6,143) = 6.0$, $p < 0.0001$).

The interaction plots in Fig. 12.5 show that, for the low target force, mean errors are much smaller in the presence of auditory (A) or audio-tactile (AT) feedback, and somewhat smaller with tactile-only feedback (T) than with no-feedback (N). For the

---

[1] The relatively low participation number of musicians as well as non-musicians reflects the exploratory character of tactile experiments with pianists as far as one decade ago. Later, they have consolidated into more robust methodologies, including the participation of more musicians when necessary—see, e.g., Sect. 12.6.

[2] performed by *aligned rank transform*, the nonparametric equivalent to factorial within-subjects analysis of variance

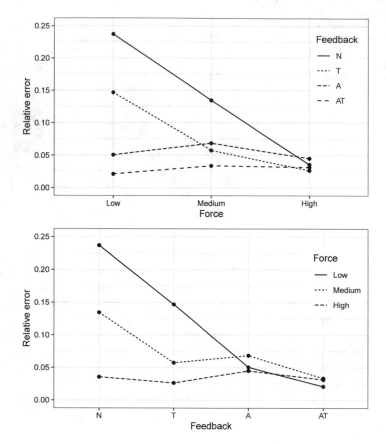

**Fig. 12.5** Interaction plots. Top panel: mean relative errors at the three target forces, presented for each feedback condition. Bottom panel: mean relative errors at the four feedback conditions, presented for each target force level

medium target force, mean errors decrease in case of no-feedback (showing that the task becomes increasingly easier for higher forces) and with tactile-only feedback (T), whereas with auditory or audio-tactile feedback (A, AT) they did not change much from the low target force. For the high target force, however, the results are almost equivalent at all feedback conditions.

The results generally show that the addition of vibrations to auditory feedback may improve performance in musical finger-pressing tasks, enabling subjects to achieve memorized target forces with higher accuracy.

## 12.4   Vibrotactile Recognition of Traditional Musical Scales

The harmonium, visible in Fig. 12.6 (left), is played in both Western and Oriental music using scales that belong to the respective tradition. Musicians and also listeners with a normal understanding of music immediately recognize the ethnicity of a scale. In fact, the human ear is especially accurate in assessing the intervals existing between the fundamental frequencies of musical notes.

Does a haptic counterpart of scale recognition ability exist, result of a tactile frequency identification process musicians have internalized as part of their practice on an instrument? And, if recognition does not occur, would they be able to at least discriminate between different ethnicities? If either answer was positive, then musical vibrations would prove to be active carriers of spectral information capable of supporting, or even substituting, an especially important component of the musical message coming from an instrument.

Western and Indian notes have fundamental frequencies that in general do not match; furthermore, such intervals between notes differ depending on the scale. As a result, clearly audible discrepancies exist between Western and Indian musical scales, and then between different scales belonging to the same ethnicity.

The stimuli for the experiment [48] consisted of two Western (*C natural* and *A minor*) and two Indian (*Raag Bhairav* and *Raag Yaman-Kalyan*) scales played on the harmonium in the setup of Fig. 12.6 (right) by an Indian performer living in Europe. After listening to the four scales without touching the instrument during a training session, participants in a tactile recognition test were sitting on the left side of the same setup with their hands on the harmonium. At every trial, they were exposed to a train of vibrations corresponding to the sequence of notes belonging to a scale played by the performer. At the end of it, they had to decide whether the vibration was reporting about a Western or Indian scale, and to which one of the two.

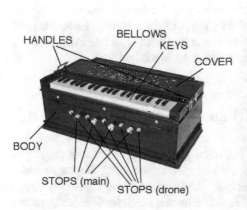

**Fig. 12.6**  Left: the harmonium. Right: experimental setup

**Table 12.2** Individual subjective performance

| Subject typology | Western participants | | Indian participants | |
|---|---|---|---|---|
| | Recognition of tradition | Recognition of scale | Recognition of tradition | Recognition of scale |
| A—teacher of music | 7/16 | 4/16 | 12/16 | 12/16 |
| B—teacher of music | 11/16 | 9/16 | 13/16 | 11/16 |
| C—amateur musician | 15/16 | 12/16 | 13/16 | 8/16 |
| D—professional musician | 16/16 | 12/16 | 10/16 | 7/16 |
| E—professional musician | 13/16 | 11/16 | 10/16 | 5/16 |
| Overall recognition | 62/80 | 48/80 | 58/80 | 43/80 |
| Overall percentage | 77.5% | 60% | 72.5% | 53.75% |
| Chance percentage | 50% | 25% | 50% | 25% |

During the test, they neither wore headphones emitting masking noise nor could they observe the playing action, thanks to a panel standing amid the harmonium body, avoiding the performer and participant from seeing each other.

The test was performed by a native group of Italians and then repeated in India. The two groups of participants, identical in number, were selected so as to have comparable levels of musical knowledge and performing skills. Results are listed in Table 12.2: They reveal the ability of both groups to recognize the ethnic origin with no significant differences between groups. Limited to specific subgroups, i.e., Western performers and Indian music teachers, the specific scale was recognized as well. The surprisingly high performance shown by our participants suggests the existence of a well-developed tactile memory for tones and/or note scales in musicians, a possible result of musical instrument training. However, the support during the task of nearly masked auditory cues of pitch bypassing the headphone insulators, or traveling from the hands to the cochlea through bone conduction, in principle could not be excluded. Similarly, scale-dependent temporal nuances biasing the recognition of the stimuli might have been unconsciously introduced by the performer during playing. In spite of its limited control, this experiment nevertheless represented an interesting starting point for the study of the role of touch in musical scale recognition.

## 12.5 Perception of Plucked Strings

*Keytar* is a plucked-string instrument interface [17]. Its software was developed within the Unity3D development engine. While running on a PC, Keytar provides real-time auditory, visual, and haptic feedback to the player who controls a virtual plectrum through a Phantom Omni robotic arm with one hand, while selecting notes and chords with the other hand (see Fig. 12.7, left). An accurate haptic rendering of the interaction point was made possible by modeling each string as a queue of

**Fig. 12.7** Left: Keytar. Right: particular of the plectrum-string interaction point

short cylinders with alternating radius, and then by characterizing the contact of the plectrum using physical parameters which, due to the elastic behavior of the string, fall within the operating range of the Phantom Omni (see Fig. 12.7, right). This way, the robotic arm not only reproduces the elastic response of the plucked strings, but also some fine-grained dynamic textures arising between the colliding plectrum and the vibrating string. The sensation of rubbing the string during plucking is further enhanced by a realistic noise of frictional contacts coming from the servo-mechanisms of the robotic arm, while they are continuously switched on and off by the collision detection software module. The overall virtual environment defined an especially convincing reproduction of string plucking [45].

In a virtual reality experiment [44], twenty-nine participants on average having 8.2 years (SD = 8.3) of regular practice on a music instrument were asked to first pluck the strings of a real guitar, and then to wear an Oculus Rift CV1 helmet displaying an electric guitar and a plectrum in a nondescript virtual room. Twenty-one such participants in particular reported being able to play one or more stringed instruments. Interaction with the plectrum was made possible using the robotic arm controlled by Keytar, furthermore, the collision detection module controlled also a vibro-tactile actuator standing below Phantom Omni. This active stand was used to produce additional vibrations independently of the kinesthetic feedback. On such a setup, a within-subjects study compared four different haptic conditions during plucking: no feedback (N), force only (F), vibration only (V), and force and vibration together (FV).

Each participant was exposed to every condition, in randomized order, for approximately 20 minutes each. On every condition, first all six strings were plucked twice in a randomized order by the guidance of a visual marker emphasizing the string to pluck; then, participants were encouraged to freely interact by both plucking each string individually and strumming the entire string set. When one condition was completely tested, each participant evaluated four metrics on a Likert scale (see Fig. 12.8): overall perceptual similarity with the real instrument (from completely different to identical); stiffness similarity between virtual and real strings (from much lower to much higher); overall realism of the virtual instrument (from strong disagreement to

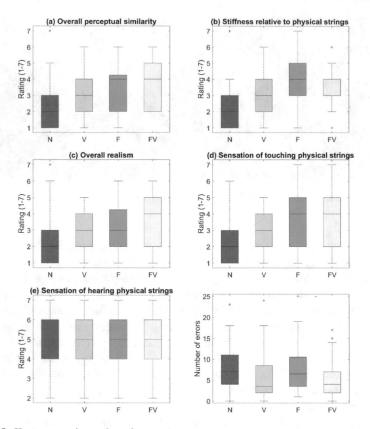

**Fig. 12.8** Keytar: experimental results

strong agreement); touch realism of the virtual strings (from strong disagreement to strong agreement); effects of haptic cues on sound realism. At the end of the test each participant was additionally asked to choose his/her preferred condition. Finally, the errors made on plucking a wrong instead of a visually marked string during the part of the test involving individual strings were logged.

Results suggest the existence of significant effects of haptic feedback on the perceived realism of the strings. Further considerations can be drawn from the specific histograms [46]. By contrast, as can be seen from the left histogram below in Fig. 12.8, no effects on sound realism were measured. The lesson to take home from this experiment, hence, is that increasing the haptic realism of a virtual musical instrument in principle has no effects on its perceived auditory quality.

## 12.6 Piano Playing

A different lesson was instead learnt from an experiment in which the realism of the interaction with the musical instrument, in this case a piano, was pushed to its limit [18]. The piano keyboard in fact offers a controlled experimental setting, as the performer can only hit and then release one or more keys with one or more fingers while the rest of their body is disconnected from the instrument. This setting permitted to design a task in which auditory and haptic feedback could be delivered separately and independently. Furthermore, the intensity of both feedback channels is a reliable function of the key velocity which, in turn, is driven by the pianist's finger. Under these experimental premises, Yamaha's Disklavier pianos in particular offer two specific advantages: first, they can both record and mechanically reproduce the action of a pianist on all keys; secondly, they can be automatically switched between normal operation and a *silent* mode. When this mode is set, all strings are decoupled from the respective key hammers in ways that the instrument produces no sound, meanwhile conveying the same haptic feedback as to when the performer also hears the instrument.

The group of participants was split into two independent subgroups. Either subgroup performed on a grand Disklavier model DC3 M4 (in Padova, Italy) or on an upright model DU1A (in Zurich, Switzerland). During the tasks, the acoustic and silent modes were randomly switched across trials, letting the participants receive either natural or no steady vibrations from the keys after the initial percussive event. In both configurations participants via insulated headphones received the same auditory feedback, consisting of piano sounds synthesized by Modartt Pianoteq 4.5 digital piano software which was set to simulate a grand or an upright piano, and was driven in real time by the respective Disklavier's Musical Instrument Digital Interface (MIDI). The synthetic sounds were equalized so as to match those of the corresponding piano, by positioning a KEMAR mannequin visible in Fig. 12.9 (left), where the setup is shown during the calibration procedure. Figure 12.9 (right) shows a typical train of vibrations reaching the pianist's finger when the piano was operating in acoustic mode: the initial percussion event preceding the vibrations coming from the strings is evident in this figure.

Participants performed first a playing task and then a rating task. The former is relevant for this chapter. Three note ranges were considered separately across the keyboard, labeled low (keys below D3), mid (keys between D3 and A5), and high (keys above A5). Participants could play freely, within one range at a time, to compare the quality of the instrument in the presence and absence of string vibrations following the initial percussive events. Twenty-five professional pianists, mostly classical and a few jazz, took part in the tests: 15 on the upright and 10 on the grand piano (the slight imbalance in group sizes was due to varying easiness of recruitment in the two locations). Their average age was 27 years and their average piano experience was 15 years. Using a manual control, they could switch at their convenience between two setups, X and Y, associated with the silent and acoustic modes of the Disklavier. The difference between the two setups was not explained to them.

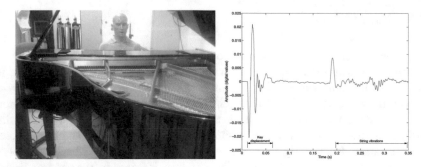

**Fig. 12.9** Left: setup calibration. Right: acceleration signal measured on the key surface (note A2; MIDI velocity equal to 12; grand piano)

**Fig. 12.10** Results with errorbars ±SE. Positive values signify preference for the vibrating mode. X-axis presents ratings for dynamic range, loudness, richness, and naturalness at low (A0-D3), mid (D3-A5), and high ranges (A5-C7) (l, m, and h, respectively). Preference was rated in full range only

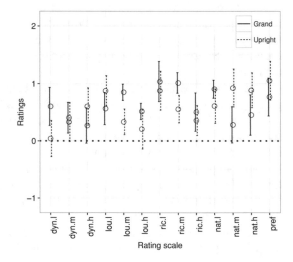

The task was to compare the setups on a Likert scale (from "X much better than Y" until "Y much better than X") with respect to the following attributes: dynamic range, loudness, richness, naturalness, and preference. The first four were rated separately in the low, mid, and high ranges, while the preference rating was given considering the entire keyboard. Participants were given definitions of the attributes and informed that dynamic range, loudness, and richness were mainly related to sound, whereas naturalness and preference could also be related to touch. A laptop finding place next to the piano displayed a set of sliders that were accessible at any moment to pianists for rating such attributes.

Results are shown in Figs. 12.10 and 12.11, suggesting a general preference for the vibrating mode. Since this preference was not explicitly linked to a specific attribute, two principal components, PC1 and PC2, were discovered to account for 80% of the variance. PC1 had the highest positive correlations with richness, naturalness, and preference; PC2, less powerful, was associated with dynamic range and loudness, which conversely decrease as naturalness and preference increase.

**Fig. 12.11** Quality rating profiles projected onto the first two principal components. Subjects were segmented a posteriori according to positive/negative rating on preference. Ellipses enclose 68% of subjects in each group

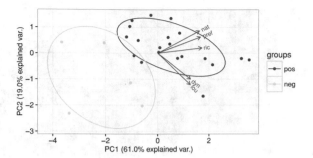

Analysis of Lin concordance correlation coefficients revealed a subgroup of seven subjects whose inter-individual consistency was negative. It was observed that most of them belonged to the group of five subjects who gave a negative preference rating. Therefore, participants were segmented a posteriori based on a positive versus negative preference rating. As seen in Fig. 12.11, the negative group differs from the majority of participants in that their ratings are negative on both principal components; in fact, while both groups gave rather similar ratings for dynamic range and loudness, their mean ratings for richness, naturalness, and preference are nearly opposite to each other. The conclusion was that approximately 80% of the participants preferred the vibrating setup and perceived higher naturalness and richness from it. Why the remaining 20% did not perceive any benefits from vibrations could not be thoroughly explained; however, in that group were two subjects who performed significantly under average in a vibration detection experiment related to this study. Notably, the negative group also included some jazz pianists. They reported performing frequently in small ensembles where digital stage pianos are used, which lack the natural vibrotactile feedback found on acoustic pianos.

At any rate, after completing the test in Zurich, the experimenter asked each participant what may have caused the difference between the setups: Interestingly, only 1 out of 15 participants could pinpoint vibrations. Thus, while the participants generally preferred the vibrating setup, they were not actively aware of vibrations. Their unawareness testifies to the especially high level of cross-modal integration that piano sounds and vibrations achieve in a real instrument.

## 12.7  Digital Piano Playing

An effect related to what was observed on acoustic pianos was discovered to play a role with digital pianos [19]. Since electronic instruments do not vibrate except for possible mechanical perturbations coming from the internal speakers, potential additional effects of artificial vibratory feedback to perceived instrument quality, precision in timing, and dynamic performance were investigated. The setup definition required to disassemble a digital piano keyboard, and then attach two vibrotactile

**Fig. 12.12** Left: experimental setup. Right: transducer conveying vibrations to the keyboard

actuators (Fig. 12.12, right) on a stiff wooden panel which was firmly screwed below its keybed (Fig. 12.12, left).

These actuators conveyed stimuli that had previously been acquired from an acoustic piano. In parallel, binaurally recorded tones were reproduced using headphones. Such tones and vibrations had previously been calibrated to have an intensity equal to that measured on the finger and ears of a pianist performing on a Disklavier grand piano, in the same fashion as the experiment in Sect. 12.6. In particular, calibration is required to equalize the vibration signals in order to avoid unrealistic resonance peaks on the digital keyboard for certain played notes.

Eleven pianists, five females and six males, participated in the experiment. Their average age was 26 years, and their average piano playing experience was 8 years after reaching the conservatory level. Two participants were jazz pianists. Audio-tactile stimuli were produced at runtime: the digital keyboard in fact sent MIDI messages to a computer running Modartt Pianoteq 4.5 piano synthesizer and, in parallel, Native Instruments Kontakt 5 sampler in series with MeldaProduction MEqualizer parametric equalizer for playing back the corresponding vibration samples.

Perceived instrument quality was assessed by feeding the digital keyboard respectively with (A) no vibrations, (B) grand piano vibrations, (C) grand piano vibrations with 9 dB boost, and (D) synthetic vibrations. By contrast, the sound synthesis parameters were kept constant throughout the experiment. Pianists were asked to play freely while assessing the experience on five attribute rating scales: Dynamic control, Richness, Engagement, Naturalness, and General preference. During playing, at their convenience they could switch among two unknown setups, $\alpha$ and $\beta$: the former was always made to correspond to A, whereas the latter could randomly correspond to B, C, or D. The assessment was conducted by rating $\beta$ relatively to $\alpha$ during 10 minutes of piano performance, for a session that hence lasted half an hour. During each assessment, participants at any time could rate every attribute by pointing to the respective virtual slider and setting a level by clicking with the mouse on a graphical user interface that was displayed by a laptop computer at hand reach. Each slider exposed a continuous Comparison Category Rating scale ranging from −3 ("$\beta$ much better than $\alpha$") to +3 ("$\beta$ much worse than $\alpha$"). Once the quality rating

**Fig. 12.13** Results of the quality experiment. Boxplot presenting median and quartile for each attribute scale and vibration condition

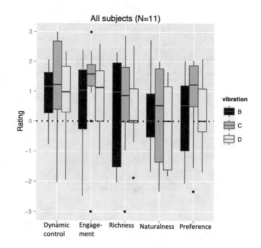

of the keyboard was over, another half an hour was spent by each participant to participate in the remaining two tests, assessing precision in timing as well as dynamic performance.

Results show that the augmented setups were generally preferred, with an emphasis on boosted vibrations (Fig. 12.13). Again, heterogeneity was observed in the data, as might be expected due to the high degree of variability in the inter-individual agreement scores. A k-means clustering algorithm was used to segment the subjects a posteriori into two classes, according to their opinion on General preference. Eight subjects were classified into a "positive" group and the remaining three into a "negative" group. The results of the respective groups are presented in Fig. 12.14. A difference of opinion is evident: The median ratings for the preferred setup C are nearly +2 in the positive group and −1.5 in the negative group for General preference. In the positive group, the median was positive in all cases except for Naturalness in D, whereas in the negative group, the median was positive only for Dynamic control in B.

Similar to what was observed in Sect. 12.6 while experimenting with the acoustic piano, low concordance between pianists exposed to vibration suggests that intra- and inter-individual consistency is an issue also while playing a digital piano. By contrast, no effect was observed on timing or dynamics accuracy in the performance tests. Taken together, these considerations point to conclude that vibrations do unconsciously influence the perceived keyboard instrument quality, however, along a direction which depends on the performer's previous multisensory experience of a specific instrument. Hence, augmenting a digital piano with the vibrations of an acoustic piano might not increase sense of quality if the performer played a digital (i.e., non vibrating) keyboard for most of the time. In parallel, haptic augmentation neither improves nor disrupts key aspects of piano performance such as timing and dynamic control.

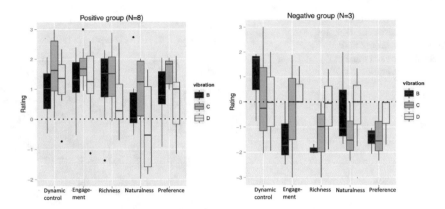

**Fig. 12.14** Differences in quality ratings between the positive (left) and negative (right) groups formed by a posteriori segmentation. Boxplot presenting median and quartile for each attribute scale and vibration condition

## 12.8 Playing Experience on a Haptic Surface for Musical Expression

A multi-touch force-sensitive surface for musical expression was equipped with multi-point localized vibrotactile feedback, resulting in the HSoundplane haptic interface [43] shown in Fig. 12.15. A subjective assessment was conducted using the HSoundplane, which measured how the presence and type of vibration affect the perceived quality of the device, as well as various attributes related to the playing experience [41].

**Fig. 12.15** The experimental setting for the HSoundplane experiment

## *12.8.1 Design*

Two clearly distinct sound presets were tested, each with three vibrotactile feedback strategies.

The pitch of the audio feedback—ranging from A2 ($f_0 = 110\,\text{Hz}$) to D5 ($f_0 = 587.33\,\text{Hz}$)—was controlled along the x-axis. The two offered sound presets were

**Sound 1**—A sawtooth wave filtered by a resonant low-pass and modulated by a vibrato effect (i.e., amplitude and pitch modulation). A markedly expressive setting, responding to subtleties and nuances in the performer's gesture.

y-axis control: Vibrato intensity is controlled along the y-axis, from no-vibrato (bottom) to strong vibrato (top).

z-axis control: The filter cutoff frequency is controlled by the applied pressing force (i.e., higher force maps to brighter sound), and so is the sound level (i.e., higher force maps to louder sound).

**Sound 2**—A simple sine wave is added with noise depending on the location on the y-axis. A setting offering a rather limited sonic palette and no amplitude dynamics.

y-axis control: Moving upwards adds white noise of increasing amplitude, filtered by a resonant band-pass. The filter's center frequency follows the pitch of the respective tone.

z-axis control: Pressing force data are ignored, resulting in fixed intensity.

The different degrees of variability and expressive potential of the two sound settings allowed us to investigate whether the possible effect depends on audio feedback characteristics. All sounds were processed by a reverb effect so as to make the playing experience more acoustic-like. Sound was provided to the participants by means of closed-back headphones (Beyerdynamic DT 770 Pro). Audio examples of the two sound types are made available online,[3] demonstrating C3, C4, and C5 tones modulated along the y- and z-axes.

Before being routed to the actuators layer, vibration signals were filtered in the $10-500\,\text{Hz}$ range by a 10th-order band-pass, so as to optimize the actuators' efficiency and consequently the vibratory response of the device, as well as to minimize sound leakage. Any residual sound spillage produced by the actuators was taken care of by the closed-back headphones carrying auditory feedback. Three vibrotactile strategies were implemented:

**Sine**—Pure sinusoidal signals, whose pitch follows the fundamental of the played tones ($f_0$ within $110-587.33\,\text{Hz}$), and whose amplitude is controlled by the intensity of the pressing forces. By focusing vibratory energy at a single frequency component, this setting aimed at producing sharp vibrotactile feedback.

**Audio**—The same sounds generated by the HSoundplane used to render vibration: the audio signals are also routed to the actuators layer. Vibration signals thus share the same spectrum (within the $10-500\,\text{Hz}$ pass-band) and dynamics of the related sound. This approach ensured the highest coherence between musical output and

---

[3] https://tinyurl.com/HS-sounds.

tactile feedback, mimicking what occurs on acoustic musical instruments, where the source of vibration coincides with that of sound.

**Noise**—A white noise signal of fixed amplitude. This setting produced vibrotactile feedback generally uncorrelated with the auditory one, ignoring any spectral and amplitude cues possibly conveyed by it. The only exception is with Sound 2 and high y-axis values, which resulted in a similar noisy signal.

The designed vibration types offered different spectral and dynamics cues resulting in varying degrees of similarity with the audio feedback, thus enabling to determine the importance of the match between sound and vibration. The intensity of vibration feedback was set by the authors in a pilot phase, aiming at two main goals: (i) sound and vibration intensities had to feel reciprocally consistent; (ii) while levels had to be overall comfortable for prolonged use, vibration had to be clearly perceivable even at low force-pressing values [42].

At each trial, the task was to play freely while comparing two related setups: they were labeled A/B in a balanced way, and differed only in the presence/absence of vibration (i.e., they shared the same sound setting). Participants could switch at any time between A and B and had to provide ratings for four attributes: *Preference*, *Control and responsiveness* (referred to as *Control*), *Expressive potential* (referred to as *Expression*), and *Enjoyment*. Ratings were given by adjusting a respective slider on a continuous visual analog scale ranging from A (left) to B (right) to reflect the degree of preference in terms of the given attribute. In case of perceived equality between A and B, the slider would be set to the midpoint. All 4 (attributes) × 3 (vibration types) × 2 (sound types) factor combinations were evaluated twice.

All 29 participants—7 males and 22 females, aged 18–48 years ($M = 25.4$, $SD = 7.1$)—were professional musicians or music students. Their main instrument was either a keyboard or a string instrument, on which they had on average 17 years of experience. Roughly one-third of the participants had significant experience with electronic musical instruments, mostly synthesizers, or digital musical interfaces.

## 12.8.2  Results

The continuous slider scale ratings were mapped to the closed interval [0, 1], where 1 indicates a maximal preference for the vibrating setup and 0 maximal preference for the non-vibrating setup, and 0.5 is the point of perceived equality. Statistical analysis was carried out by fitting a zero-one-inflated beta (ZOIB) model, whose parameters were estimated with Bayesian methods [9, 32]. Four parameters describe the ZOIB distribution: the mean ($\mu$) and precision ($\phi$) of the beta distribution, the probability of a binary {0, 1} outcome (zoi), and the conditional probability of outcome {1} (coi). The mean of the beta distribution was modeled by sound, vibration type, their interaction, and attribute. The models for the precision ($\phi$) and zero-one-inflation parameters (zoi, coi) were set to depend on vibration type, sound, and attribute without interactions.

**Fig. 12.16** Marginal effects; estimated $\mu$ parameters with 95% Credible Intervals (N = 29). **a** Interaction between vibration and sound type; **b** Effect of vibration on the evaluated attributes. 0.50 = point of perceived equality; higher values indicate preference for vibrating over non-vibrating setup

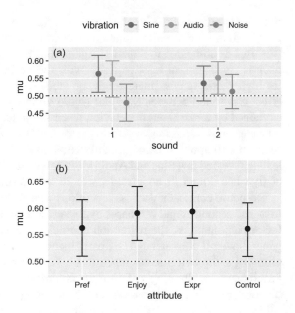

Estimates for the beta distribution means and their corresponding 95% Credible Intervals are presented in Fig. 12.16. On average, the vibrating setups were preferred to their non-vibrating versions: all mean estimates but one are above 0.50 (the point of perceived equality) as well as most of the respective credible intervals.

The model output showed the following effects.[4] The mean parameter for Audio vibration was not credibly different from Sine vibration, while Noise vibration was rated credibly lower. Sound type had a credible effect on the mean parameter ($\mu$) only in combination with Noise vibration. *Expression* and *Enjoyment* both had a rather credible positive effect, although slightly short of 95%, on the mean parameter relative to *Preference* and *Control*. However, many of the manipulated factors had credible effects on the precision parameter ($\phi$) and on the zero-inflation parameter (zoi), suggesting that even if the means are not credibly different, the shapes of the respective distributions may differ.

The main findings of this study may be summarized as follows: i) although not large, the measured effect of Sine or Audio vibration was appreciably positive. ii) Noise vibration did not credibly enhance the subjective quality of the interface as compared to the non-vibrating condition. iii) Vibrotactile feedback especially increased the perceived expressiveness of the interface and the enjoyment of playing. As appears from Fig. 12.16 (a), a more marked effect was found when vibration was more similar to the sonic feedback and consistent with the user's gesture: Indeed, Sine and Audio vibration follow the pitch of the produced sound and their intensity can be controlled by pressure. Conversely, Noise vibration—offering fixed ampli-

---

[4] Note that unlike the other studies reported in this chapter, these data were analyzed using Bayesian inference; therefore, we use the term "credible" instead of "significant" of effects.

tude, independent of the input gesture, and flat spectrum—was rated lowest among the vibrating setups. Noise vibration resulted in slightly better ratings when Sound 2 was used as compared to Sound 1: Again, that was likely because vibrotactile feedback is consistent, at least partially, with the noise-like sonic feedback produced for high y-axis values. Interestingly, no credible difference in the globally positive effect was found between Sine and Audio vibration. This may be at least partially explained by a masking effect taking place in the tactile domain toward higher frequencies, thus impairing waveform discrimination [5]. However, such phenomenon seems not to apply to markedly different signals [49]. In this regard, our informal testing revealed that Sine and Audio vibration were virtually indistinguishable, especially when Sound 1 (modulated sawtooth waveform) was selected.

Response consistency across repetitions was evaluated by modeling participants' first- and second-round responses by linear regression. Pooled over participants and factor combinations, the regression coefficient ($\beta = 0.32$, p < 0.001) indicated a general overall consistency (i.e., participants preferred the same vibrating or non-vibrating setup twice across repetitions). However, ten participants frequently preferred once the vibrating and once the non-vibrating setup in the same factor combination, resulting in regression coefficients $\leq 0$ (mean coefficient over the N = 10 subjects was $\beta = -0.19$). The remaining subjects (N = 19) instead gave consistent ratings ($\beta = 0.53$). Interestingly, the inconsistent group (N = 10) spent noticeably less time with the tasks than the reliable group (N = 19): the median length of their gestural data logs was only 62% of that of the consistent group. In order to estimate the effect of the inconsistent participants, we re-run the ZOIB model including only the N = 19 consistent subjects and finding that the main result was similar to the full dataset: only vibration type had a clearly credible effect on the estimated mean parameter. However, this way the effect is somewhat larger, as the mean estimates for vibration types Sine and Audio (with Sound 1) slightly increase, while that for Noise decreases (see Table 12.3). Also in this case, *Expression* is the highest rated attribute; its marginal mean estimate increases from 0.59 to 0.64 (see Table 12.4).

As the participants were highly skilled musicians, we believe that the recorded inconsistent responses were not due to the task being too difficult. However, as

**Table 12.3** Estimated $\mu$ parameters from the ZOIB fit (on original response scale) for the marginal effects of sound and vibration (attribute = *Preference*). N = 29: all subjects; N = 19: consistent subjects

| Sound | Vibration | Estimate (N = 29) | Estimate (N = 19) |
|-------|-----------|-------------------|-------------------|
| 1 | Sine | 0.563 | 0.604 |
| 1 | Audio | 0.548 | 0.576 |
| 1 | Noise | 0.480 | 0.466 |
| 2 | Sine | 0.536 | 0.558 |
| 2 | Audio | 0.552 | 0.550 |
| 2 | Noise | 0.512 | 0.493 |

**Table 12.4** Estimated $\mu$ parameters from the ZOIB fit (on original response scale) for the marginal effects of Attribute (sound = Sound 1, vibration = Sine). N = 29: all subjects; N = 19: consistent subjects

| Attribute | Estimate N = 29 | Estimate N = 19 |
| --- | --- | --- |
| Preference | 0.563 | 0.604 |
| Control | 0.562 | 0.594 |
| Expression | 0.594 | 0.645 |
| Enjoy | 0.591 | 0.628 |

they were not screened for individual vibrotactile sensitivity, it is possible that they did not feel vibrations equally. On top of that, we argue that rating inconsistency may be linked to the varying perceived vibration strength and audio-tactile congruence, depending on where and how the participants were playing over the interface's surface. Indeed, vibrotactile intensity perception is affected by vibration amplitude (obviously), spectral content (with a peak in the 200–300 Hz range [55]), and the exerted pressing force [42]; also, varying degrees of spectral and temporal similarity between auditory and vibratory feedback may result either in cross-modal perceptual integration or interference [60]. However, we specifically chose a free playing task in order to measure the effect of vibrotactile feedback on various aspects of the playing experience.

With regard to the coherence of specific audio-tactile combinations, although Noise vibration resulted in very uniform ratings when associated with Sound 1 ($\beta = 0.56$, p < 0.001), it produced the lowest rating consistency with Sound 2 ($\beta = 0.16$, p < 0.05). While this was obviously affected by the general tendency of ten participants toward inconsistent ratings, one may also consider the varying degree of similarity between Sound 2 and Noise vibration: at the upper range of the y coordinate Sound 2 was noise-like, while for lower y values it was increasingly sinusoidal; inconsistency might follow from having played once mostly at high y and once mostly at low y. Conversely, Sound 1 retained the same degree of (dis)similarity with Noise vibration, independent of the playing position/style. Overall, the noticed inconsistency of responses sets a future challenge for screening the participants and controlling the playing task.

## 12.9   Conclusions

Based on the reported results, we suggest that the design of future multisensory interface technologies, especially if applicable to music performance, should take into consideration the addition of advanced vibrotactile feedback. This would enable the re-establishment of a consistent physical exchange between users and their digital devices—similar to the natural relationship that musicians establish with their instrument, where the source of sound and vibration coincides—with the demonstrated potential to enhance the experience and the perceived quality of the interface. Indeed, several participants in the reported musical studies were impressed with the novelty and "aliveness" of haptic interfaces, as opposed to their experience with existing digital musical devices.

Ultimately, it is yet to be seen if and how such subjective enhancements may be reflected in the quality of playing, and musical performance altogether. Making objective measurements of these aesthetic aspects however poses a major research challenge, and the present work only scratched the surface in this direction. Instead, this will be the main object of a follow-up experiment currently in the works.

# References

1. Ahmaniemi, T.: Effect of Dynamic Vibrotactile Feedback on the Control of Isometric Finger Force. IEEE Trans. on Haptics (2012).
2. Altinsoy, M. E. in Lect. Notes Comput. Sci. (eds Nordahl, R., Serafin, S., Fontana, F., Brewster, S.) 20–25 (Springer Berlin / Heidelberg, 2010).
3. Altinsoy, M. E.: Quality of auditory-tactile virtual environments. J. Audio Eng. Soc. **60**, 38–46 (2012).
4. Banu, A., Praliyev, N., Evagoras, X.: Effect of Frequency Level on Vibrotactile Sound Detection in Proc. of the 14th International Joint Conference on Computer Vision, Imaging and Computer Graphics Theory and Applications **2** (SciTePress, Prague, Czech Republic, July 2019), 97–102.
5. Bensmaïa, S. J., Hollins, M.: Complex tactile waveform discrimination. J. Acoust. Soc. of Am. **108**, 1236–1245 (2000).
6. Brungart, D. S.: Auditory localization of nearby sources. III. Stimulus effects. J. Acoust. Soc. Am. **106**, 3589–3602 (Dec. 1999).
7. Brungart, D. S., Durlach, N. I., Rabinowitz, W. M.: Auditory localization of nearby sources. II. Localization of a broadband source. J. Acoust. Soc. Am. **106**, 1956–1968 (Oct. 1999).
8. Brungart, D. S., Rabinowitz,W. M.: Auditory localization of nearby sources. Head-related transfer functions. J. Acoust. Soc. Am. **106**, 1465–1479 (Sept. 1999).
9. Bürkner, P.-C.: brms: An R Package for Bayesian Multilevel Models Using Stan. J. Stat. Softw. **80** (2017).
10. Caclin, A., Soto-Faraco, S., Kingstone, A., Spence, C.: Tactile "capture" of audition. Perception & Psychophysics **64**, 616–630 (2002).
11. Caetano, G., Jousmäki, V.: Evidence of vibrotactile input to human auditory cortex. Neuroimage (2006).
12. Dahl, S., Bresin, R.: Is the player more influenced by the auditory than the tactile feedback from the instrument? in Proc. Int. Conf. on Digital Audio Effects (DAFx) (Limerick, Ireland, Dec. 2001), 194–197.
13. De Pra, Y., Fontana, F., Järveläinen, H., Papetti, S., Simonato, M.: Does it ping or pong? Auditory and tactile classification of materials by bouncing events. ACM Trans. Applied Perception (TAP) **17**, 1–17 (2020).
14. Ernst, M. O., Bülthoff, H. H.: Merging the senses into a robust percept. Trends Cogn. Sci. **8**, 162-9 (2004).
15. Falchier, A., Cappe, C., Barone, P., Schroeder, C. E. in The New Handbook of Multisensory Processing (ed Stein, B. E.) chap. 4 (MIT Press, 2012).
16. Fiebelkorn, I. C., Foxe, J. J., Molholm, S. in The New Handbook of Multisensory Processing (ed Stein, B. E.) chap. 21 (MIT Press, 2012).
17. Fontana, F. et al.: Rendering and subjective evaluation of real vs. synthetic vibrotactile cues on a digital piano keyboard in Proc. Int. Conf. on Sound and Music Computing (SMC) (Maynooth, Ireland, July 2015), 161–167.

18. Fontana, F., Paisa, R., Ranon, R., Serafin, S.: Multisensory plucked instrument modeling in Unity3D: From Keytar to accurate string prototyping. App. Sci. **10**, 1452 (2020).
19. Fontana, F., Papetti, S., Järveläinen, H., Avanzini, F.: Detection of keyboard vibrations and effects on perceived piano quality. J. of the Acoust. Soc. Of Am. **142**, 2953–2967 (2017).
20. Fujisaki, W., Nishida, S.: Audio-tactile superiority over visuo-tactile and audio-visual combinations in the temporal resolution of synchrony perception. Exp. Brain Res. **198**, 245–259 (2009).
21. Galembo, A., Askenfelt, A.: Quality assessment of musical instruments - Effects of multimodality in Proc. of the 5th triennial conference of the European Society for the Cognitive Sciences of Music (ESCOM) (Hanover, Germany, Sept. 2003), 441–444.
22. Glennie, E.: Hearing Essay 1993.
23. Goble, A. K., Hollins, M.: Vibrotactile adaptation enhances frequency discrimination. J. of the Acoust. Soc. of Am. **96**, 771–780 (1994).
24. Hopkins, C., Maté-Cid, S., Seiffert, G., Fulford, R., Ginsborg, J.: Inherent and learnt abilities for relative pitch in the vibrotactile domain using the fingertip in 20th Int. Congr. Sound Vib. (ICSV 2013) (Bankok, 2013), 3207–3214.
25. Huang, J., Gamble, D., Sarnlertsophon, K., Wang, X., Hsiao, S.: Feeling music: integration of auditory and tactile inputs in musical meter perception. PLoS One **7** (Jan. 2012).
26. Jack, R. H., Mehrabi, A., Stockman, T., Mcpherson, A.: Action-sound latency and the perceived quality of digital musical instruments: Comparing professional percussionists and amateur musicians. Music Percept. An Interdiscip. J. **36**, 109–128 (2018).
27. Järveläinen, H., Papetti, S., Schiesser, S., Grosshauser, T.: Audio-Tactile Feedback in Musical Gesture Primitives: Finger Pressing in Int. Conf. on Sound and Music Computing (SMC) (2013), 109–114.
28. Jiang, L., Cutkosky, M. R., Ruutiainen, J., Raisamo, R.: Improving finger force control with vibrational haptic feedback for Multiple Sclerosis in Proc. of the IASTED Int. Conf. on Telehealth/Assistive Technologies (ACTA Press, Baltimore, Maryland, 2008), 110–115.
29. Kaaresoja, T., Brewster, S., Lantz, V.: Towards the temporally perfect virtual button: touch-feedback simultaneity and perceived quality in mobile touchscreen press interactions. ACM Trans. on Applied Perception **11**, 1–25 (2014).
30. Kayser, C., Petkov, C. I., Augath, M., Logothetis, N. K.: Integration of Touch and Sound in Auditory Cortex. Neuron **48**, 373–384 (2005).
31. Kitagawa, N., Spence, C.: Audiotactile multisensory interactions in human information processing. Jpn. Psychol. Res. **48**, 158–173 (2006).
32. Kruschke, J. K.: Doing Bayesian data analysis - A tutorial with R, JAGS, and Stan 2nd (Academic Press, 2014).
33. Kuchenbuch, A., Paraskevopoulos, E., Herholz, S. C., Pantev, C.: Audiotactile integration and the influence of musical training. PLoS One **9**, e85743 (2014).
34. Landry, S. P., Champoux, F.: Musicians react faster and are better multisensory integrators. Brain Cogn. **111**, 156–162 (2017).
35. Levänen, S., Hamdorf, D.: Feeling vibrations: enhanced tactile sensitivity in congenitally deaf humans. Neuroscience letters **301**, 75–77 (2001).
36. Merchel, S., Schwendicke, A., Altinsoy, M. E.: Feeling the sound: audiotactile intensity perception in Proc. 2nd Polish-German Struct. Conf. Acoust. 58th Open Semin. Acoust. (2011).
37. Merchel, S., Leppin, A., Altinsoy, M. E.: Hearing with your Body: The Influence of Whole-Body Vibrations on Loudness Perception in Proc. 16th Int. Congr. on Sound and Vibration (ICSV16) (Kraków, Poland, July 2009), 5–9.
38. O'Modhrain, S., Gillespie, R. B. in Musical Haptics (eds Papetti, S., Saitis, C.) 11–27 (Springer International Publishing, Cham, 2018).
39. Okazaki, R., Kajimoto, H., Hayward, V.: Vibrotactile Stimulation Can Affect Auditory Loudness: A Pilot Study in Haptics: Perception, Devices, Mobility, and Communication (eds Isokoski, P., Springare, J.) (Springer Berlin Heidelberg, Berlin, Heidelberg, 2012), 103–108.
40. Papetti, S., Fröhlich, M., Schiesser, S.: The TouchBox: an open-source audiohaptic device for finger-based interaction in IEEE World Haptics Conf. (WHC) (Tokyo, Japan, July 2019), 491–496.

41. Papetti, S., Järveläinen, H., Schiesser, S.: Interactive vibrotactile feedback enhances the per-ceived quality of a surface for musical expression and the playing experience. IEEE Trans. on Haptics, 1–1 (2021).
42. Papetti, S., Jarvelainen, H., Giordano, B. L., Schiesser, S., Frohlich, M.: Vibrotactile Sensitivity in Active Touch: Effect of Pressing Force. IEEE Trans. on Haptics **10**, 113–122 (2017).
43. Papetti, S., Schiesser, S., Fröhlich, M.: Multi-point vibrotactile feedback for an expressive musical interface in Proc. New Interfaces for Musical Expression (NIME) (2015).
44. Passalenti, A. et al.: No Strings Attached: Force and Vibrotactile Feedback in a Virtual Guitar Simulation in Proc. 2019 IEEE Conf. on Virtual Reality and 3D User Interfaces (VR) (2019), 1116–1117.
45. Passalenti, A., Fontana, F.: Haptic interaction with guitar and bass virtual strings in Proc. Int. Conf. on Sound and Music Computing (SMC) (Limassol, Cyprus, July 2018), 427–432.
46. Passalenti, A. et al.: No Strings Attached: Force and Vibrotactile Feedback in a Guitar Sim-ulation in Proc. Int. Conf. Sound and Music Computing (SMC 2019) (Málaga, Spain, 2019), 28–31.
47. Perrault Jr, T. J., Rowland, B. A. in The New Handbook of Multisensory Processing (ed Stein, B. E.) chap. 6 (MIT Press, 2012).
48. Romagnoli, M., Fontana, F., Sarkar, R.: Vibrotactile Recognition byWestern and Indian Popu-lation Groups of Traditional Musical Scales Played with the Harmonium in Haptic and Audio Interaction Design (eds Cooper, E. W., Kryssanov, V. V., Ogawa, H., Brewster, S.) (Springer Berlin Heidelberg, Berlin, Heidelberg, 2011), 91–100.
49. Russo, F. A., Ammirante, P., Fels, D. I.: Vibrotactile discrimination of musical timbre. J. Exp. Psychol. Hum. Percept. Perform. **38** (Aug. 2012).
50. Sanabria, D., Soto-Faraco, S., Spence, C.: Spatiotemporal interactions between audition and touch depend on hand posture. Exp. Brain Res. **165**, 505–14 (2005).
51. Schürmann, M., Caetano, G., Hlushchuk, Y., Jousmäki, V., Hari, R.: Touch activates human auditory cortex. Neuroimage **30**, 1325–31 (2006).
52. Schürmann, M., Caetano, G., Jousmäki, V., Hari, R.: Hands help hearing: facilitatory audio-tactile interaction at low sound-intensity levels. J. of the Acoust. Soc. of Am. **115**, 830–832 (2004).
53. Shore, S. E., Dehmel, S. in The New Handbook of Multisensory Processing (ed Stein, B. E.) chap. 1 (MIT Press, 2012).
54. Stanford, T. A. in The New Handbook of Multisensory Processing (ed Stein, B. E.) (MIT Press, 2012).
55. Verrillo, R. T.: Vibration sensation in humans. Music Perception **9**, 281–302 (1992).
56. Wilson, E. C., Reed, C. M., Braida, L. D.: Integration of auditory and vibrotactile stimuli: Effects of phase and stimulus-onset asynchrony. J. Acoust. Soc. Am. **126**, 1960–74 (2009).
57. Wilson, E. C., Reed, C. M., Braida, L. D.: Integration of auditory and vibrotactile stimuli: Effects of frequency. J. Acoust. Soc. Am. **127**, 3044–59 (2010).
58. Wollman, I., Fritz, C., Poitevineau, J., McAdams, S.: Investigating the role of auditory and tactile modalities in violin quality evaluation. PLoS One **9**, e112552 (2014).
59. Yau, J. M., Olenczak, J. B., Dammann, J. F., Bensmaïa, S. J.: Temporal frequency channels are linked across audition and touch. Curr. Biol. **19**, 561–6 (2009).
60. Yau, J. M., Weber, A. I., Bensmaïa, S. J.: Separate mechanisms for audiotactile pitch and loudness interactions. Frontiers in psychology **1**, 160 (2010).
61. Young, G. W., Murphy, D., Weeter, J.: Auditory Discrimination of Pure and Complex Wave-forms Combined With Vibrotactile Feedback in Proc. New Interfaces for Musical Expression (NIME) (Baton Rouge, LA, 2015).
62. Young, G. W., Murphy, D., Weeter, J.: Haptics in music: The effects of vibrotactile stimulus in low frequency auditory difference detection tasks. IEEE Trans. on Haptics **1412**, 135–139 (2017).

# Chapter 13
# From the Lab to the Stage: Practical Considerations on Designing Performances with Immersive Virtual Musical Instruments

Victor Zappi, Dario Mazzanti, and Florent Berthaut

**Abstract** Immersive virtual musical instruments (IVMIs) lie at the intersection between music technology and virtual reality. Being both digital musical instruments (DMIs) and elements of virtual environments (VEs), IVMIs have the potential to transport the musician into a world of imagination and unprecedented musical expression. But when the final aim is to perform live on stage, the employment of these technologies is anything but straightforward, for sharing the virtual musical experience with the audience gets quite arduous. In this chapter, we assess in detail the several technical and conceptual challenges linked to the composition of IVMI performances on stage, i.e., their *scenography*, providing a new critical perspective on IVMI performance and design. We first propose a set of dimensions meant to analyse IVMI scenographies, as well as to evaluate their compatibility with different instrument metaphors and performance rationales. Such dimensions are built from the specifics and constraints of DMIs and VEs; they include the level of immersion of musicians and spectators and provide an insight into the interaction techniques afforded by 3D user interfaces in the context of musical expression. We then analyse a number of existing IVMIs and stage setups, and finally suggest new ones, with the aim to facilitate the design of future immersive performances.

V. Zappi (✉)
Northeastern University, Boston, MA, United States
e-mail: v.zappi@northeastern.edu

D. Mazzanti
Independent researcher, Genoa, Italy
e-mail: darmaz@gmail.com

F. Berthaut
University of Lille, Lille, France
e-mail: florent.berthaut@univ-lille.fr

© The Author(s) 2023                                                      383
M. Geronazzo and S. Serafin (eds.), *Sonic Interactions in Virtual Environments*,
Human—Computer Interaction Series, https://doi.org/10.1007/978-3-031-04021-4_13

## 13.1   Introduction

Making music while immersed in a virtual environment (VE) is an exciting experience. In a synthetic space designed to replicate and transcend our world, we gain the ability to become composers and performers of inventive musical pieces, that leverage unprecedented acoustical phenomena (virtual sound), mechanical phenomena (virtual interaction) and perceptual/cognitive phenomena (virtual experience). This is possible thanks to the design of virtual devices that, alike digital musical instruments (DMIs), transform interaction into sound, but also allow to channel musical expression through the peculiar features of the surrounding VE. For example, in a world where sound can be visible as well as tangible (like the one created by Lanier to host his "Virtual Instrumentation" [49]), virtual musical devices might permit not only to play notes but also to manipulate them, as they are still echoing in the air. In other VEs, their design might leverage the possibility to fly or teleport through space to create huge distributed instruments that would be otherwise impossible to manoeuver. What these apparently disparate musical applications share is *immersion*, meaning that physical equipment, virtual content and the overarching logic that binds the two are geared towards the amplification of the physical and cognitive involvement of the musician acting in the environment. Being both DMIs and elements of immersive environments, or even extending across whole VEs, we call these devices immersive virtual musical instruments (IVMIs); they typically consist of virtual representations of sound processes and parameters [11, 35], and rely on immersive multimodal technologies to support fine 3D interaction.

As it happens in the case of most musical instruments, composition or studio practice with IVMIs may be considered an end itself [88]. The musician that is immersed in the VE may experience the feeling of satisfaction typical of the completion of challenging musical tasks [58]. Moreover, in this scenario satisfaction is likely to be combined with the sense of *discovery* that characterises virtual reality (VR), as the IVMI may feature novel musical affordances [10] or, more in general, unusual sets of sensory-motor contingencies [79]. While some musical VEs are designed specifically to elicit such autotelic responses[1] [35, 72, 96], the final aim of a considerable number of musicians is to perform with their IVMI in front of various audiences and use it to create some sort of *connection* with them.

Unfortunately, the step from the studio to the stage is anything but straightforward. First of all, the rehearsal spaces of most IVMI players are not standard music studios. Before the release of consumer head-mounted displays (HMDs) and the rise of VR videogames, IVMIs were almost exclusively designed (and played) in VR research facilities, equipped with minimal audio gears like an audio interface and a mixer [10, 56, 94]. Nowadays immersive technology is more affordable and VR musicians may have access to spaces more affine to traditional music facilities [36, 53]; however, in these studios professional audio equipment still needs to be laid side by side with tracking systems, HMDs, projectors, all connected to dedicated computers. The

---

[1] We may label this kind of musical VEs with the umbrella term *installations*.

showcasing of live IVMI performances—even the simplest ones—inevitably relies on the employment of such heterogeneous studio equipment, which has to be moved to the venue and arranged on stage.

But it is not the size nor the complexity of the setup alone to qualify IVMI performances as challenging artistic endeavours. Rather, the real hurdle for VR artists comes from the nature of the required equipment. Musicians active in contemporary popular and underground music scenes are no stranger to the on-stage employment of remarkably complex setups, the most straightforward example being a generic rock band playing electric, electronic as well as acoustic instruments altogether during the same show. However, when a rock band steps on stage and the concert begins, the chosen technological setup immediately proves itself fundamental to support musical expression and to create a synergetic connection with the audience. The instruments fuse with the bodies of the members of the band and each gesture acquires a clear musical meaning; cables and speakers disappear from sight, concealed by the music and by the flashing lights, that equally immerse the musicians and the audience into a large shared audio/visual environment. Unfortunately, this *inclusive* scenario is in stark contrast with the musical experience that is delivered on average through an IVMI performance. When inside the VE, the musician fully leverages the immersive technology laid on stage to approach the IVMI's logic and control it, as if the instrument were physically there in front of them. But to the eyes of the audience, this interaction is quite cryptic, even abstract. This is due to the fact that spectators are confined outside of the VE. They see the musician assuming awkward poses and contorting themselves while handling invisible objects on a semi-empty stage. The only visible clue about the existence of the VE is the technology that surrounds the performer, which mediates the interaction between the physical and the virtual world, but tells very little about the mechanics of the latter. Without a clear view of the virtual objects and their response to interaction, what remains is just a music piece almost completely disconnected from the gestures and the physical presence of the musician.

Some may argue that the potential of immersive music extends way beyond the virtualisation of the sole performer's experience. For a moment we can forget about stages equipped with immersive gears and even venues, and rather imagine shows taking place in completely synthetic worlds, that spectators access remotely from their living rooms. This is one of the many social expressions of contemporary VR culture [62]. Showcasing a fully virtual performance surely helps the audience see the show in its entirety, and better appreciate interaction and aesthetic nuances. However, research proved that VR setups and networked technologies available today are not yet capable of providing the same sense of connection triggered by social activities set in physical reality, let alone by complex psychophysiological experiences like concerts and live performances [50].

Leveraging immersion to create a sense of connection/inclusion clearly becomes the main challenge for VR artists and IVMI designers, and the very immersive equipment they rely upon seems to get in the way. During the first experiments with IVMIs carried out in the early 1990s, this scenario was not necessarily considered a limitation to artistic expression.[2] Conversely, it was taken as an opportunity to explore a new relationship between performer and audience [49]. Immersive technology was employed to create novel musical instrumentation, but at the same time concealed this instrumentation and made the musician unable to know how this looked like to the audience. Differently from a traditional musical performance, this scenario did not elevate the status of the performer; it put performer and audience on the same level instead, providing IVMIs with a distinct aesthetic. However, while a similar peer relationship could be achieved by means of other forms of live art too [49], some emerging properties of VR appealed new media artists for their utter uniqueness [57, 98]. This caused a rapid change of paradigm and by the mid 1990s the focus of VR performances became revealing a new world, as opposed to concealing it. Immersive technology started to be praised for its potential to offer to the audience a stake in the VE, in the form of a *vicarious* experience [31]. In other words, for the first time VEs were conceived as spaces where to live an experience not only via first-person interaction (as in the case of the performer), but also by observing someone else interacting. This emphasised the importance of being able to perceive continuity between the performer's gestures and the resulting sounds and visuals, to connect with the performer, and share with them the same virtual musical experience.

Today, the design of most IVMIs and VR performances is based on the same rationale [10, 36, 41], as artists aim for shared experiences and connection with the audience. But in practice this is a costly goal. The setting up of such musical VEs requires beforehand a strong commitment to understanding both what performing music means and how VR affects action and cognition, as well as a fair amount of equipment ready at hand. Alas, in real-case scenarios mental and physical resources tend to be limited; trade-offs happen to be extremely common, either in terms of a reduction in the sense of agency and immersion of the performer (to favour the audience's side), or as an overall depreciation of what attending *live* music truly feels like (biasing the performer's role).

## 13.1.1  The Role of Scenography

The impending gap between performer's and audience's virtual musical experiences is a complex phenomenon that has to be accounted for in every IVMI performance. But how can we measure the entity of this gap? And how can we intervene to reduce it? What we suggest is to embrace a larger perspective on performance practice, by means of applying scenographic theory to the domain of IVMIs.

In theatre, cinema and television, *scenography* relates to the study and the development of audio/visual, spatial and experiential composition of performance, by taking

---

[2] Here the use of the term "experiments" does not want by any means to devalue the artistic significance of these early performances; it refers to the inability to predict the effects that such a novel technology would have had on the overall vibe of the shows and on the audiences' experience.

into account the perspective of two main stakeholders: performer and audience.[3] In the case of IVMIs, the dichotomy between performer's agency and audience connection is due to the constraints of immersive technology; nonetheless, analogous issues often arise when staging a play, filming a movie or broadcasting a live show, even if completely different sets of technologies are in use. Shots of magicians or jugglers are quite challenging for example, as the presence of one or more cameras makes it more difficult for these performers to disguise or show off their dexterous movements. A famous example consists of the crystal-ball scenes in Jim Henson's 1986 movie *Labyrinth*, where artist Michael Moschen had to juggle blindly with only his right hand in the frame while hiding the rest of his body behind David Bowie. In theatrical plays, it is the physical presence of an audience to challenge the performers instead. Actors are often compelled to face the spectators while interacting with stage props or with each other, sacrificing visual feedback/eye contact to create a sense of inclusion. One of the main aims of scenography is to account for these and similar scenarios. A well-designed scenography fully immerses the spectators in the production, eliciting emotional and rational engagement [59] while seamlessly synthesising the performers' and the audience's experiences [44].

In the context of IVMIs, the scenography of a performance may be defined as the complete setup chosen to reproduce the instrument/VE on stage, make it playable to the musician and present it to the audience. This includes (1) the technology dedicated to the immersion of the performer, like displays (e.g., HMDs, projections), tracking systems (e.g., head tracking, full-body motion capture and active/passive markers), physical user interfaces (e.g., joysticks and haptics) and sound monitors (e.g., headphones and speakers); (2) the technology addressing the audience's experience, like large screens, projected surfaces, lights and the power amplifier system; and (3) the spatial arrangement of such technologies on stage, taking into account the freedom of action required by the musician to play the instrument, as well as size and position of the stage compared to the seat area or the parterre. In line with general scenographic theory, such a practice extends across design, curation and technical development [44].

When included in the design process of an IVMI performance, the development of a specific scenography may change how the VE is experienced, starting from disentangling immersive technology from the concept of *user*. Such a term is at the basis of most—if not all—conventional design approaches to VR, which tend to represent "the human subject as an omnipotent and isolated viewpoint" [30]. The great majority of IVMIs comply with this rationale. This is the main reason why, on stage, VR technology is almost exclusively employed to immerse the musician, creating the sense of isolation that we discussed earlier in this section. As opposed, musical VEs conceived for live performances would highly benefit from the exploration of novel design approaches, possibly discarding strict user-centric solutions.

---

[3] Scenographic theory often includes the figure of the director among the stakeholders of production; to make a simpler connection with IVMI performances we omit this detail, as in most cases the artist playing the IVMI is also the composer of the piece as well as the designer of the instrument.

In this context, scenographic theory may provide valuable guidelines to support experimentation. By dedicating time to the study and the development of a proper stage setup, artists may devise new ways of employing immersive technology, in compliance with the performer–audience paradigm that lies at the core of scenographic theory [59]. In other words, by definition, a scenography has the power to turn the VR user into a performer, fostering an experience that is suitable for the entertainment of an external audience.

## 13.1.2 A New Approach to IVMI Performance

The design of a proper IVMI scenography is not an easy task though. In particular, the transition from user to performer proves to be a critical hit, as witnessed by the remarkable number of musical VEs that have been designed as instruments but never reached the stage. Indeed, despite the relatively large literature, very few works report the showcase of musical VEs in the context of concerts, for most IVMIs tend to be used as installations or research platforms, rather than as instruments for live performance [35, 47, 56, 94].

The aim of this chapter is to address this problem and combine theory and practice to facilitate the design of IVMI scenographies. To do so, we propose a set of *dimensions* specifically conceived for the analysis of immersive stage setups. Such dimensions form a set of evaluation criteria that reflect the twofold nature of IVMIs. They stem from the detailed examination of the specifics of immersive VEs, combined with the practicalities of live music performances and in particular those featuring DMIs. As a consequence, their application allows to extrapolate from a chosen stage setup the technical characteristics that affect these factors and to qualitatively evaluate their individual impact on the showcasing of a generic IVMI performance. Furthermore, when the stage setup is coupled with a specific immersive instrument, the outcome of the analysis provides quick metrics to assess the experiential gap that likely divides performer and audience, also highlighting the main causes of such a disconnection.

It is worth noting that the scope of this work extends beyond the domain of VR. As detailed in the following sections, virtual performances and scenographies often span augmented and mixed realisations too, including see-through visual displays and a combination of physical and virtual stage props. This is the reason why we are referring to *immersive virtual* musical instruments as opposed to *virtual reality* musical instruments (commonly referred to as VRMI [78]), the latter being for the most part a sub-category of the former.

The actual relationship between these two classes of musical devices appears clear in the context of the categorisation of interactive environments proposed by Milgram and Kishino [65]. The two authors introduce a single continuous axis—the "virtuality continuum"—that goes from real environments (where everything is physical) to VEs (that host synthetic elements only), and encompasses in between all kinds of environments that mix physical and synthetic entities. On such a continuum, VRMIs belong to the far end of the spectrum ("virtuality"), and are distinct from devices that rely on technologies that lie closer to the "reality" end, like for example augmented reality (AR). However, the authors point out that virtual, augmented and any other kind of mixed technology can be characterised by different levels of immersion, regardless of their location on the continuum (see Sect. 13.3.1 for a more thorough discussion about immersion and its degrees of execution). In line with this perspective, IVMIs do not belong to a single point in the continuum, rather they cut across the spectrum; they include VRMIs, AR musical devices and any mixed solution in between, provided that the design of the instrument targets immersion.

Before moving forward, we'd like to remind the reader that this chapter is an extended and revised version of a pre-existing work, published by the authors in 2014 [12]. The decision to try to improve our contribution to this challenging research and artistic field comes from a very practical consideration. Over the seven years following the original publication, VR technologies have settled in the world of videogames and consumer electronics, and today the result of this process is the emergence of a new generation of immersive instruments and performances. For the first time, musicians have access to commercial IVMIs alongside more affordable and reliable resources for do-it-yourself development, to make new music and engage with new audio/visual experiences. And as expected, this is happening both inside and outside music studios. Companies are teaming up with underground as well as mainstream artists to popularise the use of new immersive devices in performance settings, starting the exploration of innovative stage technologies to sell on the market of music and entertainment. In this vibrant scenario, the need for guidance in performance and instrument design is stronger than ever. The way we try to fulfil this need is by presenting a new set of cross-domain dimensions; by doing so, we aim at combining in one single critical perspective the practical—as well as cultural—implications that derive from the latest development of immersive musical technologies.

In line with this purpose, the rest of the chapter is structured as follows. Sections 13.2 and 13.3 discuss the main technological as well as experiential factors that play a role in the context of DMI performance and of immersive VEs, respectively. We will refer to these factors as *constraints*, a term originating from human–computer interaction [68] yet widely used in both DMI and VR literature [20, 32, 38, 93]. In particular, we embrace Magnusson's take on the subject, which deems constraints complementary to the *affordances* of an artefact/system [55]; in the context of this work, this means that by following cultural conventions and by adhering to technical and psychophysical requirements, it is possible to express at best the potential of DMIs, VEs as well as IVMIs. Starting from such constraints, in Sect. 13.4 we provide a detailed presentation of the set of dimensions we conceived to support the practice of scenographers and IVMI designers. Then, the following two sections exemplify how the dimensions may be applied to real-case scenarios. Section 13.5 analyses an assorted selection of IVMI performances spanning the last 30 years, with the aim to assess the type of experience provided to musicians and audience across all dimensions; while Sect. 13.6 shifts the focus on the future of immersive scenography, as we introduce novel stage setups and we use the dimensions to frame their potential when combined with IVMIs. Some of the solutions discussed in these two sections provide concrete examples of how to bring a musical VE to a live stage not only by using immersive VR technologies, but also by combining AR equipment/paradigms within the setup. Finally, conclusions are drawn in Sect. 13.7.

## 13.2 Constraints of the Digital Live Music Experience

DMIs are flexible tools that allow for the exploration of original musical and design practices. The vast potential granted by digital technologies makes it possible for designers and players to embrace the most daring sensing and interaction techniques, and to combine them with sound synthesis technologies that can also extend into the analog domain [61, 76]. Moreover, any mapping between musician's gestures and sound parameters can be devised almost arbitrarily, removing further limitations from the creative process [45, 91].

Unfortunately, this design freedom leads to great challenges when transferring a DMI from the studio to a live stage.[4] The type of musical exploration afforded by DMIs often manifests itself through bizarre and do-it-yourself equipment, unusual gestures, abstract sounds and idiosyncratic mapping between them. If not properly contextualised (in both a broad and a literal sense), these very distinctive features may impinge on the audience's experience of the show, as well as on the technical and expressive proficiency of the performers.

This section looks at DMIs from the perspective of live music performance. In particular, we discuss what we consider the main constraints linked to this form of expression/entertainment. Although centred on novel digital technologies, the list includes constraints that may as well inform the design of performances for traditional instruments. However, their overall impact is far more relevant when relocated within the domain of DMIs.

### 13.2.1 Stage Performance

On stage, performers need to be comfortable with their instruments. In an ideal scenario, a DMI plays the same regardless of *where* it is played, allowing the musician to build a live performance around the same affordances explored in studio and rehearsal spaces. Unfortunately, this is not always the case. Some DMIs are big and complicated, composed of parts that are difficult to assemble/disassemble or simply fragile. When dealing with such designs, the way the instrument is set up on stage often differs from the original studio configuration, forcing the performer to adapt their playing postures or even to sacrifice important visual/sound/haptic cues. Other musical systems impose requirements on the specifications of the stage itself. These include peculiar lighting, accurate microphone placement and support

---

[4] A great portion of the DMI literature discusses how detrimental the apparent lack of design limitations may be on the musical appropriation of the instrument too, but this is beyond the scope of our work.

**Fig. 13.1** López's playing at the NIME Conference 2011; despite the use of curtains and dimmed lights, the instrument's optical tracking system kept malfunctioning, forcing López to adapt the execution of his pieces to the adverse situation. Image courtesy of Alexander Refsum Jensenius

for multichannel audio playback; sometimes calibration procedures are required too, as in the case of multichannel audio or motion capture. If any of these elements is missing or merely not compatible with the DMI, some of the musical affordances and functionalities the performer grew accustomed to may become unavailable, right before the start of the show. A notable example of this contingency is the opening concert of the NIME Conference 2011. On that occasion, Carles López had to rework his performance on the fly since the adverse lighting conditions of the stage made a large portion of his Reactable unresponsive (Fig. 13.1).

Approaching the stage unprepared clearly is a hazard and not all performers have the flexibility displayed by López (his performance was a success!). To avoid this risk, it is not uncommon for DMI musicians to organise live events in their practice studios, leveraging the very spaces where the instruments were designed, built and tested [97]. Yet, the appeal of a real venue is invaluable. Creators of a musical performance involving DMIs should dedicate particular attention to the phase of the stage setup. Issues and necessities should be anticipated with care, from the most general and basic ones to the most specific and complex ones: will cables be long enough to connect the required hardware across the stage? How long does it take to calibrate and prepare the instrument? Are any of the pieces of equipment employed in the design difficult to install/use on a regular stage? Similar questions should arise early in the DMI's creation process, and could very well affect its design and behaviour.

## 13.2.2  Communication Between Performers and Audience

Communication between performers and audience is another fundamental aspect of musical performances. Often coupled with *cognition*, communication is one of the main terms in use in music psychology and emotion research to frame the experience of playing and attending a live show. In this context, communication refers to the musician sending encoded messages for the spectators to be interpreted; more specifically, these resolve into music as well as related actions conceived to trigger specific emotions in the listener/viewer [48, 71]. However, authors like Gurevich, Treviño and Fyans thoroughly discussed how the application of such a model in the domain of DMIs is quite controversial, as it does not account for experimental and improvisatory music (to name a few), nor for the non-instrumental/intellectual engagement such instruments seem to be better suited for [37, 39].

To escape diversions from the main topic of this chapter, in this work we adopt a definition of *communication* that is more akin to Bonger's discourse on human–machine interaction [17]: non-verbal and non-necessarily musical cues that define the interplay existing between audience and performers. From this perspective, communication can be analysed as a constraint, rather than as a yet-to-understand factor of music cognition.

Nonetheless, the way such a constraint is dealt with when designing a performance can still deeply influence and characterise the live music experience. Musicians should be able to perceive reactions of the audience, in order to adjust their playing and get a feeling of the ambience. For example, an improvised section could last longer or be cut short based on the hints performers can get from the audience. Or in large venues, performers could feel like getting physically closer to the spectators, or move around the stage also based on non-verbal cues. Spectators can communicate actively their emotions and appreciation to the performers via social and cultural conventions too, for example through gestures, like applauding and shouting. Symmetrically, spectators should perceive musicians' expressions, gestures and looks, which are part of their playing style and together with the sonic outcome contribute to outline the performance. To this end, stages for live performances played in front of huge crowds typically include big screens showing close-ups of the musicians.

Apart from the direct interplay between the parties, Bonger describes also another type of communication, happening in the context of "performer–system–audience" interaction. Performer and audience can indeed use the very technology setup on stage/in the venue (the "system") as a communication channel beyond sound and music. In his work, he discusses performances in which multimodality and—in particular—VR technologies are leveraged by the musicians to provide visual and haptic stimuli to single spectators, as well as multiple members of the audience. Finally, this type of communication includes the case of participatory performances, with spectators being able to use the system to input content in the performance and share information with the musicians. Some examples are the use of text messages as both sonification and literal communication means [29], or votes on the preferred type of music [92].

## 13.2.3  Music Ensemble

In performances involving multiple musicians, group dynamics are an essential aspect of both the performers' and spectators' experience. In fact, the interaction between musicians among the ensemble when playing DMIs may differ from what happens with traditional instruments. Moreover, the difficulty in understanding the musician's gestures might increase with an ensemble, as it may also be difficult for the spectators to understand who is doing what [64]. Collaboration modes in digital ensembles can be separated into cooperation, communication and organisation modes [9]. Cooperation modes, when concurrent or complementary, allow musicians to share parts of sound generation processes or even allow other musicians to play their instrument. These choices and changes can be highlighted for the benefit of the audience—or even of other musicians, if they are not involved in the sharing process. Communication modes, such as exchanging messages or gestures indications, can also be amplified for the audience, as done in [51] since they can be less visible than with acoustic ensembles. Finally, organisation modes, which allow musicians to define roles such as conductor and groups within the orchestra, are usually obvious from spatial arrangement of musicians in acoustic ensembles and might need to be reinforced for the audience of digital orchestras.

## 13.3  Virtual Environments and the Constraints of Immersive Experiences

Compared to the case of live digital music, the compilation of a list of constraints capable of informing how we experience virtuality may seem overwhelming. The design of most, if not all, live DMI performances targets the delivery of one or more musical pieces; and while the details of the chosen technological setups vary from performance to performance and from artist to artist, their employment on and off stage is always dedicated to supporting the re-creation and the diffusion of the featured music (as discussed in the previous section). Conversely, the variety of applications and scopes of systems capitalising on VR is astonishing, spanning industrial design [46], psychological and physical therapeutics [43], military training [52] and—of course—musical applications, just to name a few. From this perspective, it is quite hard to pin point all the requirements of such systems and scenarios and to address in a single discussion the contingencies relative to employed technologies and common practices.

Luckily, the literature in VR research highlights an overarching theme that is common to all VR applications, and that can be used as the lens through which to analyse the constraints affecting the users' experience of generic VEs. This theme is the search for *presence*. In particular, presence has been described as the psychological sense of "being in the VE" [84], a specific state of consciousness that ought to be experienced by VR users. In an optimal scenario, when a user feels "present" in a virtual world, they act as if the environment were real, physically and emotionally engaged in the application. Therefore, presence is targeted by all designers of VEs, regardless of the specific scope of the application or the technical details of the system. Furthermore, the concept of presence is tightly connected to disciplines like physiology, perception and psychology [60, 80, 82], making carefully designed narratives, settings and tasks necessary for it to be triggered.

In line with this scenario, we can consider constraints of VEs and all the technological and experiential factors that play a role towards the establishment and the preservation of the feeling of presence in VR applications. In this section, we gather and discuss such constraints, placing emphasis on the aspects that will have a particular significance when crossing the domain of musical performance.

### 13.3.1 Immersion

*Immersion* is a key constraint in VR. The term refers to the description of the technology used to make the user feel present in the VE [81]. Immersive VR applications are characterised by a combination of equipment and techniques, the most common being wide stereoscopic viewports, multimodal feedback, detailed graphics, high framerate and large tracking areas. Such an arsenal may sound quite heterogeneous, and in fact it is not trivial to design and combine all its components as functional elements of a robust global system. Yet, the effect that this class of immersive technologies has on presence is immediate and conspicuous such that researchers used to identify their technical specifications as the main constraints of VR [20]. But, nowadays, other immersive features are deemed fundamental too. For example those pertaining to the design of the content of the VE, and in particular of those details that grant a coherent perception of the virtual objects, the surrounding virtual world and the virtual representations of the body of the user. In technical terms, this translates into scale, perspective and alignment. On a cognitive level, this coherence relies on components such as place illusion and plausibility, i.e., the sensation that the place and events occurring are real [79]. In a musical performance context with 3D avatars, plausibility, for example, seem to be strongly linked to eye contact with the musicians [8]. Presence is also strengthened by virtual body ownership, i.e., when one perceives their virtual avatar body as their own.

As discussed in [25], the effects of all these technologies and techniques are highly interconnected with one another. Moreover, the absence or the misuse of any of them may produce immediate breaks in presence [19]. For example, in a poorly designed VR setup the user may end up pulling the cable of a tracking device, or may thrust their hand through a virtual object, revealing its inconsistency. Similar contingencies have both perceptual and physiological consequences on the users, which can be measured to determine the extent of the experienced loss in presence [86]. Hence, immersion often fulfils the role of a filter too. Equipment and design techniques can be employed to block unwanted stimuli that come from the real world surrounding the VR setup, and that are often collectively referred to simply as *noise*. These include the touch of hard boundaries of the tracking space, like sensor stands and walls [16, 67], or even the voice of people conversing close by.[5] Properly filtering noise from a VR setup is not enough to avoid all breaks in presence, but it is a good practice to minimise those caused by external reasons [80].

The strong connection between immersion and equipment means that different VR setups are characterised by more or less pronounced immersive features, regardless of the actual applications run with them. Then, the overall feeling of presence experienced by the user will depend on the specific combination of the immersive setup and the immersive design features of the software. But the role of the equipment/setting is so prominent that often times VR setups are assigned labels hinting at their intrinsic level of immersion [75]. These labels range from *fully immersive*, like the case of consumer VR headsets available nowadays and composed of HMDs, head and hand trackers, to *non-immersive*, denoting monoscopic screens and general-purpose input devices, like mice, buttons and joysticks.[6]

The case of *partially immersive* setups (also labelled *semi-immersive*) is particularly interesting for the purpose of this work. Most of these mid-tier solutions capitalise on stereoscopic monitors and stereo-projected screens, occasionally coupled with head tracking. The result is a window on the virtual world, whose size is proportional to the rendering/projection area. Hence, the smaller the window, the more likely for the elements of the VE to end up beyond the clear-cut boundaries of the visual display and disappear from sight—especially during manipulation or locomotion. This eventuality endangers presence and represents the main technological limitation of partially immersive setups. And similar risks affect AR applications too, which leverage setups belonging to the same class.

Yet, monitors and projected screens provide VR designers with the opportunity to seamlessly combine real and virtual elements in the virtual experience. For example, a large projected setup allows to perceive the real hands and body of the user literally inside the VE, along with the virtual objects that populate it (or virtual objects inside the real world, as in the case of AR). Moreover, real-world objects and props may be used to carry out virtual interaction, hence entering the domain of hybrid reality [65]. As a consequence, the overall level of immersion that is achievable when using partially immersive setups largely depends also on *reality–virtuality continuity*, i.e., the set of immersive design features aimed at generating a consistent perceptual connection between the real and the virtual world. We can consider reality–virtuality continuity as an extension of the triad scale/perspective/alignment that entangles rendering and tracking with the physical properties of real space.

AR displays can be used to cover a range of setups from partially immersive, e.g., integrating a few virtual elements in the physical space, to almost fully immersive, e.g., placing users in a virtual room or on a virtual stage. Because the physical space

---

[5] Interestingly, this happens both in the context of research experiments, during which the subject may hear comments from the investigators or other lab members, and in casual game sessions, when friends/observers support the immersed player.

[6] Indeed, when you are playing a videogame on your laptop or console, you are actually experiencing non-immersive VR!

remains visible in all these cases, AR inherits from usual performance conditions: direct visibility of the performers and other spectators, and visibility of one's own body. These setups may also amplify errors in scale/perspective/alignment provided by a 3D display. However, these displays may also restrict 3D interaction opportunities to a subset of the techniques described below if part of the physical environment remains visible (e.g., navigation in a VE might be perceptually confusing if it is not correctly designed).

## 13.3.2   3D Interaction

Immersive technologies and design features are not the only means to trigger a sense of a presence. In most cases, being able to interact with the VE encourages the user to deem the virtual world they are immersed in as real, and to forget that the experience is actually taking place in a different physical space. In other words, interaction is another powerful ally in the search for presence. The argument supporting this approach is that the reality of experience is defined by functionality rather than appearances, hence the sense of "being there" in a VE is grounded on the ability to "do" there [34, 77]. This does not mean that in an interactive system immersive technologies are superfluous or even a waste of money/resources; rather, interaction can be considered a constraint working on a different level from immersion, and both can be combined to describe VR more in-depth.

Interaction with the virtual world (what we also referenced as "virtual interaction") consists of altering the state of 3D models that populate foreground and/or background of the scene. This paradigm offers quite different perspectives—and challenges—compared to the case of interaction with 2D widgets, text and icons; for this reason, the term *3D interaction* is often used to distinguish it from the "desktop metaphor" employed in traditional personal computer environments [42]. Existing research on 3D interaction discusses an assortment of techniques, usually classified using the following categories: *selection*, *manipulation*, *navigation* and *application control* (the latter pertaining to menus and other VE configuration widgets, as a 3D extension of 2D interaction). In this section, we focus on the first three categories, as they provide a greater variety of controls with higher dimensionalities and are better suited to frame musical interaction in VEs.

Selection techniques allow users to indicate an object or group of objects in the VE. They are essential as they precede all manipulation techniques (i.e., to indicate which object will be manipulated) and some navigation techniques (e.g., to select a point of interest that the user wants to inspect). Several classifications of selection techniques have been proposed. Among them, Bowman et al. [18] classify techniques according to the object indication method (occlusion, object touching, pointing and indirect selection), activation method (event, gesture and voice command) and feedback type (text, aural, visual and force/tactile). More recently, Argelaguet and Andujar [1] proposed a set of design variables which allows for describing selection techniques according to, for example, the selection tool and how it is controlled, the control-display ratio or the disambiguation mechanism to avoid multiple selections. Most common techniques involve either a virtual ray/cone projected from the user through the environment or a virtual cursor/hand mapped to the user's hand movements.

Manipulation techniques allow users to modify the spatial transform of elements of a VE, namely rotation, scaling and translation. They can also be used to modify their material (albedo, texture and other shading properties) through virtual tools such as virtual paint brushes and 3D palettes. Other techniques focus on the modification of the shape of composite 3D structures or 3D meshes, in particular through virtual sculpting metaphors. A recent review of such manipulation techniques can be found in [63].

Navigation techniques allow users to move inside the VE. This translates to the discovery of new areas and details of the virtual world, often segueing into the selection and the manipulation of virtual objects. From a technical perspective, navigation consists of a real-time update of the user's visual feedback carried out by the rendering engine, which provides a consistent dynamic representation of all the 3D models that cross the viewport. One possible classification of navigation techniques was introduced by [54] and separates them into three categories. *General movement* comprises all exploratory displacements through the VE, for example flying or walking. The case of walking is of particular interest; this type of navigation supports natural locomotion, a solution that has a strong impact on presence [83] and whose effectiveness can be further enhanced by means of walk-in-place immersive technologies and design features [67, 73]. The second category is *targeted movement*, which includes all techniques for which the user defines a target position and orientation within the VE. These can be discrete, when jumping or teleporting, but also continuous with smooth transitions between positions, such as those proposed in the Navidget technique [40]. Finally, *specified trajectory movement* techniques allow users to define a path through the VE which is then followed with different degrees of automation.

In the context of musical expression and IVMIs, these categories of interaction techniques can and have been used for all types of gestures, including the selection of components of the instrument, excitation/production of sound and modulation of sound parameters [21]. For example, in *Drile* [10] a virtual ray technique is utilised for selecting tools and nodes of musical trees, while in Maki-Patola's VR percussion instrument [56] virtual sticks are used to trigger sounds. Techniques from the same category can be employed for both discrete and continuous controls in IVMIs. For instance, 3D navigation in *Versum* [3] allows for continuously controlling the volume of sound sources placed in the virtual environment. By changing to a discrete navigation technique, such as teleportation, one could trigger presets of sound mix, eventually playing them in a rhythm.

From a scenographical point of view, 3D interaction techniques do not all offer the same level of transparency [66], meaning that the influence of the musician on the VE can be more or less difficult to appreciate [13]. Navigation in VEs may be easily perceivable through the movements of avatars or changes in viewpoint. Manipulation and selection techniques however, especially when they involve subtle gestures (e.g., button presses, joysticks, finger poses) or complex graphical tools (e.g., sculpting or selection disambiguation), can prove more difficult to perceive and understand.

This effect can be reinforced in the case of techniques which require spatial alignment between the physical musician, or their avatar, and 3D graphical tools, for instance in the case of virtual rays techniques. In fact, a correct perceptual alignment then requires a fully immersive setup, either in VR or AR, making partially immersive setups less suited for specific interaction techniques.

The 3D interaction aspect of IVMIs constitutes one of the dimensions that we propose and is described in Sect. 13.4.5.

### 13.3.3  Collaboration and Observation

VR is not always a solo experience. Collaborative and social VEs [7, 26] are subject of extensive study, that pertains to the relation among two or more immersed users and has yielded a large number of questions and results. In this context, users interact or cooperate within a shared VE, for example to collectively design industrial products or to join a gathering from remote locations.

When users leverage direct *collaboration* to achieve a practical common task, a number of factors influence efficiency as well as the dynamics of personal interaction. Analogous to the feeling of presence described above, *co-presence* [24] can be defined as the sense of being together in the VE. It has been shown to depend to a large degree on avatar appearance, as more realistic avatars tend to elicit a stronger sense of co-presence, as well as on the level of cooperation required to complete the actual task [70]. Another important aspect of practical collaboration in VEs is *awareness* [4]. Awareness can be defined as the understanding of other users' actions within the virtual world, a concept that relates strongly to the issues of musical performances with DMIs covered in the previous section. Once again, embodiment (i.e., the provision of users with appropriate body images) has proven to have a strong impact on awareness [5]. Yet, other visual cues have also been proposed, such as a representation of the view cone of each user, signalling what is in sight and where the individual focus is.

The VR literature also discusses the case of *observation* without direct interaction. Virtual public speaking has been studied to understand the user/speaker's emotional response when performing in front of virtual audiences (immersed observers), leading to applications in psychotherapy for social phobias [85]. Moreover, other experiments focused on the observers themselves, and on the levels of presence and arousal triggered by watching virtual interaction as carried out by other users, using both immersive and non-immersive setups [22, 50]. As expected, these studies suggest that the lack of active involvement makes observers feel less engaged and less "present" in the VE compared to users. However, when both users and observers are properly immersed, witnessing real-time 3D interaction showed the potential to trigger a powerful perceptual experience, along with emotional responses way beyond the standards of non-immersive media and applications.

## 13.4 Dimensions of IVMI Scenographies

When designing and showcasing an immersive performance, artists have to take into account the full set of constraints that govern the experience of both digital live music and virtual interaction. Choosing the most appropriate stage technology to address each constraint may seem the obvious *modus operandi*, yet in a realistic scenario this straightforward approach reveals hard to apply. In first instance, some DMI and VR constraints appear to be orthogonal, meaning that good design in one domain tends to break constraints in the other. In other words, a technical solution specifically designed for musical purposes may end up hampering the device's VR functionalities and, vice versa, efforts targeting the virtual experience often degrade the pleasantness of the musical performance. Furthermore, constraints from different domains can combine, making standard technologies and common practices suddenly less effective in preserving engagement and expression.

For instance, moving to a VR audience–performer scenario, immersion deeply affects both the audience's and the musician's experience. An immersive performance acts on the audience's feeling of presence within the VE used on stage. As a consequence, the virtual instrument and all its 3D graphical components can be perceived, to a certain extent, as "real". In more practical terms, HMDs, single-user projections and head-tracking grant to the performer the level of immersion required to master the instrument, but exclude the spectators from the VE and cut direct communication between them and the performer. And the higher the performer's immersion (i.e., the more refined 3D musical interaction), the less intense the audience's experience (i.e., the less understanding and communication). As discussed in Sect. 13.5, the reverse is also true.

In this section we define the seven dimensions of performance setups of IVMIs and how they relate to the musical performance and VR constraints defined above. These can be visualised as a dimension space, as shown in Fig. 13.2.

More than instruments based on physical, gestural or 2D graphical interfaces, IVMIs may create a strong asymmetry of performance experience between musicians and spectators, depending on the display and interaction technologies used on each side. In turn this also generates different constraints, which we take into account by dedicating some dimensions to the audience experience and others to that of the performer's. For instance, the following dimensions focus on the performer's experience: *Performers Transportation, Ensemble Potential, Interaction Spectrum, Spectators Visibility*. Those targeting the audience experience are *Spectators Awareness, Spectators Transportation, Performers Visibility*. By placing them on the two sides of the dimension space shown in Fig. 13.3 one can quickly judge the asymmetry in

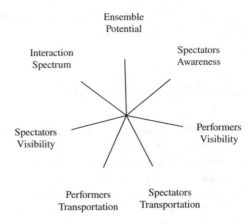

**Fig. 13.2** Dimension space to describe performance setups of IVMIs

a given performance setup. The dimension space also distinguishes between interactive aspects, in the top half of the diagram, while immersion aspects are left to the
bottom half.

The seven dimensions emerged from multiple iterations and numerous discussions, with the aim of being usable for both the design and analysis of scenographies, addressing all aspects of the audience and musicians experience through the
technical choices of performance setup.

### *13.4.1* **Performers Transportation** *and* **Spectators Transportation**

*Performers Transportation* and *Spectators Transportation* relate to the manner in
which performers and spectators are immersed in the virtual musical environment,
and to the extent to which the virtual and physical spaces intersect in a meaningful
performative fashion. In particular, it indicates if the virtual stage is integrated in
the physical space (or if it is surrounding it) and whether the setup is adequate to
play/showcase the chosen IVMI.

It includes the following (non-exhaustive) range of technological settings to display the VE:

- a single monoscopic (2D) screen
- a volumetric display in the centre of a physical stage
- a mobile/handheld augmented-reality display
- a stereoscopic screen without and then with head-tracking
- a CAVE or set of stereoscopic screens
- an augmented-reality headset
- a virtual reality headset

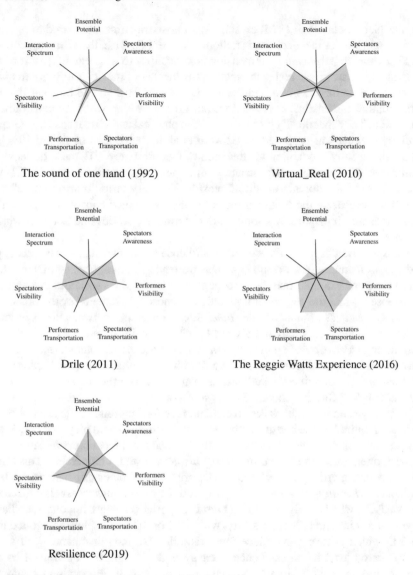

**Fig. 13.3** Dimension spaces for the analysed stage setups

Beyond visual displays, transportation also applies to auditory feedback (ranging from a monoscopic speaker to ambisonics and binaural spatialisation) and to haptic feedback, including passive solutions (like the grips on the physical controllers required to play the IVMI) as well as proper actuators (ranging from a small vibrotactile wearable to exoskeletons for large-scale kineasthetic feedback). While targeting the enhancement of the feeling of presence within the VE may help, to achieve a high *Performers Transportation* these technologies have to be combined to allow the musician to play their IVMI on stage with no extra effort, compared to practice sessions carried out in a dedicated studio/lab space. Likewise, the ultimate scope of the *Spectators Transportation* dimension is to quantify to what extent the proposed *musical* experience feels real, and whether the display of musicianship is perceived as genuine as in the case of a traditional concert setting. It should be clear that the transportation dimensions are linked to, but do not overlap with, the constraint of immersion. They specifically highlight how the physical and virtual spaces intersect, similarly to what was proposed by Benford et al. in the context of shared VEs [6]. Although partially accounting for the need to feel present in VE, these dimensions incorporate all the stage performance requirements discussed in Sect. 13.2.1 and extend them to the domain of virtual worlds. The very term "transportation" was chosen to emphasise the focus on music, which is deemed capable on its own of psychologically transporting audiences into narratives, stories and fictional worlds [28, 87].

Transportation deeply affects both the audience's and musician's experience, yet in different manners. As a result, its measure tends to be highly asymmetrical. A straightforward example may be a scenography where the spectators are wearing VR headsets while the performer uses only a monoscopic screen—or the other way around as seen in *The Sound of One Hand*. Such a difference between the experience of the two stakeholders may not always be detrimental. For example, it is hard to imagine high *Performers Transportation* in the absence of interaction. Nonetheless, VEs that do not include interactive 3D objects, but are capable of physically reaching and surrounding the audience, sensibly enhance the transportation of the spectators [95]. More in general, HMDs, single-user projections, head-tracking and active/passive haptic feedback are all elements capable of granting the level of transportation required by the performer to master the instrument and play it on stage; yet, their use may exclude the audience from the VE and cut direct communication with the performer, unless the *Spectators Transportation* level is comparable. This translates into strong crossovers between transportation and other dimensions, such as *Performers Visibility*, *Spectators Visibility* and *Spectators Awareness*. For instance, VR headsets, which likely result in a high transportation value, impose a mediated view of musicians and spectators, e.g., with a 2D or 3D live-capture integrated into the VE, which in turn may reduce their visibility. On the other hand, with a low transportation level for the audience, their awareness might be constrained by the impossibility to visually align the virtual components of 3D interaction techniques, e.g., a virtual ray, with the physical hands of the musician.

## 13.4.2 Spectators Awareness

This dimension describes how well the audience perceives the virtual and physical interactions performed by musicians on the virtual instrument, i.e., the relation between their gestures, the instrument and the resulting changes in the sound.

It can be low, for example, when a technique such as virtual ray is used for the selection of distant parts of the instrument, but this ray is either not visible at all to the audience or not visually co-located with the performer's hand. It can also be low if some physical interactions, e.g., with physical sensors, are not visually reflected in the VE and the *Spectators Transportation* dimension is high.

The problem of abstract interaction is not unique to IVMIs, yet its occurrence is intensified by the employment of immersive technologies. Much like the case of IVMI performances, spectators are often incapable of fully grasping the workings of non-immersive DMIs, nor a causal relationship between action and music. As a result, the performance runs the risk to become opaque [14, 33], even confusing [27, 89], reducing the attributed agency [13] for the audience and in turn potentially degrading their experience [23]. DMI research suggests that this is due to the very metaphor of the instrument [33], as designs favouring intellectual and cognitive skills (e.g., live-coding environments, algorithmic devices) prove more prone to trigger abstraction compared to those leveraging familiar physical gestures [37].

When *Spectators Awareness* is low, the articulation between perceived manipulations, i.e., gestures and interaction techniques, and effects, i.e., controlled sound parameters, is not visible enough and there is a risk of IVMIs being seen as secretive or magical instead of expressive [74].

In some cases, a breach into the virtual world is provided by means of screens that display the point of view of the performer. This solution may help the audience's understanding of the performance. Nonetheless, as explained in depth in Sect. 13.5, much is still left to imagination and interpretation, the reason being that the IVMI is made visible but to the eyes of the spectators is not immersive (i.e., it does not surround the audience, nor the performer).

In cases where the transportation has a different value for spectators and performers or if the interaction techniques are too subtle or too complex, it is also possible to provide dedicated visual representations of the interactions for the audience. The design of these representations should however be chosen carefully. A correct balance needs to be targeted, between too little information, which results in a degraded subjective comprehension and potentially degraded experience [23], and too much information, which can lead to perceptual and cognitive overload. In the case of individual VR headsets or shared views of the VE for the audience, this level of detail can be interactively chosen by spectators [23].

## 13.4.3 Performers Visibility *and* Spectators Visibility

*Performers Visibility* and *Spectators Visibility* correspond respectively to the level of perception of the musician(s) by the audience and to the level of perception of the audience by the musician(s). It may take the following (non-exhaustive) values:

- not visible at all
- partially (from behind, from the side, with occluded parts)

- seeing fully in a simplified manner
- seeing a detailed 3D reconstruction or facing the physical performer

This dimension has a strong impact on the performer–spectator non-verbal communication.

Many commercial IVMIs and frameworks for immersive performances make use of avatars to represent the spectators. These are usually simple and can be chosen by users. They will therefore range between a medium and medium/high visibility levels depending on the level of detail provided on the appearance, behaviour and reactions. In these setups, performers often have more detailed or more expressive visual representations than spectators.

In a setup with lower *Performers Transportation* or *Spectators Transportation*, i.e., where the IVMI is integrated in the physical space, the physical spectators and performers can be seen more clearly if they are facing each other, with the instrument displayed between them.

### 13.4.4 Ensemble Potential

The *Ensemble Potential* dimension describes the ability for the scenography to accommodate multiple IVMIs or performers.

It is low when the setup only affords a single performer, for example because a head-tracked stereoscopic display is used or because the virtual environment was designed to host a single instrument or performer.

Depending on *Performers Transportation* and *Performers Visibility*, a high *Ensemble Potential* means either that the physical space can accommodate multiple performers collaborating on the same or with different instruments, or that the VE allows for displaying and/or navigating in 3D amongst multiple IVMIs.

Scenographies with a high *Ensemble Potential* should also ensure a correct co-presence [69], for example with high values of *Performers Visibility* and can provide access to a variable number of collaboration modes [9]. This dimension also strongly relates to the inter-actors and distribution in space dimensions used as part of the dimension space proposed by Birnbaum et al. [15]. Inter-actors describe the number of musicians while distribution in space specifies how the instrument extends in the physical space, ranging from a small device to a networked instrument. *Ensemble Potential* integrates both aspects, since IVMIs can virtually expand to integrate all musicians in a single shared VE.

### 13.4.5 Interaction Spectrum

This dimension describes what range of interaction techniques is permitted by an IVMI performance setup. These include the three categories of 3D interaction techniques described above, to which we add physical manipulations, i.e., musical inter-actions performed in the physical rather than virtual space.

3D selection techniques enable various types of musical gestures [21]. Although they would typically be associated with selection gestures, i.e., picking a component of an instrument, they can also serve as excitation, i.e., generating sound, or mod-ulation gestures, i.e., changing the properties of the instrument. In fact, entering an object with a virtual ray may be used as an instantaneous excitation gesture to trigger a note, as done by Maki-Patola et al. [56]. It can also be used for continuous excitation when, for example, dragging a virtual cursor across the surface or inside the volume of virtual objects. In the context of public performances, selection techniques based on virtual rays require a high continuity (from physical hand to virtual ray) to be understandable by the audience, while virtual hands/cursors might be more tolerant (they are by definition not co-located when doing distant selection) and image-plane selection requires no (non-co-located) visual feedback.

3D manipulation techniques can be used for both excitation and modulation musi-cal gestures. Spatial transformations offer not only continuous controls from the changes in position, orientation and scale but also discrete controls, which can be used, i.e., as instantaneous excitation gestures, from collisions and intersections. Modification of appearance and shape can also serve as modulation gestures. For example, the *tunnels* of the *Drile* instrument [10] are 3D sliders which allow musi-cians to set the graphical parameters and associated sound parameters of 3D nodes of musical hierarchical structures. [66] proposes virtual sculpting as a way of setting musical parameters associated with the shape of a 3D mesh. Manipulation techniques can be distant, e.g., with 3D tools, or co-located, e.g., in the case of virtual sculpting. In both cases, however, the musician's actions and the causal link between manipu-lation and musical result [13] are made visible to the audience by the visual changes in manipulated objects on which the focus is put. Therefore the lack of real–virtual continuity in manipulation techniques might not affect the spectator experience as much as in other interaction categories.

3D navigation techniques can be used for most types of musical controls. Processes and parameters can be discretely selected before modification by entering associated volumes, such as the virtual rooms used in *Drile* [10]. Modulation of musical param-eters can be achieved through displacement in parameter spaces, either continuous with general movement techniques or discrete with targeted movements. In the same manner, excitation gestures can be achieved by mapping the relative position of vir-tual objects to the volume of associated sound processes, as done in *Versum* [3]. The impact of real–virtual continuity in the audience experience of 3D navigation depends very much on the granularity of the musician's position mapped to musical parameters. If the mapping is done according to the musician's movements within the space physically navigable, meaning that the user can physically walk to move through it, the audience understanding of the musician's impact on the sound will require a high level of real–virtual continuity. However, if the navigation moves this physically anchored space in the VE, then the performed action is directly visible to all spectators from changes in the environment only and real–virtual continuity is not as necessary.

Physical interactions constitute another category of interaction which can be made available by a specific scenography, and corresponds to controls performed in the physical space, e.g., on a control surface or an acoustic instrument. In order not to degrade the *Spectators Awareness*, these controls also need to be represented in the VE using changes in the performer's avatar or in the instrument appearance for example. Physical controllers and instruments can also be captured and rendered inside the VE.

## 13.5   Case Study: Analysis of IVMI Performances

In this section we use the seven IVMI scenography dimensions to analyse different performances and discuss their setups. This allows for practical observations on scenography and their possible variations. The performances are introduced chronologically: the section tries to give a sense of evolution and change of the medium over time, both in terms of ideas, implementation, technology and diffusion. Performances have been selected giving precedence to pioneering solutions, and preferring well-documented acts, both in the literature and on the web at large.

A visual representation of the analysis is given in Fig. 13.3, in the form of a dimension space that provides a quick overview of each performance's properties. As mentioned in Sect. 13.4, it is structured both vertically and horizontally in order to provide a quick idea of the distribution of a scenography, between interaction and immersion and between spectators and performers.

### 13.5.1   Approaching a Performance Analysis

The analyses featured throughout this section start by dissecting the essential aspects of each performance. The main objective at the beginning of the process is to isolate the atomic components defining the stage setup, the IVMI, its use and the expected behaviour of the performer(s) and audience. If the venue has some other peculiarities, it is also helpful to address them at this stage. As an example, the following are all valid questions which arise when starting the analysis process: Are there HMDs involved? Who is wearing them: the audience, the performer(s) or both? Is there a screen dedicated to the audience, how is it oriented? Is it hiding the performer from the audience, or vice versa? Beyond the visual aspect, other important questions inquire about the performance itself: How many performers are playing? How do the virtual and real instruments used on stage work? Are they easy to understand, or hindered by some design choice or technical limitation? Finally, our focus may shift to the location: Is everyone in the same physical location, or does the performance setup involve some form of telepresence? How good is the continuity between virtual and real elements on stage? What about the venue, seen from the performers' point of view? Therefore, the first part of the analysis consists of making a list of all the prominent bits which make the performance *that* performance: the resulting summary is not necessarily a technical survey. On the contrary, it can be interpreted as a synopsis of the IVMI and its stage setup, from where the actual constraints will emerge. The outcome of this summary is a quick reference to consult when evaluating the seven dimensions.

Once the fundamental pieces of the performances (and their setups) have been identified and summarised, it is possible to start discussing how they fit within the dimension space as a whole. As a preference, analyses here presented start by addressing *transportation*. *Performers Transportation* and *Spectators Transportation* act as a solid ground for building the rest of the evaluation: as specified in Sect. 13.4.1, they can easily influence other dimensions. They encompass multiple feedback channels (visual, auditory and haptic), even though they tend to gravitate towards visual feedback, which has typically a heavy impact on presence. Available technologies are also affecting this bias towards visual immersion. Nonetheless, other channels should be considered carefully when investigating these dimensions. After evaluating transportation, it is reasonable to consider *awareness* and *visibility* dimensions, which also depend on multimodal feedback. Finally, the remaining dimensions can be addressed prioritising their prominence and importance within the performance.

Plotting the dimensions is a process involving a subjective judgement, especially when it comes to choosing the exact values used to generate the dimension space. Nonetheless, the seven dimensions are designed to highlight the asymmetries and relationships existing between the different aspects of a performance. Such constraints exist independently from the chosen numerical values: this is where a careful analysis potentially moves from being mostly subjective to being descriptive of a set of existing relationships. Certain technological setups are currently intrinsically incapable of providing, for example, high transportation both on and off stage, as-is. HMDs tend to hinder visibility, projected screens can break continuity between virtual and real elements, thus affecting transportation, and so on. So, the descriptive viewpoint provided by an accurate dimension space is of great interest despite the exact values used to create the plot. A reliable IVMI stage overview can be used not only to understand and analyse an already staged performance, but also to monitor and guide the design of a new one. The performance designer(s) could address early on some limitations, e.g., if *Spectators Visibility* and *Performers Transportation* are both considered important for a certain performance, a real-time video or point cloud representing the audience could be used to improve *Spectators Visibility* when the performer is wearing a HMD while maintaining high *Performers Transportation*.

After having carefully populated the dimension space, an additional final step is that of finding a one-sentence description of the analysed performance. In this section these short descriptions can be found right at the beginning of each analysis. This final touch has at least two objectives: it implies a review of the analysis process and it guides the future reader by highlighting the performance core values.

## 13.5.2   The Sound of One Hand

*Pioneering performer's immersion for fine control.* Jaron Lanier's *The Sound of One Hand* [49] was performed for the first time at SIGGRAPH in 1992.

Multiple virtual instruments are used during the performance, with Lanier playing them in turn. Sounds and notes were generated by hand movements, as they were transmitted to the instruments using a Data Glove. The Data Glove was also used by the musician to move and reach the instruments, which were sparse all around the VE. Instruments are described by the musician as autonomous and sometimes fighting back. Lanier talked in detail about these instruments, addressing how they are created and also how they take inspiration, visually and sonically, from real-world instruments.[7] A head mounted display (HMD) was used by the artist in order to immerse himself in the VE, and therefore access the virtual instruments. This creates a setting where the musician can clearly be seen by the audience throughout the whole performance. On the other hand, it is impossible for the performer to see the audience. On stage, next to the performer, a screen was used to display a 2D projection of his point of view. This grants the spectators an access to the VE.

The primary dimension of this stage setup is *Performers Transportation*: the use of the HMD allowed the musician to perceive a consistent world all around him and to have access to fine 3D controls. However, the use of the HMD leads to the absence of *Spectators Visibility*. Conversely, *Performers Visibility* is quite high: Lanier played on stage, right in front of the audience, but he was also free to move and rotate, yet partially hiding his gestures. *Spectators Awareness* is limited since the VE and the musician were perceived by the audience as two completely separated elements, the former projected onto a screen, the latter moving on the physical stage, with no continuity between the two. Furthermore, the screen projection was 2D and it displayed the musician's point of view, resulting in an extremely low level of *Spectators Transportation*.

The *Interaction Spectrum* includes 3D manipulation and navigation. Lanier opted for a point-flying navigation technique, a choice motivated by the artist's will to have an unconstrained and skilful way to explore the VE.

The scenographic level of this pioneering setup is understandably constrained, and it mainly focuses on the musician and his interaction with the VE. About the instruments, Lanier himself states that *"They emerged from a creative process I cannot fully explain"*, and describes them as not immediately understandable, and also difficult to play. However, showing spectators a 3D projection aligned with the physical position of the musician on stage would remarkably enhance the audience's experience, providing immersion and increasing gestures continuity.

An interesting note: according to Lanier's impressions, the asymmetry between *performers* and *audience visibility* resulted in him feeling vulnerable on stage—as

---

[7] http://www.jaronlanier.com/instruments.html

opposed to what might happen when using rare and expensive technology for a performance. So, for the musician, adding this combination of dimensions generated a *"more authentic setting for music"*.


## 13.5.3  Virtual_Real

*Intense audience experience.* The Virtual_Real performance [95] was born from a collaboration between Victor Zappi and the electronic composer USELESS_IDEA. It took place three times in Genoa, in 2010.

The performance was set up inside a laboratory room, which acted as an intimate venue. At the centre of the stage, the musician could play standard hardware controllers available in front of him. A single screen was positioned on stage, at his back. The screen displayed to the audience stereoscopic images of VEs populated by 3D objects, acting as both instruments and visuals. Thanks to optical motion capture the performer could move, touch or morph these virtual objects, in order to control audio effects. Thus, the setup allowed the musician to play both standard hardware controllers and non-immersive virtual instruments in front of the audience. 3D visuals and control algorithms were designed, tested and modified based on the artist's input and ideas. USELESS_IDEA played five tracks specifically composed for the event, each associated with a different 3D choreography.

Hardware controllers used by the performer included a laptop, a MIDI controller and a small mixer. The artist's dominant hand was tracked using passive reflective markers, allowing him to trigger interactions with the VE. The immersive content was designed to be experienced by the audience: despite the impossibility to provide head-tracking for each spectator, the proportions between the projected screen size and the room size allowed the small audiences of nine spectators to enjoy a shared viewpoint, with no significant visual distortions. The audience could thus experience a stage where the performer, real items and virtual elements shared the same space (Fig. 13.4).

This performance is strongly focused towards providing an intense audience experience. As a consequence, *transportation* is highly asymmetrical, with immersion affecting the spectators exclusively. The VE and its virtual instruments are perceived by the audience as coherently superimposed with the physical stage. This leads to a high *Performers Visibility*. *Performers Transportation* is absent since the musician faces the audience and not the screen, while *Spectators Visibility* is high. *Spectators Awareness* is positively influenced by the possibility of clearly seeing the performer interacting with both real and virtual instruments. The musician's physical interfaces provide the same interaction transparency which could be expected in a traditional electronic music performance. Virtual instruments were coherently rendered with the audience's point of view, and the performer could be seen manipulating them. The sonic and visual results of such interaction were designed to be easily perceived. The *Interaction Spectrum* mainly included 3D manipulation techniques, with the performer moving and dragging objects around the VE scenes.

**Fig. 13.4** USELESS_IDEA performing *Virtual_Real*, 2010. The shot frames two spectators wearing stereoscopic goggles, required to fully appreciate the hybrid virtual/physical stage

This single-screen setup can create a strong involvement in the audience: virtual choreographies can be really convincing, and non-verbal communication with the performer can be really close to what would happen on a traditional stage. However, such an extremely audience-centric setup makes it impossible for the musician to use complex and potentially more expressive 3D interaction paradigms, thus limiting the possibilities of the virtual instrument. Slight setup modifications could generate a dual experience, in which the screen projection is dedicated to the performer, completely changing the scenographic outcome. The audience would no longer enjoy the perfect virtual/real environments consistency, while the musician would be immersed in the instrument, allowing for fine audio control.

### 13.5.4  Drile

*Immersion for both ends.* This performance was executed by Florent Berthaut in Bordeaux, 2011. The Drile instrument [10] used throughout the performance allows a musician wearing a stereoscopic goggle to execute live-looping in a 3D immersive environment. The performer uses handheld devices with pressure sensors in order to reach, excite and modulate the musical objects populating the environment. These objects are associated with the nodes of hierarchical live-looping trees, and their manipulation allows the musician to create and handle loops. Virtual rays are used to select and interact with the virtual objects.

Drile was shown on stage, thanks to stereoscopic projections. Two screens, juxtaposed, were positioned on stage, with an angle between them. One screen was

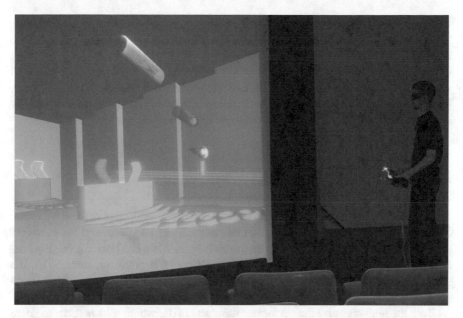

**Fig. 13.5**   Florent Berthaut performing with the IVMI *Drile*, 2011. The shot is taken from the seat area and shows the 3D musical environment being pierced by the green virtual rays cast by the performer

exclusively facing the performer, sideways. The second screen was rotated so that it could face the audience. This arrangement had the screens defining an enclosed volume on stage. Therefore, both audience and performer perceived Drile as an instrument "contained" inside this volume (Fig. 13.5). A correct perspective was granted to the performer by means of head-tracking, while a shared viewpoint was used to display the stereoscopic content on the audience screen.

This performance gives a highly symmetrical experience to the audience and the performer. *Transportation* is medium, since both parts can properly perceive the virtual instrument and the real stage while the virtual space is literally contained within the physical space. *Spectators* and *performers visibility* dimensions are quite high, since musician and spectators could directly see each other. *Spectators Awareness* is good, but hindered by the distance between the performer and the screen: virtual rays shown within the VE indicated which virtual objects the musician was manipulating, yet the instrument was operated standing one or more meters away from the screen. This distance breaks the continuity between the performer's hands and the virtual rays. The *Interaction Spectrum* relies on virtual rays for the selection and manipulation of the 3D musical elements, but without physical manipulations.

This performance setup provides proper immersion for the audience and the performer, resulting in a great scenographic outcome and potential. Having a correct perspective for both parts allows the musician to have fine control of the instrument, and the audience to have a meaningful understanding of his actions. An alternative version of this setup could use a bigger, transparent screen dedicated to the audience. This screen would be placed between the spectators and the musician, allowing to overcome the absence of continuity between the performer's hands and the virtual rays shown in the VE. Since the musician's head and hands are tracked, additional visual effects and feedback solutions dedicated to the audience could be designed. This though could negatively impact *Performers Visibility*, and should be carefully implemented to avoid a negative outcome on *Spectators Awareness*.

### 13.5.5   The Reggie Watts Experience

A *truly shared experience.* This setup is based on the possibilities offered by social VR platforms. Users wearing a headset can share a virtual space, and interact with each other through 3D avatars. The performer Reggie Watts has been a recurring host of shows taking place specifically within the AltspaceVR platform, since 2016. His shows have been labelled as *The Reggie Watts Experience* and the performer keeps exploring the possibilities given by the format to this date.

Both the audience and the performer wear an HMD, which allows them to share the same virtual space and see each other. Reggie Watts movements on stage can be tracked, thanks to full-body motion capture. He can use a microphone, controllers and effects, close to what he might do on a real stage. This kind of setup allows him to dance in front of the audience, see and address participants and move around the entire venue. The appearance of the avatars, venue and visual effects used throughout performances is designed to match the overall stylised aesthetic of AltspaceVR. Regarding the venues, different virtual spaces have been created and used, thanks to the possibilities given by the platform. Sometimes, visual effects can be seen, such as virtual fireworks, and simple, moving shapes. Tracking is available for the audience as well, based on the setup they have access to.

While wearing his HMD and tracking system, the performer can still interact with his own instrumentation, which is sometimes represented on the virtual stage by simple 3D models. AltspaceVR provides a tool which allows to host multiple instances of the same venue so that countless number of spectators can participate at the same time. Each instance can host ten participants, meaning that each member of the audience can be close to the stage. Spectators and the performer only see a limited part of the total number of participants currently present at the virtual venue. The completely virtual environment allows Reggie's voice and instruments to be spatialised so that as he moves throughout the venue, it is clear to the audience where to look for him.

These performances focus on the idea of a shared space, and *transportation* is strongly symmetrical: both the audience and the performer are immersed in the VE as if they were physically present at the same venue. *Performers Visibility* is high, even when a huge audience is participating, thanks to the possibility of having multiple instances of the same performance, each hosting a limited number of spectators. *Spectators Visibility* is high, but only for those spectators which are in the same venue instance of the performer. So, from the performer's point of view, spectators are either really close and visible or not present at all. *Spectators Awareness* is limited to what can be understood from Reggie's limbs and body movements. Thus, audience experience mainly relies on his voice, music, posture and dancing. The presence of 3D models of his gear mitigates the limited awareness, for those cases in which the performer interacts with physical instruments. His avatar can in fact be seen bending over the controllers, making it easier to understand his posture in those particular moments. Regarding the *Interaction Spectrum*, virtual instruments are absent. 3D navigation is possible for the performer and affects the spatialisation of sound, but it's not used to interact with virtual instruments.

This performance allows a direct communication between the audience and the performer. Reggie can address his spectators and interact with them. The possibility of seeing the performer moving, dancing and posing in the VE could be further explored, though. No virtual instruments are present, so the potential of the setup used to stage this performance is not completely explored yet. Virtual instruments could be added, which might be a way to create an even more compelling experience. Both the audience and Reggie share the same environment, and no perspective issues are present: this can overcome part of the limitations seen in more asymmetrical performances, and would allow a less constrained interaction design for virtual instruments. Nonetheless, the immediacy of having only the performer on stage has its own advantages: going to the extreme opposite could be detrimental to *Spectators Awareness*, and also negatively affect the spontaneous feel of the performance.

The Reggie Watts experience is part of a set of immersive performances and virtual instruments which are exploiting the growing diffusion of consumer virtual reality setups. A variety of platforms is being developed, each addressing different scenarios: immersive music making, remote participation to live events, VR dance clubs and so on. *Electronauts* is a VR instrument for beat making and jamming. The creators also showcased an augmented/mixed reality video of a session where a performer playing the Electronauts instrument jams along with other musicians (guitar and sax drums). AltspaceVR is providing a platform for performers like Reggie Watts to create shared musical experiences, and other companies aim to provide similar setups. MelodyVR allows to capture and share immersive videos from live concerts, which can be experienced on a VR HMD. Online multiplayer videogames such as Fortnite have been used to host musical performances. Even if not immersive for audience or musicians, such endeavours show a growing interest in the exploration of novel possibilities in the field of virtual musical performances.

## 13.5.6 Resilience

*A laptop orchestra with a VR Conductor.* This performance is designed for a laptop orchestra and one VR performer/conductor. Resilience [2] was performed in June 2019, at the *2019: A SLOrk Odyssey* concert at the Bing Concert Hall of Stanford University.

**Fig. 13.6** *Resilience* immersive musical performance, 2019. The conductor stands at the centre of the stage, wearing an HMD and leading the orchestra via both hand gestures and 3D interaction. Image courtesy of Ge Wang, Stanford Laptop Orchestra

The VR performer is at the centre of the stage, wearing an HMD and acting as a conductor. Surrounding him, eight performers are positioned on two separate rings. The performer's hand movements are tracked by handheld motion controllers, while the rest of the ensemble has access to tether controllers. Each performer has a laptop and speaker array. The VR performer is facing away from the audience, in the direction of an oversized projection screen. Thus, the audience has a view of the conductor, the orchestra and a 2D projection of the environment experienced by the VR performer (Fig. 13.6).

The performance was structured in three movements, with the VR conductor cueing the orchestra throughout the piece with his body movements. By using motion controllers, he sometimes also triggered flashes of lightning. The orchestra members used tether controllers to affect the movements of virtual seedlings and their visual aspect, and excite synthesised sounds. The way the performer's movements were acted out, and the timbre of the synthesised sounds changed with each piece movement. The whole ensemble at times also acted as a whole meta-instrument, performing wave gestures which were paired with movements of a wind timbre across the ensemble. When this happened, the virtual seedlings changed their direction accordingly. During the entire performance, the point of the projection shown to the audience was curated by the head movements of the conductor, which the creators have thoroughly evaluated and rehearsed. The same 2D projection was rendered on small monitors available to the orchestra performers.

In terms of fruition, this performance provides different experiences to the audience, conductor and orchestra. *Performers Transportation* is high for the conductor, who is immersed in the VR environment, while the orchestra only experiences the VE on a small monitor. The conductor entirely misses the real stage, which conversely is the main space experienced by the other performers. Because of this, overall *Performers Transportation* can be considered of medium level. *Spectators Transportation* is limited: the stage is clearly in front of the spectators, while the virtual environment is displayed on a screen from the conductor's point of view. *Performers Visibility* is high for the audience and the orchestra, while the conductor can only perceive the virtual environment. *Spectators Visibility* is high for the orchestra, and absent for the performer. *Spectators Awareness* is positively influenced by the clearly visible choreographed movements of conductor and orchestra, which are affecting the sonic outcome of the piece and the visuals of the virtual environment, thanks to the tethered controllers. This performance *Ensemble Potential* is good, as the piece is designed for a conductor and orchestra. Nonetheless, co-presence is limited for the conductor, who cannot perceive their own orchestra if not sonically.

Resilience could be described as a carefully planned laptop orchestra piece with live visuals, featuring the addition of a conductor immersed in a VR environment. Audience access to the VE is provided through a 2D projection, curated by the conductor in real time. This can be used as an expressive channel, to the expense of audience immersion, which could otherwise be improved by introducing a stereo projection with shared point of view (see Virtual_Real and Drile performances).

## 13.6   Towards the Design of Novel Scenographies

The rapid growth of consumer and professional VR technologies is offering new interesting perspectives to IVMI designers and performers. As hinted by the analyses presented in the previous section, a fair amount of stage setups have been explored over the last 30 years, leading to extremely different experiences and related dimensional spaces. Nonetheless, there is still much to experiment with and discover. Every year, technologies that once were seen only in research laboratories or during specialised scientific events become available in public and entertainment spaces, and some even populate the shelves of electronics stores. Some examples are the large immersive multi-projection systems now found in several museums and performance spaces, as well as the first wave of see-through headsets that hit the market just a few years ago. While facilitating the design of more advanced and more daring virtual experiences, these technologies embrace specifications that make them more and more compatible with digital media and—in particular—audio standards.[8] As a result, the creative horizons of VR musicians keep expanding, thrust by the embedding of devices, materials and arrangements that had never before been available to convey musical expression in live settings.

---

[8] To corroborate this argument, we would like to point the reader to the beautiful *Alt F* performance showcased at NIME 2021, during which DMIs well-known to old-time attendees of the conference were played for the first time in a fully immersive online environment!

In this section, we take the liberty to suggest three solutions that propose unique takes on the virtual musical experience and that, to our knowledge, are yet to be explored. It is important to remark that we are not going to describe scenographies per se, though. The technological and spatial composition of a virtual musical performance depends necessarily on both the instrument and the stage (Sect. 13.1.1), and refers to a precise instance (or a series of instances) of the show. As opposed, now we are about to discuss the use of immersive technologies in precise stage arrangements that encompass performers and spectators, yet without focusing on any specific IVMI or performance. In this context, the dimensions allow us to carry out an analysis of the *potential* of these stage setups, in terms of their ability to accommodate various categories of musical instruments and to create impactful scenographies for/with them. At this point, it should also be clear to the reader that no solution is perfect and the setups we are about to introduce are no exception.

### 13.6.1   Co-located Antithetical Immersion

We start with something relatively easy to achieve, at least from a purely technological perspective. Let us consider what appear to be two antithetical immersive solutions, in particular those used in *The Sound of One Hand* and *Virtual_Real* (Sects. 13.5.2 and 13.5.3). The former features HMD and Data Glove to give the performer full access to the VE (high *Performers Transportation* and wide *Interaction Spectrum*), though limiting *Spectators Transportation* and *Spectators Awareness*; the latter leverages exo-centric 3D projections that convincingly merge virtual and physical world to the eyes of the audience (remarkable *Spectators Transportation* and *Spectators Awareness*), at the cost of *Performers Transportation* and *Interaction Spectrum*. Although often used separately (e.g., [36, 90]), these immersive setups can be combined to balance out most of their individual shortcomings.

In practical terms, what we envision is a stage where headsets are used by performers[9] and stereoscopic projections are designed for the audience. This scenario co-locates on the same physical stage immersive technologies that differ in structure and target, allowing to display the VE and interaction from two distinct perspectives simultaneously: the one of the performer (as rendered on the HMD) and the one of the audience (as rendered on the screen). This permits to reach high values of transportation for both performer and audience, and strong *Spectators Awareness*. Furthermore, such a setup provides access to all 3D interaction techniques, making it compliant with a variety of IVMIs and leading to the design of scenographies characterised by a broad *Interaction Spectrum*. Unfortunately, the use of headsets makes the visibility dimensions quite asymmetrical, yet scales quite well in case of ensemble performances.

---

[9] As discussed in Sect. 13.3.1, headsets combine an HMD with tracking and input devices.

## 13.6.2   Augmented Workspace and Spatial Paradox

The second setup that we propose promotes a rather "unorthodox" experience of the space that performer and spectators share. Right at the beginning of this chapter (Sect. 2), we mentioned the possibility to play with the scale of the VE in paradoxical ways, the most common example being virtual instrumentation that exceeds the physical size of the stage (e.g., [49]). Now we take a step in the opposite direction. We describe a solution to make music with a virtual world in miniature, that can fit the hands of the performer, but is still capable of surrounding a full audience!

The inspiration for this concept comes from artist Hicham Berrada and his work *Présage*. Berrada filmed a 360 view of the inside of a small water tank, while pouring coloured chemicals into it; he then scaled up the video to fit a large multi-projection installation, where spectators could experience a stroll at the bottom of the lively tank. Our take on this setup replaces the water tank with a medium to small-sized VE, populated with musical objects and embedded in the performer's workspace via an AR headset (like the Microsoft HoloLens). In a separate room, the audience is hosted inside an immersive stereo-projection system; here, the same VE is scaled up of two or more orders of magnitude and rendered as if the seat area/parterre were inside of it, facing the performer. Furthermore, stereo-cameras can be easily installed on both sides of the setup so that the AR workspace could include a miniature volumetric render of the audience and the stereo-projections could showcase the titanic body and gestures of the performer.[10] The result is a paradox, a non-existing shared space where musicians, spectators and virtual objects can be huge or tiny, depending on the beholder.

This unusual setup may support the design of scenographies that excel in most dimensions, in particular those pertaining to transportation and visibility. The main drawbacks may though come in terms of low *Ensemble Potential* and *Interaction Spectrum*. Indeed, sharing the AR workspace between more than two performers may reveal problematic while the overall spatial design aligns well only with specific interaction techniques and IVMI metaphors.

## 13.6.3   Double-Sided Virtual World

We conclude our review of proposed stage setups with a technically challenging yet visually impressive solution. The aim of this last entry is to employ a single VR/AR technology to immerse both performer and spectators, while they are physically present in the same venue. By leveraging the *Pepper's ghost effect*, an acrylic semi-transparent screen can be set up to obtain a double-sided reflective surface that splits

---

[10] The seat area maybe even virtually embedded in one of the movable parts of the instrument, turning the execution of a piece into a lively ride for the audience; this type of extremely embodied musical experience would likely cause a high occurrence of motion sickness, but who are we to define the boundaries of artistic expression?

the stage from the seat area and forms two distinct windows on the virtual world—one for the musician and one for the audience. The screen has to be installed at the edge of the stage with a 45 degree horizontal tilt so that one of its sides leans towards the spectators. Then, two projection surfaces are placed above and below it; projections reaching the top surface are reflected on the audience's side of the semitransparent screen, while projections directed to the bottom surface are reflected on the musician's side. Such a setup minimises interference between the two reflections so that both performer and audience can use the screen to have a clean stereo-view of the VE, from their own perspective. The way the VE is rendered on the two sides may even differ in level of details or content! Furthermore, portions of the screen not reflecting any light maintain their see-through nature. This allows to include physical props within the VE or, vice versa, to augment traditional musical gears with virtual widgets.

In our 2014 work [12], we described a prototype scenography based on this doublesided setup, built and tested in a VR laboratory. Despite the obvious advantages of working in a controlled setting as opposed to an actual stage, that experience highlighted the effort required to install the screen apparatus and to calibrate it along with a tracking system. Nonetheless, once in place the setup revealed quite remarkable capabilities. Both sides of the stage can support 3D visuals, tracking and multimodal feedback without interfering with each other, hence leading to very high peaks of *Performers* and *Spectators Transportation*. As previously mentioned, interaction is potentially extremely varied (wide *Interaction Spectrum*) and easy to understand (high *Spectators Awareness*), with the caveat that the playing of the IVMI must happen in the space between the musician and the audience. But where this setup excels are the visibility dimensions; thanks to the semi-transparent screen the physical bodies of both musician and audience can be completely visible to one another, much like the case of a traditional musical performance. The only clear limitation concerns *Ensemble Potential*, for the employment of such a complex projection-based setup makes it extremely difficult to immerse more than one musician on stage at a time.

## 13.7  Conclusion

In this chapter, we investigated the scenography of immersive virtual musical instruments. We first reviewed the constraints of both immersive virtual environments and digital musical performances. From these, we derived seven dimensions for the design of scenographies of IVMIs. We finally demonstrated how this dimension space can be used to analyse past performances and how it can inform the design of new ones.

We also believe that this dimension space may result in an opportunity to improve the quality of IVMI scenographies. Scenographers may employ the dimensions to intervene in the most critical details of the stage setup, and choose technologies and spatial arrangements that make the performance as inclusive as possible, without the need to modify the instruments' metaphor. Moreover, the proposed approach to IVMI performance practice has the potential to influence instrument design too. For example, when the topology of a venue imposes too many constraints to build a proper scenography, the instrument designer may use the dimensions as a set of guidelines to adapt the IVMI to the encountered limitations.

In similar eventualities, the outcome of the dimensional analysis carries important design feedbacks that might extend even beyond the specific stage scenario. Maybe the metaphor designed for the IVMI is simply too complex/idiosyncratic to result comprehensible to an external audience, whether or not the venue is suitable for the showcase of immersive performances; in other cases, it might be the specific combination of some of the parts of the instrument's metaphor to hinder the transition from user to performer—for example, an interaction technique that is not compatible with the chosen visualisation paradigm. So, another scope of the dimensions is to preventively foster this kind of analysis, and push the designer to question the nature of their musical VE (i.e., instrument or installation?) during the very design phase.

We can see multiple extensions of our dimension space, which would allow for (1) a stronger integration of the various perceptual aspects in a performance and (2) refinements in the analysis to handle the complexity of performance scenographies. First, the dimensions that we proposed, in particular *transportation*, tend to focus on the visual immersion of both the audience and performers, i.e., the choice of display technology. While presence in a virtual environment and the experience of musical performances are very strongly impacted by the visual perception, other modalities are also essential. Our dimensions could therefore be refined to take into account the auditory and haptic transportation and the interactivity for the audience.

Second, in this chapter, we chose to use the word scenography to describe technical design choices. In this regard, a possible refinement of our dimension space would be to distinguish between *stage setups*, which can be informed by the dimensions, and the development of the setups into shared musical experiences (i.e., actual IVMI scenographies!), which require further discussion, and potentially an even more qualitative analysis approach. However, given a set of choices, the diversity of potential implementations remains very high. In fact, the relationship between constraints and the outcome of a performance is even more complex and more counter-intuitive than what one would expect. Skilled scenographers may carefully pay attention to the direct consequences of design decisions across virtuality and music, yet the strong entanglement among the constraints (and the different stakeholders) may make any prediction quite inconsistent. For example, it is hard to suspect that replicating on stage the same exact setup used by the musician to rehearse in studio could be detrimental to the outcome of the performance. Such a design approach would preserve the intimacy with the instrument developed by the performer over hours of practice (DMI constraint, Sect. 13.2.1) and it would reinforce the level of immersion that is achieved on stage (VE constraint, Sect. 13.3.1); yet, it may clash with how the actual IVMI lends itself to a live stage realisation, as well as with venue specifics, audiences' expectation and—always present—miscellaneous contingencies. As a consequence, the term "scenography" as intended in this work does not equal a predictable experience.

# References

1. Argelaguet, F., Andujar, C.: A survey of 3D object selection techniques for virtual environments. Computers & Graphics **37**, 121–136 (2013).
2. Atherton, J., Wang, G.: Curating Perspectives: Incorporating Virtual Reality into Laptop Orchestra Performance in Proceedings of the International Conference on New Interfaces for Musical Expression (2020), 154–159.
3. Barri, T.: Versum: audiovisual composing in 3d in (2009).
4. Benford, S., Bowers, J., Fahlén, L. E., Greenhalgh, C.: Managing mutual awareness in collaborative virtual environments in Proceedings of VRST (1994), 223–236.
5. Benford, S., Bowers, J., Fahlén, L. E., Greenhalgh, C., Snowdon, D.: User embodiment in collaborative virtual environments in Proceedings of CHI 95 (Denver, Colorado, United States, 1995), 242–249.
6. Benford, S., Greenhalgh, C., Reynard, G., Brown, C., Koleva, B.: Understanding and constructing shared spaces with mixed-reality boundaries. ACM Transactions on computer-human interaction (TOCHI) **5**, 185–223 (1998).
7. Benford, S., Greenhalgh, C., Rodden, T., Pycock, J.: Collaborative virtual environments. Commun. ACM **44**, 79–85 (7 July 2001).
8. Bergström, I., Azevedo, S., Papiotis, P., Saldanha, N., Slater, M.: The plausibility of a string quartet performance in virtual reality. IEEE transactions on visualization and computer graphics **23**, 1352–1359 (2017).
9. Berthaut, F., Coyle, D., Moore, J., Limerick, H.: Liveness Through the Lens of Agency and Causality in Proceedings of NIME (2015).
10. Berthaut, F., Dahl, L.: BOEUF: a unified framework for modeling and designing digital orchestras in International Symposium on Computer Music Multidisciplinary Research (2015), 153–166.
11. Berthaut, F., Desainte-Catherine, M., Hachet, M.: Drile: An Immersive Environment for hierarchical live-looping inNewInterface for Musical Expression (Sydney, Australia, June 2010), page 192.
12. Berthaut, F., Desainte-Catherine, M., Hachet, M.: Interacting with 3D Reactive Widgets for Musical Performance. Journal of New Music Research **40**, 253–263 (2011).
13. Berthaut, F., Zappi, V., Mazzanti, D.: Scenography of immersive virtual musical instruments in VRWorkshop: Sonic Interaction in Virtual Environments (SIVE), 2014 IEEE (Minneapolis, United States, 2014).
14. Bin, A., McPherson, A., Bryan Kinns, N.: Skip the pre-concert demo: How technical familiarity and musical style affect audience response in NIME '16: Proceedings of the 2016 conference on New interfaces for musical expression (2016).
15. Birnbaum, D., Fiebrink, R., Malloch, J., Wanderley, M. M.: Towards a dimension space for musical devices in Proceedings of the 2005 conference on New interfaces for musical expression (2005), 192–195.
16. Boletsis, C.: The new era of virtual reality locomotion: A systematic literature review of techniques and a proposed typology. Multimodal Technologies and Interaction **1** (2017).
17. Bongers, B.: Exploring Novel ways of interaction in musical performance in C&C '99: Proceedings of the 3rd conference on Creativity & cognition (ACM, Loughborough, United Kingdom, 1999), 76–81.
18. Bowman, D. A., Hodges, L. F.: An evaluation of techniques for grabbing and manipulating remote objects in immersive virtual environments in SI3D '97: Proceedings of the 1997 symposium on Interactive 3D graphics (ACM, Providence, Rhode Island, United States, 1997), 35–ff.
19. Brogni, A., Slater, M., Steed, A.: More Breaks Less Presence in Proceedings of Presence 2003: The 6th Annual International Workshop on Presence (2003).
20. Bryson, S.: Approaches to the successful design and implementation of VR applications. Virtual reality applications, 3–15 (1995).

21. Cadoz, C. in Les nouveaux gestes de la musique (Éditions Parenthèses, 1999).
22. Calvert, S. L., Tan, S.-L.: Impact of virtual reality on young adults' physiological arousal and aggressive thoughts: Interaction versus observation. Journal of applied developmental psychology 15, 125–139 (1994).
23. Capra, O., Berthaut, F., Grisoni, L.: All you need is lod: Levels of detail in visual augmentations for the audience in The 20th International Conference of New Interfaces for Musical Expression (2020).
24. Casanueva, J., Blake, E. in Virtual Environments 2000 85–94 (Springer, 2000).
25. Cho, D. et al.: The Dichotomy of Presence Elements: The Where and What. in VR (IEEE Computer Society, June 26, 2003), 273–274.
26. Chung, D.: Something for nothing: understanding purchasing behaviors in social virtual environments. Cyberpsychology& behavior 8, 538–554 (2005).
27. Collins, N.: Generative music and laptop performance. Contemporary Music Review 22, 67–79 (2003).
28. Costabile, K. A., Terman, A. W.: Effects of film music on psychological transportation and narrative persuasion. Basic and Applied Social Psychology 35, 316–324 (2013).
29. Dahl, L., Herrera, J., Wilkerson, C.: TweetDreams : Making Music with the Audience and the World using Real-time Twitter Data in Proceedings of the International Conference on New Interfaces for Musical Expression (Oslo, Norway, 2011), 272–275.
30. Davies, C.: OSMOSE: Notes on being in Immersive virtual space. Digital Creativity 9, 65–74 (1998).
31. Davies, C., Harrison, J.: Osmose: towards broadening the aesthetics of virtual reality. SIGGRAPH Comput. Graph. 30, 25–28 (4 Nov. 1996).
32. Dickey, M. D.: Brave new (interactive) worlds: A review of the design affordances and constraints of two 3D virtual worlds as interactive learning environments. Interactive learning environments 13, 121–137 (2005).
33. Fels, S., Gadd, A., Mulder, A.: Mapping transparency through metaphor: towards more expressive musical instruments. Organised Sound 7, 109–126 (2002).
34. Flach, J. M., Holden, J. G.: The reality of experience: Gibson's way. Presence 7, 90–95 (1998).
35. Gelineck, S., Böttcher, N., Martinussen, L., Serafin, S.: Virtual Reality Instruments capable of changing Dimensions in Real-time. Proceedings Enactive (2005).
36. Graham, R., Bridges, B., Manzione, C., Brent, W.: Exploring pitch and timbre through 3d spaces: embodied models in virtual reality as a basis for performance systems design. in NIME (2017), 157–162.
37. Gurevich, M., Cavan Fyans, A.: Digital Musical Interactions: Performer- system relationships and their perception by spectators. Organised Sound 16, 166–175 (02 June 2011).
38. Gurevich, M., Marquez-Borbon, A., Stapleton, P.: Playing with constraints: Stylistic variation with a simple electronic instrument. Computer Music Journal 36, 23–41 (2012).
39. Gurevich, M., Treviño, J.: Expression and its discontents: toward an ecology of musical creation in Proceedings of the 7th international conference on New interfaces for musical expression (2007), 106–111.
40. Hachet, M., Decle, F., Knodel, S., Guitton, P.: Navidget for Easy 3D Camera Positioning from 2D Inputs in 3DUI '08: Proceedings of the 2008 IEEE Symposium on 3D User Interfaces (IEEE Computer Society, Washington, DC, USA, 2008), 83–89.
41. Hamilton, R.: Collaborative and competitive futures for virtual reality music and sound in 2019 IEEE Conference onVirtualReality and 3D User Interfaces (VR) (2019), 1510–1512.
42. Hand, C.: A survey of 3D interaction techniques in Computer graphics forum 16 (1997), 269–281.
43. Hodges, L. F., Anderson, P., Burdea, G. C., Hoffmann, H., Rothbaum, B. O.: Treating psychological and phsyical disorders with VR. IEEE Computer Graphics and Applications 21, 25–33 (2001).
44. Howard, P.: What is scenography? (Routledge, 2019).
45. Hunt, A., Kirk, R.: Mapping strategies for musical performance. Trends in Gestural Control of Music, 231–258 (2000).

46. Jayaram, S., Vance, J., Gadh, R., Jayaram, U., Srinivasan, H.: Assessment of VR technology and its applications to engineering problems. J. Comput. Inf. Sci. Eng. **1**, 72–83 (2001).
47. Johnson, D., Tzanetakis, G.: VRMin: Using Mixed Reality to Augment the Theremin forMusical Tutoring in Proceedings of the International Conference on New Interfaces for Musical Expression (NIME-17), Copenhagen **33** (2017).
48. Juslin, P.N.: Emotional communication in music performance:Afunctionalist perspective and some data. Music perception **14**, 383–418 (1997).
49. Lanier, J.: The sound of one hand. Whole Earth Review (1993).
50. Larsson, P., Västfjäll, D., Kleiner, 50. M.: The actor-observer effect in virtual reality presentations. CyberPsychology & Behavior **4**, 239–246 (2001).
51. Lee, S. W., Freeman, J., Colella, A., Yao, S., Van Troyer, A.: Collaborative musical improvisation in a laptop ensemble with LOLC in Proceedings of the 8th ACM conference on Creativity and cognition (ACM, Atlanta, Georgia, USA, 2011), 361–362.
52. Lele, A.: Virtual reality and its military utility. Journal of Ambient Intelligence and Humanized Computing **4**, 17–26 (2013).
53. Lyon, E. et al.: Genesis of the cube: The design and deployment of an hdlabased performance and research facility. Computer Music Journal **40**, 62–78 (2016).
54. Mackinlay, J. D., Card, S. K., Robertson, G. G.: Rapid controlled movement through a virtual 3D workspace in ACM SIGGRAPH computer graphics **24** (1990), 171–176.
55. Magnusson, T.: Designing constraints: Composing and performing with digital musical systems. Computer Music Journal **34**, 62–73 (2010).
56. Mäki-Patola, T., Laitinen, J., Kanerva, A., Takala, T.: Experiments with Virtual Reality Instruments in Proceedings of the 2005 International Conference on New Interfaces for Musical Expression (NIME05), Vancouver, BC, Canada (2005).
57. Malpas, J.: Place and the Problem of Landscape. The place of landscape: Concepts, contexts, studies, 3–26 (2011).
58. McDermott, J., Gifford, T., Bouwer, A., Wagy, M. in Music and humancomputer interaction 29–47 (Springer, 2013).
59. McKinney, J., Butterworth, P.: The Cambridge Introduction to Scenography (Cambridge University Press, 2009).
60. McMahan, A. in, 67–86 (Routledge (New York), 2003).
61. McPherson, A. P., Zappi, V.: Exposing the scaffolding of digital instruments with hardware-software feedback loops. in NIME (2015), 162–167.
62. McVeigh-Schultz, J., Márquez Segura, E., Merrill, N., Isbister, K.: What's It Mean to" Be Social" in VR? Mapping the Social VR Design Ecology in Proceedings of the 2018 ACM Conference Companion Publication on Designing Interactive Systems (2018), 289–294.
63. Mendes, D., Caputo, F. M., Giachetti, A., Ferreira, A., Jorge, J.: A survey on 3d virtual object manipulation: From the desktop to immersive virtual environments in Computer Graphics Forum **38** (2019), 21–45.
64. Merritt, T., Kow,W., Ng, C., McGee, K.,Wyse, L.: Who makes what sound?: supporting real-time musical improvisations of electroacoustic ensembles in Proceedings of the 22nd conference of the computer-human interaction special interest group of Australia on computer-human interaction (2010), 112–119.
65. Milgram, P., Kishino, F.: A taxonomy of mixed reality visual displays. IEICE TRANSACTIONS on Information and Systems **77**, 1321–1329 (1994).
66. Mulder, A. G.: Design of virtual three-dimensional instruments for sound control PhD thesis (Simon Fraser University, Canada, 1998).
67. Nilsson, N. C., Serafin, S., Nordahl, R.: Establishing the range of perceptually natural visual walking speeds for virtual walking-in-place locomotion. IEEE transactions on visualization and computer graphics **20**, 569–578 (2014).
68. Norman, D. A.: Affordance, conventions, and design. interactions **6**, 38–43 (1999).
69. Nowak, K. L., Biocca, F.: The effect of the agency and anthropomorphism on users' sense of telepresence, copresence, and social presence in virtual environments. Presence: Teleoperators & Virtual Environments **12**, 481–494 (2003).

70. Pinho, M. S., Bowman, D. A., Freitas, C. M.: Cooperative object manipulation in immersive virtual environments: framework and techniques in Proceedings of the ACM symposium on Virtual reality software and technology (ACM, Hong Kong, China, 2002), 171–178.
71. Poepel, C.: On interface expressivity: A player based study. in NIME **5** (2005), 228–231.
72. Prpa, M., Schiphorst, T., Tatar, K., Pasquier, P.: Respire: a Breath Away from the Experience in Virtual Environment in Extended Abstracts of the 2018 CHI Conference on Human Factors in Computing Systems (2018), Art10.
73. Razzaque, S., Swapp, D., Slater, M., Whitton, M. C., Steed, A.: Redirected walking in place in EGVE **2** (2002), 123–130.
74. Reeves, S., Benford, S., O'Malley, C., Fraser, M.: Designing the spectator experience in Proceedings of the SIGCHI conference on Human factors in computing systems (ACM, Portland, Oregon, USA, 2005), 741–750.
75. Rose, T., Nam, C. S., Chen, K. B.: Immersion of virtual reality for rehabilitation-Review. Applied ergonomics **69**, 153–161 (2018).
76. Rossmy, B., Wiethoff, A.: The Modular Backward Evolution-Why to Use Outdated Technologies. in NIME (2019), 343–348.
77. Sanchez-Vives, M. V., Slater, M.: FROM PRESENCE TO CONSCIOUSNESS THROUGH VIRTUAL REALITY. Nature Reviews Neuroscience **6**, 332–339 (2005).
78. Serafin, S., Erkut, C., Kojs, J., Nilsson, N., Nordahl, R.: Virtual Reality Musical Instruments: State of the Art, Design Principles, and Future Directions. English. Computer Music Journal **40**, 22–40 (2016).
79. Slater, M.: Place illusion and plausibility can lead to realistic behaviour in immersive virtual environments. Phil. Trans. R. Soc. B **364**, 3549–3557 (2009).
80. Slater, M., Linakis,V., Usoh, M.,Kooper, R., Street, G.: Immersion, presence, and performance in virtual environments: An experiment with tri-dimensional chess inACMVirtual Reality Software and Technology (VRST 1996) (1996), 163–172.
81. Slater, M., Pertaub, D.-P., Steed, A.: Public speaking in virtual reality: Facing an audience of avatars. IEEE Computer Graphics and Applications **19**, 6–9 (1999).
82. Slater, M., Steed, A.: A Virtual Presence Counter. Presence **9**, 413–434 (2000).
83. Slater, M., Usoh, M., Steed, A.: Taking Steps: The Influence of a Walking Technique on Presence in Virtual Reality. ACM Trans. Comput.-Hum. Interact. **2**, 201–219 (Sept. 1995).
84. Slater, M., Usoh, M., Steed, A.: Taking steps: the influence of a walking technique on presence in virtual reality. ACM Transactions on Computer- Human Interaction (TOCHI) **2**, 201–219 (1995).
85. Slater, M., Wilbur, S.: A framework for immersive virtual environments (FIVE): Speculations on the role of presence in virtual environments. Presence: Teleoperators & Virtual Environments **6**, 603–616 (1997).
86. Slater, M. et al.: Analysis of Physiological Responses to a Social Situation in an Immersive Virtual Environment. Presence **15**, 553–569 (2006).
87. Strick, M., de Bruin, H. L., de Ruiter, L. C., Jonkers, W.: Striking the right chord: Moving music increases psychological transportation and behavioural intentions. Journal of Experimental Psychology: Applied **21**, 57 (2015).
88. Swift, B. in Music and human-computer interaction 85–99 (Springer, 2013).
89. Trueman, D.: Why a laptop orchestra? Organised Sound **12**, 171–179 (2007).
90. Vincs, K., McCormick, J.: Touching space: Using motion capture and stereo projection to create a "virtual haptics" of dance. Leonardo **43**, 359–366 (2010).
91. Wanderley, M. M., Depalle, P.: Gestural control of sound synthesis in Proceedings of the IEEE (2004), 632–644.
92. Wu, Y., Zhang, L., Bryan-Kinns, N., Barthet, M.: Open symphony: Creative participation for audiences of live music performances. IEEE MultiMedia **24**, 48–62 (2017).
93. Zappi, V., Brogni, A., Caldwell, D. G.: OSC Virtual Controller. in NIME **10** (2010).
94. Zappi, V., Mazzanti, D., Brogni, A., Caldwell, D.: Concatenative Synthesis Unit Navigation and Dynamic Rearrangement in vrGrains in 9th Sound and Music Computing Conference (2012).

95. Zappi, V., Mazzanti, D., Brogni, A., Caldwell, D. G.: Design and Evaluation of a Hybrid Reality Performance. in NIME **11** (2011), 355–360.
96. Zappi, V., McPherson, A.: Hackable Instruments: Supporting Appropriation and Modification in Digital Musical Interaction. Frontiers in ICT **5**, 26 (2018).
97. Zappi, V., Pistillo, A., Calinon, S., Brogni, A., Caldwell, D.: Music expression with a robot manipulator used as a bidirectional tangible interface. EURASIP Journal on Audio, Speech, and Music Processing **2012**, 1–11 (2012).
98. Zhai, P.: Get real: A philosophical adventure in virtual reality (Rowman & Littlefield, 1998).

# Index

**A**

Acoustic invariants, 56
Active inference, 21
Actor-network theory, 21
Adaptability, 120, 128
Additive synthesis, 64
Adversarial design, 25
Aerodynamic sounds, 67, 82
Agency, 20, 54, 59
Agential cuts, 20
Agents, 36
Algorithmic music composition, 191
Ambisonics, 83, 160, 171
Archipelago, 8
Artificial intelligence, 25, 37, 125
Attention, 305, 323, 327
Audio coding, 102
Audio quality, 67, 119, 136, 146, 154
Audio samples, 60
Audio-tactile experience, 313, 354
Audio-visual experience, 78, 170, 271, 309, 319
Auditory digital twin, 14, 22
Augmented interaction, 210, 252, 354, 417
Auralization, 78, 159
Authenticity, 79, 149
Avatar, 6, 22, 196, 202, 204, 240
Awareness, 37, 202, 210, 221, 239, 398, 402

**B**

Balance, 224
Balance board, 228
Beamforming, 160
Beam tracing, 100
Bidirectional impulse response, 87
Binaural recordings, 119, 162

Binaural rendering, 116
Binaural room impulse responses, 10, 162
Binaural synthesis, 119, 151, 158, 199, 284
Bodily interaction, 223
Body, 221, 275
Body ownership, 54, 59
Breaking sounds, 67
Break in presence, 18, 79, 153

**C**

Clarity, 91
Cocktail-party effect, 25, 306
Coherence, 28, 31, 57, 305
Colavita effect, 307
Collaborative music making, 196, 238, 245
Collaborative sonic interactions, 238
Collaborative spaces, 33, 191, 209
Communication, 250, 392
Complex scenes, 93, 118, 157
Computational auditory models, 123
Computational cost, 65, 79
Computer graphics, 100
Conductor, 191, 414
Consciousness, 327
Co-presence, 37, 398
Creative spaces, 187, 207
Cross-modal enhancement, 307
Cross-modal transfers, 307
Cross-talk cancellation (CTC), 164
Crumpling sounds, 66
Cybersickness, 30, 273
Cyborgs, 19

**D**

Defamiliarization, 223

Design guidelines, 186, 203, 262, 399
Design typology, 188
Diegetic sounds, 51
Digital audio workstation (DAW), 191, 270
Digital transformation, 14
Directional audio coding (DirAC), 102, 159, 171
Directional impulse response, 86
Directional transfer function, 123
Direction of arrival, 86, 159
Direct sound, 90, 160
Direct-to-reverberant ratio, 91
Distractor task, 338
Distributed user interface, 183
Doppler Shift, 82, 272
Dummy head, 116, 120, 162, 282, 367
Dynamic scene geometry, 93
Dynamic sound sources, 93

**E**
Early reflections, 90, 160
Echo threshold, 90
Ecological acoustics, 56, 310
Egocentric audio, 13
Egocentric vision, 15
Embodiment, 18, 59, 205, 208, 239, 312
Enaction, 16, 58, 354
Enactive potential, 35
Energy decay relief (EDR), 97
Engagement, 387
Entanglement, 20, 28, 34
Envelopment, 91, 331
Estrangement, 223
Everyday listening, 56
Everyday sounds, 52, 358
Externalization, 17, 169

**F**
First-person point of view, 15, 204, 224, 274, 386
Flow, 331
Foley Art, 58
Footstep sounds, 60, 310
Front-back confusion, 30, 134, 167, 169

**G**
Gamification, 129
Geometric acoustics, 99
Gestalt, 128
Gestures, 392
Green's function, 85

**H**
Haptics, 224, 273, 354
Headphone compensation, 169
Headphone reproduction, 83, 150, 161, 173, 230, 355
Head-related transfer function (HRTF), 10, 81, 83, 116, 162
Head-tracking, 30, 163, 169
HRTF accommodation, 128
HRTF learning, 128
HRTF modelling, 121
HRTF–non-individual, 128, 282
HRTF personalization, 83
HRTF selection, 125
Human-computer interaction, 20, 184, 221, 389

**I**
Image sources, 104
Immersion, 28, 29, 153, 320, 394
Immersive analytics, 36
Immersive music, 194, 385
Immersive potential, 327
Immersive tendency, 34, 328, 339
Immersive virtual musical instruments, 388
Individualisation, 118, 167, 326
Interaction design, 19, 220, 273, 280
Interactive audio systems, 183
Interaural level difference (ILD), 116, 161
Interaural time difference (ITD), 116, 161
Intersensory biases, 307
Interviews, 228, 288
Intra-action, 13, 21

**J**
Jitter, 54

**K**
Kinaesthetic thinking, 312
Knowledge diffraction, 25

**L**
Latency, 54, 273
Learning interface, 191
Level of detail, 68, 119
Liquid sounds, 67
Listener, 30, 86, 119, 127, 148, 288, 322, 326, 328, 339, 369
Localisation, 118, 167, 170, 249, 271, 283, 285

Localisation tests, 131
Loudspeaker reproduction, 83, 150, 158, 164, 336

**M**

Machine learning, 124
Magical interaction, 31, 185, 273
Marble hand illusion, 313
McGurk effect, 309
MIDI controller, 367, 370, 409
Mixed reality, 199, 389, 395
Mixed structural modelling, 126
Mixing metaphors, 270
Modality appropriateness hypothesis, 311
Modal synthesis, 65, 71, 230
Monad, 35
Morphological parameters, 123, 125
Motion analysis, 18, 208
Motion capture, 208, 310, 409, 412
Motion sensors, 23, 163
Motor learning, 225
Movement, 36, 208, 220, 227, 261, 405
Multi-modal experiences, 238, 281, 322, 371, 392
Multi-modal simulations, 269
Multisensory integration, 33, 54, 306, 308, 354
Musical experiences, 199, 357, 363, 384, 390
Musical instrument, 314, 367
Musical listening, 56
Music production, 185, 269

**N**

Narrative, 12, 16, 192, 322, 323
Near-field acoustics, 81
New interfaces for musical expression, 8, 184, 272, 372, 391
Numerical simulations, 101, 120

**O**

Object-based rendering, 84
Open Sound Control (OSC), 284

**P**

Parametric pinna model, 123
Parchment-skin illusion, 313
Participatory design, 25, 224
Perceptual evaluation, 127, 286
Performance environment, 191, 386
Personal space, 33, 252, 356

Perspectives, 223
Physical modeling, 64
Physics-based synthesis, 64
Pinna, 121
Place illusion, 30, 59, 153, 324, 330
Plasticity, 128
Plausibility, 79, 151
Plausibility illusion, 32, 54, 57, 153, 324, 330
Post-phenomenological thinking, 13
Precedence effect, 90
Precomputation, 102, 105
Presence, 5, 57, 152, 254, 329, 393
Procedural audio, 33, 62
Proprioception, 59, 129
Provotyping, 25, 37
Proxemics, 33, 205
Proximity, 68, 91, 170
Pupil dilation, 137

**Q**

Quality of experience (QoE), 148, 328, 366, 368
Quantified self, 23

**R**

Ray tracing, 104
Reaction time, 18, 333
Real-time rendering, 78, 280
Reflexive intentionality, 20
Rehabilitation, 225
Reinforcement learning, 26
Responsiveness, 314
Reverberation, 91, 97, 166
Rolling sounds, 66, 221, 310
Room acoustics, 78, 135, 150
Room divergence, 170
Room impulse response (RIR), 10, 159
Room-portal decomposition, 100, 104
Rubber hand illusion, 59

**S**

Sandbox system, 192, 196
Scalar wave equation, 85
Scenography, 386
Scraping sounds, 66
Selection and manipulation, 184, 396
Selective attention, 137
Sense of self-location, 59
Sensorimotor contingencies, 59, 312, 384
Sensory misalignment, 223

Sequencer, 196
Shared experiences, 33, 238, 386
Six degrees of freedom (6DoF), 157
Social experience, 186, 209, 239
Social presence, 239, 245
Social virtual reality, 183, 199, 239, 398, 412
Solid sounds, 66
Soma design, 220
Somaesthetics, 18, 221
Somatosensory feedback, 354
Somatosensory stimulation, 355
Sonic experience, 193, 354
Sonic interaction design, 6, 220
Sonic interactions in virtual environments
    (SIVE), 9, 21, 181, 220
Sonification, 224
Sound and music computing, 8, 182
Sound field analysis and synthesis, 158
Sound propagation, 80–82, 85, 252
Soundscapes, 192, 221, 332
Sound source modeling, 50, 60, 80
Sound spatialization, 81, 83, 115, 220
Source directivity, 87
Spaces/places, 206, 311
Spatial audio production, 199, 211, 275
Spatial design, 182, 193, 205, 252
Spatial hearing, 17, 122, 161, 271
Spatial user interface, 183
Spectral cues, 116, 161
Spherical harmonics, 83, 173
Spritz
    (simulation), 29
Storytelling, 25, 323
Subjective measurements, 146, 332
Synesthesia, 308
Synthesizer, 373

T
Tangible user interface, 209, 240, 281, 360
Technological mediation, 17, 19, 152, 183,
    227, 330
Teleportation, 32, 202
3D annotations, 243, 251
3D interaction, 32, 183, 184, 384, 396, 410
3D projection, 408
3D scan, 120
Touch, 59, 225, 354
Training, 129, 356

U
Ubiquitous and pervasive computing, 35

V
Vector-based amplitude panning (VBAP),
    160, 171
Ventriloquism effect, 170, 271, 307
Video-games, 51, 137, 191, 322, 324
Virtuality continuum, 27, 388
Virtual reality music instrument, 185, 192,
    272, 388
Visual cues, 243, 271, 275, 307, 336, 404
Visual dominance, 310
VR audio hardware and software, 69, 103,
    174
VR hardware and software, 30, 391, 400

W
Walking, 15, 32, 66, 227, 305
Wave acoustics, 101
Wave field synthesis (WFS), 160
Wearables, 226

Printed in the United States
by Baker & Taylor Publisher Services